D0999280

WORLD PHYSICAL MAP

THIS REGISTRATION CODE GIVES YOU ACCESS TO

B Ebook | InQuizitive | History Skills Tutorials | Map & Primary Source Exercises | **©** Student Site

FOR *The Webs of Humankind,* Volume One, Seagull Edition

ACTIVATE YOUR REGISTRATION CODE!

1) Scratch the foil to view your code

2) Go to digital.wwnorton.com/websseagullv1
3) Follow the instructions to register your code

A code can be registered to only one user. Used codes are nontransferable and nonrefundable.

For more help, see the back of this card.

What if my code is scratched off?

You can purchase access at
digital.wwnorton.com/websseagullv1

What if I need more help?

For additional support, visit **support.wwnorton.com**

ISBN 978-0-393-41752-4

9 780393 417524

90000

THE WEBS *of* HUMANKIND

A WORLD HISTORY

SEAGULL EDITION

Volume One

JOHN McNEILL

THE WEBS *of* HUMANKIND

A WORLD HISTORY

SEAGULL EDITION

Volume One

W. W. NORTON & COMPANY

Independent Publishers Since 1923

W. W. Norton & Company has been independent since its founding in 1923, when William Warder Norton and Mary D. Herter Norton first published lectures delivered at the People's Institute, the adult education division of New York City's Cooper Union. The firm soon expanded its program beyond the Institute, publishing books by celebrated academics from America and abroad. By midcentury, the two major pillars of Norton's publishing—trade books and college texts—were firmly established. In the 1950s, the Norton family transferred control of the company to its employees, and today—with a staff of five hundred and hundreds of trade, college, and professional titles published each year—W. W. Norton & Company stands as the largest and oldest publishing house owned wholly by its employees.

Senior Editor: Steve Forman
Editor: Justin Cahill
Senior Associate Managing Editor: Melissa Atkin
Manuscript Editor: Alice Vigliani
Senior Associate Editor: Gerra Goff
Assistant Editors: Lily Gellman and Angie Merila
Cartographic Editor: Charlotte Miller
Copyeditor: Marne Evans
Managing Editor, College: Marian Johnson
Managing Editor, College Digital Media: Kim Yi
Director of Production, College: Jane Searle
Media Editor: Carson Russell
Media Project Editor: Rachel Mayer
Media Associate Editor: Alexander Lee
Media Assistant Editor: Alexandra Malakhoff
Photo Editor: Stephanie Romeo
Photo Researcher: Lynn Gadson
Associate Art Director: Jillian Burr
Permissions Manager: Bethany Salminen
Permissions Specialist: Josh Garvin
Layout Artist: Brad Walrod/Kenoza Type, Inc.
Cartographer and Illustrator: Mapping Specialists—Fitchburg, WI
Manufacturing: Transcontintental Interglobe Inc.—Beauceville, QC

ISBN for this Edition: 978-0-393-41755-5

The Library of Congress has cataloged another edition as follows:

Names: McNeill, John Robert, author.
Title: The webs of humankind : a world history / J. R. McNeill.
Description: First edition. | New York : W. W. Norton & Company, [2021] |
    Includes index.
Identifiers: LCCN 2019045123 | ISBN 9780393979114 (hardcover)
Subjects: LCSH: World history—Textbooks. | Human ecology—History—Textbooks. |
    Globalization—History—Textbooks.
Classification: LCC D20.M4843 2021 | DDC 909—dc23
LC record available at https://lccn.loc.gov/2019045123

W. W. Norton & Company, Inc., 500 Fifth Avenue, New York, NY 10110

wwnorton.com

W. W. Norton & Company Ltd., 15 Carlisle Street, London W1D 3BS

1 2 3 4 5 6 7 8 9 0

This book is dedicated to families: especially the one into which I was born, the one that Julie and I created, and the one that is the community of historians at Georgetown University—students and teachers, past and present.

ABOUT THE AUTHOR

 **J. R. McNEILL** studied at Swarthmore College and Duke University, where he completed a Ph.D. in 1981. Since 1985 he has taught at Georgetown University, in the History Department and School of Foreign Service, where he held the Cinco Hermanos Chair in Environmental and International Affairs before becoming University Professor in 2006. He has taught roughly 3,000 Georgetown students in courses on world history, international relations history, and environmental history.

McNeill's books include: *The Atlantic Empires of France and Spain* (1985); *The Mountains of the Mediterranean World: An Environmental History* (1992); *Something New under the Sun: An Environmental History of the Twentieth-Century World* (2000), co-winner of the World History Association book prize and the Forest History Society book prize; *The Human Web: A Bird's-Eye View of World History* (2003), co-authored with his father, William McNeill; and *Mosquito Empires: Ecology and War in the Greater Caribbean, 1620–1914* (2010), which won the Beveridge Prize from the American Historical Association. His latest book, *The Great Acceleration: An Environmental History of the Anthropocene, 1945–2015*, appeared in 2016. He has edited or co-edited 15 other books, including two volumes of *The Cambridge World History* (2015).

In 2010, McNeill was awarded the Toynbee Prize for "academic and public contributions to humanity." In 2014, the World History Association awarded him its annual prize for achievement in that field; in 2019, the American Society for Environmental History presented him with its Distinguished Scholar Award. The Royal Netherlands Academy of Arts and Sciences awarded him the Heineken Prize for history in 2018. In 2011–2013, he served as President of the American Society for Environmental History, and in 2019 as President of the American Historical Association. He is a member of the American Academy of Arts and Sciences.

CONTENTS IN BRIEF

CONTENTS

States as Social Systems • The Emergence of States and
Rulers • The Twin Challenges of Complex Society

PART 2

Regional Webs and Their Fusion into
the Old World Web

MAPS

FEATURES

The Webs of Humankind Seagull Edition offers two text features that reinforce and enrich the book's presentation of world history. They are meant to support student work with primary sources and strengthen their engagement with world history questions.

The first is a primary source feature called **Considering the Evidence**, which appears in every chapter. Authored by Daren Ray (Auburn University), Considering the Evidence presents text documents and images of art and artifacts for analysis by students. Each box includes a contextual headnote and study questions. The primary sources all shed light on the events and developments of each chapter.

The second feature, **The Human Web**, is a map feature that combines text and maps to illustrate webs of interaction at key periods. Each volume of the textbook offers three Human Web features. Each one is built around a central map of an important web, including an introductory headnote by J. R. McNeill and study questions based on the feature and the chapter reading.

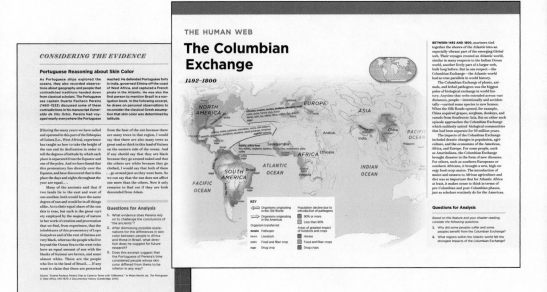

FEATURE CONTENTS

PEDAGOGY

The Webs of Humankind Seagull Edition presents a set of pedagogical features intended to guide introductory students through the chapters and support their understanding of world history.

All chapters open with a list of **Focus Questions** that correspond to the major section headings in the chapter. These questions, which appear also in the relevant running heads at the tops of pages, are meant to alert students to the key developments in each section. All chapters also open with a **Chronology** of major events and an **immersive narrative vignette** to draw students into the reading. The chapters end with a summary **Conclusion** and a **Chapter Review** page that includes **Review Questions** and a list of the **Key Terms** (with page references) that appear in bold in the chapter. A **Further Reading** list compiled and annotated by J. R. McNeill appears at the end of the book, along with a **Glossary** including definitions of all key terms and a pronunciation guide.

The author also collaborated on the art program, which includes more than 350 images, and more than 150 original maps, all with captions by the author.

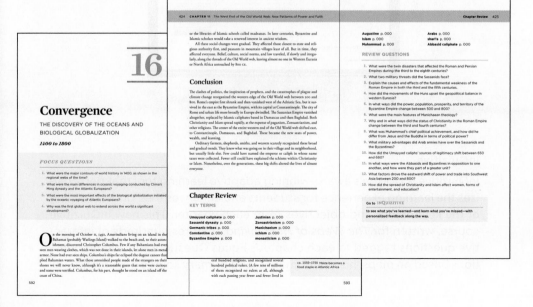

DIGITAL RESOURCES FOR TEACHING AND LEARNING

W. W. Norton has a long history of delivering robust and carefully designed digital resource packages to support teaching and learning. The resources described here have been built from the ground up—with guidance and input from active world history instructors—specifically for use with *The Webs of Humankind* by J. R. McNeill.

RESOURCES FOR STUDENTS

The following resources are available using the access card at the front of this text.

InQuizitive

InQuizitive is Norton's award-winning adaptive learning tool that personalizes the learning experience for students and enhances their understanding of the key themes and objectives from each chapter. This new InQuizitive course, written for *The Webs of Humankind*, features hundreds of interactive questions tagged to each chapter's Focus Questions—including questions based on maps, historical images, and primary source documents—all of which are delivered in an engaging game-like environment with detailed, answer-specific feedback. InQuizitive can be integrated directly into your existing learning management system for easy student access.

▶ **Increased student scores by 16%**

In efficacy studies, when history students completed InQuizitive activities prior to taking a summative quiz, their quiz grades increased by an average of 16 percentage points. Go to www.wwnorton.com/inquizitive for more information.

History Skills Tutorials

The History Skills Tutorials are interactive, online modules that support student development of key skills for the world history course—such as analysis and interpretation of primary source documents, images, and maps. With interactive practice assessments, helpful guiding feedback, and videos with John McNeill modeling source analysis, these tutorials teach students the critical analysis skills that they will put to use in their academic and professional careers. These tutorials can be integrated directly into your existing learning management system for easy student access.

Primary Source and Map Exercises

Building from the critical analysis skills developed in the History Skills Tutorials (above), a series of assignable Primary Source Exercises and Map Exercises provide students the opportunity to practice these skills in every week of the course. Each exercise includes 5 to 10 interactive questions based on documents, images, and maps found in the chapter reading. These exercises can be integrated directly into your existing learning management system for easy student access.

Student Site

The online Student Site offers additional study and review materials for students to use outside of class. Resources include:

- An Online Reader features over 100 additional primary source documents and images, with introductory headnotes, sample short-answer questions, discussion prompts, and activity ideas for easy assignability.
- Author videos featuring John McNeill help students understand the webs of interaction that shape world history.
- Flashcards invite students to review the key terms from the textbook.
- Chapter outlines give students a detailed snapshot of the key topics of each chapter.

Ebook

Norton Ebooks give students and instructors an enhanced reading experience at a fraction of the price of a print textbook. Students are able to have an active reading experience and can take notes, bookmark, search, highlight, and even read offline. Instructors can add notes for students to see as they read the text. Norton Ebooks can be viewed on—and synced among—all computers and mobile devices. Features in the ebook include:

- Enlargeable maps and art
- Embedded videos
- Pop-up key term definitions

RESOURCES FOR INSTRUCTORS

All instructor resources are available for download after free registration at

wwnorton.com/catalog/instructor-resources

Resources for Your LMS

Easily add high-quality Norton digital resources to your online, hybrid, or lecture courses. Get started building your course with our easy-to-use integrated resources; all activities can be accessed right within your existing learning management system. The downloadable file includes integration links to the following resources, organized by chapter:

- Ebook
- InQuizitive
- History Skills Tutorials
- Primary Source Exercises & Map Exercises
- Student Site Resources

Test Bank

The Test Bank features more than 1,500 questions—including multiple choice, true/false, and short-answer questions—aligned with the chapter's

Focus Questions. This bank of quiz and exam content provides multiple avenues for comprehension and skill assessment.

Norton Testmaker brings Norton's high-quality testing materials online. Create assessments from anywhere with an Internet connection, without downloading files or installing specialized software. Search and filter test bank questions by chapter, type, difficulty, learning objectives, and other criteria. You can also customize questions to fit your course. Then, easily export your tests to Microsoft Word or Common Cartridge files for import into your LMS.

Instructor's Manual

The Instructor's Manual contains:

- Detailed chapter summaries
- Chapter outlines
- Discussion/forum prompts
- Lecture ideas
- Sample responses to Questions for Analysis in the text, and more

Lecture and Art PowerPoint Slides

The lecture PowerPoint slides combine chapter review, images, maps, and lecture notes, and are easily customizable. Art PowerPoint slides and JPEGs are available separately for every image and map in the text. Alt-text is provided for each item.

PREFACE

How did our world get to be the way it is? Why are some parts of the world so much richer than others? Is gender inequality universal, or have societies ever existed without it? Why are empires, so common throughout most of world history, so rare today? Why in both the Americas and Eurasia—which developed in isolation from each other—did many early cities feature monumental architecture, grid patterns, and open public spaces? When and why did slavery begin, and why, after thousands of years, was it abolished almost everywhere in the nineteenth century? What role has climate change played in history, and has that role changed in recent decades?

The study of world history can provide answers to big questions like these. Almost any variety of history can help explain how and why societies have changed over time. However, world history (or global history—I make no distinction between the two terms) is a special kind of history. It is not the sum of all history: it is in fact more than the sum of its parts.

WHAT IS DISTINCTIVE ABOUT WORLD HISTORY?

World history is comparative: it helps distinguish what is commonplace from what is distinctive about societies. In the early chapters of this book, we will notice that places where people raised crops that store well were much more likely to develop kingdoms, empires, and other states than places where people relied on crops that spoil too quickly to be stored and distributed. An important pattern like this would be harder to see if we were looking at the histories of China, India, Africa, and South America separately, without comparison. So too with several religious movements of the sixteenth and seventeenth centuries. The Protestant Reformation in Europe, the birth of the Sikh religion in India, and the Shi'a Islamic revival in seventeenth-century Iran all emphasized personal relationships with divinity, and valued intuition over institutions in matters of faith. Comparing these (as Chapter 18 does) suggests a common pattern despite the different contexts.

World history is also selective. Because the past is virtually infinite, all historians must choose what to include in their accounts and what to leave out. World historians must be more selective to avoid having their subject become a giant jumble of facts. World history tends to foreground parallels, contrasts, and connections among societies rather than the details of national history. So, for example, Chapter 9 considers the impact of iron working on both northern Europe and sub-Saharan Africa after 1000 BCE. In Africa, iron making and iron tools tended to bring societies closer through trade, but in northern Europe it had the opposite effect, weakening linkages. A world historical lens on international politics similarly shows that on every continent in the sixteenth and seventeenth centuries a handful of big empires grew much larger, eliminating hundreds of smaller states. In Chapter 19, we see that this was not an accident but a result of faster flows of new technologies and techniques of warfare through a globalizing world.

In the process of being selective, world history can also highlight the global trends that are distinctive across long stretches of time. For thousands of years, powerful states saw fit to build and maintain empires as long as their power lasted. But after 1960 or so, the idea of empire lost its appeal, and ever since the powerful have preferred to avoid formal empires. That is a historically unique development, although not necessarily a permanent change. On even longer time scales, we can see, as Chapter 29 explains, that the modern rise in greenhouse gas concentrations in the atmosphere has been faster—by far—than any other such rise in the historical or geological record. These two examples of distinctive, and even peculiar, aspects of our own period are best understood in the long sweep of world history.

THE APPROACH OF THIS TEXTBOOK

This book differs from most world history textbooks in a few ways. It has one author, not several, which has been hard on that author but might be good for the reader because it raises the odds of achieving a consistent viewpoint and framework. I hope I have achieved that because it might compensate for the chief disadvantage of a single-authored world history: no author can know everything. I do not have the same command of human evolution, ancient Chinese history, medieval Russian history, or modern U.S. history that specialists in these fields have. However, I have taught world history for decades and learned a fair bit along the way, not least from my students. I've also written global-scale histories before, mainly environmental histories. This book reflects my own background as a historian, giving frequent attention to matters of geography and environment.

This book features a particular framework for understanding world history. Having an effective framework is essential because it helps organize information and put it into a context—avoiding that giant jumble of facts. The framework here is based on the concept of webs of social interaction.

It's an approach that, I hope, will provide readers with a strong sense of the connectedness, but also the contrasts, of world history—and in an easily accessible way.

THE WEBS OF HUMANKIND: AN OVERVIEW

People always and everywhere have been connected to others. These connections have taken many forms, ranging from kinship and friendship to economic exchange and military confrontation. In all such relationships, people exchanged information and used it to guide their future behavior. They often also exchanged technologies, religious beliefs, artistic visions, trade goods, food crops, violent threats, lethal infections, and much else. These exchanges shaped what people could do and could imagine. When exchanges and connections became regular, I call them webs of interaction.

For most of human history—from the dawn of our species' existence some 300,000 years ago until roughly 13,000 years ago—our ancestors lived in a very loose, far-flung human web. Their communities were normally small migratory bands that only occasionally mixed with others. That way of life only rarely presented them with the stimulus of new ideas and objects to consider. By later standards, the pace of change in arenas such as technology or social organization was glacially slow. This doesn't mean nothing happened, though: this was the time when humans invented religion and language, and migrated from their place of origin in Africa to settle every habitable continent. These were momentous changes, even if they happened extremely slowly.

Beginning around 13,000 years ago (or roughly 11,000 BCE), a handful of changes occurred that encouraged the weaving of much tighter webs of interaction. While the loose and far-flung human web continued in the background, new, tighter webs developed where people began to settle into permanent, sedentary communities. Sedentary life in those times worked best beside a seashore with abundant edible marine life (as on the coasts of Japan, for example) or amid wild grasses that yielded reliable and nutritious seeds (as in what is now southeastern Turkey). Some of these now-sedentary people domesticated wild animals and plants, converting them genetically into livestock and crops, respectively. Farming, the first evidence of which comes from Southwest Asia, encouraged larger communities, denser populations, and more vibrant, if still local, interactive webs—"local" here means several villages and a few thousand people. Changes in technology and social organization now came more rapidly than before.

Around 5,500 years ago (3500 BCE), much bigger and tighter webs formed when people first clustered together into cities, and then built networks of cities linked by regular trade and communication. This too happened first in Southwest Asia, specifically in what is now southern Iraq. But it didn't take long—a thousand years at most—before cities and regional webs linking multiple cities emerged elsewhere—in northeast Africa, South Asia, and East Asia, and by 200 CE in the Americas, especially in Meso-america and the Andes region of South America. Each of these regional webs, between roughly 2500 BCE and 200 CE, would grow to contain a few million people, dozens of cities, and thousands of villages. Within these emerging webs, changes in ideas, technologies, and social structures came faster than before, and faster than among people not connected to webs. Cities—nodes in these larger webs where people with different outlooks, religions, skills, and technologies rubbed shoulders every day—became hothouses of innovation and adaptation.

Mainly through the expansion of long-distance trade, those urban-based webs gradually linked up to one another. The biggest one formed between the Nile and the Ganges, and the next biggest in East Asia. By roughly 200 CE, sprawling webs of interaction spanned continents. By far the biggest, called the Old World web in this book, was anchored at either end by China and Egypt, stretching over most of Eurasia and North Africa. (Scholars often refer to Eurasia and Africa as the Old World, a usage I adopt because human occupation of those continents predates that anywhere else.) In 200 CE, it encompassed tens of millions of people living in cities and villages especially along rivers such as the Huang He (Yellow River), the Yangzi, the Ganges, the Indus, the Tigris and Euphrates, and the Nile. All of these rivers served as sources of irrigation water and arteries of transport, per-mitting more productive farming, larger food supplies, more people, more trade—and more frequent and sustained interaction of all sorts. The Old World web eventually—by 1400 CE—grew to include almost everyone living within a space the edges of which were Japan and Java in the east, and Iceland and West Africa in the west. At the time, that area included at least three-quarters of humankind, or more than 200 million people.

Smaller but still sizeable regional webs grew up elsewhere. In Africa, the northeastern region along the Nile and the Red Sea coast was enmeshed in the Old World web early on—by 1500 BCE if not before. Elsewhere in Africa, much smaller webs developed, especially along the Niger River in West Africa. That one merged with the Old World web by about 800 CE, mainly through the trans-Saharan trade routes that linked North Africa and West Africa as never before.

In the Americas, local webs developed based around irrigation agricul-ture, the first of them starting as early as 3000 BCE in the Andes. Bigger regional webs formed in the Andes by about 100 CE and another in Meso-america by about 200 CE. Both the Mesoamerican and Andean webs grew, but intermittently with many reversals. The outer threads of these two webs by 1450 CE extended far across the Americas and linked both continents very loosely through trade and migrations.

In Oceania, as people sailed from what is now Indonesia out to remote Pacific islands, a process that began around 2000 BCE, they formed thin webs linking island communities, bringing thousands of people into contact with one another over vast distances.

In character, these smaller webs bore many similarities to the Old World web: they were held together by trade, travel, and communication, and clusters of people—whether in cities or tightly packed villages—served as key nodes for the transmission of ideas, goods, and everything else. But in size, the Old World web, from its beginning around 200 CE, always outstripped all others.

A GLOBAL WEB

Beginning in the fifteenth century, breakthroughs in transport and communication fused all these webs into a single global one. Breakthroughs in ship design and in information storage, especially printing technology, contributed to a bigger breakthrough: sailors accumulated enough information to crack the code of the planet's winds and currents, enabling them to navigate the deep oceans much more securely than ever before. That launched an era of intercontinental navigation that wove the world's coastlands together into a global web. Beginning with Chapter 16, which overlaps both volumes of the text, this Global web is the main story of the book.

This new Global web triggered thorough-going and accelerating changes in the sixteenth through the eighteenth centuries, the first of which I call biological globalization. Infectious diseases such as measles and smallpox spread to populations with no acquired immunity, especially in the Americas and on Pacific islands, cutting populations by 50 to 95 percent. Sailors and ships also carried crops to new environments. Potatoes, for example, native to the Andes, gradually became part of the diet in northern Europe, and eventually in China and north India as well. Maize, originally from Mexico, became Africa's most important crop.

The Global web brought changes that extended far beyond biological transfers. New information and ideas from the four corners of the Earth led people to reconsider long-cherished beliefs, altering religious landscapes in Europe and Asia, as Chapter 18 details. The variety of political formats in which people lived diminished as small polities gave way to growing empires. The productive techniques and technologies that underpinned industrialization spread widely within decades after their introduction during the eighteenth and nineteenth centuries, reflecting the accelerating flow of information characteristic of the Global web. So too with new ideas about freedom, justice, and sovereignty that underlay political revolutions around the world, from the United States and France in the late eighteenth century to Mexico, Russia, and China in the early twentieth.

Throughout the last 150 years, with telegraphs, telephones, and networked computers, the Global web has grown tighter, its communications faster, its linkages stronger. Cities, which were home to about 10 percent of humankind in 1800, by 2010 accounted for more than half of the world's population. Today, almost everyone lives within a single, unified, global-scale web of interaction, competition, and cooperation. Different people experience this differently, but almost no one (aside from a few thousand people deep in rain forests) lives outside it.

WEB MAKING: A GLOBALIZING PROCESS

The long process of web making over thousands of years is in effect a globalizing one. The first webs launched a long-term trend—with reversals—toward greater connectedness. In this sense, world history has a direction to it. Several motors drove the web-making process. Among them were the economic advantages of specialization and exchange, which inspired trade. The desire of monarchs, whether Macedonian kings such as Alexander the Great or Chinese emperors such as Han Wudi, to expand their power and influence also extended the reach of webs. So did the ambition of missionaries to spread their religions. Merchants, monarchs, and missionaries weren't trying to extend webs—they didn't think in these terms at all. But their ambitions and actions had that effect. So did the routine movements of travelers, pilgrims, refugees, soldiers, sailors, pastoral nomads, and everyone else who moved around, interacted with strangers, and—unintentionally—helped to build sustained webs of interaction.

The long-term trend of webs growing, tightening, and consolidating was far from consistent. At times, when empires fell apart, plagues swept through, or trade routes shifted, contacts and connections might languish and webs unravel. This happened after the fifth century CE in western Europe when the Roman Empire fell. Webs might also fray as a result of deliberate choices, as in East Asia in the late eighth century CE when the rulers of China's Tang dynasty decided to reduce foreign contacts of all sorts. The complete disappearance of webs occurred often on local scales, probably more often in the Americas than elsewhere. But bigger webs, although they often frayed or shrank, rarely disappeared altogether and normally rebounded within a century or two, as happened in East Asia after new dynasties replaced the Tang.

The expansion of webs was often a brutal process. It frequently involved warfare and epidemics. Both occurred at once in many cases—as, for example, after Christopher Columbus's voyages of the 1490s when the Americas

Major Webs of World History

NAME AND EXPLANATION	LOCATION	APPROXIMATE DATES
Human web This refers to the faint and intermittent ties that have linked all, or almost all, humans throughout our species' entire career. But its connections were weak compared to the tighter local and regional webs, and to the Global web of the last five centuries.	Everywhere people have lived, except in the few cases where groups became genuinely isolated	From human origins ca. 300,000 years ago until today
Southwest Asian web This formed in the Tigris-Euphrates valley beginning about 5000 BCE. It extended into surrounding uplands by 3500 BCE, lasting until 2500 BCE when it was subsumed into the Nile-Indus web.	Mesopotamia and neighboring areas	5000 BCE to 2500 BCE
Nile-Indus web This was an expansion of the Southwest Asian web to both the east and the west.	From Egypt, and at times its southern neighbor Nubia, across Southwest Asia to the Indus valley	2500 BCE to 1500 BCE
Nile-Ganges web A further expansion across north India.	From Egypt across Southwest Asia and north India	1500 BCE to 200 CE
East Asian web Originated in China but extended to neighboring societies.	North and central China, with strands reaching into Korea, Japan, Central Asia, and northernmost Vietnam	1000 BCE to 200 CE
Old World web This is the fusion of the East Asian web and the Nile-Ganges web, with extensions into Europe and Africa.	From Senegal and Scotland in the west to Japan and Java in the east, including the Indian Ocean world	200 CE to 1500 CE
Andean web This formed in South America from the Moche and Tiwanaku cultures.	From the Altiplano in Bolivia to the coasts of Peru, straddling the high Andes	100 CE to 1500 CE
Mesoamerican web This developed with the interactions among the Maya, the Zapotecs, and Teotihuacán.	Central and southern Mexico and the Maya lands of Yucatán and northern Guatemala	200 CE to 1500 CE
Global web This is the fusion of the Old World web, the American webs, and all other local and regional webs.	Global, but tiny uncontacted communities deep in rain forests such as Amazonia remain outside it.	1500 CE to the present. It began to take shape with oceanic voyagers in the fifteenth and sixteenth centuries and is still tightening in the twenty-first.

were firmly linked to the Old World web. Newly introduced diseases in combination with warfare killed tens of millions of people in the Americas. Peoples who had lived outside of webs, such as the indigenous populations of the Americas, Australia, Polynesia, or Siberia, often suffered heavily for a century or more once they became entangled in webs.

As a rule, the expansion of webs, especially the Global web in recent centuries, has worked to reduce cultural diversity. The number of languages spoken has fallen by about half since 1500, while English, Spanish, Hindi, Arabic, Chinese, and a few others have acquired more speakers. The number of legal traditions too has declined: more and more people live under fewer and fewer legal systems, many of them now based on English common law or Islam's code of shari'a. Farmers' fields feature fewer strains of wheat, maize, and rice than they did 100 years ago, partly because farmers now have more information about which crop varieties yield best in their environments.

The table at left summarizes the main webs featured in this book. Many smaller ones that involved thousands, but not millions, of people are left out of the table. The dates are given in round numbers and are approximate because webs formed and merged gradually, with no sharp beginnings or end points.

ORGANIZATION OF THE BOOK

With the globalizing process of web making at work throughout, this book takes a largely regional organization in Volume 1 and a largely global one in Volume 2. The schemes of regionalization it adopts change as the world changed, reflecting the formation, and occasional decay, of webs. So, for example, "Africa" in some periods is treated as a continental unit, but at other times regions of Africa appear as parts of larger maritime webs. In Chapter 13, the coasts of eastern Africa are presented as a key element of a region called the Indian Ocean world. In Chapter 21, parts of Africa appear as components of a different region, the Atlantic world, united by trade, travel, and exchanges among the coastlands of the Americas, Europe, and Africa. The book often avoids the vocabulary of regions as we typically see them today. A conventional regionalization of the world takes the continents as regions, with a few additions such as "Middle East" and lately "Asia-Pacific." In emphasizing webs of interaction, this book minimizes the projection onto the past of today's conventional regions. So there is no "Middle East" until the twentieth century here, and no "Latin America" until the nineteenth century. It is worth noting too that in this world history some of the most important regions are defined by water, not land. There is no perfect way to regionalize the globe for all time periods. The different regionalization schemes used in this book reflect the changing reality of web connections among people in the past.

PARTS AND PERIODS

This book is divided into six parts, each of which corresponds to a period of time.

Part 1 (Chapters 1–3) takes on the longest sweep of time, from human origins to about 1500 BCE. For most of this period, all people lived in Africa. When some migrated to other continents, beginning about 70,000 years ago, we follow them wherever they went, which included every habitable continent by 12,000 BCE. Part 1 is global in the sense that it considers the experience of the entire human population. The very thin and faint web uniting our entire species endured despite the inter-continental wanderings of peoples.

Part 2 (Chapters 4–10) deals mainly with the period between 3500 BCE and 200 CE and shifts to a regional scheme of organization. It addresses the emergence of regional webs in parts of Eurasia, Africa, and the Americas, as outlined in the table above. In so doing, it examines the rise of cities, states, organized religions, and stratified, hierarchical societies. In places such as China, India, or Egypt—among others—these millennia also saw the formation of durable cultural traditions anchored in religion. By 200 CE, several regional webs in Eurasia and North Africa had fused into the single, sprawling Old World web. Chapter 9 pairs two places not often drawn together for comparison: northern Europe and sub-Saharan Africa. They were similar in that they stood on the frontiers of the big webs in the millennia before 200 CE. Among the resulting commonalities were smaller polities, a slower pace of technological change, and better health than that of people living in the larger webs. Slowly, though, they too became entangled in the Nile-Ganges web and, eventually, the full Old World web. The Americas and Oceania, the focus of Chapter 10, remained autonomous, unaffected by the formation of the Old World web until well beyond 200 CE. So this chapter continues up to 1000 CE, by which time a big web linking both North and South America had taken shape.

Part 3 (Chapters 11–15) maintains a regional organization and takes up the centuries between 200 CE and 1400 CE—and in one chapter to 1500. Most of it is devoted to developments within the Old World web, in East and South Asia, Africa, and Europe. It deals with several aspects of the maturation of regional webs—such as improvements in transport and navigation, and the accelerated spread of cultural traditions such as Buddhism, Christianity, and Islam. The final chapter of Part 3 returns to the Americas and Oceania, each of them still standing apart with no significant links to the Old World web until 1492 in the Americas and about 1770 in Oceania. Both built, or extended, webs of their own, which developed in accordance with prevailing conditions: the vast distances of the Pacific, for example, rewarded the navigational skills that islanders developed, while the paucity of domesticable animals in the Americas encouraged agriculture that did not require plowing. Yet strong, thought-provoking parallels existed between the societies in the Old World web and those of the Americas—as, for example, in the relationships between religious and political power, or the prevalence of gender inequality.

With **Part 4** (Chapters 16–20), the book becomes global in scope again because the links connecting every large population strengthened so much between 1400 and 1800 with the weaving of the Global web. Chapter 16, a pivotal chapter that ends Volume 1 and begins Volume 2, focuses on the convergence of the world's webs into a single Global web and the wave of biological exchanges that followed. This biological globalization set some of the basic conditions for world history in the next centuries, mainly through major shifts in agriculture and population. The connections of the Global web meant that the oceans no longer separated peoples as much as before. The histories of Angola and Brazil, as we see in Chapter 17, were firmly linked by a slave trade that established African culture in much of Brazil. As we see in Chapter 19, the effective use of guns in sixteenth-century Japan illustrates the effects of the Global web in distributing techniques and technology around the world. In Chapter 20, we see that the histories of China and Mexico developed a tie through transpacific trades in silver, silk, and porcelain routed through the Philippines. Part 4 considers the comparatively sudden changes resulting from this surge of globalization in the realms of ecology, ideas and culture, economies, and political competition.

With one exception, the chapters of **Part 5** (21–25) are also global in scope and organized by theme. They span the centuries between 1620 and 1920. The exception is Chapter 21, which is devoted to political revolutions in the Atlantic world—Africa, Europe, and the Americas. Collectively, these Atlantic revolutions were momentous enough, and their legacies global enough, to merit treatment as a unit unto themselves. The balance of Part 5 considers fundamental changes such as industrialization, the near-elimination of slavery and other forms of forced labor, and the rise of such political trends as nationalism and imperialism. It also treats some major political revolutions—in part, efforts to resist imperialism and industrialization—in India, China, Mexico, and Russia. Its main theme is the many political and social realignments and revolutions encouraged by the formation, and tightening, of the Global web. It seeks to find some balance between global currents and local factors in explaining these turbulent times.

Part 6 (Chapters 26–29) takes on a mere century and a half, from 1870 to the present—an era of accelerating globalization and episodes of fierce resistance against it. Maintaining the pattern of chapters that are global in scope and focused on themes, it takes up international politics more than earlier parts do, including two world wars, the Cold War, and decolonization. It also explores the global economy, particularly the rapid rise of East Asia; global ecological shifts including recent climate change; and social and cultural transformations such as migration, urbanization, or the rise of globalized popular music and sport. The pace and scope of global integration in this last century and a half is extraordinary, and many peoples and communities found the rapidity of changes wrenching or the direction of change unwelcome. Part 6 explains why the pace was so fast and the process so disruptive.

CONSIDERING THE EVIDENCE OF WORLD HISTORY

One last point to bear in mind before the story begins. Understanding history is like assembling a challenging jigsaw puzzle. Some of the pieces clearly fit together in obvious ways. Most of them don't, and it is not easy to know what to make of them. Many of the pieces are missing, hidden under the rugs of time. All this means that history is an exercise in creating plausible interpretations from incomplete evidence.

One needs to use imagination disciplined by evidence to arrive at a reliable reconstruction of the past. It is evidence—written texts, works of art, archeology, oral traditions, historical linguistics, and now also genetic analysis—that helps us figure out what is plausible and what isn't, what arguments to accept and what to reject. Among the skills history teaches are the abilities to assess evidence thoughtfully and to recognize when the evidence is insufficient or contradictory, making strong conclusions difficult.

When multiple pieces of evidence seem to be saying the same thing, and especially when different types of evidence harmonize, we can be more confident of our conclusions. So, for example, when linguistic evidence, genetic evidence, and pottery fragments all suggest that people from West Africa filtered into central and southern Africa beginning roughly 1500 BCE, we can be confident that something historians call the Bantu migration took place—even though there is not a single written document that says anything about it. If pottery were the only evidence, we could not be sure about the migration—people can trade pots over long distances, one person to the next, without migrating. If we had only the genetic or the linguistic evidence, we would have only the fuzziest idea about when the migration occurred.

For the deeper past, we have fewer written records, and none more than 5,000 years old. In some places—the Americas, Oceania, and most of sub-Saharan Africa, for example—written records are non-existent or at best extremely rare until 500 years ago. In these situations, other forms of evidence such as archeological remains or genetic analysis become much more important in underpinning interpretations of the past.

Keep in mind too that written documents almost always reflect the viewpoints of adults rather than children, men rather than women, rich rather than poor, powerful rather than weak, and literate rather than illiterate. In archeology, as well, we are likelier to find the remains of royal palaces built of stone than peasant huts made of thatched reeds. Historians (and other scholars) have shown some ingenuity in overcoming these inherent biases, "reading against the grain" as historians often put it. But these asymmetries of information remain, and it is important to remain aware of them.

Sifting, evaluating, and interpreting incomplete and sometimes contradictory evidence, and evidence of different types, are crucial intellectual skills. The study of history, and especially world history, hones those skills. As Ziauddin Barani, a scholar of the fourteenth century writing in Persian but working in India, said: "I have not observed such advantages from any branch of learning as I have from history." The branches of learning have changed since his day, as a grounding in history would lead you to expect, but he could still be right.

ACKNOWLEDGMENTS

During the years devoted to researching, writing, and revising this book, I have accumulated deep debts to many people. First to acknowledge are those to my former students who have read parts of the text and suggested improvements: Kwabenah Akuamoah-Boateng, Dan Brendtro, Adrienne Kates, Michelle Melton, Ani Muradyan, and Michael Samway. Then various classes of History 007 and History 008 in recent years, under-graduates who collectively made thousands of (anonymous) comments on a first draft of the book. Because the book is written for students, their feedback proved enormously valuable. I also wish to thank—enormously—Robynne Mellor and Javier Puente, who worked as teaching assistants in my world history classes and provided their own advice on drafts of the book. And Benan Grams, a PhD student who helped me with medieval Arabic passages.

I am fortunate to have family members willing to share their unvarnished opinions of my prose. These include Katriona McNeill and Patrick McNeill, Mairead MacRae, Leila Meymand, and especially my sister and brother-in-law Ruth McNeill and Bart Jones. They read every word of every chapter and were not stingy with their advice. My sister taught me to read before I went to school and ever since, it seems, has felt a responsibility to improve my facility with the English language. When she read my PhD dissertation, she wrote that it could be improved if I added 20 commas per page, and it would hardly matter where I put them. I must have taken her suggestion too strongly, because when she read this book she said I should remove most of its commas. My wife, Julie Billingsley, also read passages and suggested, tactfully, that I should try to make the book more amusing.

Another family member earned my deepest thanks although he never read a word of this book. In his final years my father, William McNeill, never failed to ask me when I would finish it, which spurred me along. Debating with him how best to present the big picture in our short, co-authored book, *The Human Web: A Bird's-Eye View of World History* (2003), influenced the thinking behind this book more strongly than anything else—other than my years teaching world history.

Several professional colleagues also earned my deep gratitude. Three experienced world history teachers helped shape my understanding of how to introduce the subject to students: Alan Karras of the University of California and Merry Wiesner-Hanks of the University of Wisconsin–Milwaukee, with both of whom I served for several years creating and vetting questions for the Advanced Placement world history examination; and the late Jerry Bentley of the University of Hawaii. Rick Potts of the American Museum of Natural History, an expert in human evolution, helped me avoid missteps in the first chapter. At the Foundation for Civic Space and Public Policy in Warsaw, Poland, professors Spasimir Domaradzki, Maciej Janowski, Dariusz Kołodziejczyk, and Jan Szemiński critiqued parts of the manuscript, correcting some of my misconceptions especially about central and eastern European history. My colleagues in the History Department and Walsh School of Foreign Service at Georgetown University have contributed to my education in countless ways over the past 30-plus years. Their insights, perspectives, knowledge, and encouragement have enabled me to come to grips with world history in ways unimaginable to me without their help.

I wish to acknowledge as well the superb work of a team of colleagues at W. W. Norton, beginning with Steve Forman, who has patiently supervised the entire project from start to finish, read multiple drafts, and made thousands of valuable suggestions—of which I probably should have taken more than I did. Lily Gellman was invaluable in her orchestration of myriad details in the publishing process. Alice Vigliani, the excellent manuscript editor, improved and tightened my prose and eliminated some of those extraneous commas to which I am now apparently prone. Charlotte Miller, our outstanding cartographer, created an ambitious map program with insight and vigor, and politely tolerated my endless suggestions for revisions. Gerra Goff and Stephanie Romeo were creative and resourceful in building the extensive illustrations program. Melissa Atkin brought order to the puzzle pieces of the book as project editor. Jillian Burr, our brilliant designer, created beautiful book and jacket designs. Sarah Bartley gave us timely advice from the perspectives of marketing and sales. Carson Russell, our media editor, planned and implemented the important digital resources that support the book; and Jane Searle, our production manager, kept this big train running on schedule.

REVIEWERS OF THE FIRST EDITION

Other professional colleagues, most of whom I have never met, have also worked wonders for this book. World history teachers and scholars from many colleges in the United States and abroad have read draft chapters and made useful suggestions:

Anthony Barbieri-Low, University of California, Santa Barbara
Hayden Bellenoit, United States Naval Academy
David Biggs, University of California, Riverside
Beau Bowers, Central Piedmont Community College—Levine
Kevin Brady, Tidewater Community College—Chesapeake Campus
Gary Burgess, United States Naval Academy
Annette Chamberlin, Virginia Western Community College
Stephen Chappell, James Madison University
Katy Clay, Shippensburg University
Sean C.D. Colbert-Lewis, Sr., North Carolina Central University
Phyllis Conn, St. John's University
Judith Davis, Three Rivers College
Peter De Rosa, Bridgewater State University
Eric Dursteler, Brigham Young University
Gregory Ference, Salisbury University
Allen Fromherz, Georgia State University
Denis Gainty, Georgia State University
Jessica Gerard, Ozarks Technical Community College
Rachael Goldman, Rutgers University
Noah Goode, Central Piedmont Community College—Levine
Andrew Goss, University of New Orleans
Candice Goucher, Washington State University
Hans Hägerdal, Linnaeus University
Sarah Hamilton, Auburn University
Ann Hardgrove, University of Texas at San Antonio
Matthew Herbst, University of California, San Diego
Carsten Hjort Lange, Aalborg University
Stephanie Holyfield, Wesley College
Paul Stephen Hudson, Georgia State Perimeter College
John Hyland, Newport University
Joanna Jury, Georgia State University
Sofia Laurein, San Diego City College
Jess LeVine, Brookdale Community College
Scott Lloyd, University of Arkansas
Anthony Makowski, Delaware County Community College—
   Marple Campus
Harold Marcuse, University of California, Santa Barbara
Matthew McCoy, University of Arkansas—Fort Smith Campus
Ian Miller, St John's University—Queens Campus
Elizabeth Milliken, Mount Hood Community College
Philip Misevich, St. John's University
Lance Nolde, California State University, Channel Islands

Hosok O, Dixie State University

Annette Palmer, Morgan State University

Alejandro Quintana, St John's University—Queens Campus

Daren Ray, Auburn University

Charles V. Reed, Elizabeth City State University

Thomas J. Rushford, Northern Virginia Community College—
    Annandale Campus

Ruma N. Salhi, Northern Virginia Community College—
    Annandale Campus

Christine Senecal, Shippensburg State University

Michael Seth, James Madison University

Emily Story, Salisbury University

Barbara Syrrakos, City College of New York

Peter Utgaard, Cuyamaca College

Evan Ward, Brigham Young University

Molly Warsh, University of Pittsburgh

James Webb, Colby College

Andre Wink, University of Wisconsin

Jennifer Winters, Northern Virginia Community College—
    Annandale Campus

In a book that aims to explore the history of the world from the origins of humans until today, there are sure to be more than a few lapses. Those are all my fault and no one else's.

J. R. McNeill, *Georgetown University*

THE WEBS *of* HUMANKIND

A WORLD HISTORY

SEAGULL EDITION

Volume One

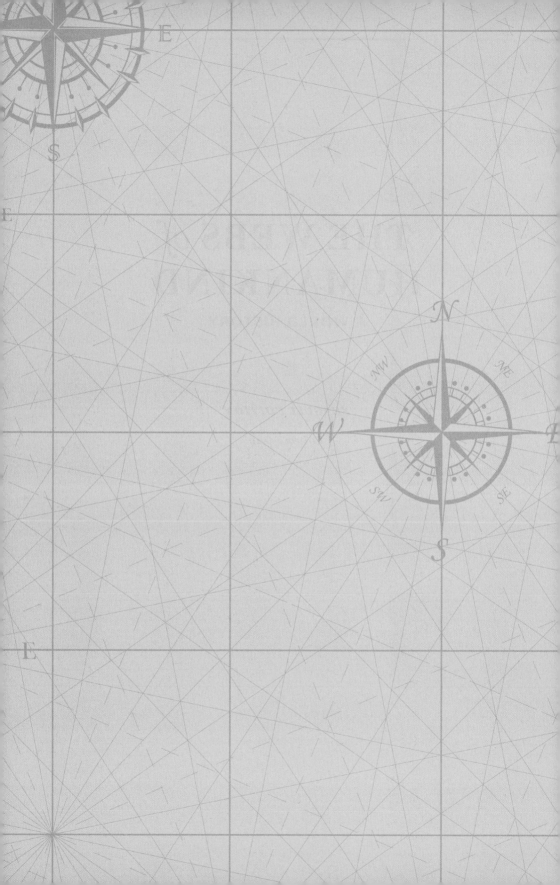

THE FIRST 99.93 PERCENT OF HUMAN HISTORY

Part I (Chapters 1 through 3) of this book deals with the history of humans and our hominin ancestors up until about 5,000 years ago. That means it covers about 97 percent of the history of our species, *Homo sapiens*, and about 99.93 percent of the history of hominins. (Hominins are our branch of the family of apes, which diverged from the ancestors of today's chimpanzees about 7 million years ago.) The two most important things to know about this long stretch of history are that nobody knows much about it because the evidence is so scanty, and that cultural and social changes came slowly by the standard of more recent history. A third point, but a less important one, is that there is no satisfactory way to slice up the first 99.93 percent of human history into periods that fit the facts everywhere around the world.

Sources of Evidence

Here's how we know what we *think* we know about the long stretch of time, 7 million to 250,000 years ago, during which our hominin ancestors evolved into modern humans. Our information mainly comes from the study of very ancient bones and stone tools. Systematic archeological work in what may be the cradle of humankind, East Africa, began in the 1930s. Only a few thousand artifacts from that long period have been dug up and analyzed, and those artifacts are—inevitably—a biased sample. Bones, teeth, stone tools, and a few footprints survived, but no soft tissues, no wooden tools, let alone any evidence of our remote ancestors' mental world. Moreover, the artifacts all come from only a few sites where conditions were dry enough to allow preservation. Dating of these artifacts is imprecise, which makes for contentious debates among specialists.

Since 2004, a few remarkable new discoveries, explained in Chapter 1, have re-written the story of human evolution. And you should expect more discoveries in the years to come. Archeology for any period is a bit like a challenging jigsaw puzzle with most of the pieces missing. It can only provide fragments of the full picture. Fortunately, there are other ways to get at the remote human past.

Ever since the deciphering of the human genome began in the 1990s, a new form of evidence about human history has rapidly become available. The study of ancient genetic material is now known as paleogenomics. The distribution of certain varieties of genes can tell us much about human origins and migrations—for example, that the humans who left Africa about 100,000 years ago probably were few in number, probably only around 100 to 1,000 individuals. All non-Africans in the world are descended from those few.

A weak link in paleogenomics is chronology. Scientists make assumptions about the rate of genetic mutations over time in order to try to date events in the past, such as the exodus from Africa. But the margin of error in such estimates is considerable. Archeology is usually better than paleogenomics for dating things.

Another way to make inferences about what life was like among the earliest humans is to examine current societies that maintain the same general way of life followed by early humans: foraging, hunting, and (in places) fishing. Anthropologists have studied such groups carefully in recent decades to make educated guesses about the human condition 50,000 or 100,000 years ago. Their observations suggest, for example, that our ancient ancestors spent only a few hours each day foraging and hunting their food, and that they enjoyed a lot of leisure time. This anthropological approach is instructive, but it's also just as unreliable as any other because it's hard to know which social traits have changed the most and which the least over such long spans of time.

Archeology, paleogenomics, and inference based on current forager-hunters are the three main sources of information about early humans and other hominins. Even when used together, the three methods leave lots of interesting questions unanswered. So these chapters are—regrettably but necessarily—peppered with words such as *perhaps* and *probably*.

Slow Change

The second important thing to remember about this long span of history, beyond the uncertainty, is that change was slow in early human societies. The genetic evolution of our ancestors and our own species took place over thousands of generations, with only imperceptible change from one generation to the next. Cultural evolution was also slow. The record of changes in tools is the best evidence of this. As Chapter 1 explains, tools showed very little change until roughly 50,000 years ago. And even then, in what is sometimes called a cultural revolution, the pace of change remained glacial by today's standards. In thinking about history before about 15,000 years ago, we have to contemplate immense stretches of time that were marked by strong continuity in culture.

Problems of Periodization

Scholars divide up this immensity of time in a few different ways, none of them truly satisfactory. Some scholars use the term *prehistory* to refer to the entire human past before the invention of writing (which occurred roughly 5,000 years ago). This book doesn't use the term on the grounds that there are now so many ways to learn about the human past that the invention of writing is no longer the watershed moment that it once seemed. The term *prehistory* is going out of fashion, and deservedly so.

Natural scientists generally use terms that come from geology, and they divide the last several million years into epochs such as the *Pliocene* (5.3 million years ago to 2.6 million years ago) and the *Pleistocene* (2.6 million years ago until 11,700 years ago). This book rarely uses these terms and confines them to discussion of matters such as climate shifts.

Other scholars, especially archeologists, divide up the distant past based on the materials used to make tools and weapons. Thus they refer to a *stone age*, eventually followed in some places by *bronze ages* and *iron ages*. This scheme emphasizes certain aspects of archaic peoples' lives—tool technology—over others. The main advantage of using this scheme is that evidence for tool technology shows up well in the archeological record. This book employs a version of this terminology in its early chapters and refers to the Paleolithic and Neolithic eras.

The Paleolithic literally means "old stone age" and in this book refers to the time span from the first appearance of stone tools anywhere until the first evidence of farming anywhere (about 2.6 million years ago until about 13,000 years ago). *The Neolithic* means "new stone age" and in this book refers to the time between the earliest sign of agriculture anywhere about 13,000 years ago and the first appearance of cities anywhere about 5,000 years ago. Note that specialists in archeology use these terms to mean different slices of time in different places, typically depending on local dates for the first tool use, agriculture, and cities. So, for example, the Neolithic began later in Southeast Asia than in Southwest Asia. This book will not use *Paleolithic* or *Neolithic* to mean different periods for different places.

This difficulty of terminology reflects the strong local and regional focus of archeologists and the weakness of global perspectives. Because they do painstaking local work, without which we would know almost nothing about the deep past, archeologists don't need terms for time periods that will work everywhere around the globe. That is why we don't have a satisfactory vocabulary for thinking about deep history in general and its periodization in particular.

Chapters 1 and 2 explore the ancestry and evolution of the human species, which took its—our—approximate shape about 250,000 years ago. They also cover our colonization of the globe from about 100,000 to about 13,000 years ago, and our cultural evolution along the way. Chapter 3 focuses on the more rapid cultural change that led some of our ancestors to settle down, farm, and—about 5,000 years ago—start to create cities, governments, writing, and other features of human societies that govern our lives today. In each chapter of Part 1, as throughout the book, we are concerned with the connections among human communities and how those grew to become webs of interaction.

Last Hominin Standing

BECOMING HUMAN

FOCUS QUESTIONS

1. What significant events led to the emergence of human ancestors?

2. What were the major traits and skills that distinguished our species, *Homo sapiens*?

3. What were the major characteristics of the hominin species most closely related to us?

4. How did the global migrations of *Homo sapiens* contribute to increasing cultural and genetic diversification?

5. In what ways did human culture change dramatically in the late Paleolithic period?

In 1974 in Ethiopia, a pair of paleontologists (scientists who find and interpret fossil remains) decided to take an unusual route back to their camp. Walking through a gully, they spied what looked like an arm bone resting on the ground. A moment's inspection told them they had happened upon a relative, perhaps an ancestor, of the human race. In camp that evening, the paleontologists celebrated the find with their French and American teammates, and because the Beatles song "Lucy in the Sky with Diamonds" was playing on their tape machine, they named the skeleton to which the arm bone belonged "Lucy."

CHRONOLOGY

ca. 66 million years ago Asteroid hitting Yucatán Peninsula causes massive extinction event

ca. 6 million–4.5 million years ago Bipedalism evolves

3.2 million years ago Lifetime of the hominin Lucy

2.6 million years ago Paleolithic period begins

ca. 2.5 million years ago First evidence of tool use

Between 2 million and 120,000 years ago Language emerges

ca. 1.5 million years ago *Homo erectus* emerges

Between 1.5 million and 500,000 years ago Hominins first control fire

ca. 400,000 years ago Neanderthals emerge

ca. 300,000–200,000 years ago *Homo sapiens* emerges

ca. 190,000 years ago *Homo erectus* goes extinct

ca. 130,000 years ago Last ice age begins

ca. 100,000–65,000 years ago *Homo sapiens* migrates out of Africa

ca. 90,000 years ago Flores Island "Hobbits" appear; late Paleolithic cultural revolution begins

ca. 75,000 years ago Mount Toba erupts

ca. 50,000–30,000 years ago Neanderthals, Denisovans, Flores Islands "Hobbits" go extinct

Lucy was a marvelous discovery. Paleontologists and other specialists hunting for early human remains generally count themselves lucky to find a tooth or a finger bone. But after two weeks of digging and scratching, the paleontologists who found Lucy's arm bone uncovered hundreds of bone fragments, amounting to about 40 percent of her skeleton.

Lucy was a young adult female who died of unknown causes about 3.2 million years ago. She stood about 3′7″ (1.1 m) tall and weighed about 65 lbs. (30 kg). Her feet, pelvis, and spine were astonishingly human-like, but her cranium, teeth, and jaw more ape-like. She walked upright and probably ate mostly fruits, vegetables, and leaves. Her hands suggest she was good at climbing trees. Her braincase was in the average range for modern chimps, only one-third the size of your brain. She is classified as an *Australopithecus afarensis*, a species of hominin that lived in what is now Ethiopia and Kenya about 4 million to 3 million years ago. (The term **hominins** refers to humans, all extinct branches of humans, and all our ape-like ancestors over the last 7 million years.) After touring the world's museums for several years, Lucy now makes her home in a climate-controlled vault in a museum in Ethiopia's capital city of Addis Ababa. Lucy's bones provided more new information about human origins and evolution than any previous find, but her skeleton contained only fragments of the human story.

It's disconcerting to admit it, but we are, all of us, descended from a very ancient mammal that looked something like a modern tree shrew—a small, slender, furry creature. And like all earthlings, our ancestry ultimately extends back to single-celled creatures resembling pond scum. It was highly unlikely that the course of biological evolution should have produced modern humans. If, somehow, the epic could start up again, it almost certainly would turn out differently—just as human history, if magically replayed, would almost certainly not produce Aztecs or Buddhism or the Constitution of the United States. Biological evolution, like human history, was and is full of chance. Nonetheless, biological evolution did produce us, and it's instructive to think about how that unlikely turn of events happened.

This chapter deals with the story of human origins, the migrations of people from their original African home to the far corners of the Earth, and the fabric of life during the period scholars call the Paleolithic. It ends with the burst of cultural change that occurred near the end of the Paleolithic, roughly 70,000 to 15,000 years ago. During the Paleolithic, even though people were few and widely scattered, they retained connections that spanned the inhabited world. As we will see, there is reason to suppose that even when transportation meant walking and communications technology consisted only of speech, a slender and faint web embraced all our ancestors.

ca. 50,000–12,000 years ago Massive megafauna extinctions

ca. 45,000 years ago *Homo sapiens* enters Europe

ca. 40,000 years ago *Homo sapiens* reaches Australia and Tasmania

ca. 30,000 years ago *Homo sapiens* reaches China and Japan

ca. 23,000–14,000 years ago *Homo sapiens* reaches the Americas

13,000 years ago Paleolithic period ends

12,000 years ago Last ice age ends

Life on Earth

The human story goes back to the origins of our universe, which scientists now think happened in the **Big Bang** some 13.8 billion years ago. In this mysterious moment, time, space, and energy somehow began. The universe started out hot (trillions of degrees), dense, and smaller than an atom. Ever since that initial moment, the universe has been cooling and expanding. It reached the immense size of a galaxy in a fraction of a second. Protons, neutrons, and electrons—the building blocks of all matter, including our bodies—appeared in the first few minutes. Within the first 300,000 years after the Big Bang, most of these building blocks had formed into atoms of hydrogen and helium. Gravity collected these atoms into stars, and the stars into galaxies such as the Milky Way, which includes our sun and billions of neighboring stars.

The sun and our solar system, Earth included, took shape about 4.6 billion years ago. Then, in a process for which no consensus explanation yet exists, life emerged on Earth about 3.8 billion years ago, perhaps in the hot thermal vents under the oceans. For most of its career, life on Earth was dull, lived by single-celled organisms sloshing about in the seas. Not until about 1.2 billion years ago were there multi-celled organisms, and no

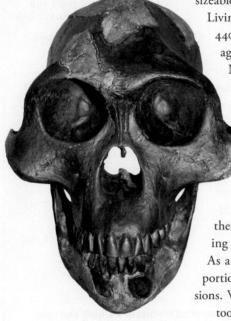

Lucy The skull of Lucy, an early hominin, indicates a brain size comparable to that of modern chimpanzees.

sizeable animals until about 600 million years ago. Living things climbed onto dry land to stay some 440 million years ago, and by 240 million years ago dinosaurs and small mammals walked Earth. New forms of life were appearing faster now, because life on land evolved in response to more variable conditions than in the sea.

Life anywhere on Earth was risky business. Every now and then an asteroid, meteorite, or something else hurtling through space smashed into the planet. Volcanoes rumbled and belched forth fire and toxic gases. The continents slid here and there, slowly crunching into one another, opening and closing seas and raising mountain chains. As a result of these and other hazards, large proportions of life on Earth went extinct on five occasions. Whenever this happened, biological evolution took new directions. On the last such occasion, when an asteroid slammed into the northwestern Yucatán Peninsula in Mexico about 66 million years ago, the shock from its impact opened a crater the size of Belgium or Maryland. It ignited fires that consumed much of the planet's vegetation, and it raised a veil of dust that blocked sunlight and chilled the Earth. All land animals bigger than a medium-sized dog went extinct, including all dinosaurs and most other reptiles. The meek inherited the Earth. Among the meek were small mammals, such as the ancient tree shrew that is our ancestor.

Within a few million years, there were many new kinds of mammals, creatures that couldn't have gotten their start had dinosaurs still trodden the Earth. The first primates (the extended family of primates comprises all monkeys and apes, including humans) soon emerged. By 35 million years ago, creatures that looked like modern monkeys had evolved, and some 15 million years later, ancient apes appeared. From genetic evidence, it now seems that the last common ancestor of humans and chimpanzees lived around 7 to 5 million years ago. Although we still share 98.4 percent of our genetic material with chimps, even 1.6 percent can make quite a difference. The chimpanzee ancestors stayed in forest habitats and eventually evolved into the two modern chimpanzee species. Human ancestors adapted to changing climate and ecology by fleeing the forest for what was slowly becoming the East African savanna. This is now a land of plentiful grass, scarce water, and only occasional trees; but 5 million years ago, it was a mosaic of forest, shrubs, and grassland.

Our Hominin Ancestors

A bewildering variety of hominins roamed the African earth over the last 5 million years. Early hominins had brains, and probably habits, more like chimpanzees' than like ours today. Fossil hunters have found about 18 different species of hominin, each with a double-barreled, tongue-twisting name such as *Australopithecus afarensis*, Lucy's species.

Regrettably, we don't know much about how our own species evolved over the last 5 or 6 million years. We don't know whether it happened gradually or in comparatively sudden leaps. We don't know when the various steps took place, and we don't know why it happened. The evidence is still too spotty. But there are a few things we can say with some assurance about the evolution of humans. It surely happened in Africa: the earliest remains of hominins have been found mainly in Chad, Ethiopia, and Kenya. Human evolution happened over hundreds of thousands of gener-

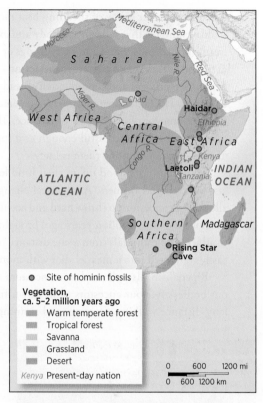

African Vegetation and Hominin Fossil Sites The location of belts and patches of forest, grassland, and desert have changed considerably over the time in which humankind evolved. Hominin remains are mainly found in what were savanna zones, and it is likely that most of our hominin ancestors' history took place there.

ations, until, by about 300,000 to 200,000 years ago, our species, ***Homo sapiens***, had definitively emerged somewhere between the areas of modern-day Morocco and Tanzania. And the first big step toward the emergence of our species was standing upright.

Bipedalism

One of the crucial distinctions, and apparently the earliest, that separates our recent ancestors and ourselves from other apes is that we stand and walk upright. **Bipedalism** evolved about 6 to 4.5 million years ago. It may have been a result of climate change—drier conditions that expanded the savanna and made upright posture more rewarding by affording a better vantage point from which to see opportunities and dangers. It may have developed as a way of shedding heat more efficiently by reducing the amount of midday sunlight that falls on the body and exposing it to more wind. Bipedalism also freed the forelimbs (hands) to carry things or pick fruit from bushes and trees. For one or several of these reasons, **natural selection**—the process through which genetic traits helpful for survival and reproduction spread over many generations, enabling species to better adapt to their environment—favored bipedalism in hominins. It also favored the development of a fine sense of balance. The first bipedal hominins were short and small-brained, but successful enough as a species to survive for over 2 million years. The most famous among them is Lucy.

After hominins stood up on their hind legs, they eventually became good throwers, walkers, and runners. Anatomical changes, especially to the shoulder, gradually allowed our ancestors to throw hard and accurately. This new skill, which seems to have developed about 2 million years ago, brought many advantages, including the ability to attack edible animals from a safe distance by pelting them with rocks. Safer hunting easily translated into a meatier diet with more protein and fats.

Bipedalism also allowed our ancestors to run better. Many of the changes in our bodies after our ancestors came down from the trees resulted from selection for long-distance walking, trotting, and running prowess: loss of body fur, proliferation of sweat glands, longer legs, narrower waists, arched feet (which provide extra spring) with short toes, neck ligaments that keep our heavy heads from jolting, shoulders that allow our arms to swing free, knees and ankles that serve as shock absorbers.

Thanks to all these bodily changes, humans could (and can) jog long distances in warm weather better than any other animal. Good marathoners today can outrun a horse over 26 miles. While the fastest human sprinters are almost turtle-like over short distances compared to other animals of our African homeland, fit humans can outlast anything on the savanna, even antelopes, mainly because we can keep cool more efficiently by sweating.

Hominin Ancestors These *Australopithecus afarensis* footprints, preserved in volcanic ash over 3 million years ago, show that our ancestors had a foot structure like ours, enabling them to walk upright. These are the footprints of two adults and a child and, at right, an ancestor of the horse.

As they became good distance walkers and runners, our ancestors could cover more ground; gather, hunt, and scavenge much more food; and sustain larger groups. Improved mobility brought new selective pressures for better memory of terrain, better communication, and better social coordination for actions like getting and sharing food and for defense against predators or rivals. Hominins that somehow were a little better at these tasks stood a much better chance, in the long run, of surviving and reproducing. In this way, bipedalism may have helped stimulate bigger and better brains even as better running and throwing allowed a richer diet that could feed such brains. In short, our bodies probably evolved primarily to jog for hours under the hot sun, while our brains probably evolved to handle complicated social situations.

Big Brains

Our brains are big, complex, and capable. Lucy and her hominin kin had brains the same size as those of modern chimpanzees—much smaller than ours. For *Homo sapiens*, the ratio of brain size to body size is three times bigger than is normal in the animal kingdom. Our big brains are also amazingly complex, possibly the most complex structures in the universe, with 100 billion cells and perhaps 80,000 miles of pathways linking cells to one another. The neural connections in the brain of a 20-year-old, if laid end to end, could wrap around the Earth at least three times.

The size and complexity of our brains come at a cost. Our brains are energy guzzlers: we devote 20 to 25 percent of our metabolism to keeping them well supplied with oxygen and nutrients; other mammals use about 5 percent. Big-brained hominins needed lots of high-quality food rich in proteins and fats. Some small-brained apes can survive by foraging for fruits, roots, berries, and the like. But for big-brained hominins, this sort of diet was insufficient. Our ancestors had to take the risks associated with hunting animals or scavenging the kills of other predators for fats and protein, unless they lived somewhere with abundant fish and shellfish. They had to become hunters and scavengers as well as foragers.

Big brains also require more cooling. An overheated brain doesn't work properly, and a big one is more difficult to keep cool than a small one. Overheating was a real risk under the African sun, especially for those who needed to trot for hours on end after antelope, gazelle, or wildebeest. The evolutionary answer to this problem was nearly hairless skin with plenty of sweat glands, which had become standard equipment on some hominins by about 1.6 million years ago. Humans are by far the sweatiest of primates, and together with horses by far the sweatiest of creatures. The importance of sweat as the body's equivalent of engine coolant meant that our ancestors needed to drink plenty of liquids, walk efficiently between water sources, and have a good sense of where to find water. Even so, they couldn't afford to venture far from water—a real constraint in many environments.

Big brains—or skulls big enough to house big brains—carry another cost as well: they make childbirth hazardous for mothers. Before modern medical interventions, about 1–3 percent of births killed the mother. That usually resulted in the death of the infant as well. With these costs, big brains had to offer great advantages; otherwise, natural selection would have made sure we don't have them. The greatest advantages of big brains were the ability to form larger social groups and the imagination to invent tools, harness fire, and develop language. All these achievements were related, but we'll look at them one at a time.

Social Cooperation Bigger brains probably allowed our ancestors to capitalize on the advantages of mobility and bipedalism by organizing tighter, more cooperative, and possibly larger groups. Individuals with brains that could recognize the rewards of cooperation and sharing, and organize more cohesive groups, enjoyed better survival chances. Through teamwork, they could reap benefits from more efficient foraging, scavenging, and hunting.

Improved teamwork made it possible to coordinate foraging strategically over larger territories, assigning specific roles to group members. Teamwork also enabled people to hunt bigger animals with greater safety by fixing a plan of attack. Better coordination raised the quantity of food available, and improved cooperation meant that less food went to waste. No single hunter, not even a team of hunters, could eat a two-ton hippo before its meat began to spoil. But if they shared it with others, confident the favor (or an equivalent) would one day be returned, no meat need go bad. Sharing food strategically—which other primates scarcely do at all, except mother to infant—radically improved everyone's survival chances, because even the best foragers and hunters have bad days. Moreover, keeping others who were inefficient foragers and hunters alive allowed the most efficient food-getters to concentrate on getting food rather than doing other chores. Early hominins figured out that a society could benefit collectively from specialization and exchange.

In short, bigger brains permitted greater social cooperation, and tighter social units in turn promoted bigger brains. Both processes allowed a dietary shift toward more meat—the proteins and fats that, in turn, fed bigger brains. Humans are by far the most cooperative of primates. Ants and bees cooperate intricately by instinct. We do it more as a result of culture—the collective habits, skills, and achievements that we transmit from one generation to the next, which only creatures with big brains can develop.

Pair Bonding Bigger brains may also have complicated the hominin social scene—specifically, what scholars call mate selection. Chimpanzees live in small social groups in which dominant males keep a harem of several females and respond violently to any rival male's attention toward harem members. Male chimps are much larger than female chimps, a pattern that prevailed among early hominin species as well. To judge by the available skeletons, females on average weighed about 60 to 75 percent as much as males among our early forebears. Like chimps, these early hominins also probably lived in small hierarchical groups in which females reproduced with one dominant male and most males had no offspring.

But at some point a different pattern evolved. About 1.5 million years ago, one hominin species (early ***Homo erectus***, called by some scholars *Homo ergaster*) emerged in which males and females were closer in size. This may have signaled the beginning of male-female pair bonding, an arrangement in which couples enter into long-term partnerships. Today, pair bonding is characteristic in most human societies, in one species of small ape called gibbons, and in a few distantly related species, mainly birds. With pair bonding, all males have a good chance at securing a mate and reproducing. They can coexist less violently, live together in larger social groups, and find it rewarding to take a durable interest in one female and offspring—which male chimps decidedly do not.

To the extent that males cared for their children, they helped their species to prosper. Among other ape species today, mothers get comparatively little help and must breast-feed their offspring for six or seven years. They then cease providing for their young soon after the young are weaned. Hominins, however, gradually evolved a system in which the young were weaned earlier, and caring for toddlers was shared by mothers, grandmothers, aunts, older sisters—and even males who could be enticed into helping with the children. This evolving arrangement translated into higher fertility, because adult females who aren't breast-feeding are far more likely to conceive than those who are breast-feeding. This approach possibly led to higher infant and child survival rates, because the incapacitation or death of a mother didn't automatically doom her children. In this way—perhaps—hominins out-competed other less cooperative apes by helping mothers raise the young.

If comparative male-female body size is any guide, then early *Homo erectus* (or *Homo ergaster*), who lived 1.9 million to 1.4 million years ago in eastern and southern Africa, was the pioneer of greater sexual equality. Subsequent hominin species all showed narrower differences in size between males and females. Among humans today, males on average are 17 percent heavier and 8 percent taller than females. Greater physical and social equality between the sexes and pair bonding rewarded better brains, because navigating the social scene so as to get and keep a good mate, or to trade up for a better one, was—and remains—a mentally challenging process. Beyond tracking social relations, there are three other crucial skills that our ancestors' outsized brains proved useful for: toolmaking, fire management, and language.

Toolmaking The first evidence of tool use dates to about 2.5 million years ago, before the hominin brain had grown much. Early tools were chipped from stone and used for cutting and smashing—actions that were probably helpful for getting at bone marrow, a rich source of protein. Toolmaking required imagination and dexterity, and perhaps over time toolmaking hominins developed these traits, stimulating further refinement of their mental capacities. (Incidentally, archeologists think most early toolmakers were right-handed, from patterns in the chipped stones. About 90 percent of humans are right-handed today.) Stone tools available more than 2 million years ago enabled

Hand Axe Hand axes found in northern France were likely used by *Homo erectus* to butcher the carcasses of large animals. This one dates to 800,000 years ago.

hominins to cut meat better than a sharp-toothed lion and dig up roots and tubers better than a sharp-tusked warthog.

Once good stone tools were invented, tool technology stagnated. For nearly a million years, hominins used the same sorts of tools, made in the same ways. Then, around 1.6 million years ago, a new generation of tools was invented—notably, a double-sided hand axe, which was good for butchering large animals. These served, with virtually no modification, for another million years—until a mere 500,000 or 300,000 years ago. One variety of archaic humans, *Homo erectus*, wandered out of Africa all the way to Southeast Asia, but everywhere they went their hand axes looked just like the ones their distant cousins used in Africa. Archaic humans were conservative in their culture and technology.

After about 400,000 years ago, that conservatism slowly waned and a few innovative ideas spread. These included attaching wooden handles to stone tools, using projectiles as weapons, and applying pigments as decoration. The evolution of the hominin tool kit apparently came in occasional leaps more than in slow, steady modifications. If the links between tools and brains were strong (better brains, better tools; better tools, better food, better brains), then perhaps the evolution of the brain sometimes came in leaps as well.

Control of Fire Other primates, notably chimpanzees, use primitive tools such as sticks to probe holes in the ground at spots that might contain tasty insects. But only hominins have ever controlled fire. Control of fire was probably more important as a cultural accomplishment than the invention of stone tools; but because it shows up poorly in the archeological record, we know much less about it. We have only the haziest idea when hominins first came to control fire. It may have been as recent as half a million years ago, or as long ago as 1.5 million years. Control of fire was so useful that it probably spread quickly. With fire, our ancestors could keep warm in colder climates, which opened higher latitudes and higher elevations to them. They could keep dangerous animals at bay—especially at night, when big cats, for example, had the advantages of keener smell and better night vision. They could brandish fire to scare carnivores away from their kills or to aid in their own hunting. They could burn whole landscapes, turning forests into grasslands to attract tasty herbivores—in effect, converting natural vegetation into good habitat for animals they could eat, and therefore, good habitat for themselves. And, perhaps most important, with fire our ancestors could cook.

Cooking increased the amount of food available. Scorching or smoking meat delays its decay. Cooking kills some bacteria, neutralizes some toxins, tenderizes tough fibers and meats, and alters the chemistry of molecules in ways that ease human digestion. Today's chimps and gorillas have much larger intestines than we have, and they can digest a wider range of raw organic materials than we can. They don't need to cook. But about 60 percent of their food intake is needed just to provide the energy for chewing and digesting. Cooking enabled our ancestors, in effect, to outsource and speed up digestion, thus requiring less elaborate stomachs and intestines. Thanks to cooking, they no longer needed big jaws and large teeth either.

The harnessing of fire probably had social consequences as well as dietary ones. Managing fire—finding fuel, stoking a flame, keeping it under control—required cooperation. It was a skill that had to be taught carefully to the young. Groups that managed fire probably developed a stronger solidarity because if they didn't cooperate successfully, they couldn't keep fire under control. Fire-wielders might even have sent rudimentary messages by smoke signals, even before speech emerged. The usefulness of fire is reflected in its universality: every human group, however remote, has used it—although some (generally, isolated groups confined to islands) could only preserve fire, not make it.

Language If anything our remote ancestors did proved more important than harnessing fire, it was developing language. Other species have systems of communication: for example, bees transmit information by dancing, and ants do so by releasing chemical scents. Chimpanzees use about 30 different calls to communicate. Only humans have fully developed language, capable of communicating abstract meanings. The average American 20-year-old knows roughly 40,000 words, although most people regularly use only about 4,000 of them. They can combine those words to transmit an almost infinite number of meanings.

Language is a biological adaptation as well as a cultural one. In order to speak, our ancestors had to develop peculiar anatomical features, such as a long and low larynx, which is absent elsewhere in the animal kingdom. Our ancestors' brains, as well as their larynxes, evolved so as to permit us to speak and understand language. Indeed, this is partly what human brains are *for*, and why they're wired the way they are. Between ages one and four, healthy humans learn to understand and speak whatever languages surround them, without being taught. That is a large part of what makes us human; no other creatures can do it.

The ability to use language, even if it began as a simple code with minimal grammar or syntax, conferred great advantages. It allowed the sharing of practical information (e.g., "lion behind bush") that improved survival chances. As language evolved and improved, it permitted groups to plan hunts in detail, work out quarrels peacefully, and teach skills to youngsters with greater efficiency. Language, like fire, was so useful that those groups who had it, even in rudimentary form, enjoyed great advantages over those without. So those without language either acquired it or vanished.

No one knows when language emerged or how long it took to do so. Some skeletal evidence suggests it might have begun 2 million years ago. Many scholars think it developed only with our own species, *Homo sapiens*, between 200,000 and 120,000 years ago, and a few think it was more recent than that. We will probably never know when this most extraordinary of human achievements arose. But because all human groups around the world speak, it's safe to say that the capacity to do so arose before humans left Africa roughly 100,000 years ago.

Of the traits and skills that distinguish our species, bipedalism came first. After that, developments got more complicated. Bigger brains, bigger social groups, and toolmaking perhaps came together and reinforced one another. Fire management and language also favored the development of bigger brains and bigger groups. Although the chronology of these developments remains unclear, it is likely that the biological evolution of the traits and the cultural evolution of the skills that make us human overlapped in time and collectively encouraged one another.

Our Closest Cousins

Of the 18 or so hominin species that at one time or another inhabited the Earth, only one remains. Our family tree is a bushy shrub with all but one of the branches now dead. Most of those extinct species lived and died out long ago in Africa. A few, like our own species, left Africa for Eurasia (the large landmass spanning Europe and Asia). But unlike *Homo sapiens*, the other hominins, including *Homo naledi* (see page 17), went extinct. The last of our close relatives, the three varieties of humans known as Neanderthals, Denisovans, and Flores Island "Hobbits," disappeared between 50,000 and 30,000 years ago.

Neanderthals

Neanderthals, so named because their remains were first found (in 1856) in the Neander River valley in Germany, lived from about 400,000 to about 40,000 years ago in Europe, Siberia, and southwestern Asia. They evolved from a hominin species, *Homo erectus*, that migrated out of Africa nearly 2 million years ago. We—*Homo sapiens*—also descend from *Homo erectus*, which went extinct only about 190,000 years ago and was one of the longer-lived branches of the human family. So we are remote cousins of Neanderthals.

Neanderthals flourished in an Ice Age environment, adapting to it both genetically and culturally: they were compact, heat-retaining, heavy-limbed, powerful creatures,

CONSIDERING THE EVIDENCE

Our Cousin Neo

In 2013, paleontologists began excavating nineteen hominin skeletons from the Rising Star cave in South Africa. The reconstructed skull of the most complete skeleton, named Neo by the scientists, is shown here. At an estimated 100 lbs. (45 kg) and 4'10" (1.2 m) in height, Neo was shorter than modern humans and had a much smaller brain—closer in size to the brains of *Australopithecus afarensis* like Lucy than hominins in our genus, *Homo.* Yet his brain was shaped more like ours, suggesting that he may have been able to use language. His hands, legs, and feet suggest that he was fully bipedal, but scientists usually link the shape of his hips and curved fingers with species from millions of years ago. So it was surprising when scientists confirmed that Neo lived 300,000 years ago, about the same time that our *Homo sapiens* ancestors first appeared in Africa. It's possible that Neo's species, *Homo naledi*, encountered early *Homo sapiens*, as our cousins the Neanderthals and Denisovans did.

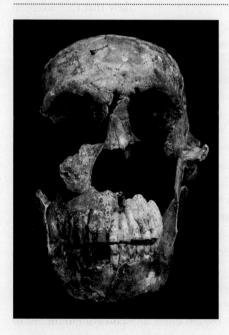

Questions for Analysis

1. Sequencing events in time helps historians to understand how people and communities influenced one other. Neo's skeleton dates to a time when *Homo sapiens* was one of several human species, including Neanderthals, Denisovans, and Flores Island "Hobbits." Most of our *Homo sapiens* ancestors lived far to the north of Neo's *Homo naledi* community. However, if they did happen to meet, do you think they would have recognized each other as human? Why or why not? How might they have cooperated and competed with each other?

2. Some scientists have suggested that the caves where Neo and other *Homo naledi* skeletons have been found were burial chambers because they required intentional effort to access. The scientists argue that such burials prove that *Homo naledi* was human, but others disagree because the caves contained no objects usually found in human burials. What does burial reveal about the way in which early humans likely imagined their world and their community? Assuming that *Homo naledi* communities did bury their dead, is that enough to consider them human? Explain your response.

3. Besides burial, what tools or other kinds of artifacts described in this chapter would help scientists to prove that *Homo naledi* possessed modern human behaviors?

Neanderthal Culture
This geometric pattern etched on the wall of a cave on Gibraltar, at the southern tip of Spain, was probably created deliberately by a Nean-derthal—perhaps as a map or a symbol of the people who lived in the cave, suggesting that Neanderthals were capa-ble of abstract thought.

on average about 30 percent heavier than modern-day people and with braincases larger than ours. Skeletons indicate that males on average stood about 5′5″ (165 cm) and weighed about 145 lbs. (66 kg), and females about 5′1″ (155 cm) and 120 lbs. (54 kg).

More is known about Neanderthals than any other extinct hominin, mainly because they lived in Europe, where far more archeological work has been done than in Africa or Asia. They hunted big game with stone-tipped spears and foraged for berries, nuts, roots, and fruits. They buried their dead, which may mean that they had religious beliefs. In 2014, archeologists found the first clear example of Neanderthal art: some scratchings on the wall of a cave in Gibraltar that are at least 39,000 years old. Nean-derthals, it seems, were capable of abstract thought. Whether or not they had language, or how much they had, is controversial; but expert opinion currently is skeptical about their linguistic attainment. Almost all Neanderthal tools (among those found so far) remained close to where they were made, suggesting that the Neanderthals had only small trade networks—if any. Genetic evidence suggests their total population never exceeded a few thousand.

Neanderthal life was tough and cold: they lived out in the open when not in caves, and they didn't live long. To judge by surviving skeletons, none managed to last beyond age 45. Their skeletons show many broken bones and possible indications of cannibalism. DNA evidence suggests that they were highly inbred, which is perhaps not surprising since they lived in small bands and rarely encountered strangers. Ice Age life grew colder for them about 39,000 years ago, owing to a giant volcanic eruption in what is now southern Italy that darkened skies for about three years and may have nudged them closer to extinction.

The last of the true Neanderthals lived in what is now Spain about 39,000 years ago, but Asians, Europeans, and Native Americans today are all, genetically speaking, about

What were the major characteristics of the hominin
species most closely related to us?

19

1 to 4 percent Neanderthal. Africans carry a much smaller genetic inheritance from Neanderthals, well under 1 percent. (They acquired that via migrations of Eurasians back into Africa, starting about 8,000 years ago.) Neanderthals vanished, but almost all of us are in small part Neanderthal.

Denisovans

We have other extinct cousins called Denisovans, named after a cave in Siberia where archeologists found some remains. Careful study of their genome (the full set of genes of an organism) suggests that the Denisovans were more closely related to Neanderthals than any other (known) species of hominin. Like Neanderthals, they were stocky and well suited to cold conditions. Denisovans probably lived in Siberia and throughout East Asia for a few hundred thousand years. They had enough culture to make bone needles as of about 41,000 years ago, before any other branch of humans started sewing. The human population today that is genetically closest to the Denisovans lives in East and Southeast Asia. The genetic overlap shows that somehow, somewhere, Denisovans and *Homo sapiens* encountered one another and interbred. So Denisovans, like Neanderthals, went extinct, but their genes live on in many humans today.

Hobbits

The most remarkable of our recently extinct cousins is *Homo floriensis*, popularly called Hobbits after the imaginary creatures in J.R.R. Tolkien novels. They were tiny folk, a little over 3 ft. (1 m) tall on average. Their remains were discovered on a cave floor on an Indonesian island, Flores, in 2003. Only a single skull and parts of nine skeletons have been found, so generalizations remain questionable. But it seems likely that they were the last of a very old pre-human lineage, isolated from all other hominins for thousands of generations. They lived on Flores as early as 90,000 years ago and shrank to their small stature under the pressure of natural selection. (Miniature mammals of many sorts have evolved in island habitats, where lower food requirements are an advantage.) They went extinct about 50,000 years ago, perhaps without any contact with *Homo sapiens*, unlike Neanderthals and Denisovans. Once the Flores "hobbits," Neanderthals, and Denisovans had disappeared, *Homo sapiens* was the last species of hominin standing anywhere on Earth, as far as we know now.

The Migrations of Homo Sapiens

We—the last of the hominins—are an upstart species. The fossil and genetic evidence suggests that our species appeared between 300,000 and 200,000 years ago in North

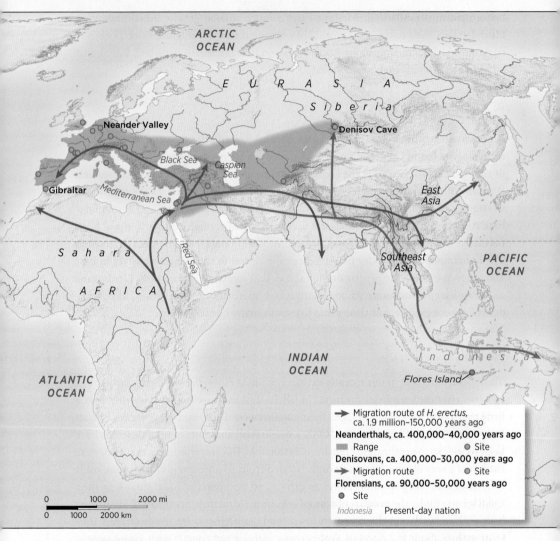

Our Closest Cousins, 400,000–30,000 Years Ago Among the closest relatives to our species are three hominins, the last ones to go extinct, known as Neanderthals, Denisovans, and Florensians or Flores Island "Hobbits." Just how they are related to us is unclear, but they and we might be descendants of *Homo erectus*, the first hominin species to migrate out of Africa.

and East Africa. We are also wanderers. Within Africa, groups of *Homo sapiens* migrated south, starting more than 80,000 years ago. Others went west a little later. These wandering groups had spread out over Africa by 25,000 years ago. In the thinly populated continent, some groups became isolated from the rest for thousands of years, which helps explain why African populations today exhibit greater genetic diversity than all other humans combined.

Out of Africa

At some point between 100,000 and 65,000 years ago, other wandering *Homo sapiens* trekked out of Africa and began to colonize parts of Eurasia. A run of dry weather in northeastern Africa about 74,000 to 60,000 years ago might have motivated them to try their luck further afield. There is as yet no archeological evidence speaking directly to this migration. But somehow they traveled, either on foot via Egypt and the Sinai Peninsula or by island-hopping across the southern Red Sea to the Arabian Peninsula. In those Ice Age days, sea level was much lower than today and the Red Sea less of a barrier. Once the wanderers crossed to Asia, they seem to have headed along the shorelines eastward toward India. They then split up and spread out.

One set of human migrants drifted eastward. They soon reached New Guinea and Australia, landmasses that were then united as a single continent owing to the lower sea level of the Ice Age. Getting there from the Asian mainland still required a sea journey of at least 60 miles (100 km). This voyage implies a considerable technological and logistical competence, as well as high tolerance for risk. The first Australians were surely a plucky lot. They continued on southward to Tasmania by about 40,000 years ago, but stopped short of Antarctica, leaving it uninhabited.

Other *Homo sapiens* entered Europe from southwestern Asia around 45,000 years ago. These new Europeans, according to genetic evidence, are the ancestors of 75 to 85 percent of contemporary Europeans. They soon encountered the depths of the last ice age and—not unlike their

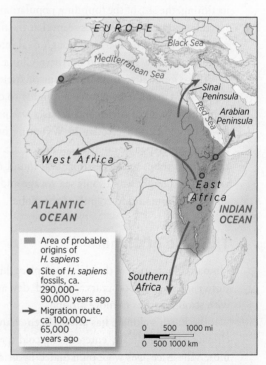

Early Human Migrations within and out of Africa, 300,000–65,000 Years Ago Our own species evolved somewhere in East or northern Africa by roughly 300,000 years ago. Tiny populations of early humans migrated into southern and West Africa as well as into Southwest Asia. Accurate dating of these migrations remains a challenge, but the evidence suggests that the exodus from Africa occurred between 100,000 and 65,000 years ago.

more affluent descendants today—headed for Spain and southern France in search of balmier climes. Other human groups walked into the frigid expanse of Siberia, attracted by the abundance of large, tasty mammals such as woolly mammoths, whose hides were as useful as their meat. Groups of humans also headed into what is now China and Japan, arriving about 30,000 years ago.

Some people moved still further afield. The last chapter in these epic migrations brought people to the Americas—possibly as early as 23,000 years ago, certainly by 14,000 years ago. They came to Alaska from Siberia via a broad land bridge exposed by the lower sea levels. They might have walked across it, or perhaps paddled rafts along its southern coast. Once in the Americas, they apparently spread out quickly, reaching Chile no later than 12,000 years ago. The archeological, linguistic, and DNA evidence concerning the human discovery of America is not consistent, so arguments rage about its timing, the size of the founding population, and whether they came all at once or in several separate waves. It does seem that the first Americans are most closely related to peoples of southern Siberia, although rival interpretations maintain their cousins were from what is now Korea and northern China.

These long, slow migrations out of Africa and throughout the world no doubt experienced many setbacks. As of roughly 50,000 to 75,000 years ago, the total human population in all of Africa and Eurasia was probably only a few hundred thousand— fewer people than live today in Wyoming or Newfoundland. It was an uncrowded world in which people rarely encountered strangers. It was full of lethal risks too. Some migrating groups guessed wrong and found themselves in deserts. Others attempted what they thought was a short sea voyage and never saw land again. But slowly, in fits and starts, humankind colonized the globe.

The Role of Climate

Human colonization of the globe took place during the last ice age, which lasted roughly from 130,000 to 12,000 years ago. Cold, dry, and fickle climate presented our ancestors with strong reasons to move around.

The Earth's climate has always been changing. For the past 3 million years or so, climate has periodically entered long cold spells that last on average 100,000 years or more. These ice ages were punctuated by brief interglacial periods lasting generally a mere 10,000 years. An ice age typically brought great expansions of polar ice sheets and mountain glaciers, colder temperatures everywhere, and dryer conditions in most places. The ice age that began around 130,000 years ago hit a particular cold snap starting about 24,000 years ago; today's Chicago and Glasgow were under ice sheets thicker than skyscrapers are tall. That big chill ended abruptly about 12,000 years ago.

The last ice age was not only much colder and dryer than modern climate, but also far more unstable. Periods of sudden cooling or warming might occur, with swings of 9 to 18 degrees Fahrenheit (5 or 10 degrees Celsius) over a few centuries. The slender

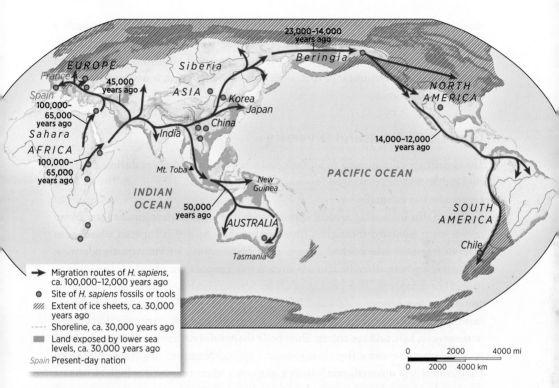

Early Human Migrations throughout the World, 100,000–12,000 Years Ago When humans first left Africa, they soon spread out in all directions, taking advantage of the lower sea levels during the last ice age. The voyages to Australia and New Guinea were the only ones that required rafts or boats, although it is possible that the rapid migrations along the western coasts of the Americas also took place by sea.

evidence suggests these swings were smaller in Africa than elsewhere. But everywhere the incentives to migrate, either to avoid the worst of the cold and drought or to take advantage of warming and moisture, were often strong.

With so much water frozen into ice sheets, our wandering ancestors enjoyed the advantage of lower sea levels during the Ice Age. This gave people more land to work with—the equivalent of a bonus continent the size of North America. It was possible to walk from Korea to Japan, from Britain to France, or, as we've seen, from Siberia to Alaska.

The most challenging moment of the last ice age came around 75,000 years ago when a giant eruption occurred at Mount Toba, a volcano in what is now Indonesia. The eruption spewed enough dust and ash into the skies to block sunlight for years, and it may have lowered global temperatures by 10 to 30 degrees Fahrenheit (5 to 15 degrees Celsius). It's likely that this catastrophe played havoc with plant and animal life, and it may have brought the human species close to extinction: DNA evidence suggests that at around this time our ancestors' numbers were reduced to 10,000 or so—only a little more than the populations of endangered species such as pandas or tigers today. The Toba event was unique. But the last ice age contained numerous cold spells and severe droughts, a circumstance that surely rewarded migration, innovation, learning, and communication.

Genetic and Cultural Diversity

The experience of migration to all the continents except Antarctica during a time of cold and fickle climate changed *Homo sapiens*. It made our ancestors more diverse, both genetically and culturally.

Recall that by moving around within Africa, the small populations of early *Homo sapiens* often separated themselves from one another. As with all species whose populations fragment into isolated groups, early *Homo sapiens* within Africa underwent considerable genetic diversification, with each small population adapting genetically to its local environment. That process of diversification continued in the small group or groups that left Africa for Asia and Europe. They also spread out, grew isolated from one another, and diversified enough genetically so that humans eventually developed a range of skin, hair, and eye colors. Their body shapes also diversified. People who lived in colder places benefited from being stockier (as had Neanderthals), because a stocky build retains heat more efficiently than a lean one. Others who lived at high elevations developed genetic adaptations to a low-oxygen environment.

The genetic diversity of the entire non-African human population, however, remains smaller than that among Africans themselves, a result of what in population genetics is called a founder effect. All non-African peoples of the world are descended from a few groups of African emigrants—probably (to judge by genetic evidence) between 600 and 10,000 people. So despite all the globe-trotting that took people to places as far apart as Europe, Australia, and the Americas, people of non-African descent today remain less genetically diverse than Africans.

The opposite proved true with respect to cultural evolution because culture can change faster than genomes. The variety of environments that those emigrants from Africa encountered stimulated changes in culture. By 30,000 years ago, people outside of Africa had developed more diverse behaviors and tool kits than were found within Africa. For example, people needed more clothing when they got to higher latitudes, so they learned how to use animal furs and skins to keep warm. They learned how to sew small bits of fur into big patchwork cloaks. They also found in most of Eurasia, especially its chillier parts, that there were fewer nutritious plants to gather than in warmer climates, but that hunting big game was far easier. The big animals in Africa had had time to evolve defenses against clever, fire-wielding, spear-throwing team players, because humans took so long to develop these skills. So animals there instinctively kept their distance from *Homo sapiens*. But outside of Africa, big animals had no such experience, so they naively allowed humans to approach and surround them. As a result, people outside of Africa often developed cultures with a larger role for big-game hunting and a smaller role for gathering roots, nuts, and berries. Artistic styles and the variety of languages spoken multiplied outside of Africa. So our ancestors' wanderings after leaving Africa led eventually to vast cultural diversity among peoples with only modest genetic diversity.

This saga of cultural, and to a lesser extent genetic, diversification as people spread out across the globe testifies to the weakness of webs of interconnection prior to 15,000 years ago. When people lived in small bands and rarely encountered other groups, they had limited opportunity to learn from and exchange with strangers. Over time, these groups grew apart. As we shall see, that trend eventually reversed itself as stronger webs multiplied the opportunities for exchanges.

Paleolithic Culture

The word ***Paleolithic*** means "old stone age." It began 2.6 million years ago with the first stone tools and ended about 13,000 years ago. For most of that time, cultural change came very slowly compared to that of more recent times. People were few in number and rarely experienced the challenges of meeting strangers with different ways. Great uncertainties cloud our understanding of Paleolithic society and culture. Most of what we know comes from the last 50,000 years of the Paleolithic.

The Hazards of Daily Life

One advantage of those uncrowded times, it seems, was that early *Homo sapiens* did not often indulge in interpersonal violence: of the 6,000 skeletons available for examination from times before 20,000 years ago, only one betrays signs of death via weapons. One likely explanation for the sparse evidence of violence is that Paleolithic people didn't lose much by running away from a fight. Aside from bands that settled around a reliable resource, like a shellfish bed, people were normally on the move in search of food. They rarely had to fight to preserve access to food, and they probably had a weaker sense of territorial possession than do modern chimps.

But Paleolithic life had its hazards. Hunting big animals, probably exclusively a man's job, involved routine, if small, risks of injury or death. Childbirth brought larger, if less frequent, dangers for women. Anyone too big to carry and too feeble or injured to walk when it was time to move on was an encumbrance to a mobile group—and was presumably abandoned to a solitary and probably short life on his or her own. Small children, if too numerous or troublesome, often met the same fate, as they do in modern mobile hunting and foraging societies. But it's noteworthy that archeologists have found in what is now Pakistan the remains of one young woman with severe birth defects who could only have survived to young adulthood with constant care from others.

Social Structures

Paleolithic people lived in unstable bands of roughly 20 to 80 individuals, sometimes as many as 150—much larger than the social groups of chimpanzees or, in all probability, hominins of any other species but our own. These bands were composed of a few closely related families, and often a sprinkling of unrelated people as well. Groups could easily fragment as a result of quarrels. Stragglers normally would have wanted to join up with a band, especially in places where big-game hunting was the dominant way of life: it was much more efficient, and safer, to hunt in groups.

Like their hominin and probably pre-hominin ancestors, Paleolithic people had a very strong sense of who belonged to their group and who did not. Indeed, our species still has a powerful tendency to divide the human population into "us" and "them," and to build strong bonds with one's group—which helps explain the emotional satisfactions of activities such as team sports.

These small bands occasionally met up with other groups with whom they could swap goods, information, and young people of mating age. In this way, they created bonds of mutual obligation and kinship and also formed new families. Women tended to join their mates' bands, to judge from DNA evidence. Within and among small bands, people cultivated one another's good will by extending kindnesses, giving gifts, and doing favors. Individuals who did this cannily emerged as influential, and in this way they insured themselves against temporary misfortune. As one modern Inuit (Eskimo) put it, "The best place for [an Eskimo] to store his surplus is in someone else's stomach." The same attitudes and behaviors survive today; they can be observed in any workplace, residential neighborhood, or college dorm.

Late Paleolithic people lived a mobile but in many ways low-stress life. Those who roamed the grasslands of Eurasia or East Africa, thickly populated by large herbivores such as mammoths, deer, or gazelles, lived largely by hunting. People living by, or periodically visiting, seashores ate plenty of fish, mussels, crabs, clams, and seaweed. These groups were in the minority, however. In most places, Paleolithic people got most of their food by gathering fruits, berries, nuts, roots, and seeds, supplemented by hunting and scavenging. Everyone accumulated a refined understanding of their local ecosystems, learning the characteristics and habits of dozens of species of plants and animals. They generally didn't have to work hard to acquire all the food they needed—probably about four to six hours per day on average. This left plenty of time for talk, instruction of the young, song and dance, and sleep. Paleolithic people also lived healthy lives (at least, by the standards of later populations), having few infectious diseases and getting plenty of exercise through their daily activities.

A Late Paleolithic Cultural Revolution

At some point late in the Paleolithic, technology and culture began to change a little faster. The sparse archeological remains found so far can support different conclusions, but it looks like the process began in Africa about 90,000 years ago and in Eurasia maybe 50,000 years ago.

Demographic Change Part of the reason for the technological and cultural revolution was likely demographic. Paleolithic people before about 50,000 years ago didn't live long by today's standards. Scanty evidence suggests the odds of making it to age 15 were about 60 percent. Judging from the evidence contained in fossil teeth, it seems that over the long haul, hominin and human populations lived longer, meaning that they contained larger proportions of people who survived to age 30 or so. But then about 50,000 to 15,000 years ago, the proportion of older people increased more than fourfold. With more "old" people (age 30 and up) around to help look after small children, women could bear more children and more babies survived, bringing a surge in population. Human population grew rapidly in the late Paleolithic, and perhaps an unprecedented abundance of helpful grandparents was part of the reason. At a guess, the world contained some half a million people as of 50,000 years ago, but perhaps 2 to 6 million people by 15,000 years ago. It remained an uncrowded world.

The lengthening of life expectancy added to the cultural dynamism of Paleolithic society. With more grandparents around to help teach the young, the efficiency of communication and learning increased, helping to account for the accelerated technological and cultural change evident in the archeological record.

Population growth had a similar effect. The mental horizons of people expanded through more frequent contacts with strangers. Living one's entire life within the same group of 20 to 80 people wasn't as stimulating as occasionally meeting up with other bands. The frequency of such encounters climbed with population growth. When people got the chance to learn from a wider array of strangers, new ideas were hatched at a faster rate. This helps to explain a pattern we saw earlier: the long conservatism in toolmaking followed by the sudden emergence of new styles of tool manufacture.

Technology and Art After 50,000 years ago, not only did tools evolve more quickly than before, but entirely new inventions appeared faster. By 39,000 years ago, Paleolithic people—at least, those living in one cave in Germany—had a musical instrument, a pipe carved from a swan's bone. They sewed garments with needles by 30,000 years ago. The bow and arrow appeared about 30,000 to 25,000 years ago and spread almost everywhere by 20,000 years ago. People started making nets, probably for fishing, about 25,000 years ago. The first fishhooks, ropes, and knife blades appeared around the same time. People now made things out of bone and antler as well as of stone.

Further evidence for the idea of a cultural revolution at some point late in the

Paleolithic comes from the world of art. In what is now South Africa, geometric patterns etched into a clay called ochre and beads made out of snail shells appeared at least 70,000 years ago. Some rock shelters in Namibia (in southern Africa) bear animal images that might be 30,000 years old. The first figurine of a human form with an animal's head, the so-called Lion Human (Löwenmensch) found in a cave in Germany, dates from 35,000 to 40,000 years ago. In southern France and northern Spain over 38,000 years ago, artists started decorating more than a hundred caves with paintings, mainly of hunted animals. In Indonesia, there's a stenciled image of a human hand that appears to be 40,000 years old. Paleolithic people seem to have engaged in cave and rock-shelter art in only a small part of the human realm in Europe, Africa, Indonesia, and Australia—although more might yet be found one day.

The first surviving evidence of humans depicting the human form, dug out of a cave in southern Germany in 2008, is a 40,000-year-old figurine of a woman carved from a mammoth tusk. These innovations in art—beads, painting, figurines—may signal big changes in human mental worlds: perhaps greater self-consciousness, greater abilities in language, a new sense of the supernatural.

All these changes—demographic, technological, and artistic—whenever and wherever they began, likely reinforced one another. Older and larger populations, organized in bigger groups, helped to bring more innovations to technology and art, while new technologies helped more people to live longer. The new art may have helped them to enjoy life more and may have reflected tighter social bonds formed around spiritual beliefs.

The Lion Human The first known representation of an animal or a human is in fact both: a 35,000- to 40,000-year-old ivory figurine with a human body and a lion's head (perhaps a representation of a deity), found in present-day Germany.

A Spirit World: Shamanism The mental world of Paleolithic peoples is difficult to penetrate, but it's possible that during the late Paleolithic people began to extend their notions of kinship and reciprocity into a spirit world. They envisioned supernatural power not as abstract but as specific, located in important objects around them—certain trees, animals, or rocks. People forged connections with these supernatural agents through various rituals that probably featured music, dance, trances, and possibly mind-altering drugs. They reached out to spirits through gifts offered in the form of sacrifices. They also believed the dead were transported to a spirit realm, a notion powerfully reinforced by dreams, in which one can, after all, see the departed. People began to bury the dead with objects that were intended to help them in the next world. This loose set of religious beliefs and practices is often called **shamanism**. In some societies, including isolated indigenous peoples in Amazonia and Siberia, shamanism survives today, making it by far the most durable variety of religion in history.

It is worth pondering what religion did for Paleolithic human society. There is evidence that groups with religion were likelier to grow, sustain larger-scale cooperation, and withstand the risks of Paleolithic life slightly better than others. Religion enhanced group solidarity: those human groups with religion generally found it easier to act together toward a common goal than those without it. This improved their odds of survival and reproduction. It's even possible that over tens of thousands of years human brains adapted so as to become increasingly willing to believe in an unseen spirit world, just as our brains became adapted to enjoy group solidarity.

The emergence of religion also shows growing connections among people throughout Africa and Eurasia before 15,000 years ago—a modest tightening of the faint web binding all humankind. Shamanism existed in different forms, but many of its rituals and practices—dance, drugs, and sacrifices, for example—spread widely. The performance of such rituals held in common probably made it easier for strangers to mingle peacefully. So shamanistic religion both thickened the web of human interaction during the late Paleolithic and provides us with evidence of its workings.

One example of Paleolithic human connectivity in the spiritual realm comes from scholars who collect folk myths. Tales of hunters and animals turned into constellations of stars appear widely in Africa, Asia, and among Native Americans. There are at least 47 versions recorded featuring different animals and constellations but following the same storyline. As people migrated around the world with their myths and beliefs, they changed them gradually to make sense in new environments. Slowly, the myths diverged—as did languages, tool kits, and other forms of culture. Yet the basic form of these myths, linking people with the heavens, remained a common human heritage.

The late Paleolithic cultural revolution strongly suggests heightened levels of interaction among our ancestors by 50,000 and especially by 15,000 years ago. The pace of change in tool design, art, and religion is likely the result of more frequent encounters with strangers whose ways were slightly different and inspired people to rethink their habits.

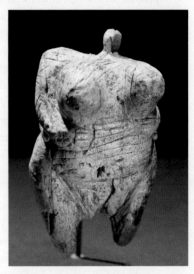

"Venus of Hohle Fels" This three-inch-tall statue, recently discovered in Germany, is a stylized representation of a woman carved from a mammoth tusk. Its exaggerated proportions may indicate it was used as a fertility object.

Environmental Impacts With improved technology, greater numbers, and stronger social solidarity owing to the late Paleolithic cultural revolution, our species acquired additional power over the plants and animals with which they shared the Earth. Despite their belief in the supernatural qualities of living things, Paleolithic people devastated parts of their environment. Their most important environmental impact came in altering vegetation through repeated burning of landscapes, which people did wherever conditions were suitably dry, as in East Africa and Australia. The goal of burning was to promote populations of useful plants and animals that would re-colonize burnt ground—grasses with edible seeds, for example, or tasty grazing animals such as gazelles. The "natural" vegetation that has prevailed in Australia over the past 50,000 years is actually made up of fire-tolerant species that can flourish amid frequent burning. Paleolithic Australians relied on these species, and on the animals, such as wallabies and kangaroos, that thrived on the vegetation that sprang up in the aftermath of a burn.

The second great environmental impact of Paleolithic peoples was a surge in extinctions. One of the less pleasant facts about our ancestors is that when they first reached new lands, mass extinctions among large mammals and birds soon followed. Around the world, between 50,000 and 12,000 years ago, about 65 percent of the genera (families) of big mammals were swept into the dustbin of natural history. The biggest wave of extinctions followed when humans first arrived in Australia, in the Americas, and on countless small islands. There were fewer extinctions in Eurasia, and fewer still in Africa. Most specialists think these extinctions resulted from human over-hunting: Paleolithic peoples were efficient hunters, and as they left Africa for different lands, they found many of the big mammals of Eurasia, Australia, and the Americas unsuspecting, easy prey. Climate change may also have contributed to some extinctions.

Mass extinctions had important long-term consequences, because in Australia and the Americas especially they reduced the number of potentially domesticable animals. With almost no wild animals that could be tamed, bred, and raised in captivity, the original human populations of Australia and the Americas had more limited food supplies and sources of muscle power than people elsewhere. As we will see in Chapters 3 and 4, peoples with domesticated animals such as horses, cattle, sheep, goats, and pigs enjoyed important advantages.

Conclusion

It is important to remember that we still know very little about the human history of the deeper past. For long stretches of that history, the useful fossils are so few that they would all fit in the back of a pickup truck, far outnumbered by the scholars studying them. A new find or two could generate radically new interpretations and drive some current ideas to extinction. The work on genetic evidence is still recent; in the years ahead, new findings will change prevailing understandings of our deep past.

All of our history until the last 100,000 years took place in Africa. Our remotest hominin ancestors lived in East and North Africa, in unstable environmental conditions that rewarded adaptability. Bipedalism, big brains, and culture helped make some species of hominins flexible enough in behavior to survive, and at times to flourish. Those species that didn't have big brains and culture—tools, fire, and language especially—died out, although it is humbling to note that some of these extinct species lasted far longer than we have so far. Our own species, *Homo sapiens*, appeared about 300,000 to 200,000 years ago and gradually spread out across most of Africa. Following the path of some earlier hominins, a few of our own branch wandered out of Africa, opening a new chapter in human history perhaps as early as 100,000 years ago.

Human Hands Red-stenciled outlines of hands appear on the wall of a cave in Indonesia. The images are dated to around 40,000 years ago.

Homo sapiens is the only remaining hominin. All others went extinct more than 30,000 years ago. Our branch proved more adaptable to changing environments, better able to bear and raise plentiful children, and more imaginative in our culture than any other. As a result, we are the last hominin standing.

On the whole, the period from 100,000 to 15,000 years ago was one of expansion and differentiation in human history, and of accelerating cultural change. Our ancestors colonized almost the entire globe, braving deserts and rain forests, and even making short sea voyages. Their numbers increased, in large part because of this occupation of new regions and habitats. Those who colonized Eurasia continued to live in small groups, sometimes very isolated ones, so that their languages and cultures quickly diverged. Those who stayed in Africa also grew in number but—obliged to respond to fewer unfamiliar environments and somewhat less scattered geographically—maintained their old cultures more successfully.

All humans, wherever they lived, shared some cultural traits. They all used language and fire from the time our species originated. They made and used similar stone tools. They all developed, or acquired, religion and art by 40,000 years ago, and in some cases long before. Some of these similarities, such as the use of fire, merely represent the continuation of very ancient practices. Others, like the bow and arrow, were innovations, and their eventual use by almost all human communities is evidence of links among those communities.

At a more basic and biological level, *Homo sapiens* remained a single species. Even when humans were very few, living in small bands, and scattered thinly over most of the globe, sporadic interactions kept them loosely in contact with neighboring groups and indirectly in touch with the entire species. A faint and slender web connected all our Paleolithic ancestors.

|||||||||||||||||||||||||||||||||||||||||||||||||||||||||||||||||||||||||||||||||||||||||||||||||||||||||||||||||||||||||||||||||||||||||||

Chapter Review

KEY TERMS

Lucy p. 6

hominins p. 6

Big Bang p. 7

Homo sapiens p. 9

bipedalism p. 9

natural selection p. 10

Homo erectus p. 13

Neanderthals p. 16

Paleolithic p. 25

shamanism p. 28

REVIEW QUESTIONS

1. How did the asteroid that hit the Yucatán Peninsula 66 million years ago facilitate the evolution of our ancestors?

2. What is the significance of bipedalism in hominins?

3. What were the main advantages of large brains?

4. Why was the control of fire so important to hominin development?

5. How does the development of language set *Homo sapiens* apart from other species?

6. What assumptions can we make about Neanderthal culture based on archeological evidence?

7. How did the unstable climate of the last ice age encourage human migration?

8. Why did the populations that moved out of Africa become culturally diverse?

9. In what sense was there a cultural revolution during the late Paleolithic period?

10. What changes in Paleolithic human societies did the emergence of religion bring?

11. What were the two biggest environmental impacts of Paleolithic humans?

12. What are the main reasons that *Homo sapiens* is the last hominin standing?

Go to INQUIZITIVE

to see what you've learned—and learn what you've missed—with personalized feedback along the way.

Settling Down

DOMESTICATION AND AGRICULTURE

30,000 to 6,000 years ago

FOCUS QUESTIONS

1. How did the gradual emergence of a warmer, more stable climate contribute to changes in human life?

2. What factors contributed to the emergence of the earliest settled communities?

3. Why was domestication a major landmark in human history?

4. What were the major characteristics of the first transitions to agriculture around the world?

5. In what ways did agriculture spread from its points of origin to adoption throughout most of the world?

6. What were the main effects of the transition to agriculture on human life and culture?

In 2008, archeologists dug up the floor of Hilazon Tachtit cave in Israel. There they found the 12,000-year-old remains of a burial feast for a 45-year-old female shaman. She was buried in high style, with tortoise shells under her skull and pelvis, and gazelle horn, an eagle's wing tip, some chalk, and a human foot all placed around her. These and other burial objects led the archeologists to infer that she was a religious specialist of great reputation. The feast in her honor was a special occasion. The menu featured fish; meat from gazelles, foxes, and snakes; and no fewer than 80 roast tortoises—enough food for several dozen people. The guests tossed their leftovers over

CHRONOLOGY

ca. 30,000–18,000 BCE First domestication of dogs

ca. 25,000–10,000 BCE Mammoth hunters flourish

ca. 15,000–9000 BCE Magdalenian culture flourishes

ca. 12,500–9500 BCE Natufians flourish

ca. 11,000 BCE First transition to agriculture and plant domestication in the Levant

ca. 11,000–9000 BCE First domestication of goats and sheep

10,700–9700 BCE Younger Dryas

9700 BCE Holocene begins

ca. 9000–7000 BCE Göbekli Tepe

ca. 8500 BCE First domestication of pigs

ca. 8000–7000 BCE First domestication of cattle; transitions to agriculture in China's Yangzi and Huang He river valleys

ca. 7000 BCE Jomon culture settlements in Japan

ca. 6000 BCE Settlements in North America; crop domestication begins in Mesoamerica

ca. 5000 BCE Transition to agriculture in Southeast Asia

ca. 4500 BCE First domestication of chickens

ca. 4000 BCE Domestication of llamas

ca. 4000–3000 BCE Domestication of potatoes and manioc

ca. 3000 BCE Transition to agriculture in Africa

ca. 2500 BCE Transition to agriculture in North America

the body of the deceased woman. Someone then placed a big stone slab on top. No other burial from the time shows anything like the elaborate care lavished on this one.

The people who held the feast and buried the shaman are called **Natufians**. They flourished from about 12,500 to 9500 BCE. The Natufians lived in settled villages of 100 to 150 people with round houses dug into the ground. Their tool kit suggests they were in contact with people in northernmost Africa and acquired shells from Egypt's Nile valley. They used obsidian that came from hundreds of miles away in Anatolia (modern Turkey). They hunted gazelles and gathered wild cereals. They invented the world's first sickles for harvesting cereals, and they used bowls for grinding grain. At some point, they started sowing their favorite cereals and eventually became farmers, producing their food rather than finding it. They were among the pioneers of sedentary lifeways and—as far as we know—the world's pioneers of agriculture.

The pioneer of Natufian studies was Dorothy Garrod. Born in England in 1892, she earned an undergraduate degree in history from Cambridge University in 1916. After her three brothers and her sweetheart died in World War I, the despondent Garrod went to the Mediterranean island of Malta to figure out what to do with her life. There she became fascinated by ancient artifacts, and soon returned to England to study archeology. Garrod found some Neanderthal remains at Gibraltar in 1925, which at a stroke made her an accomplished archeologist of the Paleolithic. In 1929, she began digging at Shuqba Cave, 20 miles (30 km) northwest of Jerusalem. She assembled a team of researchers, mostly women—a first in the history of archeology. Her team began the documentation of Natufian culture.

In 1939, much to her surprise, Garrod was appointed to a prestigious professorship in

How did the gradual emergence of a warmer, more stable
climate contribute to changes in human life?

35

archeology at Cambridge University. She was the first woman ever to hold any professorship at the centuries-old university. Like her subject, the Natufians, Garrod was a pioneer in her own right.

Back in the Paleolithic, as we've seen, history unfolded at a leisurely pace. Over the first several tens of thousands of years of human history after the emergence of language, all people lived in approximately the same sorts of social units, and they all lived mobile lives focused on foraging, hunting, and, in places, fishing. Environment and culture changed with the onset of the Ice Age and its violent climatic fluctuations, with new tools, and with the invention of art. People spread out over the Earth. But the basics of their lives remained much the same.

As the last ice age waned and climate continued to warm, people who formerly wandered in search of food began in several sites to settle down. In multiple places they also began to domesticate animals. And in the final landmark transition considered in this chapter, people invented agriculture at many times in many places. Farming spread widely, changing the basics of life irrevocably. By our twenty-first-century standards, this sea change came slowly. By the standards of Paleolithic history, it came as suddenly as a tsunami.

The End of the Last Ice Age

The coldest part of the last ice age came about 26,000 to 23,000 years ago. Then a slow global warming—a planetary defrosting—began. It coincided with the appearance in a few spots around the globe of settled communities and prepared the way for transitions to a new way of life: farming.

Retreating Ice and Rising Sea Levels

By 20,000 years ago, thanks to slow global warming, the great ice sheets covering northern Siberia, half of Europe, and a third of North America had begun to melt back. Vegetation crept northward into the soggy landscapes that were now free of ice. Wildlife and people followed. Almost everywhere, climate started slowly to improve from the human point of view. In Africa and South Asia, where aridity more than cold had constrained human endeavor during the Ice Age, conditions grew wetter as well as warmer. Deserts, like the northern ice sheets, retreated, opening new land for plants, animals, and humans. The changes took place too slowly for anyone to have noticed but were large enough to help human population to grow a little faster during the final stages of the Paleolithic.

Some ground was lost while climate warmed. Sea level rose because of melting glaciers, which drowned coastal plains and pushed people inland, if only by a few inches every year. Indonesia, Britain, and Japan eventually became the archipelagoes we know today, cut off from the Eurasian landmass. Rising seas separated Taiwan from mainland China, Tasmania and New Guinea from Australia, and Newfoundland from North America.

Usually, the rising seas claimed low-lying lands slowly; but whenever rising waters overtopped a ledge or broke through an ice-dam, epic floods resulted. According to one theory, the Black Sea, formerly an immense inland lake, filled up with Mediterranean seawater splashing over the sills of the Dardanelles and Bosporus with the force of 200 Niagara Falls. In the span of a single year (perhaps around 7400 BCE), the former shores of the inland lake were flooded and a larger, saltwater Black Sea was born. It's possible that the great flood sagas, such as those in the Epic of Gilgamesh (the first known story, written in Mesopotamia about 2100 BCE) or in the Bible's Book of Genesis, derive from folk memories of such events. But scholars don't know: the archeological evidence isn't conclusive, and the flood stories may have nothing at all to do with the forming of the Black Sea.

As of about 6000 BCE, the melting was almost over and sea level was close to where it is now. Over 15,000 years, it had risen by 430 ft. (130 m)—about the height of a 25-story building. With these environmental changes, the human population expanded, spreading out into formerly ice-covered northern (and mountain) zones and into former deserts, even as people had to abandon former coastlines and retreat inland. Far more land had been gained than lost thanks to the defrosting.

The Younger Dryas

The Ice Age had one last shiver in it. Between 12,900 and 11,700 years ago (10,900 to 9700 BCE), another brutally cold and dry spell hit the Northern Hemisphere. It is called the **Younger Dryas**, named for a tundra flower that turns up often in sediments from that time. It probably resulted from a massive outflow of fresh water from an ancient North American lake (Lake Agassiz, centered on what is now the Canadian province of Manitoba and larger than all the Great Lakes put together) that had formed from glacial meltwater during the warming. When those waters broke through into the North Atlantic, they suddenly made it less salty, changing the Atlantic Ocean's circulation pattern and plunging the Northern Hemisphere back into the deep freeze for more than a thousand years.

The Younger Dryas seems to have been coldest around the North Atlantic, in Europe especially. In Europe, the summers were 9 to 13 degrees Fahrenheit (5 to 7 degrees Celsius) cooler, and in winter more like 18 to 21 degrees F (10 to 12 degrees C) colder—the difference between sweatshirt weather and parka weather. The change apparently came on suddenly, within a decade or two, which is unusual in the annals of climate change, and made adjustment especially challenging. As during ice ages, in the Younger Dryas conditions were dry throughout the Northern Hemisphere as well as colder. In the tropics, so far as anyone can tell, the Younger Dryas was mainly dryer.

The Younger Dryas came as a catastrophe for people, animals, and plants that had been getting used to warmer and wetter conditions.

Emergence of a More Stable Climate

But when the Younger Dryas ended, the forecast was good: the warmth and wet returned, and more important still, the chaotic flickering so characteristic of the Ice Age climate came to an end—or at least a long interlude. From the end of the Younger Dryas until now, a roughly 11,700-year period known as the **Holocene** (from ancient Greek meaning "wholly recent"), climate has been remarkably stable. We of course regard our weather as unstable and unpredictable, and over short time spans it is just that. But Holocene climate fluctuates much less than climate did during the last ice age. In particular, the probability of extremely cold winters far outside the statistical norm was significantly reduced after the Younger Dryas. This relative stability of climate made it much easier for people to settle down in one place and rely on the plants that grew there. When and where climate fluctuated chaotically, people had to stay on the move. With the stability of Holocene climate, they could become sedentary with less risk.

Sedentary Societies: The First Permanent Settlements

While their cousins were still roaming the world, a few people began to settle down. In several places around the globe, they began to do so at roughly the same time. The first few formed settlements toward the end of the Ice Age, and then more followed after the end of the Younger Dryas. The best places to settle were along the migratory routes of nutritious beasts: let the food come to you, rather than chase after it.

Food Sources and the Earliest Settlements

People could do this only in a few places—for example, alongside the salmon rivers of the North Atlantic and North Pacific. Salmon swim up rivers to spawn in seasonal mass migrations that allow anyone with a net, the appropriate knowledge, and hand-eye coordination

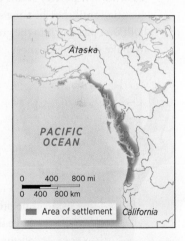

Range of Human Settlement in Pacific Northwest Coastal Region, ca. 6000 BCE Among the best places in the world to pursue sedentary cultures were spots along the Northern Hemisphere rivers that salmon use on their annual migrations. Once people figured out how to preserve salmon by smoking or salting the fish, they had a year-round food supply.

as good as a grizzly bear's to stand beside a stream and harvest a year's food supply in just a few weeks. The salmon runs are reliable and abundant in certain rivers, especially those from Alaska to northern California. This Pacific coastal region provided an ideal environment for **sedentary** life, and by about 6000 BCE—to judge from archeological remains—people had begun to settle down along several salmon rivers in western North America. Salmon harvesting also played a large role in the food supply of early post-glacial settlers of Scandinavia and the British Isles, but Atlantic salmon rarely run in the same profusion as their Pacific cousins, and therefore provided a poorer basis for sedentary life.

Jomon Culture   On the western shores of the Pacific, in Japan, sedentary life also emerged in what archeologists call the **Jomon culture**. (In Japanese, the name refers to the rope-pattern decoration on pottery characteristic of this culture.) By about 7000 BCE, these people had found it possible to settle down, especially on the Pacific coast of east-central Japan, blessed with plenty of shellfish, fish, acorns, and chestnuts. They collected these foods but also hunted deer and other animals. The Jomon were among the first inventors of pottery in world history, even though they had no kilns or potter's wheels—they made their pots by hand and fired them in bonfires. Their earliest pottery seems to be about 13,000 years old, but they didn't make it in quantity until they became sedentary in their way of life. They lived in oval houses built over pits dug into the ground, and they used chestnut wood (among other types) to make dwellings, canoes, and shoes. They may even have planted chestnut trees. The Jomon attained an unusually high population density for a foraging people.

Jomon Pottery The characteristic rope pattern is visible on this Jomon pot.

Göbekli Tepe   Recent archeology has turned up a curious case of sedentary or semi-sedentary life in southeastern Turkey at **Göbekli Tepe**. About 9000 BCE, semi-settled people (meaning they spent most but not all of each year in one spot) started doing something that no other pre-farming people anywhere on Earth did: building a large stone temple. Using only stone tools, they quarried blocks of stone weighing as much as 10 to 20 tons; dragged them several hundred yards; carved boars, ducks, snakes, and other wild animal shapes into them; and assembled them into a temple. These people had no draft animals. They needed at least 500 individuals working together to lug such big blocks of stone, and they fed themselves without agriculture. Göbekli Tepe is, as far as we know, a unique case of monumental architecture created by a hunting and foraging people.

The best guess is that Göbekli Tepe is a religious site and gathering place built by semi-settled villagers who inhabited a landscape abundant with wild wheat, the result in part of warm and lush conditions that prevailed following the Younger Dryas. The choice of the site may have had something to do with its location between the plains of Mesopotamia and the mountain passes that gave entry into Anatolia. It stood beside trade routes. But by 7000 BCE, the site was abandoned—indeed, purposely buried in rock and debris—

Göbekli Tepe Archeological excavations at Göbekli Tepe have revealed the monumental stone buildings that people built at the site.

until archeologists started scratching around in the twentieth century. Nobody knows why people abandoned it. The temple at Göbekli Tepe shows that semi-settled people could organize their efforts on a substantial scale. Since 95 percent of the site remains to be excavated, we should expect to learn much more in the years ahead.

Mammoth Hunters of Ukraine The best places to settle down were beside salmon rivers, along coastlines rich with shellfish, or on rare patches of land flush with edible wild plants. A more dangerous and less reliable environment for settlement was along the migration routes of big mammals, such as the now-extinct wooly mammoths. Huge, shaggy beasts related to elephants, mammoths could provide hunters with plenty of food as well as leather and wooly clothing—the height of Eurasian fashion during the depths of the Ice Age.

The earliest evidence of sedentary lifestyles anywhere comes from the mammoth hunters of Ukraine, the region to the north of the Black Sea. They may have been only semi-sedentary, spending a few months at a time in the same place—no one knows for sure.

Scholars use the term *mammoth steppe* to refer to the region south of the glaciers, from France to eastern Siberia, where during the Ice Age summer grasses sustained sprawling herds of mammoths. As the Ice Age waned, the mammoths drifted northward, allowing skilled mammoth hunters to follow and flourish in otherwise forbidding landscapes. Mammoths probably migrated with the seasons along well-worn paths, especially river valleys. This made them easy to find and enabled teams of spear-wielding hunters and their families to stay put, especially after they learned to dig pits in the autumn and freeze meat for later roasting during the bone-chilling winters.

The mammoth hunters ate mammoth meat to stay alive, and to stay warm they lived inside shelters made of mammoth bones and skins. Around 27,000 years ago—during a cold phase of the last ice age—they began to build houses using mammoth tusks, ribs, and leg bones as the equivalent of construction timber. Carefully arranged and covered with hides, these materials made cozy dwellings against the cold. Archeologists have found about 70 of these mammoth-bone huts. The largest is over 190 ft. (60 m) long and 16 ft. (5 m) wide and must have housed scores of people. Whether people lived in this mammoth-mansion year-round is unclear. By 15,000 years ago along the Dnieper River in today's Ukraine, clusters of mammoth huts developed—perhaps history's first villages.

The mammoths died out 12,000 years ago. One likely explanation is that mammoth hunters were too skillful and killed off their favorite prey. It's also plausible that warmer climate opened habitats to other herbivores, such as deer, that competed successfully against mammoths for edible vegetation. The huts of these inventive hunters were abandoned, to be discovered by archeologists only in the twentieth century.

Magdalenian Culture The mammoth hunters weren't alone in settling down to make a living off of herds roaming the steppe. To their west between 18,000 and 12,000 years ago lived groups of reindeer hunters known to archeologists as the **Magdalenian culture**, named after a particular rock shelter in France—although the Magdalenians left archeological remains scattered between Portugal and Poland. These people hunted reindeer with the same general approach used by mammoth hunters: intercepting seasonal migrations. In staking out migration routes, they became at least semi-sedentary. Like the mammoth hunters, they varied their diet by hunting deer and wild horses too. They supplemented their meals with whatever nuts, fruits, and berries they could find

Lascaux Caves On the walls of caves at Lascaux in France, the Magdalenian people, a semi-sedentary culture, made vivid paintings of the animals—deer, horses, bulls—that provided them with sustenance.

in their chilly surroundings. Edible plants were rare, but the Magdalenians were clever and bold. They ate partially digested reindeer lichen (a small, bushy-looking fungus) scooped out of the stomachs of freshly killed reindeer.

Settled or semi-settled life allowed new possibilities unavailable to peoples constantly on the move. Some Magdalenians in what is now France and Spain spent at least part of their time in caves, including the famous ones at Lascaux, where they painted some of the most stirring images known to history. The salmon eaters of North America staged rituals known as potlatch, which included competitive feasting and gift giving in quests for social status. The mammoth hunters accumulated jewelry, statuettes, baskets, and needles, and they seem to have pioneered a society stratified by social class: burials as well as house sizes indicate that some people had far more accumulated wealth than others. In the several spots where settled life became feasible at the end of the Ice Age, cultural revolutions took place: people had more leisure time to create new art, tools, and rituals, and they no longer had to limit their possessions to an amount they could conveniently carry.

Sedentary Communities and Cultural Change

The scattered sedentary or semi-sedentary communities were hubs of social and cultural activity, loosely connected by the movements of mobile hunting and foraging peoples. In effect, the mobile peoples served as the threads on the very faint web of interaction that kept almost the entire human race in sporadic contact. The settled and semi-settled communities served as hubs of innovation. Their cultures grew more elaborate not only because they stayed put for all or most of the time, but also because they received influences from distant communities through contacts with mobile hunters and foragers. The mobile peoples—still the demographic majority even as recently as 8000 BCE—could serve as messengers, transmitting, for example, technologies such as the bow and arrow.

Sedentary life, paradoxically, spurred the mobility and exchange of objects. Before any groups had settled down, everyone had pretty much the same small set of tools and clothing, and more or less the same skills with which to make them. People didn't have much else. Nobody carried trade goods around because they didn't know when they might meet up with others, and they rarely met others who didn't already have the same few items. But with the advent of sedentary life, people created more, and more varied, objects—tools, ornaments, maybe different kinds of clothes. Mobile people of the late Paleolithic could count on finding food, water, shelter, and probably a warm welcome at fixed places, so they had good reason to carry around rare things that other people really wanted. Among those items were flints for making fire, shells for decoration or cutting tools, and obsidian, a hard rock that can be fashioned into an excellent cutting edge.

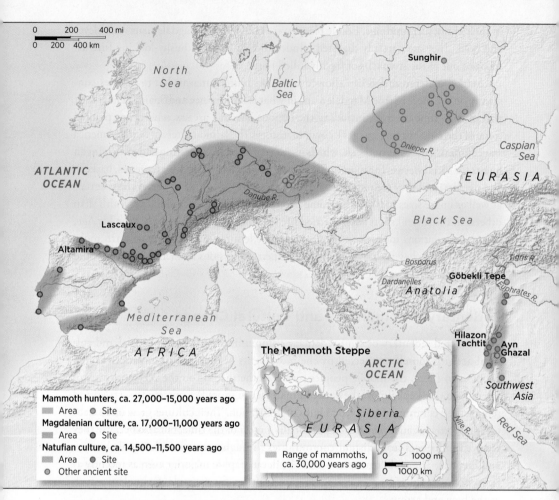

Sedentary Cultures of Europe and Southwest Asia, 27,000–11,000 Years Ago Mammoth hunters and Magdalenians settled astride the migration routes of big game animals, a strategy analogous to that of people in the Pacific Northwest who settled along salmon rivers. The Natufians, in contrast, like the Jomon, found a location with abundant local food sources.

These items often show up in archeological sites far from their points of origin, giving evidence of long-distance trade. For example, at an archeological site in Jordan (Kharaneh IV), where sedentary or near-sedentary people lived 19,000 years ago, scholars have found shells used as ornaments that came from the shores of the Indian Ocean, more than 1,200 miles (2,000 km) away. No doubt traders also carried more perishable goods that haven't lasted. In short, sedentary life created a class of mobile traders who built webs of communication and exchange among communities of settled folk.

Domestication

While some Ice Age foragers and hunters of Eurasia made long strides toward settled life, others achieved something equally momentous: the partnership between humans and dogs. We call it the domestication of dogs; but if they could think about such things, dogs might see it as the domestication of humans. In any case, it was the first domestication in history, a mutual accommodation.

Domestication is a complicated subject, with two main parts: the domestication of animals and the domestication of plants. Together, they represent a major landmark in human history: the transition between finding one's food and producing one's food.

The Process of Domestication

The domestication of plants involves the genetic modification of cultivated plants through human selection. People can cultivate (i.e., sow and harvest) wild plants. But when they consciously select certain seeds over others to sow in order to harvest more plants with desired characteristics, and do this consistently for many years, inducing genetic changes in the plants, the process is called domestication. In some cases of domestication, plants evolve that depend on humans for their propagation because their seeds don't disperse on their own. A corn (maize) cob is one example, the result of genetic modification over thousands of years and now the world's third most important food crop.

The domestication of animals also involves genetic modification through human actions. People can sometimes keep wild animals as pets, although it doesn't work well for most adult animals. However, when people breed animals in order to achieve offspring with desired characteristics—for example, tameness or small size—and do this consistently across many generations, they are domesticating animals. They can create versions of animals that couldn't survive without human aid, such as poodles.

Dogs: Humankind's First Friend

Dogs evolved from wolves over thousands of years. Just how, when, and where this began is unclear. All specialists think it happened somewhere in Eurasia. The latest genetic evidence suggests it occurred between 32,000 and 20,000 years ago. Dog skulls show up at mammoth-hunter settlement sites by 15,000 years ago.

No matter how it began, the dog-human partnership was a mutually profitable one. Dogs provided people with hunting help, compensating for our poor sense of smell. Unlike wolves, dogs bark upon the approach of unexpected animals, which gave people warning against surprise attackers. And dogs offered loyal companionship, including furry warmth on cold Ice Age nights. In dire circumstances, people could also eat their dogs.

In return, people provided dogs with food (or hunting help, as the dogs might see it), and sometimes protection and shelter. Dogs with cooperative people got a more reliable food supply, including access to big game such as mammoths that dogs could scarcely hope to bag by themselves. Over time, a genetic selection occurred for dogs that worked well with humans—dogs that showed loyalty, accepted human commands, and could read human gestures and expressions. At the same time, a cultural selection took place for human groups that worked well with dogs, training, breeding, and protecting them, and eating them only in times of need. Some specialists suggest that the dog-human partnership worked so well, and began so early, that the canine-human team out-competed Neanderthals, who didn't keep dogs. If so, "man's best friend" was among the Neanderthals' worst enemies.

By 14,000 years ago, people had grown fond enough of dogs to include them in human graves. Hunting peoples—especially those operating in forests, where sight is impeded and a good sense of smell is all the more useful—came to revere good hunting dogs. From Europe to Japan, some dogs were buried with full honors, which might consist of deer antlers, hunters' tools, or colorful stones.

The dog-human team spread rapidly and became nearly universal. The Ainu, a people in Japan's northernmost island of Hokkaido, even taught their dogs to catch salmon for them. When the first humans trekked into the Americas, their dogs trotted along too. Today, for every wolf on Earth, there are more than 3,000 dogs. For dogs, domestication has been a tremendous success. It's been a success for humans too.

Grasses

The domestication of dogs was the first of many. Dozens of animals and hundreds of plants proved susceptible to domestication. Almost all these domestications took place in remote times before written records, but archeologists can often tell the difference between wild and domesticated species from the remains of seeds and bones, and geneticists can tell wild and domestic species apart.

Like dogs, certain grasses—wild ancestors of cereals such as wheat, barley, rye, rice, and maize—in effect took advantage of human needs to become much more biologically successful, and much more prevalent over the face of the Earth. Those grasses with seeds that didn't easily fly off the stalk were most likely to be gathered, stored, and then planted by humans. If we consider the process from the grasses' point of view, humans became domesticated animals toiling away to increase the domain of grasses. Let's look at some other crucial cases of domestication connected to the emergence of agriculture.

The Origins of Agriculture

As we've seen, the first settled societies appeared in scattered locations around the world, and the first domestication—of dogs—occurred somewhere in Eurasia. The first farming community—both sedentary and based on domestication—probably appeared in the Levant, along the eastern shore of the Mediterranean and its hinterland, about 13,000 years ago (11,000 BCE). The **Levant** forms the western edge of the Fertile Crescent, which encompasses a boomerang-shaped zone in Southwest Asia from the Red Sea northward along the Rift Valley and the Jordan River valley, curving around to the middle and southern reaches of the Tigris and Euphrates. The latest evidence suggests the possibility that several farming communities popped up here and there throughout the Fertile Crescent at roughly the same time. After farming got under way in the Fertile Crescent, agriculture soon emerged independently in several other parts of the world.

Favorable Conditions

As the Ice Age gave way to warmer and damper climate, both before and after the Younger Dryas, plant life flourished. Forests overgrew steppe and scrubland, deserts retreated, and rivers rose. In many locations, these were favorable trends for people, enabling some groups to settle down and live off newly abundant local plants and animals. In many spots in Southwest Asia, for example, there were now plenty of acorns, almonds, and grasses with edible and storable seeds. Grasses ancestral to wheat and barley spread like weeds with the changing climate, and their seeds provided 50 times more calories than a person burned in gathering them. Gazelles and other tasty herbivores provided meat. The scant evidence suggests that population across Eurasia rose, perhaps quintupling from 16,000 to 12,000 years ago, as climate warmed and foraging became easier. In a few favored locations, including the Levant, the locally abundant food made it possible for foragers to settle down.

Settled Populations Settled populations tended to grow far faster than mobile ones. Parents didn't have to lug children long distances and so were less inclined to try to prevent their birth or abandon babies. Where people collected the seeds of wild grasses, they could mash the seeds into gruel and feed it to babies, weaning infants from their mothers' milk at a younger age. Since lactating women are much less likely to conceive, early weaning meant that mothers became fertile again sooner. The intervals between births tended to be shorter among settled people than among mobile ones.

But population growth among the settled folk gradually caused difficulties. More hunting thinned the numbers of big animals. In the Levant, for example, archeologists have found that people were

Processing Food This 11,000-year-old mortar and pestle from the Natufian culture would have been used to grind seeds or grains into powdery, edible forms. Sedentary peoples had the time and could create the tools necessary to process foods that couldn't be eaten otherwise.

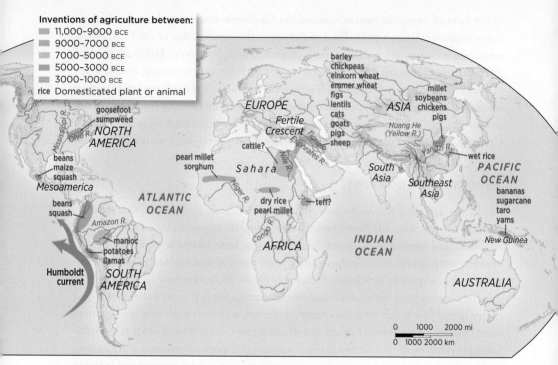

Inventions of agriculture between:
- 11,000–9000 BCE
- 9000–7000 BCE
- 7000–5000 BCE
- 5000–3000 BCE
- 3000–1000 BCE
- rice Domesticated plant or animal

Inventions of Agriculture, 11,000–1000 BCE After living from foraging, fishing, and hunting for more than 250,000 years, humans invented agriculture at least seven times, and probably more, after the end of the last ice age. The earliest of these occurrences, as far as we know, took place in the Fertile Crescent of Southwest Asia.

hunting smaller and smaller animals as time went on—fewer gazelles and more rabbits. In many parts of the world, the standard solution for food shortage remained practical: walk somewhere else. But for settled folk with accumulated possessions, lots of small children, and perhaps spiritual and emotional commitments to preferred places, this approach was less practical. Instead, people intensified their quest for food, especially in circumscribed places such as the Levant (located between a rising sea and a desert), the Nile valley in Egypt (surrounded by desert), and China's Yangzi valley (surrounded by steep hills). Rather than walk elsewhere, they foraged for a wider variety of plants, hunted more kinds of animals, and began to work spreading the seeds of preferred plants such as wild wheat and rice. Such efforts probably took place elsewhere as well, but the archeological record is so spotty that no one knows for sure.

Intelligence and Climate Not long ago, scholars used to wonder why everyone didn't take up farming. Now scholars wonder why anyone did. Farming turns out to involve more work than foraging and hunting, and it usually results in worse nutrition and worse health. Yet after more than 200,000 years without bothering to farm, shortly after the end of the Ice Age humans undertook at least seven transitions to farming on four continents. This seems most unlikely to be a random turn of events. Two important factors may help bring us closer to an understanding of what triggered the change: intelligence and climate.

Turning to a way of life that brings poorer nutrition and health yet requires more work may not seem a hallmark of intelligence, yet it surely did take intelligence to notice which plants grow best in which sorts of places, which ones yield easily edible seeds, which seeds store well, and so forth. Developing this sort of knowledge required communication—language—as well as powers of observation, memory, and reason. So it couldn't have happened before modern, intelligent, language-wielding humans were on the scene.

Depending on when language emerged, there were either no or very few such humans around before the onset of the last ice age 130,000 years ago. During that ice age, conditions were too dry or too cold for agriculture outside of tropical locations, sharply reducing the chances that people would make a transition to farming successfully. And within tropical latitudes, the yield from foraging, hunting, and fishing was usually sufficient, so people didn't bother with domesticating plants. The existence of intelligent, language-bearing humans living outside of lush environments yet enjoying interglacial climate, then, seems a likely prerequisite for transitions to agriculture. That might explain why no transitions to agriculture took place before the retreat of the ice.

The Pivotal Role of Women   One thing most scholars agree on is that agriculture in its earliest stages was women's work. As far as we know, in most hunting and foraging societies women and children specialized in gathering useful plants for food, medicines, or fibers. Adult women presumably were the most knowledgeable about the habits of helpful plants. Although there's no direct evidence for this, women presumably pioneered the transition from merely collecting plants to deliberately sowing the seed of desirable types of plants, and the further transition to sowing the seed of specific, individual plants with desirable characteristics. It seems highly likely, then, that one of the hallmark transformations of the human condition began with a change in women's approach to the task of getting food for their families.

Other Conditions   Two further conditions for the emergence of agriculture also seem sure. First, only

Women's Work This ca. 4000 BCE statue from the Negev Desert in present-day Israel shows a woman carrying a pot, reflecting the role women played in procuring food and water in sedentary communities.

sedentary people would try to farm. Roving bands had no good reason to plant seeds, or save seeds for next year, since they couldn't be sure they would come back to their plantings or that others might not reap their harvest first. The only other species that cultivate—those termites and ants that raise fungi—are also sedentary. Second, in every case, agriculture developed gradually over several centuries, and the people involved didn't know they were undertaking a momentous shift. They were tinkering, experimenting, trying to improve their food supplies or reliability, or perhaps just trying to hold on to what they had in worsening circumstances.

The First Transition to Agriculture: The Fertile Crescent and the Levant

The **transition to agriculture** that scholars know the most about is probably the earliest. It occurred in Southwest Asia, somewhere in the Fertile Crescent, probably on its western edge in the Levant, just inland of the eastern shore of the Mediterranean. Archeological evidence suggests that the earliest plant domestications took place here beginning around 11,000 BCE. Thereafter, more and more humans increasingly relied for their food on specific sorts of grass seed.

The Fertile Crescent isn't really crescent-shaped, and much of it wasn't especially fertile in soil nutrients. But it supported potentially domesticable food plants such as wheat and barley, and several domesticable herd animals such as sheep and goats. And the region offered fine gradients of climate owing to the interplay of air masses and elevations. People didn't have to walk far to move from one microclimate to the next. This could have contributed to plant domestication by enabling people to go only a little ways to take a plant out of its natural range and place it where it needed human help to reproduce.

The Fertile Crescent The first transition to agriculture (as far as we know) took place somewhere in the boomerang-shaped region encompassing the valley of the Tigris and Euphrates Rivers and the coast of the eastern Mediterranean Sea. The earliest evidence of farming we have at present comes from Abu Hureyra.

The Natufians: Environmental Refugees After a few millennia in which climate grew warmer and wetter, the sudden shock of climate

change in the form of the Younger Dryas cold snap hit around 10,700 BCE. For mobile people, this was a challenge, but one that they could meet by walking to warmer latitudes. For settled peoples, it was a crisis. One such people was the Natufians.

With the onset of the Younger Dryas, the 100 or so plants that the Natufians relied on became less reliable. The gazelles, sheep, horses, deer, and boar that they liked to eat grew rare because the grass and shrubs the animals fed on became scarcer. Populations of settled folk declined, and many of them became, in effect, environmental refugees, crowding into oases and riverbeds where there was still enough moisture and warmth for plant growth. (Some Natufians became migratory, although they continued to return to old villages, which they used as cemeteries.) The refugees may have brought seeds with them and sowed them in new settings. In one such location, Abu Hureyra on the Euphrates River in what is now northern Syria, there is spotty archeological evidence of cereal cultivation—not yet domestication—undertaken by Natufians from as early as 11,000 BCE.

As climate cooled down and dried out with the Younger Dryas, food plants withered. Gazelles and other hunting targets grew scarce. The Natufians increasingly sowed einkorn, emmer, and barley—wild grasses that would still yield a harvest in dry conditions. Over generations, they chose to sow and harvest the plants that yielded best. They probably also selected for softer husks, which made getting at the seed easier. With their choices they were slowly creating new plant species, including what we now call wheat and rye.

Figs, Cats, Goats, and Sheep Soon after domesticating cereals, peoples of the Fertile Crescent began to cultivate and then domesticate figs, chickpeas, peas, and lentils. They also domesticated wild animals, with cats perhaps coming first. Genetic evidence suggests that Arabian wild cats are the ancestors of today's pet cats. Around 11,000 to 8000 BCE, when the Natufians were keeping piles of grain, they indirectly created paradises for mice. The lucky mice gorging themselves on stores of Natufian grain attracted wild cats, which ate the well-stuffed mice. Natufians connected the dots: more cats, fewer mice, more grain. Their protection of cats over centuries produced increasingly domesticated cats, comfortable with humans and good at protecting grain by catching mice.

The domestication of goats and sheep began between 11,000 and 9000 BCE, soon after the first plant domestications. People captured juveniles, raised them, and protected them from predators. Like dogs, wild goats and sheep had (and have) a social structure, and most animals follow a leader. Human herders in effect replaced the dominant rams as leaders of the flock. Once people controlled which animals reproduced and which ones did not, they could breed for desired characteristics such as docility, thick wool, and abundant milk. By killing the most defiant males and allowing only the more docile ones to breed, people gradually produced more submissive sheep and goats. They did the same with pigs starting around 8500 BCE, and cattle a few centuries later. The most important farm animals in most of the world—pigs, cattle, sheep, and goats—were created from wild ancestors through domestications undertaken between 11,000 and 7000 BCE in Southwest Asia or, in the case of cattle, possibly northeastern Africa.

Cultural Change Some fundamental cultural changes came along with the transition to agriculture in the Fertile Crescent. Settlement size grew. Houses changed from an oval shape to a rectangular one as mud bricks came into use. People developed pottery for storing grain and liquids by about 7000 BCE. New burial practices emerged in which people lived in houses with their ancestors buried underneath. Skulls were used for home decoration, perhaps implying some sort of ancestor worship. And people fashioned clay figurines that are interpreted as mother goddesses and presumed to represent a fascination with fertility and sexuality.

By 6000 BCE, farming had taken firm root in many places in the Fertile Crescent. People had transformed several wild species into domesticated ones. They had acquired and shared knowledge of how to manage these new species. They learned when to plant and reap, which types of soil to use, how to manage flocks and herds, use animals' manure to boost the growth of food plants, and discipline themselves to the daily and seasonal routines of farming. They may also have learned to share less widely and keep more within family units—that is, to consider crops, animals, tools, and so forth as private property. A new economic and cultural configuration had emerged, a blueprint of sorts for billions of people as yet unborn.

China

So far as we know, the next transition to agriculture took place in China beginning about 7000 BCE. It happened entirely independent of developments in the Levant. There were actually two transitions to agriculture in China: one each in the basins of its two biggest rivers, the Yangzi and the Huang He (Yellow River). As elsewhere, the transition from wild plants to genuinely domesticated ones in China took thousands of years. It is still poorly reflected in the archeological record, so the chances are good that new finds will revise our understanding in the future.

The Yangzi Valley In the valley of the **Yangzi River**, people began to domesticate rice by 7000 BCE if not before. Wild rice exists in many varieties, including some that grow in swampy terrain. These were the ancestors of many of the wet rice varieties cultivated in China today. They yield far more grain per plant, or per patch of ground, than the wheat or barley of Southwest Asia. But they also take much more work to cultivate. Rice shoots must be transplanted when only a few weeks old, and to achieve maximum yields they must be raised partly underwater. Natural seasonal flooding could do this in a few favored places, but elsewhere it required arduous labor. People had to level their land by building "terraces," divide it into small patches marked off by little ridges of earth, divert stream or lake water onto these terraced paddies (or padis) at certain times of year, and drain them at others.

Wet rice agriculture often required cooperation among large numbers of people. They had to share water somehow. The vast labor needed to terrace sloping land and prepare it for planting required many hands. These considerations offset the crop's enormous yields somewhat and slowed its spread. The first communities substantially dependent on rice farming appeared near the mouth of the Yangzi about 4500 BCE.

Chinese Pottery A red-clay pottery vessel (ca. 6000–5200 BCE) from a site in northern China rests on three legs, which might have allowed it to be placed over a cooking fire.

The Huang He Valley In northern China, where rainfall was spotty and rice impractical, agriculture began with millet by 7000 BCE, then soybeans and a handful of other crops by about 6000 BCE. Millet, the most important crop, remained only a small part of people's diets until well after 5000 BCE. Wild food sources predominated until perhaps 3000 BCE. Many parts of northern China have highly fertile loess (windblown) soils that yield excellent crops if enough rain falls. When and where rain didn't fall, starvation threatened. This provided strong incentive to manage water carefully, as with rice cultivation along the Yangzi. Chickens and pigs were domesticated in northern China by 4500 BCE if not before. This was the second domestication of pigs, after the first in Southwest Asia.

One of the distinctive features of the development of agriculture in both river basins of China is that pottery marked the first step in the long process. Some recent archeological finds suggest that pottery preceded the domestication of rice and millet by nearly 10,000 years. Pre-farming peoples in East Asia developed a tradition of boiling and steaming their food in pots. With good pots, the storage of rice and millet was easy and the logic of relying on them improved. The more people relied on these crops, the more likely they were to start down the path toward domestication.

Southeast and South Asia

Somewhere in Southeast Asia, another independent transition to agriculture took place. Good evidence suggests that people on the island of New Guinea domesticated sugarcane, bananas, and root crops such as yams and taro by at least 5000 BCE and probably earlier. They used wetlands and patches of surrounding forest in the eastern highlands in a form of agriculture often called swidden, which involves farming for a few seasons at one spot and then moving one's operation to another nearby. They didn't domesticate any animals but eventually acquired chickens and dogs from mainland Southeast

Asia. New Guinea's may have been the only independent transition to agriculture in Southeast Asia, but we can't be sure.

On the Southeast Asian mainland, sedentary villages and pottery preceded farming, as in China. The first evidence of farming dates from about 2500 BCE, and it probably represents an introduction from South China rather than an independent transition. Pigs and chickens were the important animals domesticated, and rice was the central crop.

It's quite possible, however, that Southeast Asians made a transition to agriculture, or several, before the documented case in New Guinea, maybe even before it happened in China or the Levant. Some domesticable plants don't normally leave traces that last over millennia, unlike rice, wheat, and barley grains. So all we can say with assurance is that there was one transition to agriculture in Southeast Asia, on New Guinea, by 5000 BCE if not before—and that the odds are good that we know only a fraction of the truth of the matter.

In South Asia, people took up wheat farming as early as 7000 BCE and rice farming by 6000 BCE. The strongest evidence at the moment suggests that these were imported introductions of agriculture to South Asia rather than independent transitions.

Africa

The story of early agriculture in Africa is sketchy because archeologists have done much less work there than elsewhere. Africans probably domesticated cattle, perhaps in Egypt, as early as 6000 BCE. For a few millennia after that, they refined their cattle-keeping ways and spread the practice into suitable parts of the continent, but as far as we know they didn't yet domesticate plants. In this respect, Africa followed a different path from most parts of the world, where either the plants came first or both came more or less at the same time.

Then, beginning about 3000 BCE, another independent transition to agriculture took place in Africa. It apparently happened at about the same time in several spots on the southern edge of the Sahara. Millet, sorghum, and dry rice (different varieties from the rice grown in East Asia) were the chief crops. As in the Fertile Crescent, climate change was probably a key factor motivating the transition to agriculture in Africa. After 8000 BCE, the Sahara grew wetter with regular summer rains. It hosted grass and wildlife—even lakes and hippopotami. People lived among the lakes, fishing, foraging, and hunting. As in East Asia, they developed pottery before domesticating plants, perhaps by 9000 BCE. They tended to boil their food into stews and porridges, in contrast to the tradition that prevailed in Southwest Asia in which grains were ground up and baked into bread and meat was roasted.

The Sahara region began to dry out about 4500 BCE. Lakes and wetlands began to shrink, depriving Saharan peoples of some of their best environments for foraging and fishing. With less food to go around, they faced pressures similar to those in the Levant when the Younger Dryas hit. They crowded into the remaining lakeshores, just as the

CONSIDERING THE EVIDENCE

Crocodiles in the Sahara

The Sahara desert might be the last place you'd expect to find a crocodile. Water has been scarce in the Sahara for thousands of years, but between 8000 and 4500 BCE it was a green place full of lakes and rivers. It attracted people who hunted hippos, elephants, and antelope, speared catfish with stone harpoons, and did their best to avoid the crocodiles. In addition to life-size paintings and carvings of animals and themselves, these people left behind ivory jewelry and pottery. The first humans to enter the Sahara eventually became sedentary hunters and fishers, living alongside lakes until the climate shifted again and forced them out. The crocodile engraving below is locatd in the Messale plateau in southwestern Libya and dates back at least 10,000 years.

Questions for Analysis

1. Carving such large images into rock faces would have taken much time and work. What do these efforts suggest about the role of large game animals in the culture of the people who created these images?

2. How did life in the "green" Sahara compare to that of the Magdalenians in Europe, who painted scenes of wildlife in caves like Lascaux during the last ice age?

3. Some scholars suggest that rock art served a religious purpose. Does this example give any evidence for that? Explain your response.

Natufians had sought refuge in oases and next to riverbeds. Since the Saharan lakes were all shallow, they expanded and shrank considerably with the rains, which made soils around their edges often moist and suitable for growing plants. It was on these lake edges that Africans first began to domesticate and raise millet, rice, and sorghum.

In what might have been yet another independent transition to agriculture, people in the highlands of Ethiopia began to raise different crops before 1000 BCE—maybe long before. The main one was a cereal called teff, still today grown mainly in Ethiopia. Teff does well at mile-high altitudes, in dry conditions, and provides a nutritious payload of minerals and protein. It is still uncertain whether the domestication of teff occurred independently or in imitation of one of the nearby earlier transitions to agriculture.

South America

The archeological record is also thin in South America, so we don't know much about the transition to agriculture there. Some scholars think it began with horticulture (the raising of vegetables or fruits in garden patches) in the lowland rain forests of what is now Colombia as early as 9000 BCE. Scattered evidence exists for domesticated plants in what is now Colombia, Ecuador, and Peru between 8000 and 4000 BCE. There is firmer evidence for squash and bean domestication, as well as the existence of small villages, along the coasts of Ecuador and Peru after about 3000 BCE. Squash and beans alone cannot support human populations, but on these coasts people lived next door to the Pacific's Humboldt Current, one of the world's richest marine provinces. Teeming with fish and offering a hunting ground for millions of seabirds, the Humboldt Current provided the coastal peoples of Peru with plenty of fish and birds' eggs to eat.

But the Humboldt Current sometimes flowed weakly, thinning the fish and bird populations. During El Niño years, the fishing was poor and the incentive to seek other food sources was strong. It could be that the revival of El Niño after about 3000 BCE, a response to a general warming trend in the Pacific, provided a climate-change trigger to the emergence of agriculture here, as other climate changes seem to have done in the Levant and in Africa.

Potatoes, first domesticated in highland Peru between 3000 and 2000 BCE, could serve as a staple crop, a staff of life like rice or wheat and unlike squash and beans. Potatoes yield well in terms of calories per acre and also provide a healthy variety of vitamins and minerals by themselves. When people in the Andes learned to freeze-dry potatoes to make an easily storable and portable foodstuff, called *chuño*, they acquired the basis for exchange and accumulation of foodstuffs that rice, wheat, or maize provided elsewhere in the world.

Manioc, also known as cassava, is a root crop native to South America that was first domesticated in the western part of Amazonia's rain forest no later than 4000 BCE. It provides plentiful calories but little else in the way of nutrition. But if raised by people who also fish, hunt, and forage, it could provide a reliable food supply. It fares well in poor soils and withstands drought better than most crops. So in South America at least one, and perhaps more, independent transition to farming took place.

Mesoamerica and North America

In Mesoamerica—roughly the region between Costa Rica and northern Mexico—crop domestication began perhaps as early as 6000 BCE. Squash, beans, and especially maize formed the basis of Mesoamerican agriculture. Thanks to human selection, maize evolved from a small wild plant called *teosinte* to become the staple of life in much of the Americas. Over thousands of years, maize farmers chose to plant those varieties of *teosinte* that grew bigger, matured faster, and had other desirable traits. Scholars debate just where the domestication of maize began, but most argue for western Mexico.

We may never know just when and where maize was domesticated, but we know that it mattered for the societies that relied on it. Dried maize stores very well, making it—like rice, wheat, barley, and freeze-dried potatoes—a basis for accumulation and exchange. Maize also yields richly in calories, although it lacks niacin (a form of vitamin B and an essential human nutrient), so people who rely on it heavily often suffer from deficiency diseases. Farmers grew it widely in the Americas. It became a significant food in Peru by 2000 BCE at the latest, and in what is now the southwestern United States at about the same time. Farming spread across the North American continent, arriving as far as eastern Canada about 1,000 years ago.

Archeologists have also found evidence for an independent transition to agriculture in the heartland of North America. By about 2500 BCE, people living in river floodplains of what is now Ohio, Kentucky, Tennessee, and Illinois were raising plants such as sumpweed and goosefoot. These people are

Domesticating Maize Millennia of careful cultivation went into developing strains of corn (right) that were bigger and more nutritious than wild *teosinte* (left).

sometimes called mound builders because they piled up earth into mounds, presumably in connection with ceremonies of some sort. They lived in small villages until they acquired maize from Mexico (about 800 CE), which enabled their populations and the scale of their settlements to grow quickly. We'll return to them in a later chapter.

One important feature of the transitions to farming in the Americas is that animals hardly figured in the story. In the Andes, people domesticated llamas about 4000 BCE. But nowhere did they have animals they could use for traction, like the oxen and horses of Eurasia. People had to do all the work of farming themselves. And nowhere did domestic animals, or their milk, form a significant part of people's diets.

The archeological and genetic record concerning the transitions to agriculture elsewhere around the world is slender. We don't even know how many independent transitions there were, although the best guess is eight in all. But we do know that the turn to agriculture spread widely and began a sea change in the human condition.

The Spread of Agriculture

From its several points of origin, agriculture spread far and wide. The cereal culture of the Fertile Crescent, the rice culture of China, and the maize and beans culture of Mesoamerica diffused farthest and gave rise to the world's most influential and widespread farming systems. The Fertile Crescent farming system spread along the northern shores of the Mediterranean into Anatolia and Greece. Between about 7000 and 4000 BCE, people carried it from Anatolia to the British Isles. It moved eastward too, into northwestern India by perhaps 7000 BCE. Meanwhile, on a small scale, the rice-based system of the Yangzi apparently spread westward into the Ganges valley of northeastern India by about 6000 BCE, although some scholars maintain that rice was independently domesticated there. The rice system also spread to mainland Southeast Asia after about 2500 BCE. Maize culture spread from its Mesoamerican home both northward and southward, and became the staple food of most farmers in the Americas by 1000 BCE.

While those three farming systems cast the longest shadow in world history, they weren't the only ones to spread. In Africa, the cultivation of millet and sorghum spread southward from its origins in the Sahel (the belt of semi-arid land on the southern edges of the Sahara) into parts of West and Central Africa. Highland Ethiopia's teff-based farming system, however, scarcely expanded beyond its homeland. The same was true of the high Andes tradition of potato farming, which (until after 1500 CE) barely spread at all. Manioc, however, first cultivated in the forests of Amazonia, proved a good traveler throughout the damp lowlands of South America and, by 500 BCE, was raised in the small islands of the eastern Caribbean.

Farming spread in two main ways. First, farmers sometimes displaced foragers, pushed them off fertile lands, and extended their own domain. Second, the idea of agriculture sometimes spread: people who hadn't formerly practiced it learned about it and imitated the practice of others.

Expansion by Displacement

Farmers could often displace foragers through violence. Food production allowed greater densities of population. Bigger groups normally prevailed over smaller ones in violent contests. Moreover, the bigger social groups became, the more likely they could support specialists in weapon making and the arts of violence. People who had the skills to make good farming tools could also make good weapons. Foraging bands, even those that included skilled hunters, couldn't consistently withstand the collective pressure that farming peoples could bring to bear.

Infectious Disease Farmers could also displace foragers and hunters without even trying—through infectious disease. Because farming folk lived side by side with herd animals, their bodies gradually came to host microbes whose ancestor-microbes had routinely lived in sheep, goats, cattle, or dogs. Some of these species-jumping microbes caused deadly diseases among humans. Influenza comes from pigs and ducks. Smallpox may derive from some rodent-borne virus. Camels donated a common cold virus. In all, about 60 percent of the infections that human bodies host came originally from

In what ways did agriculture spread from its points of
origin to adoption throughout most of the world?

57

other animals. Over many generations, in what must have been a painful process with many mini-epidemics along the way, the immune systems of farming folk became increasingly resistant to these microbes. Indeed, when infectious diseases were constantly present, only those individuals with robust immune systems survived childhood. Their own children, in turn, would be likelier to have robust immune systems, or at least immune systems attuned to the risks posed by sedentary life among animals and animal-derived diseases. In effect, a new selection process was at work among farming peoples—selection for disease resistance.

Hunters and foragers didn't normally face this grim pressure. As long as they kept their distance from farmers, they stayed healthier than sons and daughters of the soil. But if they came into prolonged contact with farmers, disaster routinely followed. Their immune systems hadn't built up resistance to the infections now common among

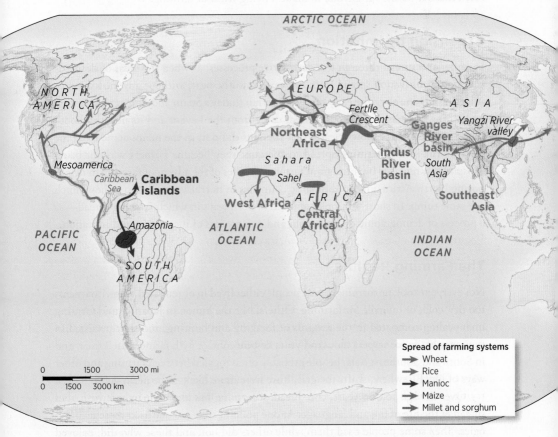

The Spread of Farming Systems Of the several transitions to agriculture, three in particular developed into farming systems that spread especially widely: those based on rice in East Asia, wheat in the Fertile Crescent, and maize in Mexico. Other crops and farming systems spread less widely. In every case, the spreading took thousands of years.

farmers, and they sickened and died at appalling rates. This process has happened again and again in more recent times, and it's extremely likely that it happened early in the history of the expansion of farming too, although the archeological evidence for it is slender. It's highly probable that greater vulnerability to new human infections cost foragers and hunters terribly, clearing the way for further expansion of farming.

Environmental Change In some environments, farming probably spread because it indirectly ruined landscapes for hunters and foragers. The daily activities of farmers often depleted the nearby wild herds on which hunters depended. Farmers' own herds and flocks munched and trampled their way over the countryside, reducing the availability of forage plants for wildlife. Farmers often set fire to vegetation to prepare the ground for their own plantings. By pursuing their own subsistence methods, farmers often made it harder for anyone to make a living without farming.

Expansion by Imitation

Farming also spread through less destructive processes, as when the ideas of domestication and cultivation spread from one person to the next, without anyone killing or infecting anyone else. The early crops of Iberian (today's Spain and Portugal) farming, and all the animals that farmers raised, came from the Levant and its neighborhood. But genetic evidence shows clearly that Iberians did not, in the main, come from the Levant. The idea of farming spread to Iberians: they became farmers without being substantially replaced by immigrant farmers. Studies of the advent of farming to neighboring North Africa, and to the Baltic countries in northeastern Europe, show much the same thing. In short, examples abound of both ways in which farming spread—as a process of demographic displacement and as a process of inspiration and imitation.

The Farming Regime

Not everyone took up farming. Some people either lived in or retreated to environments too dry, cold, or infertile for farming. Others, like the Jomon in Japan, found farming unappealing compared to the rewards of foraging and hunting, and they persisted in their way of life for several thousand years despite contact with farmers. In Africa, and in South and Southeast Asia, people probably often toggled between farming and other ways of life. Elsewhere, shifts to agriculture were more likely to be permanent.

Over the last 10,000 years, the spread of farming has almost matched the earlier spread of the use of fire and language. At one point in time, no one used these technologies. Then some people used them while others did not; and those who did, enjoyed great advantages against those who did not. Eventually, fire and language came into use by all people. This point may yet come with respect to agriculture too, although to this day in the Arctic, and in several moist tropical forests, people survive who neither practice agriculture themselves nor eat its products. These hunters and foragers now account for less than 1 percent of humankind.

The Impact of Transitions to Agriculture

The transitions to farming and its subsequent spread brought fundamental and durable consequences for human communities. Human populations increased even as people grew unhealthier. New expressions of culture in arenas such as religion, architecture, and pottery also emerged.

Effects on Population

The most basic advantage of farming, and the reason for its widespread practice, is that it enabled far more people—10 to 100 times as many—to live on the same amount of land as did hunting and foraging. Farming women had more babies, at more frequent intervals, than the women of hunting and foraging peoples. Although those babies died in droves from infections, the number of children still grew. This conferred the advantages of superior numbers on farmer folk in any competitions with hunters and foragers.

No censuses were taken during the Paleolithic, and the available evidence for early human populations is scanty. The table below shows one plausible reconstruction. If these numbers are anywhere close to accurate, they show the revolutionary demographic implications of the spread of farming in the millennia after 8000 BCE.

Health Effects

Along with the advantages that account for its spread, farming carried costs. These costs emerged gradually so that the first farmers in any locale didn't suffer from them—at least, not all at once. Remember that adoptions of farming probably took place over hundreds or even thousands of years during which people practiced foraging, hunting, and farming, with the role of farming expanding over time. The more fully dependent people became on farming, the more prominent its costs became.

Diet and Stature Farming folk ate a narrower diet than foragers and hunters. Depending heavily on a few staple foods left them at greater risk for

Global Population Estimates

YEAR	POPULATION	RATE OF ANNUAL INCREASE
40,000 BCE	600,000	n/a
8000 BCE	6,000,000	0.003%
3000 BCE	20,000,000	0.014%
1500 BCE	100,000,000	0.053%

Source: M. Perrault, "85 milliards d'humains plus tard" (2003).

poor nutrition from a lack of key vitamins or minerals. They ate less meat and got less protein, which probably accounts for the smaller stature of farming people compared to their pre-farming ancestors. Skeletal remains from sites between Ukraine and North Africa indicate that late Paleolithic men on average stood 5'8" (177 cm) tall, and women 5'4" (166 cm). In the last thousand years before agriculture—the period when game was growing scarce and climate colder and dryer—their average stature shrank by 2 inches (5 cm). During the first millennium after the origins of farming, they shrank faster, by another 2 to 4 inches (5–10 cm).

Disease Farmers were sicker as well as smaller than their hunting and foraging ancestors. The shift to agriculture was a gigantic stride backward for human health. Among the reasons for this is that farming folk, like all sedentary people, lived amid their own garbage and wastes. Moreover, they often deliberately handled human and animal feces to use it as fertilizer. They suffered heavily from gastrointestinal diseases carried by worms and other parasites, which one might collectively call diseases of sedentism.

Farming communities also suffered from what one could call diseases of domestication. As we've seen, many human diseases derive from domesticated-animal diseases. Half of these come from dogs, cattle, sheep, and goats. Even chickens and cats have donated some of their infections to their human masters. As these infections evolved into human diseases, babies in farming communities in Eurasia and Africa (not in the Americas, which hardly had any domesticated animals) increasingly were born into hazardous microbial environments teeming with influenza, smallpox, mumps, tuberculosis, tetanus, and a host of other killing diseases.

Farming invited diseases from other sources as well. As we've seen, stored grain attracted rats and mice, putting farming communities at enhanced risk for hemorrhagic fevers and other nasty infections carried by rodents. There are about 35 human diseases derived from rats or from the fleas and ticks that live on rats. And where farmers cleared forest, and especially where they allowed water to accumulate, they created new habitat for malarial mosquitoes, another dangerous disease vector. Malaria, one of humankind's worst scourges, seems powerfully correlated with farming environments—at least, where climates are warm enough for the relevant mosquitoes. In Africa and Asia, it seems to have taken firm hold among humans soon after they took up farming, although it probably wasn't unknown before.

Children and Women All these diseases made life for farming folk, especially children, far more hazardous than for hunting and foraging peoples—at least, for those who could stay away from disease-bearing farmers. Farmers had far more babies than did hunters and foragers, but their disease environments also killed them faster. If anyone had known these facts of disease history, they would have avoided agriculture like the plague. But they didn't know.

Our old friends the Natufians show that some of the health costs of taking up farming fell mostly on women. The Natufians left more skeletons than most people, giving archeologists an opportunity to calculate life expectancies. After the Natufians shifted to agriculture, men lived longer than before but women less long. Two likely reasons for this gender difference are that death by violence and hunting accidents (more likely to befall men) decreased as people took up farming, but that death in the act of giving birth became more common as fertility rates rose. The routines of work among farmers also left telling marks on Natufian female skeletons. They show signs of stresses in their knees, wrists, and backs from the endless kneeling and bending required for grinding grain. In general, the transition to agriculture made people shorter, sicker, and more likely to suffer from acute malnutrition—and in most cases, the effects were worse for women than for men.

The Self-Domestication of Humans

Here is a final reflection on what settling down and taking up farming meant for human bodies. At the same time that our ancestors were domesticating dogs, grasses, sheep, and goats, they were—equally unknowingly—domesticating themselves. Their bodies became smaller and weaker. Survival came to depend less on strength and physical courage, and more on the ability to get along with others and accept one's place in a hierarchy, the same sort of docility that humans appreciated in goats and sheep.

Gracialization In some respects, this process of self-domestication may go further back: **gracialization**—the evolutionary process by which skeletons became thinner, smaller, and lighter—began in Eurasia as early as 40,000 years ago. Earlier skeletons show much stronger legs among mobile hunters and foragers than among later farmers, and more powerful right arms on most males, perhaps a result of throwing rocks and spears. Gracialization suggests a gradual process of selection for traits other than brute strength.

Gracialization in recent millennia (since 40,000 years ago) has gone furthest among Africans and Asians. It has gone least far among the isolated populations of Tierra del Fuego at the southern tip of South America (they only arrived there 12,000 years ago at the earliest) and Australian Aborigines. This suggests gracialization is ongoing and recent, and connected to the emergence of bigger social groups. Survival and reproduction within the bigger groups made possible by sedentism and farming favors the sociable, the politically skilled, the good cooperators and clever deceivers—as well as those with strong immune systems. In short, sedentism and farming encouraged the evolution of a wily political animal no longer as reliant on strength and stamina.

Selection for Docility So as our ancestors were domesticating other species, they were also domesticating themselves through genetic selection. Farming in particular selected for people who would accept both the repetitive routines of farming life and their place in a social order in which only a few could be near the top. Farming began a process that selected against defiance and for docility in humans as well as in farm animals. This process is still ongoing after 10,000 years.

At the same time that our bodies and minds evolved so as to fit the demands of the farming life, we created cultures that help us endure numbing routines and social subordination. Cultural adjustment to the demands of farming eased the pressures for genetic adjustment. And our cultures evolved quickly in response to the risks and rewards of farming, as much of the rest of this book will show. Even in the first few thousand years after the transitions to farming, major cultural shifts occurred. Let's look briefly at some of these.

Changes in Human Culture

The transition to agriculture is one of the great transformations in the history of the human species. Raising one's food as opposed to collecting or hunting it brought broad cultural changes. It required people to submit to laborious routines, but it allowed enormous expansions in cultural richness and diversity. Mobile hunters and foragers around the world had only a few, very similar tools, the same social structures just about everywhere, and—as far as we know—roughly the same sorts of ideas about nature and spirits. By later standards, there wasn't much cultural diversity during the Paleolithic, because mobile people had to carry their culture with them. With sedentary farming, all that changed.

Energy The most fundamental change brought by farming was an energy revolution. Like cooking long before it, or the harnessing of fossil fuels long afterward, farming vastly increased the amount of energy available to human communities. The added calories that farming made available brought a dramatic change in demography, as we have seen. Now people died at faster rates than before; but babies were born even faster, and populations grew more quickly than at any previous time, thanks to the fertility of farming families.

The Social Unit Transitions to agriculture also changed the basic social unit: from the mobile band of perhaps 30 to 80 people, to farming families. These weren't necessarily nuclear families of just two parents and their children. Many agricultural societies recognized family units of three generations or groups of cousins. Bigger family units were useful for some kinds of farm work. Moreover, many farming societies clustered into villages where hundreds of people gathered together, forming another, larger, looser social unit. In global terms, until the rapid urbanization of the last 30 years, the farming village remained the characteristic human settlement and social environment.

Daily Routines Farming brought big and long-lasting changes in daily routines. Farming people normally had to work more days and longer hours every day than did hunters and foragers. Preparing the ground for sowing or planting was laborious, even with the help of fire and domestic animals. Planting, weeding, watering, and harvesting all required long hours of tedious work. So did threshing, preparing, and cooking grains. Grinding grain, where that was practiced, took even more time and effort. Farmers had far less free time than foragers and hunters did.

Social Units This Neolithic rock art found in present-day Algeria depicts a small group of people of different sizes, possibly adults and children within a larger farming community.

Religion Farming brought changes in religion too. Most farming communities placed an emphasis on fertility and found ways to revere it. They also came to locate their gods in the skies as much as in animals, trees, and rocks. This gave greater scope for religious specialists—priests—who could study the heavens and give advice about when to plant and harvest. Unlike migratory birds or flowering plants, humans have no innate sense of when in the year to perform certain tasks, but agriculture in most settings required that farmers act with a precise understanding of changing seasons. Religions acquired ever more features that connected them to the annual rhythms of farm life.

Cultural Diversification With farming came cultural elaboration in other areas as well. New styles of architecture emerged, owing in part to new materials such as bricks. Pottery became larger, more widespread, and more intricate in design. Art, tools, and weapons grew more diverse and elaborate. People could make these advances not because they had more time to spare but because they were staying put in one spot, and the efficiency of food production allowed a tiny minority to engage in creative activities.

A basic similarity in social structure underlay this cultural diversification. Agricultural society allowed social stratification of a sort unseen in mobile bands or even among sedentary foragers. Farming opened more opportunities for the accumulation of wealth, both through clever exchanges and through violent intimidation and seizure. This broad pattern of heightened stratification was fundamental to farming societies. It emerged in both Eurasia and the Americas, between which there was no contact during this period, as well as in Africa. Later chapters will explain the forms it took.

Conclusion

With the domestication of plants and animals, *Homo sapiens* for the first time became the dominant mammal on Earth. Over the four-billion-year history of life on our planet, several species (and groups of species such as the dinosaurs) have enjoyed their moments in the sun. Despite being well adapted to the conditions of their time, sooner or later they all went extinct, usually in consequence of some major environmental change to which other species adjusted more quickly and successfully. Is human dominance only the latest in this long line, or are we so clever that the pattern will change?

Given its tremendous importance in human history and its nearly universal adoption by human groups, the transition to agriculture may appear to be an inevitable stage in the progress of humankind. A century ago, most scholars who thought about such things believed just that. But it was not. Remember that the first transition didn't happen for more than 200,000 years of human history. It took place only after the climate changes at the end of the last ice age and the gradual growth in numbers of clever hunters. If big game had remained plentiful and foraging opportunities abundant, there probably would have been no incentive to experiment with the cultivation of plants.

The transitions to sedentism and agriculture are among the crucial turning points in human history, ranking with the harnessing of fire, the emergence of language, and (later) the adoption of fossil fuels. The big changes at the end of the Paleolithic are clearly momentous in their long-term consequences but hazy in their causes. Climate shifts probably played a role, and perhaps population pressure did too. What else might have been involved we just don't know. We do know that after the domestication of dogs more than 20,000 years ago, the first flurry of domestications and probably the first genuine transition to farming took place in the Levant, soon before 10,000 BCE. And we know that several other transitions to agriculture took place over the next few thousand years on every inhabited continent except Australia.

The development of sedentism and farming had important consequences. They included faster population growth, worse health, and new directions in religion and other forms of cultural expression. These trends all shaped farmers' lives, and those of non-farmers too, fairly soon after farming took root.

One other trend, slower to develop but with powerful long-term effects, is noteworthy. With farming, population grew more rapidly, communities became larger, and eventually the networks among communities grew denser than before. Farming communities formed nodes in the fragile and faint webs of humankind, connected to one another mainly by more mobile peoples such as foragers and hunters. After the transitions to farming, the world became more densely settled, with more well-worn routes among settlements and more regular contacts among communities. In a few places, such as the Fertile Crescent and the lower Yangzi valley, people, settlements, routes, and communication were much denser than elsewhere, and highly interactive local webs emerged. In most places, population was still sparse, settlements rare, routes and communication intermittent. It would be another 5,000 years after the first farming communities took shape before large-scale webs of interaction emerged with sustained long-distance linkages.

Chapter Review

KEY TERMS

Natufians p. 34

Younger Dryas p. 36

Holocene p. 37

sedentary p. 38

Jomon culture p. 38

Göbekli Tepe p. 38

Magdalenian culture p. 40

domestication p. 43

Levant p. 45

transition to agriculture p. 48

Yangzi River p. 50

gracialization p. 61

REVIEW QUESTIONS

1. Why was slow global warming after about 18,000 BCE a benefit for humans?

2. How did accessibility to food sources affect where the first sedentary and semi-sedentary people lived?

3. Why did sedentary life spur the development of tools and other objects?

4. Describe the process of domestication with examples of animals and plants.

5. What were the most important conditions for the first transition to agriculture?

6. Approximately where and when did the domestication of the most important farm animals occur?

7. Why do you think agriculture developed independently in different parts of the world?

8. What were the two main ways in which farming spread far and wide?

9. How did the transitions to agriculture impact human population and health?

10. In what sense was the development of farming an energy revolution?

11. Is the development of agriculture an inevitable stage in human progress? Explain why or why not.

Go to INQUIZITIVE

to see what you've learned—and learn what you've missed—with personalized feedback along the way.

Building Complex Societies

9000 to 1500 BCE

1. What were the main characteristics of life in early farming villages?

2. What were the main characteristics of herder societies?

3. What was the significance of the major farmer migrations in Eurasia, Africa, and Polynesia?

4. How did the spread of farming and herding change human biology, culture, and the environment?

5. What characteristics did the first cities, states, and complex societies all share?

6. Why did the first faint webs of connection begin to develop at this time?

In 1991, hikers in the Ötz Valley near the mountainous border between Italy and Austria came upon a frozen corpse protruding from glacial ice. Medical examination revealed that "Ötzi the Iceman" was well preserved for his age: 5,300 years old. When he died, Ötzi was about 45 years old, elderly by the standards of his time. He stood 5′5″ (160 cm) tall and weighed about 110 lbs. (50 kg). He was brown-eyed, wore his hair long, and sported a shaggy beard and tattoos of small dots.

Few corpses have aroused as much scientific interest as Ötzi's. The contents of his stomach showed that he had eaten two balanced meals within eight hours of his death: deer and mountain goat meat, roots, fruits, and wheat bran, perhaps eaten as bread.

Pollen ingested with his last meals indicated that he died in the springtime. Clues in his fingernails suggested he had been sick three times in the six months before his death. Chemical analysis of his tooth enamel revealed he had grown up nearby, and slight deformations of his leg bones and pelvis indicated he did a lot of walking in hilly terrain. Genetic evidence showed he suffered from something similar to Lyme disease and was lactose intolerant (meaning he couldn't digest milk or dairy products). His hands were smooth, suggesting he didn't regularly handle rough objects and may have been a trader or a shaman.

Ötzi the Iceman was a sharp dresser, sporting an array of animal skins. His boots—bearskin soles with deerskin uppers—were so elegant that many researchers suppose he came from a society with specialist cobblers. He wore a striped goatskin vest, a calf-leather belt, goatskin leggings, and goatskin underwear. He topped it all off with a bear-fur cap.

Ötzi carried an axe with a precision-crafted blade of almost pure copper, an expensive material. Like his elaborate dress, this suggested that Ötzi may have been prosperous. He also had with him a sewing kit, a fire-starter kit with fungi and flints, a modest medical kit including some natural antibiotics, a small dagger held in a sheath, a deerskin quiver with 14 arrows, and an unfinished bow.

Ötzi needed his weapons. He had bruises and cuts on his legs, hands, and chest, implying hand-to-hand combat. DNA analysis of blood found on his body and clothes indicates that others, whether friends or enemies, were wounded with him. The fight apparently took place shortly before his death. Someone shot an arrow into his back that sliced through his shoulder blade, severed an artery, and lodged under his armpit. Enfeebled by the wound and several bruises on his skull, he froze to death.

His murder remains a very cold case. Who killed Ötzi? Why was he walking near a mountain

CHRONOLOGY

Between 8000 and 5000 BCE Lactose-tolerance genetic mutations occur in some people in West Africa, East Africa, northern Europe, Southwest Asia

ca. 7500 BCE Çatalhöyük settlement begins

By ca. 7000 BCE Jericho is home to around 2,000 people

ca. 7000 BCE Pottery appears in the Fertile Crescent

ca. 6000 BCE Mesopotamians develop the potter's wheel; large-scale smelting operations begin

ca. 5000 BCE Herding becomes a full-time specialization

ca. 4800 BCE Domestication of horses

ca. 4500 BCE Pottery appears in North America

ca. 4000 BCE Eurasia's Indo-European migrations begin

By ca. 3500 BCE Steppe people ride horses

Between 3500 BCE and ca. 1500 BCE Complex societies emerge in Mesopotamia, Egypt, Indus valley, China, Mesoamerica, Andes

ca. 3500 BCE Large-scale irrigation begins; Mesopotamian smiths begin making bronze; first wheels, axles, plows, and donkey caravans appear; pottery appears in South America

ca. 3300 BCE Lifetime of "Ötzi the Iceman"

ca. 3000–2500 BCE Bantu-speakers migrate within West Central Africa

ca. 3000 BCE People begin to use sails efficiently

ca. 2000 BCE Domestication of camels

ca. 1500 BCE Lapita migrations begin

ca. 1500 BCE–500 CE Bantu-speakers migrate into East and southern Africa

ca. 500 CE Polynesians reach Hawaii and Easter Island

ca. 1200 CE Polynesians reach New Zealand

pass and carrying so much gear? How did he get into a fight, and why was he shot in the back? Was he a trader heading over the mountains? Was he a traveling shaman? Was he fleeing from someone? Despite the remarkable ingenuity of the many scientists who have pried into Ötzi's secrets, even locating some of his living relatives in Austria, we have no answers.

The first half of this chapter will focus on the world that Ötzi knew, one that developed after farming had begun to spread and before there were any cities—in other words, the millennia known as the Neolithic. In Southwest Asia, this world lasted from roughly 10,000 to 3500 BCE. But in sub-Saharan Africa and Polynesia, for example, it started later and comes forward much closer to the present, in some particulars to about 1000 CE. The second half of the chapter considers the emergence and character of cities, states, and complex society—defined when we get there—with special attention to some common features among early complex societies, including social hierarchy, writing, and metallurgy. The chapter concludes with observations on the enduring challenges to complex societies and the intriguing parallels among them.

Early Farming Villages

As we saw in Chapter 2, farming gradually spread from its several lands of origin. In most parts of the world, early farmers clustered together in villages. These weren't entirely new: a few favored locations had supported villages of hunter-foragers or fisherfolk before farming. With farming, villages soon became the new norm, the basic cell of human society, and the typical human habitat. Most of your ancestors over the past 8,000 years probably lived in farming villages.

Village Society

Farm villages usually contained several dozen to several hundred people. As a rough rule, most adult men worked preparing fields, planting, tending, and harvesting crops. Adult women often tended and harvested crops too, and took primary responsibility for grinding grain, fetching water and fuelwood, and minding small children. Recent studies of bones of women from farming villages in central Europe after 5000 BCE imply a strenuous work load: they had upper-arm strength equal to today's elite female rowers. Children by the age of five took part in farm routines, fetching wood and water, and weeding fields. These roles varied from place to place with the crops and technologies used and the prevailing cultural traditions and beliefs.

Solidarity beyond Kinfolk Farm villages were made up partly of kinfolk. But some people lived close by others who weren't their kin, and a new social category—neighbor—acquired importance. People in villages had to find ways to live harmoniously with others unrelated to them, which until then hadn't been a large part of human experience. Forging bonds of solidarity with non-kin was especially important when big tasks needed doing, such as building a wall around one's village. Villages that were subject to attack by strangers depended on solidarity among neighbors for survival.

The earliest farm villages, it seems, were composed of near equals. Old social hierarchies continued, based on age and gender and inherited ultimately from the deep hominin past. As in all societies, some people were held in higher esteem than others for their abilities. And settled farmers could own more than mobile people. But the opportunities for accumulation of wealth remained modest in early villages. Most families enjoyed roughly the same standard of living as their neighbors. This rough equality narrowed the scope for envy and jealousy, which are never far below the surface in human societies. Customs and rituals that emphasized community over individuals helped smooth over potential jealousies. Early villages developed festivals, often anchored by events in the agricultural calendar such as harvest time. Most villages today still have such celebrations.

Maximizing Fertility One feature of village life—noted in Chapter 2—was large numbers of children. Whereas hunter-foragers contrived to limit their fertility, farmers usually tried to maximize it. Roughly half of all babies died before their fifth birthday in farming villages. Parents wanted to be sure of having adult children to help out as they aged, so they eagerly welcomed births. Analysis of burials around the world suggests that women in early farming villages, on average, had two more babies in their lifetimes than did their forager ancestors. Just about all farming peoples scorned or pitied childless men and women. This cultural preference for lots of children remains strong today where village life prevails, although it tends to vanish within two generations in the context of city life.

Pottery and Its Uses Another characteristic of settled village life was pottery. Mobile people rarely used pottery because pots are heavy and break easily in transport. Typically made of clay and baked, at first in bonfires and later in small ovens called kilns, pots became essential household items in farm villages. As we saw in Chapter 2, the first pottery predated farming in a few places in East Asia, appearing as early as 18,000 BCE. Elsewhere, people generally settled down before taking up pottery. In the Fertile Crescent, for example, pottery appeared only around 7000 BCE, millennia

CONSIDERING THE EVIDENCE

Jomon Pots and Potters

Pots, bowls, cups, and other vessels are so common today that it's difficult to appreciate how revolutionary pottery was at first for storing and preparing food and liquids. Farmers produced most of the pottery that archeologists find, but some of the earliest pots yet found were made about 15,000 years ago in Japan by foraging and fishing people whom we call the Jomon. These people used at least some of their pots to cook salmon that passed along the northwestern shore of Japan to spawn. The pots were formed by hand without the aid of a potter's wheel and were hardened in an open fire rather than inside a kiln. In later centuries, Jomon potters decorated their work with braided ropes (*jomon* in Japanese), but earlier vessels had more varied decorations, such as hatch marks, indentations, and bored holes. Most Jomon pots were left undecorated. Historians and archeologists often analyze variations in decoration, method of manufacture, and location of pottery fragments to trace movements of people and the expansion of material culture.

Questions for Analysis

1. Like all tools, pottery improved humans' ability to manipulate the environment. What could they do with pots that was difficult to accomplish with animal skins, stone tools, or baskets made from reeds? In what ways was pottery an energy technology?

2. Do you think the Jomon people might have used the vessel pictured here for cooking or storing? Why or why not?

3. How can pottery help reveal the migration or expansion of cultural groups?

after the first villages. It existed by 4500 BCE in North America, where the earliest finds are in Georgia and South Carolina, and by 3500 BCE in South America. Each of these inventions of pottery was independent of the others.

Pottery answered villagers' needs. Pots made it easier to store seeds, food, and liquids. They were useful for cooking, enabling people to make stews and soups with otherwise tough-to-digest foodstuffs. By boiling tough meat or fibrous beans all day, people could make meals that even toddlers and toothless elders could eat. So pottery expanded the range of potential foods, and in this way helped improve nutrition and life expectancy.

Pottery also served as a means of artistic expression. Although most pots were purpose-built and artistically bland, sometimes people lavished care on pottery. Certain styles were based on the shapes of objects, such as the rope-coiled pattern of Jomon pottery in Japan or the inverted bell-shaped pottery, called beakerware, in fashion in western Europe after 3000 BCE. Other styles became possible once pottery glaze was developed, allowing potters to use more colors and to paint designs on their pots.

Pots were extremely useful but hard to make in quantity until about 6000 BCE, when Mesopotamians developed the potter's wheel. (Mesopotamia encompasses the basin of the Tigris and Euphrates Rivers in modern Iraq.) By spinning wet clay, one can quickly fashion it into desired shapes. The potter's wheel was the Neolithic equivalent of the modern assembly line: using it, potters could make hundreds or thousands of nearly identical bowls.

The Risks of Village Life

In Chapter 2, we saw that early farmers suffered from a handful of new diseases that were the result of settlement and farming. Village life, especially farming, also carried other risks, one of which was attack by strangers.

The core of the problem was that villagers, unlike foragers and hunters, had much to lose by running away from a fight. Farming folk used agricultural tools and storage vessels, usually pottery, and lived in carefully constructed dwellings. In some places, they had domesticated animals. They couldn't flee at a moment's notice without losing almost everything. So when raiders descended on them, they often chose to stand and fight. Many of the skeletons of men from early villages show fractures of the left forearm, an indication that they had parried blows from weapons such as clubs—although whether wielded by marauding strangers or irritated neighbors we cannot tell.

Fickle weather posed another risk. Village farmers couldn't gather up everything they valued at a moment's notice if floodwaters threatened to engulf them. Some of the early village walls—at Jericho in

Death by Violence A reconstruction of the site in the Alps where Ötzi the Iceman was found. Not only was he carrying weapons, but his remains suggest that he had sustained battle wounds—evidence of the violence that could occur in farming villages.

the Jordan River valley, for example—may have been built to deflect floods as much as to repel attackers.

In most locations, crop-killing drought was a more worrisome risk than flood. Villagers developed methods of ensuring water supplies when rains didn't suffice, typically by irrigation—diverting water from lakes, streams, and rivers to their fields and gardens. In long droughts, however, even irrigation channels might run dry, leading to hunger and perhaps starvation.

The risks and concerns of village life, whether from one's fellow humans or from the caprice of the weather, affected culture. To judge from art, architecture, burials, and other snippets of evidence, early villagers developed religious practices that emphasized fertility—of the soil, their animals, and themselves. In dry lands, rain deities became popular. Symbols of fertility—bulls or pregnant women, for example—decorated countless village homes. In a world where babies died so often, where crops withered without warning, it made sense to worship fertility in its various forms.

Some villagers also developed ancestor cults, a widespread practice wherever people lived in the same place over many generations. Villagers hoped their departed ancestors could intervene with supernatural powers and protect them against the hazards of their world. Worship of ancestors and attachment to their places of burial made villagers even more reluctant to flee in the event of attack, drought, or flood.

The Advantages of Village Life

Despite these risks, and the toll of disease discussed in Chapter 2, the populations of farming villages grew faster than those of hunters and foragers. In favorable spots, the village way of life could feed 100 times as many people per acre as could hunting and foraging. Clusters of villages formed in favored places such as the soft alluvial soils of riverbanks or deltas, or the light, windblown loess soils (loamy with small-grain clay or silt) of northern China and central Europe. The distribution of people over the face of the Earth, always uneven, became more so with the spread of farming villages. At a rough guess, the world contained 6 million people at the dawn of agriculture (or the start of the Neolithic, ca. 10,000 BCE) and 20 million by the time the first cities appeared (ca. 3200 BCE), most of them living along rivers. The spread of village farming was the main innovation that allowed such population growth.

Jericho and Çatalhöyük In ideal locations, villages could contain a few thousand people. Jericho, for example, located near a series of freshwater springs and a supply of salt—a commodity in great demand as a food preservative—seems to have been home to some 2,000 people by 7000 BCE. Larger still was Çatalhöyük, a village in south-central Anatolia. Founded around 7500 BCE, it attained a size of perhaps 6,000 or 8,000 residents. It was a well-watered site, with rich alluvial soils and a supply of obsidian. A black volcanic glass, obsidian made good, sharp edges for tools and weapons. It was also a

Architectural Advances Both of these sites are indicative of the new kinds of architecture embraced by settled agricultural communities: The Tower of Jericho (*left*) was built around 8000 BCE and measures 30 feet (9 m) in diameter and nearly 28 feet (8.5 m) high. The foundations of the 9000-year-old village of Çatalhöyük (*right*) reveal how thousands of residents lived in houses and farmed over a fairly sizable area.

valuable trade commodity: exports of obsidian contributed to Çatalhöyük's prosperity. The village houses were all similar, made of mud brick with no doors but with openings in their roofs, perhaps intended for better defense against enemies. Its people lived off their wheat and barley farming; sheep, goat, and cattle raising; and a little hunting. Men and women seem to have enjoyed similar nutrition, a sign of relative gender equality. Despite its size, Çatalhöyük was not a city: it had no public buildings or temples, no public spaces or plazas, and no signs of a ruling elite.

Shifting Agriculture Most early farmers didn't live in large villages like Çatalhöyük, and some didn't live in settled villages at all. Especially in forest zones without good soils, shifting agriculture often made more sense than permanent village settlement. **Shifting agriculture**, also called slash-and-burn or swidden, involved cutting and burning a clearing, farming it for a few years (usually three to ten), and then moving on to start anew elsewhere. At first, swidden farmers obtained good yields because the ash from burned forest contained abundant nutrients for their crops. But as nutrient supplies dwindled and weeds grew up, it paid to head elsewhere and repeat the cycle. These people typically mixed their farming with a fair bit of hunting and foraging in surrounding forests. Shifting agriculture was the most practical way to farm in much of the world. In some places, it still is.

Once people became farming villagers, they tended not to change their ways. Dense populations required food production. The archeological record shows few cases in which farming communities reverted to hunting and foraging. In this respect, the history of early farming shows a clear tendency: many communities shifted from food collection to food production, and few shifted the other way, giving up farming. This did happen occasionally, though—probably more often in the forest zones of Africa and Southeast Asia than elsewhere—because farming in moist tropical forests with the crops available then was not clearly preferable to hunting and foraging.

Herders lived off animals

Some environments, such as arid scrubland and semi-arid grasslands, couldn't support much in the way of food crops. To survive in these parts of the world, people had to live off animal products. Sheep, goats, cattle, donkeys, horses, camels, yaks, reindeer, llamas, and other domesticated grazing animals can turn grass or shrubby vegetation into meat, milk, wool, hides, horn, bone, and dung. With enough skill, people could make these animal products into food, clothing, tents, tools, weapons, and fuel. Domestic grazing animals expanded human reach into new environments and enriched human life.

People who live mainly off their animals are called **herders** or pastoralists, and their way of life is called pastoralism. How pastoralism originated is unclear, but it was probably an offshoot of early farming. Tending animals requires specialized skills, and herders at first were people who acquired these skills and used them on lands that were either temporarily or always unused for agriculture. Herding likely became a full-time specialization only after 5000 BCE or so. Most scholars think herding arose first on the fringes of farming communities in Mesopotamia. It might also have evolved as a full-time specialization on the southern edges of the Sahara, in the belt of semi-arid land called the African Sahel, perhaps around 4500 BCE. Millions of people in Africa and Asia live as herders today.

It's convenient to divide people into fixed categories and to think of farmers and herders as separate groups, as we do here. But in practice, the line between the two was sometimes fuzzy. Farmers often kept animals and might take them out to graze on nearby grasslands for a few weeks. Herders might settle for a few months and grow some crops. People might shift back and forth between farming and herding, depending on weather or other factors. But more often than not, farmers and herders regarded themselves as fundamentally different and preferred their own company.

Herder Lands and Livestock

The domain of herders was primarily the grasslands and scrublands of Eurasia and Africa. In Australia and Oceania, there were no grazing animals capable of domestication, so there were no herders. In the Americas, herding as a way of life didn't exist because only llamas and alpacas could be domesticated among large animals, and since they were useful in farm work, farmers raised them. In sub-Saharan Africa, herders concentrated in the Sahel and grassy parts of eastern and southern Africa. In moister African lands, their range was restricted by a livestock disease carried by the tsetse fly.

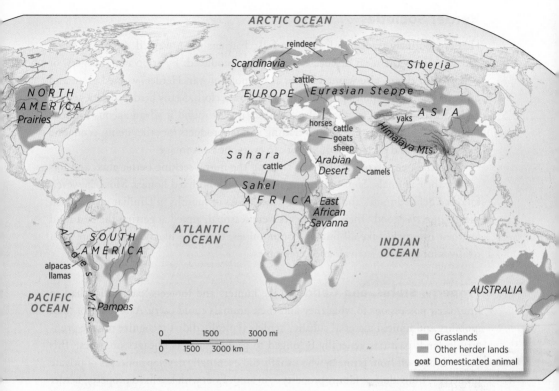

Grasslands and Pastoralist Lands, ca. 5000–1500 BCE Well after the domestication of herd animals, people in several parts of the world came to use natural grasslands for their herds and flocks as a full-time, and sometimes nomadic, way of life. Pastoralism was much more important in Eurasia and Africa than in the Americas or Australia, where suitable animals were rare or absent entirely.

In the zone from northwestern Africa to northeastern China, pastoralism became a common way of life, especially on the broad grasslands known as the **Eurasian steppe**.

Eight different animals supported herder societies. Some were found almost everywhere, but others had narrow ranges. Yaks, for example, were herded at high elevations in the Himalaya and the Tibetan Plateau but nowhere else. Reindeer herding has been confined mainly to Scandinavia and Siberia. Camels, first domesticated around 2000 BCE, were wondrously adapted to the arid conditions of North Africa as well as Southwest and Central Asia. In sub-Saharan Africa, most herders focused their attention on cattle, although they might keep sheep and goats as well. In Southwest and Central Asia, sheep and goats were the preferred livestock, but herders also raised cattle, donkeys, and eventually horses and camels. On the Eurasian steppe, herders kept sheep and goats too, and sometimes cattle and Bactrian (Central Asian, two-humped) camels as well. On the broad steppe lands, herding came into its own only with horse domestication.

Herder Societies

Herders routinely traded with farming folk. Farmers often wanted the hides, wool, and sometimes the meat or cheese that herders produced. By 2000 BCE, farmers, or at least their rulers, also wanted horses as weapons of war. Herders wanted grain and other foodstuffs, weapons, pots, baskets, and woven cloth. Many herder societies could make all these things for themselves, but often they found it advantageous to focus their efforts on raising animals and trading animal products for other items: economic specialization and exchange could work to everyone's advantage.

Herders spent all or part of their time on the move, seeking better grass and forage for their animals. Some were true nomads with no fixed homes. Most, however, followed defined routes and settled for a few weeks or months in familiar places when the grazing was good. Their movements were seasonal, aimed at getting the best food for their livestock. Like all human communities, they also liked to congregate with relatives for periodic festivals and ceremonies.

Property, Status, and Gender Like hunters and foragers, pastoralists had to limit their possessions to what they and their animals could carry. As a result of their mobility and limited material culture, herders typically didn't recognize private property in land; pastures generally belonged to groups such as lineages or tribes. This marked them off from farmers, who usually did eventually develop concepts of private property—individual or family property—in land. Even with less fixed property, herder society exhibited status hierarchies. Status among herders rested in part on individual and family achievements—feats of fertility, war, and endurance, for example. In part, it rested on the size of one's herds, the main form of wealth. It could also depend on ancestry: different families and clans enjoyed differing levels of prestige.

Herder societies normally observed sharp distinctions between male and female roles. Boys were raised to herd, fight, and if they had horses, ride. Courage, endurance, and defense of personal and family honor were highly prized male virtues. Girls were raised to do chores around tent or hut; to cook, sew, and mind babies and toddlers. Some women in Central Asia around 500 BCE were buried with weapons, perhaps an indication of warrior roles or of high social status. Women often handled commerce, especially when menfolk were away.

Small Numbers, Large Impact Herding supported much smaller, and more scattered, populations than farming. The reasons for this difference were, first, that farmers ate plants while herders ate animals that ate plants, giving them access to only about one-tenth of the energy per unit of area available to farmers. Second, herders' lands were normally less fertile to begin with, limiting the nutritional support for larger animals. Herder populations were limited by conditions, not preference. They revered fertility in soil, animals, men, and women no less than farmers did.

Herder Lifestyles Rock art from Tassili n'Ajjer in present-day Algeria depicts life in a cattle-herding tribe. Women and children work close to huts and tethered animals at the left of the scene, while a few men tend cattle in the fields beyond.

Despite their smaller numbers, herders often terrified farming folk. Where and when they mastered horses, their enhanced mobility gave them a great military advantage. They could attack when and where they pleased, and then fade away into the steppe or desert. They often operated what today we would call protection rackets—in effect, trading promises to forgo violence in exchange for grain or other goods. Conflict with farming communities usually took place on small scales, as raids rather than warfare.

Through their mobility, raiding, and trading, herders played an outsized role in world history, strengthening the strands of connection among settled folk in Eurasia and Africa, spinning additional threads of the world's webs. In the Americas and Australia, where pastoralism didn't develop until recent centuries, the process of web building was slower.

Farming Societies on the Move

While herders played an outsized role in linking populations over long distances in Eurasia and Africa, migrating farmers occasionally had the same effect. Sometimes they moved into uninhabited spaces, but at other times they pushed other people off the lands they wanted. Either way, they spread the village way of life and, where villages became clustered together, built new and tighter, if local, webs of exchange.

Most of the farmer migrations of the period before 1000 BCE were small in scale and lost in the mists of time. To minimize the problem of scanty evidence, we will look at some farmer migrations that lasted for millennia and left comparatively good traces through archeology, genetics, or historical linguistics. This will take us momentarily into later periods of history.

Eurasia's Indo-European Migrations

On occasion, farmers and their ways spread like slow-motion starbursts in multiple directions. There is linguistic evidence of such an event in the common roots of what became Germanic, Slavic, Romance, Celtic, Iranian, and several Indian languages. Migrations likely brought a single ancestral language into Iran, India, and Europe. Although there's no consensus, most specialists think such migrations began north of the Black Sea about 4000 BCE, when the onset of colder and drier climate may have triggered migrations.

The Indo-European migrations, which extended into westernmost China as well, seem in most cases connected to the spread of farming. Many words, notably for items related to agriculture, are sufficiently similar in Indian and European languages to indicate common origin. The word for "yoke," a wooden crosspiece fastening two oxen together so that they can pull a plow, is one example. In Sanskrit, a language of ancient India, it is *yuj*; in ancient Persian, *yog*; and in Latin, *iugum*. Similar variants exist in most other Indo-European languages. Archeological and genetic evidence supports the idea of a starburst migration of farmers into Europe and India.

As is often the case in migrations, young men seeking to establish themselves may have led the way. The Indo-European migrations were probably not ones in which men, women, and children all picked up and moved. Genetic evidence suggests that women were much less likely to have migrated. It also suggests that the immigrants to Europe and India had more success than local men in passing their genes on to future generations. This implies that the newcomers enjoyed higher status, supporting the notion they were farmers and more prosperous than other men.

Farming people from Southwest Asia also migrated into Africa. (This is how Africans acquired their tiny proportion of Neanderthal genes.) A 4,500-year-old male skeleton, called Mota after the Ethiopian cave in which it was found, tells us so. When compared to modern African populations, Mota's remains indicate considerable admixture of Eurasian DNA. The imported DNA reached all but the

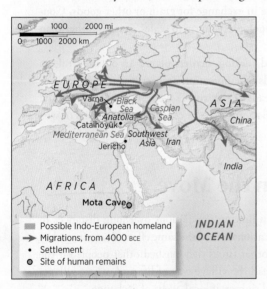

Indo-European Migrations, ca. 4000–1500 BCE
Evidence from historical linguistics, archeology, and genetics indicates that farmers and herders originating somewhere north of the Black Sea spread out widely over western Eurasia. In most cases, they settled among foraging and hunting folk and either replaced them or absorbed them.

most isolated populations of East Africa, implying that immigrants from Southwest Asia were both numerous and highly successful in transmitting their genes to later generations. But the evidence from Mota's mortal remains cannot tell us how that happened.

Overall, the linguistic, archeological, and genetic evidence combine to suggest a starburst migration of farming people originating roughly 4000 BCE north of the Black Sea. Different groups moved in different directions—into India, Europe, and on a much smaller scale, northeastern Africa and westernmost China.

Africa's Bantu Migrations

Later farmer migrations shaped African history much more deeply. **Bantu** is a language group of about 600 related tongues, now spoken widely in East, central, and southern Africa by hundreds of millions of people. Yet Bantu-speaking populations show the lowest genetic diversity within Africa, implying a small and comparatively recent founding population—another starburst that occurred around 3000 BCE.

Bantu-speakers originated in the Cameroon-Nigeria border region. In two main pulses they spread out, first within their region (ca. 3000–2500 BCE) and then into much of East and southern Africa (ca. 1500 BCE–500 CE). We know nothing about why they moved. They went slowly, reaching what is now South Africa about 1000 CE. Later Bantu migrants had better tools and weapons than the prior populations in central and southern Africa. They were skilled at cultivating yams and bananas, which do well in rainforest settings, and some of them became herders of cattle at some point along the way, probably in East Africa. With these skills they became increasingly successful colonizers, especially once they got south of central Africa's rain forests, which are challenging environments for farmers.

The migrants also had a secret

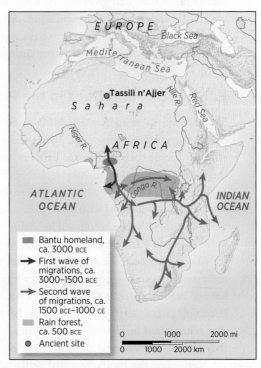

Bantu Migrations, ca. 4000 BCE–1000 CE Speakers of Bantu languages, who originated somewhere near the border of today's Nigeria and Cameroon, spread out into central Africa's equatorial forests, East Africa's savanna lands, and southern Africa's woodland and grassland mosaics. The Bantu were farmers and either displaced or absorbed most of the people they encountered on their migrations.

weapon. They were more malaria-resistant than the pre-existing central and southern African populations. Genetic evidence shows that these local populations had minimal experience with malaria before Bantu-speakers trickled in. Bantu-speakers and their ancestors, in contrast, had lived in intense malaria environments for many generations in West Africa, an experience that had ruthlessly selected for malaria resistance. On top of that, their staple food, yams, included chemical compounds that fight malaria. When Bantu-speakers moved into central, East, and southern Africa, they brought malaria with them. The mosquitoes that transmit malaria, not suited to dense forest, thrived in the agricultural clearings. The Bantu-speakers—quite accidentally—created dangerous environments for others in which they themselves could survive more successfully than anyone else.

Genetic evidence suggests that Bantu-speakers both replaced and absorbed the existing populations of central, East, and southern Africa. More specifically, it implies that migrant men had great success in passing their genes on to future generations, whereas the indigenous male populations did not—and that women of all backgrounds increasingly had their children with Bantu-speaking men. This is similar to the pattern revealed in the Indo-European migrations into Europe and India.

Polynesian Migrations in the Pacific

While Bantu-speaking farmers slowly made their way across a continent, Polynesians made their way across an ocean. Their distant ancestors came from islands of the westernmost Pacific such as Taiwan. Farmers, probably speaking a language ancestral to those of modern Southeast Asia, spread out from the Asian mainland into the islands of the western Pacific by 2000 BCE. Here they stayed put for a while, not venturing further out to sea—and with good reason. The Pacific covers about one-third of the globe and has only a few thousand habitable islands in it, most of them tiny. Those who sailed the open Pacific had to know what they were doing.

About 1500 BCE, the ancestors of today's Polynesians—often called Lapita after their style of pottery—began to sail over immense distances and settle formerly uninhabited islands. By 1200 BCE, some had reached Samoa and Tonga. A thousand years later, Polynesians settled the Marquesas Islands in the central Pacific, and by 500 CE they had arrived in Hawaii and on Easter Island. It took until about 1200 CE before they settled New Zealand, the final frontier of Polynesian settlement.

Navigating the Pacific required skill and courage. Polynesians used big wooden dugout canoes with outriggers for stability. The largest could fit a hundred or more paddlers, but all canoes used sails on the open sea. They often sailed in fleets. The Polynesian voyagers learned to get their bearings from the stars, read the patterns of ocean waves and swells, and find land by watching the flight patterns of birds. They recorded geographic information on maps made of reeds and shells. Unlike the Indo-Europeans and the Bantu, the Polynesians couldn't simply walk to their new lands.

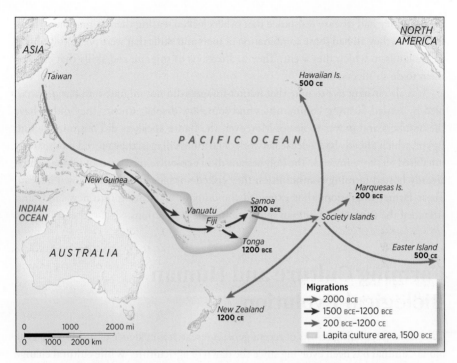

Pacific and Polynesian Migrations, ca. 2000 BCE–1200 CE Migrating in dugout canoes, small numbers of Pacific peoples spread out over immense distances, often heading out into the unknown, and settled hundreds of previously uninhabited islands. New Zealand acquired its first human population about 1200 CE, the last big place on Earth to be settled.

This extraordinary epic of exploration and colonization, like the Bantu and Indo-European migrations, was a movement of farmers. The Polynesians took their favorite crops—taro (a starchy root crop), and coconut and breadfruit (both tree crops)—wherever they went. They also brought their domesticated animals, mainly chickens, pigs, and dogs. These fellow passengers helped them colonize a few hundred Pacific islands, most of which didn't offer abundant food. On islands with coastal lagoons, Polynesians enjoyed an initial bonanza of fish and shellfish. After they depleted the lagoons, and where no lagoons were present, they farmed to survive.

The Dynamism of Farming Society

The Indo-European, Bantu, and Polynesian migrations show the dynamism of farming populations. Their ways of life gave them certain characteristics that encouraged them to spread into lands that had no farmers or, in the case of the Polynesian islands, no people at all. First, their populations tended to grow and provide streams of young people seeking their futures. Second, at least in some cases such as the Bantu and malaria, they had disease resistance that others lacked, easing their migrations. Third, as farmers, they all had some combination of tools and skills that were previously absent in the lands to which they went. They had reasons to migrate and skills that enabled them to do so successfully.

It is also instructive to note that hunter-foragers did not migrate into terrain occupied by settled farming communities and somehow displace them. They didn't have the numbers and power to do so. Moreover, the Bantu speakers did not migrate into Egypt, which already had a dense network of farming villages; they moved into sparsely inhabited territory instead. The Polynesians didn't colonize the coasts of China, which already hosted farming communities; they risked voyages into the unknown instead. These farmer migrations thus extended the domain of farming into new lands and stretched the thin web of human interaction in new directions.

Farming Culture and Human Biological Evolution

One of the fascinating results of recent genetic research is evidence of just how fast the human animal has been evolving since the dawn of agriculture. While cultural change has outstripped biological evolution in shaping our lives, human biological evolution has probably sped up since Paleolithic times. This is a result of new and sometimes rigorous selective pressures favoring the survival and reproduction chances of some people, and their genes, over others. By and large, it was the farming way of life that imposed these new pressures.

For example, after settling down in agricultural villages, humans' chances of survival and reproduction depended more than ever on having a good immune system. Durability as a long-distance walker no longer counted for so much. In most of Africa, farming brought more malaria, and therefore intense selective pressure spreading genes for malaria resistance. That is the origin of the sickle-cell trait that protects some people from the nastiest variety of malaria but raises the odds of suffering from anemia.

Likewise, the Polynesian cultural practice of voyaging changed Polynesian bodies through a process of genetic selection. Long voyages in open canoes across empty ocean with little food may have favored those Polynesians with genes for thriftier metabolisms—more able to withstand the stresses of cold and hunger. This process of genetic selection may be connected to the high risk for diabetes among Polynesians today: a thrifty metabolism was useful for their ancestors but is no longer necessary now that food is easier to come by. The genetic adaptation carries costs without the former benefit.

Genes and culture affect one another: ever since the advent of farming, we have been remaking animals, ourselves, and our culture all at once, and faster than before.

How did the spread of farming and herding change human biology, culture, and the environment?

83

Raising Cattle A rock art painting from Somaliland in East Africa shows a person milking a cow. East Africa was one of the key regions where lactose tolerance and cattle keeping helped people to survive in challenging environments.

Geneticists now think there are hundreds of genetic mutations that spread in response to cultural shifts in the last 10,000 years. With village farming, people changed their environments and cultures, and indirectly changed themselves biologically. Let's look at some of the ways they did so.

Cattle, Milk, and Lactose Tolerance

Cattle domestication changed the human animal. It led to the emergence of the ability among some adult humans to digest animal milk. About one-third of the world's adults today can digest milk.

Most people lose the ability to digest milk after about age five. They stop producing an enzyme that assists in breaking down lactose, a form of sugar found in milk. Before 8000 BCE, everyone was "lactose intolerant." But between about 8000 and 5000 BCE, at least four different genetic mutations took place—in West Africa, East Africa, northern Europe, and Southwest Asia—whereby some people kept producing the key enzyme beyond childhood.

These mutations provided an advantage among cattle keepers. Cows' milk is rich in protein and nutrients. In landscapes not suited to crop farming, milk drinkers could get higher quality nutrition more reliably than could anyone else. In northern Europe, where farming was difficult, after about 3000 BCE it seems the selective pressure for lactose tolerance was especially high, resulting in ever larger numbers of these mutant, milk-drinking humans. Today, almost everyone whose ancestors lived there can easily digest milk all throughout their lives. Ireland has the highest proportion of lactose-tolerant people anywhere in the world.

Mutations among cattle keepers in Africa achieved the same effect. In parts of East Africa, most people whose ancestors had kept cattle can digest milk as adults. In West

Africa's Sahel, some pastoral peoples also have high proportions of lactose-tolerant adults. In both East Africa and the West African Sahel, where water is often scarce, milk drinking was useful not only for nutrition but also for avoiding dehydration.

People who developed lactose tolerance avoided some nasty waterborne diseases too. Cattle, camels, sheep, and goats can absorb moisture from the grasses they eat, drink water swimming with microbes that would make humans sick, and then turn all that into a healthful liquid for humans. They are water purifiers.

The lactose-tolerance mutations were so advantageous that they spread everywhere people kept cattle, and to some extent where they kept camels, sheep, and goats. The most recent of the mutations permitting milk-drinking adults took place in Southwest Asia, perhaps Arabia, after 3000 BCE, and probably only after the domestication of camels (whose milk is also good to drink). People in Central Asia, where keeping sheep and goats was common, today show a moderate rate of lactose tolerance. Most of them can easily digest cheese and yogurt, which have less lactose than milk. But in East and Southeast Asia, southern Europe, and most parts of Africa, none of these mutations spread widely, so adults didn't drink milk. In the Americas, where early people had no domesticated animals other than dogs, there was no advantage to lactose tolerance at all.

The history of milk drinking is a case of ongoing genetic change in the human population in response to human culture. An innovation in culture—cattle keeping—opened the way to an innovation in the human genome, and each reinforced the other: the more lactose tolerant people became, the more likely people were to keep cattle and drink milk; and the more they kept cattle, the stronger the selection became for lactose-tolerance genes. By the standards of genetic shifts, this one swept through human populations very quickly—in just a few thousand years, suggesting strong advantages for milk drinkers in environments good for cattle.

Milk drinkers are not the only ones whose bodies adjusted to new dietary possibilities that resulted from cultural changes. At some time in the past 15,000 years, residents of the Arctic, people known as Inuit, developed a genetic mutation that allows them to metabolize quantities of whale, seal, and fish meat, which are rich with fatty acids, and yet keep their bloodstreams free of unhealthy levels of those fatty acids. Their migration into places such as northern Canada and Greenland, in which there was precious little to eat other than fish and whale blubber, created a strong selective pressure favoring the spread of this adaptation, which is rare in other human communities. Once again, cultural change dovetailed with biological change in human bodies.

Horse Domestication

The domestication of horses, like the emergence of lactose tolerance, opened new spaces to denser human settlement. As with the earlier domestication of dogs, this one proved to be a durable partnership. Humans deliberately selected for preferred characteristics in horses. When they succeeded in genetically altering horses so as to make them useful to human societies, they—unintentionally—created a cultural selection for societies that were good at managing horses.

Wild horses live in small groups with one stallion, five to seven mares, and their young offspring. Mares routinely accept guidance from stallions or lead mares. Stallions, in contrast, are uncooperative and violent. Genetic evidence shows that today's tame horses are descended from many mares but from very few, perhaps only one, stallion. Taming mares wasn't so difficult: they usually accept human guidance willingly. Taming a wild stallion took extreme courage and persistence.

Horse domestication probably happened somewhere on the grassy steppes between the Black and Caspian Seas around 4800 BCE. The reason people tried to tame horses initially was to eat them or to drink their milk and blood. People ensured that the most docile and obedient mares had the most offspring; and as a result, over hundreds of generations horses grew tamer and easier to control.

Horses are much better than cattle or sheep at surviving hard winters because they will paw at snow to find grass and will kick through ice to get water. On the chilly steppes, herds of horses were more reliable food sources than flocks of sheep or herds of cattle, which couldn't survive the winters if not carefully fed by humans. A cold snap on the steppe lasting a few centuries around the period 4200–3800 BCE might have helped spread the practice of domesticating horses.

Eating horses allowed people to survive cold winters, but riding horses allowed them to do much more. By 3500 BCE at the latest, people on the steppes had learned to ride horses, launching a partnership at least as important as the earlier one with dogs. The curious fact that horses and humans can sweat profusely, which no other animals can, meant they were made for each other. Horse and rider can exercise for hours on end without overheating, even in warm climates.

The advantages of riding for horsemen were tremendous. Horsemen could herd two or three times as many sheep or cattle as could someone on foot, and could also hunt much more efficiently. They could steal animals and abduct women and children

Horse-Rider Partnership A fourth-millennium BCE cave painting found in present-day Algeria shows a confrontation between a swordsman on horseback and a spearman on foot. Societies that had horses held military advantages over those that did not.

from rival groups more easily. After 2500 BCE, where grass was abundant and horses thrived—which at this time meant much of western and central Eurasia—no human group could last long without becoming skilled riders and horse-breeders. People who exploited the economic and military potential of the horse managed to amass wealth and power on a scale formerly impossible. The rise of the horse-rider partnership led to the rise of greater social stratification, which is evident in changes in goods buried in the graves of prominent men.

The importance of horses goes further. Before horse domestication, the steppe grass-lands posed a daunting challenge to people, like seas before sailboats. On foot, people could scarcely hope to find enough food and water to cross the sea of grass. Domesti-cated horses made the steppe accessible—indeed, they transformed it from a barrier to a highway, just as sailboats did to seas. Transport and travel on these grasslands ultimately brought all the cultures of Eurasia and North Africa into contact with one another, forming a giant web, as we shall see in some detail. So the genetic changes in horses as they became domesticated, and attendant cultural change in horse-using societies, altered the patterns of world history.

New Ecosystems, New Species

In addition to changing the human genome and human culture, farming and herding changed the planet. Early farmers, we must remember, inherited environments already in flux. Their ancestors had used fire liberally to clear forest and had probably spear-headed the accidental extinction of many large mammals everywhere they went. On top of those human-induced environmental alterations, climate shifts led to vegetation changes. Thanks to the warming after the last ice age, early farmers faced a world of expanding forests, shrinking ice caps, and disappearing tundra—although all these changes came so slowly that no one understood what was afoot.

Against this background of both natural environmental change and the ongoing alterations caused by hunter-foragers, early farmers added their weight to the balance. Through domestication, they created several new species of plants and animals, as we've seen. Herding and farming meant spreading these chosen species far and wide at the expense of others, now considered weeds and pests.

In other words, farmers and herders created new ecosystems—pastures and farmlands—as well as new species. Tame cattle and sheep roamed over far greater spaces than their wild forerunners ever did. Maize, rice, and other cereals also covered far more space than their wild predecessors had.

Early farmers, without plows and draft animals, found grasslands too difficult to cultivate. They preferred riverbanks, lake edges, or cleared forestland. Across Eurasia, early farmers gradually cleared forests in river floodplains, using fire and axe. They also cleared patches here and there in deep forests. Once they harnessed strong animals, such as oxen or water buffalo, and invented plows (around 3800 BCE), farmers found it worthwhile to farm heavy or damp soils. Early farmers also assaulted forests in the Americas and sub-Saharan Africa. In both settings, they typically either practiced shifting cultivation in forest zones or used the soft soils of riverbanks.

The environmental impacts of early farmers were surely of greater scale than that of hunters and foragers in the vicinity of villages, where fields were cleared, fuelwood gathered, and domestic animals grazed. But the environmental consequences of early agriculture, before cities and states, were small compared to what was yet to come.

The Emergence of Cities, States, and Complex Societies after 3500 BCE

The advent of farming also made possible the emergence of new political forms and much bigger social units, which brought still more radical changes in turn. This section explains the emergence of cities and states, first created during the fourth millennium BCE and still with us today. They became the social contexts in which more and more people lived, and which produced ever more ideas, technologies, and other forces shaping human history. Their emergence was simultaneous with what social scientists call complex society. The development of all three—complex society, states, and cities—accelerated the building of larger webs of interconnection.

What Are Cities, States, and Complex Societies?

These three related innovations in the structure of societies shaped world history from 3500 BCE onward. They require some definitions. **Complex society**, in the language of the social sciences, means a large-scale social unit with an elaborate division of labor, pronounced social hierarchy, hundreds of different social roles that people can fill, and institutions to regulate exchanges among individuals and among groups. Every society, even a hunting and foraging band, is *complicated*, with intricate networks of social relations; but in this specialized sense, not every society is *complex*. Complex societies usually developed together with states and cities.

A **state** is a territorial unit and political community with a formal government. States are easy to identify. They employ office-holders who govern according to set rules (bureaucrats), specialists in the administration of justice (judges), and masters of the arts of violence (soldiers). States claim for themselves a monopoly on the legitimate use of violence. They extract goods, labor, or money from a subject population through taxes and conscription. States, except for the most nakedly coercive, also have ideologies—sets of ideas that justify their existence and operations. State ideologies have typically been based in religion. An effective ideology can enable the rulers of a state to harness the willing support of their population, without frequent resort to coercion.

It's not easy to draw a sharp line separating a city from a town or big village. But in general, a **city** contains the elaborate division of labor and social hierarchy of complex society, and it is distinguished by dense living quarters, open public spaces, and imposing public buildings. Cities feature trade and exchange, and institutions—usually, markets—that bring buyers and sellers together. Villages, at least big ones, may have some of these features, but never all.

Cities are central to world history because they are hothouses of innovation and exchange. They are the densest parts of interactive webs. In cities, unlike villages, people regularly dealt with strangers, provoking adoption and diffusion of new techniques, technologies, and ways of thinking. The dense living quarters of cities also facilitated the faster exchange and evolution of disease organisms.

As we've seen, by 7000 BCE a world of farming, herding, and villages had begun to emerge in Eurasia and Africa. A parallel world would soon emerge in the Americas, although without herding. In all of these villages, scores or hundreds of people living side by side experienced life very much as their neighbors did. They all took part in the tasks of agricultural life. Aside from roles specified by age and gender, there was little economic specialization or social stratification. Exchanges took place, as in all societies, but were usually a matter of reciprocal gifts rather than market transactions. This was not complex society.

In 3500 BCE, the world had no cities. Then, in six places around the world, something new evolved: urban life and complex society. These six places were Mesopotamia, Egypt, the Indus valley, China, Mesoamerica, and the Andes. Two of these places, Egypt and the Indus valley, may have acquired some of the habits of complex society from neighbors—specifically, Mesopotamia. But for the most part, these were all autonomous transformations. Every other complex society in the history of the world derives, directly or indirectly, from one or more of these original six. By 1500 BCE, the world contained hundreds of cities. Only 1 to 2 percent of the human population lived in cities, but the most powerful people did.

In the chapters to come, we'll explore these complex societies in greater detail. Here let's consider three widely shared aspects of early complex societies: (1) their underlying economic base, especially irrigation agriculture; (2) the social and political implications of cities and states; and (3), two basic tools that shaped the development of cities and states—writing and metallurgy.

Economic Bases of Early Complex Societies

The development of complex societies depended on farmers growing more food than they needed so that other people—soldiers, artisans, bureaucrats, and priests who did not produce food—could eat.

Oxen and Plows This painting on the wall of an Egyptian tomb shows a farmer driving oxen, which pull a plow to till the soil—one of the many innovations that enabled Egyptians to practice agriculture in an arid climate.

Plow Agriculture Where people had domesticated strong animals, they could use them to pull heavy things. Oxen and water buffalo—the tractors of the pre-modern world—proved especially adept at pulling plows through the soil. The earliest plows came into use soon after 3800 BCE in Mesopotamia. They quickly appeared in Egypt too, and possibly in China—estimated dates for the advent of **plow agriculture** in northern China range from 3000 to 500 BCE. Chinese plows differed enough in design from those used in Southwest Asia that many scholars think they were independently invented.

The first plows were made of wood, suitable only for soft ground. They scratched a shallow furrow in the soil, preparing it for planting. But they allowed farmers to cultivate up to five times as much land as they could without oxen and plows. Soon plows acquired metal tips, and later metal plowshares, which turned soil over, uprooted weeds, and brought deep-seated nutrients to the soil surface. These plows could work heavier soils, including ones moistened by irrigation. Whether by diffusion or by independent invention, between 3500 and 1500 BCE, plows became routine farm equipment in North Africa and Eurasia.

But in sub-Saharan Africa, Australia, and all of the Americas, there were no plows until much later—in most cases, because there were no animals suited to pulling them. Instead, farmers used hoes or digging sticks. On steep, rugged terrain, digging sticks worked better than plows. Without plow agriculture, it was harder for farmers to generate enough surplus food to support city life and complex society. Where this developed without plows, as in Mesoamerica, Peru, and along the bend in the Niger River in Africa, the needed surplus came from intensive human labor and irrigation.

Irrigation Among the perennial hazards of farming are drought and flood. Providing crops just the right amount of water at just the right times was at first a matter of luck. No doubt the earliest farmers quickly learned to carry water-filled skins or pots to their crops. But big fields required **irrigation**—that is, the construction of artificial channels to carry water from lakes, rivers, or streams to thirsty crops.

We don't know when or where irrigation began. Some patchy evidence from the Levant and northern Mesopotamia suggests the presence of small irrigation works before 7000 BCE. But irrigation remained small-scale until about 3500 BCE, after which it appeared, via diffusion and independent invention, in suitable zones throughout Eurasia and North Africa. In the Americas, it began around 1900 BCE. The technologies of canals, ditches, dikes, and dams were simple enough in principle even if laborious to build, so it's plausible that irrigation emerged independently in many places.

Irrigation had dramatic consequences. First, it raised per-acre yields by five or ten times. With this enormous expansion of farming productivity, the world's food now increasingly came from a few pockets of irrigated farmland, surrounded by much less productive zones of rain-fed farming and herding, and by even broader zones where people collected and hunted food rather than growing it. Lands suitable for irrigation became distinctive, a new sort of agro-ecology capable of feeding far more mouths than any other landscapes on Earth. Irrigated landscapes not only raised grain yields but also served as nutritious aquariums swimming with fish, frogs, snails, and other protein-packed delicacies. In particular, irrigation produced abundant *surplus* food, enabling societies to support far more people who specialized in other things, from pottery to philosophy.

Second, even as successful irrigation fed many more mouths, it also needed many hands. Digging and maintaining canals, ditches, and reservoirs, and building dikes and dams, took enormous coordinated effort on a scale beyond what families alone could provide. Families and neighbors had to band together to build irrigation systems and make collective decisions on who would do what and when. Most irrigation schemes began as grassroots efforts, but over time religious and political authorities, and also rich landowners, usually stepped in to coordinate the necessary tasks. The greater the degree of coordination achieved, the larger the scale irrigation could attain. So irrigation favored the emergence of religious and political leaders, and in turn, successful leaders favored the extension of irrigation. Where irrigation prevailed, it co-evolved with social complexity: neither was a necessary pre-condition for the other, but each encouraged the development of the other.

Everywhere it developed, irrigation farming raised yields, generating surplus food that supported denser populations and more specialists. These were the conditions for the emergence of cities. Almost every early city was fed by irrigation agriculture.

Drawbacks of Irrigation Farming Along with its role in shaping social development, irrigation brought great vulnerabilities. Enemy armies, even a band of brigands, could easily destroy dikes and dams, ruining fields and starving those dependent on their bounty. Moreover, large-scale irrigation rested on the sustained cooperation of thousands of laborers—a fragile thing. Whenever that cooperation broke down, irrigation systems fell to ruin in short order through lack of maintenance. Societies dependent on the food surpluses delivered by irrigation agriculture became vulnerable to interruptions in the production and delivery of that surplus. In a loose way, we can liken the adoption of irrigation to modern societies' adoption of oil as their principal fuel: both technologies allowed enormous expansion of economic activity, the production of more and cheaper food, and therefore larger populations. But both added new sources of vulnerability as well.

With respect to human health, irrigation carried additional risks. Irrigated landscapes invited certain diseases, such as schistosomiasis, which is spread by snails, and malaria, which is spread by anopheles mosquitoes. People who engaged in irrigation agriculture in Eurasia and Africa probably carried heavier parasite loads and hosted more infections than anyone else, and consequently often couldn't work at full strength. In the Americas, where neither schistosomiasis nor malaria existed until much later, any health penalty of irrigation was much smaller.

Environmental Impacts The most significant environmental impact of plowing and irrigation was on the soil. Animal-drawn plows enabled people to slice deeper into the earth. Upturned and loosened soil eroded easily. Over centuries and millennia, wherever people engaged in plow farming they suffered problems of soil erosion and nutrient loss. The process of soil erosion was highly visible and could be combated to a degree by measures such as building terraces. Nutrient loss was invisible but sometimes happened fast enough that people could see the result in the form of lower yields within their lifetimes. They typically understood this as the land becoming "tired," which led ancient farmers to seek ways to renew soil fertility.

The most effective solution to nutrient loss was the use of manure on fields. Where farmers had livestock, they could graze their animals on nearby pastures, pen them at night, collect their manure, and spread it on fields. In effect, this strategy collected nutrients from a broad area and concentrated them where they did the most good for humans—one of the chief contributions to human welfare made by livestock. Where farmers didn't have animals, as in Mesoamerica, or had few, as in East Asia, they relied more on "night soil," or human excrement, as fertilizer. Another attempted solution was prayer: most early farmers, and most irrigation-based societies, worshipped earth deities whose portfolios included soil fertility. These were usually goddesses, such as Bhumi in India or Brigid in Ireland.

Irrigation agriculture brought damaging salinization of soils. Irrigation with poor drainage—which describes most irrigation—left soils waterlogged and brought dissolved salts up to the surface. As water evaporated from the soil surface, the salt content remained. Where waterlogging was common and evaporation intense, accumulated salt in topsoil layers eventually created white crusts. Only a few plants, and no useful crops, can flourish in salt-encrusted soils. In the *Epic of Gilgamesh*, a long narrative poem written around 2100 BCE in Mesopotamia, the gods turn soils white, perhaps a reference to salt encrustation.

The emergence of cities introduced a new peril to farm soils. In village agriculture, nutrients traveled from soil to plants to people and back to the soil again in a fairly closed system. Few nutrients disappeared altogether in the process. Cities, however, imported nutrients in food but didn't necessarily return them to farmers' fields. Most cities were built on rivers, which operated as convenient sewers carrying excrement and its soil nutrients to the sea. As a result, cities threatened to undermine the systems of agriculture and nutrient flows that supported urban life itself.

Cities and States as Social Systems

Irrigation farming fed the growth of cities, and growing cities made new social orders possible. Where tens of thousands of people clustered together, they developed specialized skills and institutions that helped them live together in peace. Cities needed institutions to administer justice, oversee defense and war against outsiders, organize taxation, and manage other aspects of public affairs, often through organized religion.

Social Inequality City life made social inequalities larger and more visible. In villages populated by farm families, status was based mainly on age, gender, individual achievement, and sometimes ancestry. In cities, there were added layers of stratification based on wealth, occupation, and social class.

Social Stratification City life led to a proliferation of social roles and hierarchies. A Mesopotamian stone carving from around 2600 to 2300 BCE shows many laborers preparing and serving a feast to some dignitaries, who eat while being entertained by musicians (bottom left).

Early cities typically had a ruling elite of specialists in government, religion, and commerce; they worked mainly with their thinking and communication skills, not with their hands. Beneath this elite stood a class of people who worked with skilled hands—smiths, carpenters, builders, stonemasons, potters, weavers, spinners, brewers, and musicians. Many in these latter occupations were women. Cities typically also had a class of unskilled male laborers who worked with their backs—stevedores, cart-pullers, animal drovers, water-carriers. Sharing the lower rungs of the social ladder were people who worked with disagreeable materials—handling manure or night soil, or tanning animal hides. Almost all early cities also had slaves, most of whom did manual labor. Some slaves had skills that enabled them to work as smiths or even scribes—specialists in writing, an honored occupation in mostly illiterate societies. Cities also normally had an underclass of people without regular work—beggars, thieves, and prostitutes. An elaborate social hierarchy like this posed acute problems of social harmony, which officials in government and religion strove to solve.

Disease Early cities were also cesspools of filth and infection that killed people faster than others were born. Only continuing in-migration from villages kept cities from shrinking. Disposing of human and animal excrement, carcasses of dead animals, residues from tanneries, offal from butcher shops, and other unhealthy wastes threatened human health. Few cities had clean water supplies, and all teemed with pathogens preying on tightly packed human populations.

<u>**Crowd diseases**</u> in particular afflicted cities, and especially networks of interacting cities. These infections, mostly derived from diseases of herd animals, need big populations to stay in circulation because the pathogens provoke immunity in people who survive a bout. Crowd diseases such as the smallpox, mumps, and pertussis viruses became childhood diseases when circulating in large populations. Interconnected cities had enough people, in frequent enough face-to-face (to be more precise, breath-to-breath) contact, to maintain perpetual circulation of lethal infections. Everyone encountered these infections in childhood, and those who survived became immune or resistant. A society needed several hundred thousand people regularly breathing in one another's germs to make them endemic (always present) rather than epidemic (infrequently present). These diseases took a terrible toll on children.

Crowd diseases made cities, as well as complex societies of interlinked cities, extremely dangerous not only for their own children but also for adults who had grown up in more isolated places. In demographically smaller societies, with less breath-to-breath exchange of viruses, these infections were usually absent. That was good for the survival of children; but when these infections appeared as epidemics, they killed adults and children alike—a catastrophe. In this way, interacting networks of cities, if they contained enough people, were reservoirs of lethal infections that at any time could leak out into surrounding smaller communities and cause epidemics.

Enslaved Labor These characteristics of cities meant that complex societies constantly needed more laborers. They needed them to toil in the fields that fed the cities and to do the most disagreeable jobs in the cities themselves. To meet the demand, the rulers of states normally resorted to enslaving people within reach who didn't have the means to defend themselves. Or they organized slave trades, buying people from more distant lands who had been captured to meet the need for labor. Most cities and states thus gave rise to violent slaving frontiers, either just beyond their own borders or farther afield. After the rise of cities and states, the hunting and foraging peoples of the world, and stateless farmers too, lived in greater fear of capture and enslavement. For self-defense, they retreated into mountain forests, deserts, and swamps, where slave raiders and slave traders would not easily find them.

The Emergence of States and Rulers

The world had no states before 3500 BCE but scores of them by 1500 BCE. Wherever dense populations existed—mainly in lands of irrigation agriculture—opportunistic, forceful, and charismatic people saw the chance to set themselves up as rulers. In order to succeed they needed the means to reward followers and intimidate others, and in order to stay successful they needed an ideology to convince people that it was right that some should toil while others did not. Effective ideologies normally consisted of claims to divine status for rulers or to their special power as intermediaries to the gods or ancestors.

Most early states were monarchies. Kings, and occasionally queens, made the final decisions on important matters. Bureaucrats and soldiers carried out royal commands. To retain the loyalty of these agents of royal power, kings had to show themselves worthy of their thrones. They had to reward bureaucrats and soldiers with food, goods, war booty, or captives. They had to claim royal ancestry, because kingship was always hereditary. Kingship was also always sacred. Kings typically professed to be the sons of gods and always claimed divine support, if not divine powers. They officiated at religious rituals, which were often sacrifices (of animals or humans), emphasizing that sacred and political authority were one and the same. Kings and their households showed off their power and wealth through displays of stunning jewelry and art, fancy clothes, and magnificent palaces.

As of 1500 BCE, no more than 2 percent of the globe's land surface was controlled by states. But owing largely to irrigation agriculture, perhaps half of the world's population lived in areas controlled, or partly controlled, by states. Over time, more and more states emerged because people without a state needed one to protect them from conquest and enslavement by existing states.

The Development of Writing   Almost all complex societies developed writing as a means of preserving and transmitting information. The development of writing—a system of abstract images to represent either the countless ideas that can pass through human minds, or the many sounds that human voices can make—was a major human achievement. Yet people had managed without it for more than 200,000 years. Writing—like telephones, email, and Facebook—is a networked technology of little use to anyone until other people are using it too. So how and why did writing develop?

The answer lies in the demands of complex society. The first customers for information stored in writing were states and merchants. States that depended on thousands of inhabitants to pay taxes needed a way to monitor and record who had paid and who hadn't. Merchants needed writing to track their numerous transactions and debts.

Whatever the format and whatever its original purpose, writing proved to be fundamental to history over the past 5,000 years. Writing and reading made possible much faster accumulation of knowledge and, indeed, the creation of new knowledge and belief. A reasonable case can be made that writing is the second most important innovation, after agriculture, since the origins of language. In later chapters, we'll examine specific features of writing as it developed in Mesopotamia, Egypt, China, India, and Mesoamerica.

Metallurgy Another important tool that played a role in state making was **metallurgy**—the working of metal ores first into metals and then into useful objects. The important metals for this chapter are copper and bronze; iron had revolutionary effects in Eurasia and Africa, but only after 1500 BCE. In the Americas and Oceania, metallurgy remained of trivial importance until far later, after 1500 CE.

Early Writing One of the earliest known examples of writing for the purposes of accounting comes from Mesopotamia. This tablet, dated to around 3200 BCE, contains pictographic symbols that correspond to specific quantities of certain goods—including, perhaps, cereal grains such as wheat.

All metals come from the earth, and most are chemically or physically bound up with rock in ores. They require processing, often smelting with fire, to separate metal from rock. Smiths used high temperatures to make metals pliable enough to hammer into useful shapes. They applied even greater heat to melt metals into liquid that could be poured into molds. To generate heat, they burned wood or charcoal in enclosed spaces called forges. Smiths also learned how to combine metals into useful alloys. Smiths were highly skilled men—there is no evidence of female smiths until recent centuries.

The earliest evidence of metalworking comes from the Paleolithic, but metals weren't important anywhere until about 6000 BCE. The first smelting operations on a large scale occurred, remarkably, in southern Mesopotamia, a region with no useful ores and not much wood for fuel. Soon after 6000 BCE, smelting developed elsewhere in Southwest Asia and in southeastern Europe, mainly in upland regions where both ores and wood were abundant. Copper, tin, and lead were among the easiest metals to work. Ötzi the Iceman, to judge by chemical analysis of his hair, lived some of his life around copper smelters in the Alps.

Metallurgy acquired much greater importance at about 3500 BCE, when smiths in Mesopotamia started to make **bronze**, an alloy of copper and tin. Bronze was a harder metal than any yet in use, good for axes, armor, and weapons as well as ornamentation. Since tin and copper aren't generally found together, bronze making always involved long-distance trade of tin, much the rarer of the two metals. So bronze was always expensive and became a favorite ornament of the rich and powerful. By 2000 BCE, bronze-making skills had spread widely in Eurasia and North Africa.

Bronze quickly became important to states and rulers. It made much better

Using Bronze A display of bronze knives found in present-day Iran, and dated to around 2000 to 1000 BCE, represents only a small range of the many items that could be made from the versatile and durable material. Knives could serve as tools, as weapons, or as luxury items to signify status.

weaponry than stone or any other available metal. Those who could control its supply held a military advantage over everyone else. Most early states in Eurasia struggled to acquire the tin and copper needed to make bronze weapons and armor. They set out either to conquer upland regions where the ores were found or to establish trade links. Few states without bronze could survive for long anywhere near others that had it. Bronze in Eurasia was a bit like fire, language, and farming everywhere: those with it enjoyed advantages over those without it, and those without it either acquired it, were conquered, or fled from those who had it.

The Twin Challenges of Complex Society

In Chapter 2, we tried to account for the emergence of agriculture at least seven times between 11,000 and 4000 BCE after more than 200,000 years without it. The appearance of complex society presents a broadly similar problem. It arose independently in at least four places, and probably six: Mesopotamia, Egypt, the Indus valley, China, Mesoamerica, and the Andes. In all these places, it came several thousand years after a transition to agriculture. And in each case, complex society shared many of the same features: irrigation agriculture, cities, markets, states, monumental architecture, armies, and bureaucracies. Almost all shared kingship, writing, and metallurgy too.

Could it be accidental that such a similar socio-technological package evolved a few millennia after each transition to agriculture? It can't be inevitable: people practiced farming for millennia in most of sub-Saharan Africa and North America without proceeding to develop cities, states, or writing. But it's also not random—not by a long shot. Complex societies showed so much uniformity because they all faced two main challenges: attack by neighbors and civil strife within. They all had to develop practices, beliefs, technologies, and institutions to equip themselves to address these two problems.

Threats from Without and Within Defense against unfriendly neighbors, whether skilled and violent horsemen or organized in a state with an army, was a matter of survival for complex societies. To create the means of protection, complex societies generally organized as states. Kingship, armies, metallurgy, and other practices—even writing—contributed directly to the goal of self-protection. Ideologies of social solidarity, religious emphasis on fertility, and technologies of irrigation agriculture contributed indirectly to a society's ability to defend itself.

The other main problem for complex societies was conspicuous social inequality. The quest for status may be innate among humans, as it is among chimpanzees; but simple human societies, as we've seen, are relatively egalitarian. In complex society, however, the difference between kings and slaves was much greater than the difference between leaders and followers in any hunting-foraging band or village—or chimpanzee troop. This chasm expanded the scope for envy, jealousy, rivalry, division, and conflict within any given society.

All complex societies that endured developed cultures that persuaded people to accept, even if only resentfully, enormous inequalities. (In later chapters, we'll examine some of these cultures in detail.) Religions played the leading role in convincing the toiling masses that it was proper that they should sweat and suffer while others lived in comfort. They justified kingship and elite power, keys to the survival of such unequal societies. To be sure, soldiers used violence (or threats of violence) when needed to keep the masses in line and societies stable. Architects designed awe-inspiring monuments to remind everyone of rulers' authority. Rituals and ceremonies of social solidarity, including examples of public generosity on the part of elites, also helped to keep the lid on.

The twin problems of complex societies were closely related. To be strong in the face of threats from neighbors required some measure of inequality because rulers needed to equip and train warriors—which, if it required expensive equipment, made for a social structure with warrior elites. But too much inequality could become a source of weakness and division: the downtrodden might welcome defeat at the hand of outsiders on the theory that nothing could be worse than the rulers they had. This helps to account for the unstable nature of politics in most examples of complex society: states and dynasties came and went even if the underlying structures of societies remained much the same. States lasted longest, by and large, when and where effective ideologies united elites and commoners and on those occasions when and where trade, technology, or conquest allowed a society to enjoy an expanding economic pie.

The First Big, Faint Webs

By 5000 BCE, if not before, village farmers made up most of humanity. There were still hunter-foragers, of course, and in areas inhospitable to farming—deserts, steppes, and dense forest zones—they might well have outnumbered farmers at that time. But globally, farmers accounted for ever larger numbers and spread their ways with each passing century. As the world became dotted with farming villages and inhabited by ever more people, it knitted itself together into interactive webs faster than before.

Trade and Technology

Although villages could be self-sufficient for a time, producing their own food, fuel, and other basic commodities, most could not always do so. To acquire commodities beyond the basics, many villages linked to one another, and sometimes to distant sources of high-value goods, like the obsidian of Çatalhöyük or the salt of Jericho. Precious goods might be traded, one village to the next, over distances of hundreds of miles. For example, a farming center in the lower Indus valley region, Mehrgargh, acquired shells from the Persian Gulf and turquoise from Central Asia as early as 6000 BCE.

Wheeled Carts Trade in bulk goods was limited to easily navigable rivers and coastlines until someone invented the wheel. The earliest evidence of wheels and axles dates to around 3500 BCE and turns up in several places more or less at once—Poland, the Balkans, the Caucasus, and Mesopotamia. It's possible that people re-invented the wheel shortly after it was invented, or the technology may have spread quickly because it was so useful. Oxen pulling wheeled carts could move ten times the load that a beast of burden might carry. By 3000 BCE, people on the steppes of western Eurasia probably lived in animal-drawn wheeled carts—the first mobile homes. On flat land, oxcarts became a crucial technology, smoothing movement and exchange. In rugged lands, the wheel had little use. Its invention and spread, therefore, contributed to the unevenness of the Eurasian economy: a boon to level lands, especially the clusters of villages in the already well-populated floodplains of Mesopotamia, Egypt, and the Indus, but of no value in hilly country.

Donkey Caravans At about the same time that the wheel made its debut, people in Southwest Asia and Egypt started transporting goods in donkey caravans. Although much less efficient on flat land than wheeled transport, strings of donkeys could navigate uneven terrain. They helped to link uplands, where timber and useful ores were more common, to the more densely populated lowlands. By and large, pack animal transport developed earlier and more fully in Southwest Asia than anywhere else. In East and

Southeast Asia, river transport loomed larger. In Africa south of the Sahara, river transport and human porterage proved more practical than beasts of burden, which suffered heavily there from a livestock disease. In the Americas, there were no suitable beasts of burden outside the Andes, where llama caravans played much the same role that donkey caravans did in Southwest Asia.

Beyond these economic links, villagers interacted with their neighbors in nearby settlements through regular festivals and ceremonies, and at times in efforts to defend themselves against invaders from afar. Families sought marriage partners for sons and daughters in neighboring communities—it was always prudent to have kinfolk a day or two away in case something went

Trading Luxury Goods The elephant shown here was carved of the rare stone lapis lazuli and mined in Afghanistan. The trade of this valuable commodity extended across Southwest Asia into North Africa.

wrong in one's own village. So for social as well as economic reasons, villages formed ever tighter, if tiny, webs of interaction with neighboring villages.

The First Regional Webs

The first regional webs in Eurasia and North Africa began to appear by around 5000 BCE, even before cities and states. Rivers were central to this web-building process. Water transport, even on mere rafts or canoes, was far cheaper than on land. The frequency of interactions with distant villages was far greater for people living along navigable rivers. Where these rivers linked up to seaborne transport networks and to local overland routes, villages became especially interactive and interconnected. Examples of such locations include the mouth of the Nile in Egypt and the Tigris-Euphrates in southern Mesopotamia.

Two technological developments soon spurred on the development of regional webs in Eurasia and Egypt. The first was the combination of horse domestication and the wheel, which gradually made it easier to transit broad grasslands after 3500 BCE. The second occurred by roughly 3000 BCE, when people from the Persian Gulf to the Pacific began to learn how to use sails efficiently, making seaborne and upstream river-borne transport more practical. It took many more centuries for people to learn the best routes and the ideal ways to rig sailing vessels. These two technological changes eased human trade and travel in Eurasia and North Africa, and helped prepare the way for bigger, thicker, regional webs to form—as we will see in later chapters.

After 3000 BCE, writing as well as transport technologies eased the development of regional webs. Record keeping enabled merchants to operate more reliably over long distances by keeping track of who owed how many bolts of cloth or baskets of rice. And it enabled states to recruit, feed, and equip larger armies and extend their authority over larger territories.

Web Expansion from the Top Down The expansion of these regional webs also derived from the wishes of people involved, especially powerful people. Village and rural elites benefited from involvement in larger networks. If they could get farmers or herders under their influence to produce goods that cities wanted such as grain or leather, then in exchange they could enjoy the fruits of urban craft production—fine clothing, dazzling jewelry, effective weaponry. Rulers normally sought to collect rents or taxes from more people to maximize their income. When they could, they spread the worship of their preferred gods widely. Such goals were attractive enough that rulers everywhere routinely used their armies, priests, and wealth to break down centers of resistance to their authority. They extended their states, founded new cities, and in so doing spread webs of interaction.

Web Expansion from the Bottom Up Web building, to a lesser extent, also resulted from the daily activities of petty traders, sailors plying unfamiliar seas, refugees escaping from wars, slaves taken from their homes, soldiers posted to faraway lands, and countless others who introduced their accustomed ways in new places. The metals that were traded over long distances were passed from trader to trader in little towns; after all, big trade networks consisted of lots of smaller networks. Sailors, soldiers, refugees, and slaves—anyone traveling or living far from home—occasionally introduced to their new communities novel ways of worshipping, cooking, dyeing cloth, decorating pots, or fletching arrows. Without intending anything of the sort, they too brought communities into closer economic and cultural contact, simply by traveling or living away from home.

As a result of the routine activities of common people and the ambitions of the powerful, fewer villages retained the autonomy of earlier times. Instead, people found themselves entangled in larger webs, entranced by the culture of cities, enmeshed in complex society—and subject to the authority of states.

Webs and the Durability of Knowledge

Although webs grew bigger and tighter, the whole process was fragile and occasionally reversed. Webs could break down under the impact of epidemics and famines that reduced population sharply. Pirates and brigands could stop traffic on seas or steppes. But usually these proved to be temporary interruptions, and patient effort guided by the self-interest of elites and the daily routines of people traveling far from home normally rebuilt torn webs.

With the advent of dense populations, complex societies, cities, and states, the likelihood of a lasting breakdown in webs dwindled. During the Paleolithic, when people were few and spread out, disasters could eliminate skills and knowledge. An example is the case of the native Tasmanians. Tasmania, now an island the size of Indiana or Maine, was part of the Australian mainland until rising seas filled the Bass Strait about

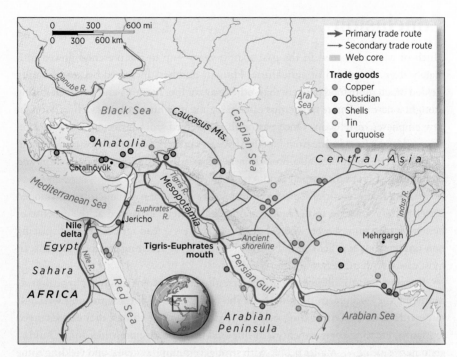

Trade Routes and the First Regional Webs, ca. 5000–3500 BCE Trade routes in South-west Asia, especially those involving Mesopotamia, acquired more and more traffic after 5000 BCE, well before any cities or states emerged. Gradually thickening connections came to form a thin web that by 3500 BCE extended loosely to the Nile and to the Indus.

10,000 years ago. At that time, fewer than 4,000 people lived on the new island. No one had boats capable of crossing the strait, so the Tasmanians were isolated. They gradually lost the capacity to make items such as fishhooks and sewing awls (big needles). They could no longer fish or make clothing. They even lost the ability to make fire.

This small story shows the penalty of small numbers. When those Tasmanians who knew how to make fishhooks died, they hadn't passed on their knowledge to enough other people to ensure its perpetuation. Useful knowledge was lost because it wasn't stored in enough different brains.

In large regions such as Mesopotamia, Egypt, China, or Mesoamerica, however, once dense populations, complex societies, and regional webs were in place, such cultural losses couldn't happen. Population density meant that skills diffused readily to large numbers of people. Interactive webs enabled people far away to learn of every new skill or technology, and some of them would adopt it or alter it to fit their circumstances. With writing, information could survive outside of people's brains altogether, and live on beyond any individual's death. Innovation and learning became more cumulative inside the webs. The losses that Tasmanians experienced only happen among small, isolated populations—of which there were ever fewer as complex society, cities, states, and webs spread.

Conclusion

Much of what happened in the past 10,000 years—up to the present—flowed ultimately from the spread of agriculture. Human numbers increased because farming yielded much more food per acre than other ways of life. Farming and livestock raising brought a new and more dangerous disease regime into human history. They brought new emphases in religion. Once pastoralism diverged from farming, a new tension emerged in the broad zone from North Africa to northern China between herders and farmers. That divergence also brought a new basis for economic specialization and exchange—of crops for animal products.

Farming communities reproduced faster; hosted more nasty microbes; fashioned better pottery, textiles, tools, and weapons; and thereby expanded at the expense of hunter-foragers almost everywhere. Sometimes farmers spread agriculture by displacing non-farmers, but at other times they spread farming by teaching it to non-farmers. In most cases, both processes were involved.

Farmers, and to a lesser extent herders, altered the biological and physical environments they occupied, pushing back the boundaries of forests, turning wetlands into gardens, and exterminating wildlife. In doing all these things, they also changed humanity, creating environments that imposed new selective pressures on the human genome, resulting in smaller people with stronger immune systems, and yielding some local adaptations such as the ability to digest milk in adulthood.

Perhaps the most important thing farmers did, although no one at the time recognized it, was to produce food efficiently enough to create a surplus. The surplus food could support smiths, potters, weavers, warriors, traders, and priests—specialists who concentrated their talents on single pursuits, and so developed new skills and, in turn, a greater economic surplus. This bigger surplus production permitted the creation of cities, states, and complex society.

History sped up and grew more complicated after the shifts to agriculture. For over 200,000 years, people had lived as hunters and foragers until, almost in a flash, they developed agriculture in several places between 11,000 and 4000 BCE. Once some people had taken up farming, population tended to grow faster and more people tended to live more closely together. This sped up interactions to the point where, again almost in a flash, another crucial transformation took place.

Starting just about the time Ötzi the Iceman lived, complex society began to emerge across Eurasia and North Africa. Between 3500 BCE and 1500 BCE, elaborate division of labor and social hierarchy, cities and states, irrigation agriculture and herding, metallurgy and writing, all appeared in Egypt, Mesopotamia, the Indus valley, and China. Complex society with all the trappings developed in the Americas too before 1500 BCE, and specifically in Mesoamerica and the Andes.

All these trappings—divine kingship, irrigation, cities, markets, states, armies, bureaucracies, monuments, writing, and so forth—looked broadly similar in every setting. This conformity wasn't so much a matter of imitation, although there was some of that among Egypt, Mesopotamia, and the Indus, but rather a set of effective responses to the two foremost challenges faced by complex societies: attack by strangers and internal discord driven by inequality.

The formation of complex societies, cities, and states kick-started the emergence of big, regional webs. Elites in complex societies had good reason to try to extend their political control, commercial operations, and preferred religions. By doing so, together with the ordinary activities of ordinary people, they extended the interactive webs to new territories and tightened the existing links of culture, trade, and politics.

Chapter Review

KEY TERMS

shifting agriculture p. 73
herders p. 74
Eurasian steppe p. 75
Bantu p. 79
complex society p. 87
state p. 87

city p. 88
plow agriculture p. 89
irrigation p. 90
crowd diseases p. 93
metallurgy p. 95
bronze p. 95

REVIEW QUESTIONS ◆ = answers

1. How did the needs and desires of people in settled village societies differ from those of people in mobile societies?

2. What were the risks and advantages of village life?

3. Why did people turn to pastoralism for survival in arid scrubland and semi-arid grasslands?

4. What was the relationship between herder societies and farmers?

5. What characteristics of farming societies encourage migration?

6. Describe how culture and biology affected each other in the cases of cattle and horse domestication.

7. What were the three important features that complex societies often shared?

8. Why do complex societies often rely on plow agriculture and irrigation?

9. How did access to bronze confer military advantages?

10. Why do complex societies in different regions share many of the same traits?
11. What was typically the purpose of religion in complex societies?
12. What technologies spurred regional connections in Eurasia and Egypt?

Go to **INQUIZITIVE**

to see what you've learned—and learn what you've missed—with personalized feedback along the way.

REGIONAL WEBS AND THEIR FUSION INTO THE OLD WORLD WEB

3500 bce to 200 ce

U nlike the first three chapters, which take on the development of humans and their early societies across the world as a whole, Chapters 4 through 10 approach world history regionally. They deal with similar themes in several different settings around the world. The most crucial themes include the formation of regional webs of interaction and the spread of complex and hierarchical societies and states. The web-making process, introduced here, will stay with us as the key impetus for globalization, weaving together localities, regions, and then the entire world.

Part 2 carries the human story up to 200 CE. The major exception comes in Chapter 10, which treats the history of the Americas and Oceania up to 1000 CE.

Developing Webs

The logic behind choosing 200 CE is that by this date large parts of Eurasia and northern Africa had developed strong and steady enough connections so as to be considered a single, sprawling web of human interaction, called here the Old World web. Although patchy in places, and here or there unraveled for centuries, this web linked most of humankind—perhaps as much as 70 percent. It represents the fusion of earlier webs that developed first around Mesopotamia, then Mesopotamia together with Egypt, and the Indus and Ganges valleys in India. While those regions were growing in population and connectivity, in East Asia something similar was under way centered on northern China. An East Asian web was emerging, and by 200 CE it had linked up with those to its west to form the Old World web. This process was pushed along by the emergence of big, powerful states—notably Achaemenid Persia, the Han Empire in China, and the Roman Empire around the Mediterranean Sea. But millions of anonymous merchants, muleteers, and missionaries also helped this integration along by pursuing their daily routines. So did millions of silk spinners, silver miners, and shipbuilders whose labor created goods that inspired trade and travel.

Regions outside the Web

The logic behind ending the chapter on the Americas and Oceania in 1000 CE (rather than 200 CE) is that these places followed their own traditions and trajectories outside the Old World web. The web fusion that took place in Eurasia and North Africa did not involve or affect them. Moreover, we know much less about their history because they had no writing before 200 CE and almost none as late as 1000 CE. Archeology, ancient DNA, and historical linguistics are all we have to go on here. In Oceania, people built seaborne webs over formidable distances, but those webs touched on thousands, not millions, of people. In the Americas, societies built mainly terrestrial webs over vast distances and rugged terrain, involving at most a few million people. As late as 1000 CE, the biggest and most influential of these societies remained smaller in scale than the big ones within the Old World web. So it's fair to say that over this period the Americas and Oceania remained isolated from the main centers of human population and interaction.

That was less true for most of Africa and Europe. Parts of those regions, such as Egypt, took part in big regional webs very early on, and by 200 CE sizeable parts of northeastern Africa and southern Europe had become deeply entangled in the Old World web. But at the same time, broad regions of Africa and Europe stood on the frontiers of the web. They weren't as isolated as the islands of Oceania or the plains of North America, but nonetheless they were unentangled, free to follow their own traditions and trajectories without much interaction with the cultures and empires of China, India, Southwest Asia, or Egypt.

Regional Variety, Common Themes

So in Part 2 we see how the most populated parts of the world, from Egypt to China, developed up to 200 CE and how they slowly forged links among themselves. We also see regions on the frontiers of this process—large parts of Africa and Europe—as they evolved up to 200 CE. And finally, we see other regions, the Americas and Oceania, that stood far outside this giant process of Old World fusion.

In the Indian folk tale about the blind men and the elephant, each man touches only part of an elephant and describes what he feels. One, who touches only the tail, says an elephant is like a rope. Another, who touches only the trunk, claims an elephant is like a tree branch. In approaching world history regionally, as we do here in Part 2 (and will again in Part 3), we risk the same confusion, failing to see the trends of human history as a whole because we focus on one part of it at a time.

So even though each chapter deals chiefly with one or at most two regions, most chapters also address some common themes to help keep the bigger picture in mind. We will be concerned with how societies organized themselves politically and how states expanded their territories. We'll look at the spread of big, multicultural empires. We'll examine how cultures structured social relations. And we will chart the formation and development of influential traditions such as religions and systems of thought. These chapters also address health and disease, military techniques and technologies, agriculture and animals. And all of these chapters address the slow and unsteady process of web building.

4

The Southwest Asian Web

MESOPOTAMIA AND THE INDUS VALLEY

3500 BCE to 200 BCE

FOCUS QUESTIONS

1. What conditions contributed to the development of the Southwest Asian web?
2. What were the distinctive characteristics of culture, society, and politics in Mesopotamia?
3. What made the culture of the Indus valley cities so remarkable?
4. What links were there between the cultures of Mesopotamia and the Indus region?

A ncient **Sumer**, in today's southern Iraq, developed a lively literature of myths, poems, and epics. One poem, called "Enki and the World Order," details the feats of the god Enki as he arranges everything to suit Sumer. Written down around 2100 BCE, the poem celebrates Sumer's thriving trade with lands to the south on the Persian Gulf (Magan and Dilmun) and to the east in the Indus valley (Meluha).

> Let the lands of Meluha, Magan and Dilmun look upon me, upon Enki. Let the Dilmun boats be loaded with timber. Let the Magan boats be loaded sky-high.

Let the boats of Meluha transport gold and silver and bring them to Enlil, king of all the lands....

Sumer... land of heaven and earth, trailing glory, bestowing powers on the people from sunrise to sunset: your powers are superior powers, untouchable, and your heart is complex and inscrutable. Like heaven itself, your good creative force [?], in which gods too can be born, is beyond reach. Giving birth to kings... giving birth to lords who wear the crown on their heads....

Then Enki proceeds to the land of Meluha and its rich resources:

Black land, may your trees be great trees!... Chairs made from them will grace royal palaces! May your reeds be great reeds....May your bulls be great bulls, may they be bulls of the mountains! May their bellowing be the bellowing of wild bulls of the mountains! The great powers of the gods shall be made perfect for you!...May your birds all be peacocks! May their cries grace royal palaces!...Land, may all you possess be plentiful!

The poem celebrates the superiority that Sumerian rulers and subjects alike claimed for themselves. In this it resembled much of the art and literature from ancient Mesopotamia (and elsewhere), which consisted mainly of boasts about the greatness of rulers and gods.

In a more unusual vein, the poem details trade flows, suggesting that Sumer imported goods from the shores of the Persian Gulf and the Arabian Sea. It offers an inventory of products from Meluha, including bulls and peacocks, which prompts scholars to think Meluha was in the Indus valley. Meluha's big trees would have come from the flanks of the Himalaya and been floated down the Indus River before becoming furniture in Sumerian palaces. The gold and silver likely came from today's Afghanistan, north of the Indus valley.

CHRONOLOGY

ca. 7000 BCE Farming begins in upper Indus valley

ca. 6000 BCE Farmers settle floodplain of Tigris and Euphrates Rivers and begin small-scale irrigation

ca. 3500–3000 BCE City of Uruk emerges and flourishes

ca. 3400–3300 BCE Writing begins in Uruk with cuneiform

ca. 3200 BCE Signs of irrigation appear in lower Indus valley

By 3000 BCE Mariners regularly sail the Indian Ocean

By ca. 2600 BCE Five main cities arise in Indus valley

ca. 2340–2150 BCE Rule of Akkadian Empire

ca. 2300 BCE Poem "Enki and the World Order" is written

By ca. 2300 BCE Farmers use a water-lifting device, the *shaduf*; Mesopotamia and Indus region are linked through contact

ca. 2200–2100 BCE Prolonged drought occurs

ca. 2100 BCE Epic of Gilgamesh is written.

ca. 2000 BCE Salinization begins to ruin fertile Mesopotamian land

ca. 1900–1700 BCE Indus valley cities fall apart and are abandoned

1792–1750 BCE Reign of Hammurabi, king of Babylon

By 1500 BCE Warriors use chariots in Egypt, Mesopotamia, Iran, India, China

ca. 1200 BCE Advent of high-quality iron

ca. 1200–800 BCE Mounted archers using composite bows become widespread

911–609 BCE Height of Assyrian Empire

ca. 900 BCE Solomon's temple in Jerusalem becomes center of Hebrew religion

By ca. 700 BCE Slavery is widespread in Southwest Asia and Egypt

ca. 75 CE Last use of cuneiform

This text is one of the clues that shows how interconnected the two river valleys—the Tigris-Euphrates of Mesopotamia and the Indus—had become by the late third millennium BCE. A handful of Indus valley products, unearthed by archeologists in Mesopotamia, confirm these links.

Each river valley was itself the central avenue of a system of trade and travel routes that extended hundreds of miles, linking farming areas to pasturelands, and to upland zones rich in timber and minerals. In the case of Mesopotamia, its links connected it to Anatolia, the Levant, Egypt, and the Iranian plateau. The Indus's tendrils extended into Central Asia, especially Afghanistan, and much of western India. These two riverine webs merged in the third millennium BCE to form the Southwest Asian web—the first big regional web in world history. The next chapter considers the extension of that web to the Nile valley in northeast Africa and the Ganges valley in northern India.

This chapter examines two of the core components of the Southwest Asian web, Mesopotamia and the Indus valley. Since we know far more about it than about the Indus valley culture, Mesopotamia draws more attention here. Mesopotamia also bequeathed more to the future than did the culture of the Indus. Firm bonds linked Mesopotamia and the Indus, but the complex societies they spawned differed in many respects, as we shall see.

Threads of Connection in Southwest Asia

Because networks of trade and travel held the Southwest Asian web together, we will begin with geography focusing on Mesopotamia, the Indus valley, and their vicinity.

Rivers

The life-giving rivers of Southwest Asia rise in mountain regions that served (and still serve today) as water towers for the whole region, reliably squeezing rain and snow out of passing clouds. The twin rivers of Mesopotamia, the Tigris and Euphrates, flooded every spring with snowmelt from the highlands of eastern Anatolia. The flood carried an annual gift of water and fertile silt to the lowlands—a gift that made farming and cities possible in central and southern Mesopotamia, which is mainly desert. Farther east, the Indus brought a similar gift as its spring flood tumbled down from the Tibetan Plateau and the western Himalaya. With ample sunshine and a fresh coating of nutrient-rich and well-moistened silt, the river valleys invited people to farm. Once people mastered the necessary irrigation techniques, the result was bountiful agriculture, and soon thereafter dense populations, urban life, and complex society.

Connecting Uplands and Lowlands The highlands provided more than water and silt to the populations that crowded into the river valleys. Without nearby forests, the cities and villages in these valleys had to import wood from the nearest mountain ranges—the Taurus, Zagros, and Himalaya, all crowned with tall forests. Mesopotamia had to import most of its metals as well, from upland Anatolia, Iran, or farther afield. As a result, each valley's population had reason to build and maintain linkages to distant uplands—linkages that over time evolved into webs. By 3500 BCE, this binding of upland and lowland in Southwest Asia was well along, and Mesopotamia was the center of its own emerging web. That became true several centuries later of the Indus valley as well.

These developing webs stretched—tenuously—across dry scrub, steppe, and desert land in between the river valleys. The general lack of water confined the scattered farming settlements mainly to oases. Rainfall was sufficient, however, to support grazing animals and herders on lands of grass and scrub vegetation. The herders provided leather, meat, and other animal products to the cities and villages of the river valleys in exchange for grain, cloth, and other items the herders couldn't easily make themselves. During the fourth millennium BCE, trade links increasingly bound the sparsely populated steppe lands, like the uplands of Iran and Anatolia, to the dense populations of Mesopotamia. A similar process occurred several centuries later along the Indus.

Maritime Threads and the Monsoon

Both of these nascent webs had maritime threads. People and goods moved not only along the rivers and donkey tracks, but on the sea as well. Mesopotamia stood at the head of the Persian Gulf, a body of water that was easy to navigate and that connected to the much larger Arabian Sea. The Indus valley lay adjacent to the Arabian Sea itself. Mariners took to these waters early, and by 3000 BCE were regularly sailing along the coasts and learning the patterns of the Indian Ocean monsoon.

The **Indian Ocean monsoon** is so important to world history that it merits a geophysical explanation. Eurasia is by far the biggest continent, so its interior, far from the moderating impact of oceans, gets very hot in summer and very cold in winter. This regular seasonal pattern generates strong and reliable winds over South Asia and the Indian Ocean that blow northward in summer and southward in winter. The regularity of the monsoon made the Indian Ocean comparatively easy to sail. On its western side, the monsoon linked western India, Southwest Asia, and Egypt to the East African coast. On the ocean's eastern side, the winds linked Southeast Asian islands to

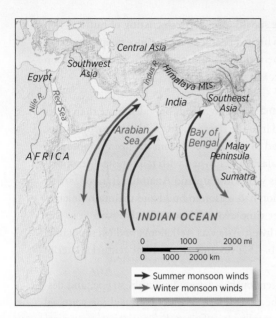

The Indian Ocean Monsoon Steady and predictable winds characterize the Indian Ocean north of the equator. This geographical and climatological feature helps explain the early development of sailing technology and maritime trade and travel involving people from Egypt to India.

the mainland. Essentially, the monsoon made the Indian Ocean into the first large, interactive seascape in the world.

No other region on Earth matched the corridor between the Indus and Mesopotamia for the combination of easy river and seaborne transport, and suitable animals and forage for land transport. This helps explain why people here were among the first to develop the systematic social and economic interactions of complex society, cities, and states, and the first to create regional webs. While occasional exchanges between the Indus and Mesopotamia date back at least to 6000 BCE, after 2500 BCE regular trade connections by river, land, and sea linked the two river valleys and their surroundings together as the Southwest Asian web.

Environmental Challenges: Drought and Disease

The complex societies of Mesopotamia and the Indus valley, and the big regional web that they were forming in the third millennium BCE, faced two great environmental challenges: drought and disease. Occasionally, the rain and snow didn't fall in the mountains and the rivers didn't rise. Without the annual flood, irrigation agriculture failed and the specter of starvation haunted these lands. The worst of these climate shocks, a prolonged drought lasting for about a century after 2200 BCE, drastically reduced population everywhere from the Indus to Mesopotamia to Egypt. Trade fell off, weakening or unraveling the threads that connected these regions. But, as with every such catastrophe, after the drought population and connections eventually recovered, even if specific kingdoms and cultures disappeared.

Epidemic disease was the second great enemy of peoples living in the fertile and populous river valleys. The problem lay in the density of human population, the prevalence of irrigation, and the frequent contact of people with herd animals. Working with, and often in, irrigation ditches promoted the spread of snail-borne diseases such as schistosomiasis and mosquito-borne ones such as malaria. Living in tight quarters eased the spread of breath-borne infections such as smallpox. The populations of Southwest

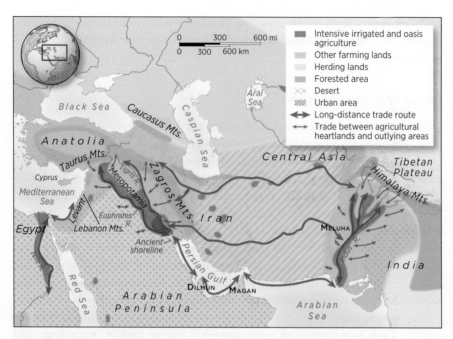

Emerging Webs of Southwest Asia and Egypt, ca. 3500–3000 BCE The great rivers of the Indus, Tigris-Euphrates, and Nile valleys provided the geographic basis for growing webs of interaction by 3000 BCE. Donkey caravans and wheeled carts helped people to transport goods across the dry steppes and deserts between the rivers.

Asian valleys gradually built up resistance to many communicable diseases, turning some infections into childhood (endemic) diseases to which adults carried resistance or full immunity. But this process—which no one at the time understood—took many centuries of recurrent epidemics to achieve.

Over time, the bounty of irrigation agriculture prevailed over droughts and epidemics, and population grew. In the Indus valley, archeologists have found over 1,000 settlements, including two major cities. Mesopotamia at times had dozens of cities with populations of 10,000 to 80,000. While estimates are rough, each river valley as of 2000 BCE held about 3 million people (and neighboring Egypt's Nile valley another 1 to 2 million). The dense population and urbanization of these river valleys made the region (including Egypt) the world's demographic center of gravity for a long time. From 3000 BCE until 500 BCE, it hosted between one-quarter and one-third of the global population.

Mesopotamia

Mesopotamian history stretches over several millennia. Here we'll look closely at the early stages before 2000 BCE, when most basic patterns were formed. The availability of abundant ancient texts, inscriptions, and art allows a much more confident depiction of society and religion in **Mesopotamia** than has been possible for any other society to this point.

Irrigation Agriculture

The emergence of complex society in Mesopotamia depended on the bounty of irrigation agriculture: grain farming, mainly wheat and barley.

The earliest evidence of irrigation in Mesopotamia suggests it began on a small scale at about 6000 BCE in the floodplain of the **Tigris and Euphrates Rivers**—at that time a mosaic of wetlands, braided river channels, and shifting islands of silt. Snowmelt from the mountains of eastern Anatolia spurted through the river channels in springtime, briefly filling the floodplain with life-giving water. However, the water came at the wrong time of year for grain crops such as wheat and barley. To grow grain in Mesopotamia's dry climate, one had to plant it in the fall and harvest in the late spring. Summer was too hot and dry for plant growth. Farmers had to figure out how to store the floodwaters from springtime until just before fall planting.

Topography helped them out. The Euphrates normally runs at a higher elevation than the Tigris, so it was possible to cut channels in the east bank of the Euphrates and let gravity carry water to fields between the rivers, and then use the Tigris to drain off any excess water. But southernmost Mesopotamia is so nearly flat that directing water by gravity was a fine engineering art. Yet farmers mastered it and throughout the length of Mesopotamia produced enough grain to feed cities, armies, priests, and bureaucrats as well as themselves and their families.

Mesopotamians invented a water-lifting device, the *shaduf*, a bucket attached to the end of a pole that rests on a lever and has a counterweight on the other end. The device, in use by 2300 BCE, allowed irrigation of small areas at higher elevations than

Irrigation In this stone carving dated to around 695 BCE from Nineveh, a city in Mesopotamia, workers use a *shaduf* to lift water out of a river.

the local water source. It was useful for a grove of date palms, for example, but less so for grain farming.

In Mesopotamia, irrigation exacted its normal price. After several centuries of intensive farming, salinization forced farmers to abandon wheat in favor of barley, which is more salt-tolerant. But this adjustment didn't solve the basic problem. Beginning by 2000 BCE, if not before, salinization sapped the agricultural potential of much Mesopotamian land so that even barley yielded poorly, if at all. In a tragic irony, ancient Mesopotamians often fought wars over scraps of territory while salt ruined broad expanses of their otherwise fertile soils.

Uruk and the City-States of Sumer (3500–2500 BCE)

The Sumerian city of Uruk lay in what is today southern Iraq, where a channel of the Euphrates flowed across a flat plain just inland from the head of the Persian Gulf. It is here that archeologists have found the first evidence of urban life, state apparatus, monumental architecture, and writing. Uruk was the first of several Sumerian city-states. (A city-state was a small state consisting of a city and its surrounding farmland.)

Society and Economy Beginning around 3500 BCE, Uruk emerged among the smaller, mud-brick villages that dotted southern Mesopotamia. At first, its people grew barley, herded sheep and goats, and fished in nearby marshes. They traded with people to their south, on the shores of the Persian Gulf, and with others to their north, along the Euphrates. Uruk's merchants organized donkey caravans into the uplands of western Iran, where wood, metals, and other goods could be obtained. Uruk stood at the confluence of maritime, river-based, and land-based merchant networks and exerted economic sway over a growing region. Soon its people started building big structures out of imported limestone—first temples, then temple-palaces. Called **ziggurats**, and dedicated to local gods, they were visible for many miles around in the flat Sumerian landscape. (The tower of Babel described in the Bible was a ziggurat.) Uruk grew to be a full-fledged city in a century or two.

Uruk at its biggest, between 3400 and 3000 BCE, covered about half a square mile, the size of a small college campus. About 50,000 to 80,000 people huddled inside its walls, and most toiled in surrounding barley fields. They believed that their work fed gods, and that gods—if satisfied—protected them from bad weather, floods, sickness, plunderers, and other perils.

A remarkable surge of technological creativity helped make Uruk's growth possible. Between 3800 and 3100 BCE, plows came into use in Mesopotamia, multiplying the area farmers could till. Potters' wheels after 3500 BCE allowed the mass production of clay pots, one of Uruk's chief exports. Wheels and wagons were in use by 3100 BCE, extending the area from which it was practical to transport grain, pots, woolen cloth, and other bulky items. All these inventions advanced the social process of specialization and

Appeasing the Gods A detail from a limestone vase from Uruk, dated to around 2900 BCE, shows people making offerings, including a valuable bull, to the fertility goddess Inanna, who they hoped would ensure the viability of their crops.

exchange, helping Sumerians—especially potters—refine their skills, create wealth, and extend their trade networks.

These potters, weavers, and hardworking farm families supported a priestly elite, specialists who claimed to know how to keep the gods happy. The priests accepted a share of the wheat, barley, dates, onions, beans, peas, and fish that Uruk's people produced. They kept it in temple storehouses, eating some of it themselves, using some in sacrifices to the gods, and saving the rest for feasts, for the poor, and eventually for an army. They also fed it to potters and weavers, whose pots and cloth the priestly elite distributed and traded. Control of this surplus food, pottery, and cloth was a crucial source of priestly power, but ultimately that power rested on the popular belief that only the priests could keep the gods contented. As Uruk's temples became temple-palaces, its priests became priest-kings.

Religion helped ordinary Sumerians to accept their hard life. So did beer. Barley, which yielded abundantly on the soils of Sumer, could be brewed into beer. Women took responsibility for brewing, done in the home. Sumerians had some 70 varieties of beer and drank it day and night. It was healthier to drink beer than to drink the water around their fields and cities, which was normally contaminated by animal and human feces. As one Sumerian proverb had it, "He who does not know beer, does not know what is good."

Warring City-States A few centuries after the emergence of Uruk, similar social, political, and religious arrangements prevailed in several other city-states elsewhere in Sumer. Each one had its own king and preferred gods. City-states often went to war with one another, obliging citizens to build walls and refine their fighting skills. They fought with bows and arrows, spears and shields, inventing new armor (such as metal helmets) and weapons (such as battle axes) at a remarkable rate. By 3000 BCE, Sumer had become a university of war. Peasant farmers did most of the fighting. Priest-kings led from the front and often died in battle. Nevertheless, a roster of Sumerian monarchs claims that an early one, Alalgar, king of Eridu, ruled for 36,000 years, later matched by Dumuzu, and topped by Enmen-lu-ana, who lasted 43,200 years on the throne. Perhaps the reigns seemed that long to their subjects.

Culture and Writing While Uruk and its neighbors were battling it out, Uruk's cultural influence spread far and wide. Its styles of architecture, bowls, and mosaics have turned up in archeological digs in Iran, Syria, and Egypt. Perhaps Uruk had colonies in all these lands; certainly, Uruk exported manufactured items in exchange for timber and metals. So far, only a small fraction of ancient settlements have yielded their treasures to the archeologists' trowels, and much more remains to be learned.

Uruk's most important cultural legacy was writing. As far as we know, writing began here. The earliest examples date from about 3400 to 3300 BCE. They are cuneiform: scratches made with dried reeds on wedge-shaped pieces of wet clay, which were then baked so as to become durable. Most early examples seem to be records of merchant accounts, a type of bookkeeping. They indicate quantities of goods, such as "14 sheep temple," which might mean that someone gave 14 sheep to a certain temple. There isn't much contextual information in early **cuneiform**—presumably, it was already known to writers and readers. As Uruk grew as a commercial economy and a city-state, the value of written records to merchants, rulers, and bureaucrats grew as well.

Early Sumerian cuneiform was both pictographic and logographic, meaning that the symbols were either pictures of things or representations of words. Sumerians used several hundred symbols, at times up to 1,200, and many surviving documents are the equivalent of spelling lists: guides to how to write things. It was hard to learn several hundred symbols, so only specialists—scribes—did so. Ordinary folks remained illiterate. So did most merchants and kings for whom written information was highly useful. In Sumer in those days, it was so tedious to learn to read and write that it paid to hire someone to do it for you if you could.

Despite its imperfections, cuneiform worked well enough to serve for some 3,000 years. Early cuneiform was by later standards very rudimentary writing: it didn't include verb tenses or prepositions. You just had to know if the sheep had already gone or were still expected to go to or from the temple. It was almost like texting exclusively with

Cuneiform This cuneiform tablet, dated to around 3000 BCE, records the allocation of beer to a workforce. The symbol for beer is the upright jar with a narrow, pointed base—in profile, as here, almost a triangle. Beer was the drink of choice in Mesopotamia; it was probably much healthier to drink than water drawn from the lower Tigris-Euphrates. Brewing was done at home and was considered women's work, like baking.

emoji and no words. Like later forms of information technology, cuneiform got better over time, capable of communicating more efficiently by using more symbols for sounds and fewer for ideas or words.

Cuneiform spread widely among the neighbors of the Sumerians in Southwest Asia, who adapted it to their own languages. At least 15 languages were written in cuneiform throughout its long career, which lasted until around 75 CE (the last remaining tablet had to do with astronomy). And thousands of the inscribed clay tablets survive until this day, more than any other form of writing until printing. Modern scholars gradually figured out how to read cuneiform, enabling us, miraculously enough, to read words spoken and written nearly 200 human generations ago—even if we have no idea how the Sumerians pronounced them.

Gilgamesh   The masterwork of cuneiform literature is the ***Epic of Gilgamesh***, the oldest surviving epic poem in world history. According to Mesopotamian legend, one of Uruk's kings around 2600 BCE was named Gilgamesh. In the poem, Gilgamesh and his friend Enkidu decide to slay a ferocious monster guarding a cedar forest, in order to "establish forever a name eternal." They succeed in their quest, reduce "the forest to a wasteland," and return victorious. Gilgamesh wins the love of Ishtar, a Sumerian goddess of love, sex, and war, but spurns her, which together with the destruction of the forest earns him and his friend the anger of the gods. Their curse leads to Enkidu's death. Forlorn, Gilgamesh refuses to leave his friend's corpse for seven nights. When a worm falls out of Enkidu's nose, Gilgamesh gives up his vigil. After wandering the world in fruitless search of the secret of eternal life, Gilgamesh returns home to Uruk and concludes that he must be satisfied with the fate of mere mortals. He may not have established a name eternal, but at 4,600 years and counting, his renown is more long-lasting than most fame-seekers can expect.

The *Epic of Gilgamesh*, which covers 12 cuneiform tablets, was first written down around 2100 BCE, more than half a millennium after the king's supposed life. Although the characters resemble superheroes and monsters abound, the narrative illuminates some aspects of Sumerian life. It indicates the value of timber, gold, and silver. It refers to livestock and lawsuits, boats and baked bread. It also explores eternal human questions about the purpose of life, the nature of happiness, friendship, divine power, and the proper response to the fact of mortality. It is the mother of all literature, from Tolstoy to Tolkien and beyond, and its script, Sumerian cuneiform, was the most important information revolution since the emergence of speech.

The World's First Empire (ca. 2340–2150 BCE)

The city-states of southern Mesopotamia came and went with the fortunes of war and the shifts in river channels. They were all monarchies, led by rulers who claimed divine authority. Few if any contained more than 100,000 people. They never united among themselves, but around 2340 BCE they were forcibly united by **Sargon of Akkad**. Sargon pioneered a new political format—empire—that became standard in Mesopotamia for millennia to come, and routine in world history.

Sargon of Akkad According to legend, Sargon was born to a priestess and an unknown father and, like Moses in the Bible, placed in a reed basket and put afloat on a river. A gardener found the abandoned infant and raised him to work in an orchard. Somehow (the legends invoke divine intervention) after this unpromising start, Sargon became king of a small city-state called Kish. He built the world's first professional army of full-time soldiers and conquered all of Mesopotamia from the shores of the Persian Gulf to the foothills of the Taurus Mountains. He reigned for about 56 years.

Mesopotamia in Sargon's day was culturally diverse. It was a land of two main languages—Sumerian-speakers in the south and Akkadian-speakers in the north. Each city had its favorite gods. Sargon founded a new capital, Akkad (also known as Agade), which archeologists haven't found but suspect might lie beneath modern Baghdad. It lay in the linguistic frontier zone between Sumerian-speakers and Akkadian-speakers. Sargon was tolerant on religion: he prayed to several gods. He based his approach on performance: he worshipped those gods who seemed to help him and ignored those who didn't deliver.

Trade and Power Political power in Mesopotamian kingdoms hinged partly on access to trade goods, and Sargon was an architect of interaction who promoted long-distance trade. Inscriptions reveal that ships from the Indus valley ports and Oman (on the Arabian Peninsula) docked at Akkad in his time. Sargon expanded trade to the west and north, bringing timber from the Levant (Lebanon and Syria) and minerals from what is now southeastern Turkey under his control. Previous Mesopotamian states had relied exclusively on trade to procure timber and minerals. Sargon went further by establishing control over the territories from which they came. Thereafter, he could command his underlings to provide these essential materials.

It proved more difficult to obtain the luxury products such as lapis lazuli (a prized and striking blue stone) or gold that came from lands not under Sargon's control. Such items were important for displays of royal wealth and for the appropriate decoration of statues of the gods. Kings by Sargon's time also needed copper and tin, the ingredients of bronze. These metals had become, like timber, strategic materials. Bronze made better weapons and armor than any other metal yet in use, and control of bronze supplies had helped make Sargon's army the scourge of Mesopotamia.

For the purpose of obtaining the trade goods on which royal power rested, Sargon built on a Mesopotamian tradition: weaving cloth. His royal workshops employed hundreds, maybe thousands, of women who wove linen and wool into garments valued in foreign markets from the Nile to the Indus. The wool came from steppe pasturelands good for raising sheep and goats. Herders, often children, and weavers, always women, working on the king's account helped to secure the luxury imports with which Sargon could buttress his authority. His was a commercial as well as a military empire. As one Mesopotamian text put it, "The houses of Agade [Akkad] were full of gold . . . and silver, the city was full of music, and the quays where the boats docked bustled." His empire helped integrate larger and larger spaces, encompassing more and more people, into a broad web based on Mesopotamia.

The Empire's Collapse   Sargon's empire did not long survive his death. His daughter, Enheduanna, an accomplished poet whom Sargon appointed as both governor and high priestess of the moon god in the conquered city of Ur, wrote an account of her city's fall to local rebels. She had to flee "like a swallow," which shook her faith in the moon god. More rebellions followed, and the empire crumbled. Sargon's grandson rebuilt it, but thereafter it all fell apart again—for reasons unknown.

The prolonged region-wide drought that began around 2200 BCE probably contributed to the collapse of Sargon's Akkadian Empire. Archeological evidence suggests that in neighboring Palestine the population fell by 80 percent. The water level in the Dead Sea, to the west of Akkad, fell by 110 yards (100 m) from 2200 to 2100 BCE. Lakes in Iran, to the east, dried up. Akkad's trading partners were suffering, no longer able to provide Sargon and his inner circle with the goods—tin and copper, for example—that underpinned their rule. Only the well-irrigated land in Mesopotamia remained productive, and there starving flocks driven by desperate herders clattered into the fields, damaging crops. One such pastoral group from northern Syria, the Amorites, seems to have played a large role in dismantling the Akkadian Empire.

A Sumerian text titled "The Curse of Akkad," composed about a century after the abandonment of Sargon's capital, explicitly refers to a lack of rain.

> *For the first time since cities were built and founded,*
> *The great agricultural tracts produced no grain,*
> *The inundated tracts produced no fish,*
> *The irrigated orchards produced neither syrup nor wine,*
> *The gathered clouds did not rain, the masgurum* did not grow.*
> *At that time, one shekel's worth of oil was only one-half quart,*
> *One shekel's worth of grain was only one-half quart. . . .*
> *These sold at such prices in the markets of all the cities!*
> *He who slept on the roof, died on the roof,*
> *He who slept in the house, had no burial,*
> *People were flailing at themselves from hunger.*

---

* "Masgurum" is an as-yet-unidentified crop.

The sharp and prolonged drought affected all of Southwest Asia and brought several states to ruin. In Mesopotamia, it helped to end the century-long interlude of political unification that Sargon and his family brought about. For the next 13 centuries, no one could unify Mesopotamia for long.

Disunity after Sargon Sargon's short-lived achievement appealed to kings ever after. In Mesopotamia after 2100 BCE, as in Egypt after 2600 BCE and China after 200 BCE, rulers and many of their subjects considered unity to be natural and desirable. In Egypt and China, as we will see, unity was more consistently attained than in Mesopotamia.

That was not for lack of trying. Ambitious rulers of Mesopotamian city-states often made bids for empire and tried to pose as Sargon's natural successors. Their claims to power hinged on controlling the rich alluvial farmlands of Sumer and—because

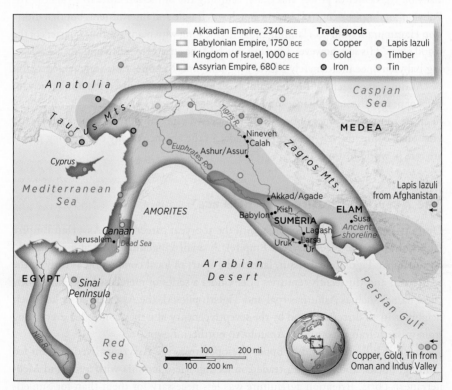

Empires of Mesopotamia after 2340 BCE The agricultural surpluses of Mesopotamian agriculture undergirded three main imperial states over the next 1,800 years. The Akkadian Empire was the first true empire in world history. The Assyrian Empire was the first to unite the rich farmlands of Egypt with those of Mesopotamia.

of Mesopotamia's lack of timber and minerals—the northern reaches of the Tigris and Euphrates where copper, silver, and other metals could be found. Ur, in Sumeria, flourished for a century, then was overrun. Other city-states such as Lagash, Kish, and Ashur conquered a few neighbors, made a brief run at empire under a lucky or skilled king, and then faded. As one Sumerian poet put it,

> *Ur was given kingship, but no eternal reign was she given,*
> *From time out of mind, from the foundations of this land*
> *and the multiplying of its people,*
> *Who has ever seen a reign of kingship that endured uppermost for long?*

Babylon In the eighteenth century BCE, one city, Babylon, suddenly conquered north and south and formed another Mesopotamian empire under a king named Hammurabi. A master of both tactical alliance and treachery, **Hammurabi** (r. 1792–1750 BCE) made Babylon the center of power and trade, eclipsing the Sumerian cities to its south. The Babylonian Empire's control over the north was fragile and intermittent, but that didn't stop Hammurabi from proclaiming himself "the king who made the four quarters of the world obey." His son, however, soon lost much of the empire to rebels and invaders, leaving Babylon once more merely a local kingdom, and Mesopotamia fragmented again.

At times, monarchs of Mesopotamia's divided states recognized the mutual advantages of peace. Through alliances and the exchange of princesses as brides, they managed to create temporary zones of peace and prosperity, especially in the period 1400–1300 BCE. Such comparatively peaceful interludes in the absence of any overarching power are rare in world history.

The Assyrian Empire (911–609 BCE)

Disunity prevailed in Mesopotamia until the 300-year career of the **Assyrian Empire** (also known as the Neo-Assyrian Empire). A small kingdom, based at a stronghold on the upper Tigris called Assur, launched a spurt of local conquering as early as the fourteenth and thirteenth centuries BCE. Under a series of merciless kings (with merciless names such as Ashurnasirpal and Tiglath-pileser), the Assyrians assaulted their neighbors in all directions, and by the seventh century BCE they controlled everything from western Iran to southeast Anatolia to northern Egypt.

In their hilly homeland of upper Mesopotamia, the Assyrians lived off rain-fed farming, flocks, and a caravan trade connecting Mesopotamia with Syria and Mediterranean ports. Irrigation agriculture was less necessary for them than for Sumerians farther south in Mesopotamia. The Assyrians raised horses, which inhabitants of southern Mesopotamia did not, and this helped them develop a formidable army with cavalry and chariot corps as well as infantry. They had easy access to metal ores. Their economy was well suited to supporting their military.

Iron and Assyrian Success A large part of Assyrian military success came from the labor of countless ironsmiths. Bronze remained the most important metal to rulers and would-be rulers in Southwest Asia until the advent of high-quality **iron** about 1200 BCE. In Anatolia, people were working iron by 2000 BCE, but it took several centuries for them to make tools and weapons that anyone preferred to bronze. Iron ore is more common than copper and tin, the components of bronze, but it is harder to work. Ironsmiths had to heat, hammer, and re-heat ores at just the right temperatures to get good metal. They had to build a furnace for each smelt, pack the ore just right amid layers of charcoal, and pump the right amount of air in with a bellows for hours on end. Iron requires much higher temperatures than bronze to smelt and shape. So the constraint on iron use wasn't the availability of ores, as with bronze, but of fuel and, above all, of specialized knowledge.

By 1200 BCE, well-wrought iron was far cheaper than bronze and for many purposes better, accounting for its widespread adoption in Southwest Asia and southeastern Europe. (Iron came into common use in India by 800 BCE, Egypt by 700 BCE, and China by 600 BCE.) It made good plowshares and sickles, improving the productivity of agriculture, especially of cereal crops. It also made good armor and weapons. With iron tools, states could feed more people. With iron weapons, they could field larger armies of well-armed men. The Assyrians, the first people to realize the potential of cheap iron, built their empire on iron, horses, and brute force.

The Art of Intimidation In the process of building their empire, the Assyrians acquired a reputation for extreme brutality, partly because they boasted of it. Their atrocities may not have been unique, but their delight in recounting them in gruesome detail was. When Assurbanipal (r. 668–627 BCE) chose to teach a lesson to Elam, a state in western Iran that had supported a rebellion led by his brother, he flattened

Intimidating Art Assurbanipal's palace displayed stone reliefs like this one to boast of Assyria's military strength. Dated to approximately 645 BCE, this relief shows Assyrian soldiers attacking an Egyptian city, killing some of its inhabitants and taking others as captives.

CONSIDERING THE EVIDENCE

The Banquet Stele of Ashurnasirpal II

When Ashurnasirpal II (r. 883–859 BCE) ascended the throne, the Assyrian Empire was only a few decades old, but his predecessors had ruled the city of Assur for around 1,700 years. In order to elevate his stature among generations of famous kings, he relocated the Assyrian capital from Assur to Calah (now Nimrud). The Banquet Stele, named for the 10-day feast that celebrated the city's renovations, announced his achievements to the empire.

Ashurnasirpal is the king whose fame is power!

I took over again the city of Calah ...I heaped up a new terrace measuring from the water level to the upper edge 120 layers of bricks; ...to proclaim my heroic deeds I painted on [the palace] walls with vivid blue paint how I have marched across the mountain ranges, the foreign countries and the seas, my conquests in all countries....

I brought in people from the countries over which I rule...who were conquered by me personally...I settled them there in the city of Calah.

I dug a canal...straight through the mountains; ...I provided the lowlands along the Tigris with irrigation; ...

I collected and planted in my garden...the trees and plants raised from seeds from wherever I discovered them....

its capital and took the extra step of planting thorn bushes in Elam's fields. Sennacherib (r. 704–681), responding to a rebellion in Babylon, boasted that he "completely destroyed it by flooding and left it like an open field," leaving no man, woman, or child alive. He even plundered its soil, carrying it away to Assur, his capital city. Other Assyrian kings proudly described the flaying of enemies, the bonfires of their captives, the piles of rebels' skulls, and so forth. They sometimes blinded captives and set them loose so they could spread the word of the horrors that resulted from

I erected...temples...which did not exist [in Calah] before; I rebuilt... temples of the great gods...[and] presented them with golden jewelry and many other precious objects which I had won as booty.

I organized the abandoned towns which during the rule of my fathers had become hills of rubble, and had many people settle therein; I rebuilt the old palaces across my entire country in due splendor; I stored in them barley and straw.

I killed 450 big lions; I killed 390 wild bulls from my open chariots in direct assault as befits a ruler....

I added land to the land of Assyria, many people to its people.

When I inaugurated the palace at Calah I treated for ten days with food and drink 47,074 persons, men and women,...from across my entire country, also 5,000 important persons, delegates from [other] countr[ies], also 16,000 inhabitants of Calah from all ways of life, 1,500 officials of all my palaces, altogether 69,574 invited guests....

I did them due honors and sent them back, healthy and happy, to their countries.

Questions for Analysis

1. The inscription on the stele claims that fame is power. What did Assyrian kings like Ashurnasirpal II do to ensure they were famous in their lifetimes and would be remembered by later generations?

2. The detailed numbers lend a sense of accuracy to the inscription. Do you think everything on the stele is an accurate portrayal of Ashurnasirpal II's deeds? Explain why you may have doubts about some parts but not others.

3. From your reading of the chapter, you know that trade was important to Assyria and other parts of Mesopotamia. Why do you think trade isn't mentioned in the Banquet Stele? What does this omission suggest about how Assyrian kings viewed their responsibilities as government leaders?

Source: James B. Pritchard, *The Ancient Near East*, Vol. 2: *A New Anthology of Texts and Pictures* (Princeton, 1975).

resisting Assyrian power. Intimidation is always a component of governance; the Assyrians raised it to a fine art.

Even their artwork was intended to intimidate. Assyrian kings went to great lengths to get suitable stone to build grandiose cities, palaces, and defensive walls. They inscribed their monuments with terrifying boasts, part of a long tradition of Mesopotamian rulers. Assurbanipal, for example, referred to himself as "ferocious dragon, conqueror of cities...the king whose command disintegrates mountains and seas." He departed from tradition when he added boasts about his skill in solving mathematical problems and deciphering problematic texts in ancient languages.

The Assyrian Empire was much larger and more multicultural than those built by Sargon or Hammurabi. To cope with the tensions that diversity brought, the Assyrians began systematically relocating populations. Millions of people had to uproot and move. Tribes were scattered in order to undermine their solidarity. Hill peoples were moved to the plains and deprived of their horses. Kings sought, with some success, to encourage an Assyrian identity among their diverse subjects and to inspire loyalty to the throne. Assurbanipal II, upon completion of a gargantuan palace, threw a 10-day party for (the sources claim) 69,574 guests. Assyrian kings also created a royal messenger service and built a system of guardhouses and wells along roads and tracks, all in the service of integrating a diverse empire.

Like every empire, the Assyrian one eventually declined and fell. In 612 BCE, the Medeans, originally a confederation of pastoralists from northwestern Iran, sacked Nineveh, the Assyrian capital, and together with their allies destroyed everything they could touch—Assyrian-style. With Assyrian power shattered by 609 BCE, the city of Babylon recovered its position and briefly became the dominant power in Mesopotamia—until the Persians arrived in 535 BCE.

Patterns of Mesopotamian Politics

There were some underlying patterns to the repeated rising and falling of states and empires. The whole region of Mesopotamia alternated between periods of fragmentation and unity for a reason. Each arrangement had its beneficiaries and its advantages. Unity improved conditions for trade and usually helped repel invaders such as mobile pastoralists from the nearby steppe grasslands. Fragmentation allowed more men to enjoy the charms of being king. If foreign invaders loomed, the odds of Mesopotamian elites banding together and accepting an overlord improved. If there were no threatening invaders, elites preferred to go their own way, rebel against central authority, and set up their own smaller kingdoms. So, part of the rhythm of unification and fragmentation in Mesopotamia came from the action of foreigners in neighboring lands, mainly pastoral tribes from the steppe.

Another source of this cycle of unity and fragmentation was internal. It was hard to maintain unity because local chieftains were quick to start up their own states if they saw a chance. Even rulers as strong as Sargon or Hammurabi constantly had to repress rebellious subjects. Lesser kings failed to win over rebels and saw their empires fragment. But sooner or later, an ambitious, skilled, ruthless king would come to power somewhere and start conquering his less formidable neighbors. Thus the Mesopotamian region swung back and forth between unity and fragmentation, often briefly parked somewhere in between.

The Prevalence of War Throughout the centuries, from soon after the first establishment of Sumerian cities, violence frequently wracked Mesopotamia and nearby lands. Mesopotamian societies were often militaristic and dominated by army men. This was especially true after the time of Sargon, before which priests had often exerted more authority than soldiers. The prevalence of war and armed force resulted in part from the inability of anyone to dominate the entire region for long.

A second explanation for the pattern of routine violence and militarism, which contributed to the first, was the proximity of mobile pastoralists. On the Iranian plateau and in Syria, steppe grasslands supported herding peoples. They gradually mastered horsemanship and developed the skills to fight from the saddle. As we've seen, mounted pastoralists regularly traded with nearby farming peoples, but they could also make war when and where they chose. If they perceived weakness among the farming folk and their protectors, it often served as reason enough to attack. When herder groups were numerous, as after a string of years with good rains, they might like the odds of war. When they were desperate, as in times of drought, they might feel they had no choice but to attack, having nothing left to trade.

Horse-Drawn Chariots Let's zoom out briefly to look at the bigger picture of which Mesopotamian politics was a part. Two technologies of war helped shape the balance between pastoralists and agrarian states throughout Eurasia. The first was the horse-drawn war chariot. It initially gave an edge to pastoralists, mainly because they had the skills and space to raise, manage, and train plenty of horses.

Chariots appeared in western Asia around 2100 BCE and spread quickly throughout Eurasia's suitable lands. By 1500 BCE, warriors in Egypt, Mesopotamia, Iran, India, and China had adopted them. Chariots were difficult to build and use. The proper technique involved controlling horses with reins while standing on a mobile platform and hurling a javelin or loosing an arrow at one's enemy. When done well, it proved to be a formidable and intimidating way of warfare. Eventually, two- and three-man chariots appeared, allowing driver and warrior to specialize in their tasks.

Chariot warfare became an aristocratic way of war: only a few well-off people could afford the expense of good chariots and spare the time needed to master the skills. Pastoralists, although they had plenty of horses, usually lacked wood and skilled carpenters, so they could rarely field large numbers of chariots. But few were better than none, and pastoralists dominated militarily when and where no one else could deploy lots of chariots. Rulers of agrarian states, in contrast, usually found it hard to get enough horses. But since after 1500 BCE no ruler within reach of Eurasia's pastoralists could expect to survive long without a corps of charioteers, where possible kings paid the price for horses and chariots in sufficient quantity to keep pastoralists at bay.

Chariots helped shape the politics of Eurasia from their invention until about 500 BCE. Agrarian states across Eurasia, from Egypt to China, either adopted chariot warfare

Mesopotamian Chariot Warfare This fragment of a stone relief from the palace of Assurbanipal in Nineveh, dated to around 645 BCE, depicts the Assyrian army's use of a chariot in battle.

quickly or were conquered by peoples who had mastered it. Chariots became standard burial goods for kings and grew prominent in the myths and religions of Indians, Persians, the ancient Hebrews, Egyptians, and Greeks.

The Composite Bow The second important step in military technology was the adoption of the composite bow, made from pieces of wood, bone, and horn glued together. Like the chariot, it was hard to make and use. It required strong and flexible wood, horn from water buffalo or oryx (an antelope), sinew from antelope or deer, glue (also made from animals), and very precise craftsmanship. To shoot arrows with a composite bow required considerable muscular strength. Unlike the chariot, the composite bow was an innovation that pastoralists could easily make for themselves.

The composite bow's origins are hazy, but they probably date back to about 1500 BCE. Its importance came only after continual refinements made the bow better and better, tipping the military balance in favor of mounted archers from around 1200 to 800 BCE. The key to this shift lay in the bow itself, which was shorter but much more powerful than an ordinary bow. Composite bows enabled horsemen to shoot arrows at enemies hundreds of yards away and gallop out of range of ordinary bows while preparing for their next shot. As with chariots, agrarian states had to adopt the new technology or be overrun by pastoralist groups who mastered it.

The more formidable the pastoralists became, thanks in part first to chariots and then to composite bows, the stronger the incentive for agrarian peoples to band together for defense. This process of change in military technology and the power of pastoral peoples helps explain why agrarian states grew larger over time, culminating in giant empires in Persia and China, as we will see.

The Scale of Warfare Let's zoom back in on Mesopotamia. Farmers, increasingly, had to submit to rule by soldiers to avoid being plundered by steppe pastoralists. When not fighting off pastoralist raiders, brutal rulers such as Sargon and Sennacherib used their men and skills to amass more territory for themselves and crush rebellion by members of their own royal families or disaffected local leaders. The scale of warfare, like the scale of states, grew over time: Sumerian armies numbered in the thousands; Assyrian armies in the tens of thousands.

By the standards that prevailed in the Southwest Asian web, Mesopotamian political life was eccentric. It was unusually violent compared to life in the Indus valley or, as we will see in the next chapter, Egypt. It was more directly affected by the politics, fortunes, and military technologies of pastoral peoples in neighboring regions such as Iran or Syria. In Mesopotamia, it was a lucky peasant farmer who never heard the beating hooves of horses from the steppe or the clash of spear on shield.

Gods and Goddesses, Priests and Priestesses

Everyone in Mesopotamia lived in an unpredictable world shaped by violent politics and forces of nature that worked in mysterious ways. They explained this unpredictability, as people elsewhere had done, in spiritual terms. Their version emphasized gods of the sun and moon, earth and sky, water and storm, as well as specialists in love and war. Sumerian gods, with a few alterations, made sense to Akkadians, Babylonians, Assyrians, and others in Mesopotamia. Conquerors, beginning with Sargon, found it made good politics to embrace these gods, so they gradually became standard throughout Mesopotamia.

The Roster of Deities Enlil/Ellil was in charge of choosing kings and decreeing the destinies of people and gods, as well as sharing responsibility for regulating floods. He was the father of several other gods but was ultimately subservient to An/Anu. The gods were all related in one way or another. The only female among the top gods was Inanna/Ishtar, perhaps the most popular of all. She was responsible for power, combat, love, sex, fertility, and beauty. She went in for casual sex, treated men and male gods as disposable, and enjoyed provoking them to combat. The gods all had their own personalities and tendencies, although quick temper and jealousy were a family trait.

A host of more-local gods joined this rowdy family of deities. Each city typically had its own god responsible for its protection. Marduk, for example, was the god of the city of Babylon. When Babylon built an empire, Marduk-worship expanded with it.

A Temple Economy According to Mesopotamian myths, the gods created humans because they were tired of the drudgery of doing farm work, grinding grain, and baking for Enlil.

Mesopotamian Gods and Their Associations

SUMERIAN NAME	AKKADIAN NAME	RESPONSIBILITIES AND ASSOCIATIONS
Utu	Shamash	Sun, justice
Nanna	Sin	Moon
An	Anu	Sky, creation
Ishkur	Adad	Storm, war
Enki	Ea	Water
Inanna	Ishtar	Love, sex, war
Enlil	Ellil	Fates of individuals

They were about to kill him when one of them had the bright idea of creating humans to do all the work. The main job of humans was to see to the care and feeding of the gods.

Temples, shrines, and statues of the gods served this purpose. Priests oversaw a temple economy that produced food for the priesthood and for sacrifices to the gods. Sacrifices of animals or food were typically burned before statues of gods, who drew nourishment from the smoke and smell of the burnt offering. Temples owned farmland: one Mesopotamian king granted 200 square miles (520 sq. km) for a temple to Inanna/Ishtar. Workers employed by temples—often enslaved war captives—raised crops, tended animals, baked bread, brewed beer, and carved statues. In return for their labor, they got a ration of bread or beer and a place to sleep.

The Priesthood Priests and priestesses, or the laborers they commanded, kept temples and statues clean and properly guarded against thieves. They divined the will of the gods by examining the entrails, especially the livers, of sacrificed animals and by watching the movements of heavenly bodies. They kept careful records of the shapes and sizes of animal livers and of shooting stars and eclipses. These divinations were of the utmost importance, because knowing the will of the gods helped one make the right choices in life—which crops to plant where, whom to marry one's children to, whether to launch a war or sue for peace.

At regular intervals, priests and priestesses organized festivals that often involved carrying the statue of a local god to a neighboring town in a gesture of friendship, sealed with feasting, dancing, and drinking. They also oversaw burials of important people and preparations for the afterworld, which in Mesopotamian texts was described as a grim, grimy place, full of dust: nothing to look forward to at all (unlike the Egyptian version, as we will see).

The priesthood enjoyed considerable authority, prestige, and wealth, especially in the early centuries in Sumer, before the militarization of Mesopotamia. Even in Assyrian times, however, the army chieftains had to share power with the priests. Kings had to build temples and worship devoutly, as publicly as possible, to shore up their legitimacy. And amid their boasts of greatness and brutality, they usually included a few phrases about being the favorites of the gods. Power in Mesopotamia—as would become common in world history—consisted of an alliance between throne and altar.

Astronomy and Mathematics The prominence of divination in Mesopotamian religion led to the precocious development of astronomy and mathematics. Babylon acquired a particular reputation for math and science. Although the effort put into reading goat livers led to no practical applications, studying the heavens did. Babylonians learned how to predict eclipses and devised a lunar calendar. They used a base 60 system (ours is base 10) for mathematics and worked with fractions, square roots, and exponents. Babylonian math and astronomy improved over time and became impressive

Great Ziggurat of Ur This famous ziggurat, a temple-palace dating from around 2100 BCE and dedicated to the moon god Nanna, was almost 100 ft. (30 m) tall. The photograph was taken during archeological excavations in the 1930s that revealed the temple.

enough that foreigners from Egypt to India adopted much of it. Our minute, hour, and 360-degree circle are legacies of the Babylonians' base 60 system. They were good at calculating the area of irregularly shaped fields, and highly skilled at the architecture of monumental building—temples, palaces, and fortifications. Less useful, but very important to them, was astrology. Kings and commoners often believed that people's fates could be read in the stars, and they chose to schedule weddings, invasions, and other important events only after due consultation with astrologers. Generally, ordinary people, except those employed by priests, did their worshipping at home, with smaller statues of the gods they preferred, and left higher mathematics to the priestly class.

The Ancient Hebrews and Monotheism

One important cultural and religious innovation occurred on the edges of the Mesopotamian world: the emergence of a novel spiritual outlook among a then-obscure tribe we know as the ancient Hebrews or Israelites. Throughout Southwest Asia, gods were numerous, resembled humans, and behaved more or less like elite humans with superpowers. They competed for power, status, honor, love, and sex. They didn't care much about human fates, but they used humans to advance their own agendas. And they were best approached through the intervention of priests, who knew the arcane rituals—usually involving sacrifices of animals or food—that improved the chances of a successful appeal to divine power.

The ancient Hebrews, although surrounded by this general understanding of spirituality, came to see divinity differently. They created a dissident, minority tradition within the larger Southwest Asian, and mainly Mesopotamian, religious sphere.

Monotheism According to traditions written down about 450 BCE in scriptures that were compiled into the Hebrew Bible, the ancient Hebrews were led out of bondage in Egypt, wandered in the Sinai, and settled in the land of Canaan (the southern Levant).

Along the way, they accepted a vision in which there was only one supreme god, Yahweh, who was concerned that justice and morality should prevail among humans—at least, among his chosen people. If the Israelites followed his rules in their everyday lives, he would protect them; protection was a role expected of all gods everywhere. However, this pact between a *solitary* god and believers constrained by religious laws was a new departure in world religion, and the first lasting example of **monotheism**.

Once in Canaan, the ancient Hebrew tribe gradually formed a kingdom. It conquered the settlement of Jerusalem, where one king, Solomon, built a temple that became the focal point of Hebrew religion in the late tenth century BCE. It was here, in particular, that Hebrew religion became fully monotheistic and its variety of rituals and practices more or less standardized.

The Ancient Hebrews and Their God The ancient Hebrews were few, poor, and weak and often buffeted about by the great Mesopotamian powers of the day. An Assyrian ruler deported thousands of them in the mid-eighth century BCE. Babylonians sacked the temple in Jerusalem in 586 BCE and carried off Jewish leaders to Babylon in imitation of the Assyrian policy for undermining the identity of unreliable groups. Yet through it all, the ancient Hebrews retained Yahweh as their god.

Yahweh was all-knowing and all-powerful, generous to his people when they behaved according to his instructions, but spiteful and jealous when they did not. In fact, the ancient Hebrews had great difficulty living up to Yahweh's standards and often worshipped Babylonian gods—called idols in the Hebrew Bible. Their leaders sometimes found it expedient to cooperate with the earthly powers in Babylon or Assyria. These failings gave rise to a tradition of prophets, priests, and scribes who railed against the shortcomings of other priests, kings, and people in general. Uncompromising scolds, the prophets were unloved in their day. But they shaped the tradition of Hebrew religion and sharpened its emphasis on ethical conduct as an overriding human responsibility.

Yahweh's commitment and his terms (the basis for Jewish law) were revealed in scriptures so complex and contradictory that experts might argue endlessly over points of interpretation. Expertise in the understanding and explanation of scripture became a point of honor for the ancient Hebrews—among men and boys, at least. Weekly gatherings to observe rituals and discuss textual interpretation became routine. This weekly observance is the root of our weekend.

Judaism, as we now call it, marked a significant departure from prevailing religious practice in Southwest Asia. It not only insisted on monotheism and strongly linked the ethics of daily life to religion, but it held that a single divinity ruled Earth, with no tie to a certain city. The ancient Hebrews' religious vision endured, and large parts of it, especially its core of ethical monotheism, proved sufficiently attractive to survive the ages and inform the belief and practice of Christians and Muslims—in other words, about one-third of the world's population today.

Society, Family, and Law

Ancient Mesopotamia is the earliest society for which we have abundant evidence of social life and daily affairs. Like all complex societies, Mesopotamia had social hierarchies. These generally became more pronounced over time as the division of labor grew more refined and militarism more entrenched. By Hammurabi's day (eighteenth century BCE), a tripartite social structure was enshrined in law. At the top stood the landowning class, and at its apex were the rulers and priests. In the middle were free but landless, and usually poor, people—artisans, scribes, petty merchants, and ordinary farmers. At the bottom were slaves. The hierarchy had some flexibility, as class structures normally do. If one had to sell off one's land, one's status slipped with the transaction. Slaves could be freed and acquire property. The free, when desperate, might sell themselves or their children into slavery. A man could also legally sell his wife into slavery, but she could not sell him.

Slavery and Peasant Labor While slavery on a small scale had existed in most agricultural societies for thousands of years, it became common first in Mesopotamia. Mentions of it appear in early Sumerian texts. Law codes from the time of Hammurabi refer to slavery. Enslavement was often punishment for unpaid debts. It was the usual fate of war captives. But one could also be born a slave: the status was hereditary. Over the centuries, slavery became more common, a result of both the demand for routine labor in fields and workshops and the supply of captives in ceaseless raids and conquests. Terms for "slave" in Mesopotamian languages implied foreign-ness. Slavery became widespread by the eighth century BCE, when large-scale conquests by the Assyrians generated streams of captives.

All that slaves produced belonged to their owners. Most slaves worked in households. Female slaves spun, wove, and served as concubines for prosperous men. Male slaves performed manual labor too and were sometimes trained as craftsmen—cobblers, carpenters, or smiths, for example. A lucky few who were skilled in cuneiform kept accounts for merchants. On occasion, masters might permit loyal and clever slaves to go into business for themselves, accumulate money, buy other slaves, and perhaps buy their own freedom.

Landless peasants, the largest class by far, did most of the farm work. A good chunk of what they

Unfree Labor A stone relief from the palace of the Assyrian king Sennacherib at Nineveh shows how that palace was likely built: dozens of forced prison laborers, guarded by soldiers, chisel stone from a quarry and carry it to the construction site.

produced went, as rent and taxes, to the landowners, temples, and states. Their precise status is unclear: they weren't slaves, but not entirely free either. They normally met their obligations in kind, with grain, fish, wool, dates, and so forth, but might instead perform military service or labor on irrigation works, fortifications, palaces, or temples. The urban population included all manner of craft workers, unskilled laborers, and peddlers.

Marriage and the Family The surviving evidence is long on the legal aspects of marriage, most of it drawn from the reign of Hammurabi in the eighteenth century BCE. People of all classes expected to marry as teenagers. As in most societies, in ancient Mesopotamia marriage, normally monogamous, was an alliance between two families for the purpose of having children, including a legal heir. There was often a formal contract between families concerning property arrangements. This contract specified "gifts"—both the bride-price (a sum given by the groom's family to the bride's) and the dowry (a sum paid by the bride's family to the groom's). Breaking a marriage engagement brought big fines. If a groom died before his wedding, his bride would ordinarily be married to one of his brothers. If a wife died, her husband expected a refund of the bride-price or else a sister of the wife as a substitute bride. Widows normally continued to live with their husband's family, supported by their children. A husband might divorce a wife who bore no children, but he had to negotiate with his wife's family to do it. However, wives who neglected their household duties or insulted their husbands might be divorced more freely. Adultery was a serious offense: women, and in some societies men, if judged guilty might be killed for it. By Assyrian times, brides and married women wore veils, which unmarried women were prohibited from doing.

Some poems and artwork reveal that passion and love occasionally blossomed within marriage. Babylonian love poetry (sometimes relating to marriage) could be unabashedly romantic and shamelessly explicit. A stanza from a twenty-first-century BCE poem, the earliest surviving love poem in history, gives some sense of a bride's passion:

> *Bridegroom, let me caress you,*
> *My precious caress is more savory than honey,*
> *In the bedchamber, honey-filled,*
> *Let me enjoy your goodly beauty,*
> *Lion, let me caress you*

A later Sumerian poem speaks of an enduring passion: "Though she has already borne me eight sons, she is still ready to make love." Throughout ancient Mesopotamian history, figurines of erotic scenes were popular artwork displayed in temples and homes, and placed in graves to accompany the departed.

Not all marriages were happy. A Sumerian text includes a husband's lament: "My wife is down at the temple. My mother is down at the river. Here I am starving. Whoever has not supported a wife and child does not know what it's like to have a leash through one's nose." One Assyrian woman wrote to her husband, presumably a traveling cloth merchant: "Why do you keep writing me that the textiles I send you are no good? I'm the one who makes every effort to produce and send you textiles so that with each caravan you make at least ten shekels [a unit of money] of silver." Money worries divided many a Mesopotamian couple.

The point of marriage was to have children—ideally, sons, and lots of them. Many infants and mothers died in childbirth, and perhaps half of all children never made it to age five. So parents who wanted someone to look after them when they grew feeble needed many children. A woman who had many sons enjoyed a boost in status. But fathers enjoyed full legal rights over children. Raising children was a married woman's main job. Most kids, especially girls, had no schooling but learned their skills within their family.

For the elite, formal schooling existed from at least 2500 BCE. Its chief goal was to teach writing and reading. A cache of clay tablets from the eighteenth century BCE tells us almost all we know about Mesopotamian schooling. Most students were boys, probably ages 10 to 15, the sons of scribes, rich businessmen, or government and temple officials. Families had to pay for their sons' schooling. Teachers specialized in subjects such as math, writing, music, or field surveying. A specialist in discipline beat the students with canes for offenses such as speaking out of turn. After Sargon's time, students had to learn cuneiform in both Akkadian and Sumerian, which would take several years. They did

Veiled Woman This Sumerian statue from the third century BCE was found in a temple of Ishtar in the region of present-day Syria. A seated woman wears a headdress with a veil, as many brides and married women did—especially by Assyrian times.

it by rote memorization and endless copying on clay tablets. Records indicate a few female scribes—very few—in the long history of Mesopotamia, but how they learned to read and write is unknown.

Law and Hammurabi Mesopotamian kings claimed special powers bestowed by gods and took responsibility for administering divine justice on Earth and enforcing laws. The earliest laws known to history are Sumerian, set forth by kings and no one else, on behalf of the gods. Some date to the twenty-fourth century BCE. The fullest picture of Mesopotamian law comes from a black stone stele (a tall slab used as a monument) erected by Hammurabi in the eighteenth century BCE. It is often described as a law code, although its 282 laws are a disorganized jumble, not comprehensive, and may merely be intended to show that the king took his duty as purveyor of justice seriously.

Sumerian and Babylonian laws dealt with crime and punishment, but also with wages and prices, inheritance, and other economic matters. They do not advance principles but are invariably specific, following a regular format: if such-and-such happens, then the penalty will be such-and-such. If a doctor blinds a patient, the doctor shall have his hand cut off. If a boatman loses a cargo, he must pay for the cargo and the boat. If a wife is a spendthrift, she will be thrown into the river.

Penalties were strict: either fines or bodily harm. There was no imprisonment. The early Sumerian laws usually prescribed fines, such as 60 shekels (maybe four years' wages for a commoner) for breaking someone's leg. Hammurabi and the Assyrians especially went in for mutilation as punishment. Stealing, burglary, or adultery earned the death penalty. A priestess who entered a tavern would be burned alive. A son who struck his father would lose his hand. A man who kissed another man's wife, Assyrian law prescribed, would have his lower lip sliced off with an axe.

Hammurabi's laws show how the tripartite class division of Mesopotamian society worked in practice. People were far from equal before the law. Punishment not only fit the crime, but also fit the relative status of the victim and criminal. It was a more serious offense to cause injury to a social superior than to a social inferior. If you stole from the palace or temple, you had to pay back 30 times the goods heisted. If you stole from a commoner, the fine was one-third as much; and if you couldn't pay, you were put to death. At the same time, fines were bigger for the landed class than for the poor. In the prologue to his list of laws, Hammurabi claims his purpose is to "protect the weak from the strong." Perhaps in prescribing these penalties he was preventing harsher ones. But it looks like the main purpose of his laws, as of those promulgated by other kings, was to uphold the authority of fathers within families, protect the property of those who had any, and maintain social hierarchy.

Hammurabi's Laws This eighteenth-century stele, on which Hammurabi's laws are written, has as its most prominent aspect the frieze in which the king (left) receives the laws from the god Shamash, asserting Babylonian justice to be divinely inspired. The laws themselves are written in cuneiform below.

There were judges in Mesopotamia, but no lawyers or juries. One represented oneself in Sumerian, Babylonian, or Assyrian courts. In villages, respected elders would serve as judges whenever a case came up. In the cities, and for serious cases, royal appointees who specialized in justice would preside. When a panel of judges couldn't come to a verdict, they sometimes referred cases to a higher power. The accused would be thrown into a river:

if he or she drowned, or seemed sure to, that indicated guilt. If the accused bobbed to the surface and made it to shore, that revealed innocence.

Some traces of Mesopotamian law, as well as astronomy, religion, technology, art, and literature, remain with us today. The practices and culture of Sumer, Babylon, and Assyria proved highly influential in their time and spread along the routes of the Southwest Asian web and eventually beyond. Today, our concepts of marriage, kingship, and calendrical time, as well as our habit of writing—even certain board games such as checkers—are all echoes of ancient Mesopotamian culture.

The Mysterious Indus Valley Societies, ca. 2600–1700 BCE

One of the places touched by Mesopotamian culture was the Indus valley and its complex urban society. Its history is one of the compelling mysteries of the ancient world. No one can read the writing it left behind, and no one knows why urban society along the Indus River vanished—although theories abound.

The **Indus River** runs nearly 2,000 miles (more than 3,000 km) from Himalayan glaciers to the Arabian Sea. It splashes through deep gorges in the mountains, then slows down in the Punjab (meaning "Five Rivers"), acquiring the water of tributaries before weaving through the arid region, called Sind, near the sea. Even the summer monsoons bring almost no rain to Sind because it's flat and the rain clouds push farther north, piling up against the Himalaya and dumping torrential rains on the mountain slopes. The Indus carries a tremendous silt load, twice that of the Nile. Eons of silt deposits have built up the river's banks so that in Sind it flows above the level of the surrounding plain. Like the Huang He (Yellow River) in northern China, the Indus changes its course now and then during big floods. The river stays in its bed and is easily navigable in winter, but not in summer when monsoon and snowmelt floodwaters swell the flow five- or tenfold.

The annual flood of the Indus and its burden of fertile silt made its floodplain and valley a good place for farming. In Punjab, people could farm in a limited way without irrigation. Farming in the upper Indus valley, with barley and wheat, began about 7000 BCE. Subsequently, farming and villages spread out over the Indus basin. Most experts believe that farming techniques were transplanted to the Indus valley from the Fertile Crescent.

In the lower Indus valley—in Sind—farmers needed to irrigate. Signs of irrigation appear in the archeological record starting around 3200 BCE. We have no way of knowing whether Indus farmers developed irrigation on their own or learned of it from somewhere else. They raised wheat and barley, as Mesopotamian farmers did, and on approximately the same annual rhythm. As elsewhere, the development of cities and complex society along the Indus rested on the high yields of irrigation agriculture.

Cities of the Indus, ca. 2600–1900 BCE

By about 2600 BCE, five main cities had arisen in the Indus valley. The largest, Mohenjo Daro and Harappa, housed perhaps 20,000 people (some archeologists say 50,000 for Mohenjo Daro) at their height a few centuries later. Each site covered around 200 to 250 acres (80 to 100 hectares), or the equivalent of 200 football fields. Unlike the higgledy-piggledy layout of cities of Mesopotamia, those in the Indus valley had a regular design on a grid pattern. These were the first planned cities in world history. The main thoroughfares were laid out almost precisely north-south and east-west. The cities' buildings were made of baked mud brick. New, painstaking, and highly standardized styles of pottery, bead making, and metalworking appeared. The Indus cities developed a strong craft tradition, especially in stoneworking. Their artisans knew how to make bronze but rarely did so, perhaps because copper had to come from afar. A system of writing emerged, used for inscriptions on seals made of a soapstone called steatite. This was a sudden transition to complex, urban society, similar to Uruk's in Sumer 500 years before.

Cultural Unity The cultural unity visible in the archeological remains is remarkable, considering that the five big cities stood far apart. The nearest pair were separated by 175 miles (280 km), roughly the distance between Cleveland and Detroit or Houston and San Antonio. Sumerian cities, by contrast, were often only a long day's walk from one another.

Each Indus valley city had a lower town, divided into rectangular blocks; an elevated inner city, built on a mound and surrounded by walls; and a sprawling warehouse or granary complex adjacent to the river by which the city sat. Houses typically had bathrooms with sit-down toilets, and earthenware drainpipes encased in brick walls. Mohenjo Daro had a water tank, perhaps used for ritual bathing, about half the size of an Olympic swimming pool and an average of one well for every three houses. The **Harappans**, as the Indus River populations are often called, paid more attention to the problem of clean water—separating wastewater from drinking water—than any urban population anywhere until about 170 years ago. The Indus cities all used the same script, the same weights and measures, and the same shells and beads for ornamentation. Even their bricks were the same size.

Transport and Trade This cultural unity rested on a regional network of transport and communications. There is archeological evidence of riverboats, which would have moved up and down the navigable waters of the Indus. A second crucial component of this network was wooden ox-carts, which do not survive in the archeological record except as models or toys made of durable clay. Mesopotamian societies used ox-carts, and it's highly likely that those along the Indus did as well. The invention or refinement of ox-carts was probably necessary for urban development along the Indus, because it allowed more efficient hauling of harvested crops from farm to riverbank, and from there to the granaries and storehouses of the cities.

As in Sumer, this local network of overland transport was linked both to a riverine system and to a maritime one—in fact, to the same maritime system, that of the Arabian Sea and its monsoon winds. Mesopotamian texts mention Indus traders and trade goods such as timber, stone, animals, and ivory. Mesopotamian archeological sites yield Indus seals, as well as lapis lazuli. Lapis lazuli came from Afghanistan, probably via the Indus and sea routes. A city that archeologists regard as an outpost of Harappan culture existed in Afghanistan, near the main supply of lapis lazuli. Some copper came from Oman on the Arabian Peninsula. Ivory and other goods

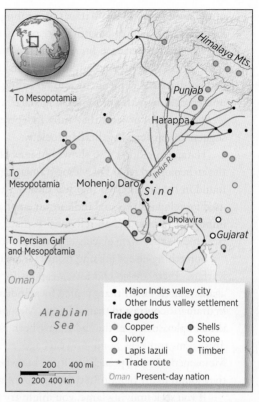

Indus Valley Settlements, ca. 2600–1900 BCE In and around the Indus River, urban societies developed after 2600 BCE with growing overland and maritime links to Mesopotamia. No one can read the script used in these cities, so much about them remains mysterious despite a century of archeological work.

came from the western shores of India. For luxury items at least, the Indus peoples traded far and wide, and funneled some of what they acquired to Mesopotamia. Unfortunately, neither texts nor archeology can tell us what the Indus traders accepted in exchange from Mesopotamia, but woven cloth is a strong candidate.

The Mysteries of Harappan Culture Just how the integrated urban society of the Indus originated is entirely unclear. Most of the archeological sites show evidence that previous settlements were burned and rebuilt in a grander, more orderly style. Could this mean that warfare and conquest brought complex society to the Indus? Could it instead represent the arrival of some new ideology, to which gridded cities and sanitation were important? No one knows.

There are other mysteries concerning Harappan culture. All other complex societies of the ancient world show traces of a ruling class in palace architecture, big statues, luxury grave goods, or boastful inscriptions, and usually all of the above. None of this existed—or has yet been found—for the Indus. The biggest statue so far discovered is the size of a flashlight. Could Harappan culture, unlike almost all the others, have had no sharp social hierarchy and no ruling elite? No kings? Was there a remarkably unified culture with no overarching state? Were the cities linked in some empire, in a confederation, or were they fully independent politically? The archeological traces suggest an unusually egalitarian society.

Harappan culture also shows no signs of organized religion. In sharp contrast to the archeological record of Mesopotamia, Egypt, and Mesoamerica, nothing has been found in the Indus cities that was clearly a temple. Perhaps the water reservoirs were used for religious rites and indicate an emphasis on cleanliness and purity, which were important in later Indian religions. Perhaps the presence of figurines of animals and trees means they were objects of worship. No one knows.

Something else is missing from Harappan archeological sites: signs of violence or warfare. There are no chariots, weapons, or armor. The walls seem built for defense against floods rather than human foes. Indus valley art includes no scenes of warriors, in dramatic contrast to that of Egypt, Mesopotamia, China, and Mesoamerica. Could the complex society of the Indus have been peaceful, unlike all other ancient societies? This seems unlikely. Some 60 years ago, scholars thought that the ancient Maya (in Mesoamerica) was a peaceful culture; but when they cracked the code of Maya writing, they found many bloodthirsty boasts about battles and conquests.

If you seek undying fame, you might try decoding the Indus valley writing system and unlocking its secrets. The Indus valley script appears on stone seals, pots, bits of bone and ivory, and a few copper and bronze items. Unlike the hieroglyphs of Egypt and the cuneiform of Mesopotamia, it wasn't written on walls, statues, clay tablets, or tombs—although at one Harappan site, there is an example of writing with stones affixed to what was probably a wooden signboard. Some 3,700 inscriptions have been found so far, but about 40 percent of them are duplicates. It could be that most writing was done on perishable surfaces—palm fronds, for example, or wood slabs—that have decayed over the centuries. The inscriptions often appear together with images of big animals: rhinos, elephants, tigers, cattle, and even imaginary ones such as unicorns—but never horses, which people of the Indus didn't have, although their trading

Indus Seals A seal from Mohenjo Daro, dated to around 2500 to 2000 BCE, bears the image of an elephant as well as symbols in the Indus script, which scholars are still unable to decipher.

partners in Afghanistan surely did. Most scholars think there are about 400 symbols in all. People have been working hard on the Indus script for about 80 years now, but Indus writing may remain a mystery for some time to come.

The Disappearance of the Indus Cities, 1900–1700 BCE

The greatest Indus valley mystery of all is what happened to its urban society. Around 1900 BCE, after thriving for seven or eight centuries, it fell apart. By 1700 BCE, the cities were abandoned, the writing stopped, the oceanic trade dried up, the careful and standardized craftsmanship of jewelry, pots, and tools vanished. Village life persisted, and settlements grew more numerous to the south and east of the most urbanized districts of the Indus. But something happened to make city life either impossible or unappealing. At Mohenjo Daro, it seems to have happened suddenly. Dead bodies were hastily buried. Caches of valuables were left by their owners. What happened to cause this collapse?

Maybe it was disease. The carefully laid out drains, the countless bathrooms, the systems of water tanks and wells in Indus cities all testify to skillful hydraulic engineering and unrivaled attention to sanitation. Maybe this somehow broke down, and cholera, typhoid, or some other waterborne diseases got into the drinking water and ravaged city populations. Perhaps malaria, spread by mosquitoes that flourish amid stagnant water, swept through. Some of the skeletons from the last days of Mohenjo Daro show signs of malaria.

There is good geo-archeological evidence for earthquakes and shifts in river channels. This might have separated the cities from their hinterlands and trade routes, making it expensive and impractical to transport food from farm to city. City dwellers may have migrated elsewhere rather than starve, leading perhaps to the increase in the number of villages.

Climate change likely was involved. After 2200 BCE, the whole region of Southwest Asia grew more arid for a century or more, and the summer monsoon over South Asia weakened—as it does from time to time over the millennia, owing mainly to solar cycles. Soil samples imply that vegetation patterns were changing, and perhaps agriculture became less rewarding as water grew scarce and the silt-bearing floods became unreliable.

Maybe deforestation and greater flooding took a toll. Baking all those bricks required fuelwood, and so did metalworking and pottery. Perhaps the Punjab region lost much of its former forest cover, leading to increased erosion. Soils and vegetation that had formerly absorbed floodwaters were lost, so floods became more violent. Piled-up silt formed deltas and marshes in the lower Indus, inhibiting waterborne trade and improving habitat for malarial mosquitoes. But the evidence for massive flooding is poor, and people living in the Indus were used to periodic flooding.

Maybe outsiders caused the decline. Generations ago, most archeologists believed an invasion from the north ended Indus civilization amid a blaze of destruction. This almost certainly did not happen—although a couple of centuries after the end of Harappan city life, migrants from the north did pass through.

Maybe trade with Mesopotamia fell off as a result of the strife that followed the collapse of Sargon's empire, and people from Gujarat (a region to the southeast of the Indus) took over the maritime trade. Beginning around 2000 BCE, drought-resistant African millets were grown in Gujarat, making it possible to harvest two crops annually there. The new crops raised its ceiling for population, wealth, and power and enabled elites there to dominate long-distance trade that had formerly sustained the Indus cities. (How African crops got there is another, smaller mystery, but an indication that the trade and travel links of the Southwest Asian web could extend to East African shores.)

Maybe all these things occurred, or maybe it was something else entirely that the experts haven't thought of yet. In the unlikely event that the decline of Harappan culture had a single cause, the best bet would probably be disease. But to judge by the decline of every other culture, city, or state that we know anything about, the likelihood is that several things came together at the same time, or one immediately after another; probably none of these alone could explain the decline, but several taken together may have overwhelmed the resilience of urban society in the Indus valley.

In any case, the disappearance of urban culture and complex society in the Indus valley remains mysterious. Something similar happened in Peru and in the Maya lands of Mesoamerica, as we'll see later. In general, complex society and urban culture, once developed, usually stay intact. In Mesopotamia, Egypt, and China, for example, the tradition of complex society lasted, uninterrupted, from its origin until today. That is the rule; the fate of the Indus valley cities is the exception.

Formation of the Southwest Asian Web

Links between Mesopotamia and the Indus region began by at least 6000 BCE. Their farm tools and crops are similar. Both regions had a long tradition of baking grains into bread and roasting meat, as opposed to the cooking traditions prevalent in most of China and Africa, in which foods were more often boiled and prepared in porridges and stews. Long-distance trade in luxury goods intermittently connected the two regions too. But the volume and velocity of exchanges increased in the mid-third millennium BCE after cities emerged in both settings. Both valleys hosted complex urban societies with their own trade networks, their own riverine webs that extended tendrils in all directions. Those tendrils intertwined by 2500 BCE and quickly grew to form a trunk route across the Arabian Sea with its predictable winds so beloved of sailors. As the poem "Enki and the World Order" suggests, by the end of the third millennium BCE the twin rivers of Mesopotamia—the Tigris and Euphrates—and the

Indus River had become linked in a single sustained web of contact, trade, and cultural influence.

Trade

Trade links left the strongest evidence of these connections, both in texts and in archeological sites. The Indus valley exported timber from the Himalayan foothills above Harappa to the treeless cities and villages of southern Mesopotamia. Indus merchants also traded stone beads, gold dust, and Central Asian lapis lazuli. In exchange, the Indus cities must have imported perishable things—perhaps cloth or food—because the archeological record shows no sign of Mesopotamian objects, with the possible exception of silver items. Most of this Indus-Mesopotamian trade probably went through middlemen based in ports along the Persian Gulf

Indus Weights and Measures Standardized weights and measures enabled traders from the Indus valley to exchange consistent quantities and values of goods, allowing for the efficient operation of the trade network.

in places such as Oman, where Indus weights and measures were used, and Bahrain. But inscriptions from the time of Sargon show that Indus ships also docked in Akkad in the twenty-fourth century BCE. The Mesopotamia-Indus web presumably included many other dimensions. Surely they exchanged diseases, for example, something about which archeology and surviving texts have nothing to say.

Land and Water

Several features of the entire region between the Indus and the Levant proved especially helpful in promoting this sort of connectivity, both on land and on water. First, the region supported good beasts of burden for land-based transport. Donkeys, and later horses and camels, could carry heavy loads. Moreover, the floodplains along the Indus, Tigris, Euphrates, and lesser rivers could provide forage for caravans with animals. Caravans could also carry a day or two's supply of grain and some water for pack animals, allowing them to get from one grassy spot to the next across an intervening desert.

Second, the rivers themselves were easy to sail, with minimal rapids and few waterfalls. The Indus, Tigris, and Euphrates all offered seasons in which the winds were strong enough and currents weak enough to enable boats to move upstream as well as down. Once sailing vessels existed, these rivers became inexpensive two-way highways. Third, the surrounding seas—the eastern Mediterranean, the Persian Gulf, and the broad Arabian Sea—offered favorable conditions to sailors. Their winds were remarkably predictable, thanks mainly to the annual monsoon pattern. These geographical features help to explain why the world's first big regional web formed in Southwest Asia.

Conclusion

Mesopotamia developed complex society first and maintained it far longer than the Indus valley. Archeology and textual evidence is much richer for Mesopotamia than for the Indus valley; in particular, some of the languages of Mesopotamia can be read by modern scholars, while that of the Indus cannot.

Mesopotamia's political history featured a series of mainly short-lived states and empires. All were agrarian and, until the Assyrians, based on the irrigation agriculture of the Tigris-Euphrates floodplain. All were hierarchical, led by elites who were either religious or military specialists, and sometimes both at once. Over the centuries, Mesopotamian societies became more militaristic. Soldiers increasingly wielded more power than priests and played a larger role than in most other early complex societies. As they became more militaristic, Mesopotamian states relied more heavily on slavery for labor. They were the first societies in world history in which slavery played a substantial role. Usually Mesopotamia was politically fragmented, and often its cities engaged in warfare with one another. But under Sargon in the mid-third millennium BCE, Hammurabi 500 years later, and under the Assyrians in the early first millennium, the whole region attained a temporary unity.

Mesopotamian culture and religion spread among its neighbors. The power of its states lent a certain prestige to its languages, literature, art, science, and religion. Everywhere from Egypt and the eastern Mediterranean all the way to the Indus valley felt Mesopotamian influence.

The Indus valley cities of Harappa and Mohenjo Daro remain mysterious compared to the cities of Mesopotamia. But diligent archeological work has revealed some extraordinary features. First is the high degree of cultural unity among the various settlements, demonstrated by artistic and architectural styles. We don't know if that unity was politically imposed or, more likely, voluntary. Second is the obsession with water and its cleanliness, unique for the time. Indus cities achieved a standard of urban water supply and wastewater management that wouldn't be matched until as recently as 170 years ago.

The biggest mystery surrounding the Indus valley cities is their disappearance. The interpretation that best fits the scanty evidence is that their populations migrated to the east as other centers took over the long-distance trade routes. Epidemics, river channel shifts, and adverse climate change could have provoked such a migration.

The Indus cities and those of Mesopotamia formed the urbanized core of the Southwest Asian web. The societies on its western and eastern frontiers, anchored in two other river valleys, the Nile and the Ganges, were much less urbanized. But they too became nodes in the web.

Chapter Review

KEY TERMS

Sumer p. 108

Indian Ocean monsoon p. 111

Mesopotamia p. 114

Tigris and Euphrates Rivers p. 114

ziggurats p. 115

cuneiform p. 117

Epic of Gilgamesh p. 118

Sargon of Akkad p. 119

Hammurabi p. 122

Assyrian Empire p. 122

iron p. 123

chariot p. 127

monotheism p. 132

Indus River p. 137

Harappans p. 138

REVIEW QUESTIONS

1. Which natural features of the Tigris, Euphrates, and Indus River valleys made them attractive for human settlement?

2. Why were drought and disease sometimes disastrous for river valley populations?

3. What were the costs and benefits of irrigation agriculture?

4. What needs spurred the invention of writing?

5. In what way was Sargon of Akkad a trailblazer?

6. What are the advantages and disadvantages of bronze in comparison to iron?

7. Describe how chariots and composite bows impacted the balance of power between Eurasian agrarian states and pastoralists.

8. How did early Judaism differ from prevailing religious beliefs and practices in Southwest Asia?

9. How did Hammurabi's law codes reflect the social structure of Babylon?

10. In what ways do remnants of the Harappan culture reflect a society much different from other societies of its time?

11. What are the two most extraordinary features of Harappan culture?

12. What three big geographical features promoted connection between Mesopotamian and Indus valley societies?

Go to INQUIZITIVE

to see what you've learned—and learn what you've missed—with personalized feedback along the way.

5

From Nile to Ganges

AN EXPANDING WEB

3000 BCE to 200 BCE

FOCUS QUESTIONS

1. What features of Egyptian life account for its high levels of political and cultural unity?

2. What do the religious texts of the Ganges basin peoples tell us about their society, culture, and politics?

A text known as the Lansing Papyrus (ca. 1800 BCE) surveys the occupations of ancient Egyptian society and offers advice for young men:

> Love writing, shun dancing; then you become a worthy official. . . . Befriend the scroll. . . . It pleases more than wine. Writing . . . is better than all other professions. It pleases more than bread and beer, more than clothing. . . . It is worth more than an inheritance. . . . Young fellow, how conceited you are! You do not listen when I speak. . . .
>
> See for yourself with your own eye. The occupations lie before you. The washerman's . . . limbs are weak, [from] whitening his neighbors' clothes every day. . . . The maker of pots is smeared with soil. . . . His hands, his feet are full of clay; he is like one who lives in the bog. The cobbler mingles with vats. His odor is penetrating. . . . The merchants travel downstream and upstream. They are as busy as can be, carrying goods from one town to another. . . . The scribe, he alone, records the output of all of them. By day [the peasant] cuts his farming tools; by night he twists rope. Even his midday hour he spends on farm labor. . . . He does three plowings

with borrowed grain.... Now the scribe... surveys the harvest. Attendants are behind him with staffs.... One says [to the peasant]: "Give grain." "There is none." He is beaten savagely. If you have learned about the peasant, you will not be able to be one.

Come, [let me tell] you the woes of the soldier, and how many are his superiors: the general, the troop-commander, the officer who leads, the standard-bearer, the lieutenant, the scribe, the commander of fifty, and the garrison-captain.... He is hungry, his belly hurts; ... He is called up for Syria. ... There are no clothes, no sandals.... His march is uphill through mountains. He drinks water every third day; it is smelly and tastes of salt. His body is ravaged by illness. The enemy comes, surrounds him.... He is told: "Quick, forward, valiant soldier! Win for yourself a good name!" His body is weak, his legs fail him.... His wife and children are in their village; he dies and does not reach it. ... Be a scribe, and be spared from soldiering!

The author, no doubt a scribe himself, disdains hardworking washermen, cobblers, potters, merchants, peasants, and soldiers. Only the scribe has it easy. The text lays bare the division of labor in Egyptian society, something of the hierarchy among social classes, and delivers a full dose of condescension directed against everyone who is not part of the literate bureaucratic elite. The author addresses only men, taking it for granted that the profession of scribe would not include women.

Literacy was rare everywhere 4,000 years ago, and much rarer among women than men. Along the Ganges River after about 1000 BCE, the literate were mainly male religious specialists known as Brahmins. Most of them, like the author of the Lansing Papyrus in Egypt, looked down on everyone who lacked education and refinement. Like him, they sometimes served as bureaucrats,

CHRONOLOGY

ca. 3000 BCE Development of hieroglyphs

ca. 2950 BCE Narmer/Menes unifies Egypt through conquest

2575–2125 BCE Egyptian Old Kingdom

ca. 2500 BCE Reign of Khufu; construction of Great Pyramid at Giza

2010–1630 BCE Egyptian Middle Kingdom

ca. 1700 BCE First use of Chinese rice in Ganges basin

ca. 1700–1500 BCE Hyksos rule of Egypt

1539–1069 BCE Egyptian New Kingdom

ca. 1500 BCE Complex society emerges in Ganges valley

ca. 1100 BCE *Rig Veda* is written down

ca. 1000 BCE Caste system takes shape in Ganges basin

ca. 1000–800 BCE Inhabitants of Ganges basin acquire iron tools

After 800 BCE Small kingdoms emerge in Ganges basin

ca. 712–664 BCE Kush controls most of Upper Egypt

ca. 664 BCE Egypt becomes Assyrian vassal kingdom

525 BCE Persians conquer Egypt

ca. 500 BCE Jainism takes shape

ca. 500–400 BCE Siddhartha Gautama, the Buddha, is born

By 400 BCE Classic Hinduism evolves

321–230 BCE Height of Mauryan Empire

ca. 268–230 BCE Reign of Ashoka

400 CE Last use of hieroglyphs in Egypt

and their standing and authority came from their position within a state as well as within a religion. The precise nature of social stratification differed from one society to the next. But in all the complex societies, from the Nile to the Ganges, stratification and inequality were dominant facts of social life. All societies had to develop ways to deal with the tensions they brought.

This chapter considers the complex societies that emerged in the valleys of the Ganges and the Nile. It dwells on social structure, religion, and state and empire building. In the case of Egypt, where the textual record and the harvest of archeology are far richer, it also reflects on foreign relations, the economy, and health.

The chapter also considers these societies as components of the world's first big web. The Southwest Asian web formed initially in Mesopotamia and surrounding lands. As we saw in Chapter 4, seaborne trade to the Indus expanded and thickened it. The societies of the Southwest Asian web also had connections farther afield—with Central Asia, some coastlands and islands of the eastern Mediterranean, and Egypt. As these links solidified over time, the Southwest Asian web by 2500 BCE became something larger: a Nile-Indus web. It incorporated the societies along the Nile and Indus river basins as they became ever more connected to the circuits of Southwest Asia and the Arabian Sea.

Gradually, over the next thousand years, as new settlement and new linkages developed in northern India, the Nile-Indus web expanded into a Nile-Ganges web. Integral parts of this enlarged web, the societies of the Nile and Ganges were also frontier regions. To the east, south, and north of the Ganges, and to the west and south of Egypt, the web shaded off into more thinly populated lands with societies that, as of 200 BCE, remained only intermittently affected by the trends within the Nile-Ganges web.

Egypt, 3000–200 BCE

Herodotus, the renowned fifth-century BCE Greek historian, wrote: "I will speak at length about Egypt because there is no other land like it." Egypt had several distinctive geographical features. For the last 5,000 years, Egypt has consisted of broad expanses of sandy and rocky desert where almost no one could live, split by the narrow river valley of the Nile and its lush, muddy delta, where almost every Egyptian lived. Rainfall was negligible. The **Nile River** flows more than 4,000 miles (nearly 7,000 km) northward from its source at today's Lake Victoria, in East Africa, to its delta near the Mediterranean Sea. The Nile has several shallow rapids, called cataracts, that posed obstacles to navigation. Yet, despite climatic and geographical constraints, Egyptians were among the first people anywhere to create cities, states, and writing. As far as we know, only Sumerians preceded them—and not by much.

Egypt had a political peculiarity too. After about 3000 BCE, Egypt was usually a unified state—in sharp contrast to Mesopotamia, the Ganges valley, probably the

Indus valley too, the Chinese river valleys, and almost every other center of population in the ancient world until 200 BCE.

The Nile itself helped shape this political peculiarity. Its annual flood with loads of fertile silt from the Ethiopian highlands made its banks and delta the most durably productive farmland anywhere in the ancient world. The Nile also served as a two-way highway. Its current flows north, while for most of the year winds blow south: boat traffic could move either up or down the river easily north of the First Cataract. Water transport was so cheap and efficient that Egypt didn't need roads. Once people figured out how to exploit the annual flood, farming with the same techniques and crops worked well throughout Egypt. These characteristics of the Nile made Egypt easier to unify than most other lands, and when it fell apart, it was easier to re-unify. Herodotus called Egypt, with some justice, the "gift of the Nile."

Whether it was politically united or not, Egyptians conceived of their country as divided into two parts. The southern part—the Nile valley—was a narrow ribbon of life only 4 to 20 miles (6 to 30 km) wide and 600 miles (900 km) long, roughly the area of New Jersey. The northern part—the delta—was twice as large. In 4000 BCE, it was a triangle of shifting river channels, mud banks, and reed beds teeming with geese, ducks, herons, and other wildfowl, and home to crocodiles and hippos. It was, however,

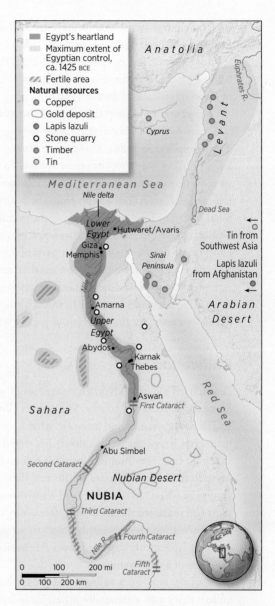

Ancient Egypt, ca. 2575–1069 BCE Ancient Egypt, a united kingdom more often than not after 2950 BCE, was simultaneously part of Africa and the Mediterranean world. A narrow ribbon of life, villages, towns, and cities in one of the driest parts of the world, Egypt was the "gift of the Nile." In most years, Egypt produced surplus food that it exchanged for metals, timber, and other items that were hard to come by in Egypt.

undergoing transformation into a cultivated and irrigated landscape. As we'll see, the extent of southern Egypt varied, as its rulers enjoyed fluctuating success in conquering territory upriver. But Egypt's heart remained the Nile delta and valley north of the First Cataract. Scholars refer to southern Egypt as Upper Egypt; northern Egypt, the region of the delta, is called Lower Egypt.

Egypt was politically distinctive in another way that geography helps to explain. Whereas people living along the other big rivers hosting complex societies—the Tigris-Euphrates, Indus, Ganges, or Huang He—often had much to worry about from invaders sweeping into their valleys, Egyptians were comparatively secure. The surrounding desert provided a formidable barrier against outsiders, so there were only two practical ways into Egypt: from the north or northeast either by sea or across the Sinai desert; or from the south along the middle reaches of the Nile and the land called **Nubia**. Egypt suffered comparatively few invasions and devoted far less of its wealth and effort to self-defense than did other parts of the ancient world. Political unity meant that Egyptians were rarely fighting one another, and geographical barriers meant that they rarely had to fight invaders. This combination of unusually fertile soil and unusually low defense requirements is unique in world history. It made Egypt a wonderful country to live in—at least, for the 1 percent of society who commanded the labor of all the rest.

Unification

People lived along the Nile for thousands of years before complex society took shape. From about 9000 BCE to 5500 BCE, wetter climate enabled people to live among lakes and rivers, grasslands and forests in what is now the Sahara desert. After 5500 BCE, climate grew drier, the Sahara slowly became desert, and people crowded into the Nile valley. At first, they hunted abundant fish and wildlife and collected edible plants. To judge from the few skeletons of this era, these were violent times in the Nile basin. By 5500 BCE, wheat, barley, peas, and lentils were prominent crops. By 3500 BCE, Egyptians had mastered the art of irrigation along the Nile, had built farming villages, and were harvesting enough surplus food to support a social elite. Elaborate burials with precious lapis lazuli imported from Afghanistan and gold from Nubia testify to the existence of a dominant class.

By 3300 BCE, a few villages had grown into towns. Each town identified with an animal deity and presumably prized its independence. But independence didn't last. A process of consolidation, probably violent, quickly followed. Soon there were only two or three polities. At around 3100 BCE, rulers of a city in Upper Egypt called Abydos managed to unite all the towns and countryside from the Nile delta in the north to Aswan, a city near the First Cataract, in the south. Thereafter, the kings of Egypt, eventually called **pharaohs**, wore a double crown symbolizing Upper and Lower Egypt. The Egyptian kings chose Memphis, near today's Cairo, where the delta and the Nile valley meet, for their capital.

Narmer and His Successors   From then on, Egypt was usually unified, and for Egyptians it became normal to think that it *should* be unified. The first ruler of all Egypt, known as both **Narmer** and Menes, probably completed unification through conquest around 2950 BCE. (Incidentally, he was the only ruler in world history to be mauled to death by a hippo.) No texts illuminate this early period of Egyptian history, so scholars rely on archeology and artwork such as the so-called Narmer Palette, which seems to show the king about to bash someone's skull. It's unclear whether that was intended to represent historical events or to establish the principle that Narmer would deal harshly with enemies. Beneath Narmer stand two long-necked animals, perhaps lionesses, whose intertwined necks, bound by leashes, may represent the union of Upper and Lower Egypt and Narmer's control over both. The motif imitates a Sumerian cylinder seal, providing evidence of cultural links between Egypt and Mesopotamia. Narmer's successors ruled Egypt for nearly 3,000 years.

This long era is conventionally divided into three periods of political unity—the Old Kingdom, the Middle Kingdom, and the New Kingdom (see table on next page). Each of these is subdivided into dynasties following a scheme invented by a third-century BCE Egyptian historian-priest named Manetho. In between the three kingdoms are the Intermediate Periods, when unity broke down. There were about 33 dynasties and roughly 170 pharaohs in all. One could create chronologies of Egyptian history based on pottery styles or climate shifts, but Manetho's scheme, which emphasizes the significance of Egyptian unification, is still preferred by experts despite its uncertainties.

The Egyptians created the world's first stable monarchy and more or less invented hereditary kingship. The first kings, of the Early Dynastic Period, were understood as both divine and human, children of Ra, one of the sun gods. The kings cruised up and down the Nile every other year, dispensing justice, conducting an agricultural census, and extracting grain and other goods from every community. Little is left of their

King Narmer The Narmer Palette features scenes of battle with mythical creatures and an illustration of Narmer (large figure at left) as the warrior king who conquered and unified all of Egypt.

Periodization of Ancient Egypt

PERIOD	DATES
Pre-dynastic Period	to 2950 BCE
Early Dynastic Period	2950–2575
Old Kingdom	2575–2125
First Intermediate Period	2125–2010
Middle Kingdom	2010–1630
Second Intermediate Period	1630–1539
New Kingdom	1539–1069
Third Intermediate Period	1069–664
Late Period (Assyrian, Kushite, Persian rule)	664–332
Macedonian and Ptolemaic Period	332–30 BCE

Source: The dates before 664 BCE are approximate, and some are disputed. Those used here follow Toby Wilkinson, *The Rise and Fall of Ancient Egypt* (2010), xiv–xxiii.

legacy except their mud-brick tombs at Abydos, and for the last king, Djoser, a small pyramid. We know next to nothing about the first kings or of Egypt in their time. However, beginning with the Old Kingdom, around 2575 BCE, we know a surprising amount.

Agriculture and the Economy

Ancient Egypt was one of the most densely populated places on Earth. Most people lived in the delta in farming villages.

Farming and Irrigation The foundation of ancient Egypt was farming. Every year, upward of 90 percent of the population took part in the sowing and harvesting of barley, wheat, and a few vegetable crops. They also raised flax, from which linen cloth was made, sesame (for its oil), and eventually a variety of fruits and grapes. All these crops came originally from Southwest Asia. The delta region also specialized in livestock, especially oxen used for traction.

Irrigation, annual silt deposits, and ceaseless toil made ancient Egypt the richest agricultural land anywhere in the world. No fallow period was needed to restore fertility to soils because the annual summer flood brought a coating of rich silt. The technologies and methods of Egyptian farming changed little over 3,000 years, once the techniques of irrigation were mastered. Basin irrigation, used along the Nile, involved capturing part of the floodwaters behind earthen berms, or embankments, and releasing water to crops as needed over the following months. During the New Kingdom, an irrigation device called the *shaduf* was developed to help in the watering of gardens and vegetable plots. Later, waterwheels called *saqia* improved irrigation efficiency and added 10 to 15 percent to Egypt's cropland. But in general, under Egyptian conditions, little incentive existed to experiment and innovate in agriculture. Tried and true routines brought huge surpluses in most years.

All land belonged, in name at least, to the pharaoh. His agents took a share of the harvest in kind (Egyptians didn't use money before 300 BCE) and shipped it to central distribution points. From there grain went to the court, the bureaucracy, temples, far-flung garrisons, and royal enterprises such as mines. Large parts of the economy were state-run. Markets played only a small role in Egypt compared to Mesopotamia. Transport was by boat or donkey until camels came into use around 200 BCE. Egyptians didn't need wheeled carts much because riverboats and barges could go just about anywhere goods had to go except around the cataracts. Nile shipping made the transport of grain easy in normal times, so local famines were rare. Moreover, pharaohs typically kept a reserve of grain to use against hunger where needed. Nine years out of ten, the river's flood was neither too low nor too high, grain ripened, pharaohs took their cut, and the people still had enough to eat.

Low Niles and Famines Big famines were also rare in Egypt, but impossible to prevent if harvests failed throughout the country. Royal granaries might hold a reserve good for a few months—maybe enough to get most of the population through one bad harvest. But consecutive bad harvests brought starvation. There was nowhere else to turn to for food. Importing it from Mesopotamia would require overland travel and be too costly. Nubia and other lands dependent on the Nile would themselves have too little food in years when Egypt's harvest was poor.

The most frequent cause of a bad harvest was a low Nile flood that brought too little water and silt to Egypt and Nubia alike. Periods of sustained drought in Ethiopia's mountains brought repeated "low Niles," which spelled disaster for Egypt. Around 2300 to 2200 BCE, several low Niles helped to bring the Old Kingdom to an end: without surplus grain, the pharaohs had nothing to distribute to their followers, their moral authority evaporated, and support for the state withered away amid starvation and chaos.

About 1210 to 1100 BCE, recurrent low Niles helped to bring down the New Kingdom. On both these occasions of dynastic change, searing droughts afflicted the whole of northeastern Africa and Southwest Asia, making it unlikely that people whose crops failed could get food from elsewhere. This misfortune spanned the entire web from the Nile to the Indus, brought about by a large-scale disturbance in climate patterns that lasted for decades. But when the gifts of the Nile began to flow once more, agricultural abundance and re-unification of Egypt soon followed.

Scribes and Smiths Ancient Egypt had crafts and industries as well as farms. In the desert outside the Nile valley, there were copper and gold mines and stone quarries, where unlucky men toiled in miserable conditions. Potters, weavers, smiths, and boatmen worked in many villages and every town. Women in most rural households spun linen cloth out of flax. In bigger towns, there were also stonemasons and scribes.

Only 1 to 2 percent of the population could read or write, almost all males. The few who mastered writing were professional scribes, most of whom worked at the court in service of pharaohs, who were usually illiterate. It was great work if you could get it, as the Lansing Papyrus made clear. But learning to write took five to ten years of hard

Hieroglyphs This excerpt from The Book of the Dead attests to the quantity of pictographic symbols a scribe would need to memorize and interpret—even in papyrus manuscripts, such as this, which usually employed a more simplified form of hieroglyphs than that used for stone inscriptions.

study. The Egyptian writing system, called **hieroglyphs** ("sacred carvings"), developed beginning about 3000 BCE, possibly influenced by the Sumerian cuneiforms. It reached full complexity by 1500 BCE, when it comprised some 1,000 symbols—a lot to memorize.

Hieroglyphs can represent either sounds or words, and they can be written left to right, right to left, or top to bottom. Simplified versions developed, but even they were hard to learn. Priests used an easier version called hieratic script, for example, and after 700 BCE an even easier one, called demotic script, served for daily transactions. Hieratic and demotic were often used for the less formal texts—letters, bills of sale, poetry—that were written on papyrus, a thick and absorbent paper made from the stems of a reedy plant that grew in the Nile delta swamps. Stone inscriptions used the more formal hieroglyphs. The last use of hieroglyphs in Egypt came around 400 CE, by which time Egyptians had turned to alphabets.

Smiths were comparatively rare in Egypt. The techniques and technologies of metallurgy changed only slowly, as with agriculture, and Egypt had some copper and gold but little else in the way of useful ores. Egyptians adopted bronze for some weapons and tools beginning around 1600 BCE. They were late turning to iron, which they used sparingly before 670 BCE, perhaps because working iron requires much charcoal or fuelwood, always scarce in Egypt. Neighbors in Southwest Asia and to the south in Nubia used iron in greater quantities at earlier dates than Egyptians did.

Trade Egypt was normally self-sufficient in food and in most other necessary items—but not all. With few sturdy trees, Egyptians had to trade for timber, which came mainly from the shores of the Levant. With the advent of bronze weaponry, Egypt had to import tin, also from Southwest Asia. Perhaps its most important import was gold, that favorite metal of ancient monarchs. Egypt had its own gold mines in the desert east of the Nile, but imported plenty from Nubia, to the south, and perhaps from elsewhere in Africa. The pharaohs' desire to secure access to timber and metals from abroad shaped their foreign policy.

Egypt and Its Neighbors

Egypt's most important trading partners were its near neighbors. To the south, upstream along the Nile, was Nubia. To the northeast, across a stretch of desert, stood the societies of the Levant and Mesopotamia.

Nubia and the Levant   South of the First Cataract lay the land called Nubia. Nubians were farmers, cattle herders, and fisherfolk living along the Nile. When pharaohs were strong, they sought to control Nubia, pushing Egypt's frontiers south. From the time of the Old Kingdom if not before, they occasionally mounted expeditions to seize Nubian slaves, ivory, ebony wood, cattle, animal skins, and above all, gold. During the Middle Kingdom, Egyptians managed to drag riverboats around the Nile's cataracts to launch assaults on Nubian towns and conquer parts of the country. But Nubia always reasserted its power south of the Second Cataract, if not all the way north to the First. Nubians often worked for Egypt as mercenary soldiers (they were renowned for their archery skills), especially during the Middle Kingdom.

When Nubian kings were strong and pharaohs were weak, they traded for Nubia's ivory and gold. And when Egypt was divided and at its weakest, Nubian rulers pushed out Egyptian garrisons and traders, and took control of the fortified posts at the First Cataract. Once, around 712–664 BCE, a Nubian state called Kush controlled most of Upper Egypt for half a century and Kushite kings became Egypt's pharaohs.

But that was exceptional. Most of the time, Egypt exploited Nubia through greater military power and better knowledge of the value of goods in the wider world. Pharaohs frequently boasted of their savage treatment of Nubians: Senusret III, in the nineteenth century BCE, for example, wanted people to believe he had "carried off their women . . . poisoned their wells, driven off their bulls, ripped up their barley and set fire to it." Pharaohs preferred reputations as brutal rather than merciful rulers—at least, as far as Nubians were concerned.

Over the millennia, through war and peace, Nubia provided vast quantities of goods that helped sustain the refined tastes of Egypt's elite. At the same time, Nubia's elite, especially the royal houses of Kush, took on attributes of Egyptian culture. They came to speak the Egyptian language and use Egyptian hieroglyphs in inscriptions. They adopted the worship of Egyptian gods—especially Amun, a major god in Thebes and eventually in all of Egypt, and built temples to him in the Egyptian style. They

Nubia Depictions of Nubians speak to their relationship with their Egyptian neighbors. In this frieze from an Egyptian temple (ca. 1490 BCE), a group of Nubians are shown as mercenary soldiers whose archery skills could aid the Egyptian army.

wanted to be buried with Egyptian-style funerary goods, and after 750 BCE or so, Nubian rulers began to build small pyramids.

Surplus grain and Nubian gold enabled Egypt to trade for timber and minerals from the Levant and elsewhere in Southwest Asia. Here too, exceptionally strong pharaohs occasionally preferred to exercise control over territory, installing garrisons in Palestine and Syria and sometimes as far afield as Mesopotamia in order to secure access to timber and metals. Weaker pharaohs might make peace with the dominant power in Southwest Asia, hoping to ensure access to trade goods. When Egypt was truly weak or divided, it couldn't keep "miserable Asiatics" (as one Egyptian text put it) from infiltrating the northeastern delta or perhaps even invading Egypt—as in the case of the Hyksos.

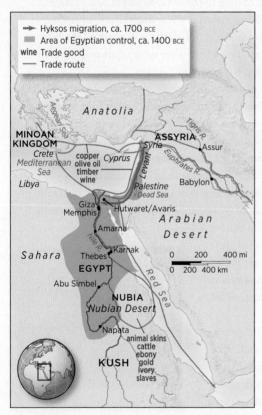

Egypt and Its Neighbors, ca. 1700–600 BCE In addition to trade links, Egypt after 1700 BCE was increasingly involved in politics and war both in Nubia to the south and in the Levant. Politically speaking, after the Hyksos intrusion, Egypt was tightly enmeshed in a web of interactions with its nearest neighbors and occasionally further afield.

The Hyksos Starting in the eighteenth century BCE, the **Hyksos** either invaded Egypt militarily or infiltrated as peaceful migrants. They probably came from what is now Lebanon, spoke a different language than Egyptians did, and worshiped different gods. The Hyksos were skilled in the latest military technique, chariot warfare (unknown in Egypt), and the arts of horsemanship. They also had bronze weapons, composite bows, and body armor, all new to Egypt. So armed invasion is plausible, but so is a peaceful movement into an Egypt suffering from famines and divisions. Soon after 1700 BCE, the Hyksos took the Egyptian capital of Memphis.

Hyksos rule (ca. 1700–1500 BCE) brought Egypt stronger connections to the trading world of the eastern Mediterranean. They built a large port in the northeast delta—Hutwaret (also called Avaris)—to handle the trade with Southwest Asia and the islands of Cyprus and Crete. Wine, olive oil, copper, and timber flowed into Egypt from Cyprus and the Levant. Egyptian artwork began to show—for a few decades, at least—influence from the Minoan kingdom on the island of Crete. Egyptian technologies, especially of war, came to resemble those in use in Mesopotamia. As Egypt became more tightly integrated with Southwest Asia after 1700 BCE, the linkages of the western edge of the Nile-Indus web thickened—not long after those of the eastern edge, the Indus valley itself, had weakened.

While the Hyksos dominated the delta, and at times as far south as Thebes in Upper Egypt, Nubians made incursions from the south. Egypt seemed about to disappear, gobbled up by neighbors. But soon, and surprisingly quickly, Egyptian pharaohs based in Thebes turned the tables first on the Nubians and then on the Hyksos, and drove them out of Egypt. Perhaps a string of good harvests lifted their fortunes to the point where they could finance bigger armies. Perhaps they learned the arts of chariot warfare and the making of bronze weapons well enough to oust their neighbors. In any case, the tighter links to Southwest Asia remained.

A Regional Power During the Middle and New Kingdoms, when Egypt was usually strong, it was often a major player in the international relations of Southwest Asia, raiding and invading rather than suffering raid and invasion. Pharaohs fought the various powers of Mesopotamia and Syria from time to time. One, Tutmose III, campaigned annually in the Levant for nearly 20 years running. The pharaohs' aims, in addition to looting and ensuring access to metals and timber in Southwest Asia, included making names for themselves as glorious leaders. The ideal career for a pharaoh of the Middle or New Kingdom featured victories in both Nubia and Syria, followed by peace and a spree of monument building. Warfare and diplomacy, as well as trade and cultural exchange, linked Egypt to Southwest Asia, as to Nubia, more strongly after 2000 BCE than before and, by and large, more strongly still with each passing century.

Disdain for Foreigners Egyptian elite culture included a vigorous chauvinism directed against foreigners. People from Palestine and Syria were often referred to as animals or disdained as shepherds. Other foreigners, especially "wretched Kushites," were also held in contempt. Unlike most monarchies, the Egyptian pharaohs rarely used royal daughters as tools of diplomacy. About 1500 BCE, one Mesopotamian king, following cultural tradition, hoped to boost his standing by negotiating for a pharaoh's daughter in marriage. He was rebuffed with the remark that pharaohs never sent

Race in Egypt A relief from around 1250 BCE of the pharaoh Ramses II conquering other peoples shows the range of skin tones that Egyptians used to visually represent foreign peoples.

their daughters to marry foreigners. Elite Egyptians, although highly chauvinistic about their language and culture, welcomed those who mastered it. Foreigners who became culturally Egyptian married freely with native Egyptians and had as good a chance of enjoying high status and power as anyone else. A few foreigners did rise into the elite.

In the nineteenth and twentieth centuries CE, some scholars of ancient Egypt tried hard to prove that Egyptians were representatives of either a white or a black race. Either argument would have puzzled ancient Egyptians. In their art, they depict four different shades of human: Libyans (from Mediterranean coastlands west of Egypt) were the fairest; people from Palestine and Syria a yellowish-brown; Egyptians a reddish-brown; and Nubians black. Women were always portrayed a few shades lighter than men, perhaps indicating that they either were, or should be, less often outdoors in the sun. In their texts, ancient Egyptians took no interest in skin color or physiognomy. The variations among humankind that mattered to them were cultural.

Egyptian disdain for foreigners grew harder to maintain as Egypt's power waned. After the eighth century BCE, Egypt was more often weak than strong in comparison to its neighbors. We've seen that Nubian kings ruled Egypt for half a century. They were driven out not by Egyptians but by Assyrian invaders from northern Mesopotamia, whose iron weapons and mass armies made them masters of much of Southwest Asia. Egypt, dependent on distant sources for iron and without a reliable supply of horses, had no military answer for Assyrian power. After 664 BCE, for half a century Egypt lost its autonomy and became an Assyrian vassal kingdom. And in the sixth century BCE, a new power arose, Persia, which in 525 BCE ended Egyptian self-rule for many centuries to come. More invasions and rule by foreign elites followed.

Pharaohs and Monuments

Of the roughly 170 pharaohs from Narmer's time onward, two were women. The female pharaoh we know most about, Hatshepsut, came to power by marrying a pharaoh—her half-brother—who died a few years afterward. She at first served as regent for her infant son, but then claimed full powers for herself. Hatshepsut proved to be a highly competent pharaoh for 20 years until her death about 1458 BCE. She often had herself depicted in official artwork as a muscular man with a beard and referred to as "son of Amun," an indication of ancient Egyptian expectations of pharaohs.

Hatshepsut A statue of Hatshepsut created during her reign depicts the pharaoh with a masculine body and a beard. In her hands, she carries vessels for making offerings to the gods.

Maat The main duties of pharaohs were to oversee Egypt's irrigation system and ensure a good harvest, defeat Nubians and other neighbors when necessary, and keep the temples properly supplied and the gods satisfied. As Egyptians saw it, the pharaohs' primary role was to maintain *maat*, a concept that embraced justice and truth as well as order. Pharaohs could fulfill this responsibility only through proper mediation with the gods—a crucial duty of almost every ancient monarch anywhere. There were two final duties: to have a son suitable for succession and to build monuments to oneself. To achieve the former, pharaohs usually married several women, frequently including their sisters, and most pharaohs had liaisons on the side. To build monuments, they conscripted labor and materials in gargantuan quantities. Suitable monuments included temples with boastful inscriptions recounting their achievements in life and above all an impressive tomb worthy of a divine, or at least semi-divine, king. Egyptian religion, as we'll see shortly, took the concept of an afterlife to heart, much more so than Mesopotamian peoples did.

Pyramids For tombs, pharaohs of the Old Kingdom came to prefer **pyramids**. In the Old Kingdom, Egyptians believed that only pharaohs would experience an afterlife. Since afterlife was eternal, preparations for it were exacting. Early pharaohs arranged to have servants, pets, and dwarves (they had a fascination with dwarves) killed by strangulation and buried with them. One king had 600 people sacrificed to keep him properly attended in the afterlife. By 2600 BCE, pharaohs had stopped human sacrifice and instead stocked their tombs with *shabti*, or miniature statues of people, and things they might need in the afterlife. And they started conscripting thousands upon thousands of peasants to build giant pyramids to serve as pharaonic tombs.

Khufu, also known as Cheops, reigned for 20 years around 2500 BCE. He oversaw the construction of a pyramid that, at 481 ft. (147 m), remained the world's tallest building for 4,300 years, until completion of the Eiffel Tower in Paris in 1889. The Great Pyramid at Giza—just outside of today's Cairo—is built of 2.5 million blocks of stone weighing about 2 tons each. It took a minimum of 10,000 men—some say 25,000—working day and night to satisfy Khufu's megalomania. If his labor force worked every single day of his 20-year reign, they would have had to place a block of stone every 4 minutes. They worked with great precision under the direction of skilled engineers: the base is nearly perfectly flat, and its four sides are within 1/20 of a degree of alignment with the four points of the compass.

Scholars used to think that legions of slaves built the pyramids. But it seems that slavery was rare in Egypt before the New Kingdom, and the unlucky army of laborers was made up of conscripted peasants. If, as experts believe, Egypt as a whole contained about 1 to 2 million people during the Old Kingdom, and only males above age 14 were conscripted, then during Khufu's reign 2 to 10 percent of adult male Egyptians were drafted to build pyramids. The few skeletons that survive show evidence of many accidents and arthritis of the joints. What these men thought about pushing and pulling

Pharaonic Monuments The pharaoh Ramses II built this monument to his own greatness as part of a temple complex in southern Egypt around 1250 BCE. The enormous statues of Ramses emphasize his status, likening him to a god.

huge blocks of limestone up ramps to ensure a suitable afterlife for the pharaoh is unrecorded.

After the Old Kingdom, pyramids gradually went out of style, in part because of the expense. The last of the pyramids, a mere 2 percent the size of Khufu's, was built in 1745 BCE. Later pharaohs devoted their subjects' labor to erecting other kinds of monuments, temples, obelisks, stelae, and statues of themselves; these far outnumber pyramids. Some involved moving stone blocks weighing 1,000 tons—using only muscle power. The pharaohs employed stonemasons to carve messages into these monuments, most of which record their great deeds. These were platforms for pharaonic propaganda rather than launching pads for the afterlife. In this respect, the pharaohs' behavior grew less distinctive and more like that of rulers elsewhere.

Every pharaoh wanted to undertake a program of monument building, but not all could afford it. The biggest programs occurred during periods of peace, especially during the Old Kingdom. In effect, pharaohs had to choose between foreign wars and monument building; doing both at once was usually too costly in manpower terms. But during the Middle and New Kingdoms, several pharaohs began their reigns with wars in Nubia or the Levant. When these wars went well for Egypt, they burnished royal reputations and brought home loot that made it easier to finish pharaonic careers with magnificent monuments. When foreign wars went badly for Egypt, pharaohs built fewer monuments.

Religion

The fundamental purpose of religious practice in Egypt, as in Mesopotamia, was to win the favor of the gods. They, after all, were believed to control the elemental forces of the universe. Careful attention to rituals was needed to ensure that they would continue to bestow blessings—the warmth of the sun, the life-giving waters of the Nile—upon those who honored them properly. As it did in all ancient states, religion also underpinned the power of Egypt's rulers. The pharaohs claimed to have unique access to the gods, and some of them claimed to be gods themselves. Most Egyptians probably accepted these claims—at least, when order prevailed and the Nile's flood didn't fail.

Gods What we know about Egyptian religion comes from a handful of texts and a lot of archeology, almost all of which speaks only to the experience of the elite. In the Old Kingdom, every Egyptian village and town had its own gods, usually associated with a particular animal and represented by a stylized image of that animal or the animal's head on a human body: for example, a falcon (Horus, associated with kings and the sky), a wolf or jackal (Anubis, associated with preparation for the afterlife), a cat (Bastet, originally a goddess of warfare, later the protector of cats). Some peasants honored gods who specialized in helping people through trials such as childbirth. Many relied heavily on Isis, goddess of the home and fertility, at least by the time of the New Kingdom. Magic and charms surely played a big role in popular religion. Humble folk often carried amulets, small pieces of jewelry thought to ward off evil spirits.

By and large, ancient Egyptian deities were benign and helpful, bringing warmth, water, fertility, and other blessings. However, one, called Set or Seth, eventually became associated with chaos and deserts. A popular myth held that he killed his brother Osiris and chopped up the body to prevent anyone from carrying out the appropriate funeral rites. Another, Hathor, was goddess of joy and erotic love, fate and divine vengeance, and drunkenness. In one myth, the sun god Ra grew irritated with humankind's evil conduct and assigned Hathor the job of punishment. She took to it with relish and by the end of the day had killed half of the people on Earth. Ra managed to trick Hathor and save humankind, and Egyptians eventually associated Hathor with motherhood and childbirth.

Over the centuries, gods could change their responsibilities, merge with one another, or disappear—just as in the pantheons of Mesopotamia or, as we'll see, the Ganges basin. Egyptians had no formal scripture, no holy texts invested with divine authority. Their religious texts were more like guidebooks, with instructions on how to perform rituals and how to ensure an afterlife. Theirs was a living, evolving religion, less constrained in its mutations than many others for which sacred scriptures exist.

With the arrival of the Hyksos in the eighteenth century BCE, Egyptian religion acquired features borrowed from the Levant. Some Egyptians, especially in the delta, began to worship Baal, a Semitic god. A cult developed devoted to Astarte, a goddess

Major Egyptian Gods

NAME	IDENTITIES, RESPONSIBILITIES, AND ASSOCIATIONS
Ra	Sun; pharaohs
Amun	Patron god of city of Thebes
Amun-Ra	Sun, air; a fusion of Ra and Amun, considered the most powerful of gods during the New Kingdom
Hathor	Kindness, motherhood, love; Nile flood; often considered mother of Ra
Isis	Motherhood; mother of kings; originally associated with Hathor
Osiris	God of the afterlife; husband of Isis
Anubis	Death, embalming, underworld
Thoth	Writing, mathematics, wisdom, magic, the moon; patron of scribes and priests

based on the Babylonian Ishtar who in Egypt became a war goddess. Egyptians in the delta started to bury dead infants in clay jars (called amphora) from Palestine. In religion, as in trade, the Hyksos occupation brought Egypt closer to Southwest Asia, tightening the Nile-Indus web.

The Afterlife Elite Egyptians placed great stock in the afterlife. At first, only pharaohs could attain it. To arrive in good condition, one needed to be mummified and provided with all manner of grave goods, tools, weapons, and servants. Mummification alone took up to 10 weeks and required skilled morticians who removed a corpse's organs (except the heart) through narrow incisions. They took brains out in small pieces through the nasal cavity. After this, they had to dry the body with salts and wrap it in linens. Egyptians believed that elaborate funerary rituals had to be carefully carried out to ensure passage into the afterlife.

During the First Intermediate Period, just after the Old Kingdom, a democratization of the afterlife took place, associated with an emphasis on Osiris as lord of the afterlife (he had formerly been a god of farming). Egyptians came to believe that anyone who followed the necessary procedures was eligible to make the journey to Osiris's domain, not just pharaohs. It was beyond the means of ordinary folk, but those who could afford it normally took the necessary steps, and understandably so. The afterlife was eternal, one was always young and healthy there, and food, drink, and sex were always available. If you took the precaution of including a *shabti* of a human laborer among your grave goods, in the land of Osiris it would do all the manual labor that might be needed, ensuring an afterlife of leisure.

During the Middle Kingdom, Egyptians developed a concept of the final judgment: you could only gain entry to the land of Osiris with a good moral transcript. The dead, including pharaohs, could plead their case to a panel of gods, but that wouldn't help if they flunked the real test: their heart, which contained all the evil they had done in

Shabti Important people were buried with dozens of *shabti* figurines—like this troop, found in a tomb from 500 BCE—who would perform all necessary domestic labor for the dead person in the afterlife.

their lives, was weighed in a scale against the feather of *maat*—the concept of truth, justice, and order. Only those with minimal evil in their hearts could pass to the land of Osiris. Others, whose hearts outweighed the feather of *maat,* had their beings forever destroyed by the goddess Ammut, devourer of the dead. Whether this new concept constrained immoral behavior or not is uncertain, but it placed responsibility for one's eternal fate squarely upon the individual.

An important text, the Book of the Dead—a collection of magic spells and religious recommendations in use by 1500 BCE—offers some guidelines on how to pass the ultimate test. All would go well if one lived so as to be able to make a declaration to Anubis like this:

> I have not done falsehood against men, I have not impoverished my associates, I have done no wrong in the Place of Truth, I have not learnt that which is not, I have done no evil, I have not daily required labor in excess of what was to be done for me, my name has not reached the offices of those who control slaves, I have not deprived the orphan of his property, I have not done what the gods detest, I have not slandered a servant to his master, I have not caused pain, I have not made hungry, I have not made to weep, I have not killed, I have not turned anyone over to a killer, I have not caused anyone's suffering.

Like every durable faith, Egyptian religion evolved over the centuries, absorbing foreign influences and adapting to changes in society.

Akhenaten In the fourteenth century BCE, a pharaoh of the New Kingdom, Amenhotep IV, tried to change Egyptian religion by using his authority to impose monotheism. After a few years on the throne, he led a religious revolution, forbidding worship of gods other than his favorite, Aten, the sun disk and a manifestation of the sun god Ra. He had references to other gods scratched out of Egypt's temples, and he diverted resources from all other cults to that of Aten. He changed his own name to Akhenaten ("living spirit of Aten") and founded a new city, today's Amarna, dedicated to Aten.

Just what lay behind this radical departure in Egyptian religion is unclear. Akhenaten had himself depicted differently from all previous pharaohs, who always appear as young, athletically built, and serene. Akhenaten's physique is less imposing, and he and his wife, Nefertiti, are shown in homely scenes. Nefertiti in some representations appears with the trappings of a pharaoh, leading scholars to suppose that she may have been a co-regent with Akhenaten. All this novelty proved unpopular with the priesthood and did not long outlive Akhenaten himself. Most of his monuments were torn down, defaced, and re-used by his successors. A few scholars suggest that Akhenaten's religious revolution provided the basis for the monotheism that infuses Judaism and Christianity (the first evidence of Judaic monotheism came about two centuries after Akhenaten, as we saw in Chapter 4). Akhenaten's son, incidentally, was Tutankamun, the famous King Tut, an insignificant pharaoh who died as a teenager and whose only distinction

Akhenaten A wall relief depicts Akhenaten and Nefertiti playing with their three daughters while the sun's rays shine Aten's blessings on them.

was that his tomb was among the very few never robbed before archeologists got to it in 1922.

Egyptian religion had the effect of justifying pharaonic rule. The great mass of Egyptians led lives of unremitting toil that supported an opulent and often slothful courtly life for pharaohs and their families. The fact that Egyptians rarely rose up in revolt against this arrangement suggests that the ideology of divine kingship convinced almost all Egyptians almost all the time that things were as they should be. The common folk may have been intimidated—that was part of the purpose of monumental architecture—but they were more ideologically intimidated than physically. There is little evidence within Egypt (as opposed to lands that Egyptians conquered) of the sort of apparatus of repression used by Assyrian kings, for example.

After a long and successful career, Egyptian religion faded away—but it didn't vanish without a trace. After 300 BCE, Egyptian beliefs and rituals were influenced by Greek and Roman religion. Later, most Egyptians became Christians and then later still, Muslims. But even today, modern Egyptians observe festivals originally offered in honor of Osiris.

Health and Society

At the time of the unification of Egypt around 3100 BCE, the entire country contained perhaps 300,000 people. During the Old Kingdom, population reached 1 to 2 million and in prosperous moments of the New Kingdom, about 3 million. People's lives were short by our standards, filled with suffering and disease. Few reached age 40, and the average life expectancy for those who made it past toddlerhood was about 30 years. A large proportion died between ages 2 and 4. With high death rates, Egyptians, like all ancient farming peoples, tried to have big families. Some texts refer to contraceptives, including honey and crocodile dung, but few Egyptians used them.

Disease Disease lay at the heart of life for ancient Egyptians at least as much as for other ancient peoples. Since the Nile, like other rivers along which people clustered, served as both a sewer and a source of drinking water, gastrointestinal ailments were common. Peasants who waded for long hours in irrigated fields usually had schistosomiasis, a debilitating illness spread by worms that are carried by snails. Skeletons testify to the existence of tuberculosis in perhaps a quarter of all Egyptians. No doubt ancient Egyptians hosted some crowd diseases—infections such as smallpox that can circulate indefinitely among large enough populations. Many skeletons show evidence of malaria, probably widespread in Egypt, or of hookworm. Malnutrition was routine among the masses. A celebrated pharaoh of the thirteenth century BCE, Ramses II, in contrast, suffered from hardening of the arteries, likely reflecting a meat-rich diet. Pharaohs, according to texts, ate meat often, including such delicacies as cranes, antelopes, and hyenas. Hatshepsut, the female pharaoh of the New Kingdom, who died at about 50 years of age, was obese. She, like most Egyptians, had worn-down teeth, a result of eating food containing dust and sand.

Ancient Egypt had doctors and a number of detailed medical texts. Egyptian doctors specialized in the treatment of specific diseases and parts of the body. Specialists in eye ailments were in demand, as one would expect in a population subject to wind-blown Saharan dust and sand. Surviving Egyptian texts suggest doctors could deal with wounds and broken limbs fairly well, but—like everyone else—had no clue what to do with malaria or tuberculosis. In any case, doctors only treated the top 1 percent in Egypt; everyone else trusted to luck, the gods, and home remedies.

Social Hierarchy Egyptian society was as hierarchical and unequal as human societies get. Pharaohs enjoyed a degree of authority rarely equaled elsewhere. The main threats to their position came from provincial elites and their own extended families, which often included several wives eager to see their sons on the throne and many sons and nephews hankering for a turn as pharaoh. So palace intrigues and occasional coups d'état were the essence of court politics.

An elite of powerful families surrounded the king and court, together making up perhaps 1 percent of Egyptian society. Provincial elites ran temples and estates throughout the country. Some of them amassed great wealth. Most were literate and took part in the high culture of Egypt. Artisans, normally illiterate, made up another small percentage of the population. Cities such as Memphis, Thebes, and Abydos were home to many artisans, scribes, temple priests, construction workers, beggars, and thieves; city residents accounted for less than 5 percent of the population. Close to 95 percent of Egyptians worked the land.

In one sense, Egypt was a society of immigrants. Its first settlers had wandered in from the Sahara. From the Old Kingdom onward, Egypt absorbed Nubians from the south, as slaves, mercenaries, laborers, and—as we've seen—as conquerors of the southern part of the country. After the New Kingdom, foreigners referred to as Libyans drifted in to the delta from the west, dominated some areas, and set up their own dynasties. Others came from Southwest Asia, sometimes as shepherds hoping

Immigrants A group of warriors dressed in the tunics and sandals of Semitic nomads asks permission to enter Egypt in a tomb painting from the nineteenth century BCE. This evidence may indicate the presence of ancient Hebrews in Egypt during the period.

their herds might nibble on the Nile delta's lush vegetation, sometimes as conquerors like the Assyrians. Egyptian texts indicate a few ancient Hebrews migrated to Egypt too, although they left no archeological trace. Almost all of these immigrants were "Egyptianized": they or their children learned the local tongue, came to worship the local gods, and conformed to the conventions of Egyptian culture and society. And, as immigrants generally do, they changed Egypt a little by bringing their own traditions, beliefs, artistic styles, and cooking habits with them.

The Nile valley and delta, like Mesopotamia and—as we'll see—the Ganges, was a magnet for people looking for work, food, and opportunity. All neighboring lands were poor compared to these river valleys. And the river valley environments were so unhealthy that societies in Egypt, Mesopotamia, and the Ganges often needed immigrants to take the place of the sick and the dead. The newcomers probably died at even faster rates than the native-born, but they kept coming, sometimes willingly, sometimes as slaves.

Family Life Family life in Egypt was similar to that in other ancient agrarian societies. As usual, the available evidence overwhelmingly concerns elite families and largely comes from texts authored by men until after 300 BCE. Elite women took responsibility for the domestic sphere and supervised squadrons of servants. Some texts remind men not to criticize or interfere with their wives' conduct of a household. Arranged marriage was the norm, typically around ages 12 to 14 for females and 18 to 21 for males. Divorce was possible. Women could own property and conduct trade on their own accounts. By and large, elite women didn't work outside their homes, although a very few served as priestesses. None seem to have worked in the state bureaucracy. By the seventh century BCE, marriages often included contracts that safeguarded the property of individuals, both men and women.

Children were numerous and often sickly. When healthy, they played with dice, knucklebones, dolls, and board games. They swam in the Nile, wrestled, and boxed. By age five or six, they spent much of their time working alongside their parents and older siblings. Children were beloved, regarded as gifts from the gods, but discipline could be tough: parents often beat their children to improve their behavior. That apparently didn't always work. One lad studying to be a scribe earned this report card: "[Y]ou neglect your studies and think only of pleasure. You wander through the streets, stinking of beer." Inheritance was typically equal among all children, male and female. One document from the New Kingdom shows a mother named Naunakht playing favorites among her offspring, cutting out of her will those who she felt had treated her poorly.

Gender and Class Most Egyptian women spent their adult lives tending to children, weaving cloth, baking bread, and preparing other foods. They and their families lived in humble mud-brick houses. Artwork from the Old Kingdom shows women winnowing grain—although later art shows only men doing this chore. Other images suggest that women also harvested flax and gleaned fields (gleaning involves picking up loose seeds or kernels after a harvest). Some women worked as domestic servants in elite households. Almost no women, even members of the elite, could read or write.

Class trumped gender in some respects. Elite women could command male servants, but lower-class males couldn't command elite women. Texts suggest that occasionally lower-class men could rise in government service and join the elite. Beautiful lower-class women might be recruited for the royal harem. But the great majority of people died in roughly the same circumstances into which they were born—again, much as in other agrarian societies.

There is one last point to consider about social class in ancient Egypt, one that will come up again in other contexts. The written sources about Egyptian life indicate a strong preference for social stability and order. They portray the Intermediate Periods as dark ages. From the point of view of toiling peasants, however, periods when the state was weak might have been the best of times, not the worst. After all, the state when weak had less power to extract a share of the harvest from peasant families. And fewer men were conscripted for foreign wars or building sprees.

Egyptian society developed in a context of tightening links to its neighbors. The whole Nile valley north of the Fifth Cataract formed something of its

Women's Work This statue of a woman grinding grain on a stone mill from around 2500 BCE provides a vivid example of the daily labor that Egyptian women performed at home.

own web by 2500 BCE, thanks to the ease of transport along the river. The Nile's links to Mesopotamia and indirectly to the Indus meant that a far larger Nile-Indus web was under construction by 2500 BCE and was firmly in place after Hyksos rule around 1500 BCE. By that time, people along the Ganges were beginning to build another complex society in northern India—in effect, another eastern expansion of the web.

The Ganges Basin, the Vedas, and Early India, 2000–200 BCE

Before their collapse, the Indus valley cities had stood at the easternmost edge of the web that stretched from the Nile to the Indus. As they declined, a slow frontier movement of people wafted across northern India. Many settled in the forested plains of the **Ganges basin**. These rich alluvial lands could support dense populations and numerous urban centers, provided farmers had suitable crops, tools, skills, and sufficient organization to undertake irrigation.

Most of what we know about the people of the Ganges basin (or the Gangetic plain) comes from religious texts—in sharp contrast to what we know of people in the ancient Indus, Egyptian, or Mesopotamian societies. As we've seen, the material remains of Indus valley, Egyptian, or Mesopotamian cities and villages allow us to make strong inferences about agriculture, trade, crafts, art, and architecture. With respect to the early history of the societies of the Ganges, scholars working from Sanskrit texts can reconstruct something of the spiritual and social world, but less of ancient economic life along the Ganges.

Indo-Aryan Migrations and Vedic Peoples

From around 1500 BCE, the Ganges valley became the cradle of a new Indian culture and complex society. Just how this happened, and the degree to which it involved migrant populations from outside India, are fiercely contested among specialists and political partisans in India today. The textual, archeological, linguistic, and genetic evidence is not consistent. But it looks as if pastoralist migrants from Central Asia and Iran, mainly men, filtered through mountain passes and into Punjab and the upper Ganges beginning around 2000 BCE. They spoke an Indo-European language, closely related to Iranian tongues, that evolved into Sanskrit, the sacred language of Hindu religion. The migrants called themselves *arya*, which originally meant "people from Iran" but in Sanskrit came to mean "noble." Scholars generally call them Indo-Aryans or Vedic peoples.

The newcomers to north India were herders, skilled in cattle raising and equestrian warfare. The migrants brought horses and war chariots to India, as well as new gods and rituals, often built around fire and animal sacrifice. They merged with people departing the declining settlements of the Indus valley, and together they forged a new culture, one often called Vedic after the religious texts they created—the **Vedas**.

The Gangetic plain to which Indo-Aryans and early Vedic culture came had a scattered population of foragers, hunters, and shifting cultivators as of 1500 BCE. They used mainly stone tools. Dense forests, nourished by the monsoon rains, covered most of the land.

By 1200 to 800 BCE, archeology suggests, incoming migrants had occupied the upper Ganges. They practiced their traditional cattle raising and, increasingly, settled agriculture. They gradually expanded eastward to the middle and lower Ganges, taking up rice farming as they went. The further east they moved, the more their language, Sanskrit, incorporated features of existing north Indian languages.

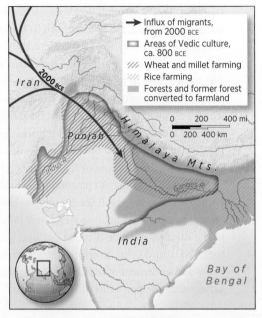

Ancient North India, ca. 2000–800 BCE Like certain other river basins before it, the Ganges came to host an interactive web of thousands of villages engaged in irrigated farming of grain crops—typically wheat, millet, or rice—in the millennium after 2000 BCE. People in these villages developed a distinctive religious tradition involving elements of ritual practice brought by migrants from Central Asia and Iran. That tradition evolved into Hinduism.

Their communities were led by religious specialists; kings and states came only after about 800 BCE. What held them together was a sense of kinship, of superiority over local folk, and a high culture encapsulated in songs and poems—the Vedas.

The Vedas

The four Vedas are the earliest extant examples of literature in Sanskrit and the oldest sacred texts of the Hindu religion. The Vedas—*veda* means "wisdom"—say they were composed by sages just "as a skilled craftsman makes a chariot." Modern scholarship says they were oral traditions recited for many centuries before being written down and may have originated as early as 1800 BCE. Memorizing the *vedas*, which include many thousand verses, required deep devotion. Their contents include hymns, myths, magic spells, and rules for carrying out rituals properly.

The earliest, the *Rig Veda*, probably dates from about 1500 to 1200 BCE as an oral tradition. People wrote it down no earlier than 1100 BCE. It shares similarities with a sacred Iranian epic, the *Avesta*, both in language and in the stories it tells. Much of its dialogue is spoken by women. It recounts the exploits of some 33 gods, most of whom were responsible for features of nature such as the sun or rivers. To stay on their good side, people had to offer them sacrifices, usually of animals ranging from bees to elephants but most often livestock. The gods in the *Rig Veda* undertake heroic and violent deeds, prize horses and cattle, and indulge in drinking, gambling, and sex. Their behavior reflected the values and self-image of a male warrior elite. In these respects, the gods of the *Rig Veda* bore strong similarities to the gods of Iran and Mesopotamia and contrasted with those of Egypt.

The early Vedas depict pastoral peoples in the process of taking up farming. Cattle raiding, horse racing, and sheep and goat herding figure prominently, but there are references to plows and fields as well. They portray a society without much specialization in the division of labor (beyond age and gender) and without villages or towns. The later Vedas (and other Sanskrit texts), composed after 800 BCE when farming loomed larger and settlement of the Ganges valley was moving eastward, show a more complex society with the first hints of urbanization.

Gender and Family Life From the Vedas and other texts, we can get some idea of family and gender relations in ancient north India. Women have speaking roles in some early Vedic hymns, and in one a young wife is invited to speak publicly. Another refers to a "learned daughter," implying that education wasn't entirely limited to males. Women could take part in religious rituals. They could boast unblushingly about their sexual prowess. Nonetheless, the Vedas also contain plenty of misogynistic views, and over time it seems the situation of women deteriorated. Later texts connect women with

Indo-Aryan Equestrians These stone figurines, dated to around 2000 BCE, suggest the importance of horses to the early Vedic peoples.

evil. One from the eighth to sixth century BCE, the *Shatapatha Brahmana*, declares: "The woman, the Sudra, the dog and the crow are falsehood." (A Sudra was a low-status person in the Hindu caste system, as we'll see shortly.) The *Law of Manu*, from about the third century BCE, portrays women as in all things dependent on fathers, husbands, and sons. The north Indian case is one of several in which the independence of women diminished as pastoral societies took up farming and created states.

Households were normally composed of multiple generations all under the authority of one senior male—a father or grandfather. Sons took part in farm work and religious rituals. Daughters took responsibility for preparing food and other household chores. All women were expected to marry, subordinate themselves to their husbands, and ideally produce sons who could perform proper funeral rites and sacrifices. Husbands were urged to honor wives and give them specific clothing and foods as gifts on holidays. Widows could not remarry (widowers could). Marriage was usually monogamous, but polygamy was not unknown. Property was held by families and perhaps by large extended families—clans—but not by individuals. Later Vedic texts sometimes consider wives as their husbands' property. Families belonged to clans and tended to live together with their kin in the same villages. Most of these social arrangements were common in ancient agrarian societies.

Social Divisions Parts of the Vedas are hardly any easier to understand than the undeciphered Indus valley script. But some sections are more straightforward, such as the story of Purusa (also spelled Purusha), the primeval giant, the "cosmic man" from whose body the world and its social order was built. Here is a condensed version, from the *Rig Veda*.

> *Thousand-headed is Purusa, thousand-eyed, thousand-footed. Having covered the earth on all sides, he stood above it the width of ten fingers.*
> *Only Purusa is all this, that which has been and that which is to be. He is the lord of the immortals, who grow by means of [ritual] food.*
> *When [the gods] divided Purusa, how many ways did they apportion him? What was his mouth? What were his arms? What were his thighs, his feet declared to be?*
> *His mouth was the Brahman [caste], his arms were the Rajanaya [Ksatriya caste], his thighs the Vaisya [caste]; from his feet the Sudra [caste] was born.*
> *The moon was born from his mind; from his eye the sun was born; from his mouth both Indra [war] and Agni [fire]; from his breath Vayu [wind] was born.*
> *From his navel arose the air; from his head the heaven evolved; from his feet the earth; the [four] directions from his ear. Thus, they fashioned the worlds.*

This excerpt allows a glimpse into the social divisions of ancient India. The most basic division, as ancient Indians saw it, was among the various castes—a social hierarchy created and sanctioned, like the moon, the sun, and the earth, by the gods.

Caste, Hierarchy, and Early Hinduism

The early migrants who drifted into the Ganges basin divided society loosely into rulers, priests, and producers. But they apparently had no rigid distinctions. Once settled, they gradually developed a four-tier hierarchy, the basis of the **caste system** that was taking shape around 1000 BCE.

Early Caste System   At the top stood priests, or Brahmins; next came rulers and soldiers, or Kshatriya; then peasants and traders, or Vaishya; and at the bottom of the hierarchy, slaves and artisans, or Sudra. Caste status was hereditary: your caste was the same as your parents' caste. It's notable that genetic admixture from Central Asia is found much more frequently among people of the Brahmin caste than among other Indians. This suggests that the migrating newcomers became religious specialists above all else—and that Brahmins generally obeyed the religious law that they should marry only fellow Brahmins. By 500 BCE, north Indian society was far different than that of a millennium before: more complex, more hierarchical, more agricultural—and more like that which already existed in Mesopotamia and Egypt.

Brahmins were held to be the most ritually pure, the least "polluted," and were expected to wear white clothing. The Sudras' black garb symbolized their impurity. But there were people who ranked even lower, people who had no caste at all, such as those who worked with hides and leather, which were considered ritually impure. They were called untouchables (and today are often known as *dalits*). Brahmins in particular tried hard to avoid them. Dozens of sub-castes eventually evolved within this four-tier structure. Doctrines and habits emerged that prohibited different castes from intermarrying or even eating together.

The Vedas and later texts spelled out the duties and privileges of all castes and provided justifications for the system as a whole. Brahmins preserved—and altered—the Vedas as oral traditions long before they were written down. It's reasonable to suppose that the position of Brahmins improved over time thanks to their role as custodians of the Vedas. All ancient agrarian societies, including those of Mesopotamia and Egypt, had systems of social rank based on birth. The north Indian caste system, embedded in the texts and laws of early Hinduism, made social rank unusually explicit. The system proved more durable than most. It still matters in India today.

Classic Hinduism   By 400 BCE, Vedic religion, with its emphasis on caste, ritual, and sacrifice, evolved into **classic** (or Brahminical) **Hinduism**. Its character is known to us partly through sacred texts such as the Upanishads, some 200 densely philosophical treatises probably composed between 800 and 100 BCE. Believers understood the tangible world to be illusion, a mere reflection of an eternal, pure, spiritual world. Ascetic meditation on this hidden but eternal world joined, and in cases replaced, animal sacrifice as the mark of religious specialists.

To the core Vedic beliefs, classic Hinduism added a powerful moral idea, the doctrine of the endless migration of souls: one's soul persists through cycles of birth and death, re-birth and re-death, and appears as living flesh in incarnations determined by one's moral conduct, or *karma*. As the *Chandogya Upanishad* put it, "Those who are of pleasant conduct here will enter a pleasant womb, that of a Brahmin, Kshatriya, or a Vaisya. But those who are of stinking conduct here will enter the womb of a dog, a pig, or an untouchable." Release from these cycles of re-birth and suffering is possible only if one performs one's duties consistently and attains true self-knowledge. (Different traditions within Hinduism understand this concept of release, *moksha* in Sanskrit, differently.) Brahmins stood closer to release than anyone else, owing to their accumulated moral record through previous incarnations.

Hindu believers also developed a notion of time that was as central to their faith as the moral code and cycle of re-birth and re-death. Like many peoples, Hindus came to believe in a golden past in which people had carried out religious obligations carefully and had behaved more ethically. They believed that time divided into four ages, in each of which morality, virtue, and religious observance (*dharma*) successively declined by a quarter. The present age, called Kali ("discord" in Sanskrit), is the worst, in which wickedness, ignorance, and conflict flourish. The Kali age precedes the destruction of the world, after which the cycle will begin again with another golden age. The current Kali age, according to conventional calculations, began on January 23, 3102 BCE, and has about 427,000 years left to run. That may seem a long time, but it's nothing compared to the time elapsed since the current cycle began, according to Hindu texts, a little over 155 trillion years ago. Hindu theology required formidable arithmetic skills to calculate the immensities of time.

Like the moral codes of other enduring religions, Hinduism provided a potent logic for accepting one's circumstances. One could hope for a better future life if one fulfilled one's duties and accumulated good karma. It was a religious idea that made social inequality and personal suffering easier to bear. Almost all complex societies with stark social hierarchy developed ideas that blunted envy and soothed suffering.

Ordinary people took comfort in several routines of worship. Anyone could appeal to any god at any time if feeling the need. On a daily basis, parents (normally fathers officiated) performed small sacrifices of rice, barley, or ghee (a form of butter) to one or more gods preferred in their household. Households also observed carefully prescribed rituals at key moments in life: birth, naming, first exposure to sunlight, first food, puberty, marriage, and above all, death. More publicly, male Brahmin priests undertook ritual sacrifices at holidays and festivals under the open sky (only after about 300 CE did temples become common). In addition, Hindu believers expressed their devotion by visiting pilgrimage sites associated with various gods, most of which lay along the banks of the Ganges. Eventually, the most important of these sites became Varanasi, where one could wash away one's sins in the river.

The Hindu pantheon was (and is) a crowded one, especially because each deity had

Vishnu A sixth-century CE relief from a Hindu temple in what is now Karnataka, southwest India, depicts the popular god Vishnu in the form of a boar.

many manifestations and equivalents. For example, Vishnu, preserver of the universe and humankind, had alternate forms as Rama or Krishna. Different traditions within Hinduism saw (and see) divinity differently, so depending on how you count there are only one, dozens, or thousands of gods and goddesses. In the early texts such as the *Rig Veda*, the most frequently mentioned are Indra, responsible for storms and warfare, and Agni, god of fire. The more popular deities of later Hinduism, such as Vishnu and Shiva, didn't figure prominently in the early Vedas. Each deity could help with specific problems, so if you needed an obstacle to some enterprise removed, you appealed to Ganesh, the elephant-headed son of Shiva; if your father was dying, you prayed to Rama; and if you wanted to enjoy good fortune, you turned to the goddess Lakshmi.

Hinduism took its enduring shape along the Ganges between 1000 BCE and 400 BCE. It is a particularly rich and variegated religious tradition, partly because it has had time to evolve in multiple directions, and partly because it has had few formal institutions to enforce conformity. Hinduism is today one of the world's great religions, accounting for about one-sixth of humankind.

Rice, Power, and the Mauryan Empire

The people who developed Hinduism found, along the Ganges, fertile soil for the creation of complex society, states, and cities. As along the Tigris-Euphrates and the Nile, religion and politics were intertwined here.

By 1000 BCE, the inhabitants of the Gangetic plain followed a mixed economy of herding and farming. The *Rig Veda* has more references to pastoralism than to agriculture, but it includes mentions of plows, oxen, irrigation, rice, lentils, and more. The upper reaches of the Ganges could support wheat and millet cultivation. The lower (and more easterly) section of the Gangetic plain suited rice.

Growing rice required different knowledge and skills from those needed for wheat, and the beginning of rice farming in India presumably indicates contacts with China, the homeland of rice cultivation. Texts are silent on this point, but genetic evidence from rice suggests that Ganges rice farmers began using seeds from China about 1700 BCE.

Everywhere along the Ganges, farmers faced two obstacles. The first was the dense forest that they had to cut and burn. Their acquisition of iron tools, beginning around 1000 to 800 BCE, eased the task of clearing forests. The second obstacle was the management of water. The Ganges swelled with summer rains brought by the Indian Ocean monsoon. The river's floodplain had many swamps. The rains came at inconvenient times for wheat and barley, the leading crops of northwest India. Farmers along the upper and middle Ganges needed to drain swamps and build irrigation networks, comparable to what had been done along the Nile, Indus, or the Tigris-Euphrates, for the benefit of agriculture. The same was true on the lower Ganges: rice farming required careful water management too.

Small Kingdoms After 800 BCE or so, the farming communities of the Gangetic plain were numerous enough and produced enough surplus food that a more specialized division of labor emerged, and with it, cities. Riverside markets grew into river port towns. Clusters of smiths and carpenters grew into manufacturing centers.

Charismatic leaders used surplus wealth—mainly foodstuffs that stored well, such as rice—to attract and reward followers. Specialists in politics and violence, usually of the Kshatri caste, successfully challenged the priestly caste for social leadership, even as they depended on the endorsement of priests to establish their authority. Small kingdoms, the first states in the Ganges valley, began to sprout when chiefs and rulers converted moral and spiritual authority into territorial control. The many new kingdoms fought one another frequently and rose and fell rapidly, often within the lifetime of a single warlord.

Magadha Then, in the fifth century BCE, a warlord managed to conquer far and wide and create a much larger state in the Ganges basin. This state was called Magadha. The scanty evidence suggests that Magadha's power rested on the spread of iron tools and rice farming in the Ganges basin, which produced enough surplus food to support a professional army, religious specialists, literate bureaucrats, artisans, and all the skilled personnel a state needs. Its rulers were not from the Kshatri caste, an obstacle to legitimacy that they overcame with military prowess.

Magadha's expansion rested in part on military innovations involving coordination of the "four-limbed" army, consisting of infantry, horse cavalry, chariot corps, and war elephants. The first mention of war elephants—uniquely important in South Asian history—comes in fourth-century BCE texts. Pachyderm power (which involved capturing elephants in forests, taming them, and training them to trample enemies) became a crucial component of political success in India. Even the most experienced and best-trained foot soldiers felt helpless (and rightly so) when faced with charging elephants. One indication of their value is that a Central Asian king traded the entire region of today's southern Afghanistan plus much of what is now Pakistan and eastern Iran, as well as one of his daughters in marriage, to an Indian prince for 500 war elephants.

Chandragupta Maurya That Indian prince was Chandragupta Maurya. He was a soldier of fortune of obscure origins, allegedly from a family of peacock tamers. He managed to overthrow the Magadha rulers, conquer neighboring states, and unite all of north India into the **Mauryan Empire**. By 321 BCE, for the first time, the valleys of the Indus and the Ganges were under the same rule, enabling a great expansion of trade and specialization in the division of labor.

A foreign diplomat, Megasthenes, left a portrait of the Mauryan Empire as of about 298 BCE. It survives today only in fragments quoted or paraphrased by other authors. Some of it was fanciful—men who could outrun horses, women who gave birth by age six, men with ears so large they used them as blankets. Some of it is overly optimistic—no famines, no slavery, almost no theft. But much of it is plausible. The Mauryan state had a powerful professional military that included an elite imperial bodyguard composed of women archers. The state controlled the supplies of horses, imported from Central Asia, and elephants. It maintained a sizeable bureaucracy and tax collection unit, and controlled trade up and down both the Indus and the Ganges. Its population was composed mainly of farmers growing rice, wheat, barley, and other crops. Its society, according to Megasthenes, was organized into seven occupation-based castes (Megasthenes included herders, artisans, bureaucrats, and judges as separate castes). This was a society far more elaborate than that described in the early Vedas and as complex as that of Mesopotamia or Egypt.

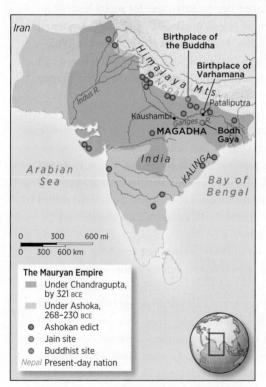

The Mauryan Empire, 321–230 BCE The Mauryan Empire rose and fell quickly, lasting roughly a century. It was the first state in South Asia to unify both productive river basins, the Ganges and the Indus. Its leaders welcomed religious diversity, while ruthlessly commanding surplus grain and other tribute from much of South Asia.

Kautilya The Mauryan Empire in Chandragupta's day (he died in 297 BCE) also had one of the cagiest political advisers ever to walk the Earth: Kautilya, whose book of advice for kings and princes, *The Arthashastra*, was found inscribed on palm fronds just over a century ago. Kautilya wrote in a most practical vein with little reference to the supernatural. His manual of statecraft contains practical advice on everything a king might need to survive and prosper in a world of pitiless political competition. He advised his boss on how to out-maneuver rivals, relying on spies,

CONSIDERING THE EVIDENCE

Death and Taxes in the Mauryan Empire

Megasthenes was a Greek diplomat who visited India during the expansion of the Mauryan Empire. His original writings, like many historical texts, have been lost, but later writers had preserved fragments of his observations as quotations in their own works.

Besides describing India's caste system, Megasthenes reported on the administration of justice, geography, and the training of war elephants. In the following excerpt, he describes the work of India's royal officials in their capital city.

Some superintend the rivers, measure the land, as is done in Egypt, and inspect the sluices . . . so that every one [*sic*] may have an equal supply of it. The same persons have charge also of the huntsmen, and are entrusted with the power of rewarding or punishing them. . . . They collect the taxes, and superintend . . . the woodcutters, the carpenters, the blacksmiths, and the miners. . . . Those who have charge of the city are divided into six bodies of five each. The members of the first look after everything relating to the industrial arts. Those of the second attend to the entertainment of foreigners. . . . They escort them on the way when they leave the country, or, in the event of their dying, forward their property to their relatives. . . . The third body consists of those who inquire when and how births and deaths occur, with the view not only of levying a tax, but also in order that births and deaths among both high and low may not escape the cognizance of Government. The fourth class superintends trade and commerce. Its members have charge of weights and measures, and see that the products in their season are sold by public notice.

No one is allowed to deal in more than one kind of commodity unless he pays a double tax. The fifth class supervises manufactured articles, which they sell by public notice. What is new is sold separately from what is old, and there is a fine for mixing the two together. The sixth and last class consists of those who collect the tenths of the prices of the articles sold. Fraud in the payment of this tax is punished with death.

Questions for Analysis

1. What sorts of activities did the government of the Mauryan Empire keep track of, and why? For which offense was the death penalty reserved?

2. What similarities did Megasthenes notice between India and Egypt? What similarities do you notice, both in this excerpt and in the chapter?

3. Does Megasthenes's status as an outsider make it more or less likely that his description of India's society is accurate? Who do you suppose he got his information from?

Source: J. W. McCrindle, *Ancient India: As Described by Megasthenes and Arrian* (London, 1877).

deceit, and ruthlessness as needed. He made recommendations for coping with potential assassins within one's family. Some of his advice for kings is useful for students today: cultivate the intellect by association with learned elders; avoid daydreaming and addiction to drink, lust, or gambling; schedule 90 minutes a day for recreation and contemplation. However, Kautilya also imprudently recommended only four and one-half hours sleep per night.

Ashoka   The Mauryan Empire conquered far and wide under Chandragupta's son and grandson. Ashoka, the grandson, was one of world history's most unusual rulers. He took the reins in about 268 BCE and added territory through conquests in eastern India. When his armies slaughtered thousands upon thousands of one tribal people, the Kalingas, Ashoka, full of remorse, suffered a spiritual crisis. When walking through a corpse-strewn battlefield, he allegedly said:

> What have I done? Is this a victory? What's a defeat then? Is this justice or injustice? Is this gallantry or a rout? Is it valor to kill innocent children and women? Did I do it to widen the empire or for prosperity or to destroy the other's kingdom or splendor? Someone has lost her husband, someone a father, someone a child, someone an unborn infant.... What's this debris of the corpses? Are these marks of victory or defeat? Are these vultures, crows, eagles the messengers of death or evil? What have I done!

We know about Ashoka's anxieties because he had dozens of inscriptions carved on rocks and pillars scattered around India. Ashoka's spiritual crisis—probably a quest for self-purification—took the form of deepened commitment to the tenets of Buddhism, a new religion with a strong ascetic streak. His rock and pillar edicts urge his people to avoid animal sacrifice, practice non-violence toward all people and animals, respect all faiths, and love justice and fairness. Ashoka had roads built, wells dug, shade trees planted, and in general sought to promote the welfare of people under his rule. He renounced wars of expansion—although in one of his edicts he warned a forest people not to resist his authority. His principles, after his conqueror's remorse, were about as far from those of Kautilya as a ruler can get. Like most people, he didn't always live up to his principles, and in one of his rock edicts he admitted that despite his efforts his palace kitchen still killed two peacocks a day and often a deer as well. It's a rare ruler who inscribes his own moral failings in stone.

Ashoka's pillars were erected all over India except for the far south. But he probably didn't fully control all that territory. The Mauryan Empire was more likely a collection of cities and rich agrarian hinterlands under direct imperial rule, with stretches of uncontrolled mountainous and forested land in between. When Ashoka died around 230 BCE, the Mauryan Empire soon fragmented. Its last remnant disappeared in 187 BCE, after which India once again became an arena of small states, often at war among themselves.

New Indian Religions

While Chandragupta Maurya, Ashoka, and their successors were gaining and losing empires, a religious revolution was overtaking India. The Vedic traditions that had evolved into Hinduism acquired new rivals. In the middle of the first millennium BCE, many people in north India were experimenting with novel approaches to faith and ritual. They found some aspects of Hindu practice unappealing.

Dissent and Social Change The most enduring of these spiritual experiments were Buddhism and Jainism. Like Hinduism, from which they are offshoots, both were (and are) religions of renunciation, in the sense that their doctrines emphasize the rejection of earthly desire. If one could abandon desire and cease all actions harmful to other life forms, one might achieve release from the endless cycle of re-birth and re-death, and attain a state of infinite understanding and bliss that Buddhists call *nirvana* (akin to the Hindu *moksha*). This ideal required pious Jains to follow a path of non-violence, truthfulness, non-acquisitiveness, and, for monks and nuns, celibacy. Pious Jains will not knowingly kill even a mosquito. Hindu sacrifice of animals and other Vedic rituals offended Jains and Buddhists alike. They had no use for Brahmins, nor for caste.

An even more radical departure from Hindu belief arose at the same time. Charvaka was a school of thought that rejected all spirituality including soul, afterlife, and karma, denied the authority of all sacred texts and priests, and claimed that the only reality is the one people can perceive.

Buddhism and Jainism, and other creeds and philosophies that didn't last as long, such as Charvaka, arose as dissent from Vedic religion and revolts against the social order. That order was changing after 500 BCE as iron tools and rice cultivation spread in north India. Larger food surpluses encouraged the emergence of more and bigger cities, mainly along the Ganges. Kaushambi (also spelled Kosambi), for example, a commercial center on a tributary of the Ganges, attained a population of roughly 36,000 by 500 BCE. River trade burgeoned, and people were accumulating more wealth, including some for whom their caste status was an irritating constraint. Many felt that Brahmins and Kshatriyas didn't deserve their exalted position and that animal sacrifice was wasteful and cruel. City life generally inspires people to question the established social order. Cities along the Ganges had that effect.

Roots of Jainism The slender textual and archeological evidence suggests that Jainism took shape after the sixth century BCE. One of its great proponents, Varhamana (also known as Mahavira), starting at age 30 wandered for 13 years as a naked beggar before achieving enlightenment and spreading his wisdom throughout the Ganges plain. He took his ascetic principles so seriously that he starved himself to death. Jainism, despite its demands on believers, acquired many followers in the early years of

Jainism Built in the fifteenth century CE, the Jain temple at Ranakpur in western India is one of Jainism's most important religious sites.

the Mauryan Empire. Chandragupta himself took an interest in Jainism, supported its monasteries, and by some accounts late in life devoted himself to that religion. Jainism, like Buddhism, appealed to merchants and artisans, who didn't enjoy high status in Hindu culture. Its rejection of all forms of killing made it unsuitable for farmers, hunters, fisherfolk—indeed, anyone inclined to squash a bug. A demanding faith, it remained a minority creed in India, confined mainly to cities and towns, and never spread much beyond India. But it continues to be influential among modern India's business and financial elite.

Roots of Buddhism Buddhism in many ways offered a more accessible, less demanding path than Jainism. **Siddhartha Gautama**, the Buddha (the Enlightened One), was born a Kshatri caste prince in what is now lowland Nepal sometime in the sixth or fifth century BCE, a rough contemporary of Varhamana. Spurning his privileged inheritance, he wandered for years, including a visit to the city of Kaushambi, trying to understand the sorrows and sufferings of the world. According to tradition, enlightenment came to him after he sat for 49 days beneath a pipal tree (a variety of fig) in Bodh Gaya, a village in north India. Sorrow and disappointment, he realized, spring from desire; and if one could abandon all desire, one could find a path to wisdom and contentment, escape the endless cycle of re-birth and re-death, and achieve nirvana.

Institutions and Beliefs Buddhist doctrine is recorded in several texts, some purported to be the words of the Buddha himself, others to be writings of his followers. These began as oral traditions, like the Vedas, but eventually were written down in a language called Pali, similar to Sanskrit but more in use by common people. Unlike Hinduism, Buddhism built an institutional framework with monks and monasteries at the center. Monks took primary responsibility for maintaining, and modifying, Buddhism's spiritual heritage. Buddhism probably invented monasteries: communities set apart from society as a whole in which monastic membership replaced family and other social ties, and everyone devoted themselves to religious exercises. Monasteries also trained missionaries who could explain the insights of the Buddha to anyone willing to listen. This formed another contrast with Hinduism, in which there was little missionary work. Supporting monasteries financially was good for anyone's moral balance sheet, and dozens of them flourished.

Buddhism, like Jainism, held particular appeal for merchants and entrepreneurs. It didn't recognize the caste privileges of priests and warriors. While its doctrines encouraged asceticism and begging among monks, it also legitimated the quest for riches. One text credits the Buddha with these words:

> *Whoso is virtuous and intelligent,*
> *Shines like fire that blazes,*
> *To him amassing wealth, like a roving bee*
> *Its honey gathering,*
> *Riches mount up as an ant-heap growing high.*
> *When the good layman wealth has so amassed*
> *Able is he to benefit his clan.*

The layman who has amassed wealth can support not only his clan, but his local monastery as well.

The core beliefs of Buddhism evolved over time. Although for most Buddhists there is no god, some of the Buddha's followers eventually awarded him divine status—against his wishes. Within four or five centuries of his death, Buddhism split into two main doctrinal camps, called Mahayana (or the Greater Vehicle) and Theravada (the Lesser Vehicle). They differ on just what is required for enlightenment. The Mahayana view holds that anyone can attain nirvana and can do so in one lifetime if one tries hard enough. Theravada Buddhists believe that only monks and nuns can achieve enlightenment; everyone else first has to be re-born as monk or nun. Mahayana became the majority sect and today is dominant in Tibet, China, Japan, and Korea. The Theravada school is more important in Southeast Asia and Sri Lanka. Each is by now subdivided into many smaller sects.

Buddhism and Jainism weren't for everyone. Pastoralists needed to kill animals. Anyone who cherished fire rituals, animal sacrifices, the Vedas, or caste privileges wouldn't admire Buddhism or Jainism. They emphasized an ethical commitment to all humankind rather than privileges and constraints based on caste status.

Buddhists and Jains found the question of whether or not women could achieve enlightenment a divisive one. The voices recorded in the relevant texts are all men's. The Buddha himself at first thought women should stay at home, but later he decided they could become devotees as nuns, if always subordinate to monks. Remarks attributed to him (although perhaps the work of his followers) castigate women as by nature envious, greedy, unwise, and sensual—common notions at the time. Buddhist sects differed as to whether women could attain enlightenment as women, or whether they first must be reincarnated as males. None of the Buddha's 547 past lives, as recorded in Buddhist tradition, were lived as a female, even those he lived as an animal. Jains, for their part, debated for 1,500 years whether women could attain enlightenment, an issue that turned on whether or not life as a naked beggar was required; all parties agreed that was out of the question for women.

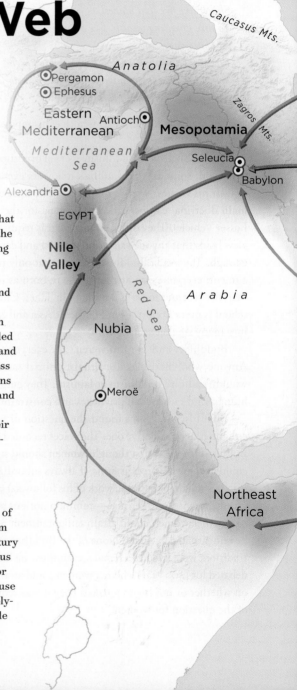

THE HUMAN WEB

The Nile-Ganges Web

200 BCE

POLYBIUS (ca. 200–ca. 118 BCE), a Greek historian, recognized some of the globalizing changes under way in his time. But the integration he observed was only part of a longer trend that extended to larger spaces. Beginning with the exchanges among Mesopotamian cities going back at least to 3000 BCE, a slow process of web building took hold that eventually spanned the entire area between the Nile and the Ganges river valleys.

Countless people spun this web through their actions. Traders trudged, rode, or sailed from city to city, carrying food, cloth, salt, and hides. Soldiers and refugees streamed across territories. Monks and sages spread religions such as Zoroastrianism and Buddhism far and wide. Travelers also transferred technologies and pathogens along routes that by their actions they were fusing into the first large-scale web in human history.

The regions of this web were in at least intermittent and indirect contact with one another by 200 BCE, and often in sustained and direct contact. Egyptian artwork made of lapis lazuli, a turquoise stone imported from Afghanistan, had become a sought-after luxury among prosperous Egyptians before Polybius was born. War elephants, first developed for military advantage in India, had come into use in Greece by Polybius's time. History, as Polybius observed, had become an organic whole throughout the Nile-Ganges web.

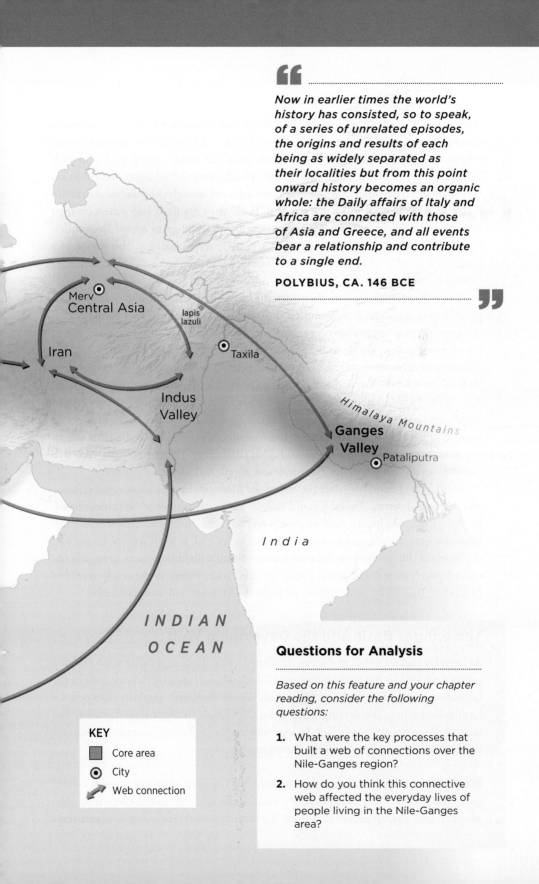

> Now in earlier times the world's history has consisted, so to speak, of a series of unrelated episodes, the origins and results of each being as widely separated as their localities but from this point onward history becomes an organic whole: the Daily affairs of Italy and Africa are connected with those of Asia and Greece, and all events bear a relationship and contribute to a single end.

POLYBIUS, CA. 146 BCE

Merv
Central Asia
lapis lazuli
Iran
Taxila
Indus Valley
Himalaya Mountains
Ganges Valley
Pataliputra

India

INDIAN OCEAN

KEY

Core area
City
Web connection

Questions for Analysis

Based on this feature and your chapter reading, consider the following questions:

1. What were the key processes that built a web of connections over the Nile-Ganges region?

2. How do you think this connective web affected the everyday lives of people living in the Nile-Ganges area?

Religious Pluralism Hinduism, Buddhism, and Jainism (and some less prominent creeds) competed for followers in the Mauryan era and beyond. Competition among religions usually breeds innovations—often, ones that make a creed more accessible and appealing, and so it was in north India. Hinduism and Buddhism evolved forms that emphasized devotion to *bodhisattvas*, who achieved enough enlightenment to attain moksha or nirvana but by choice stayed in the human realm to help others on their way. Many Indians came to believe that some deities could grant release from suffering directly, freeing people from the slow ascent via reincarnations. This notion of a faster track to release had obvious appeal, but for some people the more arduous route seemed the only true one.

These three religions, with their literature, art, architecture, and moral codes, all spread widely throughout India and a little beyond—along some but not all the strands of a growing web. Sometimes they spread with the assistance of rulers such as Ashoka, but often without, propelled by the power of moral example. Except for Buddhism, they did not have missionaries. In the early centuries CE, as we'll see, maritime connections took Indian religion, art, and architecture to newly forming royal courts in Southeast Asia. Trans-Himalayan routes followed by traders and the occasional missionary carried Buddhism to Tibet and eventually to China. Indian religions didn't make much of an imprint in Southwest Asia. Although more strongly connected to India than almost anyone else, people there found their own gods satisfactory. The existence of strong web connections did not guarantee the movement of religious ideas and culture.

Political fragmentation after the end of the Mauryan Empire encouraged cultural and religious diversity. No king could enforce any orthodoxy over the Ganges basin, let alone the whole Indian subcontinent. Over the centuries, India experienced a few brief moments of unification—the Mauryan Empire and, as we'll see, the Gupta and the Moghuls. But more often than not it was politically divided, helping to explain the rich religious pluralism of India. Yet, at the same time, owing to the steady spread of Hinduism, Buddhism, and Jainism, all India shared broad cultural similarities.

The Ganges Basin and the Developing Web

As complex society, cities, and states developed along the Ganges after 1000 BCE, the region deepened its ties to the wider world. Its strongest links, by far, extended to the northwest, toward Iran and Southwest Asia. To the northeast, the Himalaya posed a formidable barrier. The developments along the Ganges in effect extended what had been a Nile-Indus web into a Nile-Ganges web beginning faintly around 1500 BCE and firmly in place by 300 BCE with the Mauryan state.

Biological Links The connections between the Gangetic plain and the wider world took many forms. On a biological level, north India acquired several crops from elsewhere. Wheat and barley had come long ago from Southwest Asia, and rice came from

China by 1700 BCE. Millets and sorghums came from northeast Africa, presumably by maritime trade routes, and were in use by 1000 BCE. North India acquired horses from Iran and Central Asia by 2000 BCE and sustained a horse import trade ever after. There's evidence of Indian cattle breeds as far west as Syria by 1500 BCE, and by Mauryan times India exported war elephants to kings in Southwest Asia. Beyond these biological links for which good evidence exists, there was also the almost certain exchange of pathogens such as smallpox, which arrived in north India after 1000 BCE from Central and Southwest Asia.

Culture, Trade, and Conflict On a cultural level, as we've seen, north India imported language and religious practices from Iran, and over time melded that with local forms into Sanskrit and Hinduism. Two of the early Hindu epics contain a flood story that resembles the Mesopotamian one and that of the Hebrew Bible. By the time

Buddha of Bamyan An enormous stone Buddha carved into the side of a mountain in Afghanistan in 554 CE testifies to the spread of Buddhism beyond India. It was destroyed by the Taliban in 2001.

of the Mauryans, artistic motifs flowed back and forth between north India and Iran: capitals on columns of the Mauryan palace in Pataliputra resemble Iranian and Greek capitals. Elephant sculpture appeared in Iran and Syria after 300 BCE.

In terms of trade and technology, north India's links to Southwest Asia were especially strong. Chariots came from Iran. Iron working came from either Southwest or Central Asia. North India imported jade and horses from Central Asia, and woolen cloth from Mesopotamia. It exported gold, elephant ivory, honey, indigo (for making dyes), and wood to Mesopotamia and Persian Gulf ports. The Mauryan Empire maintained flourishing caravan routes to the northwest by land and maritime routes across the Arabian Sea. It had weaker trade connections to the east, into the Bay of Bengal, and to southernmost India.

Finally, on a political level, Mauryan armies fought frontier wars with various powers in Southwest Asia. In addition, Ashoka sent diplomatic embassies to Syria, Anatolia, and as far as northwest Greece in search of allies. The Mauryans introduced to India a new element of statecraft—minted coins, a practice borrowed from Southwest Asia.

Conclusion

In this chapter, we've seen two expansions of world history's first big web, which had initially formed around a core area of Mesopotamia and the Indus valley. Connections with Egypt, although they began long ago, took hold around 2500 BCE and solidified with the arrival there of the Hyksos (1700–1500 BCE). As those links were firming up, new ones with north India were developing. Migrations into the Ganges valley paved the way for stronger connections between north India and Southwest Asia after 1500 BCE, and the rise of the Mauryan state by 300 BCE solidified those links, consolidating what was now a Nile-Ganges web.

The complex societies that formed along the Nile and the Ganges lay on the frontiers of this newly expanded web. To the east of the Ganges, and to the west and south of Egypt and Nubia, populations were sparser and their connections to the wider world weaker. So it makes sense to see the region from the Nile to the Ganges as a giant web in full operation by 300 BCE. It extended threads—intermittent links—into the adjacent parts of Africa and Asia, and as later chapters will show, into Mediterranean Europe.

The two frontiers of the Nile and Ganges showed contrasts and commonalities. Along the Nile after 3100 BCE, unity was frequent and came to be regarded as natural. Along the Ganges, political disunity was the rule. In both places—as in all complex societies—sharp social and political hierarchies prevailed. Along the Ganges, but not the Nile, these hierarchies became formalized in a caste system.

Religion underpinned both social systems. Although pharaohs liked to boast of their brutality against foreigners, there is little evidence of systematic resort to violence as a tool of government within Egypt. India's Mauryan emperors likewise did not shrink from slaughtering foreigners, but rarely found it necessary to butcher their subjects. Along both the Nile and the Ganges, rulers generally succeeded in winning moral authority through religion and, in effect, alliance with priests—a pattern we've seen before in Mesopotamia and will see again elsewhere.

The underlying philosophies of Egyptian and Indian religion were quite different. Egyptian religion had no endless cycle of re-birth from which one could only find release by fulfilling one's duties meticulously. The pantheons of Hinduism and of Egyptian religion bore only passing resemblance to one another, although both had many gods with specific responsibilities and powers. Both had loose connections to Mesopotamian religion, in one case by way of the Levant and in the other through Iran. Despite the differences in detail, religious life along the Ganges and the Nile both served to ease the suffering and salve the resentment of the poor and downtrodden—the great majority of the population in both places.

Chapter Review

KEY TERMS

Nile River p. 148

Nubia p. 150

pharaohs p. 150

Narmer p. 151

hieroglyphs p. 154

Hyksos p. 156

pyramids p. 159

shabti p. 162

Ganges basin p. 168

Vedas p. 169

caste system p. 172

classic Hinduism p. 172

Mauryan Empire p. 176

Siddhartha Gautama p. 180

REVIEW QUESTIONS

1. How did the Nile contribute to Egypt's political unification?

2. Explain "low Niles" and their social and political consequences.

3. Describe Egypt's relationship with Nubia when Egyptian pharaohs were strong, and when Nubian kings were strong.

4. What was *maat*, and how did the pharaohs maintain it?

5. How did the Egyptian understanding of the afterlife change over time?

6. Why did Egypt both attract and need many immigrants?

7. Define the four primary tiers of the early caste system in India.

8. In what key ways did classic Hinduism evolve from Vedic religion?

9. What were the two biggest obstacles facing farmers in the Gangetic plain?

10. How were Jainism and Buddhism linked to dissent and social change?

11. How was the Ganges valley linked biologically, culturally, politically, and through trade to Mesopotamia?

12. What were the main similarities between the complex societies that emerged along the Nile and the Ganges?

Go to INQUIZITIVE

to see what you've learned—and learn what you've missed—with personalized feedback along the way.

Building the Old World Web

PERSIA, GREECE, AND THE HELLENISTIC WORLD

600 BCE to 200 CE

FOCUS QUESTIONS

1. In what ways was multiculturalism a strength of the Achaemenid Empire?

2. How did political fragmentation contribute to the dynamism of Greek culture?

3. How was Alexander the Great able to establish a vast empire?

4. How did a developing market culture connect people within the Nile-Ganges web during the Hellenistic age?

Webs of connection are sometimes visible in images. A coin (see p. 190) from what is now eastern Afghanistan, in the second century BCE, displays an image of Hercules, a hero from Greek myth, with his club and lionskin. One side of the coin shows Greek writing that says "of King Demetrius," and the other shows a profile of the king. He seems to be wearing an elephant head, complete with tusks and trunk, as a hat.

Another image (see p. 190) comes from eastern Pakistan and was carved in stone during the first or second century CE. It shows the Buddha in human form, wearing a halo and a toga-like garment draped over both shoulders. This is striking: the earliest Buddhist art usually depicts the Buddha abstractly, and when he's shown in human form, he's wearing a loincloth, not a toga. Every fold and wrinkle of the toga is carved with great skill. How should we understand this?

These are examples of Greco-Buddhist art. As we will see, armies that were culturally Greek invaded Central Asia in the fourth century BCE, led by a young Macedonian king, Alexander the Great. Over the next several centuries, Greek language, culture, religion, and artistic styles spread in and among cities in what is now northern Pakistan, Afghanistan, and westernmost China. Local people, who were mainly Buddhist, adopted these styles. They built new Buddhist temples with columns that would have looked at home in a Greek temple. They carved reliefs of bodhisattvas surrounded by Greek gods or figures from Greek myth. They fused Greek and Buddhist traditions, myths, and styles. And they continued to do so for about a thousand years after Alexander the Great's invasion.

Greco-Buddhist art allows us, in effect, to see the formation of a bigger, thicker web of interaction extending from the Mediterranean through Central Asia and into China. This chapter explains how the process happened. It presents the history of the first superpower in world history—a Persian state that stretched from India to Egypt and for two centuries pursued policies that helped to integrate that vast space economically and culturally. And it recounts the political, intellectual, and commercial traditions of the ancient Greeks, which the conquests of Alexander the Great spread throughout this vast region.

The Achaemenids of Persia

For 3,000 years after the emergence of complex societies in Southwest Asia, the broad region from Egypt to north India remained a political patchwork. Even the Assyrians with their giant armies and iron weapons couldn't conquer so

CHRONOLOGY

ca. 2500–1400 BCE Minoan palace culture of Crete

By 2000 BCE Introduction of sailing boats in eastern Mediterranean

ca. 1900 BCE Earliest example of alphabetic writing

ca. 1500–1200 BCE First traces of Greek language and culture

ca. 1400 BCE Mycenaeans occupy Crete

ca. 1000 BCE Phoenicians begin writing with alphabet

ca. 1000–900 BCE Founding of Sparta

ca. 700 BCE Song-poem *Iliad* is written down; Greeks develop the *polis*

559–530 BCE Reign of Cyrus II

ca. 559–330 BCE Achaemenid imperial rule

522–486 BCE Reign of Darius

508/7–322 BCE Athenian use of democracy

490–480 BCE Persian Wars

486–465 BCE Reign of Xerxes

ca. 470–399 BCE Lifetime of Socrates

431–404 BCE Peloponnesian War

427–348 BCE Lifetime of Plato

384–322 BCE Lifetime of Aristotle

356–323 BCE Lifetime of Alexander the Great

331 BCE Alexander the Great founds Alexandria

323–31 BCE Hellenistic age

311 BCE Seleucid dynasty emerges

247 BCE–224 CE Height of Parthian dynasty

The Hellenistic World A coin issued by the ruler of Bactria (located in what is now Afghanistan) features an image of Hercules and the king's name in Greek, indicating the far-reaching spread of Greek language and culture.

Greco-Buddhist Art Trade and communication links could lead to the fusion of Mediterranean and Asian cultures: here, a representation of the Buddha from first- or second-century Central Asia depicts him wearing a toga with folds like those that appear on Greek statuary.

vast a space. Then, in an astonishing shift in pattern, an obscure dynasty from what is now southwestern Iran managed to unify the whole region in just a few decades in the middle of the sixth century BCE. This dynasty is called the **Achaemenids** (or Achaemenians). At their height, they ruled over about 20 to 30 million people—roughly 20 to 30 percent of humankind. Only one state in world history—China's Ming dynasty (1368–1644 CE)—ever ruled a higher proportion of the human race.

Compared to the Assyrians or Egyptians, we don't know much about the Achaemenids. Greek historians such as Herodotus, whose home city of Halicarnassus was controlled by the Achaemenids, are among our best sources. His *Histories* is mainly a narrative account of the empire. But Herodotus included tall tales for entertainment value, and he knew only the western part of the empire well. He depicted the Achaemenids as a decadent, despotic foil against which to highlight the virtues of the Greeks. The Achaemenids themselves left royal inscriptions and tens of thousands of cuneiform tablets in several languages. They shed light mainly on economic and social issues. Archeology supplements these written sources.

The Rise of the Achaemenid Dynasty

The Achaemenids arose from a people called Persians, who hailed from the foothills of the Zagros Mountains and the western Iranian plateau. Before they acquired an empire, their language—an Indo-European tongue—was not written, and they had scant urban tradition and no monumental architecture. Starting in 559 BCE, however, under a king named Cyrus II, they built an imperial state that eclipsed any previous ones in size and power. This imperial state conquered all the major powers from Egypt to northwestern India. It was the first superpower in world history.

Cyrus II must have been both a lucky and a skilled military commander. He toppled local monarchs, then swung west into Anatolia (Asia Minor) and conquered Lydia, a kingdom that pioneered the use of coins and was known for its wealth. In 539 BCE, Cyrus took over Babylonia and all of Mesopotamia, cagily presenting himself as the chosen instrument of Marduk—the god of the city of Babylon—for the liberation of oppressed peoples. He is warmly remembered in the Old Testament's books of Ezra and Isaiah for ending the Babylonian captivity of the ancient Hebrews and restoring them to Jerusalem. In a public inscription, he boasted of his respect for religious traditions. Whatever his other merits, Cyrus had a shrewd cultural policy—not unlike Sargon's 1,500 years before—by which he embraced the religions of the people he conquered, encouraging the defeated to adopt him as their rightful king. He died on campaign in Central Asia in 530 BCE.

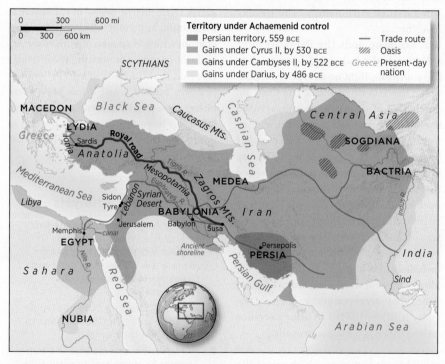

Territory under Achaemenid Control, 559–486 BCE A Persian dynasty that took the name Achaemenid became the world's first superpower in the sixth and fifth centuries BCE, uniting the oases of Central Asia with the riverine societies of Mesopotamia and Egypt. Its borders stretched from the Nile to the Indus, but through imperial policies and the daily routines of merchants, travelers, soldiers, and many others, the Achaemenid Empire consolidated and extended the web stretching from the Nile to India.

CONSIDERING THE EVIDENCE

Herodotus on the Persians

Like other Greek writers, Herodotus intended his *Histories* for performance. He interrupted detailed accounts of wars and revolts by sharing with his Greek audiences odd tales and other information about customs among Persians, Egyptians, and other people. Later writers accused him of making things up for entertainment. Yet, in his description of Persian customs below, Herodotus carefully distinguishes between what he saw and what others told him during his travels around the Mediterranean Sea and along the Nile in Egypt.

131. The customs which I know the Persians to observe are the following. They have no images of the gods, no temples nor altars, and consider the use of them a sign of folly. This comes, I think, from their not believing the gods to have the same nature with men, as the Greeks imagine....

132. To these gods the Persians offer sacrifice in the following manner: they raise no altar, light no fire, pour no libations; there is no sound of the flute, no putting on of chaplets, no consecrated barley-cake; but the man who wishes to sacrifice brings his victim to a spot of ground which is pure from pollution, and there calls upon the name of the god to whom he intends to offer.... The sacrificer is not allowed to pray for blessings on himself alone, but he prays for the welfare of the king, and of the whole Persian people, among whom he is of necessity included.... When all is ready, one of the Magi comes forward and chants a hymn, which they say recounts the origin of the gods. It is not lawful to offer sacrifice unless there is a Magus present.

...

135. There is no nation which so readily adopts foreign customs as the Persians. Thus, they have taken the dress of the Medes, considering it superior to their own; and in war they wear the Egyptian breastplate. As soon as they hear of any luxury, they instantly make it their own....

...

140. Thus much I can declare of the Persians with entire certainty, from my own actual knowledge. There is another custom which is spoken of with reserve, and not openly, concerning their dead. It is said that the body of a male Persian is never buried, until it has been torn either by a dog or a bird of prey. That the Magi have this custom is beyond a doubt, for they practise it without any concealment.

Questions for Analysis

1. Herodotus is careful to note the lack of fire, music, and altars in Persian worship. How does he explain the differences between Greek and Persian religious practices?

2. How did adopting customs from other people help the Persians to strengthen their empire?

3. Herodotus suggests that the burial custom he describes may be a rumor. Should historians include information that they think may be untrue? Why or why not?

Source: *The History of Herodotus*, Vol. 1, ed. and trans. George Rawlinson (New York: 1861).

Cyrus's son, Cambyses II, continued the Persian expansion. He conquered Egypt in 525 BCE and made himself pharaoh. Like many an earlier pharaoh, he tried to conquer Nubia but failed. Like his father, he ruled through local elites and folded local religion into his ruling ideology. With their conquests, the Persians held the two richest regions in the world at this time: Mesopotamia and Egypt. They also nominally controlled many other lands from Anatolia to Central Asia, although much of the region was pasture, home to nomads who rarely paid tribute to anyone. The empire of Cyrus and Cambyses was a loose one. Its size made it a hard empire to rule.

The Achaemenid Empire (ca. 550–330 BCE)

The empire contained farmers, herders, and city-dwellers of many ethnicities and religions. It included peoples accustomed to ruling themselves, and many who regarded the Persians—plausibly enough—as upstarts. Stitching together all these constituencies was a challenge. Revolts popped up in Cambyses's time, during one of which he died in mysterious circumstances. A few months later, in 522 BCE, his lance-bearer, **Darius**, then about 27 years old, pulled off a coup d'état. He claimed descent from a Persian king named Achaemenes, and from this point forward the Persian kings were called Achaemenids.

The State An empire this large required good communications, bureaucracy, and armed forces. Darius, whose talent lay as much in consolidation as in conquest, was equal to the challenge. Early in his long reign (r. 522–486 BCE), he had to put down revolts left and right. He then added new territory along the Indus River and the North African coast as far west as Libya, and chased a nomadic confederation, the Scythians, north of the Black Sea. To project power over such distances, Darius adopted a system of mounted couriers and post stations, pioneered on a smaller scale by the Assyrians. His system made it possible to carry information quickly throughout his empire from the banks of the Nile to those of the Indus. (Herodotus found this especially impressive and wrote, "Neither snow, nor rain, nor heat, nor dark of night prevents these couriers" from their appointed rounds, a phrase adopted over 2,000 years later by the U.S. Post Office as its motto.) To make the courier system fully effective, Darius had roads and bridges built throughout the empire. One of the important routes was a "royal road" connecting the cities of Sardis in western Anatolia and Susa in western Iran. Horsemen clattering along this road could transmit messages over 1,500 miles (2,500 km) in about 12 days. The Achaemenids even developed a system of mountaintop bonfires to send information faster still.

Darius supplemented his communications system with a carefully crafted bureaucracy. He solidified his rule by building on an inherited structure of provinces (called satrapies) with hand-picked governors (satraps) who were usually ethnic Persians. Each satrap had to furnish a specified amount of gold or silver, extracted from conquered peoples, to the Achaemenids. Satraps had to maintain roads and provide soldiers when Darius wanted to launch a campaign. Persians, although liable for military service, paid no taxes. The Achaemenids allowed local traditions to continue and local elites to retain some power—as long as they supported the dynasty.

Darius also organized his army crisply, forging a tight hierarchical force integrating infantry and both light and heavy cavalry. Many rulers before Darius had fielded infantry and light cavalry, meaning horsemen typically armed with bow and arrow. Darius's **heavy cavalry** was an innovation: big, strong horses able to carry riders, weaponry, and armor—precursors to the steeds of medieval European knights, almost as terrifying as Indian war elephants, and capable of charging and often trampling anyone in their way. Darius's army, like his bureaucracy, was multiethnic but Persian at the top. According to Herodotus, Darius's elite unit, known optimistically as the "The Immortals," numbered exactly 10,000. When a man was killed, another instantly was promoted to take his place.

Darius was an innovative ruler. However, governing such a big empire also required reliance on tried-and-true methods. He included in his imperial management playbook techniques such as the construction of monumental architecture and the use of religion as political ideology. In the grand tradition of Mesopotamian monarchs, Darius built a new ceremonial city, Persepolis, in southwestern Iran. His minions leveled a sloping hillside and erected palaces and temples made of precisely cut stone, all behind a triple wall, the height of which reached 40 ft. (12 m) according to ancient authors. Persepolis also had an elevated water storage tank and sewage tunnels dug through rock. Darius spared no expense to make Persepolis an awe-inspiring monument to his rule. He used artistic motifs, such as griffins—mythical beasts with the head of an eagle and the body of a lion—that symbolized strength, power, kingship, and perhaps the fusion of cultures.

Since no clear rule of succession existed, palace intrigues and power struggles among royal sons were routine. According to Herodotus, royal wives maneuvered to get their sons into power—their political conniving struck Herodotus as a sign of Persian decadence. Aspirants to the throne and newly installed kings often killed their brothers to consolidate their position. All this was normal for monarchies without fixed rules of succession, and although it led to frequent political crises and occasional civil wars, it was a system that ensured no weaklings came to power.

Achaemenid kings had to prove themselves as politically ruthless and militarily capable. They led their troops into battle personally. They increasingly relied on mercenaries: soldiers of shifting loyalties who fought for whoever paid best. Mercenaries—many of them Arabs, Indians, Central Asians, and Greeks—were hired from the edges of the empire. These hired soldiers played something of the same role with respect to Persia as Nubians did to pharaonic Egypt: they provided military manpower but occasionally, when their loyalty strayed, proved to be a thorn in the imperial side.

Achaemenid Religion Like all other monarchs, Darius found ways to use religion to secure his power. Cyrus had enlisted the Babylonian deity Marduk on his behalf, and Cambyses exploited Egyptian divine kingship in his own interest. Darius and later Achaemenids linked their regime with the worship of a god named **Ahura Mazda**, an all-knowing and benevolent creator who with human help would eventually vanquish evil and darkness. The Ahura Mazda rituals were similar to those described in the *Rig Veda*, involving fire ceremonies and sacrifices conducted outdoors. Unlike the practices of earlier religions in Southwest Asia, temples played no major role in Ahura Mazda worship.

The creed of Ahura Mazda was only one of several in circulation in the Achaemenid Empire, but in Darius's time its priesthood, called the Magi, came to occupy a privileged position. Darius supported the priesthood and it supported him. Thereafter, Ahura Mazda, in the official version, selected the ruler from the Achaemenid clan, and that ruler served as the god's regent on Earth, responsible for embodying and enforcing morality and truth. (Herodotus wrote that the Persian elite trained their sons in only three things: archery, horsemanship, and truth telling).

Darius and his son Xerxes (r. 486–465 BCE) each left inscriptions claiming that they punished people who worshipped other gods. Xerxes boasted of murdering them. But if they did persecute people who didn't revere Ahura Mazda, it had little effect. The old Mesopotamian and Egyptian gods retained their followers. Scattered documents mention at least a dozen gods other than Ahura Mazda invoked by Achaemenid kings. So, Persia remained a multireligious society, and the Achaemenids, like Mesopotamian rulers before them, adapted to religious practice in lands they conquered, even if they preferred Ahura Mazda over all other deities.

Techniques of government both new and old enabled Darius, and his son Xerxes, to preside over a stable order and growing prosperity in Persia. Revolts were few and always suppressed. With the exception of a few decades in the fourth century BCE when they lost hold of Egypt, the emperors maintained control over the richest agricultural heartlands, Egypt and Mesopotamia.

Agriculture and Trade The Persian Empire grew stronger still, thanks to improvements in agriculture. Rice from India joined the crop mix, allowing higher yields than other grains could provide, especially in the swampy settings of, for example, Mesopotamia. Darius and Xerxes expanded the networks of irrigation, particularly *qanats,* the underground irrigation tunnels that are still in use in parts of Iran. They extended the cultivation of alfalfa, useful especially as nutritious feed for horses and indispensable to the big steeds of the Persian heavy cavalry. Alfalfa was also good for fixing nitrogen from the air into the soil, which improves crop yields of all sorts; planting a field one year to alfalfa and the next year to wheat raised the food supply. With more *qanats* and more alfalfa, the Achaemenids addressed two of the problems that most constrained

Qanat Throughout Persia, extensive systems of irrigation tunnels known as *qanats* ran underground, conveying water from underground wells to points where farmers could access it. Designing, building, and maintaining such systems required considerable engineering skill.

farming: shortages of both water and soil nitrogen (although no one at the time knew of the existence of nitrogen).

Beyond improvements to agriculture, the stability of the Achaemenids encouraged trade. Darius completed a canal begun by a pharaoh to connect the Red and Mediterranean Seas. The road system helped drive down the cost of transport for merchandise and information. Control of port cities of the eastern Mediterranean such as Tyre and Sidon opened the commerce of the entire Mediterranean to Persia, and control over desert oases in the east did the same for trade to India and Central Asia. The expanded use of Arabian dromedaries, thirst-resistant camels, allowed direct travel from upper Mesopotamia to the Mediterranean across the Syrian desert. The increased circulation of coin reduced another obstacle to commerce, because money exchanges are so much more efficient than barter. But above all, it was the political unification of the entire region from the Nile to the Indus that promoted trade. The economic integration of so many ecologically and culturally different regions inspired specialization and exchange, which for a few centuries under Achaemenid rule encountered minimal political barriers.

The Achaemenids reveled in the diversity of their empire and didn't try to homogenize it. The empire's population of 15 to 30 million remained multiethnic, multireligious, and multilingual. Darius celebrated the varying origins of materials and artisans assembled in his building program at the city of Susa: cedar from Lebanon, gold from Sardis and Bactria, lapis lazuli from Sogdiana (Central Asia), silver and ebony from Egypt, ivory from Ethiopia and Sind; stonecutters from Ionia (western Anatolia), goldsmiths from Egypt and Medea (western Persia), brickmakers from Babylonia. Their inscriptions usually appeared in three languages: Akkadian, used in central Mesopotamia, and Elamite and Old Persian, both from western Iran. Their administration was often conducted in a fourth language, Aramaic, spoken in Syria. The Achaemenids made multiculturalism a strength of their empire.

Multicultural Empire A life-sized relief carved on a hillside in Behistun (located in what is now Iran) commemorates the reign of Darius the Great. He holds a bow, signifying his kingship, and faces shorter figures that stand for conquered peoples. Beneath the frame of the image, the story of Darius's reign is written in the three primary languages of the Persian Empire: Old Persian, Elamite, and Akkadian. In this way, even official royal proclamations embraced linguistic and cultural diversity.

The basic structure of the empire remained in place for 135 years after the reigns of Darius and Xerxes. Achaemenid Persia continued to stand as the lone superpower for nearly two centuries.

The Greek World to 338 BCE

In many accounts of human history, the ancient Greeks loom large. Here they will too. Although many people ringed the Achaemenid Empire—including Scythians to the north and Arabs to the south—the one we'll discuss at this stage will be the Greeks. There are two reasons for this. First, unlike other peoples on the frontiers of the Nile-Ganges web, the Greeks burst out of their homeland, conquered Persia, and spread aspects of their culture throughout the region. Therefore, they were important in their own time. Second, they are important to our time as well. Certain of their distinctive cultural traits, detailed below, while almost forgotten for more than a thousand years, resurfaced in later times and became widely admired among European elites in the fifteenth and sixteenth centuries CE, just as those elites were embarking upon a world-girdling spurt of imperialism. Thus ideals of democracy and rationalism, for example, articulated in what was an obscure corner of the world in the fifth century BCE, profoundly affect almost everyone today. But as a starting point, it's useful to remember that in the fifth century BCE the Greeks were few in number and just one of the many peoples on the fringes of a Persian-dominated world.

Crete and Mycenae

The first traces of Greek language and culture date back to around 1500 to 1200 BCE. On the island of Crete, and later in the Peloponnese (the southernmost part of mainland Greece), a palace culture arose that owed something to the examples of Egypt, Anatolia, and Mesopotamia. The introduction of sailing boats into the eastern Mediterranean, soon before 2000 BCE, improved communications. The palaces at Knossos, on Crete, and at Mycenae, in the Peloponnese, organized artisan workshops, stored grain for distribution to loyal followers, and hosted ceremonies to underscore the majesty of kings, in the same general manner as the rulers of Egypt or Babylonia.

The palace culture of Crete is now called Minoan, after the mythical King Minos. It developed slowly, beginning as far back as 2500 BCE, when the Old Kingdom was taking shape in Egypt and urban centers were appearing along the Indus. Scanty evidence suggests its people spoke a language that was not Indo-European. Clay tablets with hieroglyphs, and a later partly syllabic writing system, called Linear A, are as yet undeciphered. The Minoans' religion, to judge by surviving artwork, featured goddesses far more than gods. Minoan art, mainly pottery and frescoes, proved appealing enough to be imitated in Egypt and in mainland Greece. Some of it, such as the possibly female acrobats risking their lives somersaulting over bulls, can be interpreted to mean that women enjoyed unusually high status in Minoan society.

Minoan Crete's prosperity, which peaked around 1600 to 1450 BCE, was based on agriculture but to an unusual extent also on seaborne trade. Crete exported olive oil to Egypt and probably enjoyed a strong position in the trade of bronze goods. Crete took part in an interactive eastern Mediterranean network linking Egypt, the Levant ports, and Anatolia. Minoan Crete suffered from earthquakes, and around 1550 BCE its northern coasts were flooded by a tsunami caused by a gigantic eruption on a nearby volcanic island.

After 1450, more calamities struck (perhaps more earthquakes), and by 1400 BCE or so Mycenaean invaders from the Greek mainland had taken over the palaces of Crete. They brought their own language, which they soon wrote in an adapted version of the Minoan script known as Linear B. Thousands

Linear A This tablet from around 1500 to 1400 BCE was found in the palace at Knossos. It is inscribed with the syllabic Linear A script in which the Minoan language was written, which scholars have yet to decipher.

of Linear B tablets dug up in Crete and in Mycenae have been decoded since the first decipherment of the script in 1952. They reveal that the writing served to record administrative business and that only a few dozen hands did all the writing. The earliest evidence of a Greek language comes from Linear B and dates to about 1500 BCE.

Greece in the next three centuries was a thinly populated region dominated by a warrior aristocracy using bronze weaponry and organized into small kingdoms. The outlook of these aristocrats is reflected in the *Iliad*, a song-poem that recounts events during the Trojan War, which occurred in the thirteenth or twelfth century BCE. (The *Iliad* was recited and sung for centuries before being written down in the eighth century BCE. Along with the *Odyssey*, it is attributed to the Greek writer Homer.) That aristocratic outlook bears comparison to the *Rig Veda*: the *Iliad*'s heroes—Achilles, Agamemnon, and dozens of others—were obsessed with honor, quick to violence, disdainful of social inferiors, and respectful of their gods.

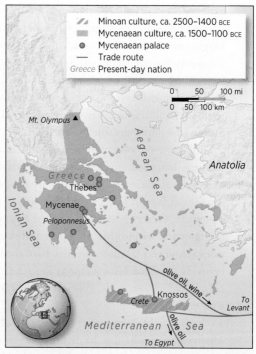

Minoan and Mycenaean Greece, ca. 2500–1100 BCE
The first inklings of Greek culture emerged on the island of Crete as early as 2500 BCE but flourished only after 1600 BCE. Its royal courts and its merchants maintained links with Egypt, the Levant, and Anatolia. On the mainland, another palace culture developed somewhat later, named for the citadel of Mycenae. Both specialized in olive oil production, and both used bronze goods and a language ancestral to Greek.

After 1100 BCE, bigger kingdoms, including that of Mycenae, fell to ruin. Small-scale polities prevailed for the next several centuries. No one could build a big one in Greece, where rugged terrain worked against centralization—unlike in Egypt or Mesopotamia, where big states now were the rule.

The *Polis* and Greek Political Culture

Instead, the Greeks, starting around 700 BCE, developed a distinctive political institution called the **polis**, a word often translated as "city-state." Sumer had had city-states, but some of the Greek ones veered onto an unusual path. Instead of a king, some Greek *poleis* had magistrates who governed for a set period of time (often, no more than one year) and were selected by citizens. Sometimes they were chosen by lot. Only adult males of the *polis* could be citizens—no women, slaves, or foreigners. This left perhaps 10 to 20 percent of the population with political rights—far more than anywhere else. Magistrates served at the citizens' pleasure and could not stay in office if they displeased a majority. So magistrates struggled to find policies acceptable to majorities rather than acting solely in their own interests, those of a royal family, or those of a few families. Self-government, even by only a subset of the total population, was abnormal among settled agricultural societies. Even among tribal societies without formal political institutions, the norm was rule by chieftains.

The sense of collective interest and identity that underlay the *polis* rested in part on the military requirements of the day. The Greek city-states, like the Sumerian ones, were often at war with one another. By the end of the seventh century BCE, the cutting edge in warfare in Greece was a formation of citizen-soldiers called the phalanx. In a phalanx, each citizen-soldier, called a hoplite, stood shoulder-to-shoulder with his neighbor and wielded his long spear and shield so as to protect men around him. This tactical unit was far more effective than the individual, aristocratic combat duels celebrated in the *Iliad*. Now weapons were cheaper (they were iron, not bronze), and each citizen had to own a set. Political rights came with doing one's duty in the phalanx with one's fellow hoplites.

Each *polis* had a powerful interest in enabling citizens to equip themselves for war, which meant not letting the divide between rich and poor grow too wide. Some of the city-states, most prominently Athens, also developed navies that enrolled the poorest classes—men who couldn't afford shield and spear. Yet they too could be citizens. This system gave even the poorest a stake in politics and at times a pride in the achievements of their *polis*. The tactical advantages of the Greek phalanx (at least, on level ground),

Hoplites An illustration on a Greek vase shows a phalanx of hoplites wielding spears and standing close together to protect their fellow soldiers with their shields.

and the political allegiances generated by the Greek *polis* were sufficient to keep the tiny Greek city-states independent for centuries. Some of them, notably Athens, conducted the brand of citizen politics that Greeks called democracy.

The connection between self-defense and self-government helped to justify the exclusion of women, even free native-born women. Beyond that, most Greeks held to the view that women were unsuited to public life. They were, it was thought, easily influenced by unruly passions and intellectually inferior to men. An Athenian playwright of the fifth century BCE, Euripides, may have recognized the illogic of the prevailing view: one of his characters says, "Of all living, thinking beings, we women are the most unlucky." Plato (ca. 427–348 BCE), the great Athenian political philosopher, suggested that women might be fit to receive the same education as males and—this was scandalous in the Athens of his day—to fight and rule. But such views were rare and never prevailed. The more common view was expressed by the Athenian political leader Pericles, who thought that a woman's reputation stood highest when no one spoke of her at all. In this respect, the ancient Greeks' outlook was conventional, broadly similar to views expressed in the later Vedas or, as we'll see, in Chinese texts of the same era.

About 30 Greek city-states founded colonies on the shores of the Mediterranean and Black Seas, beginning as early as 900 BCE but for the most part after 650 BCE. The purpose of these colonies was primarily to enhance the trade and wealth of their founding city (or "metropolis"). The colonies generally maintained cordial relations with their metropolises, sending delegations to take part in religious festivals, for example. Some of them became self-governing *poleis* in their own right while maintaining ties of trade and sentiment with their ancestral home cities. Among the most important colonies were Syracuse, in Sicily, a Corinthian outpost; Cyrene, on the coast of Libya; and Massalia, where the French city of Marseilles stands today. The colonies numbered several hundred in all, stretching from the easternmost Black Sea to the coasts of Spain. Collectively, they created an archipelago of Greek culture far beyond the Aegean, a culture that included the self-governing *polis*, Greek religion and language, and a way of life that emphasized maritime trade.

Sparta Greeks such as Herodotus prided themselves on their distinctive democracy, but democracy held sway in only a few hundred of the roughly 1,000 Greek city-states. Sparta, for example, was an oligarchy, meaning a state run by a handful of ruling families, led by kings. Founded in the eleventh or tenth century BCE, Sparta eventually ruled by far the largest territory of all Greek city-states.

Sparta was a militaristic society that held other Greeks in bondage. In the eighth century, its warriors conquered a neighboring land, Messenia, and turned its inhabitants into *helots*, a word that meant "captives" but in practice meant "slaves." Helots did the agricultural work in the lands Sparta controlled, handing over a share of the grain, olive oil, and wine they produced to the Spartans. Some also served as artisans and servants. Female helots often bore children of Spartan fathers in an officially encouraged

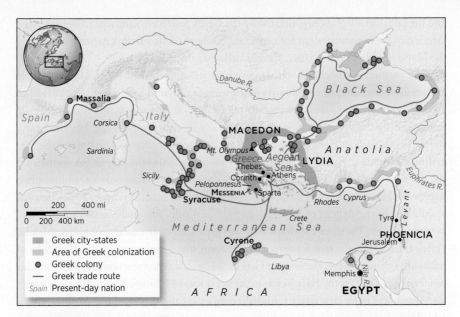

Greek Colonization, ca. 900–500 BCE Greeks were among the peoples who took advantage of the favorable conditions for sailing on the Mediterranean Sea. Greek city-states established hundreds of colonies on the shores of the Mediterranean and Black Seas, creating a tight network of trading communities by 500 BCE.

effort to top up the supply of potential soldiers. Girl babies produced in this way were probably killed.

All Spartan males at age 7 left their families to reside in a communal barracks, where they trained, at public expense, in the martial arts until age 18. As part of their preparation, the best of them were encouraged to sneak up on helots and murder them. Spartans used terror to keep helots in their place. But Spartans lived in fear that the more numerous helots (Herodotus wrote that for each Spartan there were seven helots) might rise against them, so they carried weapons at all times. They suppressed the occasional helot uprisings with unrestrained brutality. Adult male Spartans lived in barracks, even if married, until age 30. They remained on active military duty until 60, an age that few attained.

Their social system made Spartans more formidable in war than any other Greek polity. Sparta built no city walls, relying for defense on its army and its fierce reputation. That was practical partly because of the extreme training and commitment of their soldiers, and partly because every male was a warrior. Sparta had ancient Greece's only genuinely professional army. In other Greek states, the cost of armor and weaponry was such that only about one-third of the male population could afford to take part in the phalanx. Other Greeks regarded Spartan men as unusually pious, overly attuned to omens, and inhumanly restrained in their approach to wine. Spartans, who felt that real men exercised self-control, routinely humiliated helots by forcing them to drink too much wine. The highest honor for a Spartan male was glory in warfare.

For a Spartan woman, the highest honor was having sons who attained glory in warfare. Ancient authors (none of them Spartan, however) often wrote that Spartan mothers taunted and even killed their own sons if they showed cowardice in battle. Spartan girls underwent obligatory physical training too, which included running, wrestling, and javelin- and discus-throwing; they also practiced dancing and singing. In their late teens, they typically married and soon began begetting the next generation of warriors. They might accomplish this with their husbands or with other men—uniquely for ancient Greece, adultery for women was no crime in Sparta. They did no housework, nor the disagreeable parts of child rearing, which fell to helot women. They could own property in their own right, unlike Greek women elsewhere. And they had a reputation as promiscuous among other Greeks—but we should bear in mind that Greek women elsewhere typically lived in seclusion after puberty.

Spartan men launched the practice of exercising naked, their bodies coated in olive oil. As this habit spread to other Greek city-states, a cult of naked male beauty evolved, emphasizing the chiseled, muscular physiques we see in Greek statuary from this period. Greeks occasionally denigrated foreign men as being too scrawny or tubby to appear in public without clothing.

Sparta's political system was, as we've seen, an oligarchy. Its constitution stipulated that two hereditary kings would rule together, serving as a check upon one another. They worked with five executives, called *ephors,* elected for one-year terms by the citizenry. The constitution also included a select council that could veto any decisions taken by its assembly, a check upon the wishes of the citizenry. The council consisted of 28 males over the age of 60 who were elected for life by the assembly, plus the two kings. It served as a high court as well as the key lawmaking body for Sparta. The assembly could accept or reject proposed laws and policies, but it could not initiate any. Ultimately, a total of 35 men directed Spartan public life.

Like Sparta, most of the Greek *poleis* were not democratic. Some, like Corinth or Thebes on the Greek mainland or Syracuse and Rhodes on islands, were run at least from time to time by kings or upstart dictators called tyrants. But at times they also practiced a form of democracy, which Sparta never did. Because taking part in politics and debates is time consuming, those with more leisure time—both the idle rich and the unemployed—were more likely to be active citizens, while those who needed to work to feed their families often neglected their responsibilities as citizens. Where democracy went the furthest, poor men and rich men had, at least in principle, equal rights and equal voice.

Athens and Democracy Only a few Greek city-states experimented with democracy, and none took it further than Athens in the fifth century BCE. Under a written constitution drafted by Cleisthenes in 508–07 BCE, the Athenians created a political system, eventually termed **demokratia**, based on equal rights for all citizens. Cleisthenes, an aristocrat and brother-in-law of the last tyrant of Athens, wanted to break old allegiances based on kinship and locality, and focus everyone's loyalty narrowly on the Athenian *polis*. He did this by creating new political units of the city, the coasts, and the hinterlands of Athens, and according them rights to supply members to a ruling council of 500 that met to do the business of the state every day. This council was responsible to a larger assembly, in which all male citizens age 18 or older who had completed military training could sit, but only those 30 and over could speak. No man who had thrown down his shield and run from battle was allowed to speak, nor could anyone convicted of prostitution or failing to support his parents properly. The assembly of citizens, which usually met a few times a month to discuss policy, was the unit that passed legislation.

In Athens in the mid-fifth century BCE, slaves made up half the population and foreigners one-tenth. Among free Athenians, citizens—males age 18 or older—numbered some 25,000 to 40,000. About 6,000 could fit into the space dedicated to the assembly at any one time. One needed a loud voice, and it was easy for dozens of men to shout down any single speaker whom they didn't like. A show of hands served as the voting system, so everyone knew how others voted. The assembly also elected the city's military commanders, of whom there were normally 10, which led to some hapless generalship. It was an unwieldy system, often swayed by silver-tongued demagogues who promised favors or cash for support. The assembly was quick to vote for war: in the fifth century BCE, Athens was at war more often than not. Greek cities not under Athenian sway—Corinth or Thebes, for example—did not choose to imitate this constitution.

To improve it, Athenians imposed a fine on proposed legislation that didn't pass, discouraging frivolous proposals. The assembly could also vote to ostracize—that is, ban from Athens for 10 years—any individual. Men who seemed dangerously or selfishly ambitious could find themselves in exile under this system. Surviving records indicate 13 ostracisms between 487 and 416 BCE.

The Persian Wars Athenian democracy in one form or another lasted for nearly two centuries. Its greatest peril came in wars against Persia and then against Sparta. Athens in 490 BCE had taken the gamble of supporting a rebellion against Persian rule mounted by a few Greek cities in Ionia on the coast of Asia Minor. Darius responded with a punitive expedition against Athens in 490, but Athenian skill and valor at the Battle of Marathon convinced the Persians to give up and go home. Darius died in 486 while preparing another expedition against Greece.

His son Xerxes carried it out and initially had better luck. He enjoyed the support of several Greek cities and defeated those who resisted in battle. His forces occupied Athens briefly, burning the temples of the Acropolis, the citadel of the city. But his fleet lost a key naval battle at Salamis in 480 BCE, and he soon withdrew. From the Greek point of view, tiny Athens had defeated the superpower of the day, Achaemenid Persia, and preserved its experiment in democracy.

These events loom large in ancient Greek history, partly through the magic of Herodotus's storytelling. From the Persian point of view, they were merely rebuffs at the edge of the empire, costly in manpower and embarrassing in terms of prestige but far from vital concerns. In comparison, when Egypt and Mesopotamia rebelled in 485–484 BCE, Xerxes prevailed against the rebels and preserved core areas of his empire. Greece was a relatively poor land despite its mines and maritime trade, worth far less than Mesopotamia or Egypt. Failure to conquer Greece posed no threat to Persia. Even though Greece was a low priority after 480 BCE, Persian kings kept a hand in Greek affairs. They financially supported one city-state against another in a developing rivalry of alliances surrounding Athens and Sparta, and they tried to enlist both as client states of the Achaemenid dynasty.

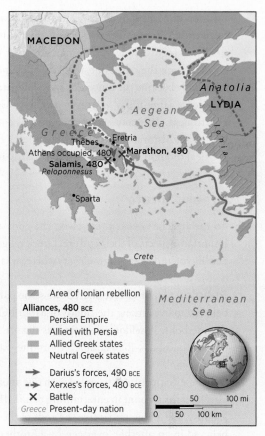

The Persian Wars, 490–480 BCE By banding together, several Greek city-states managed to resist invasion attempts mounted by Achaemenid Persia, the great power of the day. For Persia, this conflict was merely one of many on the fringes of its empire. For the Greeks, it was a matter of political and cultural survival. Persian-Greek warfare continued intermittently until 449 BCE.

The Peloponnesian War

Athens used the prestige it won in the rebuff of Persia and the wealth it acquired from silver mines to create a small Athenian empire, composed mostly of island states that couldn't resist the Athenian navy. Athens grew richer by taxing these states ruthlessly, forming in effect an Athenian maritime empire in and around the Aegean. The apparent rise of Athenian power distressed Spartan rulers, who judged it wise to attack Athens rather than allow Athenian strength to build further. The Peloponnesian War (431–404 BCE) involved most of the Greek world. Thanks in part to Persian aid, Sparta won in the end by destroying the Athenian navy.

In victory, the Spartans resisted their allies' suggestions to destroy Athens and enslave its entire population. After a brief interruption—a repressive oligarchic government subservient to Sparta—Athenians restored their democracy. But in 322 BCE, an invasion of Macedonians from the north brought this experiment in self-government to an end. A few democracies elsewhere in Greece survived a bit longer, until they were finally extinguished by the Roman conquest of 146 BCE.

Although they died out, the Athenian and other Greek experiments in democracy eventually became the touchstone for democratic movements many centuries later, and they loom large today wherever people consider democracy to be a suitable form of government. This continuing resonance is a result of the intellectual legacy of ancient Greece. Its historians and philosophers left a detailed account of Greek democracy and political thought, part of an extraordinarily influential culture.

Greek Culture

To the ancient Greeks themselves, the gods and the rituals of worship were the most important aspects of their culture. Greek religion carried influences from Mesopotamia and Egypt and, like religion everywhere, was tied up with politics.

Religion All of Greece shared the same pantheon of gods, a big quarrelsome family believed to live among the clouds of Mount Olympus. Zeus ruled the heavens with his thunderbolts. Poseidon's domain was the sea. Others took responsibility not for places but for concepts—for example, Aphrodite was the goddess of love and beauty, Athena of wisdom.

These deities often struggled with one another and meddled in human affairs, as the Greek myths recount in entertaining detail. They displayed human failings such as lust, jealousy, and anger, rather like the gods of the *Rig Veda* or of Mesopotamia. The Greeks believed in an afterlife, overseen by a brother of Zeus named Hades. They eventually came to understand the afterlife as taking one's soul to a specific place, the realm of Hades, which included agreeable destinations such as Elysium for those who had led virtuous lives, and a place of eternal torment called Tartarus, reserved for the wicked.

Greek religion contained an ethical component. Throughout the Greek world, including the scattered colonies, the gods expected humans to submit to the discipline of regular worship, pay proper respect to their elders, and extend hospitality to strangers. Worship of the gods usually involved sacrifices of sheep or other livestock intended to win the goodwill of one or another deity.

Beyond these widely held beliefs, each *polis* had its own religious identity, rituals, and bonds to specific deities. Atop the Acropolis and visible across Athens, the Parthenon was a temple to Athena, the city's favored god. Corinth esteemed Aphrodite above all others. Frequent festivals not only reinforced the bonds of gods and city, but also helped to forge a distinct identity for each *polis*. Festivals often featured athletic contests and large processions ending at a city's main temple. They offered prominent roles to women, lesser ones to children, and sometimes even to foreigners and slaves. By allowing members of those social classes with no political rights to take part in the public life of the *polis* and feel a commitment to it, religious festivals sustained social bonds within each *polis*.

Religion helped shape everyday life in the Greek world, and through the work of Greek playwrights, poets, and scholars it filtered into the broader intellectual life of literature and philosophy. As we will see, Greek religious ideas informed the world in which Christianity arose, and its intellectual culture had a lasting influence on thinkers in western Eurasia and Africa's Mediterranean lands.

Alphabets and Influence The intellectual achievement of Greece between about 500 and 330 BCE isn't easy to account for. In part, it may derive from the use of an alphabet, which made literacy easier to acquire than in most parts of the world, where scripts were more complicated. The invention and spread of alphabetic writing in Greece merits a brief detour in our discussion.

The earliest example of alphabetic writing dates to about 1900 BCE in Egypt. Representing a language spoken in Southwest Asia, probably Canaanite, this form of writing had 22 symbols that stood for consonant sounds rather than words or ideas as in all previous scripts. If Egyptian scribes saw it, they probably thought it was inelegant and inefficient: it required many symbols—what we call letters—to record just one word.

But over the centuries that followed, alphabets proved to be an appealing alternative to logographic script (in which symbols represent words) and ideographic script (in which symbols represent ideas) because readers only had to memorize a small number of symbols. By 1000 BCE or so, a trading people called the Phoenicians, based in the merchant cities of the Levant, were writing with an alphabet. From there, the idea of alphabetic writing spread westward to the Greeks, who were the first to use letters to represent both consonant and vowel sounds. That system spread in many directions as people adapted it to different tongues. The alphabet stands among the most important cultural innovations that circulated within the world's webs. The concept of alphabetic writing, although adopted in hundreds of cultures, was invented only once. Today, other than in Chinese and Japanese, alphabets of about 20 to 35 symbols are the building blocks of written language everywhere, all of them adapted from or inspired by the Phoenician alphabet.

After about 700 BCE, the use of an alphabet enabled larger numbers of people to read and write Greek. The Greeks began to write down their myths, and soon their histories and philosophy, rather than merely recording merchants' transactions and royal feats. With more people writing, the odds of brilliant thoughts being written down improved. With more people taking part in intellectual exchanges through writing, the chances of brilliant thoughts occurring to anyone improved. That can't be the whole of the explanation for the Greek achievement, however, because Phoenician cities used an alphabet and left nothing comparable to the Greek intellectual legacy.

Another part of the explanation probably lies in the combination of cultural unity and political disunity. The Greek cities shared a written language, although their inhabitants spoke several different dialects. They shared the same set of gods, military tactics, marriage customs, farming routines, poetic and dramatic forms, architectural styles, and much else. The whole of the Greek world took part in certain rituals such as the Olympic Games, begun in the eighth century BCE. It was a culturally unified space, if politically fragmented. This situation helps to explain (although nothing fully explains) the extraordinary Greek intellectual flowering in the century and a half after the Persians' retreat in 480 BCE.

Political fragmentation meant that no single king, no priesthood, no authority of any sort could stamp out experimental thinking among the Greeks. Poets, playwrights, and philosophers were often at liberty to disagree and to compete with one another for influence. New ideas flourished. Just as the laws of the *polis* guided the behavior of society, some Greeks supposed that there might be laws governing the behavior of nature. Philosophers (which meant deep thinkers of all sorts) increasingly disregarded the older explanations in which just about everything represented the will of the gods. Eventually, they crafted a much more rational explanation of human affairs.

History, Philosophy, and Rationality That progression is illustrated by accounts of Greek wars over several centuries. In Homer's *Iliad*, written down in the eighth century BCE (although recited and sung earlier), the struggles between Greeks and Trojans are manipulated by rival Greek gods. Herodotus, the Greek historian, writing in the 440s about the Greco-Persian Wars of a few decades before, gathered evidence, sifted it, formed hypotheses, but in the end also often attributed outcomes to divine wills. However, Thucydides, an Athenian general-turned-historian, in his account of the conflict between Athens and Sparta composed late in the fifth century BCE, explained events quite differently. In his work, the gods have virtually no role and people make their own history, as individuals or in groups. Thucydides sought purely human, not supernatural, explanations for the events in his history.

The rationalism exemplified by Thucydides appeared in other spheres of Greek intellectual life as well. Socrates, an Athenian philosopher and son of a stonemason, proclaimed that reasoned arguments could produce answers to life's most vexing questions about virtue, honor, and the meaning of existence. He had the misfortune to make his case just after Sparta's defeat of Athens and a brief civil war in which one of his students led the losing (pro-Spartan) faction—all of which left Athenians anxious. For Socrates's insistent moral questioning and his supposed neglect of the gods, Athenian authorities put him on trial, despite his record as a minor war hero. Socrates, charged with corrupting Athenian youth, argued that his relentless rationalism provided Athens a service, but to no avail. He was sentenced to death. A different man would have avoided this fate by leaving Athens for another city. But Socrates drank the prescribed poison and died in 399 BCE.

A flock of more fortunate philosophers made respectable livings by teaching the arts of reasoned argument. Citizens found that skill essential if they wished to be effective

Philosophical Life An illustration from an Athenian drinking cup shows two young men sharing a couch at a symposium, a gathering centered around wine drinking and conversation. The image also suggests an erotic relationship between the men common among the educated elite.

in politics or to defend themselves in lawsuits. In fact, the political format of the *polis* with its citizen assembly and the skillful use of argument reinforced one another. The philosophers with the most enduring and widespread influence were Plato (427–348 BCE) and Aristotle (384–322 BCE).

Plato came from the upper ranks of Athenian society and was the star student of Socrates. He lectured on, discussed, and wrote about philosophy for more than 40 years in and around Athens, where he created an academy for reflection on philosophical and practical problems. Having grown up in Athens as it was losing the Peloponnesian War, and having seen what the Athenian assembly did to his teacher, Plato was no friend of democracy. He recommended that the best people—meaning those with self-discipline and unmoved by luxury, dedicated to virtue, and educated in philosophy and mathematics—should rule over everyone else. He considered women worthy of education, and felt that those who mastered philosophy and math, and whose souls were suitably aggressive, could also fight and rule. He argued for dissolving the family and encouraging the best men and the best women to have sex for the purpose of producing the best offspring.

Plato was concerned by questions that ran deeper than politics. He was absorbed by the relationship between appearances, which anyone could perceive, and true reality, which he thought only those with years of systematic philosophical study could detect. He had a mystical bent too, arguing for the existence of a human soul, distinct from the body, that lived on after death. Indeed, his concept of the soul had overtones of Hindu belief in which one's ethical record held consequences for one's future existence, which might include being reborn in another body. Later religions such as Christianity and Islam carried on some of Plato's ideas on these subjects. He was a firm believer in the value of religion, and late in life he recommended that anyone spreading atheism should be put to death. Plato had an obsession with discipline, order, and virtue.

Aristotle was Plato's star pupil. He came from northern Greece but studied in Athens, in Plato's Academy, from age 17 to 37, before making his career as a teacher throughout the Greek world. He was more interested than Plato in the empirical study of reality, and he delighted in classifying objects and pointing out exceptions to rules, including his own. He pursued an extraordinarily wide set of interests, writing on ethics, botany, zoology, weather, logic, drama, music, and poetry as well as politics, law, and constitutions. He held more charitable views of his fellow Greek citizens than Plato, and thought that farmers and soldiers, for example, were worthy of political rights and capable of reasoned judgment, without the extended training that Plato recommended.

But Aristotle drew the line at uneducated tradesmen, foreigners (meaning non-Greek speakers), and women, none of whom he considered equal to the demands of citizenship. He explicitly objected to Plato's notion that women might be suited to rule. He also thought that some people, mainly foreigners, were by nature suited to be slaves because they lacked the discipline and judgment to direct their own lives. At age 40, he took a job at the court of Philip, the king of Macedon, and for seven years labored as the tutor for Philip's son Alexander. Aristotle stands among the most influential thinkers who ever lived.

Greek poets and playwrights also flourished in the world of competitive city-states. Some dramatists, especially in Athens, commented on current politics, even mocking the authorities. Such expression was dangerous in Athens but would have been impossible in a monarchy. The best example may be the bawdy comedy *Lysistrata*, written by Aristophanes and produced in Athens in 411 BCE in the middle of the Peloponnesian War against Sparta. It challenges the wisdom of the war by supposing what might happen if all the married women of Athens and Sparta refused to have sex with their husbands and lovers until the men stopped the war. In the play, the men, desperate for sex, give in and negotiate peace. (In reality, the war went on and on.) Most Greek poetry and drama, however, dealt indirectly with political events through the exploration of timeless themes of love and longing, ambition and revenge, honor and justice—often enacted in conflicts of the gods.

The emphasis on rationalism, debate, and quests for truth also affected inquiry into nature—what we now call science. Ancient Greeks developed a theory of matter based on atoms. Aristotle systematically pursued scientific truth, painstakingly gathering observations about plants, animals, astronomy, and so forth. His portrayal of the natural world was based on evidence and logic. His worldview had little room for the gods, although he allowed that something supernatural could account for the origins of the universe.

After Aristotle, who died in 322 BCE, Greek creativity ebbed somewhat, although it continued to hum for another century or more in mathematics and science, and especially in Alexandria, a culturally Greek city in Egypt. In mainland Greece, the extinction of the independent *polis* by Macedonian conquest (338 BCE) soon narrowed the scope for speculative and irreverent thought. So, perhaps, did the achievement of Aristotle, who seemed to have had the last word on so many subjects. The intellectual golden age of the Greeks did not last long, although its impact is still with us today.

Greek Intellectual Culture   Political fragmentation in the Greek world encouraged this intellectual flowering by making thinkers feel freer. As Chapter 7 will show, a similar efflorescence in Chinese thought accompanied a period of political fragmentation in ancient China. Such moments are rare. Rulers typically regard ideas as too dangerous to be free, and they use their power to constrain if not thought, at least expression. But where a common language and culture exist over a politically fragmented space, as for a while in ancient Greece and China, thinkers can speculate, argue, and interact without careful self-censorship.

The Greek philosophical tradition also answered a growing need felt far and wide in Eurasia during these centuries. Greece, like Mesopotamia in Hammurabi's time, badly needed strong ethical codes. With population growth, the rise of trade and markets, and especially the emergence of urban living with its daily encounters with strangers, Greek societies needed rules. In village settings, where everyone knew everyone else and their families, bad behavior was noticed quickly. But in the city, where people often interacted with others they didn't know, the chances of avoiding retribution for theft or violence were greater.

In the anonymous city, ethical codes carried special appeal. That helps to explain the rise of religions such as Buddhism and Jainism, which offered ethical codes and flourished among commercial communities in north India. In Greece, however, the gods didn't require, model, or even suggest responsible behavior. Indeed, in Greek myth, the gods ran amok, deceiving, tricking, cheating, and raping without remorse. Greek philosophers by the late fifth century BCE felt a need for ethical codes to help navigate the social terrain of the city, above and beyond what religion provided.

Socrates, Plato, Aristotle, and a later school of thinkers known as the Stoics—founded in Athens about 300 BCE—all offered guides to ethical conduct that had appeal in their time and in later centuries too. The Stoics emphasized virtue as the key to happiness and recommended seeking contentment through rational contemplation rather than questing after pleasures. All this is not to say, however, that carpenters, fruit sellers, slaves, sea captains, or priests behaved any more ethically after Greek philosophers wrote their treatises. Ordinary folks had at best the vaguest idea of what philosophers recommended. Rather, it is to say only that Greek thinkers found ethical questions in need of answer as never before, and some of their answers seemed so persuasive as to appeal to reflective minds from their day to ours.

Greek Market Culture

In addition to the unique *polis* and the remarkable intellectual outpouring, there is a third notable distinction of the ancient Greeks: the unusual role of markets and money in their society. Their rocky lands suited grain poorly, but olive groves and vineyards thrived. Greek city-states often had to import grain by exporting olive oil and wine, and sometimes wool, honey, pottery, weaponry, and silver too. Their proximity to the sea encouraged trade and specialization, and enabled them to rely on Egypt, Sicily, and their own colonies on the coastlands of the Black Sea for grain. Athens took this commercial orientation furthest. Its foremost marketplace, the agora, adjacent to the citadel of the Acropolis, symbolized the importance of trade and merchants in Athenian life with its location. Its arcades of shops and warehouses, clustered together, eased transactions.

The invention of coinage in Lydia (western Anatolia) sped the development of commerce from the late sixth century BCE. The prominence of commerce and especially risky sea ventures in Greek economic life led to the invention of financial instruments and contracts for loans and insurance. Ports often had rudimentary banks, and cities—especially Rhodes, off the southwest coast of Anatolia—adopted maritime and commercial legal codes that dealt with issues such as liability in the event of a shipwreck. By Plato's time, money and markets had grown so prominent that he argued states ought to control them.

Money and markets changed the way people thought and behaved. Money connected people with total strangers through multiple social networks. Its use weakened the older bonds of kinship and patronage based on social rank. Soon after money was introduced, some priests came to prefer cash contributions for temples and gods over the blood of a firstborn lamb or the first fruits of the harvest. Families quickly put money into the balance when arranging marriages, so that dowries and bride-prices were paid in cash as well as in sheep or bolts of cloth. Money provided a common denominator that encouraged people to think in terms of equivalences: a goat was worth 3 weeks' rent, or 16 poems, or half a slave, or 3 amphorae of olive oil—because all were worth the same amount of money. Sparta, incidentally, resisted the use of money into the third century BCE, clinging to the concepts of honor, valor, and ancestry after the rest of Greek society had accepted the values of the marketplace.

The combination of networks of colonies, a common culture embracing both popular religion and rational philosophy, combined with an unusually market-driven economy, made the ancient Greek world into a densely interconnected extension of the Nile-Ganges web. Ship traffic on the Mediterranean and Black Seas held it all together and linked the Greeks to neighboring communities, such as the equally maritime and mobile Carthaginians (whom we'll encounter in a later chapter).

Ancient Greece contained only 3 to 4 million people, maybe 15 to 20 percent as many as in Achaemenid Persia. That population was divided among more than a thousand small polities, none of them—not even Athens at its imperial height—powerful or rich compared to the kingdoms of Egypt or Southwest Asia. Just one of several cultures on the fringes of the Persian world, the Greeks would ordinarily not count for much. But because Greek market culture spread throughout the Nile-Ganges web in the fourth century BCE, because Greek philosophy influenced enduring religious traditions, and because of the rediscovery of Greek ideas of democracy and rationalism in later times, ancient Greece deserves an outsized place in world history. The first step in the spread of Greek influence was the fusion of Greek and Persian culture and power that took place under the command of Alexander the Great.

Alexander the Great as Persian King

The politically fragmented world of the many Greek *poleis* came to an end in 338 BCE. Macedonians, led by King Philip II and his son, **Alexander the Great**, conquered almost all of the Greek world. The Achaemenid dynasty came to an end in 330 BCE when Alexander routed Persian forces. But in a way, Alexander himself became the last of the Achaemenids and consciously tried to fuse Greek and Persian cultural heritage and military power.

Raised to Rule

Alexander was born in 356 BCE. He was raised to rule by his father, Philip of Macedon, and his mother, Olympias, a princess from Epirus in northwestern Greece. Macedon was not a city-state but a small regional kingdom, not Greek but with a Hellenized elite culture—that is, one modeled on Greek ways. It was a client state of Achaemenid Persia that rose in power with the long decline of Athens and Sparta (ca. 400–350 BCE). Philip was a political and military innovator, highly successful in kingly pursuits. He introduced the Greek phalanx formation to his army with great effect. He and Olympias saw to it that their son was prepared to follow in his footsteps.

They retained a disciplinarian tutor, Leonidas, whose idea of a good breakfast (claimed Alexander) was a long night's march. Olympias hired a second, gentler tutor who taught Alexander to read, write, and play music. When Alexander was 12 or 13 years old, Philip announced a competition for the post of tutor to the prince. The winner, an old crony from Philip's childhood, was Aristotle, a Macedonian himself, fresh from 20 years in Plato's Academy. Just what Aristotle taught Alexander is uncertain, but he likely emphasized politics, medicine (always of interest to Alexander), mathematics, philosophy, rhetoric, and poetry. By some accounts, he urged Alexander to see himself as champion of the Greeks and to treat barbarians, in which category he included Persians, as "beasts or plants." While Alexander absorbed Aristotle's wisdom, he continued to pursue the arts of horsemanship and hand-to-hand combat, in which any Macedonian king needed to excel. Then Philip in effect gave his 16-year-old son an internship as governor of part of Macedon and commander of a military campaign.

Building an Empire

Alexander helped his father acquire a small empire, incorporating most of the territory of Greece by 338 BCE. When a disgruntled bodyguard murdered Philip in 336 BCE, Alexander became king of Macedon. Power went to his head—as might be expected when a 20-year-old inherits a mighty army. Some of Aristotle's influence, however, stayed with Alexander. He carried a copy of the *Iliad*, annotated by Aristotle, with him on all his campaigns, and seems to have modeled himself on the hero Achilles in his quest for glory. When he oversaw the sack of Thebes (335 BCE) and ordered the slaughter of its adult males and enslavement of its women and children, he arranged that the house of the poet Pindar, whose verses he had learned to admire, should be spared.

Alexander had faith in his talents, no end of ambition, and an army grown accustomed to victory, glory, and loot—still the standard form of payment for ancient soldiers. Macedon's new empire, although it enfolded almost all of Greece, was still a modest state on the fringe of the Persian world. That wasn't enough for Alexander. In 336 BCE, at age 21, he chose to invade Anatolia and attack the world's lone superpower with about 38,000 men, mostly Macedonian and Greek infantry. The full-time soldiers of the Macedonian phalanx, intensively drilled in maneuvers, served as the cutting

Alexander the Great A mosaic from the first century CE depicts Alexander at the head of a conquering army. The armor reflects Roman motifs.

edge of Alexander's military machine just as they had for Philip. Alexander refined his father's military methods, in particular combining cavalry with infantry phalanxes. Like Cyrus, the founder of the Persian Empire, he invited cities to surrender peacefully and to support him, which many chose to do. Those that resisted he treated with savage violence and calculated cruelty. His improbable successes in battle after battle, often when heavily outnumbered, led retreating Persians to murder their king, Darius III, who was not performing up to expectations.

Alexander then claimed succession to the Achaemenid throne. He hunted down and killed Persians who claimed to be Darius's successor, and then accorded Darius III full funereal honors. In effect, Alexander was another usurper, like the first Darius, except he had no claim to be of the Persian royal lineage. He did marry two Achaemenid wives (one a daughter of Darius), dressed in the Persian style, and conducted himself—after razing the Achaemenid ceremonial city of Persepolis—as a Persian king.

Having captured the Persian treasury with many tons of silver and gold, he could buy, support, and hire all the mercenaries a king might want. He had coins enough to equal the budget of the Athenian empire for 200 years. He was, surely, the richest man

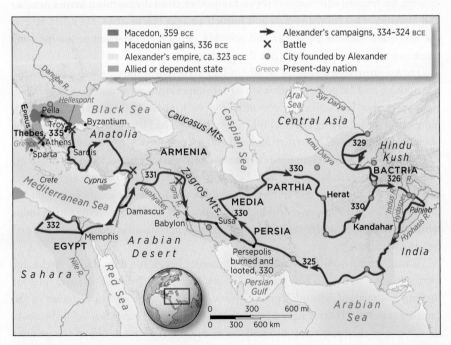

Alexander the Great's Empire, 323 BCE In a span of 15 years, a small kingdom, Macedon, conquered the Greek mainland and then, under Alexander, took over Achaemenid Persia. Alexander briefly united a space from Greece to India, but he died of fever before he could consolidate his empire. It fell apart soon after his death, but he had laid a foundation for a tighter web and more cultural integration among societies from Central Asia to the Mediterranean.

in the world. Like a good Achaemenid king, Alexander busied himself with suppressing rebellions and fighting frontier wars. He won over Egypt easily and, like Cambyses before him, arranged to be made pharaoh. But he struggled in anti-guerrilla campaigns in Bactria, roughly modern-day Afghanistan, where he married a local chieftain's daughter, Roxanne (allegedly the second most beautiful woman in Asia), improving his political position in Central Asia. In 324 BCE, Alexander oversaw a mass marriage of his Macedonian veterans with elite Persian women, which he hoped would strengthen his political position in western Asia.

A Flawed Leader

As for many people, a steady diet of success proved hard for Alexander to digest. He was growing more mercurial, grandiose, and intolerant. He named at least a dozen new cities for himself, as Macedonian kings tended to do. (They include modern Kandahar and Herat in Afghanistan, and Alexandria in Egypt). He required everyone to fling themselves to the ground upon entering into his presence, following the Persian royal custom. He boasted of descent, through his mother, from the mythical heroes Achilles and Hercules. He claimed to be a god himself and the son of Zeus. He killed several old comrades, including advisors and generals, either for subversion or for speaking truth to power, on one occasion in a drunken rage.

For his army veterans, some of whom had known him since he was a boy asking their advice and help, his petulance and self-importance were tough to take. Over eight years, they had walked 12,000 miles (19,000 km) across deserts and over snowy mountains, forded raging rivers, climbed icy cliffs, and had watched their comrades die of combat and disease. Now they had had enough conquering to burnish Alexander's legend. Many of them resented his promotion of Persians into positions of authority. In Punjab in 326 BCE, his remaining Macedonian officers finally balked. So Alexander had to skip the chance to add India to his empire, and instead he set about consolidating his rule. While Alexander still lived, the whole region from the Nile to the Indus remained united, as under the Achaemenids, although he, like them, never stopped fighting rebellions.

When, after his military successes, Alexander began to claim divine status, his former teacher, Aristotle, now back in Athens, objected. Alexander had arranged for the imprisonment of Aristotle's great-nephew, who was working as a historian of the campaigns in Asia. He threatened bodily harm to his former tutor. But before he could silence one of the most rigorous intellects in history, Alexander, one of the greatest commanders in history, veteran of eight combat wounds, died of fever in Babylonia in 323 BCE. He was not yet 33 years old.

Alexander's legend in one form or another turns up in literature and myth from Egypt to China. He appears in the Bible and the Qur'an. His body, snatched by one of his old friends and veteran commanders, Ptolemy, ended up somewhere in Egypt.

Many archeological quests have tried and failed to find it. For world history, his chief importance lies in the fact that he and his successors spread a Greco-Persian culture and more commercial ways of life throughout the vast space from the Mediterranean to the Himalaya—an area with nearly half the world's population at the time. This wasn't their purpose; it was an unintended result of their strategies to amass wealth and power.

Soon after Alexander's death, his generals quarreled over who would succeed him. Together, they took the precaution of murdering Alexander's mother, Olympias (a formidable veteran of lethal palace politics in the Macedonian court), his wife Roxanne and her infant son, and a few other members of his family. But the generals agreed on nothing else, and none managed to eliminate all rivals. In the end, they divided the empire: Ptolemy took Egypt, Antigonus got Macedon and Greece, and Seleucus claimed the Persian and Mesopotamian heartland.

Weaving the Old World Web in the Hellenistic Age

Historians use the term *Hellenistic age* to refer to the centuries of Greek and Macedonian rule in Greece, Egypt, and Southwest Asia following Alexander's death. Culturally and commercially, Alexander's successors expanded the networks of linkages they inherited, inaugurating an Old World web that embraced peoples and lands from the shores of the Mediterranean all the way to China. (The "Old World" refers to Eurasia and Africa, as opposed to the "New World" of the Americas.)

The Seleucids, the Parthians, and Trade

From 311 BCE, a new dynasty, the Seleucids, the descendants of Alexander's general Seleucus, ruled Persia. In their early years, they ruled over about 14 to 18 million people. Although much diminished compared to the realms of Alexander or Darius, the Seleucid kingdom was for a time the most powerful polity in the world. It ruled first from a capital on the Tigris (at today's Baghdad) and then from Antioch in Syria.

The Seleucids, as Macedonians and Greeks governing Persia and Mesopotamia, had a legitimacy problem they could never solve. They lost some territory in India to Chandragupta, the founder of the Mauryan Empire, and faced continual rebellion in numerous corners of their kingdom. Fully 13 of 15 Seleucid kings died by violence. But, like the Ptolemies, the dynasty that succeeded Alexander's rule in Egypt, they presided over a remarkable economic upturn and participated in a historic commercial integration of the entire Eurasian corridor.

The Seleucids sought to Hellenize their realm—that is, install Greek ways—and they succeeded in several respects. They built new cities, Antioch chief among them, with Greek features such as amphitheaters and gymnasia. They introduced Greek styles of coinage and statuary. They continued Alexander's policy, adopted from Greek tradition, of sponsoring athletic contests. They welcomed tens of thousands of Greek and Macedonian immigrants to their cities. With Seleucid patronage, Persian clergy adopted some aspects of Greek religion, and for some people Ahura Mazda merged with Zeus. The Greek language appeared on some public inscriptions.

But Hellenization could only go so far. As foreigners, the Seleucids had to conform to Persian traditions in order to win support from local elites. Even with their best efforts, frequent rebellions obliged them to rely on armed force more than the Achaemenids had needed to do. The Seleucids were often equal to that task. They combined the Macedonian phalanx with Achaemenid heavy cavalry (i.e., big horses capable of carrying armor) and added Indian war elephants to the mix. Thus their military technique was a hybrid, like the religious fusions they promoted, and probably more central to their rule.

Less obvious, but ultimately even more significant than cultural Hellenization, was the Seleucids' success in promoting commercial activity and markets—a Hellenization of sorts. The Seleucids, both by accident and by design, furthered the use of coins and markets in the economy of regions they controlled. They nurtured the linkages of long-distance trade. Chinese silks, for example, made their first appearance in Southwest Asia in Seleucid times.

The Seleucids deliberately developed the infrastructure of commerce. They built ports along the Mediterranean shore of the Levant and on the Tigris. They subsidized overland caravans by maintaining way stations (caravanserais) at regular intervals along trade routes. They adopted a uniform coinage throughout their realm, based on Athenian standards. Long-distance trade and cities such as Antioch boomed.

Seleucid War Elephants A terracotta figurine from Greece, dated to around 150 BCE, shows a Seleucid soldier mounted on an Indian elephant trampling an enemy—evidence of how the Seleucids adopted technologies and tactics from foreign lands.

The Parthians The Seleucid dynastic line lasted for two and half centuries, but Seleucid power did not. Rebels and rival kingdoms nibbled away at Seleucid territory, and by 100 BCE there was little left. But their most successful successors, the **Parthians**, formerly a group of mobile pastoralists, continued the economic and political traditions of the Seleucids and in particular nurtured long-distance connections. They set up a new Iranian state, stretching from Mesopotamia to Bactria, that lasted until 224 CE, and they maintained their end of the new long-distance caravan trade that linked China, Central Asia, India, and the Mediterranean.

The Parthians, like the Seleucids before them,

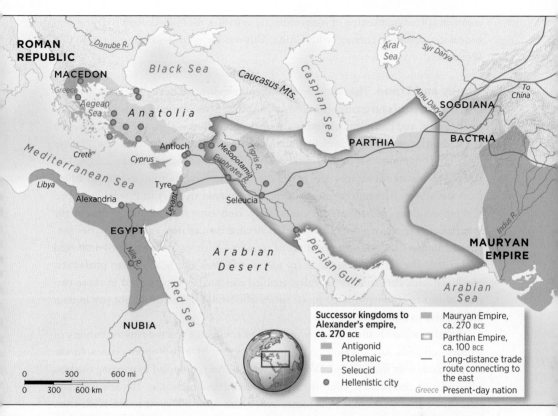

Hellenistic States, the Mauryan Empire, and the Rise of the Parthian Empire, 311–30 BCE
Soon after Alexander's death in 323 BCE, his empire fragmented and three main kingdoms resulted: the Ptolemies centered in Egypt, the Seleucids in Mesopotamia and the Persian heartland, and the Antigonids in Macedon and Greece. Ptolemaic Egypt became a center for science and literature, and together with the Seleucids built on Alexander's effort to establish Greek culture from the Nile to the Indus, a program in which creating new cities featured prominently. After the Seleucid decline, the Parthians built an empire that stretched from Mesopotamia to Bactria and the western end of India's Mauryan Empire. Like the Seleucids, the Parthians promoted trade links that stretched to India and China, the first inklings of the Silk Road.

relied upon heavy cavalry and religion to keep their subjects under control, and upon commerce and Mesopotamian agriculture for their revenues. Parthian kings supported Greek urban elites throughout their domain, especially traders whose money could easily be taxed. They found it prudent to cooperate with urban commercial elites, often Greek in outlook: many of their kings put the word *philhellenos*, meaning "friend of the Greeks," on their coins.

Over several centuries, the Seleucids and Parthians built something fundamental to world history that was a legacy both of the Achaemenids and of Alexander: a commercialized quickening of interconnections within the Nile-Ganges web and new systematic, sustained contacts with China. This was the—faint—beginning of an Old World web.

Money and Trade   The commercial awakening sponsored by the Seleucids and Parthians rested partly on transport improvements such as navigation canals and domesticated camels, and partly on cultural common denominators such as the spread of Greek as a trading language, Greek weights and measures, and Greek commercial law. Perhaps more fundamentally, it resulted from the spreading use of coined money, adopted by rulers who saw its advantages over barter especially in cross-cultural exchanges where trust was scarce. Alexander's seizure of the Achaemenid treasury in Persepolis helped this process along, as he spent his coins freely. Unceasing warfare also promoted the monetization of the region, because rulers needed mercenaries and mercenaries preferred contracts and coin to promises of plunder—although they happily indulged in that too. The extraordinary military success of Greek and Macedonian phalanxes, combined with Persian heavy cavalry, enabled mercenaries experienced in those two ways of war to command large sums: rulers who would not or could not pay in coin did not stay in power long.

Another reason behind the growing scale of commerce was the new availability of Chinese silk. Silk was a luxury good, much esteemed by urban upper classes. At the time, it came only from China. Women in western Asia competed in wearing the best silk, and men competed in adorning their wives and daughters in it. The Seleucids and later the Parthians controlled the routes over which most silk came to the Hellenistic world and had every reason to support the trade. Tolls and taxes helped provide their revenues. As the next chapter will explain, China was simultaneously building an East Asian web, which quickened the commercial economy in Seleucid and later Parthian lands.

The trade in silk, Greek market culture, and Seleucid and Parthian policy drew the hubs of Eurasia and northern Africa, from China to Egypt, into regular contact. The connecting links were made via relay trades in which goods passed from one merchant to another, along sea routes through the Indian Ocean and caravan routes across the steppes and deserts of Asia. These land routes, cobbled together from the seasonal movements of pastoralists over many centuries, are sometimes collectively called the **Silk Road**—because Chinese silk was one of the most valuable of the thousands of items traded across Eurasia.

The spread of market culture in Hellenistic times extended to agriculture as well. Before the Achaemenids, most farming in Southwest Asia was subsistence oriented, with states and priesthoods organizing the control and distribution of any surplus. During the Hellenistic age, farming became more commercial. Landowners, often members of ruling families (and some of them women), acquired bigger properties, used more slaves, fed more cities, and reaped larger profits. Whereas before, peasants had usually made decisions for themselves, with the overriding goal of avoiding crop failure and famine, now profit-minded estate owners chose which crops to sow and often preferred those that would fetch a good price to those that minimized the risk of famine.

Greek Alexandria

The career of the city of **Alexandria** in Egypt under the Ptolemies—another of Alexander's successor dynasties—exemplifies these changes in commerce and culture. The city was founded by Alexander in 331 BCE as a Mediterranean seaport, far from the former centers of power in Egypt that were along the Nile to the south. Alexandria attracted a lively merchant class, largely Greek, and other immigrant groups as well, perhaps most prominently Jews from the Levant. Its trade tightened old links between the economies of Egypt and northeastern Africa and those of the Mediterranean and Southwest Asia. Alexandria also became a manufacturing center and by 200 BCE had perhaps half a million citizens, the biggest city of its time. Its hinterland, the fertile farmland of the Nile delta, became ever more commercialized. Alexandria's merchants directed the grain surplus of the Nile delta toward urban markets of the eastern Mediterranean. They traded gold from Nubia to Seleucid (and later Parthian) Persia, where it was exchanged for Chinese silk. To judge from dozens of surviving letters written by (or for) elite women in Ptolemaic Egypt, they too occasionally took part in the commerce in goods and property, although for most of them childbirth, child rearing, and household management loomed larger among their concerns. Alexandria became a byword for wealth. One rich citizen built a lighthouse 500 ft. (120 m) tall that lasted 16 centuries before earthquakes brought it down. Its last remnants were recycled into fortifications in 1480 CE.

Like other Hellenistic kings, Alexandria's rulers patronized the arts and sciences. They built a library that housed every manuscript its directors could buy. It served as an institute for advanced study, where teams of scholars worked away at public expense. One team of 70 Hebrew linguists translated holy texts of the Jews into Greek for inclusion in Alexandria's library. Known as the Septuagint, their work is the basis of later translations of much of the Hebrew Bible. Alexandria also became a center for medical and mathematical training. One of its scholars, Eratosthenes, director of the library, calculated the Earth's circumference and was accurate within 2 percent. The Ptolemies turned

Ptolemaic Egypt A gold relief shows King Ptolemy VI, who ruled Egypt from Alexandria during the period 180–145 BCE. He is wearing the double crown of the pharaohs to make a symbolic connection to the previous rulers of Egypt.

Hellenistic Alexandria into a commercial engine, cultural hothouse, and cosmopolitan magnet for talent from near and far.

Alexandria was exceptional, but a market culture spread throughout the Nile-Ganges web. It radiated out from the cities and trade routes to thousands of villages and farms. Migrants and mercenaries moved about in ever greater numbers. So did captives sold into slavery. Scientific and religious ideas circulated a bit faster. The web of Southwest Asia and Egypt thickened and, through the contacts of the Silk Road, connected to a newly forming web of East and Southeast Asia (discussed in the next chapter) that fused into an Old World web. No record exists of any person traveling all the way from China to the Mediterranean or vice versa until a millennium after Hellenistic times. But now goods, ideas, technologies, crops, and infections, among other things, were carried the length of Eurasia far more often—and far faster—than ever before. This was among the legacies of the Achaemenids, Alexander, and Greek market culture, transplanted to Southwest Asia and Egypt in the Hellenistic age.

The political unity that Cyrus and Persian rule had brought to the region had vanished, and there was no superpower anymore. Alexander's successors couldn't hold together what Cyrus had built. But the commercial connections strengthened by Achaemenid unification and the expansion of market life under Alexander, the Seleucids, the Parthians, and the Ptolemies lived on.

Conclusion

The stories of the Persians and the Greeks were quite different: one featured a great state that unified a broad space, and the other involved many small states that quarreled constantly among themselves. Drawn together in the Hellenistic regimes that followed Alexander's conquests, they contributed to a cultural and political blend that proved to be influential from the rocky shores of the Mediterranean to the snowy mountains of Central Asia. That blend helped to tighten, and extend, existing webs and begin the process of making a more comprehensive Old World web.

Achaemenid Persia was the first superpower in world history, ruling over nearly a third of humankind. The scale of its state created new challenges for its rulers, who refined or invented technologies and techniques of power. These ranged from heavy cavalry to multicultural symbols such as griffins, a common royal motif everywhere in Southwest Asia. Like Ashoka in India, who found Buddhism a helpful way to legitimate his rule, the Achaemenids deployed Ahura Mazda worship as their core ideology while permitting other faiths. Religions that were in effect portable, not tied to any local city, rock, or tree, were much more useful to big multiethnic states such as Persia.

The tiny states of the Greek world competed ruthlessly with one another in every sense. They fought militarily. Several of them tried to amass commercial wealth, partly to be able to fight effectively. And many competed to host the most glorious thinkers, artists, and dramatists they could attract. This situation was highly unusual in world history. More often, a given region united by language and culture is ruled by a single state, which for reasons of its own power and survival limits the freedom of merchants and thinkers. The Greek city-states' stubborn disunity before Alexander's conquests in 338 BCE helps to explain the remarkable development of both commerce and culture for two centuries in Greek lands. Neither merchants nor philosophers were consistently beholden to kings. Of course, there's more to it, because not every case of political fragmentation gives rise to the equivalent of Socrates, Plato, and Aristotle.

It took the combination of Persia and Greece—brought together by the conquests of Alexander and his followers—to Hellenize and tighten links among most landscapes of Southwest Asia and Egypt. Alexander's successors, in power from Epirus and Egypt to Bactria and Sogdiana, admired Greek culture and found ways to meld it with local traditions to support their authority. Greco-Buddhist art, with which this chapter began, is an example of this cultural melding. Alexander's successors also favored the development of commerce and commercial agriculture because it helped expand their tax base. Trade, cities, crafts, and agriculture all flourished in the Hellenistic world, quickening the pace of economic life and linking cities and farms into tighter webs. Trade in the gold of Nubia and the silk of China connected these commercial webs with both Africa and East Asia. Hellenized culture did so too, as widespread artistic motifs such as the halo show. By 200 CE, a new and bigger web, an Old World web, was under construction, thanks in large part to the Achaemenids, the Greeks, Alexander, and Alexander's successors. The new trade contacts with China were links to another big web, an East Asian web, one that had been developing for thousands of years—as we will see in the next chapter.

Chapter Review

KEY TERMS

Achaemenids p. 190

Darius p. 193

heavy cavalry p. 194

Ahura Mazda p. 195

polis p. 199

demokratia p. 204

Alexander the Great p. 213

Hellenistic age p. 217

Parthians p. 218

Silk Road p. 220

Alexandria p. 221

REVIEW QUESTIONS

1. How did Achaemenid rulers regard the cultural practices of peoples they conquered?

2. How did Darius project power across the expanse of his empire?

3. In what ways did the stability of the Achaemenid Empire encourage trade?

4. What were the main characteristics of the Minoan and Mycenaean cultures?

5. Why was the Greek *polis* such a distinctive and important political institution?

6. Describe the social system that made the Spartans particularly formidable in war.

7. Why was Greek culture so rich and dynamic?

8. What was the impact of money and markets in ancient Greece?

9. What was Alexander the Great's chief importance for world history?

10. How did the Seleucids and the Parthians Hellenize their realm, both culturally as well as through money and markets?

11. How did Chinese silk contribute to the growing scale of commerce in western Asia?

12. What does it mean that Ahura Mazda worship was portable, and why was that an important feature for the Persian Empire?

Go to INQUIZITIVE

to see what you've learned—and learn what you've missed—with personalized feedback along the way.

Weaving an East Asian Web

5000 BCE to 200 CE

FOCUS QUESTIONS

1. What were the most important features of East Asia's geography and ecology?

2. What were the main features of early complex societies in East Asia?

3. What accounts for the spread of Chinese cultural influence across East Asia?

4. What were the major shared features of peoples living in the emerging East Asian web?

Things ended badly for the Trung sisters in 43 CE. They were among the millions of people who tried to resist the expansion of China at a time when the gap between Chinese power and that of China's neighbors was widening fast. Trung Trac and Trung Nhi were daughters of a prominent family in the Red River delta of what is now northern Vietnam. Chinese armies had conquered the Red River delta in 111 BCE, and it soon became the biggest population center in East Asia south of the Yangzi River. China controlled it very loosely. Its people lived by fishing, hunting, and farming, often using swidden techniques—cutting and burning forests before planting—or "farming with fire" as Chinese authors put it. The Viet, as these people are called, seemed exotic to Chinese observers: they ate strange foods, tattooed their skin, married only after a couple's first baby was born, and expected women to share in property and in family decision making. Upon marriage, men usually moved in with

CHRONOLOGY

ca. 13,000 BCE Earliest use of pottery in Japan

ca. 8000 BCE Pottery emerges in Korea

By 5000 BCE Farming exists in New Guinea

ca. 3500 BCE Shift toward complex society in China

By 3500 BCE Farming begins in Korea

ca. 1800–1500 BCE First large, walled sites emerge along Huang He River; Erlitou is largest East Asian population center

ca. 1600–1046 BCE Shang dynasty

ca. 1500 BCE Korean bronze working and dolmen building begin

ca. 1450 BCE Copper smelting begins in central Thailand

ca. 1200–1050 BCE First writing in China

1045–256 BCE Zhou dynasty

By 1000 BCE Japan acquires millet, yams, taro from East Asian mainland

ca. 800–700 BCE Introduction of iron in China

771–256 BCE Eastern Zhou rule; Warring States period

ca. 700 BCE Rice is introduced in Korea

ca. 551–479 BCE Lifetime of Confucius (Kong Qiu)

ca. 500 BCE Lifetime of Laozi; *Daodejing* is written down

259–210 BCE Lifetime of Shi Huangdi

their wives' families, and so adult sisters often lived together. The Trung sisters both married the same man, a minor local lord.

In time, the potential of the Red River delta and adjacent lands became too great for China to allow it to remain loosely governed. Its ports gave access to lucrative trade with peoples farther south, in what is now Indonesia and Malaysia. The delta itself was perfect for irrigated rice cultivation. Beginning about 1 CE, Chinese governors took a more active policy with respect to the Viet, trying to "civilize the barbarians," as they put it. This policy included building roads, developing ports, introducing iron tools and plows, and imposing higher taxes. It also involved requiring the use of Chinese language and Chinese hairstyles, and welcoming thousands of Chinese settlers. Moreover, the Chinese overlords wanted to "correct" the Viet's "betrothal and marriage procedures"—in particular, to ensure that males were masters of their own houses and that women no longer could inherit property.

When a Chinese governor executed the Trung sisters' husband for objecting to taxes in 39 CE, they raised a revolt. Rather than secluding themselves in mourning, as the Chinese thought proper, the sisters gathered thousands of Viet, organized them into armies, and captured 65 cities. The Chinese governor retreated, leaving the Trung sisters in charge of what is now northern Vietnam and a sizeable chunk of southern China. Trung Trac declared herself a queen.

Word of the rebellion led by women soon reached the Chinese capital in Luoyang. A large army descended on the Viet in 41 CE, and although it lost half its men to combat and disease, by 43 it had captured the Trung sisters. Together with several thousand leading families of the Viet, the sisters were beheaded and their skulls delivered to the Chinese emperor. The Chinese then got on with the business of "civilizing" the Viet, settling more Chinese in Viet lands, and converting the Red River delta into a productive rice bowl. For the next 900 years, northern Vietnam was, except for brief intervals, part of China.

The term *East Asia* for the purposes of this chapter means the sprawling region including all of modern China, Korea, Japan, and parts of Southeast Asia (mainly Vietnam). For the last 3,000 years, this East Asian region has been home to something like one-quarter to one-third of humankind. This chapter shows how in the millennia before 200 CE, the region of East Asia slowly knit itself together into a vast web of interaction—the East Asian web—broadly comparable to the process afoot in the region between the Nile and the Ganges at the same time.

As it did between the Nile and the Ganges, the process of integration in East Asia involved trade links, the spread of farming, the appeal of certain religions and cultures, and plenty of military conquest—Chinese armies eventually became as ruthlessly efficient as the Assyrians. However, here in East Asia, the role of one political and cultural tradition—the rich and ever-changing one we call Chinese—was much larger than that of Sumerians, Babylonians, Assyrians, Egyptians, Harappans, Persians, or Greeks, or anyone else in between the Nile and the Ganges.

221–207 BCE Qin dynasty

206 BCE–220 CE Han dynasty

ca. 1 CE Chinese governors try to control the Viet; wet rice production spreads into Southeast Asia from China

39–43 CE Trung sisters revolt and rule

By 100 BCE Silk roads link China and the Mediterranean

ca. 300–400 CE Korea and Japan adopt writing

Evolving Environments in East Asia

Before getting into the particulars of East Asian history, let's examine how its geography and ecology helped to shape the region before 200 CE.

Monsoons

East Asian climate is powerfully influenced by seasonal monsoon winds that in summer months carry warm, moist air from the tropical Pacific, and to a lesser extent the Indian Ocean, bringing plentiful rain. The southern coasts of China, for example, where mountains intercept monsoon winds every summer, get a reliable soaking of about 60 inches (1,500 mm) of rain almost every year. Inland regions of East Asia are drier. In winter, the monsoon winds reverse direction, bringing cold, dry air from Central Asia and Siberia over almost all of East Asia. Although not fully reliable, the monsoon pattern, apparently in place for the last 20 million years or so, became the foundation of East Asian agriculture. When it failed, crops withered and people starved. Many of the earliest surviving writings from East Asia express anxiety that spring rains might be too little or summer rains too strong for a good harvest.

One reason monsoons sometimes failed was the irregular shift in currents of the tropical Pacific called El Niño. For reasons no one fully understands, every few years currents of warm water that usually flow from east to west across the Pacific instead stay put near South America. This keeps water in the western Pacific cooler than usual, and the air above it both cooler and drier. When this happens, the monsoon winds bring much less moisture to East Asia. A strong El Niño spells drought for most of Southeast Asia and sometimes southern parts of China. In the past, it meant not only more fires, but also more hunger.

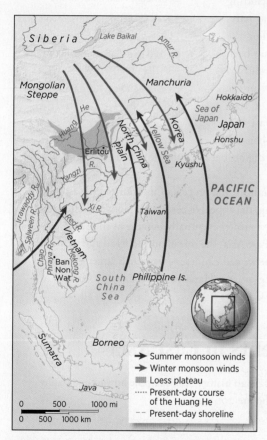

Rivers and Seas

Monsoon rainfall fed a series of rivers that formed another environmental feature important for East Asian history. Several of the world's biggest rivers flow across the region, most of them rising in the Tibetan Plateau or the Himalayas and traversing thousands of miles en route to the sea. The Huang He (or Yellow River), the Yangzi, Mekong, Chao Phraya, Irrawaddy, and Salween served as sources of drinking water, irrigation water, and fish, and as arteries of transportation.

All these rivers had dozens of tributaries, making for a gigantic network potentially available for boat traffic. The combination of navigable rivers and the adjacent seas made East Asia a strong candidate for early development of long-distance trade and transport networks—in short, for webs of

East and Southeast Asia, ca. 1800–1000 BCE The agricultural potential of East Asia depended in part on the seasonal monsoon winds that brought spring and summer rains. Some of the richest soils, important to the development of early Chinese states, lay in the loess region along the Huang He. The monsoon winds aided navigation especially in the South China Sea, helping to tie China to Southeast Asia. (Note that the lower course of the Huang He has shifted over time, and the shoreline of the sea it empties into has also moved. All maps of East Asia will show the river course and shoreline as of the date of the map.)

human interaction. The combination also made it all the more rewarding to build yet more waterways—canals linking the rivers together.

Environmental Dangers

East Asia's environment also featured earthquakes, tsunamis, typhoons, volcanic eruptions, and floods. The offshore islands, from Japan to the Philippines, are especially exposed to typhoons—tropical cyclones with high winds. They also lie across geologically unstable cracks in the Earth's crust, so they're often rocked by earthquakes and volcanic explosions. East Asians have had to learn to live with this dynamic, unpredictable, and at times dangerous environment. In Southwest Asia, by contrast, drought was a frequent risk, and earthquakes an occasional one, but tropical storms, tsunamis, floods, and volcanic eruptions were rare. East Asian societies had to organize themselves to cope with a more diverse array of risks.

East Asia 5,000 years ago was growing warmer and wetter. Alligators slithered along the Huang He (Yellow River). Most of the land was forested and dotted with lakes. Elephants, rhinos, tigers, deer, black bears, and other creatures roamed the woods. Wild water buffalo splashed through the swamps. In most of the region, human population was sparse. But here and there clusters of farming villages had formed, as we saw in Chapter 3. These clusters provided the basis from which complex societies evolved. Eventually, networks of complex societies established regular communication with one another, the beginnings of an East Asian web.

The Emergence of Complex Society in East Asia to 1000 BCE

According to later Chinese traditions, most every component of complex society in East Asia is attributable to the Yellow Emperor, Huang Di. Both god and ruler, he taught people to build shelters, grow grain, and tame animals. He invented boats, carts, the calendar, and clothing. He also instructed an associate to invent writing and wrote the first medical text. His chief wife taught people to weave silk. He reigned for a hundred years (it took some time to get everything done), and all Chinese are descended from him.

Archeologists regard matters differently. As we've seen, rice farming began in the Yangzi valley at least 9,000 years ago, and cultivation of soybeans and millet began along the Huang He at least 8,000 years ago. People living in the floodplains of these two river systems were probably loosely linked even before they started farming. After farming began, it spread from these centers, along both big rivers and into the landscapes in between, where rice and millet were raised. The emergence of complex society began along the Huang He where the river leaves the mountains for the plains.

Growing Social Stratification

To judge by burials, the early villages in East Asia were egalitarian in social structure. Remains found in grave sites imply the recognition of nuclear families within larger lineages or clans—kinship groups that might contain hundreds or even thousands of people. Chemical analysis of a few skeletons (from ca. 5000 to 3000 BCE) in the lower Huang He valley shows that males and females ate the same diet, heavy on millet but with plenty of animal protein. But we should bear in mind that new archeological finds could overturn prevailing interpretations.

Evidence from genetics and historical linguistics suggests that these villagers in what is now China were a diverse lot. They spoke a cluster of languages, many of them ancestral to a language family called Austronesian, which today is spoken mainly in Southeast Asia. The languages that we now call Chinese—Mandarin, Cantonese, and others—acquired some of their characteristics, such as tones, from these early Austronesian languages. What we now sometimes call China proper, the zone inhabited by ethnically Han Chinese, was a culturally, linguistically, and genetically diverse region.

The archeological record suggests that around 3500 BCE a shift took place toward more complex society—at roughly the same time as in Southwest Asia. Bigger settlements and more social stratification emerged in several centers between the Huang He and the Yangzi. Skeletons show evidence of more anemia and shorter life spans than in earlier eras, and more signs of violence, perhaps including human sacrifice. Over a dozen walled towns have been unearthed, several with palace-type architecture.

One cemetery shows how far stratification had developed by 2000 BCE. Most graves contain only one or two objects interred with the dead, and few contain none at all. But one, of an adult female, includes nearly 200 burial objects—ceramics, decorative stones, rings, bracelets, and pendants. Some of the graves contain goblets and pig skulls, perhaps meaning that elites confirmed their status by throwing parties and feasts for lesser folk. Ritual displays of generosity are in many cultures a way for elites to show off their status and reward their supporters.

Early Chinese grave sites also seem to show great awareness of rank and kinship, which if true would be consistent with values held in later East Asian societies. In what is now southern China, elites amassed objects of jade (a lustrous green stone), such as carved masks, taken to signify refinement and symbolize continuity across the generations.

In short, it seems that over time elites got richer and their followers more numerous. Social units were growing larger. A hefty dose of compulsion and intimidation may have been involved: centers built ever-larger fortifications—walls of packed earth—perhaps to shield elites from rebellious commoners.

Even in these early times, communities in East Asia forged long-distance links and networks. Pottery is our best evidence of these trends. Millet and rice were boiled or steamed, not ground into flour and baked like the grains of Southwest Asia, so early

Early Chinese Society
Our first evidence of complex society in China includes grave goods like these intricate jade ornaments, discovered in burials across China dating between 2500 and 2000 BCE. The presence of such luxury objects indicates the emergence of money, trade, and social hierarchy.

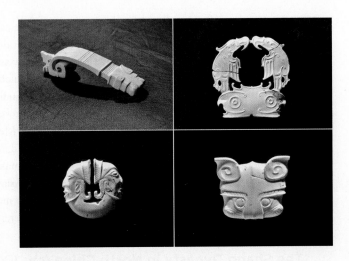

Chinese families had incentives to make durable pots. The earliest yet found, in the Yangzi valley, are nearly 20,000 years old.

Cooking pots acquired symbolic importance: handed down from one generation to the next, they connected the living with their ancestors. Similarities in pottery styles show that as early as 4000 BCE villages in China hundreds of miles apart were in contact. Decorative styles in jade ornaments also testify to early long-distance exchanges. Such connections grew far stronger after East Asian communities began to build states.

Early States

The earliest states in East Asia appeared in northern China. How this happened is unclear. Perhaps states arose from cooperative arrangements intended to manage irrigation and flood control. Rain-fed agriculture is feasible in much of northern China, including the loess region along the Huang He. But the silt load of the Huang He was so great that on its lower reaches it gradually built its bed up above the elevation of the surrounding plains (like the Indus River) and thus was prone to devastating floods.

Chinese villagers constructed levees and dams to keep floodwaters from washing away their crops and homes. Flood control infrastructure could also be used for irrigation. Chinese legends maintain that kings (now generally considered mythical) directed water control, but the scant evidence suggests that it began, as in Egypt and Mesopotamia, at the village level.

The emergence of cities in China is also a hazy story. Settlements in the loess region along the Huang He had existed for millennia before the first large, walled sites emerged around 1800 to 1500 BCE. Thereafter, cities dotted the landscape wherever irrigation allowed surplus food production. Still, two millennia later in 200 CE, under 5 percent of Chinese lived in cities. Most people lived in farming villages.

The first clear evidence of a state in East Asia is a site called Erlitou, just south of the Huang He in what is now China's Henan province. It dates to somewhere around 1800 to 1500 BCE. The site appears to have housed as many as 30,000 people, by far the largest population center in East Asia at the time. It had eight palaces for ruling elites, royal tombs crammed with expensive grave goods of turquoise and jade, paved wagon roads, and workshops for the manufacture of bronze objects.

Bronze working probably arrived in East Asia from Mesopotamia or Iran across the Eurasian steppe. The first East Asian bronze objects date from around 3000 BCE. Mass production seems to have begun at Erlitou. Bronze making became a hallmark of ancient China, not only for weaponry—as in Southwest Asia—but especially for ritual vessels used for making offerings to ancestors. The great majority of Chinese bronze work served this religious purpose, at Erlitou and elsewhere.

The Shang Dynasty in North China (ca. 1600–1046 BCE)

Erlitou might have been its own city-state, or perhaps the capital city of an early dynasty called the Xia. It's more likely that the Xia are mythical and that Erlitou was built under the **Shang dynasty** (ca. 1600–1046 BCE). The base of the Shang dynasty stood in the lower reaches of the Huang He. At times, the dynasty seems to have controlled people almost as far south as the Yangzi basin, but more often its domain was much smaller, closer to the size of a middling New England state, and the edges of its control usually fuzzy.

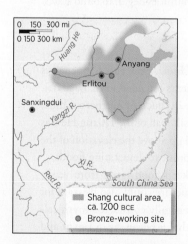

The Shang were likely one of dozens of states in East Asia, and in their time no more important than several others. Chinese tradition regards the Shang as the precursor of all things Chinese—because they had writing that evolved into the later Chinese scripts. All accounts of early East Asian history over-emphasize the Shang because we know more about them than any of their contemporaries.

The Cultural Area of the Shang Dynasty, ca 1200 BCE The Shang dynasty (ca. 1600–1046 BCE) controlled varying parts of the north China plain with its reliable agricultural surplus. Its artisans raised bronze working to a high art.

Writing The first authors of Egyptian hieroglyphs probably drew inspiration from Sumerian writing, but in Shang China writing was invented entirely anew. Although there are a few earlier pottery fragments with what might be meaningful scratches on them, the first clear-cut writing in China dates from about 1200 to 1050 BCE—the twilight years of the Shang dynasty. The Shang writing, now called **oracle bone inscriptions**, consisted of markings made on turtle shells or cattle scapulae (shoulder blades). Most of these were questions put to the gods about big decisions—what and when to plant, whom to marry one's child to, or whether to launch a war. With questions inscribed on them, the shells and bones were heated until they cracked. Then specialist diviners read the cracks as revealing the gods' answers, so people would know whether or not to proceed with their plans. No doubt this left plenty of room for artful interpretation.

The principles of Shang writing are the same as those of modern Chinese script, although all the symbols have changed. It was mainly logographic, like cuneiform and hieroglyphs, in that most symbols represented a word or idea, but a few implied a specific sound. The oracle bone writers used about 4,500 characters, one-third of which modern scholars have deciphered. Subsequent dynasties used modified scripts for purposes of state bureaucracy, literature, and the writing of history. Little survived, because they wrote on strips of bamboo rather than shell or bone. Later Chinese writers used cloth, often silk, on which they wrote with brushes and ink.

Shang Writing A turtle shell dated to around 1050 BCE is covered in writing in the logographic Shang script. It asks the gods for guidance on a military campaign.

Around 100 BCE, the Chinese invented paper, making writing easier than ever before. By mashing rags and plant fibers, such as mulberry bark, in a watery solution and then drying it, papermakers created a cheap material that preserved ink markings indefinitely. Chinese scribes developed standardized lists of characters used over wider and wider territories. Because the script was logographic, it could represent words that were pronounced in very different ways, so even though there were (and still are) several different and mutually incomprehensible languages in China, all were written in the same script. This helped keep Chinese culture cohesive and helped Chinese dynasties keep diverse linguistic regions politically unified for thousands of years—despite the continuing evolution of the Chinese script.

Like cuneiform and hieroglyphs, the Chinese writing system invented in Shang times has lasted about 3,000 years; but unlike them, it still has a future ahead of it. It's the only ancient writing system still in use. First-year university students in China today are required to know 4,500 characters, about the same number as used by Shang oracle bone writers.

Society and Economy The oracle bones and archeology reveal a stratified society. Like all complex societies, the Shang needed an agricultural surplus to support city-dwellers and elites. Although based in the dry north of China, they didn't use irrigation on a significant scale. Instead, they developed something of a plantation system, with gangs of laborers cultivating millet. They also raised wheat, the preferred food of the upper classes, and barley; both crops had been introduced to the region from Southwest Asia. Beer brewed from barley dates back 5,000 years in China. Beans and peas appeared on the menu in ordinary homes. Villagers also raised pigs, sheep, horses, and oxen.

The Shang elite was ruthless in controlling the food surplus. They ran a very hierarchical, stratified, and militarized society. Kings moved around a good deal, checking up on their domains. The oracle bones show a constant concern with warfare, especially against "horse barbarians," presumably pastoralists to the north and west of the Shang heartland. By 1200 BCE, the elite used chariots, another import from Southwest Asia introduced to the Shang by neighboring peoples from the steppe. The Shang employed chariots both as fighting vehicles and as show pieces. Every male aristocrat wanted to be buried with one.

Bronze was central to Shang religious and economic life. A giant bronze foundry at one Shang center near the modern city of Anyang covered about 2.5 acres (1 hectare) in extent. The Shang bronze workers produced enormous quantities of weaponry and even more artistic objects—chiefly, cups for ritual offerings to the ancestors. One piece weighed almost a ton (862 kg, to be precise), the weight of a good-size bull or half of an average American car. Shang bronze production was a state business. Officials organized every step: copper and tin mining, smelting, transport, and casting. To judge by grave sites, only the top rung of society owned bronzes. Common people made offerings to their ancestors with wooden or clay vessels. Shang bronzes were imitated far and wide in their time, and they still attract admiration for their craftsmanship.

The Tomb of Fu Hao Powerful evidence for the extreme stratification of Shang society comes from the tomb of Fu Hao, who lived around 1300 to 1250 BCE. She is mentioned on about 180 oracle bones. She was a king's consort and a military general—a very unusual role for a woman in ancient East Asia or anywhere else. She organized military campaigns and ran her own agricultural estates. She also handled some divination ceremonies, an honor usually reserved for kings. She had at least one son, revealed in oracle bones that express anxiety about her health at childbirth.

Fu Hao's Tomb The luxury goods found in Fu Hao's tomb include ornaments like this jade bird and elephant—two of the 755 jade items with which Fu Hao was buried.

Of the thousands of Shang tombs excavated, hers is the only one that was never looted. Here's what looters missed:

- her skeleton
- 16 other human skeletons
- remains of 6 dogs
- 468 bronze objects—weapons, bells, knives, tiger heads, mirrors, and more
- 755 jade items
- 564 bone objects, mainly hairpins
- 63 stone objects
- 11 pieces of pottery
- 5 ivory items
- nearly 7,000 fragments of cowrie shells

Her tomb shows the reverence accorded to high-ranking individuals, women included. It also attests to long-distance trade, because cowrie shells (used as money) come from warm oceans thousands of miles away.

In life, Fu Hao was exceptional as a woman exercising military and religious authority in a society that, according to oracle bones, regarded the birth of a daughter as a misfortune for parents. But in death she was less exceptional: lavish burials were normal for members of the Shang elite.

The aristocracy ruled through both intimidation and ideology. Human sacrifice figured prominently in keeping the masses in line. On occasions such as the inauguration of a palace or a temple, or the funeral of a king, hundreds of captives and slaves might be killed at a time to keep gods and ancestors happy. Several sacrificial victims joined Fu Hao in her tomb. On balance, it seems the Shang relied on intimidation more heavily than most ancient states, such as Egypt or Babylonia.

Ancestors and the Family The Shang kings, like their counterparts in ancient Mesopotamia or Egypt, also relied on ideology in the form of religion. They claimed special access to divine power and presided over divination ceremonies personally. They honored a supreme god known as Di, accessible only through esteemed ancestors. Only the king could ask the favor of Di. Lesser mortals, through their lesser ancestors, approached lesser gods. The Shang, and probably their neighbors too, believed that ancestors resided in heaven and took an active interest in the affairs of their descendants. So a family's fortunes depended on keeping its ancestors content through ritual sacrifices and offerings. Commoners paid taxes or tribute to the Shang elite, and in a sense paid taxes to their ancestors too.

Family life in Shang China emphasized hierarchy. Children and wives owed deference to fathers and husbands. Women upon marriage left their homes and surrendered membership in the lineage of their birth to join the household and lineage of their husbands. If they gave birth to sons, however, they could expect to be venerated for it—after death. Elite men could marry several wives. Shang kings often married into many important lineages, and their wives sometimes played political roles in the Shang court, as the career of Fu Hao shows. The slender evidence suggests that women of the court figured more prominently in royal politics under the Shang than in most later Chinese dynasties.

Long-Distance Trade   The presence of chariots and cowries shows that the Shang interacted with people far away. They probably did so indirectly: goods and ideas were relayed from one people to their neighbors over long distances. As we've seen, by 100 CE a Silk Road linked China and the Mediterranean; but long before that there was, it seems, a chariot or cowrie road, intermittently connecting Southwest Asia and India to China. (Recall also that Chinese rice was transplanted to India, and West Asian wheat reached China.) During the fourth and third millennia BCE, the steppe lands of Eurasia were apparently a bit warmer and wetter than they are now, and more conducive to farming. That may have eased occasional long-distance trade across Asia.

Sanxingdui and Other States   According to the official chronology, the Shang dynasty was overrun in 1046 BCE. Their successors contended that the Shang kings had grown corrupt and lost the favor of the gods. It could be that their relentless exactions and cruelties provoked more frequent peasant uprisings, giving their enemies an opening. Drier, colder weather after 1100 BCE may have undercut their agricultural surplus. Later chronicles say the Shang fell in part because the Huang He temporarily dried up.

While the Shang were building their state in north China, other states developed elsewhere in what is now China. No writing illustrates the career of Sanxingdui, a walled city to the southwest of modern Chengdu, in Sichuan province. But recently uncovered archeological evidence shows that Sanxingdui, at its height around 1500 to 1100 BCE, featured a fortified city with thick walls and moats, irrigation agriculture, and artisan workshops especially for bronze work.

Sanxingdui Among the artifacts found at Sanxingdui in southwestern China was this life-size bronze statue of a man wearing an elaborately decorated robe. The statue dates to the eleventh or twelfth century BCE.

Sanxingdui's bronze artifacts were made with a different process from those of the Shang foundries, in entirely different styles, but with equal skill. The oldest extant life-size human statue was found here, and an elegant 10-foot-tall tree of bronze. Ivory found here seems to have come from Southeast Asia, implying some long-distance trade links. Future archeology is likely to show the existence of other centers of complex society in China beyond the Shang and Sanxingdui.

Southeast Asia, Korea, and Japan

In Southeast Asia, the Korean Peninsula, and the Japanese archipelago, no major urban centers, states, or complex societies appear in the archeological record before 1000 BCE. Long after life in parts of China had come to feature states, taxes, and wars, people living elsewhere in East Asia remained mobile foragers and small-scale village farmers.

Southeast Asia As we saw in Chapter 2, Southeast Asia, if perhaps only highland New Guinea, was an early site of crop domestication. Farming existed by at least 5000 BCE in New Guinea and perhaps as early as 8000 BCE. In mainland Southeast Asia, some people had turned to farming by 2500 BCE. But populations remained very sparse.

After 3000 BCE, Southeast Asia received small streams of migrant farmers from what is now southern China. They extended the domain of agriculture, as Indo-European-speakers were doing in Europe, as Bantu-speakers were beginning to do in central Africa, and as other farming folk were starting to do on islands of the western Pacific. This was another example of a farmer migration of the sort we saw in Chapter 3. These people were speakers of Austroasiatic languages that in time evolved into Vietnamese, Khmer (spoken in Cambodia), and several other tongues. They drifted south along river valleys such as the Red, Mekong, and Chao Phraya. They substantially replaced the sparse indigenous populations and also went by sea to the Philippine and Indonesian archipelagoes. The great majority of Southeast Asians today are descended biologically from these migrants. The migrants probably brought bronze-working technology with them. Recent archeology also indicates large-scale copper smelting, in central Thailand, beginning around 1450 BCE. In all likelihood, the mining, smelting, and casting techniques came with the migrants from what would later become southern China.

The scale and consequences of farming and metallurgy in Southeast Asia remained modest. Only one archeological site, Ban Non Wat in Thailand, shows any significant social stratification. As of 1000 BCE, Southeast Asians had taken a different path from peoples in northern and central China, or Southwest Asia, with minimal social hierarchy, no state structures, and no cities.

Korea On the Korean Peninsula, complex society and social stratification also came well after 1000 BCE. Korean tradition holds that Koreans descend from the marriage of a god and a bear who had taken human female form after spending 100 days secluded in her cave eating only garlic and mugwort. Their marriage, the tradition goes, produced a son who founded a Korean kingdom around 2300 BCE.

Archeology and genetics, however, tell a less colorful tale. Koreans themselves came from Manchuria (now northeastern-most China) and the Lake Baikal region of Siberia. Most early inhabitants of the peninsula lived in small communities near the sea, harvesting fish and shellfish. The western coast of Korea features a broad intertidal zone and is one of the world's best places to find clams, mussels, and crabs. Some of these coastal dwellers were settled, some mobile. People began making pottery by 8000 BCE and were farming by 3500 BCE. Pottery styles suggest connections to both China and Japan.

After 1500 BCE, most people moved inland to fertile patches of lowland amid Korea's mountains. There they raised millet and soybeans, and lived in bigger communities, including walled towns. Farmers gradually colonized most of Korea's low-lying land, accelerating their pace after the introduction of rice from China around 700 BCE.

Korean bronze working began in the north around 1500 BCE, also introduced from China. It spread to southernmost Korea by about 700 BCE. That slow pace of diffusion, and the modest amount of bronze found by archeologists, suggests that most ancient Koreans found pottery satisfactory for their tastes and saw no reason to go to the trouble of making bronze. Jade also turns up in the archeological record, a luxury item that implies the emergence of elites.

After 1500 BCE, elaborate burials, called **dolmens**, dotted the Korean landscape. Dolmens are stacks of carefully arranged big stones, usually with three or more upright and one flat capstone, erected over burial sites. Dolmens existed in many parts of Eurasia, from western France and Ireland to Korea and Japan. Korea has nearly half the world's dolmens, erected mainly between 1500 and 500 BCE. Nobody knows why people started building them, or why they stopped, or if the structures have any connection to the dolmens of Europe, India, and the Levant. The effort required to place heavy stones above ground and the valuable bronze or jade items in the burials below are indications of social stratification. Not everyone rated a dolmen burial.

Korean Dolmens A dolmen erected approximately during the years 1500 to 500 BCE, with two upright stones and one large flat capstone, still stands in a park in present-day North Korea.

Japan The Japanese archipelago, like the Korean Peninsula, is mountainous and in ancient times was well forested. Its first inhabitants walked there from Korea 35,000 years ago when sea level was down. As we've seen, some of the world's earliest pottery appeared in Japan, perhaps as long as 15,000 years ago. Japan, like Korea, did not adopt writing until after 300 CE, so for early periods archeology provides almost all the evidence.

Japan had few people before 5000 BCE. Most of them lived in caves and practiced hunting, fishing, and gathering. After 5000 BCE, some built shelters, fished well out to sea on boats with harpoons and fishhooks, and traded a little with Korea. Their skeletons indicate they were unusually short for non-farming people: women on average under 5 feet (1.5 m) tall, and men only a little taller. There might have been a quarter-million inhabitants scattered throughout the archipelago by 3000 BCE.

After about 2500 BCE, population grew faster, villages and buildings sprang up, and more and more people took up farming, presumably introduced via Korea. Remains of houses suggest these people lived in extended, not nuclear, families. After 1500 BCE, they produced lots of clay figurines, often of plump women. These led scholars to suppose they had developed a religion with an emphasis on fertility—almost all ancient peoples worshipped fertility. As of 1000 BCE, Japan had acquired millet, yams, and taro from the East Asian mainland, and the farming way of life was spreading to most lowland regions.

At the same time, similarities among pottery styles throughout the islands imply more and more contact within the archipelago. Japan was knitting itself together, slowly, and linking to the mainland via Korea. As of 1000 BCE, it still had no rice, no writing, no metallurgy, no cities, and only modest social hierarchy. But all that was soon to come: Japan, like Korea and Southeast Asia, was too close to China to persevere for long without the trappings of complex society.

East Asia Transformed, 1000 BCE to 200 CE

In the centuries before 1000 BCE, farming, pottery, social hierarchy, cities, and states had cropped up in several places in China. These habits and institutions would continue to spread in the centuries to come with a slow, almost irresistible logic. In the presence of complex society, other societies had to become complex themselves or risk being subsumed, conquered, and perhaps exterminated. As elsewhere in the world, the nodes of dense population and interaction in East Asia—such as the Shang cities—were also nodes of wealth and power, more formidable than other agricultural regions.

This formidability, as elsewhere, consisted of cultural, military, economic, demographic, and epidemiological power. Chinese elites developed cultural traits such as writing and bronzes that elites elsewhere admired and often adopted. Chinese states (those that lasted) created efficient armies that generally swept enemies aside. Chinese agriculture, with its crop mix and irrigation techniques, produced abundant food for growing populations. And growing populations could sustain crowd diseases such as smallpox as endemic infections, dangerous to children but not to adults who had survived them.

Taken together, appealing culture, powerful armies, productive farming, and unseen biological weapons help to explain the expansion of Chinese influence in East Asia—just as they did the expansion of Mesopotamian influence in Southwest Asia.

The Spread of Chinese Influence and Its Limits

The history of East Asia after 1000 BCE features two powerful dynamics at the center of which stood north China. The first was the political and military competition that led to the unification of large spaces. The earliest example was the gradual creation of what we today call China. Later and smaller versions of similar political-military competition yielded increasingly unified political and cultural zones we can fairly call Korea and Japan. In Southeast Asia, however, nothing of the sort happened. While there was no shortage of political competition, polities remained small and no single state or handful of states succeeded in imposing rule over broad regions. This difference helps explain why cultural and linguistic diversity remained stronger in Southeast Asia than in Japan, Korea, or China.

Chinese Writing Found on the Chinese cultural periphery in northwestern China, these wooden slips from 22 CE bear writing that lists a government official's expenses—indicating the spread of both the Chinese writing system and the Chinese state bureaucracy.

The second dynamic was the forging of a cultural synthesis, one that formed first in north China and then spread throughout most of East Asia. In some places, Chinese culture spread when local people were wiped out by violence or disease (or both) and replaced by migrants from northern or central China. In other cases, local people over many generations adopted piecemeal those features of the Chinese culture—writing and bronze making, for example—that they liked or felt they required. Of course, local people altered what they borrowed to fit local circumstances; for example, Korean bronzes looked different from Chinese ones. But overall through demographic replacement and cultural change East Asia became less culturally diverse, more Chinese in its traditions and technologies, and more politically centralized.

Before seeing how these processes worked in

practice, it's important to recognize their limits. First, they worked only where sedentary agriculture was practical. On the grasslands of Mongolia, in the deserts of what is now Xinjiang, on the icy plateau of Tibet, people—although few in number and vulnerable to epidemics—found it possible to retain their political and cultural autonomy. Indeed, those on the grasslands often found they could trade and raid on favorable terms, because horses and horsemanship gave them mobility and a military formidability all their own.

To the south, in the mountainous terrain of what is now southern China, local people also found it easier to retain their autonomy if they kept to the mountains. Until well after 500 CE, these southerners usually resisted Chinese expansion successfully. Up in the hills they could stay safe; keep their own languages, gods, and traditions; and usually choose the times, places, and terms on which they dealt with lowlanders who were gradually becoming Chinese in culture, language, and political loyalty. Unlike the horse pastoralists of the northern grasslands, these hill peoples, despite sometimes legendary ferocity (according to Chinese authors), posed minimal military threat to the settled farmers of East Asia and the expansion of Chinese culture and power. They could raid from time to time, but they could not conquer.

Malaria was another check to the expansion of Chinese settlement to the south. Malaria probably entered Southeast Asia and what is now southern China with the first human migrants during the Paleolithic. It probably intensified with agriculture, because cultivated landscapes are good ones for the mosquitoes that carry the disease. Like smallpox, it killed children in droves; but for those who lived to adulthood, it posed a smaller threat. Malaria doesn't confer full immunity on survivors, but repeated bouts of the disease build up one's resistance to subsequent infection. So people who grew up in Southeast Asia or southern China had greater resistance to the disease than did those who came from the north, where colder conditions reduced the populations of relevant mosquitoes and therefore the frequency of malaria. In effect, in East Asia, malaria served as something of a shield for southern peoples against northerners.

The slow expansion of Chinese power and culture, almost irresistible in large parts of East Asia for more than a thousand years, reached its limits on the grasslands to the north and west, and in the mountains and malarial forests and clearings of the south. But within these limits, the big story in mainland East Asia between 1000 BCE and 200 CE was Chinese expansion.

The Zhou (1045–256 BCE)

The spread of Chinese cultural influence throughout East Asia was accompanied by the formation of a large state. For the last 2,000 years there has been, more often than not, a very big country we call China. The long process of building a large, durable, and unified China began with the **Zhou dynasty** in the eleventh century BCE.

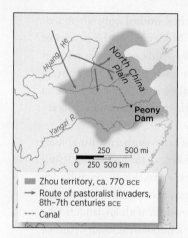

The Zhou Dynasty, 1045–ca. 600 BCE While the Zhou officially lasted until 256 BCE, the dynasty controlled a large part of the north China plain only until the eighth century BCE, after which political fragmentation prevailed for several centuries. Under the Zhou, the use of iron tools and of irrigation expanded markedly.

Consolidating Power In what would become a formula for dynastic successions, Zhou traditions depict the Shang rulers as debauched and cruel, providing just cause for the restoration of order and righteousness by the Zhou. More likely, the Zhou were the most successful of many lineages making alliances, attacking enemies, and struggling for survival and power, enabling them to push aside the ailing Shang state. The conventional dates for Zhou rule are 1045 to 256 BCE, but after the eighth century BCE they controlled only a fraction of China.

Once in control of the rich loess soils of the middle and lower Huang He, the Zhou set about consolidating their power. They supported the development of irrigation works and agriculture, enormously expanding the food production capacity of Zhou lands. The adoption of iron farm tools, which spread after the introduction of iron-working techniques from Central Asia in the ninth or eighth century BCE, had a similar effect. Irrigation and iron proved to be a powerful boon to agriculture in north China, as in Mesopotamia and north India. With more to eat, population in north China grew more quickly than before.

Like many early dynasties, the Zhou ran something like a franchising operation, allowing local leaders considerable leeway as long as they handed a chunk of their revenues, generally in grain, to the Zhou leadership. Some evidence suggests that farming under the Zhou was more a matter of family units than work gangs as under the Shang. In the idealized version, square fields were subdivided into nine smaller squares, and one-ninth of the harvest went to landowners, who forwarded some of that to their overlords. The rest belonged to those who worked the land. Rarely were things as smooth as that, though. One song recorded from the time suggests how peasants felt about their landlords:

> *Big rat, big rat*
> *Do not gobble our millet!*
> *Three years we have slaved for you,*
> *Yet you take no notice of us.*

Peasant happiness wasn't foremost among Zhou concerns. As long as enough surplus worked its way up the social hierarchy into the hands of the Zhou kings, they could maintain a military that intimidated any local lords who might be thinking about not paying up. And they could fight border wars with other states and fend off raids from the equestrian tribes of the steppe grasslands. At times, the Zhou exacted tribute from farming folk nearly as far south as the Yangzi.

The Mandate of Heaven As the Zhou solidified their power, they supported a cultural elite, scholars called *shi* who consolidated much of what is now considered Chinese culture. Some members of this cultural elite held bureaucratic positions in government for Zhou lords. Others had to work as teachers, roving from town to town instructing boys and young men in the literary arts. Collectively, this class of scholars crystallized the cultural formula often called the **Mandate of Heaven**, whereby rulers owed their position to the favor of heaven and styled themselves as sons of heaven.

Supernatural power for the Zhou did not reside in a god (like the Shang's Di), but in a more abstract entity, *tian*, usually translated as "heaven." Ancestors remained important intermediaries between the living and heaven. But human sacrifice, common under the Shang, became rare under the Zhou.

The idea of the Mandate of Heaven, which took shape under the Zhou, was the Chinese version of the widespread tendency for rulers to claim legitimacy from their special relationships with the supernatural rulers of the universe. We've encountered it in Mesopotamia and Egypt, for example. But in the Chinese variant of that claim, the support of supernatural authorities was provisional, not permanent. This provided a measure of dynastic performance that made cultural power and political symbolism all the more important: rulers had to convince everyone that they retained the Mandate of Heaven. If floods, plagues, droughts, or rebellions seemed excessive, supporters might begin to think that a given ruler or dynasty had lost the Mandate of Heaven. If their army commanders came to that conclusion, rulers were in deep trouble.

Warfare In the realm of warfare, the Zhou sponsored some important innovations. The Zhou mastered the complex tasks of integrating chariots with infantry and maintaining disciplined formations on the battlefield. By some accounts, their final defeat of the Shang featured 300 chariots. These skills made them hard to beat on the plains of northern China, although uneven terrain—common in China— negated any advantages that disciplined charioteers enjoyed. Unlike the states of Southwest Asia or north India, the Zhou did not use cavalry.

The Zhou maintained their military

Zhou Chariots The remains of horses and chariots interred with the dead in a burial pit in present-day Henan demonstrate the centrality of chariots to Zhou society.

edge until the eighth century BCE. Then local lords began to rebel and rival states grew stronger. The Zhou had reached an equilibrium of sorts. Their state had grown big enough that it had long borders to defend, and many ambitious local leaders inside their borders to co-opt or intimidate. Newly conquered lands to distribute to followers grew harder to come by, and rebellions more common. The Zhou responded with assertions of power—grander rituals, bigger bronzes, and more frequent demands for displays of loyalty. On one occasion in 860 BCE, a King Yi, fed up with lack of cooperation from a local lord, captured him and boiled him alive in a cauldron. Even this demonstration of determination couldn't solve the Zhou's problem of disunity, and by 771 they were overrun by horse pastoralists from the west. Only a remnant of their kingdom survived, called the Eastern Zhou. Later ages held up the early Zhou as a Chinese golden age of order, virtue, prosperity, and power.

The University of War: Warring States (771–256 BCE)

For 500 years after the Zhou decline, no single state could dominate China. Specialists use different designations for parts of the entire period (771–256 BCE) when the Eastern Zhou and many other kingdoms competed against one another, but the term *Warring States* captures the reality most clearly.

Economic and Social Change   With the decline of the Zhou, China became a university of war. States got good at it or were swallowed up by their neighbors. The survivors were highly inventive. They developed to a high art the technology of crossbows, which were more powerful than ordinary bows, and perfected the interplay of infantry and cavalry formations, which replaced chariots in the fifth or fourth century BCE. States relied less on hereditary rulers and more on technocratic elites, men who had proven themselves as military leaders or logistical wizards. The *shi* now became both scholars and practitioners of war.

States also needed strong economies and streams of revenue to pay for wars. Kings introduced coin money beginning in the seventh century BCE—about the same time that coins first appeared in Southwest Asia. The use of money made commerce and tax collection more efficient. Iron weaponry and farm tools spread as fast as coin money. So did the use of draft animals, such as water buffalo, and irrigation technology. Some states even allowed families to own and work their own land, and to sell it, hoping to harness private self-interest for the purpose of raising state revenues.

At the same time, some states sought to boost production themselves. Around 600 BCE, Sunshu Ao, a minister of a small state along the Yangzi River in central China, oversaw construction of what was probably the largest single irrigation operation in ancient times. The Peony Dam and reservoir irrigated about 9,300 square miles of farmland (24,000 sq. km, an area bigger than the state of New Jersey).

Despite violence and political instability, China's economy was growing more commercial and prosperous through the use of money, expanded irrigation, and experiments with private ownership of land. A sage from the third century BCE, Xunzi, took notice of the interlocking trade networks of his time:

> In the far north there are fast horses and howling dogs; the central states acquire and breed them and put them to work. In the far south there are feathers, tusks, hides, pure copper, and cinnabar; the central states acquire them and use them in their manufactures. In the far east are plants with purple dye, coarse hemp, fish, and salt; the central states acquire them for their food and clothing. In the far west there are skins and colored yaks' tails; the central states acquire them for their needs.

Xunzi portrayed a world in which the peripheral regions sent their wares to the heartlands of China between the Yangzi and the Huang He. In return, cloth, bronzes, tools, weapons, and grain presumably flowed from the center of China to the peripheries. In ways that recall fifth-century BCE Greece, but on a larger scale, commercial vitality and political strife went hand in hand in China during the Warring States period.

Chinese Currency Early Chinese coins were made of bronze and cast in a shape that resembled agricultural implements—in this image, mostly spades, although there is also a knife-shaped coin at top right. Such coins circulated widely from around 600 BCE.

The university of war promoted social change too. As rulers came to depend increasingly on experts in politics, war, and tax collection, young men of talent and ambition were able to overcome humble birth and rise to positions of power and prestige, bringing their families up the social ladder with them. The authority of aristocrats eroded, and many held their positions at the pleasure of their nominal social inferiors, the *shi*. Improvements in iron-making technology brought cheaper weaponry, so that it became possible to fit out huge armies of peasants with spears, swords, shields—even armor. The old aristocratic warriors with their expensive bronze weapons and their chariots were now—after 500 BCE or so—relics of a time gone by.

The Warring States period, and indeed the preceding several centuries, witnessed a deepening of gender inequality in China. Whereas skeletons from before 3000 BCE showed that males and females ate the same diet, later bones tell us that by 500 BCE women ate far less meat than men. Women on average now were shorter than their foremothers a few millennia before, whereas men's average heights stayed the same. Parents were now investing more in their sons than their daughters.

The university of war and the advent of iron weaponry bear some comparison to developments we've seen in Mesopotamia, north India, and Greece. Aristocracies declined in all of these regions. The geopolitical impacts in China were, however, unlike those in Mesopotamia, where one state, Assyria, took fuller advantage of the potential of mass armies and iron weaponry than all rivals and built a sprawling empire. China during the Warring States centuries was more like Greece—but on a bigger scale—with continual warfare among states and with alliance systems of roughly equal power.

Sun Tzu   The bloody chaos of the Warring States centuries suggested that the Zhou, unable to prevent mayhem and chaos, no longer enjoyed the Mandate of Heaven. But why did heaven not award its support to another ruling house that could restore peace and order? Texts from the period explored this issue and others as a new spirit of questioning—of philosophy—took root amid the destruction and gore. In this respect, too, Warring States China bore some resemblance to Greece of the fifth and fourth centuries BCE.

Among the remarkable works written during China's Warring States period was a classic of strategy attributed to **Sun Tzu** (also known as Sunzi), *The Art of War*. By tradition, Sun Tzu was a general active in the sixth century BCE, but modern scholars aren't sure he really existed. Clues in the text such as descriptions of giant battles suggest that it was written in the fifth century BCE or even later, and perhaps by several authors.

Whatever its authorship, *The Art of War* has shown extraordinary staying power and is widely read today in military and business circles. It not only explains points of military strategy and tactics, but offers insight on public administration, diplomacy, espionage, and statecraft generally. It emphasizes the importance of deception, patience, and humility in military leadership:

Warring States Art This bronze from the period of the Warring States (771–256 BCE) depicts Chinese forces in battle in northern Yunnan.

All warfare is based on deception. . . . For to win one hundred victories in one hundred battles is not the acme of skill. To subdue the enemy without fighting is the acme of skill. . . . A good commander is benevolent and unconcerned with fame.

Confucius Less widely read by business and military figures, but more influential overall, was another scholar and strategist for hire, Kong Qiu (also Kong Fuzi), or **Confucius** (ca. 551–479 BCE). He came from a down-on-its-luck military family based about 300 miles (500 km) south of today's Beijing in what is now Shandong province. As a youth, he reportedly worked odd jobs as a herdsman, clerk, and accountant. He married at age 19 and became a father a year later. He made his career as a political adviser, one of the legions of *shi*. Like Aristotle who tutored Alexander, Confucius helped train young princes. He also shared his wisdom with older ones. According to some sources, he worked many years for one warlord, but then left him and traveled around north and central China, giving advice about how rulers should run their kingdoms. As the students of Socrates had done, the followers of Confucius eventually collected some of his ideas into a book; this one was called the *Analects*.

Confucius's advice could hardly have been more different than that recorded in *The Art of War*. Confucius admitted he was "unversed in military affairs" and couldn't tell rulers how to win battles. Instead, he argued that in order to prosper and succeed, rulers needed to behave ethically toward both their ancestors and their living followers. He emphasized morality, the proper exercise of ritual (especially the reverence for ancestors), and careful study of ancient wisdom. He imagined the past, especially the early years of the Zhou dynasty, to be a better age when rulers had behaved honorably, greed had been less rampant, and sages like himself had carried more influence. In his emphasis on ethical conduct, ritual, social hierarchy, and the proper status of scholars, his views resembled those of north India's Brahmins.

Confucius saw the family as a suitable model for the state. Just as a responsible adult male ruled a family, so a king ruled a state. Unlike Sun Tzu, he insisted on truthfulness in speech, even in facial expressions. He wanted rulers to inspire their subjects through ethical, dignified conduct, rather than to rely on laws or, worse yet, bribery, deception, and intimidation. All members of society had a duty to fulfill, hierarchies to recognize, deference to pay—to fathers, husbands, elders, sages, officials, and above all the ruler. Confucius thought women had no place in public life. He mentions women only once in the *Analects*, saying they are "unpleasant" to have to deal with.

At a time when market forces were growing in China, Confucius held money-grubbing merchants in contempt. Philosophers and scholars, in contrast, merited admiration. As he put it: "The mind of the superior man is conversant with righteousness; the mind of the inferior man is conversant with profit."

Confucius died in 479 BCE, still an obscure political adviser. For the next few centuries, his thinking went in and out of fashion in China. In the second century CE, as

CONSIDERING THE EVIDENCE

The Great Learning

"The Great Learning" is from the *Book of Rites*, a compendium of Confucian teachings about ethics and rituals collected in the third century BCE. Aspiring scholars would memorize the "The Great Learning," along with a commentary attributed to Confucius's disciple Zeng Shen, before moving on to more complicated texts like the *Analects* of Confucius. "The Great Learning" encourages learners to set their politics in order by regulating their families and mastering themselves. The following excerpt is the final section of Zeng's commentary in which he discusses the proper way for rulers to acquire and manage wealth.

There is a great course also for the production of wealth. Let the producers be many and the consumers few. Let there be activity in the production, and economy in the expenditure. Then the wealth will always be sufficient.

The virtuous ruler, by means of his wealth, makes himself more distinguished. The vicious ruler accumulates wealth, at the expense of his life.

Never has there been a case of the sovereign loving benevolence, and the people not loving righteousness. Never has there been a case where the people have loved righteousness, and the affairs of the sovereign have not been carried to completion. And never has there been a case where the wealth in such a State, collected in the treasuries and arsenals, did not continue in the sovereign's possession.

...

When he who presides over a State or a family makes his revenues his chief business, he must be under the influence of some small, mean, man.

He may consider this man to be good; but when such a person is employed in the administration of a State or family, calamities from Heaven, and injuries from men, will befall it together, and, though a good man may take his place, he will not be able to remedy the evil. This illustrates again the saying, "In a State, gain is not to be considered prosperity, but its prosperity will be found in righteousness."

Questions for Analysis

1. What is the primary difference between the way a virtuous ruler and a vicious ruler use wealth?

2. Although this document doesn't mention merchants directly, what insights does it offer about why Confucian scholars held merchants in contempt?

3. In Confucian philosophy, what is the relationship between the righteousness of a ruler and the prosperity of the state?

Source: *The Chinese Classics: With a Translation, Critical and Exegetical Notes, Prolegomena, and Copious Indexes*, Vol. I, ed. and trans. James Legge (London: 1861).

we'll see below, a dynasty called the Han made his works the standard canon that all aspiring officials had to study. His influence has permeated the Chinese state and society ever since, and has seeped into Korea, Japan, and Vietnam as well.

Legalism The five centuries of war and political chaos after 771 BCE proved to be intellectually creative in other respects too. Several other philosophers offered ideas—some thoroughly at odds with Confucianism—that resonated ever after. One group advanced a grim set of principles known as **Legalism**, according to which stern laws and punishments were the only basis for a sound society, and loyalty to the state and ruler was everyone's highest obligation. As a political philosophy, Legalism put the power of the state above all other considerations and advocated a ruthless approach to building and maintaining power.

In a book compiled by his followers, Lord Shang (390–338 BCE), one of the great exponents of Legalism, maintained that "in applying punishments, light offenses should be punished heavily; if light offenses do not appear, heavy offenses will not come." In its extreme regimentation of society and idolization of the military, Legalism loosely resembled the ideology of the Greek city-state of Sparta.

Legalism took shape in the fourth and third centuries, partly in opposition to the influence of Confucian scholars—whom Lord Shang called vermin. The *Book of Lord Shang* lists "six parasites":

> . . . rites and music, odes and history, cultivation and goodness, filial devotion and brotherly love, sincerity and trustworthiness, uprightness and integrity, humaneness and rightness, criticism of the army and being ashamed of fighting.

That's actually 16 parasites in all, most of them Confucian virtues. Legalism scorned the past and any rituals that glorified it. It urged statesmen to maximize state power without respect for tradition. Lord Shang recommended intimidation as a better tool than exemplary virtue. Citizens should be rewarded for killing the state's enemies, while those who didn't report crimes committed by their neighbors should be sliced in half at the waist. Many punishments recommended in Legalist texts involved mutilation or disfigurement—a special disgrace for Chinese, who believed their bodies were a gift from their parents and should be respected as such. Tattoos, for example, were regarded as a punishment. Unlike Hammurabi in Babylonia, for whom appropriate punishments of crimes varied with the social status of victim and perpetrator, Lord Shang insisted that all be treated equally harshly before the law, even aristocrats. This principle seems to have hastened his own end: according to most traditions, vengeful aristocrats had him fastened to five chariots and torn limb from limb.

The legacy of Lord Shang and Legalism did not match that of Confucianism in China. It appealed only to China's most authoritarian and heartless rulers, although the

Qin dynasty relied upon it. Unlike other schools of thought that took shape during the Warring States period, Chinese Legalism had no appeal outside of China.

Daoism   Daoism (or Taoism) is another intellectual tradition that crystallized during the dark years of the Warring States. Like Confucianism, it has remained influential for more than 2,000 years. It draws on centuries of folk religion and Chinese philosophy, assembled into key texts such as the *Daodejing* (or *Tao Te Ching*, sometimes translated as *The Classic of the Way of Virtue*). By tradition, this text is held to be the work of Laozi, who is placed in the sixth century BCE and sometimes referred to as a teacher of Confucius. But, as with Sun Tzu, it's uncertain if there ever was a Laozi.

The heart of Daoism is the three "jewels": compassion, moderation, and humility. Daoism is full of indirection and analogy, not easily pinned down to a single set of meanings. A sample of its slipperiness appears in the first phrases of the *Daodejing*: "The Way that can be described is not the true way. The Name that can be named is not the constant name." Paradox is at its core: "Do nothing and everything is done." It has, then, multiple meanings and is easily re-interpreted at any time, which is part of the reason for its durability. At its heart, however, are messages of simplicity, humility, renunciation, and restraint—not unlike its Indian contemporary, Buddhism. Daoism had limited appeal to rulers, for whom the justifications for hierarchy found in Legalism or Confucianism seemed to provide better guidance. But educated people often found its puzzles and mysteries attractive. Daoism found eager audiences outside of China, especially in Korea, Japan, and parts of Southeast Asia.

For ordinary Chinese in these centuries, the majority of whom were illiterate peasant villagers, the doctrines of Confucianism, Legalism, or Daoism provided little direct guidance. Instead, they took their inspiration from traditions of ancestor worship mixed with combinations of local gods. For them, the centuries after the decline of the Zhou were times of violent chaos rather than intellectual achievement.

Disunity and Creativity   The university of war was also a university of the mind. The Warring States period was a dismal one in most respects, but its disunity and competition created situations in which no overarching authority could impose conformity in thought or art. China as a cultural space was so politically fragmented that rival schools of thought and styles of expression could easily co-exist. Art and music showed much more diversity than they had under the Zhou. So did medical thought and other forms of science—according to some experts, acupuncture made its debut at this time.

In some respects, Warring States China paralleled the nearly simultaneous political disunity and creative cultural explosion of both the ancient Greek world and that of north India before the Mauryan Empire. In all three cases, a community shared a language and a culture but lived amid political rivalry and chaos in which no single ruler could enforce a single creed, philosophy, or way of thought. As the sages recognized, these were terrible times to live in but wonderful times to think in.

The Qin (221–207 BCE)

In the chaos following 771 BCE, hundreds of little states flourished in the north China plain between the Huang He and the Yangzi. Within 200 years, there were only half a dozen left standing. They continued their wars until one state, the **Qin**, managed to gain control of the rich rice lands of Sichuan, in the middle Yangzi region, and tip the scales in its favor. Its rulers followed the ruthless path recommended by Lord Shang and often slaughtered entire populations whose armies had been defeated. In the late 230s BCE, the 22-year-old King Zheng launched a series of campaigns lasting 16 years and put an end to the Warring States period by conquering the Qin's last rivals in quick succession. Judging that "king" was no longer title enough, he proclaimed himself First August Emperor, or **Shi Huangdi**. For most of its history from this time forward, China was an empire.

The early career of Shi Huangdi bears comparison with that of Alexander the Great, born a century before. Both men were heirs to power in royal families and masterminded wars of imperial conquest when still young. Both met with extraordinary success, although only Alexander led troops in the field. Within nine years, Alexander had created a Greco-Macedonian empire that stretched from the Adriatic Sea to the Indus River. Shi Huangdi in 16 years conquered an area ranging from Sichuan to the mouth of the Yangzi to Manchuria.

Upon unifying most of China by 221 BCE, Shi Huangdi (also known as Qin Shi Huang, Qin being the name of his dynasty) wasted no time expanding his domain at the expense of "barbarians," meaning all people who weren't culturally Chinese. After choosing Chang'an (part of today's

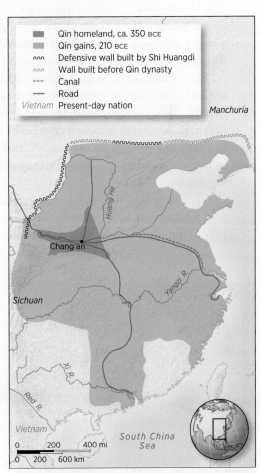

The Qin Dynasty, 221–207 BCE The Qin state, ruled for most of its duration by Shi Huangdi, was the first real empire in Chinese history. Although short-lived, it established the precedent of a large and unified China. Among its legacies was a much-enhanced infrastructure of roads and canals and a simplified written language.

city of Xi'an) as his capital, he launched campaigns in the south against peoples in what is now Vietnam. He built walls in the north to keep steppe raiders out and his people in—walls that later dynasties would extend and strengthen to the point they became known as the Great Wall of China.

Within his borders, Shi Huangdi worked to unify China in every way possible. He standardized weights and measures, coins, and even axle lengths for carts. He built canals and nearly 4,000 miles (roughly 7,000 km) of roads. He tore down city walls and melted down weapons not needed in his arsenals so that no local leaders could resist him. He simplified the written language, a useful reform when conquering linguistically diverse peoples. The Chinese characters required in his reign remained standard for almost 2,000 years until another reform occurred in the 1950s. This common written language helped ensure the long-term unity of China.

Shi Huangdi scorned the ethics of Confucianism. He tried to destroy all copies of Confucian texts and imposed Legalism as the only acceptable school of political thought. The court historian of the next dynasty, Sima Qian, wrote that Shi Huangdi took a special delight in killing off sages by burying them alive, although that could be exaggeration. In short, he consolidated his power with vigor and ruthlessness second to none, doing his best to live up to the brutal principles of Lord Shang and Legalism.

Shi Huangdi was by all accounts obsessed with immortality and feared his empire would not outlast him. When he died at age 48 or 49, in 210 BCE (perhaps of mercury poisoning from the elixirs of immortality he liked to drink), his fears were confirmed when the Qin Empire fell apart, just as Alexander's disintegrated after his death. His followers engaged in civil wars, subjects rebelled, and China seemed once more bound for disunity and perpetual war. But Shi Huangdi, although not immortal himself, had laid a firm foundation for imperial Chinese unity.

Before his death, Shi Huangdi arranged a giant mausoleum for himself. It stood roughly half the height of the tallest of ancient Egypt's pyramids. According to the historian Sima Qian, all his concubines were buried with him, as were the legions of workers who built the tomb. It was guarded by 7,000 statues of warriors, made of terra cotta, together with about 100 chariots. His mausoleum fell to ruin

Terra-Cotta Warriors Here are a few of the 7,000 soldiers and 100 horses made from terra-cotta who guarded Shi Huangdi's tomb near Xi'an. The tomb is considered one of the great artifacts of ancient China.

and remained buried and unknown until well diggers accidentally discovered it in 1974. Shi Huangdi's legacy was not his tomb, but a large and united China.

The Han (206 BCE–220 CE) and the Consolidation of Empire

In short order, a warlord of peasant origin defeated rivals and re-assembled the empire, calling himself Emperor Gaozu. He founded a dynasty in 206 BCE called the **Han**. It lasted until 221 CE, a golden age according to many subsequent Chinese. Nowadays, ethnic Chinese refer to themselves as Han Chinese.

For the Han dynasty, the number, variety, and value of written sources is much greater than for earlier periods. One of the most valuable texts, *Shiji*, translated as *The Records of the Grand Historian*, was completed in 91 BCE by Sima Qian. More than a mere tale of the exploits of emperors (although there's plenty of that), it is an insightful and analytical history, commenting on motives, social forces and conditions, causation, and other matters still of concern to historians today. In these respects, it's like the history of Thucydides—analytical as well as narrative, and still read after two millennia. Thanks to Sima Qian and other authors, we have a firmer sense of the Han dynasty than any earlier ones in East Asian history.

The Han dynasties were keen expansionists. With their capital at Chang'an (today's Xi'an), they pushed the frontiers of the reconstructed Qin state in almost all directions, south into what is now Vietnam, east into what is now North Korea, and west to the Tarim basin. Han Wudi, who reigned from 141 to 87 BCE, enjoyed tremendous success in military matters. At times he prevailed even against the pastoral peoples to the north and west, known at this time as the Xiongnu and increasingly organized in large and formidable confederations. His successes stabilized Han rule, for which he is remembered among China's greatest emperors. China was now a true empire, a gigantic state, and it approximated the borders of what we call China today.

The historian Sima Qian worked—uneasily—for Han Wudi. As a boy, Sima Qian studied ancient texts with his father, the librarian of the Han state. As a young man, he took part in imperial inspection tours with Han Wudi, who made him a senior official and adviser. As an adviser, Sima Qian became entangled in a controversy over a general who had surrendered to "barbarians." Sima Qian defended the general, provoking Han Wudi to sentence him to a fine, if Sima Qian could pay, or castration if he could not. Sima Qian could not pay and suffered the consequences. He was not kind in his judgments about Han Wudi, and as a historian he got the last word.

Population and Economy China's population grew rapidly under the Han dynasty. According to a census taken in 2 CE (the oldest surviving one in the history of the world), the Han domains included more than 57 million people living in 12 million households. The world's population at this point came to roughly 200 to 250 million,

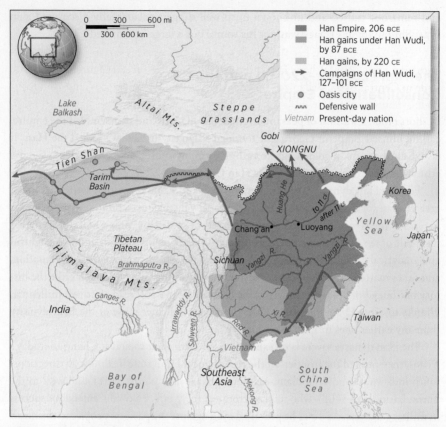

The Han Empire, 206 BCE–220 CE The Han dynasty quickly rebuilt the empire of the Qin and then, especially under Han Wudi, extended Chinese rule westward into Central Asia and to the southwest into rugged highlands. This expansion laid the groundwork for sustained contacts with western Asia and India, the basis of the Old World web.

so Han subjects accounted for perhaps one in four people on Earth. The biggest city, Luoyang, in the center of the north China plain and the Han capital after 25 CE, had about half a million people.

The economy also grew rapidly under the Han, thanks to the infrastructure built by the Qin and long years of internal peace. The Han fought endless border wars, and in both the dynasty's first and final years they faced several rebellions. But in many decades in between, and in comparison to the bloody centuries that preceded them, theirs was a peaceful time, which helped make it a prosperous time.

A small part of Han prosperity came from trade with their neighbors. As they had done for at least 1,500 years, Chinese merchants swapped grain and crafts to the north-ern pastoralists in exchange for horses, hides, furs, and other items. Now, however, they expanded their commercial horizons, especially as the emperors and their armies extended the empire. Trade thrived along the caravan routes of the Eurasian steppe and deserts, collectively called the Silk Road, linking China to Iran and the Mediterranean via Central Asia. When Han China gained control of several Central Asian oases, trade to Central Asia's Hellenized kingdoms in Bactria and Sogdiana—also Silk Road trade—flourished. Chinese silk brought big war horses, much prized by Han Wudi, from Central Asia. Precious cargoes of all sorts traveled the Silk Road routes: gems, gold, silver, salt, ivory, spices, pepper, porcelain, slaves, and much more.

Maritime trade also flourished during the Han period, expanding with Korea and Japan and extending further afield into the lands facing the South China Sea. By the first century BCE, Chinese gold and silk appeared as far south as Thailand's shores, exchanged for pearl and jade, among other goods.

The Silk Road and maritime trade of Han times helped keep the craftsmen and women (silk production was mainly women's work) gainfully employed, gave them incentives to refine their skills, and provided an easily taxable source of revenue for the emperors to fund wars and build palaces. With the expansion of traffic across Central Asia, the gigantic space from Japan to Spain was becoming a single interactive Old World web—woven in no small part by the fingers of Chinese women and girls who raised silkworms, spun thread, and made silk.

Han prosperity rested only partly on long-distance trade. The state created government monopolies over salt and iron production. When well run, they proved beneficial not only to the state treasury but to the population as well. State monopolies also controlled the making of bronze and a popular alcoholic drink. The Han tried to keep prices for important goods stable, by hoarding when prices were low and selling when prices were high, which moderated the normal price swings of markets.

Outside of a few industries, the Han encouraged production for markets and private enterprise. Paper, for writing, and porcelain, for high-end pottery, were developed as private industries. The Han required that some taxes be paid in money, motivating ordinary people to take part in a growing cash economy. By 5 CE, the treasury minted upward of 200 million coins annually. In a sense, the 500 years of internal warfare preceding the Qin and Han made China an excellent candidate for rapid economic growth once peace prevailed. Merely

The Silk Road Thanks to the Silk Road, Chinese silk was known as far away as Rome. A fresco from Pompeii (79 CE) shows a woman wearing a silk dress.

providing more peace and infrastructure, as the Qin and Han did, unleashed pent-up potential from which society and state both profited.

The large government role in the economy provoked frequent opposition. In 86 BCE, the government organized a review of the empire's economic situation, which soon led to debates among learned advisers that were recorded decades later as *The Salt and Iron Debates.* Confucian scholars regarded all commerce as suspect, an unproductive temptation to dishonesty. They felt that government officials, especially, shouldn't taint themselves with mercantile pursuits. Their notions of virtue drove them to advocate an economy based on local self-sufficiency with minimal production for market. In particular, the Confucian thinkers objected to trade with the Xiongnu, the steppe nomads to the north and Han China's most formidable military threat. However, an eloquent opponent, a minister of state, explained the advantages of trade with foreigners:

> [A] piece of Chinese plain silk can be exchanged with the Xiongnu for articles worth several pieces of gold and thereby reduce the resources of our enemy. Mules, donkeys, and camels enter the frontier in unbroken lines; horses . . . come into our possession. The furs of sables, marmots, foxes, and badgers, colored rugs and decorated carpets fill the Imperial Treasury. . . . [F]oreign products keep flowing in, while our wealth is not dissipated.

This interpretation, reminiscent of Xunzi's two centuries before, won the day. Policies favoring commerce, and state monopolies in key industries, remained in place.

Confucian Ideology Despite their statist economic policy, the Han emperors also sealed the triumph of Confucian doctrine over all rivals as the official state ideology. The Confucian emphasis on obedience and hierarchy suited emperors just fine. Indeed, Han Wudi began the practice of recruiting technocrats and bureaucrats based on their scholarly mastery of Confucian and other texts, rather than their family background. While this practice went in and out of fashion after Han Wudi's death, the Han rulers did open government careers to men (not women) of humble origins but scholarly talent. At one point, the imperial compound contained 50,000 young men studying at its Confucian academy.

Confucian education became a requirement for high office. The gradual adoption of Confucian principles as the leading ideology of the state, and the emphasis placed on mastery of Confucian texts as the best education for a government career, gave rise to one of China's distinctive characteristics: an imperial bureaucracy made up of humanistic scholars. This scholar-bureaucrat tradition, begun under the Han although formalized later, lasted until 1905 and helped to define Chinese culture.

Social Change and Gender Under the Qin and the Han, Chinese social structure gradually grew more complex. In part, this was the result of Qin and Han conquests of non-Chinese peoples. Some of these peoples assimilated to Chinese culture, but others remained ethnic and cultural minorities. A more important source of social change was the economic development discussed above. In earlier ages, China's main social divide was simple: privileged, aristocratic, and educated landowning classes above the toiling peasantry. With the emergence of more and more craft work, industry, and trade, new classes emerged.

Like the caste system in India, Confucian ideology recognized four main groups within society. But Confucianism arranged them in a different hierarchy: gentlemen-scholars (often now called literati, the class suited for government office), peasants, artisans, and merchants. This ordering reflected Confucian scorn for traders, who produced nothing. It didn't reflect the distribution of wealth or real social status. Most merchants were richer than almost all peasants, and often richer than the literati. And there were groups unrecognized in the Confucian scheme: slaves (who might have accounted for 1 percent of the population in ancient China), priests, soldiers, and women. The Confucian scheme applied to men. Women took on the status of their fathers or husbands.

Women could look forward to neither government careers nor formal education. Daughters, wives, and mothers were expected to exemplify the "Three Obediences"—to their fathers, husbands, and sons if they had any. Yet a few maneuvered their way to the center of power in the Han court. As wives or concubines of top officials, women could acquire influence. Should one of their sons attain high office, mothers might wield considerable power. When the first Han emperor died, one of his wives, known as Empress Lü, ruled as regent for 10 years, deftly engineering a succession of infants to the throne so that she might continue in power until her death in 180 BCE.

She wasn't the only woman to wield power behind the scenes. Han Wudi's mother was effectively empress during his early years on the throne. She was a commoner, called Wang Zhi, who divorced an undistinguished husband and became concubine to a prince who soon became emperor. Wang Zhi promptly bore a son, the future Han Wudi. Skilled in palace intrigue, she managed to prepare the way for her son to succeed to the throne. For several years thereafter, she exercised indirect power through the teenage emperor.

More customarily, women followed the general advice of Ban Zhao (45–116 CE) in her book *Lessons for Women*. She came from an elite family of extraordinary accomplishment. Her father and brother were historians, and

Han Lady This figurine from the Han dynasty, 206 BCE–24 CE, depicts the traditional court lady modestly dressed in flowing silk robes. Han women were expected to be obedient and domestic, though royal women occasionally wielded significant political power.

she became one herself. They lived at the Han court. In a highly unusual violation of social norms, her family arranged an education for her. She wrote poetry, the mark of an educated person, and dabbled in mathematics and astronomy. But her advice to women was orthodox in China, and broadly consistent with what Pericles had recommended for Athenian women centuries earlier. She wrote that women should be modest, obey their parents, husband, and in-laws, speak sparingly, weave, sew, cook, and keep themselves and their homes clean. She included in her book an argument for the education of girls, which she said was important so that they might better serve their future husbands. Her manual for womanly conduct remained influential for centuries.

Family life during the Han dynasty generally conformed to Ban Zhao's recommendations, although not the one about educating girls. According to the census of 2 CE, households averaged 4.7 people, implying nuclear family households. Men arranged their children's marriages, and family property was divided among sons and not daughters. Women wove, cooked, and cleaned and were expected to obey male kin. But the rapid rise of silk production gave families new opportunities to make money from female labor, which may have reduced the regret Chinese parents felt at the birth of daughters.

The Fall of the Han   Sima Qian's study of history led him to suppose that all dynasties were subject to laws of rise and fall, and the experience of the Han bore him out. After the reign of Han Wudi, successes against the Xiongnu nomads grew rare. After about 90 CE, peasant rebellions became more numerous, as mounting tax and military conscription demands became harder to bear. The Han's economic policies, helpful to the dynasty for a century or more, in the longer run allowed a few lucky and shrewd people to buy up land from less successful peasants, creating a new economic elite. That elite acquired enough political influence to avoid taxes and military service—a common pattern in world history.

As normally happens when affairs of state go poorly, court politics became more quarrelsome. Advisers, concubines, and palace eunuchs (castrated male attendants) struggled ever more fiercely for advantage, defaming and poisoning rivals—even the occasional emperor. Beginning in the Qin, China's rulers employed eunuchs in their royal households and the bureaucracy on the theory that men who couldn't have children would serve the emperor with undivided loyalty. Court eunuchs became more influential in the later years of the Han. After 184 CE, the court lost control of most of China, and in 220 CE the empire split into three warring parts.

Despite the dynasty's inglorious end, the Han, in consolidating and extending the work of the Qin emperor Shi Huangdi, left a legacy of a strong, unified, and morally legitimate state. This ideal helps explain why in centuries to come China's periods of fragmentation were comparatively brief interruptions. One dynasty followed another for the next two millennia. These dynasties oversaw the crystallization of a society and culture, based on peasant toil and ruled by educated, landed families, that we now call classical China. Its ideals remain influential in China today, and in their own time appealed powerfully to elites in neighboring lands.

Southeast Asia, Korea, and Japan

The lands adjacent to China could not escape its political power and alluring cultural example. The geopolitical expansion of the Qin and Han came at the expense of non-Chinese peoples about whom we know little. In what is now southern China, indigenous peoples retreated southward or took to the hills when faced with Qin and Han expansion. Many were killed, by violence or unfamiliar diseases, and their lands settled by Chinese. Many who survived adopted the Chinese language, assimilating to the dominant culture within a generation or two. In this way, lands that are now southern China began to become culturally Chinese under the Qin and Han. The process continued long after.

Southeast Asia Under the Han, the spread of Chinese power and culture extended into what is now Vietnam. The fertile Red River basin became a major Chinese center for 900 years after the Han took it over in the first century CE, crushing the Trung sisters' rebellion.

Before 200 BCE, all of Southeast Asia—islands and mainland—was sparsely populated. Widespread malaria was partially responsible. Villagers lived by fishing and farming. There were no cities or states of any size. As in much of Africa, political power consisted of control over people, who were scarce, not over land. It was normally a matter of charismatic individuals temporarily winning many followers whose labor they could then direct. Slavery and other forms of servitude and obligation to elites were widespread. Free women enjoyed more equal status to men in Southeast Asia than in most parts of the world, and often handled matters connected to trade and money.

A slow transformation overtook Southeast Asia when, beginning about 1 CE, irrigated rice production spread from China to lowland river valleys and deltas elsewhere. Wet rice cultivation yielded far more food per acre than any technique used before, undergirding faster growth in population. When and where people had tamed water buffalo to pull their plows through swamp and mud, wet rice cultivation was all the more productive.

More revolutionary still, rice as a grain is easily stored, transported, and hoarded. This is markedly different from the foods previously eaten by hunters, gatherers, and fishers, or by the root-crop farmers of Southeast Asia. Their foods didn't store well. If one had surplus, the best thing to do with it was throw a party, invite one's neighbors, and enjoy the prestige and good will that resulted. But with rice, people in Southeast Asia could trade food over longer distances and keep it longer. Canny people could amass food, distribute it to loyal followers, and withhold it from enemies. Priests and warriors could demand a share of the rice harvest in exchange for protection from dangers both

Wet Rice Cultivation A brick frieze dated to the period 200 BCE–200 CE illustrates the new model of irrigated agriculture in China. Farmers guide an ox and plow through a swampy field, allowing for more efficient sowing of seeds and thus more productive cultivation.

supernatural and human. Rice raised the odds of complex society and full-blown states developing in Southeast Asia.

The emergence of wet rice cultivation was even more revolutionary in Southeast Asia than in China. Substantial centers of grain production had already existed in China before irrigated rice. In Southeast Asia, irrigated rice supported the first elaboration of states and courts, extensive artisan and craft work, temples and formal religious specialists. This process was just getting going by 200 CE.

With the Han expansion, Chinese trade and culture also shaped Southeast Asia more than it had previously. Connections between China and Southeast Asia extended further south. For example, cloves from the Molucca Islands, an archipelago in today's Indonesia, reached Chinese markets by the second century BCE. Other spices from Southeast Asia came to season Chinese food as well, establishing a lasting connection that shaped Chinese cooking ever after. Vietnamese began to write their language in Chinese characters in the first century CE.

Korea Proximity to China and the emergence of irrigated rice production also changed Korea between 200 BCE and 200 CE. As in Vietnam, the northern part of Korea was conquered by the Han and substantially sinicized (i.e., drawn into China's cultural orbit). Settlers trickled in. The techniques of irrigated rice production came with them, leading to new centers of dense population. Like Vietnamese, the Korean language was first written down in Han times, in Chinese characters—even though Korean and Chinese are unrelated languages. The prestige of Chinese culture was so great that educated Koreans preferred to write in Chinese—as in the Hellenistic world educated people often used Greek in writing rather than their native tongue. The Chinese brought more refined artisanal skills, especially iron working, and helped generate more wealth, luxuries, and growing social stratification. The first evidence of slavery in Korea dates from this period (although the practice might have existed earlier). Elite burials grew more elaborate.

Koreans outside of Han control increasingly organized themselves in large clans. The clans fought among themselves, the strong devouring the weak—which helps to account for the popularity of a handful of family names in Korea such as Lee, Park, Kim, and Cho, which derive from the victors among these clans. When Han power receded from Korea at the end of the second century CE, three main kingdoms emerged, providing Korea's political framework for the next several centuries. In addition to technologies and crops from China, according to DNA studies, Koreans also acquired malaria and tuberculosis from their western neighbors at this time, further evidence of tightening linkages between Korea and the rest of East Asia.

Japan Most of the innovations that made it to Japan before 200 CE came via Korea. Around 300 BCE, bands of refugees from Korea's wars settled in Japan's southernmost big island, Kyushu. They brought bronze and iron-working skills, and irrigated rice techniques too, all of which Koreans had learned from China. Japan now began to conform more to general East Asian patterns. Population grew faster, thanks to rice and iron farm tools. Steeper social hierarchy followed, states proliferated, and wars broke out. Soon Japan acquired coinage, the potter's wheel, and much of the technology that underlay the economic growth and military prowess of the Qin and the Han, although not wheeled transport. Chinese made great use of carts and wheelbarrows, but wheeled vehicles didn't catch on in Japan until the nineteenth century CE.

Cities popped up, such as **Yoshinogari** on the southern island of Kyushu, where archeologists have found indications of weaving, bronze casting, and other crafts. Before long, Japanese states were building roads and small ships, and trading throughout their archipelago. Tighter links to mainland Asia also developed, as trade goods such as Korean-made bronze daggers and Chinese bronze mirrors uncovered at Yoshinogari attest. Chinese texts refer to "tribute" missions from small states in Japan in 57 and 107 CE, which the Japanese would have regarded as trade, not tribute, expeditions. As elsewhere, people with states victimized those without. The hunting, gathering, and fishing populations that remained in Japan were driven to the mountains and to the northern, less hospitable, island of Hokkaido.

Japan didn't develop writing until the fourth century CE, so what we know of it before 200 CE comes from archeology and writing by Japan's neighbors. Bigger and bigger tombs indicate growing social stratification. Grave goods attest to Korean influence, and also suggest some of the rituals of what would become the Japanese religion of Shinto. One Chinese text, from 297 CE, describes extreme forms of hierarchy and deference to high-ranking persons. The poor had to bow and scrape when their social betters passed by. From the Chinese point of view, however, women had it better in Japan. They were accorded more respect and could more easily enjoy leadership positions within clans. That might have been so, but it might merely reflect the Chinese author's angle of vision.

Korea and Japan, still sparsely populated lands in 500 BCE, underwent rapid changes in the centuries to 200 CE. The introduction of intensive rice techniques led to population growth and state formation. A brutal winnowing followed, whereby many states became few. In the Korean case, where iron weaponry had something of the same democratizing effect upon warfare as it had in China, by the early centuries CE three states divided the peninsula. In Japan, according to the Chinese text of 297 CE, some 30 states shared the archipelago. Meanwhile, in cultural terms, influence from China flowed into Korea and Japan, a trend that would continue for centuries. Both lands became economically linked to the ports of coastal China, an arrangement that lasts to this day.

Weaving the East Asian Web

Long before the Qin and Han dynasties, sustained interactions within what is now China marked the beginnings of an East Asian web. During the Han, this web extended into Southeast Asia, especially the northern part of Vietnam, as well as Korea and, less firmly, Japan. The most important feature of this East Asian web was the spread of intensive rice cultivation from China into Korea, Japan, and Southeast Asia, where it came to support dense settlement and more complex societies. Other parts of Chinese culture, from bronze bells to Confucian ideology, also appealed to people throughout East Asia and accordingly traveled along the threads of the web. The consolidation of this web, like all others, took place slowly and normally went unrecognized. But when ordinary people reaped wheat in north China, suffered from smallpox in Vietnam, cast bronze statues in Korea, or watched their social superiors ride horseback in Japan, they were experiencing life as shaped by the East Asian web—and increasingly its broader networks.

In 3500 BCE, the world's webs were mainly local, involving clusters of villages. Long-distance linkages were rare. But by 1000 BCE, traders and travelers had spun the Nile-Ganges web, and by 100 BCE a large East Asian web was in place. The rest of the world, as yet, had built only much smaller and thinner webs, involving far fewer people and less frequent interactions.

These two big webs, centered on Mesopotamia and China, were starting to connect while they were still forming. Among the earliest evidence for this is the movement of food crops. Crops of Chinese origin such as buckwheat, broomcorn millet, and foxtail millet turned up in Central and western Asia by 2000 BCE, and perhaps much earlier. Wheat from Southwest Asia arrived in China by about the same time, and barley well before. Chinese fruit trees—peaches, for instance—had taken root on the shores of the Mediterranean by 600 BCE.

Skills and technologies also spread across Eurasia. By 1200 BCE, the use of

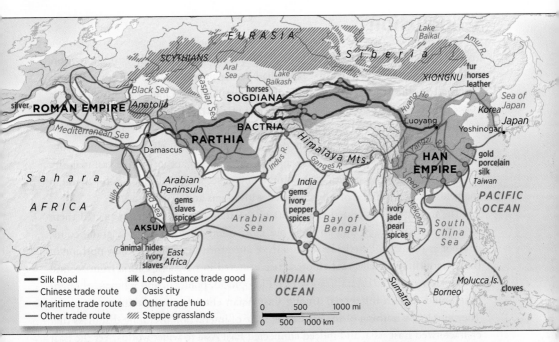

The Beginnings of the Old World Web, ca. 220 CE In the early centuries CE, thanks in part to the political consolidation and expansion undertaken by Shi Huangdi and Han Wudi, the East Asian web both grew and began to fuse with its counterpart that had stretched from the Nile to the Ganges. This fusion created a single interactive web from the Mediterranean to the East China Sea, extending as far south as the Horn of Africa and the Molucca Islands in Southeast Asia, all held together loosely by trade routes on land and sea.

chariots—a Southwest Asian invention—had reached China. Bronze- and iron-working skills, also pioneered in Southwest Asia, extended over most of Eurasia by 800 BCE. Merchant caravans passed goods to one another in relay trade all the way from the Levant to north China and back again, using the series of routes now known as the Silk Road.

Meanwhile, slender connections linked China to northern India by 500 BCE. Chinese varieties of rice were brought to India long before, but now became well established. Traders began to carry Buddhist doctrines on trans-Himalayan routes from northern India into China by the first century CE, with consequences we'll encounter in later chapters. By 200 CE, a huge transcontinental web—the Old World web—long in the making, still thin and vulnerable, had formed spanning much of Eurasia from Morocco and Spain to Korea and Vietnam. The Silk Road was its longest thread, but only one of many land routes. Sea routes linking the South China Sea, the Indian Ocean, and the Mediterranean also bound this space together.

Conclusion

By 200 CE, the East Asian region had a population of approximately 75 million, more than three-fourths of it in China. Japan had perhaps 3 million, the Korean peninsula half that. Southeast Asia, from New Guinea to Thailand, contained roughly 10 million people. Some 90 percent of East Asians lived within the orbit of states, paying taxes, tribute, or providing labor services to elites who in turn served a lord or monarch. Monarchs lived in splendor, but in constant danger too. Bureaucratic elites lived comfortably, often in royal or imperial courts, and enjoyed some modest authority. The vast majority of people lived hand-to-mouth, often hungry, never secure, despite long hours of toil in the fields and, in the case of women, often with looms and needles too.

The toiling masses feared the agents of the state but sometimes respected them too. They rebelled from time to time, but more often delivered up their grain, coins, or labor as required. Practicing the rituals of ancestor worship, they knew nothing of the extraordinary intellectual efflorescence centered in northern China from around 400 BCE onward, the crystallization of philosophical, political, and religious thought that would remain influential among East Asian elites for more than 2,000 years. They also knew nothing of the increasing scale of interaction over long distances that characterized East Asia, and indeed connected East Asia to wider worlds. Yet the East Asian web shaped their lives in ways great and small, from basic features of life such as rice as a dietary staple to trivial ones such as the bronze daggers wielded by their social superiors. To some small extent, they were experiencing life as influenced by the Old World web, just taking shape in 200 CE.

‖‖

Chapter Review

KEY TERMS

Shang dynasty p. 232

oracle bone inscriptions p. 232

dolmens p. 238

Zhou dynasty p. 241

shi p. 243

Mandate of Heaven p. 243

Sun Tzu p. 246

Confucius p. 247

Legalism p. 249

Qin p. 251

Shi Huangdi p. 251

Han p. 253

Yoshinogari p. 261

REVIEW QUESTIONS

1. What geographical and environmental features made East Asia a strong candidate for early development of long-distance trade and complex societal organization?

2. What key shifts among East Asian societies took place around 3500 BCE?

3. What is the early Shang writing called, and what was its purpose?

4. How were Southeast Asian, Korean, and Japanese societies different from those in northern and central China around 1000 BCE?

5. What two powerful dynamics defined the history of East Asia after 1000 BCE?

6. How did the Chinese Mandate of Heaven differ from rulers' claims to supernatural legitimacy in Mesopotamia and Egypt?

7. In what ways did the Warring States period trigger military innovation, prosperity, commercial activity, and social change?

8. Name and describe the three principal doctrines that arose during the Warring States period.

9. What measures did Shi Huangdi introduce to unify China?

10. What was the scholar-bureaucrat tradition introduced during the Han?

11. How did the geopolitical expansion under the Qin and the Han affect non-Chinese peoples in surrounding lands?

12. What changes occurred in Korea and Japan between 500 BCE and 200 CE, and what was the Chinese contribution to these changes?

Go to INQUIZITIVE

to see what you've learned—and learn what you've missed—with personalized feedback along the way.

The West End of the Old World Web

CARTHAGE, ROME, AND THE MEDITERRANEAN WORLD

800 BCE to 200 CE

FOCUS QUESTIONS

1. What made the Phoenician cities important players in the Mediterranean world?

2. How did Carthage rise as a sea power in the Mediterranean?

3. Why was the Roman Republic strong and stable for so long?

4. What were the major sources of stability in the Roman Empire?

About 390 BCE, before Rome was much of a city, a band of marauders nearly cooked its goose. The marauders were a tribe of Gauls, originally from what is now France but recently settled in northern Italy. They probably were on the way home from a job as mercenaries in southern Italy when they defeated a Roman army just north of the city. The surviving Romans, the story goes, scurried back into their walled city so hastily that no one closed the gates behind them. The able-bodied among them retreated to the citadel, the Capitoline Hill, and prepared for a siege. They had with them a flock of geese, sacred to the goddess Juno. Some Romans complained that the geese were better fed than they were.

The Gauls sacked and burned most of the outer city while the Romans cowered in their citadel. Then one night the attackers discovered a path up to the Capitoline Hill. As they scaled the walls of the citadel, Romans and their watchdogs slumbered unaware. But before the Gauls could murder the last of the Romans in their sleep, the well-fed sacred geese of Juno started to cackle. The Romans awoke just in time, repelled the assault, and saved their city and themselves from annihilation.

That, at least, is how Roman historians told the story. Perhaps, as some modern historians claim, the Romans saved themselves only by agreeing to turn over to the Gauls all their gold and treasure. Either way, the survival of Rome was a close-run thing. Had the geese not cackled, or the Gauls not accepted gold, Rome would have been obliterated long before it could become one of history's great empires. Without Rome, perhaps Carthage would have ruled the Mediterranean world and its legacy would loom large over the past two millennia. Little things can make a big difference in history.

This chapter follows the fortunes of two great Mediterranean empires that stood on the far western fringe of the Old World web: Carthage and Rome. Carthage, on the Mediterranean's North African coast, was founded as a Phoenician colony about 800 BCE. But within two centuries it had dozens of its own merchant colonies around the Mediterranean and soon would establish more on Atlantic coasts. As its own colonies grew more numerous and larger, Carthage gradually became something we can call an empire, held together by religion, language, trade, and the most formidable navy the world had yet seen. Unlike the empires of Sargon or Cyrus or Shi Huangdi, this one was based not on conquest of contiguous territories but on commerce and ships. It was the first seaborne empire in world history. Its traders and sailors went far toward integrating the western Mediterranean,

CHRONOLOGY

ca. 1100–1000 BCE Tyre begins to flourish

ca. 1000–900 BCE First settlements in Rome

ca. 800 BCE Carthage is founded

ca. 800–700 BCE Tyre's merchants expand operations in western Mediterranean

ca. 600–500 BCE Babylonians and then Achaemenid Persians conquer Tyre and Phoenicia

ca. 500–450 BCE Beginning of Roman Republic

ca. 350 BCE Rome stops selling slaves and has them work on farms

ca. 300 BCE Introduction of Roman coinage system; start of Roman road building

264–241 BCE First Punic War

260 BCE Rome starts building a navy

247–ca. 182 BCE Life of Hannibal Barca

218–201 BCE Second Punic War

149–146 BCE Third Punic War

100–44 BCE Lifetime of Julius Caesar

73–71 BCE Spartacus leads largest slave revolt in Roman history

49 BCE Caesar wins victory over Pompey and the Senate; rules as dictator for the rest of his life

31 BCE Marc Antony and Cleopatra kill themselves

27 BCE Rome transitions from republic to empire

27–14 BCE Rule of Augustus (Octavian)

ca. 30–33 CE Jesus of Nazareth is crucified

60–61 CE Queen Boudica leads uprising in Britain

132–135 CE Jewish revolt and the destruction of Jerusalem

161–180 BCE Reign of Marcus Aurelius

from Sicily to Spain, with the more populous eastern Mediterranean—specifically, the Levant and Egypt.

Historians of Rome call that polity a republic from its origins up to 27 BCE, and only after that date do they refer to it as an empire. But it was an empire from early on. At first it was a land empire in Italy, but eventually it became, like Carthage, a Mediterranean seaborne empire, held together by religion, language, a concept of citizenship, and an army as well as a navy. Rome in time acquired territories in northwestern Europe and Southwest Asia, but the empire's heartlands—Italy, Egypt, North Africa, Spain—all lay around the Mediterranean Sea. For most of its history, 90 percent of the population of the Roman Empire lived within a day's walk of the sea, just as Carthage's did. It turned out that the Mediterranean wasn't big enough for the two of them.

Carthage was like Cyrus's land-based Persian Empire in one respect, however: much of what we know about it comes from its enemies. If Carthaginians wrote any works of history, none have survived. Texts in Punic, as the Carthaginian language is known, mainly consist of prayers and thank-you notes to the gods. Instead, the history of Carthage comes down to us primarily through the prejudiced eye of Roman historians, who tended to see Carthage as dangerous and most Carthaginians as dishonest, corrupt, and cowardly. To a lesser extent our knowledge of Carthage derives from Greek writers, including Herodotus and Aristotle. Fortunately, archeology complements the several texts, and in recent decades it has yielded much of interest, corroborating some claims of the ancient authors and casting strong doubt on others.

Rome, in contrast, produced many histories. The textual record is extremely rich, at least on politics, wars, and religion. As usual, information about the lives of ordinary people, women especially, turns up only now and again in the written record. Archeologists have found troves of stones and bones that also illuminate the history of Rome.

So the information available is both more abundant and more reliable for Rome than for Carthage. But we shouldn't let the spotlights that historians and archeologists shine on Rome blind us to the significance of Carthage: even if often in the shadows, it lasted 700 years as a state, 1,000 years as a culture, and helped make the Mediterranean a hive of trade and cultural exchange. Indeed, by 200 CE the Mediterranean zone, thanks to Carthage and Rome, was as tightly integrated as anywhere in the world. Rome, moreover, helped to link the Mediterranean world—although thinly—to the East Asian web, creating the Old World web that encompassed North Africa and much of Eurasia, from Morocco and Spain to Japan and Java.

Phoenician Cities

The history of Carthage begins with the prosperity of the Levantine trading city of **Tyre**, and the prosperity of Tyre began with snail mucus. Tyre was one a handful of port cities along the Phoenician coast of the eastern Mediterranean. (*Phoenicia*, the Greek term for the cities of this coast, is derived from the Greek word for "purple." It's the root of the word *Punic* used to describe things Carthaginian.) Tyre flourished after the eleventh century BCE. Its merchants served as middlemen linking Egypt, northern Mesopotamia, Syria, and Anatolia. Its neighboring city, Byblos, specialized in importing papyrus from Egypt for scribes of the Levant and gave its name to books generally—and thereby to the Bible. Tyre itself specialized in the export of a maroon-purple dye extracted from the mucus of a particular mollusk, a sea snail native to eastern Mediterranean waters. The dye, used for fine cloth, was a brilliant color, didn't fade easily, and was cherished far and wide, so much so that some accounts claim it was worth 15 times its weight in gold. Its shade of purple became a symbol of royalty in parts of the Mediterranean.

Tyre, Byblos, and other Phoenician cities were part of the same cultural world as the ancient Hebrews, who called them Canaanites. They all spoke Semitic languages. The Phoenicians worshipped gods that the ancient Hebrews considered idols, but this didn't prevent business or political alliances between Tyre and the kingdom of Israel. In fact, Israel's King Solomon sold dominion over several cities to the merchants of Tyre.

The Phoenician cities were trade hubs. Phoenician sailors were among the first to recognize that you can always find north by sighting the Pole Star at night (if you're in the Northern Hemisphere). They pioneered a round-bottomed ship design that did well

Phoenician Ships This depiction of a Phoenician (sixth to fifth century BCE) sailing vessel with its characteristic rounded hull appears on a sarcophagus from the Levant.

in rough seas and were the first to coat ship hulls in tar, making them more seaworthy. These innovations, combined with their purple dye monopoly, helped the Phoenicians win a dominant position in Mediterranean trade after the tenth century BCE. In addition to purple dye, they specialized in trading metals to the metal-hungry Mesopotamian states of Assyria, Babylon, and Persia.

In the eighth century BCE, under pressure from Assyria to provide still more metals, Tyre's merchants were driven to expand their operations in the western Mediterranean—especially Spain, which was rich in tin, lead, iron, and silver deposits. Expeditions to Spain, at the other end of the Mediterranean Sea, took months. To establish a few safe havens in between, Tyre set up little colonies around the Mediterranean. One of these, established about 800 (the ancient texts imply 814), was Carthage.

Carthage

Carthage had a fine harbor and looked to the sea. But it stood firmly on land, in what is now Tunisia, among thinly scattered populations called by the ancient writers Libyans and Numidians. Somehow, Carthaginians seized or otherwise acquired land and recruited local Libyans to work those lands as sharecroppers. No doubt early Carthaginians intermarried with Libyans too. Carthage lay just a few days' sail from central Mediterranean islands such as Sicily and Sardinia, and soon its traders were active in circuits of exchange involving Greek colonies on these islands and various peoples in Italy. Carthage prospered by working these trade circuits of the central Mediterranean.

The Carthaginians also traded with a people of the central Sahara, the Garamantes, based at oases around Fezzan, in today's southwestern Libya. The Garamantes flourished from about 900 BCE to about 500 CE, living off of oasis agriculture using refined irrigation techniques, and holding a tight grip on the modest Saharan trade. Carthage probably imported gold, ivory, dates, salt, and a few slaves from the Sahara, exchanging ceramics and bronze artifacts from Mediterranean workshops. Like Egypt, Carthage and Fezzan served as funnels through which Mediterranean and African goods and influences flowed. Rock art in Garamantes centers includes images of chariots and ox-carts, implying at least knowledge, and maybe use, of these technologies. But the absence of domesticated camels, still rare in these parts until after 300 CE, severely limited the scale of trade into and out of Fezzan. These Saharan contacts with the Garamantes, all evidence suggests, were dwarfed by Carthage's links to the seaborne world of the Mediterranean, especially Italy, Sicily, Greece, the Levant, and Egypt.

A Rising City

By 650 BCE, Carthage's population reached 30,000 or so—a sizeable city for that time, although probably only one-quarter the size of Nineveh or Babylon, or Luoyang, the

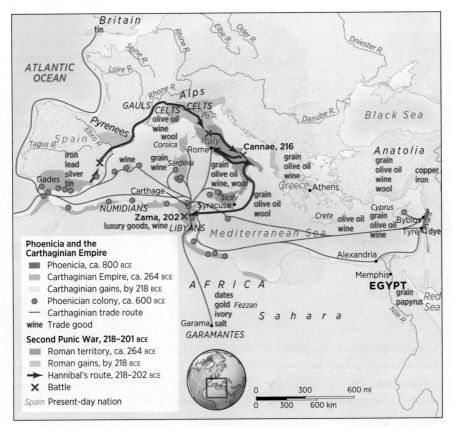

Carthage and the Mediterranean, ca. 800–200 BCE Carthage, itself originally a colony of the Phoenician city of Tyre, proved remarkably successful in colonizing the coasts of the central and western Mediterranean for more than 500 years. Although chiefly a commercial empire, it spread its cultural influence widely, especially in Spain. The rise of Roman power after 300 BCE eventually spelled the end for the Carthaginian Empire, which was finally destroyed in 146 BCE.

Zhou capital in China. At least half of Carthage's food came from overseas. It depended on trade and the grain that its merchants could get for the pottery, jewelry, ivory carvings, and bronze statuettes that poured forth from its workshops. Burial goods show that Carthage imported not just food but wool, slaves, metals, and other goods from Egypt, the Phoenician cities, Greece, Sicily, and Sardinia, among other Mediterranean lands. Carthage's artistic styles reveal the cultural influence of Egypt and Greece above all.

Despite its cosmopolitan flavor, during its first three centuries Carthage remained firmly tied to Tyre. Every year it sent representatives to make sacrifices in Tyre's temples. It retained the Phoenician language and alphabet and an enduring attachment to Phoenician names for the sons and daughters of Carthage.

Carthaginian Art Some Carthaginian art, such as this fourth-century BCE statue of a woman playing a flute (left), displays the influence of Greek artistic styles; other art, such as this sixth-century BCE bust (right), combines an Egyptian headdress with almond-shaped Greek eyes.

Carthaginians worshipped Phoenician gods, eventually preferring above all others the pair known as Baal Hammon and Tanit. Baal Hammon was a male fertility god associated with the ram, while Tanit, his consort, was a goddess of war and, like almost every other female deity, of fertility as well. Archeological findings suggest that Carthage supported a large priesthood with numerous temples. Public worship was closely coordinated with the state—as was normal wherever states existed. Carthaginian worship, as in all Semitic religions, involved frequent animal sacrifice. Before any major endeavor such as a trading voyage, sacrifices had to be made to ensure divine favor.

Greek and Roman authors accused Carthaginians of practicing child sacrifice. In fact, the Hebrew Bible contains many references to child sacrifice among the Semitic peoples from whom Carthaginians derived their religious practices. Recent archeology has unearthed funeral urns (big pots) containing the remains of babies and toddlers, some of them intermixed with animal bones. It seems that in difficult times the Carthaginian elite sometimes sacrificed their firstborn sons to Baal Hammon. Occasionally, they sacrificed multiple children from a single family.

Carthage was ruled by magistrates who held office for a fixed period. They were selected from among a handful of elite families. If Carthage ever had a monarchy, as Greek and Roman authors claim, it didn't last long. A council and an assembly worked with the magistrates, which led Aristotle to conclude that Carthage enjoyed the best possible system of government. Modern scholars regard it as an undemocratic oligarchy dominated by the merchant elite, an unusual feature in the ancient world where most elites were landowners, not traders.

State power rested, as so often, on religion and armed force. Carthage's military consisted mainly of a navy of several hundred warships, the Mediterranean's most formidable. Until the Romans built a navy, starting in 260 BCE, the main duties of the Carthaginian fleet were intimidating the Greek city-states of Sicily and attending to the endless chore of piracy suppression. The Mediterranean, with all its islands and capes to hide behind, and all its shipping to attack, was a playground for pirates except at times when someone had a strong navy. The Carthaginian navy employed loyal Carthaginian subjects, and for centuries each adult male was expected to serve in it. The army, much smaller until the later third century, consisted mainly of subject peoples and mercenaries from North Africa or Spain, men either compelled or paid to fight Carthage's wars.

A Sea Power, Sixth to Third Centuries BCE

Carthage's fortunes rose when those of Tyre fell. In the sixth century BCE, first the Babylonians and then the Achaemenid Persians conquered Tyre and all Phoenicia. In 332 BCE, Alexander the Great took Tyre and sold into slavery those of its people he didn't slaughter. Tyre's misfortunes, from the 570s BCE onward, allowed Carthage to take over the trade in metals from Spain and build its own trading empire in the western Mediterranean.

Spanish silver sustained Carthaginian power. Carthage's rulers inherited Tyre's colonies, including the settlement of Gades (today's Cadiz, on Spain's Atlantic coast), through which increasing amounts of silver flowed. At Gades and other Spanish ports, Carthaginians traded luxury goods from their workshops to local chiefs for silver. People in southwestern Spain didn't always know how valuable silver could be in the far-away eastern Mediterranean, but the Carthaginians did. Carthaginian merchants also traded along Atlantic coasts as far north as Britain, where they acquired tin. They founded settlements on Morocco's Atlantic coast. According to one Greek text, a fifth-century BCE Carthaginian navigator named Hanno managed a round trip to the mouth of the Niger River in West Africa. Whether that tale is true or not, the Carthaginians profited handsomely from western Mediterranean trade. Like all successful trading states, their fortunes rested in part in information advantages: knowing what prices certain goods might fetch in distant markets.

Carthage buttressed its financial and military strength with soft power. It spread some of its

Carthage and Spain Archeologists discovered this fourth-century BCE bust of a woman wearing an elaborate headdress and jewelry in southeastern Spain. It is believed to represent the Carthaginian goddess Tanit, indicative of Spain's close connections to Carthage.

religious beliefs and practices to the western Mediterranean. In particular, its alphabet, the Phoenician one that was comparatively easy to learn and use, appealed to people without writing. The Phoenician alphabet could be adapted for any language, as the Greeks had adapted it to theirs.

In some respects, the Carthaginians' state by the fifth and fourth centuries was a larger version of Athens: a seaborne empire sustained by a strong navy, a network of colonies and clients, financed in large part by control of silver mines and advantages in market knowledge. Carthage, like Athens, also fostered an elite culture that other peoples found attractive. But, as we've just seen, their silver came from Spain—not, as was the case for Athens, from their own backyard. So naval power was even more essential for Carthage than for Athens.

The Carthaginian economy wasn't all overseas trade and minerals. At home they developed new agricultural lands worked by Libyan sharecroppers. They specialized in fruit orchards, olives, and vines but also raised wheat and barley. They exported wine, particularly a raisin wine much admired in Italy. They must have drunk a fair bit of it themselves, because there are records of laws against the consumption of wine by slaves, soldiers, and, when on the job, judges, magistrates, and harbor pilots. Carthage's hinterland was moderately fertile but had rainfall barely adequate for most crops. So farmers raised irrigation to a high art. One Carthaginian author, Mago, probably of the fifth century BCE, wrote a detailed handbook on agriculture, unfortunately lost to us now but cited and used by later Roman authors who appreciated his insights on viniculture. By the fourth century BCE, Carthaginians occupied the northern half of modern Tunisia, and more and more of their land was worked by slaves captured in war. While Carthage is properly remembered as a seaborne trading empire, its agricultural sector was technically sophisticated and highly productive.

The Carthaginians meantime used their commercial wealth to deepen their involvement in the central Mediterranean. Their enclaves expanded in Sicily and Sardinia, bringing frictions with Greek colonies, especially the Greek city of Syracuse. To bolster its position on the Italian mainland, Carthage made a deal with the small and undistinguished city of Rome, in 509 BCE, to stay out of one another's commercial business.

Carthage in the Punic Wars, 264–146 BCE

Carthage and Rome coexisted and indeed cooperated during the fifth and fourth centuries, but that happy arrangement broke apart in the 260s BCE. The former allies eyed each other warily, each seeing the other's growing strength in Sicily as a threat. The first of the three **Punic Wars** between Carthage and Rome broke out in 264 BCE and was mainly fought at sea. Remarkably, the Romans, who had no navy of their own in 264, were routinely besting the Carthaginians in naval battles by the war's end in 241 BCE. Carthage had to sue for peace and agree to unfavorable terms.

One particular Carthaginian elite family, the Barcas, found defeat and the peace terms an affront. Men of the Barca clan (their name meant "thunderbolt") went to Spain in 237 BCE, where they led a Carthaginian conquest of local tribes. They converted the loose trading system of Carthage in Spain into a true empire—of the Barca family as much as of Carthage. In particular, they re-organized the silver mines to increase output. One Carthaginian who went to Spain was nine-year-old **Hannibal Barca**.

Hannibal's father led the subjugation of Spain. When he drowned and his heir was assassinated, it fell to Hannibal, then age 26, to command Carthaginian efforts in Spain in 221 BCE. After consolidating his personal authority, he laid siege to a client city of Rome's, inviting renewal of war. In the Second Punic War (218–201 BCE), Hannibal acquired everlasting fame as a brilliant commander.

His opening gambit was to march an army of 50,000 men and a few war elephants—small Moroccan ones, less formidable than those used in India—over the Pyrenees and the Alps and into northern Italy. Carthage no longer had the sea power to convey an army to Italy; Rome now had the stronger navy. Hannibal lost half his men on his two-month-long march, but in what is now northern Italy he recruited many warriors hostile to Rome, mostly Gauls and Celts. In a series of battles Hannibal repeatedly routed Roman armies, a feat as remarkable as the newly created Roman navy's sea victories over Carthage in the previous war. On one occasion, at Cannae in 216 BCE, his men slaughtered 46,000 Roman soldiers, the largest death toll in a single day of European warfare—ever.

The Romans, however, had more men to take the place of the fallen. Hannibal did not, and he began to lose some of his allies in Italy. Roman armies seized Carthaginian holdings in Spain, including the main sources of silver. A Roman commander then carried the war to Carthage's backyard, where Hannibal lost a climactic battle at Zama, near Carthage, in 202 BCE, which effectively ended the Second Punic War. In defeat, Carthage had to agree to pay Rome large sums of silver for the next 50 years, limit its navy to 10 ships, and disband its war elephant corps.

Roman Colonization The Roman amphitheater in El Jem, Tunisia, built in 238 CE, provides evidence of the Roman colonial presence on the site of a former Carthaginian settlement.

Hannibal, for his part, escaped the usual fate of Carthaginian generals defeated by Rome—crucifixion—and fled into exile in Anatolia, where he took refuge with Rome's enemies. There he was credited with inventing the "snakes on a boat" tactic: catapulting brittle clay jars stuffed with poisonous serpents onto the decks of Roman warships. When locals betrayed him to Roman authorities, he poisoned himself, probably in 182 BCE. His battle tactics—mobility and envelopment, but not snake launching—are still in the curriculum in military academies today.

The defeated Carthaginians returned to their trading and farming ways. They never developed the disdain for commerce that elite Romans, Assyrians, and Chinese paraded. Their success brought renewed prosperity, and by the 150s BCE they seemed, to some Romans at least, to be a potential threat once more. Rome launched the Third Punic War (149–146 BCE), which climaxed in a thorough sack of Carthage. Roman forces burned and obliterated the city, ending Carthage's career as a Mediterranean power and as a state. Most of the 700,000 people in Carthage's home territory were killed, sold into slavery, or fled, never to return. Contrary to popular myth, the Romans did not spread salt on the city and its fields to prevent anything from growing again; salt was too valuable for that.

Carthage remained deserted for a century and then became the site of a new Roman colony. Yet Carthaginian culture lived on in North Africa. In dozens of towns and hamlets in the western Mediterranean, people who were culturally Carthaginian survived despite the destruction of Carthage. The Punic language coexisted with Latin and other tongues in North Africa up until that region became Arabized in the seventh century CE. The Carthaginian alphabet, originally Phoenician, in revised forms became the basis for all writing systems around the Mediterranean.

Over the six-century career of their city and state, the Carthaginians extended and consolidated trade networks in the western Mediterranean and ratcheted up silver production in Spain. They pioneered the connections between Britain and the Mediterranean, and inaugurated seaborne contacts between the Atlantic coast of Africa and Mediterranean peoples. To judge by the number of shipwrecks found by underwater archeologists, Mediterranean trade grew fivefold between 500 and 100 BCE. Traders from many ports took part in this intensification of commerce, but Carthage (together with Alexandria) was among the leaders. The Carthaginians, in effect, created a Mediterranean world with trade links spanning from North Africa to southern Europe and Spain to Syria.

Rome from Its Beginnings to the Time of Augustus, ca. 500 BCE to 14 CE

For several hundred years, Romans told a story about their origins as descendants of Romulus. The legend, in short, is that in the aftermath of a few murders within the family, Romulus and his twin brother, Remus, were born when Mars, a god of war, raped a priestess renowned for her chastity, Rhea Silvia, who became their mother. Their great uncle tried to have the babies killed, but instead they were abandoned, suckled by a she-wolf, and raised by shepherds. Once grown up, they killed their great-uncle and then quarreled, which led Romulus to murder Remus. Romulus and his followers, feeling the need for wives, invited neighbors to a feast and at a prearranged signal abducted the guests' daughters. This story, one of several versions of Rome's origins, was written down by the fourth century BCE.

Rome's own foundation myths featured murder, rape, child abandonment, attempted infanticide, more murder, sibling rivalry, and fratricide, followed by mass kidnapping of young women. The archeological and historical record is only a little kinder to the Romans than they were to themselves. We will look at that record in some detail, because Rome proved so influential to later ages.

Roman Expansion in Italy to 264 BCE

In its early centuries, Rome was a town of no particular account. The earliest archeological evidence of settlements at Rome date from the tenth century BCE, and the first texts to mention the city are from the eighth. When the Assyrians in Mesopotamia and the Zhou dynasty in China were at their height, Rome was still a small settlement on the fringe of Etruria, the land of the Etruscans. Etruscan building styles, art, and political institutions, notably its army, influenced Rome considerably.

But in the fifth century BCE, as the power of other trading peoples—mainly Carthage and the Greeks based in Sicily—began to grow, the Etruscan towns declined. Etruscan misfortune elevated Rome in the balance, and by 450 or so Rome obliged some Etruscan towns to become Roman clients. Etruscans gradually lost their political independence to Romans, but their language and culture, like that of Carthage after its fall, survived for several centuries longer.

After subsuming the Etruscans, Rome frequently fought neighboring peoples in central and southern Italy. If the ancient authors can be trusted, Rome was at war in about 90 percent of the years between 500 and 300 BCE. Rome's fortunes in warfare improved over time for two main reasons connected to manpower: slavery and citizenship. When the Romans defeated a people, they enslaved their captives, as was normal everywhere from Central Asia to Spain. But increasingly, after 350 BCE or so, instead of selling slaves abroad for cash, they kept them at home and put them to work on Roman farms. This arrangement freed adult male Romans for warfare, and indeed the rights of Roman

Etruscans An Etruscan oil jar from the fourth or third century BCE is covered in Etruscan writing, an ancestor of the Latin (and thus our) alphabet.

citizenship required all men age 17 to 46 to serve in the army when called. With abundant slaves doing the farming, Rome, like Sparta with its helots, could put a higher proportion of its manpower into its military than did other peoples who, upon victory, couldn't resist the temptation to turn war captives into cash.

The other innovation in Rome's approach to foreign relations was to extend the rights of citizenship to some neighbors, adding further military manpower. It often came as an offer the neighbors couldn't refuse: become Roman citizens or be conquered and either slaughtered or enslaved. Roman citizenship often included exemption from taxes as well as the obligation to serve in the army, so it was an appealing offer by itself. Compared to the alternative, the offer was often irresistible, so more and more peoples of Italy became Romans.

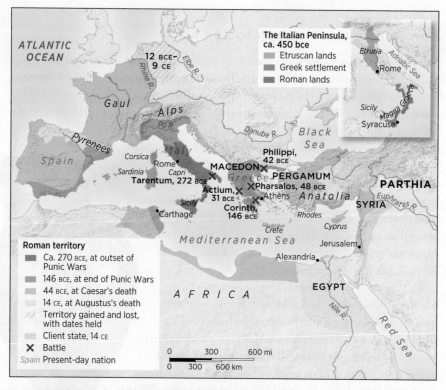

Roman Expansion, ca. 450 BCE–14 CE From its beginnings as just one of several polities on the Italian Peninsula, Rome steadily expanded. Its conquests within the peninsula were substantially complete by the 260s, when it undertook the first of three major wars against Carthage. Known as the Punic Wars, these conflicts ended with Rome in control of most of the central and western Mediterranean coastlands. Later conquests, especially in Anatolia, Syria, and Egypt, contributed mightily to the empire's wealth and population by the time Augustus took power in 27 BCE.

With these sources of manpower, Rome almost always had the biggest armies and could recover faster from losses than any rivals in Italy. Each success made Rome stronger and the next victory more likely. Between 340 and 290 BCE, just about everyone in Italy south of the Po valley had accepted Roman rule, either by conquest, by intimidation, or by negotiation.

Rome's political and military system proved its effectiveness in a spurt of conquests of the Greek cities of southern Italy between 280 and 272 BCE. These cities, collectively known as Magna Graeca, were originally Greek colonies founded during the seventh through the fifth centuries. Over time they had grown rich, powerful, and independent. When threatened by Rome and Carthage both, some wished to knuckle under, but others hired the able King Pyrrhus of Epirus to defend them. With a large army and a few war elephants, not yet encountered in Italy, Pyrrhus defeated both Carthaginian and Roman forces, becoming master of Sicily. Subsequently, he developed ambitions to match the empire of his distant kinsman, Alexander the Great. But together Carthaginians and Romans defeated Pyrrhus's forces in 272. According to one Roman author, the Romans learned that elephants were afraid of pigs and managed to panic Pyrrhus's pachyderms. He died soon thereafter when hit on the head by a roof tile hurled by an elderly woman in the Greek town of Argos—an ignoble end for a man deemed by Hannibal the greatest of all war commanders. With Pyrrhus out of the picture, the stage was set for the First Punic War, discussed above.

By the third century BCE, Rome was a large city with perhaps 100,000 people. It had begun to build a network of roads and a system of aqueducts to provide the city with clean water. The aqueducts, by reducing the toll of waterborne disease in a filthy city, helped Rome sustain its manpower advantage. And it was now in full control of almost all Italy south of the Po River, Sicily and the rich cities of Magna Graeca included, and poised for expansion overseas.

The Roman Republic

For hundreds of years following the rise of Rome in the fifth century BCE, its powerful and expanding state took the form of a republic. The institutions and politics of the Roman Republic proved remarkably resilient over those centuries, until they foundered in the crisis of the second century BCE.

Gods and Rituals As in all ancient states, religion played an important role in Roman life under the Republic. Romans worshipped many gods, some of whom were based on Etruscan deities that acquired Greek overlays over time. Jupiter, modeled on Zeus, and Mars, the Roman equivalent of Ares and god of war, stood in the front rank of the Roman pantheon. Quirinus, god of the Roman people, had no Greek counterpart but ranked third in importance after Jupiter and Mars. Poor people were especially

Religious Ritual Priestesses offer sacrifices to Vesta at a temple dedicated to the goddess in a relief from first- or second-century CE Rome.

attentive to Ceres, goddess of grain, fertility, and growth, who corresponded to the Greek Demeter. Romans even had a god for manure (Sterculinus) and a goddess for the city's main sewer (Cloacina). Romans, like Greeks, expected their gods to meddle enthusiastically in human affairs, so they sacrificed to them frequently and put great faith in omens.

Romans built an elaborate set of rituals and institutions around their gods. Part of being Roman consisted of following these rituals. Male heads of households saw to religious observance in the home, making offerings of grapes, grain, or wine to a statue of a Lar, a guardian god. Every city, neighborhood, and household, not to mention roads and ships, travelers and seafarers, had a Lar. Public rituals were the responsibility of official priests and priestesses, such as the Vestal Virgins. Girls selected from prominent families at ages 6 to 10 were taught how to maintain the cult of Vesta, goddess of the hearth. As Vestal Virgins they kept the sacred flame at Vesta's temple, fetched water from a sacred spring, and held places of honor in religious ceremonies. After 30 years on the job they retired, unless first found not to be a virgin, in which case they were buried alive. No major undertaking, least of all wars, could proceed without priests checking the omens and procuring appropriate blessings. All the important religious offices were the preserve of the social elite.

Like every religious community, the Romans adopted a few new practices now and then, but none that seemed to threaten the fabric of Roman religion and society were tolerated for long. One such, the cult of Bacchus, god of wine and ecstasy, introduced from the Greek cities of southern Italy, involved secret meetings (originally attended only by women) at which all manner of crime and political conspiracy was allegedly hatched. Seeming to get out of hand, the Bacchus cult was outlawed in 186 BCE. Roman religion helped unite Romans culturally and helped keep the elite in control.

Roman Law and Citizenship All powerful societies find a way to manage social conflict. Religion alone is rarely enough. Confucian ideology served this purpose in China, as did the democratic assembly in Athens. Like all complex societies, Rome had sharp cleavages between rich and poor, and division threatened any and all common purpose. The Roman Republic developed a series of practices and institutions that kept class conflict and civil war to a minimum until 91 BCE and checked the power-lust of successful politicians.

The first of these practices and institutions was the rule of law. Sometime about 450 BCE, Romans drew up a code of law called the Twelve Tables (it was written on 12 tablets). Its main concerns were marriage, property, debt, and the procedures of law. It also prescribed punishments for various offenses. Killing, for example, was illegal outside one's family except in cases of thieves caught in the night. Within families, the male head of household, called *paterfamilias*, technically had the legal right to kill any member of his family, a right rarely exercised. Like the Qin dynasty's laws in China but unlike the Babylonian laws of Hammurabi, Roman laws applied equally to rich and poor. The other important feature of this code was that it was written down (although schoolboys were expected to memorize it anyway). Both features helped it to endure as the basis for a tradition of law that Romans came to think was part of what made them Romans—and better than anyone else.

Another important practice in the Roman Republic was the political use of citizenship. There were several gradations of citizenship with different rights, but full citizens—always male—enjoyed the right to hold office and vote in assemblies, and freedom from most taxes. Romans used citizenship tactically to defuse social conflict and, as we saw above, to enroll defeated peoples in their legions. Citizenship could be offered in negotiations with unruly groups, as occurred repeatedly in the early years of the Roman Republic. It was used in desperation and on a large scale after a major revolt during the years 91 to 89 BCE: to avoid another war, Rome tripled the number of citizens. Since citizenship often came with exemption from taxes, Romans didn't bestow the honor casually. The forms of partial citizenship served in situations where full citizenship seemed too much to concede. Their caution notwithstanding, the Romans were much freer with the extension of citizenship than, for example, the Greek poleis or, in all likelihood, Carthage. Citizenship meant the right to take part in politics too, and it gave people a stake in the fate of Rome—even if in practice one had to live within a day's walk of the city to be politically active, because all deliberations took place there.

A Flexible Politics The third major source of Roman power and stability was the political system of the Republic, an oligarchy with just enough flexibility to bend when needed. The Greek historian Polybius of the second century BCE thought the Roman system of government, which he and others called the Roman constitution, combined the best elements of monarchy (rule of one), oligarchy (rule of the few), and democracy (rule of the many)—just what Aristotle had written about Carthage. Rome had no written constitution, but it did have institutions, laws, and traditions that for a few centuries commanded respect among its citizens and admiration among many foreigners.

Roman mythology held that their ancestors had overthrown a tyrannous Etruscan king in 509 BCE and thereafter established the consulate. True or not, sometime about 500 and no later than 450 BCE, Rome was governed by a pair of consuls, each serving for only one year—a variation on the practice of temporary rulership present also in Greek democracies and Carthage. The consuls' main duty was to lead armies in the field, and success brought glory, influence, and war booty. With two consuls always in office, the system checked the ambitions of Rome's politicians. The consuls were the most powerful men in Rome, superior to the scores of lesser magistrates charged with administrative duties.

Consuls didn't enjoy absolute power, though: former consuls and magistrates of the higher echelons, and other elite men too, sat in the Senate. Senators held office for life and weren't paid, so the Senate was full of men rich enough not to need to work. It began as a forum of 100 men who typically came from the same elite families and knew one another, and one another's families, by the time they held office. By the mid-first century BCE, the Senate had ballooned to nearly 800 members and included able and ambitious men from lesser families. Like all exclusive clubs, the Senate was a cauldron of personal ambition for status, honors, and power. Its official concerns included religious rites, issues of war and peace, and finances. The Senate's role was nominally advisory, but when it agreed on anything it was very hard for consuls not to accede to its wishes—until about 100 BCE.

The political system of the Roman Republic also included larger assemblies that approved or rejected legislation and elected high magistrates. As Rome grew larger, more offices were created: praetors, quaestors, censors, and tribunes. They too checked the power of the consuls, especially the tribunes, some of whom represented the lower classes and had the power to veto laws. The assemblies enrolled all citizens, even the poor, although through complex arrangements their voice was limited and that of the rich amplified. The system as a whole—the Roman constitution—included checks and balances and encouraged compromise. It allowed an oligarchy to remain in power but gave the ruling families the flexibility to appear to be bowing to the will of the people when that seemed prudent.

The Army   The final institution that ensured the power and stability of the Republic until 91 BCE was the army. It was occasionally called on to put down revolts. But its more important function was as a plunder machine that kept most Roman citizen-soldiers happy most of the time, even if army duty led to the early deaths of countless young men. All citizens had to serve, and the ambitious among them eagerly sought war and victory in order to advance their careers and achieve renown. (It didn't always work: at the monumental defeat of Cannae, Hannibal's forces killed 80 senators serving in the Roman army.) Roman citizens typically served in the legions—heavily armed and highly disciplined infantry units of about 5,000 men. The army also included auxiliaries, typically non-citizens, organized as both infantry and cavalry.

The poor were often needed to fill out the legions. This worked to their advantage in two ways. First, if they fought and Rome won, as it usually did, and if they survived their term of service (about a 60 percent chance), they could expect a small share of the resulting booty and perhaps some land taken from the conquered—instant advancement and a very attractive gamble for poor young men. Second, if the poor could band together and decline to serve in the army, the magistrates and senate might make political concessions. Five times between 494 and 287 BCE, Rome's poorer classes refused to work or fight, winning cancellation of debts or expanded political rights in the negotiations that followed.

With these practices and institutions, Rome managed to remain stable and become ever more powerful in the centuries after 350 BCE. However, the system began to break down shortly before 100 BCE, partly because Rome became too successful as an empire.

The Crisis of the Republic

The Roman Republic's political system worked well, and eventually too well. After winning the Second Punic War (218–201 BCE), Rome dove deeply into the affairs of the Greek peninsula. In 146 BCE, the year of Rome's final destruction of Carthage, it also crushed the city of Corinth, ringleader of Greek resistance to Roman expansion. Roman aristocrats found much to admire in Greek culture, including theater, philosophy, religion, athletic competitions, marble statuary, and architecture. As a later poet, Horace, who had studied in Athens, put it, "Conquered Greece conquered in turn the uncultivated victor." The upper ranks of Roman society gradually learned to read and speak Greek, and increasingly Rome came to resemble a Hellenistic state—although not yet a monarchy.

Further Roman conquests followed in Anatolia. The quantities of war booty now available dwarfed what earlier consuls had won in wars within Italy. Successful generals became fabulously rich overnight, and their power swelled in comparison to that of the Senate—and the law. They found it easy to bribe officials, even the whole Senate, and to put on displays that won them public adulation.

Rising Personal Power Now Roman politics became more personalized. Charismatic military heroes competed more fiercely for pre-eminence. Some aristocrats sought to mobilize the masses in their own struggles for honor and power, such as the brothers Tiberius and Gaius Gracchus. The two men, serving as tribunes, pursued radical reforms such as redistributing land and extending citizenship to large numbers of poorer Romans in hopes of gaining popular support for their quest to restore the political standing of their family. Both were murdered for their political proposals (in 133 and 123 BCE, respectively). Respect for tradition and law ebbed. Observers complained about corruption and money in politics.

After 107 BCE, a consul of humble origin, Marius, managed to get himself elected consul seven times by citing military necessity—in violation of law and tradition. Marius enacted various reforms of the army, including allowing landless men to join up, and proved remarkably successful in wars in North Africa and northern Italy. Thereafter, his armies increasingly owed their allegiance to him, not to Rome. His soldiers had less of a stake in—and probably less knowledge of—the traditions, institutions, and practices of the Roman Republic than had earlier generations. They knew their chances of getting land and a wife were better if Marius won his battles in both war and politics.

This tendency toward the transformation of Roman armies into private forces serving personal ambition was soon confirmed. Another consul, an aristocrat named Sulla, won glory and booty in wars in Anatolia. When a potentially lucrative command was awarded to a rival, he marched his army upon Rome in 88 BCE. Thus began six decades of political chaos and frequent civil war. Sulla became dictator, stuffed the Senate with his supporters, and became the law unto himself, protected by a 10,000-man bodyguard. His troops slaughtered thousands of his political enemies and confiscated property from many more. Sulla distributed land and money to his loyal soldiers.

After Sulla's power grab, there was no limit to what a successful general might seek. Sulla retired just before his death in 78 BCE. In 73, the largest slave revolt in Roman history erupted, involving tens of thousands of slaves led by a former gladiator, Spartacus. It took eight legions two years to kill or capture the rebels. Two of the generals who took part, Crassus and Pompey, used their glory to launch political careers. Soon they were joined by another military hero, **Julius Caesar** (100–44 BCE), and in a private arrangement the three divided the sprawling Republic—whose borders their legions had extended—among themselves. Quarrels followed, leading to civil wars among armies loyal to their commanders, not to the Republic.

Civil War The Republic soon collapsed. Crassus died on campaign in 53 BCE. Pompey, supported by the Senate, and Caesar, supported only by his soldiers, dueled for ultimate power. Caesar was an aristocrat from a down-on-its luck family who had joined the army at age 15 and served widely. He won glory, a reputation as a brilliant commander, and the loyalty of his legions by crushing tribes in Gaul during the years 58 to 52 BCE. In 50 BCE, the Senate summoned Caesar to Rome and instructed him to disband his army. Caesar, like Sulla before him, defied the Senate and chose to bring his troops with him.

Caesar's decision provoked civil war on the grand scale. He won in battle against forces loyal to Pompey and the Senate in 48 BCE, by which time he had a quarter-million legionnaires under his command. Chasing Pompey around the Mediterranean brought him to Alexandria, the domain of Cleopatra, last of the Ptolemies to rule Egypt. She was then a 21-year-old queen engaged in a power struggle in which she wanted Caesar's help. She got it, according to the ancient authors, after being smuggled into Caesar's quarters in a rolled-up carpet. Caesar had planned to annex Egypt to the Roman Empire, but Cleopatra changed his mind. A young woman in a hurry, she soon bore Caesar a

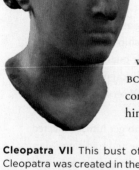

Cleopatra VII This bust of Cleopatra was created in the first century BCE and depicts her in a Greek style. She was the last ruling monarch of the Ptolemaic dynasty.

son and moved with him to Rome, despite the fact that the 52-year-old Caesar already had a wife there.

Undeterred by scandal, Caesar after 49 BCE helped himself to all offices he didn't already hold and installed his friends in the Senate. He ruled as dictator for five years, taking good care of his army veterans, extending citizenship to a few Celtic chiefs and rich foreigners who supported him, and reforming the calendar to give it 365 ¼ days through the device of leap years (which he had probably learned from Alexandria's astronomers). To accommodate calendar reform, the year 46 BCE had a total of 445 days in it, which must have puzzled ordinary folks. Caesar generously named a warm month after his clan, July. In 44 BCE he unwisely thought his situation secure enough to attend a meeting of the Senate without a bodyguard. Members of that august body, including his own brother-in-law, stabbed him to death. He was 55 years old.

Caesar ranks among the great military commanders. Those who heard him described him as a brilliant orator. He used his skills to further his own power, create a cult of personality for himself, and undermine the institutions of the Roman Republic. His supporters proclaimed him a god.

Another 13 years of on-and-off civil war followed Caesar's death. His will named a teenaged grand-nephew, **Octavian**, as his adopted son and heir. Despite a law stipulating that men had to be 42 years old to become consul, Octavian took the office when still 19. He and Caesar's fellow consul, Marc Antony, led troops against Caesar's assassins and destroyed them at Philippi, in Greece.

Octavian and Marc Antony, who were brothers-in-law, worked together for a few years but soon fell out. Antony—like Caesar before him—made a political and personal alliance with Cleopatra, who had returned home to Alexandria upon Caesar's assassination. She and Antony had three children, whom she hoped to see become rulers of the Roman world. Yet even her political skills did not suffice, and Octavian's commanders crushed their forces in 31 BCE, driving Antony and Cleopatra to suicide. Octavian added Egypt, the richest region of the world, to Roman lands.

An Empire Born Octavian was now the most powerful and richest man in the world, with the possible exception of his contemporary, the Han emperor of China. He took the name Augustus

Augustus Caesar This statue, a copy of an original made to honor Augustus during his lifetime, ca. 20 BCE, shows the emperor as the commander in chief of Rome, wearing armor covered in insignia that illustrate his military conquests.

CONSIDERING THE EVIDENCE

Hortensia's Speech

Following Julius Caesar's assassination in 44 BCE, his allies Octavian and Marc Antony seized control. They "proscribed" their enemies by executing them, seizing their property, and banning their relatives from political office. Those who escaped launched a civil war for control of Rome. Two years later, as war expenses mounted, the new leaders violated custom by taxing the wealthiest 1,400 women of Rome. Many of the targeted women—including Hortensia, their spokesperson—stormed the floor of the Roman Senate to protest the tax. The following excerpt is from Hortensia's speech. Original Latin transcriptions did not survive, but the historian Appian (ca. 95–165 CE) made a Greek translation of her speech in his history of Rome a few centuries later.

You have already deprived us of our fathers, our sons, our husbands, and our brothers, whom you accused of having wronged you; if you take away our property also, you reduce us to a condition unbecoming our birth, our manners, our sex. If we have done you wrong, as you say our husbands have, proscribe us as you do them. But if we women have not voted any of you public enemies, have not torn down your houses, destroyed your army, or led another one against you; if we have not hindered you in obtaining offices and honours,—why do we share the penalty when we did not share the guilt?

Why should we pay taxes when we have no part in the honours, the commands, the state-craft, for which you contend against each other with such harmful results? "Because this is a time of war," do you say? When have there not been wars, and when have taxes ever been imposed on women, who are exempted by their sex among all mankind? Our mothers did once rise superior to their sex and made contributions when you were in danger of losing the whole empire and the city itself through the conflict with the Carthaginians. But then they contributed voluntarily, not from their landed property, their fields, their dowries, or their houses, without which life is not possible to free women, but only from their own jewellery, and ...not by force and violence, but what they themselves were willing to give. What alarm is there now for the empire or the country? Let war with the Gauls or the Parthians come, and we shall not be inferior to our mothers in zeal for the common safety; but for civil wars may we never contribute, nor ever assist you against each other!

Questions for Analysis

1. What kind of property could free Roman women control independently of their male relatives?

2. How did Hortensia use the official exclusion of women from politics to argue for their property rights?

3. In Hortensia's view, what is the difference between the historical contributions of Rome's women to the war against Carthage and the taxes against which she is protesting?

Source: *Appian's Roman History IV*, trans. Horace White, Loeb Classical Library, eds. T. E. Page, M. A. Rouse, and W. H. D. Rouse (New York: 1913).

("the revered") and ruled from 27 BCE until his death in 14 CE. His power lay in his immense wealth, his position as Julius Caesar's heir, the loyalty of many legions, and the prestige accorded by the offices that a cowed Senate heaped upon him. Augustus too had a warm month named for him. He styled himself a son of a god (because of the deification of Julius Caesar) and the "first citizen" of Rome.

The Roman Empire was born in blood, the result of quests for personal power and public adulation on the part of Marius, Sulla, and, above all others, Julius Caesar. The checks and balances of the Republic failed when several successful Roman conquests of rich lands enabled some generals to become spectacularly rich and famous. Several of them used their riches and fame to corrupt the institutions of the Republic, make politics a matter of personal loyalties, and undermine the Roman constitution.

The Roman Empire from Augustus to 200 CE

The Roman Empire, born from political chaos, proved remarkably stable for two centuries. Augustus built on the legacy of the Republic and established enduring structures that enabled Rome to survive periods of spectacularly bad leadership for a long time. The end came slowly: a few centuries of stagnation, teetering, and slow collapse in the central and western Mediterranean. In the eastern Mediterranean, Roman rule survived in the form of the Byzantine Empire until 1453. The remainder of this chapter will explain why the Roman Empire lasted as long as it did and will carry the story up to about 200 CE.

Despite chronic bad health, Augustus lived and ruled until the age of 76, which gave him 40 years to get things done. He was among the most ruthless and conniving of Rome's rulers (a very high standard, that) and among the few to die peacefully in his bed. He arranged the murder of more political opponents than the next 20 emperors combined. He used his boundless wealth, and his two marriages, for political purposes. By the standards of monarchs he lived modestly himself, insisting publicly that he was just another Roman citizen. Indeed, he was offended by the excesses and loose morality of his fellow aristocrats and even had his daughter and granddaughter exiled for their wanton ways.

The State and the Emperors

The remarkable endurance of the Roman Empire is partly the result of Augustus's political and administrative legacy. If you want to learn how to wield near-absolute power over a gigantic organization for most of your adult life, you can do no better than to study Augustus.

Consolidation under Augustus Augustus ruled with an iron fist in a velvet glove. He maintained, or restored, the fiction of Senate power, and he permitted aristocrats enough in the way of political roles and personal wealth that they almost entirely went along with his rule. He had already killed off those most likely to resist, leaving him with a more docile flock. He rebuilt temples and theaters, making Rome an awe-inspiring architectural spectacle. In one of his rare boasts (rare by the standards of pharaohs or Assyrian kings), he said he had found Rome a city of bricks and left it a city of marble. He used his immense personal wealth, much of it derived from the annexation of Egypt, to fund public construction, including more aqueducts and fountains. He also perfected the tradition, followed by most Roman emperors, of sponsoring athletic games, religious festivals, and periodic distribution of free grain to the poor—a successful strategy for keeping a population content.

Augustus also reorganized the state administration and the army. The main thrust was to make officeholders and army commanders more dependent on the emperor's favor, a continuation of a trend begun under consuls Marius and Sulla. He re-established the census, which hadn't been taken in 40 years. He often paid soldiers out of his personal coffers to remind them where their loyalties should lie. He worked tirelessly to make sure no commander outside his family won too much military glory. He also added the so-called **praetorian guard**, an elite corps of 4,500 men, paid three times a soldier's wage, whose job was to protect the emperor. They did their job in the case of Augustus. But before they were disbanded in 312 CE, the praetorian guard had murdered five other emperors and, on one occasion, auctioned off the emperorship to the highest bidder—who offered 10 tons of gold.

The strongest testimony to Augustus's work in consolidating the Roman state is that it survived two challenges: uncertain successions and the reigns of several bungling emperors. The emperorship was not nominally a hereditary position, but most emperors tried to put a son or nephew in a position to follow in the family business. The uncertainty of succession encouraged frequent conspiracies, murders, and poisonings in the extended imperial family. Only about 30 percent of emperors died of natural causes.

Successors, Bad and Good The strong foundation Augustus laid enabled Rome to withstand the reigns of less skilled and dutiful successors. Caligula (r. 37–41 CE) squandered a full treasury in record time; insisted on being worshipped as a god; acquired a reputation for wanton cruelty and creatively perverse sexuality, often involving his sisters; opened a government-run brothel, also involving his sisters; and tried to make his favorite horse a consul. The praetorian guard killed him in 41 CE. They put in his place his uncle Claudius (r. 41–54 CE), a political wallflower who to this point had kept busy meekly writing histories. He proved to be an effective emperor, no doubt helped by his knowledge of history, until he was poisoned by his wife, who was also his niece. Much worse followed.

The track record of bad emperors was so discouraging that after 98 CE rulers often adopted promising young men as their sons, and in some cases made them co-emperors, in order to get better successors. Three formidably competent emperors, Trajan (r. 98–117), Hadrian (r. 117–138), and Marcus Aurelius (r. 161–180), came to power this way. Each was a military man who proved his worth in a long apprenticeship in the army and politics before succeeding to the emperorship in middle age; each enjoyed the support and respect of the legions; and each met with success in expanding or defending the empire's frontiers. A few capable emperors attained power through civil war or military coup—Vespasian (r. 69–79) and Diocletian (r. 284–305), for example. Both were military men who as emperors enacted effective reforms strengthening the empire.

Some emperors, like Marcus Aurelius, were paragons of self-discipline and duty. Others were not, such as the licentious teenager and religious zealot Elagabalus (r. 218–222), who came to power at age 14 thanks to the influence of his grandmother. Four years later, having witnessed his escapades and abuses of power, she then arranged his murder. Rome survived the likes of Caligula and Elagabalus in part because the praetorian guard, responsible for their safety, murdered them promptly and didn't give them the chance to reign for long.

Something of the traditions, offices, and bureaucracy of the Republic survived, although debased and personalized by consuls and emperors. Following Augustus, emperors developed a bureaucratic layer staffed by slaves and former slaves, loyal to the emperor and often of high administrative skill. The rule of law, although watered down by emperors' decrees and frequent illegality, survived in principle. So did the tradition whereby elite Romans competed for honor in the service of the state. All this helped the empire to bounce back from the frequent disastrous emperors and occasional military defeat.

In addition, bad emperors didn't make much difference in the provincial world of villages and towns. Emperors might either persecute and kill fellow aristocrats or plumb the depths of moral depravity in their not-so-private lives, and thereby earn the undying hostility of the literate classes. But that made no difference to Egyptian peasants, Spanish miners, or Sicilian shepherds. As long as they worked, paid taxes, and performed military service (as auxiliaries, because they were unlikely to be citizens), and Roman legions won most wars, Rome could survive.

Coins, Roads, Soldiers Another source of the coherence and durability of Rome was the coinage system. Beginning under the Republic about 300 BCE and continuing under the empire, Rome's mints stamped out millions of coins, using gold, silver, copper, bronze, and other metals. Although occasionally debased (by using alloys with less precious metal per coin) to pay for wars, Roman coins were accepted far and wide, even beyond the empire's borders, especially after Augustus imposed a standardization.

Reasonably reliable money spurred economic growth and commercial exchange, binding the Roman world together.

Superb infrastructure also helps explain the longevity of Rome. The road system, begun before 300 BCE, spread its tendrils under the empire. Its overall length by 200 CE stretched to 52,000 miles (83,000 km), a little more than the current US Interstate Highway System. Its main arteries were about 25 feet (8 m) wide, made of paving stones, and usually straighter than an arrow. Some of the roadbeds, and numerous stone bridges, remain in use 20 centuries later. These main roads, and many more gravel ones, sped the movement of armies and official information. Couriers could cover 50 miles (80 km) a day. Important news from the farthest corners of the empire could make it to Rome in a month or less. The Romans also built hundreds of aqueducts and sewers, which kept their cities healthier than most. Urban life on the scale it attained during the first through the third centuries CE would have been impossible without the provision of clean water. Roman engineers designed water systems that in some cases required cutting tunnels through mountain rock. Rome itself had a water system that provided about 200 gallons (800 L) per person per day, a more lavish water supply than any other big city enjoyed until recent times. Aqueducts also served to deliver irrigation water to thirsty fields. Like the Achaemenid Persian Empire, Rome lasted as long as it did partly due to investment in durable infrastructure.

The army held the empire together at least as much as did the roads and coins. The imperial army was somewhat different from that of the Republic. Under the Republic, the state raised legions as needed to make war and promised them land for their service. Augustus built a standing, professional army, paid in money. It numbered nearly 300,000 by his death. The imperial army took about 40 percent of the state's budget,

Roman Roads (Left) A section of paved Roman road built between 312 and 264 BCE in Italy testifies to the longevity of Roman material culture. (Right) As this first-century relief from Rome shows, countless laborers worked with hand tools to construct the thousands of miles of paved roads that connected the far-flung regions of the Roman Empire.

rising later to 60 percent—normal or below normal for pre-modern states. Army service lasted for 20 years, and for 25 after about 90 CE. Soldiers earned approximately 80 percent of a laborer's wage. After about 50 CE, the recruits included more and more Spaniards, Gauls, Syrians, and others from outside Italy. If they survived long enough (well under half did so), they could acquire citizenship upon retirement.

Imperial Rome also had a professional navy, created under Augustus. It cruised the Mediterranean and patrolled navigable rivers such as the Danube and Rhine, important for the defense of Rome's northern frontiers. Sailors had to serve for 26 years, after which they earned a handsome bonus and citizenship. The Roman navy stamped out Mediterranean piracy for two centuries, a feat not matched until modern times.

Early Revolts

The army's job included suppressing revolts. By the standards of most empires, these were few in Rome. Part of the reason was the brutal force that legions brought to bear against them. The Roman historian Tacitus, writing in about 98 CE, credited a Scottish chieftain with this apt summary of Roman policy toward rebellious tribes: "they make a desert and call it peace." Another reason that revolts were rare was that Rome usually found a way to make submission appealing to local elites, including allowing them cultural and religious autonomy, or perhaps Roman citizenship, if they didn't threaten Roman rule.

Revolts of the Jews But on the edges of the empire, peoples sometimes found the imposition of Roman rule grounds for revolt. Among the most threatening uprisings were those of the Jews, who amounted to perhaps 5 percent of the Roman Empire's population. The first sizeable revolt came in 66 CE in Judaea, a Roman province that included a recently created client kingdom of the Jews centered on Jerusalem. Many Jews resented Roman taxation, disrespect for Jewish tradition, and the pro-Roman policies of their Roman-appointed king. The revolt was provoked in part by a Jewish political group, the zealots, among whom extremists discouraged opposition by stabbing those Jews who seemed sympathetic to Rome. The conflict evolved into a war among Jewish factions. Its suppression required 60,000 Roman troops. Some 220,000 Jews died in a Roman siege of Jerusalem. The temple in Jerusalem, the center of Jewish community life, was destroyed in 70 CE, never to rise again.

A bigger Jewish revolt came in the years 132 to 135 CE, during the reign of Hadrian. It led to the death of hundreds of thousands of Jews, the enslavement and exile of many more, the destruction of Jerusalem, and the end of all Jewish political authority in the Roman Empire. Hadrian forbade Jews to return to their sacred city of Jerusalem and changed its name to Aelia Capitolina. He executed Jewish scholars and tried to eradicate Judaism in the empire.

These revolts, sometimes called the Roman-Jewish Wars, aimed to win autonomy

Roman Triumph A relief from the Arch of Titus (built in 82 CE) in the Forum in Rome celebrates the conquest of Jerusalem, showing soldiers with a menorah looted from the temple and prisoners captured during the destruction of the city.

for the Jewish kingdom and shield Jews from Roman power. Their suppression, and the exile of a major population of the Roman Empire, temporarily shook the Roman political landscape but ever after loomed large in the history of the Jewish people, who were scattered to the winds.

Queen Boudica Another uprising occurred in Britain in the years 60 to 61 CE, shortly after Roman legions conquered it. **Queen Boudica**, whose succession to a local throne wasn't recognized by Roman authorities, organized an assault on all things Roman in southeastern Britain. According to one Roman historian, Boudica, "tall, with flashing eyes, menacing voice, and yellow hair falling to her waist," inspired her followers to slaughter tens of thousands of Rome's supporters. The story of Queen Boudica recalls that of the Trung sisters on the edge of China's Han Empire only 20 years before. Roman troops eventually defeated Boudica, and Roman rule in Britain, like the Chinese in Vietnam, survived for centuries. Under the empire there were no massive slave revolts like that of Spartacus during the Republic.

The army itself mutinied from time to time. Frequent campaigns, sometimes in unforgiving environments such as the Syrian desert in summer, or tedious garrison duty in remote outposts, with no chance of glory, booty, or promotion, led some soldiers to think treasonous thoughts. Bad food and harsh discipline, the fate of most soldiers in pre-modern times, did nothing to change their minds. Every mutiny, however, was suppressed by loyal legions. The Romans held their army to high expectations: units showing insufficient resolve were sometimes decimated, meaning every tenth man was executed to persuade the others to shape up.

Expansion and Frontiers

When not employed crushing the occasional revolt or rare mutiny, the army's main job was extending or holding the empire's frontiers. As we've seen, from about 300 BCE the Roman polity had expanded rapidly. Even during the tumultuous era of civil wars at the end of the Republic, generals such as Pompey and Julius Caesar added or consolidated new territories.

The expansionary trend continued under Augustus. His annexation of Egypt brought rich farmland under Roman control, giving emperors surplus grain to use as a political tool. He also firmed up Roman control of the Alps and Spain, where state-run silver mines formed another crucial component of imperial power. After Augustus, the pace of expansion slowed. Emperors sometimes sought new conquests to acquire prestige and strengthen their grip on power, as Claudius did in seizing Britain in the years 43 to 44 CE, and as Trajan did along the Danube early in his distinguished reign. Trajan also extended Roman power into Mesopotamia, but his successor, Hadrian, judged it too costly to keep.

After Trajan's time, the frontiers remained more or less stable for two centuries. Most emperors had to fight little wars around the edges of the empire. Ambitious tribal leaders too might feel the need for glory and choose to attack Roman outposts.

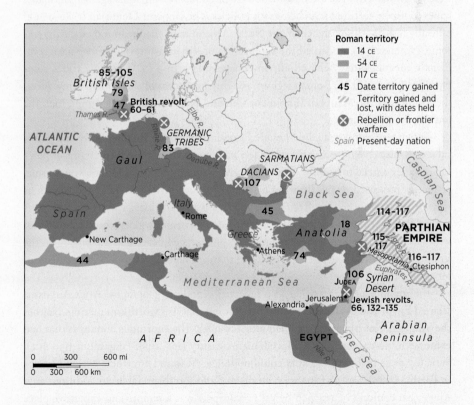

The Roman Empire, 14–180 CE After the consolidation undertaken by Augustus, who died in 14 CE, later emperors extended the frontiers especially in Britain, northwest Africa, and the eastern Mediterranean. But they often found it hard to hold what they took, and they faced frequent frontier warfare and occasional revolts.

Or whole peoples might need to flee their neighbors and calculate that fighting their way into Roman terrain was their least bad option. The most violent frontiers were, first, in Europe in the neighborhood of the Rhine and the Danube Rivers, to the east and north of which Germanic and other tribes such as the Dacians and Sarmatians roamed free. And, second, in the east along the Euphrates River, where the Parthians, an Iranian dynasty (247 BCE–224 CE) that had overthrown the Seleucids, presented a formidable foe. Roman forces tried on at least five occasions to best the Parthian Empire, but never did. Twice they captured the Parthian capital of Ctesiphon, but each time the Parthians soon recovered it.

Frontier warfare, like the suppression of revolts, was always brutal and frequently genocidal. Under the Republic, Roman generals had often enough killed all males among conquered foes, a practice far from peculiar to Rome. Allegedly Scipio Africanus, who defeated Carthage in the Second Punic War, killed all males and dogs of both genders after taking New Carthage (Cartagena in Spain) in 209 BCE. The Romans were no gentler after the establishment of their empire. Campaigns against Germanic tribes routinely featured scorched-earth policies. The emperor Domitian (r. 81–96 CE) officially forbade the existence of one North African tribe that he found especially irksome. No mercy accompanied the suppression of the Jewish revolts, as we have seen. Rome's enemies rarely behaved any more generously. In 9 CE Germanic tribes completely obliterated three Roman legions, roughly 10 percent of the Roman army. As on the frontiers of the Mauryan Empire, or Qin and Han China, politics often took the form of savage violence.

Not all was blood and gore, though: frontier policy included diplomacy and political seduction as well. Roman commanders had much to offer tribal chieftains or petty kings if they agreed to become clients of Rome, willingly accepted formal Roman rule, or merely promised to refrain from assaults. One incentive was trade goods such as wine or silver. Another was Roman support against rival tribes or petty kingdoms. A shrewd Roman frontier commander, if not fixated on military glory, could achieve a lot with bribes and diplomacy. Several emperors encouraged peace and diplomacy on the frontiers, aware that war was expensive and that war heroes were politically dangerous for sitting emperors.

The stability of the frontiers also reflected economic geography. After Augustus secured Egypt and Spain, there was much less left that was worth conquering. Neither the Sahara nor northern Europe had much to offer. The enormous bonanzas that had come with the capture of the Macedonian treasury (167 BCE), Pergamum (130 BCE), Syria (67 BCE), or Egypt (30 BCE) could no longer be found anywhere except perhaps in Parthia (Iran), and Parthia was too distant and too formidable. In addition, anywhere that couldn't be reached by water transport was a remote and expensive place to send an army and supplies. So lands beyond the Mediterranean coastlands were costly to conquer and costly to keep, despite the Roman roads and the navigability of the Rhine and Danube. Thus there were good reasons for the stability of frontiers from the time of Trajan onward.

The Economy

As a state, the Roman Empire, like the Republic, was a plunder machine. Conquests topped up the treasury, despite the lavish spending by some emperors. But the stability of the empire's frontiers after the time of Trajan paradoxically undermined Rome—slowly.

When expansion ceased, the flow of land, war booty, and slaves slowed to a trickle. Only through improvements in the efficiency of agriculture, mining, or better terms of trade with foreigners could the Romans now expand the economic pie that needed to be divided. They succeeded only modestly in these respects. A state and society built for over 400 years on periodic windfalls, in the form of rich provinces conquered or enemy treasuries seized, ran out of windfalls.

Now the state had to rely for revenue on taxes, rent on public land, and the minting of new coins. Good evidence that all this was insufficient comes in the form of the falling silver and gold content of Roman coins. Beginning in the late first century, but quickening in the late second, the official mints used less and less precious metal in each coin, enabling them to mint far more coins. This trick enhanced government revenues in the short run but invited currency inflation over the long haul. Eventually, the state refused to accept its own coins for tax payments. Taxation was inefficient and haphazard: there was little before 6 CE, more thereafter, but nothing as reliable as in Han China. Some Roman cities taxed nails, others taxed prostitutes. Sometimes officials just confiscated wealth.

Farming While the state often struggled to acquire enough revenues, ordinary people working the land often struggled to survive. In the first and second centuries CE, the empire's total population reached around 50 to 70 million, comparable to the population of Han China at the same time. Roughly 90 percent of these people lived in the countryside and followed the rhythms of farming life. These rhythms varied considerably from Egypt to England. Every province grew grain. Egypt normally harvested more than Egyptians ate, leaving a substantial reserve used for the Roman military or for distribution to the hungry; but when Egypt's crops failed, hunger stalked Roman cities. Mediterranean lands provided olive oil and wine in quantities sufficient for consumers all over the empire, from Egypt to distant Britain. Cattle, sheep, and goats grazed on lands not suited to grain, olives, or grapes.

Although Roman authors complained about the spread of latifundia, or big estates, in fact almost everywhere small farms prevailed. (This is an example of archeology correcting a bias in the textual record.) Even small farms often produced for sale as well as subsistence, conforming to the pattern—the commercialization of agriculture—of the

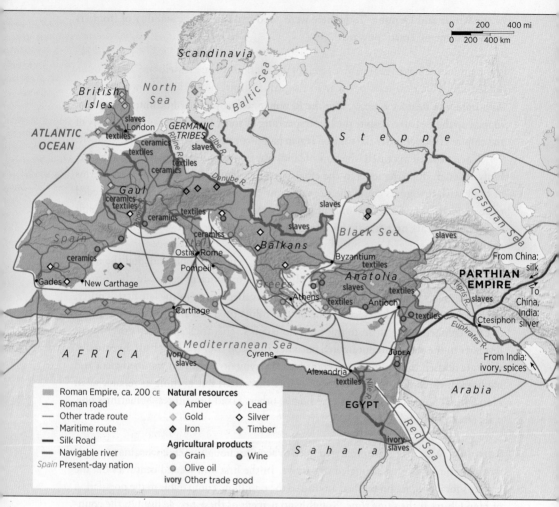

The Economy of the Roman Empire, ca. 200 CE At its height, the Roman Empire was a highly integrated economic space. Specialists produced a wide variety of goods for market exchange, and merchants shuttled around the empire, especially on its sea routes. Mining, mints, and coinage smoothed commercial transactions. For some goods, routes extended beyond the frontiers to the Sahara, the Baltic, the steppe, Persia, and even to India and China.

Hellenistic world. Under the empire, farms had to pay tax in money, so they needed to sell something to meet their obligations. The Romans made few technical improvements in agriculture, certainly nothing as helpful as the Achaemenid Empire's adoption of alfalfa. Once all the good lands were in use, it was close to impossible to expand output. Soil erosion and soil nutrient loss nibbled away at agricultural yields.

Mining Mining was ancient Rome's most important industry. Spain provided the bulk of the empire's gold, silver, and lead, and a good bit of its iron too. Britain, the Balkans, and Anatolia contributed heavily as well. Italy itself had less in the way of useful ores. Roman mines achieved remarkable levels of production in the early empire. Lead mines yielded nearly 80,000 tons per year in Augustus's time, more than the whole world would produce again for 1,700 years. Lead was used for water and sewer pipes and in pottery. Iron production outstripped that of Han China by perhaps 16-fold. But, as in agriculture, the Romans scarcely improved technologies and yields, perhaps because the plentiful supply of slaves ensured that labor in the mines was rarely short. The only notable technical improvement was a water-powered hammer for crushing ore, mentioned in one text from about 75 CE and probably not widely used.

Without technical advances, Roman mining inevitably ran into the law of diminishing returns. Lead production peaked before 50 CE, and silver about 150 CE. Gold production, most of which took place at a single mining complex in northwestern Spain called Las Médulas, tailed off by 200 CE. Reduced output of silver and gold made it hard for Roman rulers to resist debasing coinage.

Trade Trade within the empire boosted the Roman economy. Mediterranean agriculture had long been highly commercial, with some zones specializing in grain and others in olive oil or wine. The Romans continued in this tradition and expanded its scale, reaching into almost every corner of the Mediterranean. They built on the Carthaginian trade networks in the western Mediterranean, organizing even larger exports of Spanish metals. Ships bearing olive oil, wine, textiles, timber, ceramics, slaves, and more crisscrossed the Mediterranean in Roman times, shuttling among hundreds of ports large and small—as hundreds of shipwrecks attest. The pace of Mediterranean trade quickened after about 200 BCE and again with Augustus's acquisition of Egypt. Rome took part in the gradual process of commercialization that characterized the Hellenistic world, as we saw in Chapter 6.

Foreign trade mattered less to the Roman economy than farming, mining, or internal trade did. After Augustus's time, everything it truly needed came from within its broad territories. Imports consisted mainly of slaves and luxury goods. Trade links connected Rome to distant lands including Scandinavia, Russia, Arabia, India, even China and Korea. Amber, ivory, spices, and silks trickled in. They were taxed heavily (at about 25 percent), perhaps because officials sought to stem the tide of silver flowing out of the empire. Rome exported wine and pottery to northern Europe for slaves and amber, but in trade with Arabia, India, and China it had little to offer except silver.

Roman coins have turned up from Korea in the east to Ireland in the west, and as far south as Mali in West Africa. That distribution shows that the whole Eurasian world, and northern Africa too, took part in a giant web by 200 CE—the Old World web. By that time, however, as we have seen, the plunder machine and the mining that fueled the state and the economy had peaked. Thereafter, despite some energetic attempts at reform and economic stimulus, the Roman economy lurched, chugged, and slowed, never to recover its momentum.

Religion and Culture

The core of Roman religion under the empire remained the same pagan gods, rituals, and offices inherited from the days of the Republic. However, in a space as large as the Roman Empire, inevitably there were many competing religious concepts. The connectedness of the empire—the result of roads, military campaigns, shipping, and so forth—ensured that millions of people encountered novel beliefs and rituals.

New Beliefs and Practices   The first change to take hold involved the divine status of rulers, a familiar belief in Egypt and Mesopotamia. From Augustus onward, Roman emperors were regarded as gods in the empire except in Italy, where they were deified upon their death—provided they enjoyed good approval ratings. Unpopular emperors were denied deification.

Other new practices crept in as more and more people with different gods were enrolled in the Roman Empire. Some Romans, mainly women, followed a new cult of Isis, the Egyptian goddess whom they hoped would protect home, hearth, and family, and especially women in the dangerous moment of childbirth. From Persia and Mesopotamia came a mysterious religion devoted to a god named Mithra, about whom we know very little because no scriptures or revealing texts survive. But Mithraism acquired many followers in the army. A Celtic water goddess was absorbed into Roman circles in Britain and given a Roman-style temple at the hot springs near Bath, England. Emperor Elagabalus tried to convert Romans to the worship of the Semitic god Baal, but that failed to catch on. The geographical expansion of the empire brought a modest expansion to its pantheon, thanks to Roman exposure to the religions of peoples they conquered.

Christianity   One of the religious innovations that arose in the Roman Empire would eventually attain world historical importance: Christianity. Jesus of Nazareth was born in an Aramaic-speaking Jewish community during the reign of Augustus. As a young man he began to preach in the tradition of the Hebrew prophets, upbraiding the rich and powerful for their neglect of the poor and of God. His view, reported in the gospels, that it is easier for a camel to pass through the eye of a needle than for a rich man to enter the kingdom of heaven wasn't calculated to win friends in high places. His followers cast him in the role of messiah, the fulfillment of predictions concerning a liberator made centuries before by ancient Hebrew prophets. Gradually, the concept of messiah came to include the idea that Jesus was the son of God, put on Earth to show humankind the way to righteousness and salvation. Jesus's irreverent preaching irritated many influential people, who urged Roman authorities to kill him. The Roman prefect, who saw Jesus as a source of political instability, ordered his execution using a standard Roman method, crucifixion, in either 30 or 33 CE. Jesus's followers claimed he would return to oversee a reign of peace and justice that would last for all eternity. But at his death he had only about 120 followers.

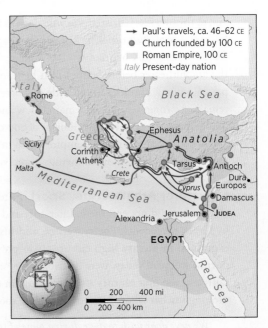

The Travels of Paul, ca. 46–62 CE After a conversion experience, Paul devoted his life to spreading the Christian faith. His itinerary reflected the existing infrastructure of roads and ports of the eastern Roman Empire of his day. He was executed in Rome around 65 CE.

That might have been the end of it, but for the relentless work of Paul (ca. 5–ca. 65 CE), a Greek-speaking Jew and Roman citizen from Tarsus, a Mediterranean port city in Anatolia. Sent to Jerusalem for his education, he vigorously persecuted Christians there until—on the road to Damascus, according to Christian tradition—a vision of Jesus changed his outlook. Thereafter, he began to preach as a Christian, enduring the beatings and persecution he had formerly dealt out. His innovation was to preach not just to fellow Jews, as Jesus had done, but to pagans, who by and large proved more receptive than Jews.

Paul also diverged from Jewish tradition by arguing that anyone could achieve salvation through faith alone, without adhering to the rituals and rules of Judaism. No elaborate dietary restrictions, no male circumcision, no adherence to Jewish law was required—just faith in God and Jesus. This amounted to a re-negotiated covenant between God and the faithful. Paul traveled about 12,000 miles (20,000 km) from town to town between approximately 46 and 62 CE, preaching his faith and founding churches. He couldn't have done it without Roman roads and shipping networks. He absorbed endless harassment from Jewish leaders, who eventually arranged his arrest by Roman authorities in Jerusalem. He insisted on being taken to Rome for trial, the right of any Roman citizen. After a two-year delay, he was tried and beheaded. His writings, recorded in the Bible's New Testament, helped to establish the traditions of Christianity.

Roman religious policy, as under the Republic, remained one of toleration except where political challenges emerged. Christianity, from the Roman point of view, seemed an obscure and curious Jewish heresy with strange beliefs and perplexing rituals that brought cannibalism to mind. Emperor Nero found it convenient to have Paul executed and to throw a few Christians to wild dogs in attempts to divert attention from his own failings. Local authorities in Roman Carthage condemned a young mother to death for converting to Christianity. The woman, Perpetua, was mauled by wild beasts in the amphitheater before being killed by a soldier in about 203 CE. But for the most part, Roman authorities found little to worry them in Christianity. While the empire remained strong, Christians remained few and unthreatening, perhaps 200,000 of the total population of 50 to 70 million as of 200 CE. They were mostly urban, petty traders and artisans. Later, when the empire began to teeter in the middle of the third century, and Christians grew more numerous, more systematic persecution would begin.

Literature, Architecture, Sport   Elite culture in imperial Rome began with religion but did not end there. Literature and architecture flourished, both influenced by Greek precedents. Poetry, satires, and histories remained the preferred modes of expression in literary high culture, as in previous centuries. Ovid's often saucy love poems, still read today, were too ribald for Augustus, who had him exiled. Martial, a satirist of the first century CE, specialized in quips, including one at the expense of a droning teacher whose lectures took place too early in the morning:

> *We next door wish to doze during some of the night hours.*
> *Total lack of sleep makes us ill.*
> *Let them out; what they pay you for screeching*
> *We will pay if only you keep still.*

The empire, like the Republic before it, also produced notable historians, political commentators, and—more than any other ancient society—agricultural writers. All writers unless rich themselves needed patrons, a role that emperors often filled. As a result, much writing was drivel meant to flatter the powerful. But the best flirted with the indistinct line of what was permitted and occasionally, like Ovid's poetry, stepped over.

Roman architecture has proved to be as enduring as Roman literature. In addition to their roads, bridges, and aqueducts, Roman engineers and architects sprinkled the landscape with temples, theaters, amphitheaters, and triumphal arches, many of which survive to this day. The precision, design, and craftsmanship involved have attracted wonder for 2,000 years. The heavy lifting, of course, was done by slaves and laborers.

Rome provided its full share of popular culture, enjoyed by rich and poor alike, and sometimes deliberately sponsored by the rich to keep the poor amused and distracted. Chariot races were the most popular sport, held in amphitheaters all over the empire. The largest, the Circus Maximus in the heart of Rome, could hold crowds of 250,000 people. (Ovid said it was a good place to meet members of the opposite sex.) Charioteers were full-time professionals, usually slaves of wealthy men who took pride in their athletic teams' achievements. Supporters bet on the races and often brawled with other fans, just like modern soccer hooligans. The crowds attracted by Roman chariot racing count as the largest for sporting events in world history to date.

Imperial Aqueducts A Roman aqueduct in Segovia, Spain, is one of many that the Romans built to transport clean water to cities throughout the empire. This one is 11 miles (17 km) long and was built around 100 CE.

Gladiatorial combat, an Etruscan tradition, was another favorite entertainment in imperial Rome. It took several forms. Professional gladiators (again, often slaves) might battle one another to the death. Their careers were normally short; one, however, a certain Publius Ostorius, allegedly won 51 bouts in a row. Sometimes amateurs, often convicts, fought one another. People fought animals. Animals fought animals. Trajan celebrated his conquests with combats in which 11,000 animals were killed, hastening the extinction of North Africa's elephants and hippos as well as Mesopotamia's lions. The emperor Domitian arranged combats in which women battled dwarves.

These and other entertainments—comic theater, poetry readings, footraces—helped keep the populace amused. Together with frequent handouts of grain, they formed the combination of "bread and circuses" that the satirist Juvenal mockingly identified as the main concern of Romans of his day (ca. 100 CE).

Society and Family

The available literary texts tell us far more about Roman aristocrats (well under 1 percent of the population) than about the lower classes. Archeological sites such as Pompeii—a city in southern Italy frozen in time by smothering volcanic ash in 79 CE—or several in Rome itself help fill the gaps.

Slavery Slaves stood at the bottom of the social pyramid. Under the empire they accounted for perhaps 12 to 18 percent of the population, more in the earlier centuries and less later when conquests slowed down. Whereas in the time of the Republic most slaves were war captives taken in Italy or Greece, now they mainly came as trade goods from lands north of the Danube and east of the Rhine. Some came from Nubia via Egypt, and others from the Black Sea shores. Rural slaves worked as farm laborers or shepherds. Urban slaves toiled as artisans, construction workers, cooks, nurses, domestics, messengers, and in some cases secretaries and tutors. The least fortunate worked in mines, where life expectancy was short, or as gladiators. Rich people owned slaves as much for the prestige it conferred as for the profit their labor might provide.

Manumission of slaves was common, more so than elsewhere in the Old World web, and too common for Augustus, who restricted it. Former slaves, or freedmen, still owed allegiance to their former masters, who owed some measure of protection to their freedmen. Freedmen became the clients of rich patrons and fit tidily into Roman social structure that way. Augustus employed some as middling officials. Freedmen often made a living through commerce, which was beneath the dignity of noble Romans. A few freedmen became wealthy businessmen, and if male they could become citizens. Normally there were limits on the social mobility of freedmen. They couldn't hold high office and couldn't marry aristocrats. The children of freedmen, however, were citizens: one emperor, Pertinax, who reigned for three months in 193 after a brilliant army career, was the son of a freedman. In time, some senators counted slaves among their ancestors.

Plebeians The majority of the people were commoners—or **plebeians**, meaning citizens not from elite families. Plebeians performed many of the same jobs that slaves did; but unlike slaves, the plebeians were paid for their work. In the city of Rome, they lived in flimsy multi-story wooden tenements. Most lived hand-to-mouth, and the emperors' periodic handouts of free grain were important to their survival. In the countryside, plebeians worked as farm laborers, often alongside slaves, sometimes as supervisors of slaves. Women specialized in spinning and weaving cloth, often done on country

Women at Home A richly colored fresco preserved at Pompeii in 79 CE shows elite women in the home, making preparations for a religious ritual.

estates (latifundia) as well as in towns. Some plebeians grew wealthy, however—either as clients of rich patrons or, for some few, on their own.

Marriage and the Family Marriage remained, as in the Republic, a property contract and, in political families, an alliance. Elite Roman men had long viewed wives, like children and slaves, as a human form of property. The senator Cato the Elder (234–149 BCE) found it shocking that women might lobby for the repeal of a law restricting lavish display of jewelry and finery, and he complained that "We rule the world and our wives rule us." He lost; the law was repealed. But that didn't change the patriarchal nature of marriage.

Toward the end of the Republic, a shift took place in marriage law and practice that allowed women to remain under the authority of their fathers even after marriage, rather than of their husbands. They could now inherit from their parents without turning property over to their husbands. This enabled families to keep their property intact even if several daughters married, and it reduced the incentive to kill baby girls. Child abandonment remained commonplace, however, as many babies were unwanted. Divorce was legal and routine among the upper classes, for whom shifting political winds might make an old alliance unhelpful and a new one desirable. Affectionate marriage was considered remarkable among the upper classes. Girls married at 13 to 16 years of age, usually to much older men.

Girls prepared for marriage from an early age. But by the second century CE, urban girls sometimes received formal education as well, learning basic literacy before marriage, when their schooling stopped. A very few women managed to participate in the lively intellectual world of Rome. Graffiti from Pompeii show that while women couldn't hold office and had no political rights, they occasionally endorsed candidates for office. Women moved about in public and didn't remain in seclusion at home,

Women in Public This first-century BCE marble relief shows two women working as butchers in a market stall, dressing and selling poultry, pigs, and rabbit.

unlike women in many eastern Mediterranean cities. They attended sporting events and spectacles, although at gladiatorial combats they were confined to the topmost seats farthest from the action.

The Roman authors of the early empire complain bitterly about the slipping moral standards of the elite. There was too little traditional virtue, too many childless marriages, and too much adultery, abortion, divorce, and vice. Women spent too much money on clothing—such as Chinese silks—that concealed too little. Augustus agreed and, like many before and after him, tried to legislate virtue and increase population. He offered tax breaks for big families and more legal rights for women with three or more children. (Augustus himself had only one child, a daughter whose scandalous adultery earned her exile.) He penalized widows for not re-marrying quickly and criminalized adultery, imposing tougher penalties for women than for men. As usual, class and rank mattered: married men could blithely have sexual relationships with women of low birth, slaves, or prostitutes. Several later emperors, not just Caligula and Egalabalus, gleefully broke all Roman sexual taboos. To what extent the masses and provincials imitated the elite in these respects is unclear, but early Christian writers found no shortage of licentiousness to rail against.

The Beginning of the End

Licentious or not, under rulers good and bad, the Roman Empire lasted for centuries after these complaints. Few emperors were better than Marcus Aurelius (r. 161–180). He came from a prominent family in southern Spain, allied to the emperor Hadrian. Young Marcus studied too much for his health, according to his biographer. He excelled in literature, oratory, and philosophy; and like Alexander the Great, he had a particular fondness for Homer's epics. Under Hadrian's patronage he began a public career, worked his way up the ladder, became consul at age 23, married well, and fathered 13 children. He was adopted by Hadrian's successor and groomed for the top job.

As emperor he was disciplined, diligent, calm, and modest. At one point he sold his palace furniture to help balance the imperial budget. He led the army in person on campaigns along the Danube and in Anatolia. His greatest character flaw was that he wrote repetitive and unoriginal philosophical treatises—a harmless defect by any standards, let alone those of Roman emperors.

But even a stalwart emperor such as Marcus Aurelius couldn't overcome the problems that now beset the Roman Empire. In 165 CE troops returning from war with the Parthians brought back an epidemic—perhaps smallpox, perhaps multiple diseases—that killed possibly 10 to 15 percent of the empire's population. The epidemic reached as far as Gaul and legions on the Rhine. The very success of the empire in building connections among far-flung places, by land and sea, created the conditions for epidemics to sear through entire populations quickly. Marcus Aurelius had to call off planned offensives against tribes along the Danube. He couldn't prevent Germanic tribes from marauding through northern Italy in 167. Italy had been safe from foreign invasion since

Hannibal nearly 400 years before, so this failure came as a shock. Marcus Aurelius was reduced to the expedient of inviting some 10,000 Germanic tribesmen to settle inside Roman territory, hoping they would prove loyal to him and fight for Rome against other tribes. Rome, which had enjoyed a manpower advantage in its wars for seven centuries, now depended on the kindness of strangers.

That was the very beginning of the end for the empire. As we will see, it was mostly downhill after the travails of Marcus Aurelius. He died without adopting a promising young man as heir and left the empire to his biological son, a disastrous choice. In a few more years Roman coins were nearly worthless, almost every general tried to make himself emperor, and civil war was as routine as in the dying days of the Republic. In 260 CE Iranian forces (under a new dynasty called Sasanians) managed to capture an emperor and treated him as a living footstool before killing and skinning him. Things had changed since the time of Augustus. And still Rome limped on.

Conclusion

Indeed, much had changed since the time when Phoenician settlers sailed forth to plant a new colony at Carthage roughly a millennium before Marcus Aurelius's death. The little colony became a seaborne empire, pioneering trade routes throughout the western Mediterranean and into the Atlantic Ocean. In the Punic Wars it lost its dominant position to a rapidly rising Rome. Colonists, traders, travelers, scholars, slaves, and soldiers now crisscrossed the Mediterranean, linking Spain to Syria and Egypt to Italy. As Polybius put it, soon after the final destruction of Carthage in 146 BCE:

> Now in earlier times the world's history has consisted, so to speak, of a series of unrelated episodes, the origins and results of each being as widely separated as their localities, but from this point onward history becomes an organic whole: the daily affairs of Italy and Africa are connected with those of Asia and Greece, and all events bear a relationship and contribute to a single end.

For Polybius, Africa meant North Africa only, and Asia meant only Southwest Asia. He was witnessing the effect of centuries of Carthaginian, Greek, and Roman integration of the Mediterranean world. By 200 CE it had become the most tightly integrated large space in the world, a Mediterranean-centered web held together by the power, economy, and culture of the Roman Empire.

But Rome did not stop there. Its soldiers, diplomats, traders, and colonists extended its political, cultural, and economic connections well beyond the Mediterranean, to the banks of the Thames, Rhine, Danube, and Euphrates. And its neighbors in Persia and Arabia sporadically carried its silver—if little else—to India. Through relay trade, its silver, and again little else, went as far as the East Asian web. Together, the Roman world and the Chinese-centered East Asian world made up the nodes of the Old World web.

‖‖‖

Chapter Review

KEY TERMS

Tyre p. 269

Phoenicia p. 269

Carthage p. 270

Punic Wars p. 274

Hannibal Barca p. 275

Julius Caesar p. 284

Octavian p. 285

praetorian guard p. 288

Queen Boudica p. 292

plebeians p. 302

REVIEW QUESTIONS

1. How was the basis of the Carthaginians' empire different from that of the empires of Sargon, Cyrus, and Shi Huangdi?

2. What seafaring innovations did the Phoenicians pioneer?

3. What prompted the merchants of Tyre to found Carthage?

4. In what ways was Carthage like Athens?

5. How did the Barca clan change the Carthaginian presence in Spain?

6. What was the legacy of the Carthaginians' empire for trade and commerce?

7. How did slavery and citizenship contribute to Rome's military success?

8. What practices and institutions minimized the outbreak of conflict and civil war in Rome prior to 91 BCE?

9. In what ways did the success of the Roman Republic's political system change Roman politics following the Second Punic War?

10. What measures did Augustus institute in the Senate, the army, the state, and for the public to ensure his power?

11. Why did Rome's frontiers stabilize, and how did this stabilization undermine Rome's economy?

12. What was Rome's response to Christianity prior to 200 CE?

Go to INQUIZITIVE

to see what you've learned—and learn what you've missed—with personalized feedback along the way.

On the Frontiers of the Old World Web

AFRICA AND EUROPE TO 200 CE

FOCUS QUESTIONS

1. What commonalities were shared by Africans and Europeans living outside the Nile-Ganges web?

2. What was distinctive about Africa's environments and early transitions to agriculture?

3. Why did Africans organize themselves into more fluid societies than peoples elsewhere?

4. What was distinctive about Europe's environments and early transitions to agriculture?

5. How was the impact of iron technology different in Europe than in Africa?

6. How did the development of Mediterranean Europe affect people in northern and eastern Europe?

Around 2900 BCE a new fashion craze took Europe and North Africa by storm. **Bell beaker ware**—clay vessels shaped like an upside-down bell and developed many centuries before—became all the rage. The first examples came from (today's) Portugal, and within a few centuries everyone from Morocco to Poland and Hungary to Ireland wanted the new pots.

In most cases, bell beaker ware spread because people valued it and learned how to make it. In most of Europe, it's found mainly along trade routes, especially those

307

CHRONOLOGY

by ca. 18,000 BCE People occupy entire African continent

ca. 9000–3000 BCE Sahara is mostly grassland with lakes and rivers

ca. 7500–6000 BCE Farming and farmers arrive in mainland Greece

ca. 7000 BCE Domestication of cattle in Africa; people occupy every area of Europe

ca. 6500–5500 BCE Farming emerges in Danube River basin and loess zones of Europe; menhirs appear

ca. 6000 BCE Pastoralism becomes dominant way of life in the Sahara

ca. 4500–2000 BCE Group burials and stone monuments spread widely within western Europe

ca. 3000 BCE Pastoralism spreads to East Africa

ca. 2900 BCE Bell beaker ware appears

ca. 2500 BCE Agriculture begins in Africa; Stonehenge is built

ca. 2200 BCE Bronze making begins in Europe

ca. 1800 BCE Iron working appears in Anatolia

ca. 1300–700 BCE Emergence of Celts

ca. 1100–1000 BCE Iron working appears in Europe

ca. 1000 BCE Rice cultivation begins in Africa; earliest uncontested evidence of iron working in Africa; states and kings emerge in Nubia

ca. 900–800 BCE Cimmerians migrate westward into Europe

along rivers and shorelines. But in the British Isles, genetic evidence suggests that arriving peoples came with the pots. The appearance of beaker ware in the archeological record coincides with the appearance in the genetic record of a new population, apparently from what is now the Netherlands. There was, it seems, an invasion of Britain by people bringing new pottery. There is no sign of violence or conquest.

Beaker ware had several uses. For families, it could hold the ashes of cremated relatives for burial. In metallurgy, it could contain super-hot molten (liquid) copper. But the primary purpose of beaker ware is evident in the many pots dug up by archeologists that retain chemical residues of beer. The introduction of beaker ware to new lands often coincided with an upsurge in the cultivation of barley—a key ingredient of beer. Indeed, it seems that the invention and spread of beaker ware is associated with the first use of alcohol in European culture.

The bell beaker ware phenomenon shows that by 2000 BCE something of a commercial and cultural web-in-the-making existed among elites in Europe. People in Poland may have been unaware of people in Portugal, but they made the same kinds of pots and used them for the same purposes. About 1800 BCE, people stopped making bell beaker ware. Beer drinking continued, but the connections among Europe's elites eventually weakened by 1000 BCE: the web-in-the-making frayed, only to be rewoven.

In Africa, as we'll see below, the invention of iron working after 1000 BCE had a broadly similar web-building effect. African communities developed a loose network of ironsmiths, as well as more long-distance trade in iron goods such as farming tools, weapons, and ornaments. Iron-bladed hoes made it easier to prepare ground for planting. The few faint webs of interaction that developed in sub-Saharan

Africa were, as in Europe, fragile and far from permanent. Sustaining webs was always easier and likelier where complex hierarchical society and states existed, such as in Southwest Asia or East Asia. However, Europe and Africa stood on the edges of the robust web uniting the lands between Egypt and the Indus. They built their own smaller and more fragile webs by 200 CE, and became increasingly linked to the more populous, more durable, and bigger web linking Egypt to India.

In many presentations of world history, Europe is not on the margins but at the center. In every account of human origins and evolution, Africa is at the center. But in this chapter, which deals with Africa south of the Sahara and Europe outside the Roman Empire, they are both at the frontiers. In the millennia between the end of the last ice age (say 12,000 BCE) and 200 CE, Africa and Europe stood in the wings, not at center stage. And they had a lot in common.

by 800 BCE Iron working is well established in eastern and central Europe

ca. 800–500 BCE Iron working reaches parts of East and West Africa

after 600 BCE Mediterranean luxury goods flow northward into central Europe

ca. 500–200 BCE Mass migration of Celts

ca. 300 BCE–100 CE Meroë thrives

by 100–450 CE Jenne thrives

ca. 300 CE Camel caravans across the Sahara begin

ca. 300–500 CE Aksum thrives

Commonalities of Africans and Europeans

People in Europe and Africa were few in number. Before farming came to Europe, its population is estimated at below 200,000 for the entire sub-continent from the Atlantic to the Ural Mountains. As almost everywhere, agriculture allowed higher population densities than did hunting and foraging. So by 3000 BCE, when farming villages dotted the landscape, Europeans numbered perhaps 1 to 2 million; and by 1000 BCE, perhaps 5 to 10 million.

For early Africa, we can only guess at population totals due to the paucity of archeological work. Even after the emergence of irrigation agriculture in Egypt, the entire continent in 1000 BCE had under 7 million people. In 200 CE, when Egypt had 3 to 5 million people and the Han Empire in China perhaps 50 million, Africa beyond Egypt had roughly 10 million. The population density of Han China was dozens of times greater than that of (non-Egyptian) Africa or (non-Roman) Europe.

Africans and Europeans, in addition to being few and scattered, lived in small-scale polities outside Mediterranean lands. Low population densities meant plenty of open space. People could wander off rather than accept the discipline and subordination required of all but a privileged few in the hierarchies of complex societies and states. Most people lived in chiefdoms or smaller units, and very few, even at 200 CE, lived

Bell Beaker Ware Culture By 2000 BCE, the same type of clay pots, shaped like inverted bells, were being used from eastern to western Europe. These beakers were found (left to right) in Spain, England, and Hungary.

within states. Their societies exhibited little of the hierarchy so pronounced in China, India, Mesopotamia, or Egypt after 2000 BCE. While the roles of men and women were clearly defined in early Africa and Europe, gender inequality was probably less sharp in most communities than in the great centers of population such as Mesopotamia or China. African and European technologies, and probably religious ideas too, changed more slowly than did those of peoples within the webs of West and East Asia.

The basic reason behind the similarities of Africans and Europeans in this period is that both regions were on the margins of the Nile-Ganges web and, to greater or lesser extent, removed from the upheavals and innovations under way there. The peoples closest to this web, in the middle Nile region or the middle and lower Danube, for example, felt powerful influences coming from Egypt and Southwest Asia—both as examples to emulate and as pressures that they wished to avoid.

Africans and Europeans were vulnerable to enslavement. Egypt, Mesopotamia, and the Roman Mediterranean—the western end of the Old World web—imported people as slaves to perform unpleasant work and to make up for the high death rates that urban life and irrigation agriculture entailed. So people close to the web, and sometimes those not so close, suffered routinely from slave raiding. Sometimes their leaders took part in slave trading to buttress their own wealth. Among Africans, those living in the upper Nile and Horn of Africa region probably ran the highest risks of enslavement and export to the cities and fields of the Old World web. Among Europeans, those around the shores of the Black Sea probably suffered most at the hands of slavers.

Europeans and Africans living farthest from the web, in Scandinavia or southern Africa, remained substantially isolated and more at liberty to chart their own course than peoples in the web. Africans and Europeans were, in general, taller, healthier, and freer than the subordinated peasants of Egypt, Mesopotamia, or China. But their societies were less militarily formidable, less resistant to many deadly diseases, and less organized for the production of surplus than those of complex societies within the world's webs.

Sub-Saharan Africa and northern Europe stood semi-isolated from the world's big webs. As we have seen, between 3500 BCE and 200 CE big webs of interaction developed between Egypt and India, and another in East Asia, with dense populations at many places and great social complexity. Taking these two big webs together, they probably accounted for two-thirds, maybe even three-quarters, of humankind at 200 CE. Everywhere else in the world was peripheral both in demographic terms and with respect to the pace of technological change and the overall volume of intersocietal and intercultural contacts. Sub-Saharan Africa and non-Roman Europe weren't fully isolated from the great webs stretching between India and the Mediterranean, but they weren't part of those webs either. They were on the frontiers, the far reaches of the interactive world. And people there were probably better off for it—at least, in terms of health and freedom from taxes and conscription.

Africa to 1000 BCE

Africa accounts for one-fifth of the world's land area. It is 4,000 miles (7,000 km) from the Cape of Good Hope to the Mediterranean Sea, and almost as far from the coasts of Senegal to Somalia's. Africa stands astride the equator: most of it lies within the tropics, and none of it extends further than 37 degrees north or south. So except at altitude, it is usually warm or hot. The great ice sheets of the last ice age never touched Africa.

Evolving Environments

About 40 percent of Africa is now desert. The Sahara accounts for most of that, but smaller deserts exist, especially in the southwest of the continent. This proportion has varied considerably with climate change over the millennia, as we'll see shortly. Rain forest accounts for another 8 percent or so of the continent, mostly in West and Central Africa. This proportion, too, has fluctuated over the long haul with climate change, and it has shrunk in recent decades through forest burning and logging. Most of Africa is, and usually has been, savanna grassland. A broad belt runs across the continent south of the Sahara, and most of East and southern Africa is also mainly savanna or mixed savanna and parkland (meaning grassland with occasional clumps of trees).

The most important variable determining the land cover is rainfall: the more rain, the thicker the vegetation. Climate changes in Africa have raised and lowered temperatures, but rarely enough to matter for human occupation. What has mattered, tremendously, are variations in rainfall. Rainfall shifts that endured for decades or centuries obliged societies to move or change their ways.

Africa is an old continent geologically, with soils that are for the most part weathered and low in nutrients. Its native plants and animals, having evolved in this environment, use nutrients sparingly. But still the agricultural potential of most African landscapes is limited by their soils. The main exceptions lie in and around the geological rift running through East Africa from the Great Lakes northward through Ethiopia. Here young rock from volcanic eruptions has weathered into rich soils.

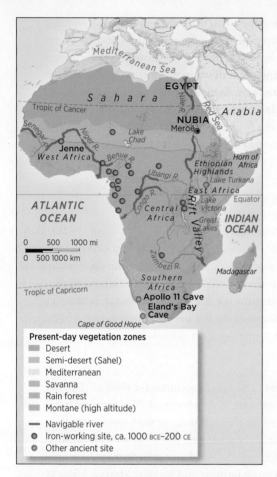

Ecological Zones of Africa Rainfall is the primary determinant of ecological zones in Africa. More falls around the equator than elsewhere. Well-watered areas supported forests, where abundant wood supplied fuel for early iron making. Over the centuries, rainfall patterns have shifted somewhat, so this current map provides only an approximation of the ecological zones in the distant past.

It is important to remember one other feature of African geography: the avenues of, and obstacles to, transport. Three big African rivers are well suited for boat traffic: the Nile, the Niger, and the Congo. They all have waterfalls or rapids here and there, as most rivers do, so it was hard to travel their entire length. But long stretches were navigable by dugout canoe. Other rivers, however, were less useful in this respect, and in the drier parts of the continent there was no alternative to walking.

Africa's coastlines are mostly sand beaches, frequently pounded by surf. With few natural harbors, bays, offshore islands, and archipelagoes to protect vessels from ocean wind and surf, there was little chance for maritime cultures to develop in Africa. People were sailing to Australia from New Guinea some 50,000 years ago, and others almost surely sailing or paddling from Siberia to Alaska, and southward along the Pacific coast of Canada some 15,000 years ago. As we've seen, Polynesians sailed the open Pacific thousands of years ago. But no such precocious maritime culture existed in early African history, except along the Red Sea linking Egypt with the Horn of Africa.

Africa before Farming and Herding

When small bands of humans left Africa about 100,000 years ago and started to occupy the rest of the globe, Africans who stayed behind were doing something similar at home. They, too, were highly mobile hunters and foragers, often settling in for a few months at one place or another, but rarely for longer periods. By 20,000 years ago, if not before, they had occupied the entire continent. Africans improved their hunting and fishing toolkits, to judge by the surviving stone evidence. They took up art, using a red ochre to decorate some rock shelters and making beads from ostrich egg shells in southern Africa. A rock painting in Apollo 11 Cave, in today's Namibia, dates to about 20,000 years ago and shows what appear to be a giraffe, a rhinoceros, and some sort of wild cat.

Like most hunting and foraging people, Africans lived in small bands connected mainly by kinship. Population density and birth rates were low, as among all hunting and foraging peoples. So they rarely encountered other human groups. When they did so, sometimes it was by design—a gathering of a clan to exchange gifts, information, and young people in marriages. Their ways of life changed only slowly. They didn't have to change quickly: Africans knew how to exploit their environments and were too few in number to imperil those environments.

Climate change—specifically, dry periods—made life harder at times. Some genetic evidence suggests that African populations fell during dry millennia such as 25,000 to 12,000 years ago. This was the last stage of the last ice age, when most of Africa was a little cooler and much drier. Lake Victoria, today the world's largest lake, vanished entirely around 11,000 BCE, and sand dunes blocked the flow of the Niger River. The Sahara crept southward about 300 miles (500 km). The savanna grasslands in West Africa shifted southward, and West Africa's rain forests shrank to a narrow coastal strip.

These were hard times. People had to move off the dried-out savannas, to forest edges, river banks, or seashores, where food supplies were more reliable. For example, at around 12,500 BCE in Elands Bay Cave in southern Africa, near the ocean, people found tortoises, mussels, seals, flamingoes, pelicans, cormorants, gulls, rock lobsters, and a variety of fish to eat. Fortunately, they failed to tidy up after themselves, leaving shells and bones galore for archeologists to study. The climate improved (for humans, at least) after about 10,000 BCE, bringing more rain more often over more of Africa.

Although they all lived by hunting, fishing, and foraging before 2500 BCE, in some ways these Africans were highly diverse. As we saw in Chapter 1, the genetic diversity among Africans today is greater than that among all other humans. That would have been true 50,000 and 10,000 years ago as well. Africans also spoke a great variety of languages. Linguists lump modern African languages into broad families but estimate that perhaps 700 to 1,000 languages are spoken today. Low population density, low levels of interaction, and lots of opportunity for isolation produce a condition favorable to the development of both genetic and language diversity.

Four language families in particular seem to have prospered and spread when the long dry spell ended and conditions improved. In northeast Africa, Afro-Asiatic-speakers lived along the Red Sea coast and by 10,000 BCE were harvesting wild grains. Nilo-Saharan-speakers, based in the upper reaches of the Nile in today's Sudan, made their living mainly by hunting and fishing. In West Africa, a group called Niger-Congo-speakers coalesced, living by collecting yams, hunting, and fishing. Last, in East Africa lived a group called Khoisan-speakers, also hunters and foragers. Today, most African languages fall into one of these four families.

Early Pastoralism

With so much savanna grassland, Africa offered good habitat for grass-eating animals such as gazelles, wildebeest, zebra, and, in places, cattle. For thousands of years, Africans had hunted them and had scavenged kills made by big cats and other carnivores. As it happens, few of Africa's grazing animals can be domesticated. They're just too feisty. But, as we've seen, one of the earliest and most important animal domestications probably took place in Africa: cattle. It probably happened about 7000 BCE somewhere in what is now Sudan or southern Egypt. And it launched a new way of life for some Africans.

From about 9000 to 3000 BCE, the Sahara, far wetter than today, was mostly grassland dotted with lakes and threaded with rivers. In the millennia after 8000 BCE, a pastoral way of life gradually took hold over much of northern Africa, based on cattle and, probably no later than 6000 BCE, also on sheep and goats introduced from Southwest Asia. These three animals would become the basis of African pastoralism ever after.

Before going any further, we must pause and reflect upon the term *pastoralist* in the African context. Evidence both modern and archeological indicates that people might practice herding as an exclusive way of life or might mix it with hunting; with hunting, fishing, and foraging; or with seasonal agriculture. Moreover, people changed their chosen mix over time, depending on climate, new technologies that made one or another pursuit more appealing, and a host of other factors. The Khoisan-speakers of southernmost Africa, for example, shifted in and out of pastoralism in response to climate shifts and other factors. So *pastoralist* is a fuzzy term and not a category in which people conveniently stayed put forever. While that is true elsewhere too, the category is probably more fluid in African history than, for example, in the steppe lands of Asia.

When the Sahara was grassland speckled with lakes, pastoralism proved appealing there. After 6000 BCE it was the predominant way of life, replacing an earlier one in which fishing featured prominently. Rock art and artifacts such as pottery show remarkable similarity in styles throughout the Sahara both before and after the shift to pastoralism, which implies high mobility and regular interaction among the Saharan peoples. Pastoralism spread into East Africa by 3000 BCE and into southern

Pastoralism This small terra-cotta model of a bull from the area of present-day Sudan dates to between 2300 and 1600 BCE. Cattle herding was central to the structure of many African societies by the late millennia BCE.

Africa around 1 CE. Throughout Africa, pastoralists kept female animals for milking. They kept a few males around to ensure the future of their flocks and herds, but they didn't for the most part castrate bulls and use them as oxen, as was often done in Asia and Egypt. Instead, most young male animals were killed for their meat. In some pastoralist societies, people also often drank the blood of their animals or mixed it with milk. Some African pastoralists (as we've seen) underwent genetic changes enabling adults to digest milk, but others did not.

Animal diseases or drought might ravage herds suddenly, so resilience was always on pastoralists' minds. It was crucial to take good care of females of breeding age. In times of drought, herders might have to move long distances. They might have to encroach on other groups' grass and water, risking conflict. They might trade or eat some of their animals, but they always tried to keep possession of some breeding stock. Although we have no evidence about it, the adoption of pastoralism by hunters and foragers must have changed ideas and practices about property and ownership in much of Africa.

The best evidence we have of social conditions among early African pastoralists comes from the area around Lake Turkana in northern Kenya. Around 3000 or 2500 BCE, sheep herders there began to bury their dead in pits carved into bedrock. This took a lot of work, and no one knows why they did it or why after 700 years they stopped. They buried some 600 to 1,000 people: men, women, and children together, carefully arranged, with modest ornamentation including, in one case, a necklace of gerbil teeth. It was apparently a rather egalitarian society, but one with a considerable capacity for working together toward a common purpose.

Early Agriculture

Chapter 2 explained the general circumstances surrounding the transition to farming in Africa. It occurred as the Sahara was getting dryer, its lakes and rivers shrinking, and its inhabitants inclined to experiment because business as usual—gathering, fishing, and hunting—was getting less rewarding. It might have occurred in several places along what is now the southern fringe of the Sahara, or it might have happened only once and spread to other environments with the same pressures. It probably began around 2500 BCE, long after pastoralism had taken hold in Africa. The first crops were sorghums and millets, which prospered in savanna conditions and withstood drought fairly well. Rice later joined the mix in West Africa, perhaps by 1000 BCE.

As with pastoralism, a few cautionary points are in order about our understanding of farming and farmers in African history. First of all, as usual, there's a great deal we don't know and probably never will know about it. The archeological record is so spotty that, for example, native African crops (pearl millet, sorghum, cowpeas) turn up in South Asian archeological sites around 2000 BCE, long before they do in East African ones—where they must have been in use before being carried to India.

Second, the transitions to farming in Africa were less decisive and important for

Women and Agriculture Reliefs on a pot made in the West African Nok culture during the sixth century BCE show women, carrying children on their backs, harvesting crops.

Africans than such transitions were for most people elsewhere. Unlike wheat or rice, African crops by and large didn't store well, so they were less suited for hoarding and trading and harder to convert into political power. This made them less practical as a basis for state making or long-distance exchanges. It also reduced the incentive to produce surplus crops. Thus Africans had less interest in spreading agriculture to every available patch of ground than did people in rice or wheat lands.

Third, African agriculture was normally women's work. Partly because of thin soils but mainly because of the absence of oxen or water buffalo, Africans outside of Egypt and Ethiopia didn't use plows. Farmers scratched the earth with digging sticks to plant their crops. It was arduous work but didn't require much physical strength, unlike handling a plow harnessed to a powerful animal.

Fourth, as with pastoralism, Africans moved in and out of farming as climate change, migrations, or other forces and factors directed. In the river valleys from Egypt to China, once people turned to agriculture their populations surged and they couldn't turn back to their former ways. They lived on ribbons of irrigated ground surrounded by desert or steppe and couldn't easily wander off to new lands. They were in an ecological cul-de-sac, committed to irrigation agriculture and its tremendous yields, with no going back. Africans lived differently, with more geographic mobility, and more fluidity and flexibility in their ways of life.

For most Africans, over many millennia, farming wasn't an attractive option. Hunting, foraging, and fishing were preferable, and there was always more room in which to do it. Farming was more work without any more reward. And it required people to stay put and defend their land against attackers, whereas foragers and hunters could walk away from conflict at little cost.

So it took quite some time for farming to spread throughout the continent. It remained rare in the Great Lakes region of east-central Africa until 1000 BCE. From there, sorghum and millets spread southward, reaching South Africa about 300 CE. In West Africa, the first archeological dates for sorghum, rice, okra, and cowpeas are around 500 BCE, although cultivation, especially of yams, might have begun much earlier without leaving a trace. By 1000 BCE, most Africans north of the equator lived as farmers or pastoralists or some mix of the two. South of the equator, hunting and foraging prevailed. Everywhere (except Egypt and Nubia), Africans lived in small groups with no states, no cities, minimal hierarchy, and unusual freedom to live as they pleased.

Africa, 1000 BCE to 200 CE

After 1000 BCE, farming and pastoralism, and various combinations of the two, continued to spread in Africa. Part of the reason for the expansion of farming was iron.

Iron Working

Before 1000 BCE, almost all Africans used tools and weapons of stone and wood, not metal. Although copper smelting appeared in Nubia by 2600 BCE and in the central Sahara by 1000 BCE, Africa has no equivalent eras to those in Mesopotamia or China when bronze was widely important for weaponry and art. Iron, however, made a big difference in Africa.

Iron making, as we've seen, is technically difficult work. It's even harder to do it if there's no tradition of working bronze, an easier process that in Asia preceded and probably led to **iron working**. In the pre-Columbian Americas, no one ever figured out how to make useful metal out of iron ore, which isn't surprising. The surprise is that anyone in the ancient world did figure it out. The earliest iron working in world history appears to be in Anatolia, begun about 1800 BCE and reaching a large scale by 1200 BCE.

Archeologists cannot agree on how, where, and when iron working arose in Africa. The raw material, iron ore, is widespread throughout the continent. The earliest uncontested archeological evidence dates from about 1000 BCE and comes from the Great Lakes region. Early African ironsmiths used different technologies from those of Anatolia, and archeologists have found no signs of iron working prior to 1000 BCE in the lands between Egypt (where, in any case, there was virtually no iron ore) and the African Great Lakes. So it's unlikely that iron working originally entered sub-Saharan Africa from Egypt. The best guess at the moment is that iron working developed independently somewhere in Africa, perhaps at more than one place, around 1000 BCE.

No matter how it arose, iron making—always men's work—spread into the easily traversed savanna zones of East and West Africa, probably by around 800 to 500 BCE, although its adoption remained spotty. Smiths carried the secrets of iron working along river routes in central and West Africa, reaching the coastal forests there no later than 500 CE. Iron working usually remained not only the preserve of men, but the preserve of certain men acting as a guild and keeping their techniques secret from others. The sons of ironworkers tended to marry daughters of other ironworkers; and especially in West Africa, iron making became associated with certain clans, in effect forming a hereditary caste. They encouraged the view that iron working involved magic powers, a belief reflected in many African oral traditions.

African ironsmiths mainly made tools such as hoes and axes. No iron weapons have turned up in early archeological sites. This forms a sharp contrast to the work of early Anatolian smiths, who made large quantities of weapons that helped the Assyrians conquer far and wide. Early Chinese bronze workers also mass-produced weaponry. In

Africa, the demand was for tools, not weapons, perhaps because stone-edged weapons were lethal enough, or perhaps because there were no big states to organize and pay for mass production.

In the forest zones of West and Central Africa, iron tools opened new possibilities. Felling trees to create a forest clearing for planting is extremely slow work when done with stone axes—so slow that almost no one bothered to do it. Iron axes, sharper and more durable than stone ones, made it sufficiently rewarding that frontier farmers increasingly slipped into the forests and hacked out clearings to plant yams. In southeastern and southern Africa there was very little agriculture at all before iron tools made it easier to clear forest and break sod.

Everywhere, iron was the enemy of trees. To make enough iron for three hoe blades took one ton of charcoal, which required about four tons of fuelwood. (Charcoal is made by heating firewood and limiting oxygen to prevent full combustion.) Iron-bladed axes allowed the felling of trees for charcoal making and the clearing of ground for farming. Open ground permitted cattle and goats to graze, which prevented saplings from growing into trees. So where iron spread, forests and woodlands disappeared, replaced by fields and pastures.

Meroë The biggest single center of iron production in ancient Africa was at **Meroë**, on the Nile in the land of Kush (today's northern Sudan). It was known to Achaemenid Persian emperors and referred to by the Greek historian Herodotus as a "great city" whose people worshipped Egyptian gods such as Amun and Osiris. Meroë stood astride the river route between Egypt and sub-Saharan Africa. It occupied about one square mile and had avenues and monumental architecture in the Egyptian style. Its prosperity rested on commerce, and at its height around the first century BCE Meroë exerted a chokehold on the export of African goods (ostrich feathers, tortoise shells, ivory, elephants, and slaves) to Egypt. Meroites gave their kings fancy burials, including pyramids, and had sizeable merchant and artisan classes—a pattern of social structure unusual in Africa outside of Egypt. They wrote in the Egyptian language until about

Meroë The prosperity brought about by iron and other trading commodities allowed Meroë to build monuments such as these pyramids and temples, dated to between 800 BCE and 350 CE. The Egyptian influence on Meroite culture is evident in their architectural style.

200 BCE and adopted some features of Egyptian religion. But they were not Egyptians. They traced descent through mothers (matrilineal descent), a social trait unknown in Egypt but common among peoples of the central and upper Nile. And they had their own language, Meroitic. Around 200 BCE their scholars invented a Meroitic script, using an alphabet of 23 characters, which no one today knows how to read.

Meroë also had abundant iron ore and woodlands. Its artisans learned the techniques of iron making from Egyptians. Meroë's iron technologies were Mediterranean and different from those used in East or West Africa. By 300 BCE—well after iron working had independently emerged farther south in Africa—Meroë was exporting iron to Egypt and other destinations. For 400 years Meroë was Africa's chief iron-making center. According to a recent estimate, it produced 5 to 20 tons of iron per year for centuries, much of which went to Egypt. By 250 CE Meroë's iron industry was a spent force, perhaps the result of a shortage of wood for charcoal. Elsewhere, especially in East and West Africa, smiths continued to make iron tools for local use. They, more than the ironsmiths of Meroë, spread iron working within Africa and opened new landscapes to hoe agriculture.

Farming and Herding Frontiers

Iron tools helped to reduce forest and spread farming and pastoralism in Africa, but iron was only part of the story. Two other factors assisted in this transition, especially in the moist tropical forest zones.

The first, which we encountered in Chapter 3, was malaria. When people brought farming to forest zones and opened holes in forest canopies, they unwittingly created good conditions for malaria outbreaks. These proved devastating to populations that lacked malaria resistance. Migrating farmers, already experienced with and resistant to malaria, inadvertently thinned the ranks of peoples who hadn't previously practiced farming, making more space for themselves and their descendants.

Bananas and other Southeast Asian crops such as taro, sugarcane, and Asian yams also sped the spread of farming, especially in East and central Africa. These crops all do well in moist climates, better than sorghum and millets. They probably arrived in Africa somewhere around 1 CE. Bananas yield abundantly and pack a lot of nutrition. They have no calcium or iron, and little protein or fat, but if eaten with a little meat now and then they provide most of what a human needs. And once a banana grove is mature, it requires little work. Women probably welcomed and encouraged the spread of bananas because they require no pounding or grinding to prepare, unlike grains and most root crops. Today, Africa grows one third of the world's bananas, and the average African eats 500 lbs. (250 kilos) of bananas per year, 25 times as much as the average American.

Plantains, another tree crop from Southeast Asia, were just as useful. They grow well in very rainy areas, such as equatorial Africa, and unlike yams don't require a forest

CONSIDERING THE EVIDENCE

The Periplus of the Erythraean Sea

In the middle of the first century CE, an anonymous, Greek-speaking merchant who lived in Egypt wrote *The Periplus of the Erythraean Sea*. A *periplus* is basically a travel itinerary for sailors, and the Erythraean Sea is what Greek-speakers of the time called the western parts of the Indian Ocean, including the Red Sea. Though written by an outsider, the descriptive notes on sailing distances, friendly ports, products, local diets, and politics offer a fairly objective view of what people were buying and selling, as well as how they used these items. The following excerpt describes how towns controlled by Aksum, such as Coloe and Adulis in modern Eritrea, attracted merchants who brought goods from as far away as Italy, Anatolia, Egypt, Sudan, and India. As merchants traded iron and cloth for ivory, tortoise shell, and other products, they drew Aksum's modest web of exchange in northeast Africa into the expanding Old World web.

On the mainland . . . lies Adulis, a fair-sized village, from which there is a three-days' journey to Coloe, an inland town and the first market for ivory. From that place to the city of the people called Auxumites [i.e., Aksumites] there is a five days' journey more; to that place all the ivory is brought from the country beyond the Nile through the district called Cyeneum [Kush], and thence to Adulis. Practically the whole number of elephants and rhinoceros that are killed live in the places inland, although at rare intervals they are hunted on the seacoast even near Adulis. . . .

There are imported into these places, undressed [unfinished] cloth made in Egypt for the Berbers; robes from Arsinoe [near Suez in Egypt]; cloaks of poor quality dyed in colors; double-fringed linen mantles; many articles of flint glass, and others of murrhine [delicately carved stone or glass], made in Diospolis [Thebes in

clearing and prepared ground. They out-yield yams by ten to one. One woman tending plantains or bananas could easily feed a large family.

With these new crops, as well as iron tools, farmers in moist tropical zones of Africa could reliably produce surplus food for the first time. Opportunities for long-distance trade by canoe along the rivers developed. Bananas wouldn't store for years, liked dried rice, but could keep long enough to be transported a few hundred miles along rivers. In the rain forests, farmers and ironsmiths built trade connections with hunters and foragers, who developed specializations as providers of honey, ivory, monkey meat, leopard skins, and other high-end goods. Population centers gradually emerged in places such as the shores of Lake Victoria.

Just how the Southeast Asian crops arrived in Africa is unclear. Linguistic evidence implies that they first arrived on the East African mainland at roughly 1 CE, presumably

Egypt]; and brass, which is used for ornament and in cut pieces instead of coin; sheets of soft copper, used for cooking-utensils and cut up for bracelets and anklets for the women; iron, which is made into spears used against the elephants and other wild beasts, and in their wars. Besides these, small axes are imported, and adzes and swords; copper drinking-cups, round and large; a little coin for those coming to the market; wine of Laodicea [in Anatolia] and Italy, not much; olive oil, not much; for the king, gold and silver plate made after the fashion of the country, and for clothing, military cloaks, and thin coats of skin, of no great value. Likewise from the district of Ariaca [in coastal northwest India] across this sea, there are imported Indian iron, and steel, and Indian cotton cloth; ... and girdles, and coats of skin and mallow-colored cloth, and a few muslins, and colored lac [resin]. There are exported from these places ivory, and tortoiseshell and rhinoceros-horn.

Questions for Analysis

1. Why would merchants be concerned about the time it takes to travel between towns or the origins of the products available at different markets?

2. How does the writer use origin, value, quantity, material, and purpose to sort the products that are available to buy and sell in northeast Africa?

3. Given Aksum's trading contacts with merchants from India and Sudan, would you consider Aksum to be part of the Old World web or some other web? Why?

Source: W. H. Schoff, ed. and trans., *The Periplus of the Erythraean Sea: Travel and Trade in the Indian Ocean by a Merchant of the First Century* (London, Bombay, and Calcutta, 1912).

via coasting voyages around the Indian Ocean. Speakers of Austronesian languages, characteristic of Southeast Asia, settled the previously uninhabited island of Madagascar around the same time. Perhaps the Austronesians brought bananas, plantains, and other crops with them on deliberate voyages of colonization, as Polynesians did in the Pacific at roughly the same time. No matter how it happened, the addition of bananas and other Southeast Asian crops to the African farmers' repertoire paved the way for agricultural expansion and population growth, especially in moist forest zones.

Bananas and plantains didn't thrive in dry or cool areas, but cattle did. Throughout much of East Africa's savanna lands, elevations are high enough that nights are cool. Cattle keepers filled these landscapes, bringing languages and culture from the Nilotic Sudan into East Africa's savannas. Gradually, cattle herders pushed farther south, bringing pastoralism all the way to South Africa. By 200 CE, farmers and herders occupied almost the entire African continent that wasn't desert. But they remained mobile except in the most fertile areas, and their numbers probably didn't exceed 10 million.

Long-Distance Trade

Like almost everyone else, Africans traded goods over considerable distances several thousand years ago. Archeologists have unearthed especially valuable stone, such as obsidian, which holds a sharp edge well, as much as 500 miles (300 km) from where it had been quarried. But logistics constrained trade in Africa. Except on river routes, people had to carry just about everything because there were no horses or mules, no donkeys except in northeast Africa, and no domesticated camels until about 200 CE. Heavy or bulky objects—rock salt, pottery, or ivory, for example—could only be transported in small quantities and locally, on people's heads or backs. Rivers and lakes (at least, after the development of boats) provided better options. The oldest dugout canoe yet found dates from about 4400 BCE, and it's plausible that by that time people were routinely gliding along the many rivers of Africa's well-watered zones. In the savannas and deserts, however, they had to walk, carrying trade items on their heads.

Metallurgy and then bananas improved the logic of long-distance trade from 500 BCE onward. Every man trying to carve out a forest clearing wanted an iron axe, and every woman digging the earth wanted an iron hoe. But iron goods were made only where ore and fuelwood, and the jealously guarded iron-making expertise, existed. As a result, many communities had to trade for iron goods. In the warm and wet parts of Africa, bananas made that easier. As noted above, they yielded so well that surplus food production became more common, and they could travel for a few weeks before rotting. All evidence, which isn't much, suggests that trade quickened throughout much of Africa after 500 BCE. The reason the evidence is sparse is that most trade goods—cloth, food, animals—decayed in the humid and acidic soils of Africa long before archeologists could find them.

Jenne A major exception to our ignorance about ancient trade is the region of the interior delta of the Niger in today's Mali—specifically, the archeological site of **Jenne** (also known as Djenne and Jenne-jeno). Here clusters of settlement developed by 250 BCE. As the Sahara and West African savanna dried out and the Niger's seasonal floods grew tamer, people, probably migrants from the Sahara itself, found the alluvial lands and braided river channels around Jenne appealing. They grew rice, sorghum, and millet in the rich riverbank soils. Nearby savanna offered grass for livestock, and the river channels yielded fish. People also made tools and jewelry from iron, although there is no iron ore nearby. It had to come by canoe along the Niger. A sprawling regional trade network developed, with merchants and markets, using the river for transport. In addition to iron wares, markets offered livestock, leather, dried fish, rice, copper, and other items. Two Roman beads are tantalizing evidence of a cross-Saharan connection as well, although there is no further evidence of this. The days of trans-Saharan camel caravans lay a few centuries in the future.

By 100 CE, Jenne had as many as 2,000 inhabitants and social complexity in the form of a division of labor among specialists in metallurgy, leather working, and other crafts. By 450 CE, Jenne had grown to cover 60 acres (25 hectares). Some scholars call it a city, others a cluster of villages. There is no archeological evidence of pronounced social hierarchy. In any case, archeology at Jenne provides a rare glimpse into a vanished world of long-distance trade and markets along the Niger River.

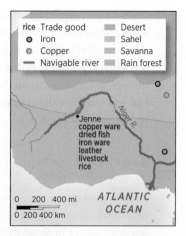

Jenne and the Niger Trade System, ca. 250 BCE The Niger River was one of the best in Africa for navigation. Canoes laden with goods glided upstream and downstream, connecting people in rainforest, savanna, and Sahelian zones. At Jenne, trade routes converged with good conditions for farming, leading to dense clusters of settlement and early development of artisan crafts.

Fluid Societies

Over the millennium before 200 CE, Africa was developing more commerce, greater specialization, and bigger, more numerous settlements. Its population was surely growing. But outside of the northeast, the region in close touch with Egypt, it retained its small-scale political and social structures. It's possible that around 200 BCE some of the iron-producing villages southeast of Lake Victoria banded together to form a state—the evidence is ambiguous at best; but if so, it lasted a few centuries and faded away. Most Africans organized themselves into more fluid societies, built on kinship, without the formal institutions and complex hierarchies of states.

In its minimal development of states, Africa resembled Europe outside the Roman lands and differed from the prevailing pattern of the river valleys and steppe lands of Egypt and the Asian webs. The simplest explanation for this divergence is sparse population. In Africa and Europe low population density, even after the spread of farming, allowed people to move whenever they wanted. Chiefs had trouble exerting authority over people in these circumstances, especially where foodstuffs were hard to store, trade, and hoard. People had better options than submitting to political hierarchy.

African agriculture, as well as low population density, encouraged fluid societies more than state building. Africans outside of the Nile Valley didn't need major irrigation works. They built small ones here and there, but usually chose adequately rain-fed lands for their fields. This, too, helped Africans remain free of overarching authority—unlike the peasants of Egypt, Mesopotamia, or China, who found priests and bureaucrats organizing their labor on irrigation canals and dikes, and making decisions about when and what to plant.

Finally, Africans didn't need to band together in large numbers for protection against equestrian raiders. As we've seen, after pastoralists mastered the arts of horse-manship and bowmanship (roughly 2000 BCE), everyone between the Levant and Korea needed organized armed forces to resist steppe horsemen. In most of Africa south of the Sahara, a disease called trypanosomiasis, carried by tsetse flies, made it almost impossible for horses to survive. So Africans, free from the threat of equestrian raiders, had less incentive than Asians to submit to rulers, taxes, and conscription and more opportunity to live in small communities of their own making.

Social Violence   African life was often violent, but not because of states, armies, and farming. Cemeteries in Africa are packed with ancient skeletons that show signs of weapon wounds. At one graveyard in northern Sudan from 12,000 BCE, fully 40 percent of the skeletons betray signs of violent deaths. An attack at a lakeshore in what is now northern Kenya in about 8000 BCE left 27 people dead. Among hunter-forager people worldwide, violent death at the hand of one's fellow man (rarely one's fellow woman) amounted to about 15 percent of all deaths and about 25 percent for adult males. Such rates of violent death probably also prevailed among African hunter-foragers, and per-haps pastoralists, before 200 CE. (For comparison, in the United States and among Americans overseas from 2001 to 2017, murders and warfare accounted for well under 1 percent of all deaths.) Pastoralists fought over water or pasture and raided one another's herds. Archeological evidence suggests that deadly encounters were usually ambushes or massacres of unarmed victims.

In the absence of states, mobile farmers in Africa often lived more peacefully than pastoralists. Battles among armed parties of adult men took place, according to some rock shelter art, but they were probably rare. In Africa, fleeing was often a viable option for anyone likely to lose a fight—even farmers, who would have to leave their crops behind. By contrast, in the river valleys of Asia and Egypt surrounded by deserts, one had to stand and fight because there was nowhere to go where refugees wouldn't die of thirst or hunger. Moreover, fleeing on foot when one's enemies rode horses scarcely improved one's chances of survival. And because there were states, people had to fight wars to satisfy the ambitions of kings. In Africa, until states emerged, farmers had no kings to obey; and with empty land at hand, they could walk away from a fight peace-fully and start farming somewhere else.

Social Identity and Hierarchy   In most of Africa, circumstances worked against the accumulation of personal wealth and power and its conversion into political strength and state formation. Small-scale politics prevailed, based on family and clan. People normally affiliated with others whom they knew or believed were their kinfolk. Clans traced their descent from a common ancestor, often awarded supernatural powers by descendants. Language groups, too, provided some basis for social identity, as did ways of life: farmers tended to regard themselves as different from, and of course better than, hunters, fisherfolk, and foragers—and vice-versa.

Social hierarchy existed, but also on a small scale. Women who worked as farmers or produced large numbers of children earned respect and status. Men who were especially good at hunting, or at raiding strangers' cattle, were admired and perhaps feared. They might acquire more wives than ordinary men, more children, and more dependents—a word that Africanist historians use to refer to people who voluntarily or otherwise attach themselves to a successful man (or more rarely, woman) for survival or perhaps a chance at betterment. Dependents might or might not be considered slaves, often an inexact category in African history. In any case, they owed deference and labor, and in the case of women perhaps sexual services as well, to someone more successful than they were. Men counted themselves rich and powerful when they had many wives, children, and dependents, and in pastoral societies when they had many cattle too. Africans generally took ancestry seriously, so that status, whether high or low, could be inherited from parents.

In Africa, as in non-Roman Europe, land was abundant and people scarce. So social power and economic wealth came in the form of control over people and livestock, rather than control over land. In China or Egypt, by contrast, land was the scarcer resource, not people, so wealth and power were expressed in the form of control over land. Africa didn't have landlords, as China, Mesopotamia, and Roman lands had; instead, it had what could be called labor-lords. Very successful Africans might have hundreds or even thousands of followers, but they normally didn't seek to convert that power into territorial states—at least, not until later periods of African history.

Early States: Kush and Aksum

In northeastern Africa, however, states developed earlier thanks to proximity to Egypt and the ease with which rulers could control traffic on the Nile. As we saw in Chapter 5, states and kings emerged in Nubia, just south of Egypt, much influenced by the pharaonic model. They built pyramids and used Egyptian hieroglyphs. In the eighth century BCE a unified Nubian state, called Kush by Egyptians, managed to conquer and rule Egypt for about 60 years. Subsequent kingdoms of Kush rose and fell, one of them, mentioned above, based at Meroë. The strength of these kingdoms was based in control of north-south trade routes in and out of Egypt, as well as land well suited to cattle raising along the Nile and its tributaries. Kings of Kush frequently provided Egypt with slaves. According to Roman authors and some images carved into stone, by 170 BCE Kush had queens either ruling in their own right or as co-regents. Meroë, which declined after 250 CE, was the last powerful Kushitic kingdom, although smaller states survived until the fifth or sixth century CE.

Kushitic Kingdoms Carvings on a first-century CE temple at Meroë picture King Natakamani and Queen Aminatore as joint rulers, both wearing crowns and carrying swords and other symbols of their authority.

The final eclipse of Kush came at the hands of another northeast African state, **Aksum** (sometimes spelled Axum), in the fourth to the fifth centuries CE. Based well to the south of Kush, Aksum arose in what is now northern Ethiopia and Eritrea, lands where plow agriculture had existed since perhaps 3000 BCE and several types of grain were cultivated on rich, volcanic soils. It was a pocket of unusually high population density. Towns sprang up by the fifth century BCE. A few centuries of higher-than-average rainfall helped Aksum to flourish. Some migrants from the Arabian Peninsula, perhaps mainly merchants, added to the cultural mix. Aksum began to specialize in the export of gold, frankincense, and myrrh, as well as rhino horn and elephant ivory. Frankincense and myrrh, featured in the gospel stories of the birth of Jesus, are fragrances derived from trees that grew in Arabia, Yemen, and Ethiopia.

Like the kingdoms of Kush before it, Aksum grew prosperous trading African products —ivory, hippopotamus hides, and slaves, to judge by the ancient authors—to Egypt, the Mediterranean world, Mesopotamia, and beyond. The dramatic surge in Egyptian population and wealth under the Ptolemies and Romans helped Aksum. Its trading towns grew, and by about 50 CE it was a genuine territorial empire controlling, perhaps loosely, lands in what are now northern Ethiopia, Eritrea, and Sudan, and at times across the Red Sea in Arabia. It also developed a naval force on the Red Sea. The narrow shape of the Red Sea made it comparatively easy for Aksum's rulers to dominate seaborne trade between Egypt and India, and the export of African goods, especially ivory, to India.

As Red Sea commerce mounted, so did the wealth and power of Aksum. Its sailors went at least as far as Sri Lanka just south of India. It minted its own coins, probably based on Roman models. Even more than Meroë or Kush, its fortunes rose with the strengthening of linkages—seaborne linkages, for the most part—of the Old World web. A Persian sage of the early third century CE referred to Aksum as one of the four great powers of the time, together with the Roman Empire, Persia, and China.

One of Aksum's rulers, according to an ancient Greek author, was conversant with Greek literature. A later king, Ezana, embraced Christianity about 325 CE, and gradually most of the kingdom's subjects did as well, which is why so many Ethiopians are Christians today. In the fourth and fifth centuries CE, Aksum enjoyed its fullest flowering. Aksum declined and fell in the sixth and seventh centuries under the impact of war with Byzantine and Arab powers, and perhaps declining rains as well.

By the time of Aksum's ascendance in northeastern Africa, Africans were developing stronger links throughout the continent. The slow transmission of farming and cattle keeping all the way to southern Africa was fully under way. Iron working was well established and had already spread widely throughout the midsection of the continent. And the domestication of the dromedary in Arabia had given rise to the ship of the desert—the camel, capable of crossing the now-desiccated Sahara. Prior to 6000 BCE, the wetter Sahara hadn't been much of a barrier to human movement and communication. As it dried out over the following millennia, though, the Sahara became a rocky and sandy wasteland separating the Mediterranean world from

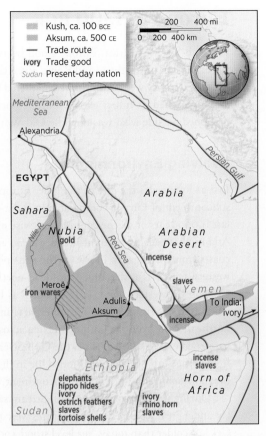

Kush and Aksum, ca. 100 BCE–500 CE Proximity to Egypt and north-south trade routes along the Nile and the Red Sea helped to spur settlement, prosperity, and social complexity in northeast African polities such as Kush and Aksum. They formed part of a trade web extending from Mediterranean shores to India, but they were cattle-raising societies as well. Aksum was also part of a political and cultural cluster including Persia and Rome, and in the fourth century CE its inhabitants began to adopt Christianity.

sub-Saharan Africa. The Nile valley pierced that barrier, and routes along the Red Sea and the East African coast also reduced the isolation of Africa from the Old World web. But as late as 200 CE that isolation remained considerable: least so for Aksum and Kush, more so for societies farther south, and almost total for southern Africa. Camel caravans across the Sahara, which started around 300 CE, would provide a new link between the emerging Old World web and Africa, bringing new commerce, new religion, new animals, and much else besides—as we will see.

Europe to 1300 BCE

Like sub-Saharan Africa, Europe stood beyond the dynamic Nile-Ganges web until the expansion of Carthage and Rome. Even then, only Mediterranean Europe became entangled in any webs until Rome conquered Gaul and Britain. And even after Rome's empire reached its fullest extent, Europe north of the Danube and east of the Rhine remained outside what was now the Old World web, sparsely populated and poor.

Evolving Environments

Just as Egypt was the gift of the Nile, Europe—best understood geographically as a subcontinent of Eurasia comparable to India—is the gift of the **Gulf Stream**. For the last 11,000 years or so, the counterclockwise movement of ocean currents in the North Atlantic has reliably brought warm waters, and warm humid air above them, to the coasts from Portugal to Norway. The sun-splashed Bordeaux wine country of south-western France is at the same latitude as northern Maine. Scotland, where palm trees grow on the western coast, is as far north as Hudson Bay. The reason these European lands aren't as frosty as their counterparts in North America is that warmth wafted northeastward from the Gulf of Mexico across the Atlantic, to Europe. When, as has happened over geological time, the Gulf Stream shuts down, Europe goes into a deep freeze. The Gulf Stream conditioned life in the European subcontinent just as much as the monsoon did in the Indian subcontinent.

During the last ice age, the Gulf Stream stopped and the northern third of Europe lay under great ice sheets. Temperatures were 10 to 16 degrees Fahrenheit (6–10 degrees Celsius) colder than today. Sea level stood 400 feet (120 m) lower than it does now. As the ice began to melt after 20,000 BCE, sea level crept up. By 8000 BCE, Ireland was an island, and Britain too by 6500 BCE. Europe had acquired its present shorelines, or very close to them, by 4000 BCE. After about 7500 BCE, its climate remained fairly stable by the standards of the past.

Vegetation belts moved northward as climate warmed. Oak and beech forest, pre-viously confined to southern Europe, inched northward into what had been steppe and soggy tundra, reaching as far as southern Scandinavia. Coniferous forest—pines, spruce, and fir—grew farther north still. The large herds of steppe-grazing mammals, which had sustained the hunters and foragers who left us the Lascaux cave paintings, dwindled. Forest creatures, such as deer, replaced them. By 6000 BCE, forests covered most of Europe except the farthest north. Whereas in Africa the key component of climate change was precipitation, accounting for the waxing and waning of the Sahara as well as the rain forests, in Europe it was temperature.

The landscape that emerged as the ice melted back had four important features that shaped Europe's history ever after. The oldest, which had been there long before the ice, were the mountains. Europe was broken up by mountain chains that posed real challenges to the movement of people and goods. There is one broad plain across northern Europe, stretching from the Netherlands to Russia, but otherwise its mountain chains fragment Europe.

The second key feature is the river system that emerged from under the ice. Fairly reliable rain and snowfall for the last 9,000 years has fed a series of rivers suited for navigation because they flowed year-round and often had estuaries that served as harbors—examples include the Po, Garonne, Seine, Rhine, Vistula, and Danube. Most were flat for long stretches, with few waterfalls or rapids. As in Africa, one could get around in the forest most easily by following the rivers. Unlike much of Africa, the density of rivers in Europe is high, making a large proportion of it accessible by river. Good river routes spanned Europe in a north-south direction, connecting the Mediterranean to the North Sea and Baltic Sea with only short land portages.

Europe's third defining geographical feature is the coastline that took shape with the rise of sea levels. Partly because of glaciations, Europe's coastline has countless indentations, fjords, estuaries, and bays that make good harbors. If Europe's coastline were straightened out, it would reach all the way around the world. One is never more than 200 miles (300 km) from the sea in western Europe, and never more than twice that in eastern Europe. The combination of a dense river network and a long, irregular coastline made Europe one of the best places in the world for water transport.

The fourth feature is the soil. In Mediterranean Europe there are pockets of good soil, but in central and northern Europe there is much more. The grinding of the ice sheets crushed masses of rock and released minerals that enriched soils. Farther south, from France to Russia, lies a band of loess soils created by the deposition of windblown dust off the ice sheets. These soils are fertile, lightweight, and easy to work, and they drain well. Early farmers, as we'll see, preferred them, as did their counterparts in the loess region of northern China.

Hunters and Foragers, 10,000 BCE to 4000 BCE

After the retreat of the ice, as forest spread over the landscape and the big herbivores disappeared, Europeans had to change their ways. Hunting in thick woodlands was far harder than on open steppe because one can't shoot arrows through thickets. And the forest animals—wild boars and deer, for example—carried less meat on them than some of the grassy steppe's gargantuan grazers had carried, so hunting became less rewarding even when it was successful. In the winters, although much milder now, there were no fruits and berries, so bad luck in the hunt meant hunger or starvation. In response, some Europeans migrated northward, following waning herds of reindeer. Others kept on the move, migrating seasonally to spots where they expected to find berries, nuts, fruits, edible roots, or animals to hunt.

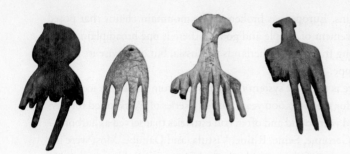

Scandinavian Settlements Artifacts that attest to the presence of coastal settlements in Scandinavia include these combs made from bone around 5000 to 4500 BCE in the area of present-day Denmark.

By 7000 BCE, people lived just about everywhere in Europe, although they usually didn't stay still for long. Reliable food supplies were hard to find. Total population probably fell markedly after 10,000 BCE, to judge by the reduced number of archeological sites found to date. Europe's forests, like Africa's, supported very sparse populations, and more forest meant fewer people.

The best solution to this food crisis, archeological evidence suggests, was to head for the coast. Europe's abundant and irregular coasts, especially river estuaries such as the Garonne's or the Rhine's, were teeming with edible life. The ambitious could hunt seals and seabirds on coastal rocks and cliffs. Fish were easier to catch, especially the salmon that made annual runs up many northern European rivers. Anyone, including small children, could pick up oysters, mussels, cockles, birds' eggs, or seaweed. At some places, the seafood harvest was so abundant and reliable that clusters of people lived year-round. At one spot in Denmark, generations of people munched away on shellfish for at least 800 years (4600–3800 BCE), leaving behind a trash pile (politely called a midden by archeologists) about the size of 75 school buses. From giant dugout canoes, these people also fished and harpooned sea mammals in the narrows between Denmark and Sweden. They, and other seaside dwellers, probably also used boats, made of animal skins stretched over wooden frames, for exploring estuaries and bays. They probably didn't venture onto the open sea. In addition to food, the seaside offered abundant salt and iodine, important for human health. As in Japan, where the Jomon culture prospered in year-round seaside settlements, so in Europe life by the sea was one of comparative ease.

Inland there were far fewer sites where permanent settlement made sense. Most appeared along rivers such as the Rhine or Danube, where trapping big fish was feasible. Perhaps the biggest inland settlement was along the Danube, at a point in today's Serbia where the river passes swiftly through a gorge called the Iron Gates. By 6500 BCE, permanent villages had sprouted here, with houses built of stone and timber. To judge by the rubbish left behind, the inhabitants ate beluga and other fish from the Danube, deer from the surrounding forest, and the occasional migratory duck or goose so unfortunate as to land in the neighborhood.

With permanent settlements inland being rare, the normal habit was to stay on the move, stopping for weeks here and there to exploit a food source—berries or acorns, for example—when it was in season. Lakes or wetlands attracted immense flocks of migratory birds such as ducks and geese in spring and fall, and consequently attracted hungry humans too. It was a precarious existence.

In this mobile world, social organization remained simple—mainly, bands of kinfolk. Opportunities for the accumulation of wealth, prestige, and power were limited, although at the Iron Gates on the Danube grave goods indicate modest social differentiation. Infants buried with precious goods such as flints or amber suggest that, as in Africa, high status could be inherited as well as earned. (Amber is fossil tree resin, good for making jewelry and scents.) Bands of loosely related kin probably gathered at regular intervals for festivals, gift exchange, and marriages—as almost everywhere among hunting and foraging peoples. Some goods also moved around a lot, whether as trade items, gifts, or possessions carried by wandering peoples. Some flints have turned up nearly 250 miles (400 km) from their places of origin.

River Communities Peoples living along the Danube in the area of present-day Serbia ate fish and other river produce—as suggested by this sandstone carving of a fish, which decorated a house in the region around 5600 to 4300 BCE.

As everywhere else, European bands sometimes ran across one another and exchanged blows rather than gifts. Perhaps 20 to 40 percent of skeletons from Europe (ca. 10,000 to 4000 BCE) show traumatic fractures and arrow wounds. The rates of violent death were comparable to those suggested by the skeletons unearthed in Africa. At one site in Bavaria (southern Germany), 37 skeletons of men, women, and children were dug up in 1908. All had their skulls bludgeoned and their heads cut off. This massacre took place about 6400 BCE.

Archeology can tell us little about the spiritual life of these mobile Europeans. A few group burials and several tiny wooden carved figurines have been found, but there is no clear idea what to make of them. Just about everything else these peoples made of wood has long since rotted away. The evidence grows far richer after 4000 BCE, when more Europeans settled down to farm and created much more in the way of durable artifacts for future archeologists to dig up.

Farming Comes to Europe

Europeans did not invent farming. To some extent, they learned it from their neighbors in Anatolia. But to a larger extent, Europe acquired agriculture because farmers from Anatolia migrated into Europe. The migrants out-competed and substantially replaced indigenous hunter-forager Europeans, just as Bantu farmers out-competed the indigenous Khoisan-speaking populations of southern Africa, and Chinese farmers out-competed hunter-foragers in what is now southern China. The precise mix of migration, replacement, and learning varies for different parts of Europe. The farther northwest one goes, apparently, the larger the role of cultural learning and the smaller the role of migration.

Southeastern and Central Europe   Farming came to Europe as part of a package consisting of the same cereals cultivated in the Levant—wheat and barley—together with domesticated animals such as cattle, sheep, goats, and pigs. It also included something not normally found in the Levant, square houses made from timber. All these things show up easily in archeology, so the chronology of the spread of farming in Europe is known with remarkable precision, far more so than the comparable process in Africa.

Farming folk migrated to mainland Greece between about 7500 and 6000 BCE. They, and their practices, moved north into the Danube basin by 6500 to 5500 BCE, by which time the process involved less migration and more imitation. By 5500 BCE, people in the loess zones of central Europe, especially Hungary, had begun to shift to farming and found it so rewarding that it spread westward at roughly 2 miles (about 3 km) per year. The loess zones quickly became a world of tiny villages amid shrinking forests. Their middens show that people had almost given up hunting by 5000 BCE. The villagers lived in multi-family longhouses as much as 100 feet (30 m) long and developed great skill as carpenters. They raised grains, peas, and livestock. The villagers of the loess regions set the pattern—farming villages every few miles—that would eventually prevail throughout most of Europe until industrialization 7,000 years later.

As farming was catching on in southeastern and central Europe, it was also spreading by sea along Mediterranean coasts. By 5400 BCE, farmsteads dotted the shores from Greece to Spain and had begun to sprout in the river estuaries of Portugal. This movement consisted mainly of tiny seaborne colonization efforts by young men who carved out farms and tried to attract or capture local women for their wives. Farming spread inland more by imitation, as in central Europe, and by 4000 BCE people had adopted it all along the Atlantic shores of Europe. The British Isles were among the last to switch to farming, but inhabitants there did so quickly between 4100 and 3800 BCE.

The Baltic   As far as we can tell, the only groups stubbornly opposed to farming lived on the shores of the Baltic. As early as 5100 BCE they borrowed pottery and some tool designs from farmers to their south. But they didn't switch to farming and weren't replaced by farmers for over a millennium, which is a puzzle given the record elsewhere in Europe. Perhaps the seafood of the Baltic was so good and plentiful that no one wanted to work hard in order to eat porridge and gruel. Skeletons show this was a time of heightened violence, so perhaps the resistance to farming took the form of military resistance to invading farmers. About 3900 BCE something—we don't know what— changed, and within a century the whole Baltic region took up farming and the raising of livestock. So between 8000 and 3800 BCE farming had spread throughout Europe, from Greece all the way to the shores of the Atlantic. That transition led to a flood of changes in Europe, just as farming's spread did in Africa.

Menhirs Mysterious changes took place in the realm of spiritual life, indicated by the practice of setting up **menhirs**—big oblong stones set to stand upright. They began to appear at about 5500 BCE in western France. The heavy stones—one of them weighs 350 tons—must have required the coordinated effort of hundreds of people to put up.

Stone monuments followed elsewhere, most famously at Stonehenge in southern England, built about 2500 BCE. People dragged or rolled its stone blocks some 140 miles (225 km) from Wales before standing them upright in southern England, suggesting a society with the capacity to organize many people around a single task. The blocks, which weigh up to 40 tons, are carefully lined up with the positions of the sun, moon, and certain stars at the summer solstice. Stonehenge stayed in use for 800 years, though what it was used for, beyond celestial observation, is unclear. Some scholars say it was a healing center, others a burial ground, still others a center for religious rites involving human sacrifice. Perhaps it was all of the above. By the time Stonehenge went up, large stone structures had sprouted throughout Atlantic Europe, from Sweden to northern Spain. Some of these, like those of Carnac in France, are dolmens, eerily similar to those erected several centuries later in Korea. But there is no evidence of contact between these dolmen-raising peoples.

In addition to stone monuments, Europe's early farmers practiced group burials, another indication of changing attitudes toward the spirit world. Gravesites tended to become fancier over time, eventually housing treasure troves of ornaments and weapons. Some had deep shafts dug into the earth. Others had sprawling mounds on top. The habits of group burials and stone monuments spread widely within western Europe between 4500 and 2000 BCE.

Other practices were spreading too, reflecting new local webs that arose in Europe after farming took root. For example, one particular mine in Brittany, in northwestern France, yielded the stone for some 2 million hand axes, used roughly between 4000 and 2200 BCE, which archeologists have found all over France, Belgium, and southern Britain. Axe-heads of a type made from jade found in the western Alps, mainly between about 4300 and 4100 BCE, have turned up from Italy to Scotland. In eastern Europe, copper ornaments from a particular mine in today's Bulgaria have been found from the Alps to the Volga. The pottery style called bell beaker ware came into vogue throughout Europe and northwest Africa after 2900 BCE. All these goods were probably not

Luxury Goods Weapons made from precious materials could be exchanged as gifts and could also symbolize prestige. These highly polished hand axes made from jade sometime between 5500 and 1800 BCE were found in northern France.

traded in the sense we understand that word today; rather, elites of neighboring societies likely exchanged them as gifts until lost, broken, or carefully buried in someone's grave.

The First Local Webs in Europe

Farming favored the development of networks of exchange in Europe just as it did in Africa and everywhere else. First of all, farmers could have, and needed to have, more material culture—more stuff—than did mobile hunters and foragers. Second, the efficiency of food production allowed some people to work as craft specialists, so skills in pottery, tool making, and weapon making improved rapidly. Improved quality made it more desirable to have such items, so the number of people making them and exchanging them grew. Third, with farming the total number of people swelled, and it was easier to know where to find them. If you wanted to secure the friendship of a powerful man, in the olden days of mobile hunting and foraging you had to locate him first, which could take months. And if you succeeded and gave him a gift in order to win his good will, he might be on the other side of a mountain range when you needed his help. In stable agricultural settings, however, you could send a messenger to a known location, invite a powerful man and his friends to a pig roast, drink beer together, and give him a nice jade hand-axe. When you needed his help, you knew where to find him.

After 2200 BCE or so, yet another factor favored the formation of webs of exchange in Europe: bronze. Recall that bronze is made from tin and copper. Tin is found only in a few places, so where bronze goods became popular long-distance networks of exchange always arose, in Europe as in Southwest Asia and China. Bronze appealed strongly to everyone, although only elites could afford it. Bronze weapons were far better than copper, stone, or wooden ones. Bronze made for handsome jewelry and ornaments because it shone brightly and could be worked into precise shapes.

Bronze goods were in such demand that new items in far greater quantities entered into Europe's circuits of exchange after 2000 BCE. These included furs from the northern forests; amber from the shores of the Baltic; horses from the steppe lands of today's Ukraine and Russia; and gold from Bulgaria, Spain, and elsewhere. Young women, too, were increasingly given as gifts to important men, either as wives or as concubines. Transactions included not only items and people, but also understandings of future obligations owed by the receiver to the giver. Gifts were investments. Poor and weak people surrendered small shares of what they could raise, often including their daughters, to more powerful men in exchange for future protection. Although no money was used, the pace of exchanges quickened over time. Sailing ships came into use, first in the Mediterranean but eventually along Atlantic shores as well. River routes became highways. Ox-carts creaked along overland tracks. With farming, most people stayed put; but with farming and bronze, European goods were on the move. Europe was knitting itself, or at least its elites, together.

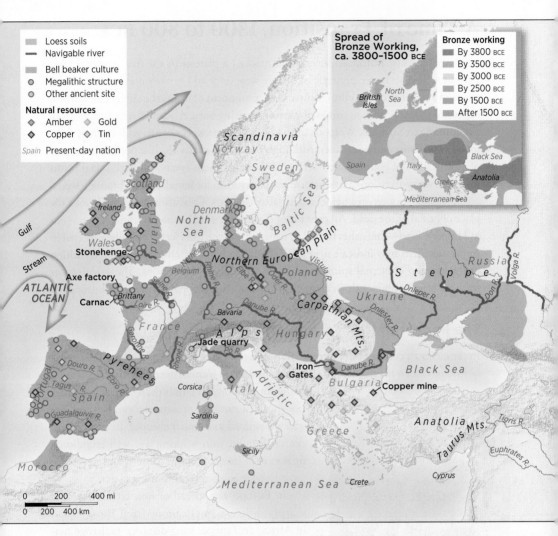

Europe, ca. 7500–1000 BCE Most of Europe is well equipped with navigable rivers that facilitated local and regional trade. With the advent of bronze artwork and weaponry after about 2200 BCE, European elites organized more frequent long-distance exchanges, binding together much of the subcontinent in its own web. The decline of bronze and the rise of iron weakened those ties.

Like Africa outside Egypt's orbit, Europe was knitting itself together in partial isolation from the much more populated, and more interactive, Nile-Ganges web. Before 1000 BCE, most Europeans, like most Africans, remained unaffected by the priests, soldiers, microbes, and other forces of complex society shaping the history of the Nile-Ganges web.

A Time of Transition, 1300 to 800 BCE

In many respects, European integration reached a plateau in the five centuries after 1300 BCE. The pervasive presence of bronze weaponry and ornamentation helped give shape to a pan-European elite culture. One component of it was the cult of the warrior, expressed in art. Bronze figurines of warriors wearing horned helmets were in style from Scandinavia to Sardinia. Weapons increasingly became works of art, with lovingly fashioned sword hilts and hand axes. Although not an especially warlike period, it was one of glorification of young male warriors. The pre-eminent symbol of high social status for males was possession of fine bronze weaponry. And for females it was bronze jewelry.

Religious life took on a new character after 1300 BCE. Cremation increasingly took the place of burial of the dead. All over Europe, the dead were burned on funeral pyres—as in Homer's *Iliad*—and ashes buried in urns. Often, the urns were carefully arranged in cemeteries. This may indicate new ideas about death and afterlife, perhaps a transition in the location of eternal spirits from an underworld to the heavens. The sun also was featured more prominently in artwork. This transition was common across Europe.

The Impact of Iron Technology

In the eleventh century BCE, Europeans began to work with iron as well as bronze. The technology came from Anatolia and first took hold in southeastern Europe. Iron was no better for weapons and tools than bronze, and inferior (in most eyes) for ornamentation. But iron ore was widespread and much cheaper. In eastern and central Europe, iron working was well established by 800 BCE. Its adoption in western and northernmost Europe came several centuries later.

Iron Working Iron began to supplant bronze as the metal of choice in Europe starting around 800 BCE. Spearheads, axes, and blacksmith's tools dated to around 500 BCE from eastern Europe indicate the variety of iron objects.

In Europe, the spread of iron technology had sharply different implications from those it had in Africa. In Europe, long-distance exchange networks had already emerged, built upon the elite's enthusiasm for bronze and the wide diffusion of farming. Iron did nothing to build these networks, and if anything, it weakened them. Iron ore could be found widely, as could wood for charcoal, so once people learned how to smelt ore and make iron, almost any community could do it. The logic of long-distance exchange, both of raw materials such as tin and of finished products such as swords or statuettes, diminished when and where iron replaced bronze. In Africa, where bronze had never mattered as much, iron working helped to build long-distance exchange networks. Moreover, in Africa the techniques of iron working remained jealously guarded secrets, whereas in Europe, as in Southwest Asia and China, prior experience with bronze meant that metalworking skills were more widely diffused. Eventually, every village had its blacksmith, and the need for long-distance exchange declined accordingly. The advent of iron in Europe shows that the expansion and thickening of webs is far from inevitable. It also shows that the same metal can have sharply different consequences in different historical contexts.

Horse Nomads from the Steppe

This transitional half-millennium saw two other important developments in Europe. One was the migration westward, as far as the Hungarian plain, of horse nomads from the Russian and Ukrainian steppe. A group known as **Cimmerians** rode in beginning in the ninth century BCE. Although domesticated horses had been in use for many centuries already, the arrival of the Cimmerians marked a new emphasis on equestrian life and a new infusion of steppe customs into the heart of Europe. In Hungary, artifacts associated with mounted warfare and horse-themed art became more common. Pottery, however, didn't change much, probably because horse nomads didn't bring much in the way of potters' skills with them. Time and again after the Cimmerians, new groups of equestrian nomads or semi-nomads would drift into eastern Europe from the steppe, each time using their military strength to gain a foothold in, and occasionally a chokehold on, societies in and around the grasslands of Hungary. As in northern China and everywhere in Southwest Asia, in eastern Europe after the Cimmerians periodic incursions by mounted peoples helped to shape politics and culture.

The Celts

The second development to note was the emergence of a loose language group in Atlantic Europe called the **Celts** (pronounced "kelts"). Celtic is part of the Indo-European language family. Just when and where it arose is controversial among specialists, but it seems to have emerged between about 1300 and 700 BCE in both central and western Europe. Whatever its origins, its speakers became more and more numerous in these and later centuries as new crops (peas, lentils, and so-called celtic beans), and increased use of livestock manure as fertilizer, improved farm yields and boosted population. In the northern reaches of Europe, the domestication of rye and oats, cereal grains that do well in chilly climes, improved the fortunes of everyone, Celts included. As we shall see, the Celts became so numerous that they soon could overrun large parts of Europe and small parts of Asia.

Trade and Instability, 800 BCE to 200 CE

In the millennium after 800 BCE, the dominant historical development in Europe was the rise of Mediterranean societies, culminating in the Roman Empire. As we've seen, by 200 BCE Roman trade and cultural influence extended into western and central Europe. By 100 CE, the Romans extended their frontier into Britain and controlled Europe west of the Rhine and south of the Danube. The rise of Roman power and culture changed things for almost everyone in Europe. The fate of people throughout Europe was increasingly shaped by their interactions with the Mediterranean societies.

Changes in Exchange Networks

The nature of trade itself changed with Europe's increased contact with the Mediterranean. Europe's exchange networks, like those in Africa, had long been confined to the exchange of gifts by elites. Powerful men swapped prestige items with one another, such as the jade axes or bronze swords we have encountered already, forming obligations to and alliances with one another. But by 300 BCE or so, the nature of exchange in Europe had begun to shift, perhaps first on the northern shores of the Black Sea. At the same time as Alexander and his Seleucid successors were monetizing the economy of Southwest Asia, a smaller-scale version of the same process was affecting Europe. Coins—at first Greek and Etruscan, then mainly Roman—came into use, spreading the concept of purchase with no social obligations attached. As in Southwest Asia and the Mediterranean world itself, this monetization helped generate economic growth and social change, notably a richer class of rich.

In contemplating the changes in Europe, it is important to remember that available evidence steers us toward Rome and the Mediterranean. For the first time we have written texts, including carefully composed histories by Greek and Roman authors as well as inscriptions on coins and the odd piece of graffiti on pots or walls. These texts, overwhelmingly, are written by, and in the languages of, the Mediterranean peoples—mainly, Greeks and Romans. The peoples of northern and eastern Europe at this time didn't use writing. In addition, the archeological evidence is slanted toward the Mediterranean, even though plenty of archeological work has been done in northern Europe. The artifacts that have survived the last twenty centuries tend to be durable goods, especially ceramic and metal ones, which Mediterranean peoples manufactured in bulk. The slaves, horses, cattle, leather, furs, and so forth traded within northern, central, and eastern Europe have left a much smaller trace in the archeological record. Genetic and linguistic evidence, so far, has not done much to redress this imbalance.

After 800 BCE in northern Europe, from the British Isles to the Baltic, the exchange networks forged in earlier millennia decayed. The abundance of local iron reduced the demand for distant supplies of bronze goods. Populations grew, in part because of the efficiency of iron farming tools and the continued spread of livestock, the new cereals oats and rye, and the practice of manuring. The British Isles, for example, had about 1 million people at the advent of iron, and 2 to 4 million by the time of Roman conquest (43 BCE). Despite this population growth, a certain localization, or disintegration, occurred in Europe before the Romans came, visible in the elaboration of more regional and local styles of pottery and weaponry, and perhaps also in the differentiation of the various forms of Celtic speech. Northern Europeans lived in greater isolation between 800 and 100 BCE. To some degree, the Celts were like the Khoisan of southern Africa in this period, geographically removed from the centers of innovation and disruption, more left to themselves than others of their continent.

Expanding Trade within Europe

Elsewhere, connections to the Mediterranean world generated new and unstable social patterns that rested on long-distance trade. After 600 BCE or so, a trickle of Mediterranean luxury goods flowed northward into central Europe. Meanwhile, close interactions on the Black Sea coasts between Greek cities and local nomads (called Scythians by Herodotus) brought similar goods into eastern Europe through Scythian migrations and trading expeditions.

Gradually, access to Mediterranean goods became essential for leaders in the heart of Europe. Their position depended on being able to distribute to their followers the beautiful jewelry, sturdy weaponry, and other goods manufactured on the Italian Peninsula or in Greek colonies. They also hosted feasts with plenty of wine to solidify their prestige and leadership. Elaborate drinking cups were an important trade item linking the Mediterranean with the European heartland, and so was drink itself. By one estimate, the quantity of Italian wine shipped to Gaul (as the Romans called what is now France) reached 2 million gallons per year in the first century BCE. The historian Diodorus of Sicily remarked at the time:

> [The Gauls] are exceedingly fond of wine. Their desire for it makes them drink greedily and fall into a stupor. Italian merchants . . . look upon the Gallic craving for wine as a treasure. They receive for wine an incredibly high price, for one amphora [jug] they get in return a slave: a servant in exchange for a drink.

Of course, the Gauls probably thought they were robbing the Roman merchants blind, giving up only one slave, of which they could always get more, for an entire amphora of wine, of which they could produce none.

To get the trade goods they wanted, European elites had to accumulate slaves, cattle, hides, furs, and other northern goods. They could sell these to Roman merchants for silver coin, which they might then use to buy their wine, weapons, and jewelry. The reach of this commercial system by 100 CE extended throughout lands under Roman control (west of the Rhine and south of the Danube) and into what is now Poland. Scattered Roman objects have been found far beyond Roman borders, in Ireland,

European Slave Trade A first-century relief from a Roman sarcophagus shows Roman soldiers taking European men, women, and children as captives. This was a common circumstance during the height of Roman power, when Europeans might be enslaved either as prisoners of war or as an export commodity.

Scotland, Scandinavia, and northern Russia; but these remote and poor lands produced little of commercial interest beyond slaves. So they remained on the outside, both beyond Roman borders and beyond the trade circuits routinely dispersing Mediterranean goods. They were the most isolated regions of Europe.

This new situation, in which trade goods from the Mediterranean and the Greco-Scythian Black Sea region loomed large, produced more than the normal political upheaval. Ambitious European chiefs competed for access to trade goods and the influence over people it brought. Securing slaves was a big part of success, so slave raiding in northern, central, and eastern Europe became increasingly popular as both a business and a political strategy. This is one of the reasons for the increasing resort to fortification and hilltop villages among Europeans, which shows up strongly in the archeological record after 500 BCE.

Commerce without personal obligation was inherently unstable, so depending on it was a risky strategy—in effect, feast or famine for chiefs. A shift in trade patterns could quickly bring the rise of one and the fall of another chief. A bad grape harvest near the mouth of the Rhone, a rash of banditry discouraging merchants—any such event—might interrupt the flow of needed goods and ruin the standing of a given chief or a cluster of them. Lest they see their followers desert them for someone else, they would make desperate efforts to seize more slaves, horses, or furs to secure the needed Mediterranean goods. Rulers in Kush, south of Egypt, faced a similar situation during the same centuries: their position hinged on control of trade goods to and from Egypt; and if trade patterns shifted, they lost the basis of their authority over supporters.

The Celtic Migrations

A second source of political unrest, which might have been linked to the instability of commerce, was the folk migrations of the Celts—movements of men, women, and children beginning in the fifth century BCE. The Roman historian Livy thought that population growth drove the Celts of central and western Europe to expand their territory. There is good archeological evidence for continued population growth almost everywhere in Europe from 800 BCE to about 160 CE. Some regions, such as what are now Poland, southern Ukraine, and southern Germany, seemed to pump out people in this period. So Livy could have been right.

But the Celtic migrations might also have been a response to the uncertainties of the new trade regime, which produced desperation as well as prosperity and power. They might also have been propelled by a social system in which young men, if they wished to distinguish themselves, win glory, and marry well, could do no better than to assault strangers, steal their cattle and perhaps women and children, and build new communities.

Whatever their motives, bands of Celts poured over the Alpine passes into northern Italy during the fourth and third centuries BCE, settling down in the rich Po valley to a life of farming and raiding their neighbors. As we saw in Chapter 8, a party of Celts managed to sack the city of Rome and came close to killing off the Roman population. The Celts remained active in northern Italy until around 200 BCE, by which time Roman power had magnified to the point where Roman armies crushed Celtic independence, sent many Celts back north to their ancestral homelands, and settled the Po valley with Roman colonies.

At the same time, other bands of Celts migrated—forcefully—southward from the Danube region. By 279 BCE some had raided as far south as central Greece. Others crossed into Anatolia, setting up a kingdom near today's Ankara. Wherever they found ill-defended cities or country estates, the Celts raided and traded for the prestige goods they had come to prize. The scale of this population movement was unprecedented in European history. Romans and Greeks retained a lasting disdain for the uncouth, unlettered, undisciplined people they called barbarians—of whom the Celts were but one.

Conclusion

In (sub-Saharan) Africa and (pre-Roman and non-Roman) Europe before 200 CE, people lived on the frontiers or beyond the big webs that were developing around the Mediterranean. Their lands were less thickly populated, and people had more room to roam. Unlike the populations of the narrow river valleys in Egypt, Mesopotamia, and China, they could walk away from men seeking to convert them into forced labor. They didn't need irrigation. With rare exception, they didn't face militarily formidable mounted nomads. So they did not need states, did not organize themselves into elaborate social hierarchies, and did not readily submit to ambitious men hoping to live like kings and pharaohs.

Africans and Europeans were, as a result, usually less constrained by taxation, conscription, and forced labor than the peoples of the webs in Egypt or Asia. But when and where populations grew and links to Egypt or Rome developed, Africans or Europeans might find themselves bartered as slaves by chiefs eager for prestige goods from the workshops of complex societies. This risk of enslavement eventually extended to almost all Europeans by the height of the Roman Empire, but in Africa not far beyond the northeastern quarter of the continent, closest to Egypt.

Although partly isolated from the world's big webs, Africans and Europeans built their own networks of trade, often along river routes. In Africa, this process accelerated with the rise of iron and the spread of new crops from Southeast Asia. In Europe, it accelerated with the rise of bronze and probably weakened—certainly in northern Europe—when after 800 BCE iron came into use, a case in which an existing web decayed.

Both Africa and Europe slowly entered more and more into the tangle of the Nile-Indus web and by 100 CE the Old World web. The distant reaches of each, southern Africa and northernmost Europe, remained but little affected. But those regions closest to Egypt, the Mediterranean, and Mesopotamia slowly changed their ways under the influence of opportunities and risks emanating from the Nile-Indus web. This process began very slowly and was certainly imperceptible to people then alive. But by 200 CE trade, artistic styles, military techniques, food crops, and diseases long in circulation in Egypt, the eastern Mediterranean, and Southwest Asia had clearly made their imprint on most of Europe and parts of Africa.

Although their circumstances and social worlds had much in common at the end of the last ice age, by 200 CE Africa and Europe increasingly differed. More of Europe showed the effects of interaction with the Mediterranean and with Asian steppe people. Its incorporation into the larger webs of humankind, although far from complete, was fuller than Africa's. It was swept up in more sustained exchanges than was Africa, outside of Kush and Aksum.

While there were several reasons for this diverging fate between Europe and Africa, the simplest ones are geographical. First, Africa is much larger than Europe, and more of it is a long way from the Mediterranean or Mesopotamia. Northeast Africa interacted regularly with the web links of the Mediterranean and Indian Ocean, and both East and West Africa were in occasional contact with the wider world. But central and southern Africa remained, before 200 CE, more isolated. Second, the Sahara, after it dried out, made a more effective barrier to communication than did the Alps or any obstacles in Europe. In time, as we shall see, geography came to matter less, and human ambition came to matter more in forming and sustaining connections among human communities.

||||||||||||||||||||||||||||||||||||||||||||||||||||||||||||||||||||||||||||||||||||||||||||||||||||||||||||||||||||||||||||||||

Chapter Review

KEY TERMS

bell beaker ware p. 307   **Meroë** p. 318
iron working p. 317   **Jenne** p. 322

Aksum p. 326

Gulf Stream p. 328

menhirs p. 333

Cimmerians p. 337

Celts p. 337

REVIEW QUESTIONS

1. What significant commonalities did Africa and Europe share between the end of the last ice age and 200 CE?

2. Explain the importance of variations in rainfall, the geological age of the African continent, and the features of African rivers for the continent's history.

3. Why were African ways of life—both pastoralism and farming—more fluid and less permanent than those of people living in river valleys between Egypt and China?

4. What three factors were essential for the spread of agriculture and pastoralism in Africa, and why?

5. What did social power and economic wealth look like in Africa and non-Roman Europe in comparison to Egypt and China?

6. Why did states develop earlier in northeastern Africa than in sub-Saharan Africa?

7. What are the four important landscape features that shaped Europe's history, and how did they do so?

8. What were the different processes by which farming spread across Europe?

9. What important cultural elements did Europeans share in the 500 years following 1300 BCE?

10. What were the effects of iron working on trade in Africa versus Europe, and why did they differ?

11. In what ways did the nature of exchange in Europe change around 300 BCE?

12. How did sub-Saharan Africans and non-Roman Europeans avoid hierarchical rule, conscription, and taxation before 200 CE?

Go to INQUIZITIVE

to see what you've learned—and learn what you've missed—with personalized feedback along the way.

10

The Americas and Oceania

BEFORE 1000 CE

FOCUS QUESTIONS

1. How did early Amerindians adapt to their distinctive environments?
2. Where and how did complex society develop in the Americas?
3. What was distinctive about the early cultures of Australia and Oceania?

One summer evening in the 590s CE, the 200 villagers of Cerén, in today's El Salvador, ran for their lives. Their village stood at the foot of a volcano, which erupted and buried the surrounding landscape under 20 feet (6 m) of ash. Cerén was frozen in time until a bulldozer sliced into it in 1976. Archeologists followed and found about 70 buildings, including homes, a communal sweat bath, and a presumed religious edifice. In their fields the villagers left maize, manioc, beans, squash, agave, cacao, guava, cotton, and other crops. In their kitchens they left clay jars full of beans, and chili peppers hanging from the rafters. No skeletons remain: all the villagers, apparently, got away in time. Culturally, Cerén was a Maya village. The Maya, as we shall see, flourished from about 200 to 900 CE in the Yucatán Peninsula of Mexico and adjacent lands.

Cerén provides detailed information about villages and households in ancient America. There's nothing like it elsewhere in the Americas, nor in Oceania. It compares, perhaps, only to Pompeii and Herculaneum in southern Italy, the Roman towns buried by volcanic ash in 79 CE. Cerén was characteristic of village life in the Americas in that it was a farming community and its inhabitants raised most of the crops important in the Americas.

This chapter begins with the earliest human migrations into the Americas at least 15,000 years ago and takes the story beyond 200 CE (in contrast to Chapters 6 through 9) all the way to 1000 CE. In some respects, 1000 CE is an arbitrary end point, but it also represents a few important transitions in the history of the Americas and Oceania. First, it roughly matches the temporary end of urbanized society in the Maya world. Second, it matches another temporary end point of urban, complex society in the Andes. Third, 1000 CE marks the point when the spread of maize cultivation in North America reached its geographic limit—and few other things in North American history mattered as much as maize. Fourth, it is when Europeans, specifically Vikings, crossed the Atlantic and dented the isolation of the Americas. And fifth, it is—again roughly—the time by which the settlement of the Pacific Islands was complete.

The Americas and Oceania are together a sprawling space. The two American continents make up 28 percent of the Earth's land surface, half again as much as Africa and almost as much as Asia. There is no clear definition of **Oceania**. Here we include Australia with Oceania. If one counts only the land and not the water between islands, Oceania amounts to less than 1 percent of the Earth's land surface—if one excludes Australia—or 6 percent if one includes it.

At first glance, the Americas and Oceania may seem an odd couple. What links them is that they represent the farthest frontiers of settlement, the last big places on Earth to acquire human populations. Beginning about 50,000 years ago, people from Asia migrated into Australia, and later into the Americas and Oceania, and for the most part never looked back. People living in these regions were, with small exception, isolated from other, larger human populations.

In a rough way, the human colonizations of the Americas, Australia, and the Pacific Islands resemble the first exodus from Africa about 100,000 years ago. In that case, people left Africa

ca. 200–900 CE Maya flourish

ca. 600 CE First migrants arrive in Hawaii

ca. 700 CE Amerindians in New England and the Canadian Maritimes acquire the bow and arrow; first migrants reach Easter Island

for Eurasia, entering worlds where *Homo sapiens* had never trod before. In these latter cases, people left Eurasia for new worlds that neither humans nor hominids had ever visited. In all these cases, people entered novel environments that offered food and other resources for the taking and that filtered out diseases that couldn't survive the new conditions. As soon as these migrants learned enough about their new lands, they prospered, grew in numbers, spread out thinly over huge spaces, and diversified culturally.

The Americas and Oceania were also worlds unto themselves. As we've seen, the large populations that lived in China, India, Southwest Asia, and around the Mediterranean were in ever greater contact with one another, so that by 200 CE they formed the Old World web. The sparse populations of southernmost Africa, northernmost Europe, and Siberia took little part in this giant network. But the populations of the Americas and Oceania stood more fully apart. They had only the most slender connections, if any, to Eurasia and Africa. Thus their histories, up to 1000 CE, followed independent tracks.

In the case of the Americas, that track showed remarkable parallels to the general trajectory of history in the lands of the Old World web. People made transitions to agriculture; developed cities and states run by priests and warriors; built monumental architecture; invented pottery, textiles, writing, calendars, and mathematics; evolved religions that emphasized concepts of sacrifice to gods and temples with elaborate rituals; created roughly the same pattern of gendered division of labor; and built up networks of long-distance trade and exchange. Indeed, by 1000 CE they had woven two substantial webs of interaction in large regions of the Americas, one in Mesoamerica and one in the Andes.

In Oceania, this broad pattern did not prevail. People either didn't need agriculture, as in Australia, or they brought it with them when they migrated from Southeast Asia. They did not invent it. They built no cities and no states until after 1000 CE. These societies and populations remained modest in scale compared to those of the centers in the Americas—and tiny compared to those of China, India, or the Mediterranean world. The peoples of Oceania followed historical trajectories of their own making. Their trajectories were different from those of complex societies in the Americas or the Old World web, not incomplete versions of those elsewhere.

The Americas: Environments and Economies

The first migrants to America, had they been more considerate of later generations, would have left big trash heaps of easily dateable rubbish for future archeologists. As it is, we have scraps of evidence and many puzzles. The best current hypothesis is that the first Americans—Amerindians*—came from Asia, somewhere in southern Siberia, and crossed to Alaska between 23,000 and 15,000 years ago. They then spread quickly along the Pacific coasts of the Americas as far south as Chile. The migration probably occurred in one or two early spurts, followed many thousands of years later by a third. The last one brought the peoples known as Inuits (or Eskimos) and Aleuts from Arctic Asia to Arctic America.

Migration and Environmental Change

This epic migration took place while North America was undergoing two major transformations. The first was the retreat of the great ice sheets that, as late as 25,000 years ago, had extended as far south as the Missouri and Ohio Rivers. The ice sheets probably obliged the earliest Amerindian migrants to go by sea as they headed south from Alaska. As the ice melted, it formed a giant lake in the heart of North America from 11,000 to 6000 BCE. The lake drained to the sea in several pulses, raising sea level by several feet each time and changing global climate. So the first migrants to North America came at a time of rapid climate change, just as the continent was defrosting.

The second transformation of this period was the extinction of many of the big mammals of North America. Some 90 genera (families) of animals went extinct around 11,000 to 9000 BCE, including mammoths, mastodons, giant beavers, and saber-toothed tigers. Possible explanations include overhunting by the first people to arrive in North America, climate change, and animal diseases. Whatever the causes, these mass extinctions fundamentally altered the ecosystems of North America. Simultaneous mass extinctions took place in South America.

In South America some 25,000 years ago, ice sheets covered the southern third of Chile and Argentina and all the Andes—about 20 percent of the continent. When the first people arrived, the ice sheets were melting back. Sea level was still rising until 3000 BCE, and Amazonia's rain forest was growing bigger—most of it had been savanna grassland during the last ice age.

The Kelp Highway Underwater forests of seaweed called kelp probably lured the first Amerindians south to Chile. The kelp beds of the Pacific coast, rich with seals, otters, shellfish, and other seafood, attracted people like magnets. Moreover, big rivers along the Pacific coast, from the Yukon to the Sacramento, were (and still

---

*There are many terms in use for the peoples who lived in the Americas before 1492 CE: *Native Americans, First Americans, First Nations, Aboriginal Americans, Amerindians, Indians, Paleoindians, Paleoamericans,* among others. Some terms are used only for one time period or region. All have supporters and critics. I will use just one term, *Amerindians*.

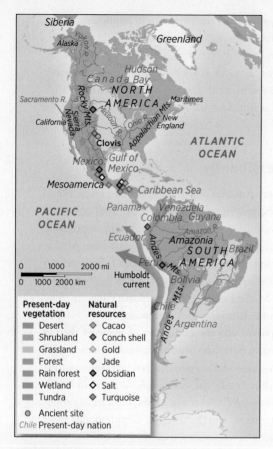

The Americas The natural vegetation zones of the Americas reflect rainfall, temperature, and soil variations. Those shown here indicate today's conditions but have been approximately the same for the past 6,000 years. The chief centers of population, Mesoamerica and the Andes, featured high ecological diversity due in large part to mountainous terrain. Because of the lack of domesticated grazing animals, grasslands in the Americas had none of the importance they carried in Eurasia and Africa.

are) highways for migratory salmon, chutes of high-protein food for anyone with a net. Exploiting kelp beds and salmon rivers is something people had already been doing along the North Pacific coasts from Japan to Alaska. So, the first arrivals in the Americas already had knowledge and skills that suited the American Pacific coastline, making it easy for them to traverse the kelp highway en route to Chile as early as 12,000 BCE.

Clovis Culture By 11,000 BCE, people had traveled almost everywhere in North America. The evidence for this is the distribution of stone spearheads called **Clovis points**, in wide use in North America (and in a few places in Central America) by 11,300 BCE. The points are nearly identical wherever they are found, indicating an early case of rapid diffusion of a useful technology—and of remarkable cultural homogeneity. Many Clovis points were discovered hundreds of miles away from the site where they were quarried. So either Clovis points were exchanged over long distances, or their users were mobile hunters—or both. Since many points are found together with mastodon and mammoth remains, it seems likely that Clovis culture included mobile hunters. Strikingly, people stopped making Clovis points only about 600 years after they started. Perhaps big game in North America had already grown scarce.

South America never had Clovis points, nor did it ever have the cultural homogeneity or the reliance on hunting that Clovis points imply for North America. People reached the southern tip of South America by 9000 BCE. The first settlers seem to have stuck to the coasts, both Pacific and Atlantic. It took longer to colonize the entire continent than in North America.

Economic Life

When people exited the kelp highway and headed inland, it took them a while to learn which plants, berries, fruits, and nuts were good to eat. Early on, away from the shorelines, the best option was to follow the big game animals. But, over centuries and millennia, early Amerindians learned in great detail how best to live in dozens of different environments. Let's see how they did it in a few places.

Foraging, Fishing, and Hunting At first, their options consisted of foraging, fishing, and hunting. In North America for the first several centuries, hunting probably played a major role in subsistence. By 8000 BCE, indications are that hunting had waned in significance, partly because most of the big game animals—mammoths, mastodons, giant beaver, horses—were gone. Foraging and fishing took up the slack.

One of the best places for foraging and fishing was California, which by 5000 BCE was the most densely populated region of North America. It offered fish, sea mammals, nuts, seeds, and acorns. California was more ecologically diverse than any similar-sized region in North America, offering plenty of food and many different types, so that if one source failed people could turn to others. People especially clustered around San Francisco Bay, which was still filling with seawater until 3000 BCE, and along the coast around today's Santa Barbara. After 3000 BCE, groups took up acorn harvesting amid the oak groves on the flanks of the Sierra Nevada.

As every squirrel knows, acorns store well and can provide calories all winter long when other foods are hard to find. Acorns are highly nutritious but require grinding, leaching, and boiling before humans can eat them, because they contain toxic tannins. The tedious labor of acorn processing was almost surely women's work. California's acorn foragers built year-round camps and even sedentary villages, some with more than a thousand people. Eventually, they were harvesting 60,000 tons of acorns per year, creating a food surplus that they could exchange for decorative shells from the Pacific coast and inland obsidian, the black, volcanic stone that holds a sharp edge.

Foraging for acorns and settling down led early Californians to have more children. When babies could eat acorn mush instead of drinking their mothers' milk, mothers became fertile again sooner after childbirth. Skeletons show shorter intervals between births, but also higher mortality among infants, children, and women of child-bearing age. Both birth

Clovis Points Archeologists have found the spearheads called Clovis points, dated from between 13,200 and 12,900 years ago, all across North America and in a few places in Central America. The nearly identical style of all these weapons suggests that one hunting culture diffused across the continent.

and death rates climbed. California's acorn eaters established a reliable source of subsistence that led to social and health changes, and commercial networks, comparable to those that followed transitions to agriculture around the world.

Amerindians in the Pacific Northwest also evolved a settled way of life without farming. This is a land of rugged mountains, jagged coastlines, tall forests, moderate temperatures, and frequent rain. The economic base here was the extraordinary abundance of migratory fish, mainly salmon, in rivers from northern California to Alaska. Permanent settlements developed by about 4400 BCE, and large villages from 1800 BCE. People also gathered berries, nuts, and fruits when the season permitted. But the key was the abundance of fish, which provided a food surplus. Smoked fish lasted for months before going bad.

This way of life permitted some people to accumulate power and wealth in the Pacific Northwest. Those who harvested more fish than others could accumulate followers and, in the case of men, have more wives and children. Elaborate burials show the rise of status differentiation. Elites were buried with spear-points, beads, carvings, and copper items. At some point, warfare and slavery became commonplace. At one cemetery site in northern British Columbia, the majority of male skeletons show signs of violence, either skull fractures or broken forearms. By 200 CE, villages built defensive fortifications, suggesting routine conflict. Population along this coast peaked around 1150 CE, after which it sharply declined for reasons unknown.

Across the continent in what is now New England and the Canadian Maritimes, Amerindians lived a more mobile and precarious existence. People first arrived here around 10,000 BCE, as the ice sheets were retreating. As in post-glacial Europe, they at first found hunting the most rewarding option. But as forests colonized the landscapes, hunting became harder and foraging for berries and nuts easier. By 7000 BCE, some people had begun seasonal migrations, congregating along rivers in the spring to exploit runs of migrating fish, and dispersing in summer for berry and nut picking. They huddled together in the hungry winter months when food often ran short. By 1000 BCE, they had cooking pots used for a wide variety of nuts, berries, roots, and seeds. They became more efficient hunters after 700 CE when they acquired the bow and arrow.

In early South America, big-game hunting was rarely if ever the main way of life. Most early archeological sites are near the coasts or along rivers. They reveal that Amerindians in these regions followed mobile lifestyles until about 3500 BCE, with great variation in subsistence strategies from place to place. On the Peruvian coast by 5000 to 4000 BCE, people learned how to fish in the rich waters of the Humboldt Current, one of the planet's great reservoirs of seafood. Along the coasts of southern Brazil, people harvested shellfish, leaving behind giant middens.

In California, the Pacific Northwest, New England, Peru, and Brazil, early Amerindians figured out ways to make a living from their varied environments. Some created settled ways of life, with fish or acorns prominent on the menu. Most moved seasonally in search of edible plants and animals. In both North and South America, coastal landscapes usually sustained the densest populations because they allowed people access to the resources of both land and sea. Within a few thousand years of their arrival in the Americas, people on both continents began to domesticate plants and turn to farming.

Farming, Americas-Style The first signs of farming in the Americas come from South American lowlands, around 9000 BCE. There is firmer evidence of agriculture in Mexico by 5000 BCE, the Andes by 3000 BCE, and the eastern woodlands of North America by 2000 BCE. In every case, these transitions were slow and unsteady. People used garden crops as just another food source together with what they might gather and hunt. Groups often farmed for a few centuries and then gave it up for reasons we can only guess at—perhaps droughts, soil exhaustion, or warfare. So the distinction between farmers on the one hand and forager-hunters on the other was fuzzy in the Americas, as in Africa, and much more so than in most parts of Eurasia.

Farming in the Americas had a few distinctive characteristics. First, it involved a completely different set of crops from those grown in Eurasia or Africa, featuring maize, squash, beans, potatoes, quinoa, and a few others. There was no rice, wheat, barley, millet, or sorghum. We'll see some of the consequences of these crops shortly.

Second, all farming work was done by human hand. Amerindians had very few domesticated animals, and in North America none of significance except dogs. In the high Andes, people herded llamas from 3500 BCE. But llamas carried loads as pack animals and didn't pull carts or plows. With no oxen, horses, or water buffalo, farmers in the Americas had no plows. They used digging sticks, as farmers did in sub-Saharan Africa, to prepare ground for planting.

Third, in many locations, people labored long and hard to improve soil and terrain for farming. In swampy lowlands, from today's Bolivia to Mexico, farmers developed **raised-field agriculture**, one of the world's most ingenious and productive farming systems. The idea is to pile up mud, muck, and organic matter into small islands in swamps or along shallow lakeshores, and then plant crops on the raised fields. This practice ensures adequate moisture even in a dry season, keeps many pesky nibbling animals away from crops, and even provides a little climate control: the surrounding wetlands moderate extremes of heat and cold, reducing the risk of crop loss. Modern experiments show that raised-field agriculture—amphibious farming, one might say— offers bountiful yield per acre. But it was a lot of work to build and maintain the raised fields—as it was in amphibious farming of the rice padis of East and Southeast Asia.

Another important, and labor-intensive, modification of farmland was the building of terraces on mountain slopes. Terracing began by 2000 BCE and was done on a huge scale in the Andes after 500 CE. The Andes are often steep, but terracing and irrigation water from melting mountain snows converted mountain slopes into fertile farmland.

Terraced Agriculture This photo, from Písac in present-day Peru, shows agricultural terraces carved into the Andes nearly 10,000 feet (ca. 3,000 m) above sea level. Farmers who worked steeply sloping land on all continents engaged in terracing, despite the enormous effort involved in both creating and maintaining terraces, because it helped prevent soil erosion and allowed easier water control. These terraces are probably from the fifteenth century, but Andean farmers built others beginning no later than 500 CE and likely before.

By 1000 CE, Andean farmers had carved out about 600 square miles (1,500 sq km) of terraced fields. A Spaniard who arrived several centuries later said the Andes looked like staircases.

Another way to improve the soil was to create patches of so-called black earth. In Amazonia, where soils are usually poor, archeologists have recently found black earth soils deliberately enhanced by careful addition of organic matter—mainly charcoal, animal and fish bones, and manure. Far more fertile than surrounding soils, black earth allowed people from about 500 BCE onward to farm productively in landscapes that otherwise would yield little. By 1 CE, Amazonian farmers had built settled villages around their black earth patches.

Intensive Farming in the Andes and Mesoamerica

In the Andes and Mesoamerica, combinations of crops eventually proved so productive, nutritious, and easy to store that they served as the basis for complex hierarchical societies and states, just as rice and wheat did in Eurasia and Egypt. These two locations became the great centers of population in the Americas.

The Andean Farming System   The heart of the Andean farming system consisted of quinoa, maize, and potatoes. Quinoa, a grain native to the Andes, does well at high elevations and yields superbly nutritious seeds. Its cultivation began around 2000 BCE. Maize is an import to the region from Mexico, but somehow it arrived as early as 5000 BCE. Andean farmers grew it on mountain terraces up to 7,000 feet (2,000 m) in altitude and down on the desert coast with irrigation water from the mountains. The most important crop was potatoes, indigenous to the Andes, grown as high up as 13,000 feet (4,000 m). Potato farming began around 3500 BCE.

This farming system formed the foundation of complex society in the Andes for three main reasons. First was its reliability. In the Andes, irrigation water came from high glaciers, which melted in the tropical sun in dry and wet years alike, reducing the impact of droughts. Moreover, farmers had three different crops they could grow at different elevations in the mountains, so if one failed for any reason, they had a backup plan.

The second important feature of Andean farming was the nutritional value of its staple crops. Quinoa and potatoes are unusually nourishing foods, with a wide variety of vitamins, minerals, and proteins.

The third and most important characteristic of the Andean farming system was that all three staple crops stored well, especially in the dry and chill mountain air. As we've seen, storable food surpluses that can be hoarded, traded, and distributed formed the basis of political power in complex societies around the world. Quinoa and maize kernels can last for months. Potatoes cannot; but at some point probably well before 1000 CE, Andean farmers learned to make *chuño* by freezing small potatoes at night, heating them up in the midday sun, and then crushing them into a pasty, tasty meal. *Chuño* can last for years without spoiling—it's among the most durable foods ever invented. Andean people also made freeze-dried llama meat, called *charqui* (from which our word *jerky* derives), which also stores well. So with these storable and portable foodstuffs, Andean farmers provided an essential requirement for states, cities, and complex societies.

The Mesoamerican Farming System In Mesoamerica, farmers developed a different intensive farming system, centered on maize, squash, and beans. As we've seen, maize—or corn, as it is also known—is the domesticated form of the Mexican grass *teosinte*. Starting at the latest by 5000 BCE, farmers produced bigger grains and taller stalks through genetic modification achieved by careful human selection. Maize lacks important nutrients but is very efficient at turning sunshine into edible calories.

Maize, squash, and beans—sometimes called the Three Sisters—seemed made for one another. Bean plants used maize stalks to climb upward. Beans (or, to be precise, microbes attached to their roots) fixed nitrogen in the soil, compensating for maize's big nitrogen requirement. Squashes helped out by spreading over the ground, denying sunlight to weeds and holding moisture in the soil. As food, beans provide the niacin and proteins that maize lacks, so they not only grow well together but also complement one another in the human diet. For more than 4,000 years, this trinity of crops has formed the heart of Mesoamerican agriculture. People in Oaxaca, in south-central Mexico, acknowledge this when they say they are *hombres de maiz*.

The Three Sisters traveled well. Like many plants, maize takes its cues about when to flower from changing day length. Mexican varieties can't grow properly in Minnesota, for example. It took millennia to develop maize varieties that would grow well at different latitudes, but Amerindian farmers gradually did it. By 1000 CE, most farmers in the Americas, from Argentina to Canada, raised maize among their crops, usually together with beans and squashes, and many made it their staple food.

In raised fields in the Maya lowlands and central Mexico, the Mesoamerican farming system, like that of the Andes, provided enough storable, portable surplus food to support the formation of states, cities, and complex societies.

Manufacturing and Trade

We've explored the subsistence strategies—ways of life—and farming systems in the Americas before 1000 CE. It remains to consider realms we can loosely call manufacturing and trade.

Textiles and Metallurgy The most important item of manufacture throughout most of the Americas was clothing. In the Andes, the most common material was alpaca wool, but cotton and even cactus fiber were used too. Andean weavers by 1000 BCE had invented on their own just about every technique in use worldwide. Men apparently sometimes wove cloth in the Andes, but everywhere else in the Americas all evidence suggests it was exclusively women's work, often done in outdoor courtyards and in the company of others. Maya weavers used hemp for everyday cloth, and cotton only for luxury. In Mesoamerica and the Andes, cloth makers found excellent dyestuffs—indigo (blue) and cochineal (red)—that yielded vivid and durable colors. They even had a purple dye made from the mucus of a snail that was a distant cousin of the mollusk so important to the merchant cities of Phoenicia.

Metallurgy mattered little in the Americas, in contrast to Africa and Eurasia. In the Andes, smiths worked copper and gold by 1800 BCE, mostly for ornamental purposes. Metal ornaments helped high-ranking people show off their importance, both in life and in death. Some burials in Peru include farm implements made of bronze or silver, too heavy to be useful as tools but just right to demonstrate one's social status. The Maya scarcely worked metals at all. Since no one worked iron, the Americas didn't experience the revolutionary impacts of that metal on farming, warfare, and politics that it wrought in Africa and Eurasia.

Trade, Cultural Exchange, and American Webs In the Americas, especially within Mesoamerica and the Andean region, people and goods were constantly on the move, creating arenas of interaction that developed into American webs.

The earliest exchanges involved food crops. As we've seen, maize spread from Mesoamerica both north and south so that by 1000 CE farmers from Quebec to Argentina raised it. People also carried sweet potatoes both north and south from their origin in Colombia or Panama, so that by 2000 BCE they flourished in warm, humid lands on both continents.

People also exchanged shells and stone over long distances. By 800 CE, the Ecuador coast, for example, hosted a thriving export business in conch shells, a luxury good. The big shells were hard to get—one had to dive 60 feet (18 m) beneath the sea—and served as ornaments for the wealthy. Traders, probably navigating coastal waters on rafts, took them as far afield as Mexico. In a world with no iron goods, obsidian had high value. Amerindians in the Ohio River valley acquired obsidian quarried in what is now Wyoming. The Maya got it from central Mexico. Jade, a stone more prized for decorative than practical purposes, was also traded over long distances, especially in Mesoamerica. Another trade good that was prized enough to be traded over long distances was cacao: in the 770s CE, people in Utah were eating chocolate made from Mesoamerican cacao beans. Conch shells and obsidian were high-value products, like tin in ancient Europe or lapis lazuli in Asia, and they provided the necessary incentives for people to knit networks of long-distance exchange.

The two centers of trade and exchange, unsurprisingly, were the two centers of population: Mesoamerica and the Andes. In the Maya world, trade and tribute involved not only obsidian but also feathers, cotton cloth, pottery, jewelry, and especially salt. The cities of northern Yucatán were well situated to produce sea salt and to trade it throughout Mesoamerica. In return they acquired goods from far and wide, such as gold from Panama and turquoise from New Mexico. In Mesoamerica, people used cacao beans as currency, an unusual choice because they don't last well. All goods went by raft, canoe, or human porter in the absence of beasts of burden and wheeled vehicles.

In the Andes, economic exchange was also common from 2500 BCE onward, but it proceeded differently. First, llamas could carry loads of up to 110 lbs. (50 kg), and to judge by artwork, they did so regularly in caravans by 200 BCE. Second, unlike in Mesoamerica, in the Andes markets and merchants played a small role. Instead, economic exchange was in the hands of political leaders, who organized llama caravans along regular routes. They bartered—there is no evidence of money—for cotton, salt, obsidian, and coca leaf. Coca leaf, from a bush that grows only in the Andes, served as medicine, aphrodisiac, and in religious ceremonies. People chewed wads of leaf to fend off fatigue, hunger, and thirst. People rarely traded for basic necessities in the Andes.

These trade patterns were part of broader webs of cultural exchange. In the lowlands of eastern South America, pottery styles were very similar over huge spaces, and new styles spread quickly. That suggests a large zone of interaction, presumably along the many navigable rivers. The practice of building mounds was even more widespread. Amerindians in California, Ohio, Venezuela, Guyana, and many points in between piled up earth to create ceremonial centers for religious rites. From Alaska to the Maya region, people used sweat baths for ritual cleansing. A team game played on special courts

Cacao Traded over long distances, cacao beans were a luxury good and status symbol across the Americas. The god depicted in this Maya statue from between 600 and 900 CE wears a cacao pod at his waist.

(discussed below) spread from southern Mexico to Arizona. So at least in a loose way, all peoples in the Americas were linked to one another—because they were linked to either Mesoamerica or the Andes.

Each of these centers of population had its own orbit, its own web. There were connections between the two—somehow maize, manioc, and the bow and arrow spread to both—but they were still slender as of 1000 CE.

Health, Society, and Culture

No one knows how many Amerindians were alive in 1000 CE, let alone in earlier times. The Americas contained perhaps 5 million people in 1000 BCE, 15 million in 1 CE, and 40 million in 1000. Even by the earliest date, the Andes and Mesoamerica held the biggest concentrations of population, home to as much as two-thirds of the hemisphere's population—thanks to the bounty of intensive farming systems.

Health   What we know about the health of Amerindians before 1000 CE comes mainly from the study of skeletons, and to a lesser extent from analysis of DNA. In global terms, people in the Americas had two great health advantages. Since they didn't live cheek by jowl with herd animals, they had none of the infections that humans elsewhere acquired from their flocks and herds. And because their ancestors had crossed to America through very cold environments, they left behind those pathogens that need warmth to survive, such as malaria. But, like everyone else, their health suffered when they settled down, took up farming, and built cities.

Health varied greatly from place to place and over time. The healthiest peoples tended to live near abundant seafood resources—for example, along the coasts of southern Brazil. Mobile peoples were also among the healthiest. The unhealthiest were sedentary farmers and—once cities developed—city folk.

Before 500 BCE, the average life expectancy in the Americas was around 34 years—high by world standards of the time. People in urbanized areas, however, lived on average only 21 to 22 years. Over time, as farming and city life spread, fertility climbed and health nosedived. Between 1 CE and 1000 CE, life expectancy averaged only about 23 to 25 years for the hemisphere as a whole. As in Eurasia, the spread of farming generally made people shorter in stature as well as shorter-lived. The main reason, probably, was a decline in animal protein in the diet as people depended more on maize and beans, and less on meat and fish.

In the eastern woodlands of North America, populations remained comparatively healthy until the arrival of maize after 500 CE, especially those living near the fishing grounds of the Great Lakes. There was an unusual decline in stature here even before the transition to farming, perhaps a reflection of diminishing game supplies. Average height shrank by 3 inches (6 cm) from 6000 BCE to 1000 BCE, more for males than females. To judge from their skeletons (ca. 600–1000 CE), peoples of the desert Southwest suffered frequent malnutrition but low rates of infectious disease.

Risks of violence, as well as malnutrition and disease, varied tremendously across time and place. Mesoamerican skeletons show violent trauma in about 6 percent of cases, low by world standards of pre-modern times. In Ecuador, rates of violence in general were also low, but higher among farming people than among others. In some Ecuadorian burials, only female skeletons show signs of violence. In the eastern woodlands of North America, rates of violence were lower still, and similar for males and females. In California, violence spiked after the introduction of the bow and arrow around 400 CE: over the next eight centuries, 10 percent of adults appear to have suffered arrow wounds. As noted above, extremely high rates of violence prevailed among males in the Pacific Northwest in the centuries before 1100 CE. As a general rule, violence became more common over time, as more people lived in permanent settlements and adopted new technologies such as the bow and arrow that enabled people to maim and kill others at lower risk to themselves.

Family and Gender For the first 10,000 years of human history in the Americas, we have scant evidence of the nature of family life or the roles of men and women. Judging from the archeological record since 1000 BCE, we can say that in most respects, gender history in the Americas looked a lot like gender history elsewhere. The best evidence available comes from artwork, burials, and skeletons.

Family arrangements ranged from small nuclear households to big extended ones. Most Amerindian societies practiced monogamy, even for elite males. The exceptions came mainly in the case of conquering states, in which successful warriors might acquire multiple wives from among the conquered. Maya kings had multiple wives, usually as a means of political alliance.

In foraging and hunting societies, women spent most of their time collecting and preparing food, raising children, and perhaps making stone tools. Social groups remained small in most cases, kin-based, and with little formal hierarchy. Some scholars surmise that because women's food collecting provided most of the sustenance for their societies, they enjoyed comparatively higher status. Among the acorn harvesters of California, for example, women probably had some say in the choice of settlement sites. Their health and life expectancy, to judge from skeletons, was equal to that of men if one discounts high mortality among women of child-bearing age.

After 1000 BCE, most women lived in farming societies. They typically made pots and jars, spun and wove textiles, collected wild foods, took some part in the work of farming, spent long hours in food preparation, and raised children. Wherever maize was the staple, women ground kernels into flour to make either tortillas or maize porridge. Their skeletons show enormous wear and tear on wrist joints, something absent in male skeletons. In maize-based farming societies, men planted crops, harvested them, hunted, and built homes and other buildings. They might also roam far and wide for purposes of trade or warfare.

Gender arrangements varied from place to place. Artwork from New Mexico (ca. 200–1000 CE) shows men and women in conventional roles, but in a few cases also shows women hunting with traps and sticks, while men hunted with spears and bows and arrows. In many cases, including New Mexico and Peru after 600 CE, artwork shows women taking part in religious ceremonies—as women did in most other parts of the world. Peruvian art also implies that men sometimes joined in textile work; and elsewhere in the Andes men were buried with spinning implements, which was rare by world standards. According to glyphs—the writing system of the Maya—a woman named Sak'k'uk ruled a city for three years (612–615 CE) until her son attained the age of 12. But women in the Americas, as elsewhere, only rarely held positions of political power.

Religion and Language Amerindians followed a variety of religious practices, but some beliefs and rituals enjoyed wide currency. Amerindians overall accepted the existence of numerous spirits and the notion of a supreme deity. The spirits were generally associated with animals, plants, rivers, mountains, fertility, death, celestial bodies, and other aspects of nature. Appeals to the spirits could be made through departed ancestors, who now lived in the spirit world, or through shamans.

The closest thing to a universal in Amerindian religious practice was shamanism. A shaman—as we've seen—is someone with special knowledge of, and access to, the spirit world. Amerindians generally communicated with the spirit world through visions, which might come through dreams, trances, or hallucinations. They often placed great importance on dreams, which might reveal the future or allow conversation with the dead.

Many Amerindian cultures also sought access to the spirit world through hallucinogenic drugs derived from plants. These might be eaten, drunk in a potion, snorted, or smoked, often together with tobacco. Peyote, a kind of cactus native to northern Mexico and the southwestern United States, provided a psychoactive drug used by shamans from at least 3000 BCE. Central American mushrooms and the Amazonian vine product *ayahuasca* also helped shamans explore the unseen. Siberian shamans had long used drugs to enhance access to the spirit world, so this practice probably came with the first arrival of people in the Americas, although the plants employed differed from place to place.

From Central America to Amazonia, shamans were often associated with jaguars. The big, powerful cats moved in the night, normally unseen. They hunted in the trees and the water, moving from one world to another, as shamans did. In some traditions, jaguars protected shamans as they approached the spirit world. Artistic motifs often put shamans and jaguars together, and sometimes show shamans becoming jaguars.

Amerindian religions, like those of most other parts of the world, also emphasized the practice of sacrifice as a means of gaining the good will of spiritual forces. Amerindians were unusual in that they rarely sacrificed crops, beverages, or—aside from llamas in the Andes—livestock. Sometimes they used humans for religious sacrifice. The Moche, who lived in coastal Peru around 200 to 600 CE, apparently sacrificed teenagers. The Maya sacrificed people by throwing them into *cenotes*, water-filled sinkholes common in Yucatán. They also decapitated people whose blood was expected to sustain the gods. It's likely that war captives provided many of the victims for human sacrifice. Maya rulers often made sacrifices of their own blood, piercing themselves with sharp tools. They hoped this would ensure good fortune for newborns or for a newly enthroned king.

Mesoamerican religion also emphasized the measurement of cosmic time. Mesoamericans developed several remarkably accurate calendars based on the perceived movements of the sun, moon, Venus, and Mars, and one, a calendar with a 260-day cycle, based—perhaps—on the human gestation period. Some calendars were used to help figure out the best days for religious rituals or coronations of new rulers. Others served to organize the agricultural years.

Human Sacrifice A Maya stone relief shows a priest holding the head of a sacrificial victim he has beheaded. The carving was created during the first millennium CE.

Shamanism, visions, and sacrifice were widespread in Amerindian religion. The sophisticated calendrics were confined to Mesoamerica.

All Amerindian languages are derived from tongues spoken in Northeast Asia long ago. Migrants from Asia may have brought one or several languages with them. As early Americans then spread out over the two continents, their contacts with one another diminished and gradually their speech evolved into a few thousand different languages. California alone had at least 74 Amerindian languages.

After thousands of years of language diversification, however, the trend reversed. By 500 CE and probably well before, certain languages such as Qechua in South America and Mayan in Central America, spread at the expense of local ones. Just as Latin spread with the growth of the Roman Empire or Chinese with the conquests of the Qin and Han, so Qechua and Mayan spread because of the political strength of people who spoke those tongues. There was nothing inherently better about these languages than the ones they replaced—just as there was nothing intrinsically better about Latin than Etruscan. This process of the spread of imperial languages was slow, and by 1000 CE thousands of languages still remained in the Americas.

States and Complex Societies in the Americas

In the Americas, as elsewhere, the development of states, cities, and complex society depended on the availability of foods that would store and travel well. As we've seen, maize and potatoes fit the bill, and that is probably why the Americas' earliest and most extensive centers of political and military power, urban life, and hierarchical society developed in the homelands of these crops, Mesoamerica and the Andes.

Mesoamerica: Olmecs and Maya

By 2000 BCE, farming villages dotted Mesoamerica. By 1000 BCE, the first signs of monumental architecture and urban life appeared, and writing evolved by about 500 BCE. As far as we can tell, most of these developments began with the Olmecs and reached a mysterious climax with the Maya.

The Olmecs, ca. 1600–300 BCE   At around 1600 BCE, in the steamy lowlands of southern Mexico at a place now called San Lorenzo, people now called **Olmecs** ("people from the land of rubber") began to build large structures such as temples, limestone-paved plazas, earthen mounds, and ball courts. The Olmecs farmed maize, beans, squash, gourds, and avocadoes in the floodplains of local rivers, gathered food including turtle eggs, and hunted for peccaries, deer, turtles, and other animals. Bones in their garbage heaps suggest that their main source of animal protein, however, was domestic dogs.

San Lorenzo had urban features such as monuments and public spaces, but its population probably never exceeded 3,000. To what extent, if any, it dominated a hinterland is unclear, but Olmec artistic motifs appeared in villages for many miles around. There is no trace of an army or a priestly caste. But something—perhaps control of trade and prestige goods such as jade and obsidian—allowed some families to dominate the rest, claim special access to the spirit realm, and become rulers. By roughly 900 BCE, San Lorenzo was abandoned. Many monuments appear intentionally smashed, so archeologists suspect organized violence, a revolution, or an invasion.

A new center of Olmec culture called La Venta, about 50 miles (80 km) away, arose around 900 BCE. It is nearer the coast than San Lorenzo and is situated in swampy terrain. Its great earthen pyramid, the first in the Americas, stands tall above a flat landscape and served as a ceremonial site.

The most remarkable feature of Olmec culture is a series of giant basalt heads, usually assumed to represent rulers of San Lorenzo and La Venta. Seventeen have been found, the biggest of which is nearly the size of an elephant. The Olmecs somehow moved stones, as large as any at Stonehenge, far from where they were quarried. This must have required the coordinated effort of thousands of people, a key sign of the degree of complexity and organization among the Olmecs. But we haven't a clue how it happened. The scraps of Olmec writing found so far, which date to about 650 BCE, shed little light. The most revealing fragment, a stone inscription deciphered only in 1993, explains that a certain "King Harvest Mountain" cut off the head of his rival.

By 300 BCE, the Olmec centers were empty. Once again, no one knows why. Village farming persisted in the region, but urban life and complex hierarchical society disappeared.

The Olmecs were the first people in Mesoamerica to develop complex hierarchical society. But some of their neighbors, such as the Maya and the Zapotecs, were moving in similar directions at almost the same time, and they all interacted through trade and perhaps military competition. The art, architecture, religion, and calendars in use throughout Mesoamerica overlapped. So it is perhaps reasonable to see the whole region together evolving toward social complexity over many centuries from 1600 BCE.

The Maya, ca. 600 BCE–900 CE People lived in the Maya lands—Yucatán and its neighborhood—for thousands of years and had taken up farming by 1100 BCE if not before. Chronically short of fresh water, the Maya landscape required a lot of work to become productive. But with enough wisely invested labor, it could be enormously productive, as it was from about 200 to nearly 900 CE.

In their origin myth, the **Maya** are made of maize, which is not far wrong. Farmers raised peppers, tomatoes, sweet potato, manioc, cotton, and cacao as well as the Mesoamerican Three Sisters. The indispensable crop for the Maya, as for the Olmecs, was maize. The Maya created a variation of Mesoamerica's amphibious agriculture with systems of ditches, drains, canals, and reservoirs to cope with seasonal water shortage and flooding. The Maya built raised fields amid their canals, replenishing fertility by piling muck from canal floors atop their fields. In hilly terrain, they also cut thousands of terraces to keep soil in place. They grew crops year-round. Maya agriculture was enormously labor-intensive.

Beyond farming, the Maya secured a little more food by hunting deer, turkeys, monkeys, crocodiles, and manatees, and collecting fruits and berries. Like the Olmec, they raised dogs for food. Those living near the coast fished and collected mollusks. Inland Maya probably stocked their canals with fish.

The Maya developed some industries that helped enrich and empower their leaders. In the northern Yucatán, Maya perfected the art of salt making by the evaporation of seawater held in ponds. They exported high-quality salt throughout Mesoamerica. Maya artisans excelled in jade carving. Harder than steel, jade isn't an easy stone to work. Maya artisans used obsidian blades and stone drills—they had no metal tools—to

CONSIDERING THE EVIDENCE

A Maya Bowl for Cocoa

Mayan glyph carvers toiled continually to record the births, deaths, ceremonies, and conquests of their kings and queens on the surfaces of their temples, plazas, and monuments. Scholars have also deciphered glyphs about lesser nobles on seemingly mundane objects that offer insights into their personal lives. Pictured opposite, for instance, is an inscribed, white stone vessel just over six inches (15 cm) in diameter and around four inches (10 cm) tall. The three glyphs along its rim record that the carving was completed on (by our calendar) August 18, 731 CE, for a "guardian-priest" named Yiban who served the "holy lord of [the land of] K'an." The carver also labeled the bowl as "cup for *ixiimte*-flavored cocoa," a potent concoction that Yiban would have prepared for his lord as part of ceremonies for communicating with the gods.

The carvings on the side of the bowl depict Yiban and his deceased parents. In the close-up "rollout" reproduction on the opposite page, Yiban's mother (center) carries the image of a god in her right arm. Her name is inscribed in smaller glyphs near her forehead as Ix-Mo', or Lady Macaw. Although Maya-carved jade made its way throughout Mesoamerica, white stone bowls were rare, prized possessions often entombed with their owners. For Yiban, this cup not only connected him to his lord and his gods, it also memorialized his parents.

Questions for Analysis

1. Why was this bowl important to Yiban and his lord? Why were similar bowls important to Maya society in general?
2. Search the Maya glyphs on the opposite page for numbers. (Hint: small circles equal one and bars equal five.) Why do you think scholars could translate number glyphs before any of the other glyphs?
3. What can historians learn from personal objects like this bowl that may not be evident from the carvings on Maya monuments designed for everyone to see?

---

carve, scrape, and polish jade into works of art. They exported jade items throughout Mesoamerica, much as bronze smiths in ancient China or Mesopotamia did in their regions. Anyone claiming elite status in Mesoamerica wanted Maya jade.

Maya trade networks contributed to the wealth and power of the elite families who dominated Maya societies. Trade links involving salt, jade, and obsidian extended to the Pacific coast of Central America and to the region around today's Mexico City—the Valley of Mexico, an excellent obsidian source.

Through extensive archeology and advances in deciphering Maya glyphs, we know much more about Maya society and politics than about the Olmecs. It seems that the

Cocoa bowl of Yiban, 731 CE

Rollout of inscriptions on the bowl This presentation of the bowl's full exterior in two dimensions shows Yiban (left), Ix-mo' (center), and his unnamed father (right). The glyphs are traced in black ink for greater readability.

Maya had Mesoamerica's most complete writing system and could write anything that they could speak. Maya scribes were at work by 250 BCE, and perhaps by 600 BCE.

By 600 BCE the Maya were also building pyramids, indicating that someone had the power to direct the labor of many others. Pyramids served as temples for religious rituals, often involving sacrifices of food, tobacco, and human life. The pyramids stood in the heart of genuine cities, which by 500 CE might hold tens of thousands of people. These cities—Tikal, El Mirador, Palenque, Copán to name a few—exercised some control over surrounding landscapes. They were territorial states, although small ones compared to what came later in Mesoamerica.

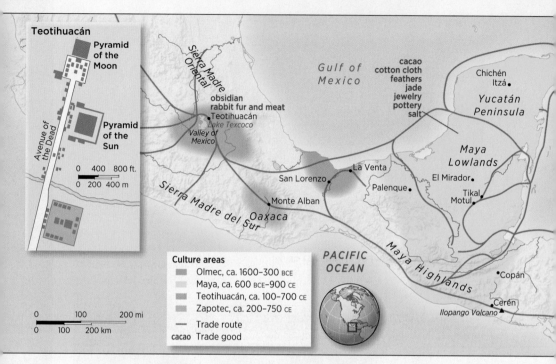

Mesoamerican Cultures, ca. 1600 BCE–900 CE Beginning with the Olmec, a succession of Mesoamerican cultures arose all based on intensive irrigated farming, often in wetlands. Some built substantial cities, none greater than Teotihuacán. Despite a lack of beasts of burden, long-distance trade and cultural exchange networks grew up, binding the entire region into its own web of interaction.

Despite common culture and language, these cities never united politically. Instead, they competed fiercely with one another. In 679 CE, for example, the city of Tikal, which might have had 50,000 people, overran a rival city, Motul. The victors composed a glyph that summarized the war: "the skulls of Motul people were piled into mountains." The Maya cities, like the fifth-century BCE Greek *poleis* or the even more ancient Sumerian city-states, competed politically, militarily, and probably commercially. That competition made the surviving polities extremely formidable with respect to neighboring villages and communities, which the bigger cities easily dominated.

The glyphs and archeology also offer a sense of the Maya social order. It was a sharply hierarchical society, at least after 200 CE, in which kings and royal lineages lorded it over everyone else. Kings and queens performed religious rituals and lived at the ceremonial temples. As with monarchs elsewhere, authority rested in part on expert access to supernatural power. Maya royalty eventually claimed to be descended from the gods. Authority also rested on prowess and leadership in war, often undertaken to acquire captives needed for sacrifices. Maya rulers were shaman-rulers, just as rulers of early complex societies almost everywhere were priest-kings. Elite families from non-royal lineages shared in power by holding offices such as judge, general, or priest. Some commoners became prosperous, either as merchants or artisans, or as artists employed by rulers.

The vast majority of Maya labored in the fields. All owed tribute to the ruler, paid as a share of the harvest, or in goods, or as labor on temples, roads, or other public works. At the bottom rung of society were slaves, often war captives who, for the moment at least, escaped being sacrificed. Orphans usually were enslaved too. We can't tell what percentage of Maya were enslaved, but considerable evidence suggests a lively slave trade throughout Maya lands. The glyphs have plenty to say about the glorious deeds and distinguished ancestry of Maya rulers, but not a syllable about slaves or commoners.

More than anyone else in the Americas, the Maya refined their mathematical skills. For them, as for the Babylonians, math was the servant of religion. With multiple calendars, the Maya needed dexterity with numbers to figure out the right day to perform a particular ritual. They used a base 20 system that included the concept of zero (also invented independently in India) and could perform calculations in the millions. By the second century CE, the Maya had devised another calendar, the so-called Long Count, which marked consecutive days beginning August 8, 3114 BCE (by our calendar), which they reckoned was the fourth beginning of creation. Their calendar even had a word (*alautun*) for periods of 23,040,000,000 days—a little over 63 million years. You couldn't be a good Maya priest without strong quantitative skills.

The Maya also elaborated the ball game that seems first to have appeared among the Olmecs and became a hallmark of Mesoamerican culture. We don't know exactly how the game was played, but it was a team game played on an outdoor court involving a hard rubber ball about the size of a grapefruit. The biggest court, at Chichén Itzá, a northern Yucatán city that had 13 ball courts, is nearly twice the size of a football field. Teams of as many as six per side wore uniforms and tried to put the ball through a stone ring, mounted vertically high up on the court's wall. They used fists, elbows,

Maya Sport The Ball Game Court at the Maya city of Chichén Itzá is over 180 yards (165 m) long. The stone rings used as goals appear midway down the court, near the top of the high stone walls surrounding it.

and hips, or maybe paddles—but not their open hands. Goals must have been as rare as in soccer. Some scholars think the game was part of divination ceremonies, used to foretell the outcome of some venture, perhaps a planned attack on enemies. Some think the game was played by captives, and the losers sacrificed. Artwork suggests rivulets of blood commonly flowed in the course of a match. Rulers perhaps encouraged the ball game as a distraction for the masses, like chariot races in ancient Rome. Archeologists have found about 1,500 ball courts so far in Mexico, Arizona, and Cuba.

The Maya flourished from about 200 CE. They suffered a devastating setback in the late 530s when the Ilopango volcano erupted, raining down ash and pumice waist-deep over much of the southern fringe of the Maya world. Within 50 to 75 miles (80–120 km) of the volcano, farming ceased for 200 years. Survivors of the blast fled north and east, toward the center of the Maya lands. But by 750 CE people had resettled the buried region, and population in the Maya region as a whole approached its maximum, perhaps 10 million—far higher than the Olmecs'.

Then beginning late in the ninth century CE monumental building and inscriptions stopped. Cities emptied, and population declined by at least three-quarters over the next 150 years. As with the Olmecs a millennium earlier, no one knows why this collapse of urban life occurred—although drought probably was part of the equation. Late in the ninth century a long searing drought, the worst in many centuries, afflicted the region. Perhaps soil erosion and nutrient loss undermined agriculture in some areas. Stepped-up warfare was likely involved. All these problems could have combined in a deadly downward spiral. The collapse of urban, complex society among the Maya is one of the great mysteries of the history of the American hemisphere, parallel in some respects to the disappearance of urban society along the Indus River 2,000 years before.

Mesoamerica: Zapotecs and Teotihuacán

Alongside the Maya, but well to their west, two other complex societies rose and fell in Mesoamerica: the Zapotecs of the Oaxaca region, and the urban population of Teotihuacán. We know less about these societies than about the Maya, mainly because they left little writing. But they interacted regularly with Maya centers, forming a lively Mesoamerican web by 200 or 300 CE.

Zapotecs in Oaxaca, ca. 200–750 CE   The Zapotecs lived—as their descendants do today—in a region of southern Mexico called Oaxaca. This is mountainous terrain, but with frost-free valleys it is ideal for maize cultivation. Farming and villages appeared by 1500 BCE here, even earlier than in the Maya lands. Most villages had defensive palisades, an indication of regular warfare. Writing emerged by 700 or 600 BCE. Their language, a descendant of which is still spoken, was different from Mayan. Scholars have yet to decipher Zapotec writing securely. What they think they can read is mainly about the heroic slaughter and mutilation of enemies by rulers, very much in the tradition of Mayan—and for that matter, Assyrian—literature. But Zapotec art shows no kings trumpeting their great deeds, and the architecture suggests a more egalitarian society than the Maya.

By 100 BCE the people of the Valley of Oaxaca had begun a successful expansion and built a city, today called Monte Alban. At its height it might have housed 15,000 to 20,000 people, rivaling most Maya centers. Its centerpiece was a leveled ridge with palaces, tombs, ball courts, and plazas. The ridge, although lacking in water, is a good defensive location, a citadel with long views in every direction. The entire Valley of Oaxaca was dotted with maize-growing villages—the Zapotecs too considered themselves children of maize—and by 500 CE may have held 100,000 people. If you like tortillas, you're in their debt, because this is the society that invented the maize tortilla.

By 750 CE, the grand buildings at Monte Alban had begun to crumble, and the city shrank in population to the size of a village, with about 2,000 residents. People dispersed to other settlements in the Oaxaca valley, and perhaps farther afield. Once again, no one knows why.

Teotihuacán, ca. 100–700 CE The last of the Mesoamerican societies we will consider, Teotihuacán, was distinctive in several ways. It was located in the Valley of Mexico, where today's Mexico City stands, at an elevation of 7,500 feet (2,300 m) and surrounded by mountains. Rain was scarce, but the Valley had several small lakes. In this environment a giant city grew up. Unlike other Mesoamerican societies, it left no evidence of real writing, ball courts, or elaborate calendars.

Around 100 BCE to 100 CE, the population of the Valley of Mexico, previously huddled around the shores of the lakes, started gathering at Teotihuacán. Soon 100,000 people, almost everyone in the Valley, crowded into the city. Careful control of a freshwater spring allowed leading families to create a big swamp with raised fields, called *chinampas*, where maize, beans, and squash thrived. The people of Teotihuacán also raised rabbits for food and fur, and they traded both to surrounding communities.

Teotihuacán had another basis of wealth: obsidian. The city lay close to the sources of the best obsidian in Mesoamerica and organized the stone's quarrying and export. Perhaps because of its obsidian business, Teotihuacán had a bigger role in long-distance trade and diplomacy than any other community in the Americas. In 378 CE, one of its leaders mounted a military expedition that dethroned the ruling house in the Maya city of Tikal, one of the two most powerful Maya centers. By 400 CE, Teotihuacán's population approached 150,000, by far the biggest city in the Americas.

Uncharacteristically for Mesoamerica, Teotihuacán had a regular grid plan, carefully laid out to awe visitors. At the heart of the city was the so-called Avenue of the Dead, with adjacent tall pyramids. The tallest, the Pyramid of the Sun, served as the main ceremonial center, atop which stood a temple used for sacrifices. The city had a sewage system, like ancient Rome and the cities of the ancient Indus. Some of the residential quarters seem to have been organized ethnically, with sections of the city

Teotihuacán The Avenue of the Dead runs through the center of Teotihuacán. The Pyramid of the Moon, constructed between 100 and 450 CE, is the city's second-largest pyramid and part of the temple complex; it appears in this present-day photo of Teotihuacán.

housing immigrants from Oaxaca, Guatemala, and other nearby regions. It was the multicultural metropolis of Mesoamerica, drawing in people from far and wide.

Although the lack of writing limits our knowledge of religion at Teotihuacán, artwork, mainly wall paintings, shows that the residents believed in the usefulness of human sacrifice. It also implies an unusual feature—the worship of a female deity, one of eight main gods. Sometimes called (by modern scholars) the Great Goddess of Teotihuacán, she is usually pictured with a bird headdress and a nose pendant with fangs. She often appears with spiders, which may associate her with the underworld. Her image appears only in Teotihuacán and places where natives of that city settled, whereas most Mesoamerican deities had followers throughout the region. Other artistic styles of Teotihuacán spread widely, and its influence stretched from Honduras to the south as far north as northern Mexico.

Then, perhaps in the 530s, the metropolis of Mesoamerica suddenly and mysteriously crashed. Central buildings burned. Its population fell to 20,000 or 30,000, still the equivalent of a big city anywhere else. A new hypothesis explains this by emphasizing cold and drought resulting from a volcanic dust veil—well documented around the Northern Hemisphere for the years 535–536. But some scholars think the city's fires and collapse came later, perhaps as late as 700, and instead see evidence of a social uprising and overthrow of the rulers.

A Mesoamerican Web These four societies—the Olmecs, Maya, Zapotecs, and Teotihuacán—show a host of strong similarities that reflect growing interaction among peoples throughout Mesoamerica. Religion, culture, farming, technology, diet, and much else give evidence of an intensely interactive web in Mesoamerica, already forming by 500 BCE and at its height around 500 CE. It survived, in attenuated form, the disasters—if they were disasters—that shrank or eliminated urban centers at Teotihuacán, Monte Alban, and throughout the Maya world.

The word *collapse* is often used to describe the sudden decline of Teotihuacán, Monte Alban, and the Maya cities. But from the point of view of survivors who didn't enjoy elite status, the word *liberation* might be more appropriate. With the end of cities and states, ordinary Mesoamerican families no longer had to sweat building pyramids and temples, pay tribute to kings, surrender sons for military conscription, and offer up victims for human sacrifice when a king's supply of war captives ran low. Instead, after the disappearance of cities, states, writing, and kings, they dispersed into the forests, farmed, hunted, and collected their food, made pottery, wove clothing—and left little trace.

The Andean World

The other great center of population and complex society in the Americas was centered in the Andes, mainly in what is now Peru and Bolivia. We know less about the people and cultures of the Andes prior to 1000 CE than we do about Mesoamericans, mainly because some Mesoamericans left writing and Andean peoples did not. Pockets of population existed here from very early on, both on the coast and up on the Altiplano, or high plateau, at 13,000 feet (4,000 m). The steep and snow-packed mountains next door to the fish-rich waters of the Humboldt Current made this a distinctive environment. It meant that people living on the western side of the mountains could move quickly from one ecological zone to another by hiking up or downhill. It was also a precarious environment because of the periodic El Niños—as we saw in Chapter 2. The biggest El Niños, which occur every few centuries, bring devastating floods that could annihilate towns.

Norte Chico and Chavín, ca. 3100–200 BCE The earliest signs of complex society in the Andes region appeared about 3100 BCE—by coincidence, about the same time as in Mesopotamia and Egypt. The Peruvian coast is perpetually foggy but almost completely without rain. About 50 rivers slice through it, tumbling out of the Andes onto the coastal plain. Between 3100 and 1600 BCE, along four of these rivers, people clustered into roughly 25 settlements, collectively known as **Norte Chico**.

One of these, called Caral, contained perhaps 3,000 people. Caral and towns like it had pyramids and earthen theaters large enough to hold several hundred people, possibly for religious ceremonies. But they had no defensive walls or any signs of war. They lived off a combination of irrigation agriculture—the only possible kind here— and fishing. Their crops featured beans and squash, but not maize. Their middens show that they ate plenty of clams, mussels, anchovies, and sardines. The Norte Chico people played music with pipes made from pelican and condor bones, but they seem to have left behind no art, statuary, carvings, or pottery.

Norte Chico is a curious case of a complex society with monumental architecture based not on a storable grain but, apparently, on dried fish. Somehow, it seems, an elite managed to control the food supply and use that power to coerce or persuade thousands of others to build pyramids, mounds, and theaters. The total population, at its height

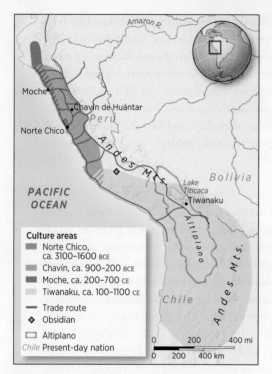

Cultures of the Andes, ca. 3100 BCE–1100 CE Complex societies developed in the Andes region based on irrigation, both on the coastal plain and at elevations up to 11,000 feet (3,300 m). Most of them exploited opportunities of steep inclines, which when terraced enabled them to raise a wide variety of crops at different altitudes. After 200 BCE if not before, llama-based transport helped bind the region into an Andean interactive web.

between 2600 and 2000 BCE, came to a few tens of thousands of people. By 1600 BCE, complex society here had vanished, and people had moved away for reasons unknown.

After the decline of Norte Chico, Andean people lived in small-scale communities until the rise of the so-called Chavín culture several centuries later. It lasted from about 900 to 200 BCE. Chavín people used irrigation to grow potatoes, quinoa, and, in smaller quantities, maize. They raised llamas for food. The main population center, Chavín de Huántar, unlike Norte Chico, stood high on the western slope of the Andes at an elevation of around 10,000 feet (3,100 m). Its central town housed about 3,000 people and included a temple complex and a big outdoor U-shaped theater. People came to Chavín from all over the Andes, presumably for religious purposes. Archeological finds suggest the religious rites included music played on trumpets made from conch shells, the use of hallucinogenic plants, and feasting on llama and guinea pig meat washed down with maize beer.

Chavín's influence stretched far and wide, to judge by the presence of its artistic motifs—snakes and jaguar heads figure prominently—on pottery and textiles occurring throughout the Andes. Chavín stone carvings show animals found only on the eastern side of the Andes, such as caimans, monkeys, and anacondas. Some obsidian tools at Chavín came from 300 miles (500 km) away in southern Peru.

The temple at Chavín de Huántar was built of limestone and granite brought from afar. That implies the coordinated labor of many people, and probably hierarchical society. Chavín burials confirm an extreme gulf between rich and poor. As with Norte Chico, there is no sign of warfare in Chavín sites.

Moche and Tiwanaku, ca. 200 BCE–700 CE About the same time that the Chavín culture fell into obscurity, roughly 200 BCE, another Peruvian people on the coast were beginning to build small cities: the Moche (or Mochicas). Like the Norte Chico people before them, the Moche combined irrigated farming—maize, squash, beans, and cotton—with the harvesting of seafood. They traded for potatoes grown in the mountains.

From about 200 CE to 600 CE, the Moche invested heavily in religious buildings, including earthen pyramids, and ceremonial objects. Political power here rested even more squarely than usual on religious authority. Graves of the elite were stuffed with precious objects, gold, silver, and items used in religious ceremonies. The poor, whose skeletons imply protein deficiency, were buried with little more than the rags they wore. The average height for adult Moche males was 5′3″ and for females 4′7″—the elite were a few inches taller, evidence of better diet.

Moche artwork, of which a good deal has survived in the form of pottery and wall paintings, emphasized religious power. Much of it shows ceremonial scenes of human sacrifice, dismemberment, and the drinking of blood. Moche sites show little evidence of war, so sacrificial victims probably weren't war captives. Perhaps the authority of the shaman-rulers was sufficient that they could sacrifice members of the Moche population. Unusually for ancient America, Moche art also shows human faces in realistic fashion. Uniquely for ancient America, much of it depicts explicit sex.

Moche centers were residential as well as ceremonial, and perhaps contained a few thousand people each at their height. The largest of them attained about 10,000 inhabitants. They all shared the same architecture, pottery, and burial styles, but probably were never politically united. By 550 CE or so they had begun to decline, and by 700 complex society here had disappeared—once again, mysteriously.

About the same time that the Moche were getting started on the coast of northern Peru, another urban society got under way. **Tiwanaku** (also spelled Tiahuanaco) was a city and an empire, connected to the Andean traditions but distinct in several ways, especially in its innovative, bountiful agriculture.

The city lay near the shores of Lake Titicaca, high on the Altiplano in what is now Bolivia. For most of the year, it's a dry, dusty, windy landscape, sunny and warm by day but chilly by night. Most rain falls in downpours between December and March. People were farming and raising llamas in the abundant grasslands before 1500 BCE. But large-scale intensive farming and city life date from about 100 CE. Early Tiwanaku shows some signs of Chavín influence in religion, and of coastal Peruvian traditions in art, but nothing from farther afield. By 500 CE, the city contained perhaps 15,000 to 30,000 people, the largest yet in the Andes.

Tiwanaku's economic basis differed from that of previous Andean centers. Llama herding was important, and control over the supply of llamas probably helped undergird the position of Tiwanaku's elite, approximately as control over supplies of horses helped some peoples in Eurasia to dominate others. Llamas weren't war animals like horses, but pack animals and a source of food and wool. Their dung was burned as fuel in a wood-short land and used as fertilizer especially for maize farming. Llamas were also important to religion and were sacrificed on important occasions. Long-distance trade, conducted in llama caravans, also supported the Tiwanaku elite. Fishing in Lake Titicaca helped feed everyone. But most important of all was the system of raised-field agriculture.

Farmers figured out how to cope with the frequent killing frosts, lack of moisture, and nutrient-poor soils by creating raised fields in the shallows along the marshy banks of Lake Titicaca. Their techniques resembled those of the amphibious agriculture of Mesoamerica. They piled up mud and muck to create rectangular islands on which they planted quinoa and potatoes. Yields were 10 to 20 times higher than farmers could get elsewhere in the Altiplano. Tiwanaku farmers maintained canals, stocked with fish, among these islands. The canal waters absorbed sunshine and warmth all day long and released it at night, keeping the immediate environment warmer and normally preventing the Altiplano's night frost from killing the crops. Recent experiments show that this form of farming in Lake Titicaca is more efficient, measured by yield per acre, than modern high-tech farming, and much more frost-proof. But, like similar systems in Mesoamerica, it took tremendous labor to create and maintain. And it depended on rain to keep the lake's water level up. Good rains after 200 CE helped float Tiwanaku farming for centuries, providing enough food for tens of thousands.

Tiwanaku, like Chavín, was a religious center. People came from near and far to take part in rituals and make their appeals to the gods in the presence of gargantuan statuary and altars. With no obvious economic or military reasons for its location, Tiwanaku's site was probably selected for its significance in some spiritual geography now invisible to us. Its monumental architecture impressed visitors and underscored the authority of its rulers. Some buildings include huge blocks of stone weighing 40 to 140 tons (bigger than the Olmec heads or pieces of Stonehenge), which were somehow transported from quarries across the lake and then dragged—without any help from animal power—several miles to sacred sites. Plenty of hard work also went into a ceremonial mound of packed earth about 430 feet (130 m) high, and stone statues nearly 22 feet (7 m) tall. The city's elite quarters also had a water and sewer system. The city was built for display, like a combination of Vatican City and Disney World, as one scholar put it.

Tiwanaku These stone walls surround the city of Tiwanaku, which flourished between around 500 and 700 CE. The anthropomorphic statue under the arch at the center of this image may have had religious significance. The heads of sacred animals and ancestors adorn the wall in the foreground.

Ordinary people must have thought highly of their priests and gods to build all this—unless they were forced to work on religious architecture and sewer drains. Residents of Tiwanaku worshipped several deities, the main one being a sun god. Priests from the elite families took responsibility for ensuring the good will of the spiritual forces, which required proper attention to rituals and ancestors. Rituals prominently featured sacrifices involving food and drink, animal and human blood; at times they required decapitating llamas or humans. As elsewhere in South America, psychedelic drugs played a big role in religious life, helping people see into the world of spirits. In this way, the shaman-rulers tried to safeguard the community against calamity and ensure the fertility of the raised fields, llama herds, and human families. Tiwanaku religion spread far and wide in the Andes and influenced subsequent Andean peoples.

At its height around 500 to 700 CE, Tiwanaku's power and economic influence reached northern Chile, lowland Bolivia, and throughout the Peruvian Andes. Its elite families had forged a fully fledged state, even an empire. There is evidence of colonization projects. The ruling class, a set of families interlocked by marriage, managed to control most long-distance trade, artisan production, and much of the food supply. Warehouses collected goods, including storable food, for distribution to those who showed sufficient loyalty to the rulers. Families produced food, ceramics, and textiles and shared them among kinfolk. There is no evidence of markets or marketplaces: political and religious authorities directed economic life beyond families and households. Tiwanaku's workshops churned out pottery and textiles for distribution throughout the region. The city imported obsidian from 200 miles (300 km) away in Peru and psychotropic drug plants from the eastern slopes of the Andes.

By 1100 CE, ancient Tiwanaku was empty. Population dispersed to small villages around the Altiplano and beyond. The leading explanation for Tiwanaku's end is protracted drought. Ice cores from nearby glaciers show reduced precipitation after 900 CE. By 1300, water levels of Lake Titicaca fell by about 40 to 50 feet (12–15 m), playing havoc with both agriculture and llama herding. With less food to distribute, the elites lost influence. Their rituals and sacrifices now seemed ineffective at bringing rain, fertility, and security, further undermining their legitimacy. Other factors too, invisible to archeology, might have played a role in the abandonment of Tiwanaku and the disappearance, for three centuries at least, of complex society on the Altiplano.

The American Webs

Farming peoples in Mesoamerica and the Andes built cities, states, and webs of interaction that by 1000 CE had attained considerable proportions. Of course, there were settlements and centers elsewhere in the Americas too. Mound builders toiled away in northern South America and southern North America. Irrigation agriculture communities developed in Bolivian Amazonia and in what is now Arizona. Some of these peoples also built substantial trade or exchange networks. Throughout lowland South America, from the Guyanas to Argentina, people on the region's rivers used the same kinds of pottery, implying sustained interaction. The mound builders of eastern North

America, especially those of the Hopewell cultural tradition (ca. 100 BCE–400 CE), exchanged obsidian, sharks' teeth, copper, and silver from Canada to the Caribbean shores. Compared to Mesoamerica or the Andes, these were thin, sparse webs of interaction, involving fewer people and no great centers of wealth and power. Some were probably fully independent webs, at least at first. Others were the farthest extensions of the larger and thicker webs centered on Mesoamerica and the Andes, as the spread of maize, ball courts, human sacrifice, and mound building indicate.

The two large webs shared many features, such as intensive agriculture and long-distance trade. They had some slender links between them, evidenced by the spread of maize, bows and arrows, and probably some techniques of copper working that in Ecuador and Mexico used similar techniques. Neither had iron working, deep-sea sailing craft, or crowd diseases—all widespread in Eurasia and northern Africa by 1000 CE, indeed by 1 CE. The Andes had livestock (llamas, alpacas) and metallurgy on a scale unknown in Mesoamerica. Mesoamerica had writing, which Andean societies did not.

Australia and Oceania

Australia and Oceania were just as isolated from the big Eurasian centers of population as were the Americas. But they were smaller spaces, with few good spots for settlement. They lacked some of the environmental features, such as domesticable large animals, that underpinned most complex societies elsewhere. More important, they were cut off from the major circuits of knowledge and innovation in the Americas and the Old World.

Australia

By the time groups of Northeast Asians had begun to migrate to North America, some Southeast Asians had already crossed open water to settle in Australia. We know even less about this colonization than about the first settlement of the Americas, but it happened at least 50,000 years ago. Sea level then was 400 feet (120 m) lower. People could walk to what is now the island of Bali. Beyond that, they had to take to the sea for about 100 miles (150 km) to reach Australia.

The first Australians, often called Aborigines, must have found their new home a strange one. They met kangaroos that were 10 feet (3 m) tall, lizards longer than canoes, carnivorous snakes that weighed as much as a man, wombats the size of rhinos, and flightless birds as heavy as a bear. Most of the big animals went extinct soon after people arrived in Australia, likely a result of hunting pressure and an increase in fire. Early Australians used fire to clear paths in the bush and to encourage the growth of species they could eat. Skillful use of fire increased the human food supply.

Soon after setting foot on Australia, people headed inland. About 50,000 years ago some had camped at Lake Mungo, now a dry lakebed. The oldest cremated human remains—Mungo Lady, as she's known to archeologists—were found here, dating to 40,000 years ago. Lake Mungo offered fish, shellfish, and waterfowl until it dried up about 20,000 years ago.

Life was hard in Australia during the depths of the last ice age. Temperatures averaged about 11 degrees Fahrenheit (6 degrees Celsius) cooler than today, and conditions were much drier. By 35,000 years ago, people had explored every corner of Australia and had made camps in all the appealing places. The end of the last ice age, about 10,000 years ago, brought wetter climate, more springs, lakes, and rivers—much better conditions for humans.

Better climate led to more people and more interaction, which helped spark a cultural revolution. It is dimly visible to us through art and archeology. Upon arrival, the first Australians had a tool kit similar to that prevailing in Eurasia 60,000 years ago. Their art consisted mainly of handprints and

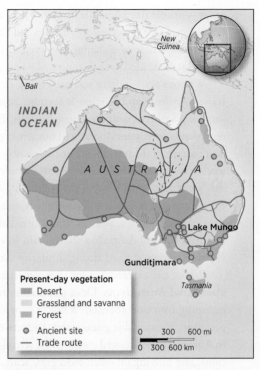

Australia The natural vegetation zones of Australia reflect rainfall and soil quality. Those shown here match today's conditions but approximate those of the last 8,000 years. Despite the challenge of aridity and the absence of pack animals, aboriginal Australians crisscrossed the continent with trade routes, carrying all goods themselves. They were almost fully isolated from human communities elsewhere in the world until 1788 CE.

modest geometric designs, some of which are still faintly visible on the walls of rock shelters. For 40,000 years they made only a few changes to their tool kit and artistic repertoire. But after about 10,000 BCE, their art shows new subjects, including hunters armed with spears and boomerangs, images of animals, and even pictures of warfare. They invented new blades and spear-points.

This cultural revolution extended to the economy. People turned more and more to strategic use of fire, sometimes called **firestick farming**. It wasn't farming in the sense of planting and domesticating species and didn't involve settlement. Australia had few plants or animals that could be domesticated. Rather, firestick farming meant the deliberate burning of landscape to promote the growth of edible plants. The purpose was to attract wild animals, especially kangaroos, that people could hunt. In addition, by about 6000 BCE in suitable places such as Gunditjmara—western Victoria today—people started to pile up stones creating weirs to trap eels and fish. They didn't domesticate eels, but they in effect raised them as one raises fish in a fishpond. The role of long-distance exchange also expanded. Pearls, flints, and quartz were valuable enough to be traded over distances of a few hundred miles.

Without texts—there was no writing in Australia—our knowledge of early Australians' culture and religion is sketchy. Some 200 to 250 related languages evolved, implying some separation among groups. But aboriginal Australian religion seems remarkably consistent. It featured numerous nature spirits and a "**dreamtime**"—a distant past when the world was born, accessible only to a fortunate few. According to this worldview, great spirits roamed Australia, creating everything one can see. Their paths are "songlines," crisscrossing the continent. All that one sees existed in spirit before it existed physically, and it will continue to exist in spirit after it is physically gone. Song, dance, ritual, stories, and law transmitted this knowledge over the generations. The animist beliefs of Australian aboriginals, like the shamanist core to religion in ancient North America, showed strong similarity across the continent.

Part of the explanation for this consistency in religion may lie in the mobility of **aboriginal Australians**. Once population reached sufficient levels, they were always bumping into one another. While it's impossible to know their numbers with any precision, a reasonable guess is that by 1000 CE there were 200,000 or 300,000 people in Australia. They moved continually, setting up camp for days or weeks in plush locations, and moving on when food grew scarce or other problems arose. They migrated seasonally to avoid the worst of wet and dry seasons, especially in eastern Australia where—over the last 5,000 years or so—El Niño cycles have often heightened the effects of flood and drought. Nowhere, it seems, did they build permanent settlements. This mobility, perhaps, helped to check the diversity of aboriginal culture and to encourage strong commonalities. It also discouraged the elaboration of material culture, because people had to carry everything with them on their migrations. They didn't bother with pottery, for example.

In some respects, we ought to consider ancient aboriginal Australians as the intellectual aristocracy of hunter-forager peoples. They survived for tens of thousands of years in a harsh land, much harsher than today, with the aid of only stone tools and fire. This required an exquisite knowledge of their environment, plants, animals, and weather.

It also required a canny knowledge of human nature and social relations, because no one could survive for long alone. Everyone had to navigate the currents of group life, securing help and cooperation through judicious use of reciprocity or threat.

The First Australians Cave art created in southeast Australia around 13,000 BCE depicts a dingo (right). Some dingoes were domesticated by ancient Australians.

And all this knowledge had to be transmitted from old to young with each passing generation.

Ancient Australians acquired the necessary knowledge without help from overseas. Some evidence exists of occasional contacts with peoples of what is now Indonesia, but only one outcome of this interaction was consequential. About 2000 BCE someone brought dogs, or perhaps just one pregnant female dog, to Australia. These were the ancestors of wild dogs, called dingoes, that joined humans as top predators in Australian ecosystems and still roam the continent. Dingoes figure in aboriginal art and lore. Some were domesticated and helped people hunt and stay warm at night. Up to and beyond 1000 CE, Australians forged their own societies and cultures, based on mobile foraging and hunting underpinned by detailed knowledge of their continent's ecosystems. Other than the import of the dingo, Australians' contact with outsiders had no discernible impact either on Australia or on the rest of the world.

Near and Remote Oceania

Southeast Asians and their descendants also first settled those parts of Oceania commonly called Melanesia, Micronesia, and Polynesia. A more useful division of the vast Pacific for present purposes emphasizes their position with respect to Southeast Asia: Near Oceania and Remote Oceania. Near Oceania consists of New Guinea, the Bismarck Archipelago, and the Solomon Islands. Remote Oceania extends as far as Hawaii and Easter Island. The biggest difference between Near and Remote Oceania is that people arrived in the former about 40,000 years ago and in the latter only 6,000 years ago.

The early history of Oceania is a history of pioneering by sea. People first arrived in New Guinea about 40,000 years ago and had settled in the Solomons by 15,000 years later. Then voyaging stopped. In Near Oceania, people could see the mountain tops of the next closest island. Once they reached the end of the Solomons chain, they couldn't see any more land and—prudently—called a halt.

After tens of thousands of years as hunters and foragers, people in New Guinea—as we've seen—made a transition to agriculture, perhaps 8,000 or 9,000 years ago. They developed irrigation and crop rotations that could support dense populations. The rugged topography of the New Guinea highlands discouraged interaction, and tremendous linguistic diversity emerged. Today, several hundred languages are spoken in New Guinea, and dozens more in the nearby Bismarcks and Solomons, where New Guinea voyagers went about 30,000 years ago. In time, New Guinea's styles of farming also spread to the Bismarcks and Solomons.

Farming in Near Oceania was always only one subsistence strategy among many. People also hunted, foraged, and fished. Outside of the cool New Guinea highlands, populations remained scattered and sparse, partly because of widespread malaria. Farming relied on root crops such as yams or taro. Most of the harvest didn't keep well, which made it hard for anyone to amass food, give it to supporters, and deny it to enemies.

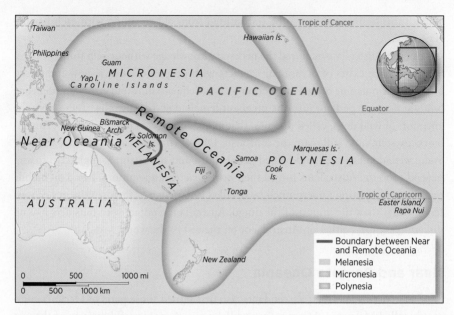

Oceania Immense distances separated the thousands of islands of Oceania, encouraging inhabitants to develop maritime skills and culture. Fishing and farming underpinned life on most islands. The division into Near and Remote Oceania more accurately reflects cultural differences and settlement history than do the older categories of Melanesia, Micronesia, and Polynesia.

Instead, people used food politically by throwing big parties and making conspicuous displays of their generosity, winning friends and supporters.

Scattered population and perishable harvests meant that in Near Oceania it was highly unlikely that any state or complex society would develop. The feast approach to cultivating political support works fine on a small scale, but it has much less potential reach than the ability to store, hoard, trade, distribute, or deny grain or any storable food. In any case, for this and perhaps other reasons, polities in Near Oceania remained small, and social complexity modest.

About 4000 BCE, a new wave of pioneers came to Near Oceania. They were Austronesian speakers and originated in Taiwan. (They were not Chinese—Taiwan had an indigenous population before it became Chinese.) The Austronesians developed seaworthy craft including 100-foot-long outrigger canoes. They acquired navigational skills far beyond those of anyone else of their time. They visited the coasts of New Guinea, the Bismarcks, and the Solomons, and some of them settled there.

About 1300 BCE, one group in the Bismarck Archipelago took things further. Known as the **Lapita** culture, and distinguished by their pottery style, they began to sail out into the open Pacific. Over the next several centuries, they settled island archipelagoes such as Fiji, Tonga, and Samoa, thousands of miles away. These were the first of the great Polynesian migrations, sketched in Chapter 3. Just about all of Remote Oceania was settled by peoples whose ancestry traced back to the Lapita culture. The island of Guam is a likely exception, however, as people there raised rice, which suggests that its settlers came from the Philippines.

Wherever they went, Pacific Islanders brought their life-support system, consisting of a handful of plants and animals. Their food crops were of Southeast Asian origin, notably yams, taro, bananas, breadfruit, and coconuts. They also brought chickens, dogs, and pigs. These were deliberate colonization attempts in which people were bringing resources with them rather than moving in hopes of finding new resources.

When settling a new island, voyagers usually found most of its natural features familiar. Reefs and lagoons offered abundant seafood. Tall islands, which in the Pacific means islands with the remnant of a volcano as opposed to low atolls, usually had flowing water suitable for irrigation. Colonization efforts typically thrived after initial adjustments, and populations rose quickly.

Many tall islands eventually supported dense populations of farming folk. For them, as for their Austronesian forebears, the central purpose in life was farming land, having lots of descendants, starting or continuing a lineage, and honoring one's ancestors. On formerly uninhabited islands, this was comparatively easy: there was no one already there to contest claims to land. In Remote Oceania, moreover, there was no malaria, the main limit to population growth in Near Oceania. (The reason is simple: the mosquitoes that carry malaria hadn't made it to the distant islands of Remote Oceania.) So populations in the Marquesas, Hawaii, and the other outposts were comparatively healthy.

Sooner or later, and it came sooner on atolls where water was often in short supply, population growth dwindled as it approached the limits of what an island could support. People quarreled over land and food, and some of them chose—or were obliged to choose—emigration as a solution. So people left, and with luck found a new island on which to settle.

Population growth encouraged not only migration but also political complexity. Especially on bigger islands such as Tonga or Hawaii, ambitious leaders with large followings found more scope to organize irrigation projects or the terracing of mountain slopes. They thereby acquired more authority and prestige, and their innovations helped to sustain, or re-start, population growth. States eventually evolved, the most notable being a kingdom on Hawaii—but only after 1500 CE.

Pacific Webs and Isolated Worlds

In those parts of Remote Oceania where islands were clustered together, networks of communication and exchange sometimes developed. By 300 CE, for example,

South Pacific Religion These stone statues, called tikis, are from the island of Hiva Oa in the Marquesas. Statues like these are found in many South Pacific cultures and are believed to represent deified ancestors.

inhabitants of the small island of Yap, in the Caroline chain, had forged links with many other islands of the western Pacific. Yapese pottery shows up in archeology on dozens of islands, and genetic data from today's populations indicate that women on other islands often had children by Yapese men. Whether these flows of pottery and genes represent a seaborne empire, a trading network, or something else entirely remains uncertain. These links centering on Yap persisted until well after 1000 CE.

Other parts of the vast Pacific, however, became isolated worlds unto themselves. Voyagers first arrived in Hawaii about 600 CE and eventually lost touch with everyone else. On Easter Island, or Rapa Nui, where settlers arrived about 700 CE, they not only lost touch with the wider world but forgot about it too: they believed they were the only people in existence.

Some tantalizing tidbits suggest that Pacific Islanders and South Americans somehow made contact long ago. The best evidence is the case of the sweet potato, a South American food crop that by 1000 CE was being cultivated in the Cook Islands, half an ocean away from the coast of Peru. Sweet potatoes cannot float or fly, and they don't have seeds that could be carried by birds. No one has ever suggested a plausible way for sweet potatoes to turn up in the Cook Islands except deliberate human action. Since the peoples of Peru used only reed boats and left no traces on islands out of sight from their beaches, the best guess is that Pacific Islanders visited South America and returned with sweet potatoes in the hulls of their giant canoes.

At the northernmost latitudes, evidence for ongoing connections between the Americas and Siberia is abundant. The Aleuts and Inuit arrived across the Bering Strait only about 3000 BCE. They stayed in touch with their Asian cousins, eventually bringing iron working, Asian-style pottery, the bow and arrow, and acupuncture to Arctic America. The bow and arrow, as we've seen, proved so useful that it spread throughout the Americas. Arctic America, in fact, was at least as connected to Arctic Asia as it was to more southerly parts of America. People moved back and forth freely from Siberia to Alaska in a circum-Arctic web based on sea voyages. Population in these frosty lands, however, remained extremely sparse.

So Pacific Islanders probably visited South America at least once, and Arctic peoples paddled back and forth between Siberia and North America. These linkages were small-scale, one-off or intermittent exchanges, nothing we could call webs of interaction, but they carried some consequences nonetheless. The sweet potato became an important crop on many islands, especially New Zealand (where it is called kumara), and the bow and arrow became an important technology for hunters and warriors in the Americas.

Conclusion

The Americas, Australia, and Oceania were the last sizable places on Earth settled by humankind. People migrated there, but their descendants had little or no contact with the rest of the world. They remained isolated from the big, dense, and interconnected populations that developed between China and Egypt until well after 1000 CE.

Nonetheless, in some places where population growth encouraged it, people in the Americas and Oceania developed their own webs of interaction. These were much larger scale in the Americas than in Oceania, involving millions rather than merely thousands of people. In the Americas, people also built their own forms of complex society. Nothing we could call complex society emerged in Australia or in Oceania until after 1000 CE. But in both Mesoamerica and the Andes, dense and hierarchical societies developed. They were founded upon distinct and highly productive farming systems that generated food surpluses that elites came to control.

People in both Mesopotamia and the Andes also created states and cities. These bore strong resemblances to states and cities elsewhere, with interlocking religious and political elites, armies, bureaucracies, and monumental architecture. But, for whatever reasons, unlike much of Asia, before 1000 CE the states and cities of the Americas rose and fell without much durable tradition. In Egypt, north India, or China, once states and cities emerged, that format of society never disappeared, even if specific cities or dynasties did. In the Americas, both complex society and webs of interaction flickered in and out of existence. In Oceania, thin webs flickered to life and then died away. In Australia, only the thinnest of webs existed. Only a few centuries later, as we shall see, all that changed.

||||||||||||||||||||||||||||||||||||||||||||||||||||||||||||||||||||||||||||||||||||||||||||||||||||||||||||||||||||||||||

Chapter Review

KEY TERMS

Oceania p. 345
Clovis points p. 348
raised-field agriculture p. 351
Olmecs p. 360
Maya p. 361
Norte Chico p. 369

Tiwanaku p. 371
firestick farming p. 375
dreamtime p. 376
aboriginal Australians p. 376
Lapita p. 378

REVIEW QUESTIONS

1. What parallels did the Americas share with centers of trade and connection in Eurasia and Africa? How was Oceania different?

2. Which two large transformations were occurring in the Americas when the first migrants arrived?

3. What features supported settled life in California and the Pacific Northwest?

4. What were the three main characteristics of farming in the Americas that made it distinctive?

5. In terms of the development of societies, why is it significant that Mesoamerica was the home of maize and the Andes region was the home of the potato?

6. In what ways were the Olmecs, Maya, Zapotecs, and Teotihuacán connected?

7. Describe the subsistence strategies of the Norte Chico, Chavín, Moche, and Tiwanaku peoples.

8. What caused the Australian cultural revolution around 10,000 BCE, and in what ways did it affect the Australian economy?

9. How did the mobility of ancient aboriginal Australians affect their religion and material culture?

10. What were the subsistence strategies of the inhabitants of Near Oceania, and how did the type of food they grew affect the development of complex society there?

11. What main trends did population growth on the islands of Oceania encourage?

12. How did the size and scope of linkages in the Americas compare to those in Oceania?

Go to INQUIZITIVE

to see what you've learned—and learn what you've missed—with personalized feedback along the way.

MATURING WEBS

200 to 1400 CE

Part 3 of this book, Chapters 11–15, traces changes in world history between about 200 CE, when durable links were first established all the way from China to the Mediterranean Sea (the Old World web), and 1400 CE, when the world's oceans were opened to routine navigation. The trans-Eurasian links of the Old World web weakened, but did not disappear, in the centuries after the Han dynasty fell in 220 CE and the Roman Empire declined. Then, in the seventh and eighth centuries, trans-Eurasian connections grew stronger again, by both land and sea, and in the thirteenth through fourteenth centuries stronger still. Although the Old World web contained perhaps 70 percent or more of humankind, it wasn't yet a truly global web. Millions of people in the Americas, southern and central Africa, and Oceania lived in smaller webs of their own making, which would link up with the Old World web, and with one another, only after 1450.

Key Themes

Several important—and interlinked—themes crop up time and again in these next five chapters. One, of central importance to the building of the world's webs, is transport and navigation. Sailors mastered the monsoon winds of the Indian Ocean as never before. Camel drivers learned how to cross the Sahara safely. The invention of the compass in the eleventh to twelfth centuries allowed people, especially at sea, to find their destinations more reliably than before.

A second theme, for which the invention of the compass also serves as an example, is technological change. People figured out how to make windmills, gunpowder, and paper during this period, and how to print texts on paper. These technologies changed the lives of ordinary people and the power of kings. Thousands learned these skills and adapted these technologies—from camel management to gunpowder to printing—as they spread throughout the Old World web.

A third theme, one to which technological change contributed, is agricultural improvement. In China, Southwest Asia, and Europe above all, diverse new farming practices after 900 CE raised yields substantially, enabling higher levels of population and bigger cities. Human numbers nearly doubled in this period, from about 200 to 250 million in the third century to about 375 to 425 million by 1450, of whom about 20 million (5 percent) lived in cities. Most of that demographic growth happened in a dynamic burst after 900 CE thanks to agricultural improvements, making the world more crowded, more urban, and more connected than ever before—especially but not only inside the Old World web.

That growth in population took place despite horrific epidemics and some disastrous climate events—a fourth theme. In the 540s, a sudden turn to cold conditions destroyed a few years of harvests. In some places, such as Southwest Asia, this climate shock was compounded by an epidemic of plague that killed millions. Seven centuries later, around 1250 a long cold spell set in that historians call the Little Ice Age—"little" compared to the ice ages of millions of years ago. It lasted until about 1850. Average temperatures fell by about 1.5 degrees Fahrenheit (1 degree Celsius) during the Little Ice Age, enough to bring more frequent harvest failures in northern lands and more searing droughts in arid ones. Then in the 1340s, bubonic plague erupted into a giant epidemic, now known as the Black Death, killing several tens of millions of people in one of humankind's most gruesome encounters with disease. The density of Eurasia's connections by the 1340s enabled the plague to spread more thoroughly, and faster, than would have been possible at any earlier time. This string of calamities—climate shocks and plague outbreaks—checked population growth temporarily, slowed the consolidation of the world's webs, and brought great suffering to millions.

A fifth theme is the simultaneous spread of certain cultural patterns—notably religions such as Buddhism, Christianity, and Islam—over sprawling spaces of the globe, mainly in Eurasia and the northern half of Africa. The strengthening connections of the Old World web enabled these religions to acquire more followers. As they did so the diversity of human religion, measured by the number of distinct religions, declined somewhat. If human cultural diversity could be reduced to a single index number (it can't!), it would show a slow increase from the dawn of humankind, as people spread out and went their separate ways, until some point between 200 and 1400 CE. Since that peak point, cultural diversity has declined. The success of a handful of religions in attracting most of humankind is the most conspicuous respect in which cultural diversity has dwindled in recent centuries.

From Regional to Global

The chapters in Part 3 explore these five themes, and more, primarily in regional contexts. Like Part 2, this one is organized mainly by region, though with the globalizing process of web integration ongoing. The chapters covering periods after 1450 are organized globally by time period and by theme. After 1450, the interactivity of the world reached such a level that an era of true global history had begun.

The West End of the Old World Web

NEW PATTERNS OF POWER AND FAITH

200 to 800

FOCUS QUESTIONS

1. How did climate change and disease affect the Sassanian and Roman Empires in this period?

2. What were the major shifts in the political landscape of the western Old World web between 200 and 800 CE?

3. How did Christianity and Islam emerge as major religions during this period?

4. What were the major economic and social changes across the Old World web in this period?

In the sixth and seventh centuries CE, two buildings capped by soaring domes rose over the landscapes of the eastern Mediterranean. Each stood as a monument to an ascendant faith and the power of a confident empire. One was Christian and Byzantine, the other Islamic and Umayyad. Christianity evolved from a fringe faith to a major religion largely through its adoption by rulers of the Roman Empire and Rome's successor state, the Byzantine Empire. Islam, a new religion forged in the seventh century, prospered in part through the efforts of the **Umayyad caliphate**, the first Muslim empire. The intertwined fates of these religions and empires form a central thread in this chapter.

The church of Hagia Sophia—Greek for "Holy Wisdom"—built between 532 and 537 CE, dominated Constantinople (today's Istanbul), the seat of the Byzantine Empire. The Hagia Sophia was at the time the world's largest building, and it remained the largest church or cathedral for a millennium. It stood on the site of earlier churches but exceeded them in every respect. Some 10,000 laborers and skilled craftsmen sweated to build the Hagia Sophia. It was an engineering and architectural marvel. Its daring dome, 182 feet (55 m) tall, seemed almost to float on air thanks to 40 arched windows that filled the church with light. Its airy interior featured towering columns of marble, hewn from quarries all over the empire. Glittering golden mosaics were soon added to the walls.

The emperor who oversaw the construction of the Hagia Sophia, Justinian (r. 527–565), built the church to symbolize the empire's unshakeable Christian faith and to demonstrate his own wealth and might. It was, like most examples of monumental architecture, an exercise in soft power, intended to inspire awe. Gazing upon the completed church, Justinian said he had outdone Solomon—a reference to the first Jewish temple in Jerusalem, which had been destroyed a thousand years before.

The Dome of the Rock stands on Temple Rock in Jerusalem—the site of the Jewish Second Temple, which replaced Solomon's temple and was itself destroyed by the Romans in 70 CE. The oldest surviving example of Islamic architecture, the Dome of the Rock was built during the years 687–691. Its base is octagonal, perhaps to reflect the Muslim belief that paradise has eight openings. Its wooden dome—the gold leaf was added later—looms 67 feet (20 m) tall, just a bit larger than that of the Church of the Holy Sepulchre in Jerusalem, built by the Roman emperor Constantine in the fourth century. Its architectural style reflected that of Byzantine churches and represented a radical departure from the spare

CHRONOLOGY

ca. 150–200 Start of shift to cooler, drier, unstable climate in Roman territory

165 Start of Antonine Plague

ca. 216–276 Lifetime of Mani

224–651 Sassanid Iran

249–260 Epidemic devastates Mediterranean populations

284–305 Reign of Diocletian

306–337 Reign of Constantine

324 Constantine establishes second Roman capital at Constantinople (Byzantium)

354–430 Lifetime of Augustine

370s Start of Hun migrations

409 Romans lose control of Britain

439 Romans lose control of Spain; Vandals take North Africa

476 End of western Roman Empire

527–565 Reign of Justinian

541 Outbreak of Justinianic Plague

570–632 Lifetime of Muhammad

622 Muhammad's flight from Mecca to Medina; year 1 in Muslim calendar

637–638 Arabs conquer Ctesiphon and Jerusalem

639–646 Arabs conquer Egypt

656–661 Civil war under Ali, fourth caliph

661–750 Umayyad caliphate

750–1258 Abbasid caliphate

Hagia Sophia The magnificent Hagia Sophia church that Justinian built in 532–537 still stands in present-day Istanbul. Converted to a mosque in 1453, it was a museum in recent times, but in 2020 reopened as a mosque.

simplicity that earlier Muslim builders had preferred. Legions of laborers from all over the Levant toiled on it, and the cost equaled seven years of tax receipts from Egypt.

The Dome of the Rock is not a mosque, and its original purpose remains unclear. The Umayyad caliph chiefly responsible for building it, Abd al-Malik (r. 685–705), surely intended to put Christian churches of Jerusalem in the shade, especially the Holy Sepulchre. He had it decorated with verses from Muslim scripture chosen to emphasize that Islam was the fullest and finest revelation of God's word. Its décor included crowns and other symbols of earthly power, a motif common in Persian and Byzantine artistic traditions. Everyone, whether Muslim, Jewish, or Christian, was supposed to conclude that Islam took precedence over other religions and that the Umayyad caliphate had replaced earlier dynasties.

This chapter concerns the tumultuous history of the western region of the Old World web, from Persia to Spain, from about 200 until about 800. It was a time when change outpaced continuity. The great empires of Rome and Persia teetered and, in most places, collapsed. Christianity spread around the Mediterranean, and then, after 630, Islam spread even faster. Politics, religion, and culture changed almost beyond recognition. Even the bedrock of societies—family life, farming routines—shifted a little.

We will consider Rome and Persia together. Their fates were closely connected, and contacts between the two empires were commonplace. Similarly, we will pair the spread of Christianity and the rise of Islam, as twin examples of the same phenomenon—the emergence of a monotheistic world religion. By now, the western region of the Old World web had become such an interactive space that it makes sense to try to see it whole.

In this period, the terms *Roman Empire* and *Persia* need some explanation. The Roman Empire split into eastern and western halves in the fourth century. Historians call the eastern Roman Empire by the late fifth century the Byzantine Empire, or Byzantium for short. Its rulers considered themselves Romans nonetheless. The term

Roman Empire here refers to the whole empire until 324 CE. After that date, I specify either eastern or western when using the term. But by 480, I use *Byzantine Empire* for the east, which was all that remained of the empire. This procedure may seem complicated, but it's the least confusing option. *Persia* means the Parthian Empire until 224 CE and thereafter the Sassanian Empire, led by a dynasty called the Sassanids. The Sassanids popularized the term *Iran* to refer to Persia. So, I will normally use *Iran* for times after 224.

Rome and Persia: Farming, Climate, and Disease

In 200 CE, the western region of the Old World web held between a quarter and a third of the world's population. The Roman Empire counted about 45 million people, down from perhaps 60 million before a nasty epidemic of the 160s called the Antonine Plague. Another 5 to 8 million lived in Persia. Neighboring lands under neither Roman nor Persian control were sparsely populated, so the grand total for the western region stood around 65 to 75 million of a global total of perhaps 200 million. As always with population figures from the pre-modern world, these estimates could be well off the mark.

In Roman territory at 200 CE, about 8 to 10 percent of the people lived in cities. Rome itself had housed 1 million residents before the Antonine Plague, maybe 750,000 in 200, and 500,000 in 400. Alexandria, in Egypt, was the empire's second-largest city, less than half the size of Rome. In Persia, the **Sassanid dynasty** founded several new cities after 224, and their Mesopotamian breadbasket contained many old ones, but even so it's unlikely that more than 10 percent of the population lived in cities.

Farming

In both empires, farming remained the staff of life. The Sassanids invested heavily in the irrigation works of Mesopotamia and encouraged farming everywhere. Archeological surveys suggest their efforts expanded farmland by 50 percent. Farmers relied on traditional crops, mainly the cereal grains of wheat, barley, and rye, supplemented by chickpeas and lentils, and orchard crops such as figs, dates, and grapes. But under Sassanid rule, some new and useful crops were introduced: apricots, olives, cotton, and sugarcane—the latter two coming from India. Rice, already grown in southernmost Mesopotamia, spread more widely in Sassanian times.

The most significant innovation in farming was the widespread use of irrigation to support alfalfa (lucerne). Alfalfa is a forage crop, highly nutritious for cattle and horses. It is probably native to Iran. It does not need irrigation but yields much better with it. Like other legumes, its roots harbor microbes that can take nitrogen from the

Commercial Agriculture Third-century mosaics from Roman Gaul (modern France) show laborers working to harvest olives and then to press them into olive oil. New and improved trade networks enabled farmers to make a living by exclusively farming this hardy tree crop.

air and lodge it in the soil, improving soil fertility for other plants. So alfalfa was grown in rotation with cereals or vegetables, and this practice raised their yields. More alfalfa meant more and better animal feed, and indirectly (via nitrogen fixation) more human food. The latter made it easier to supply cities as bulwarks of Sassanid power and culture. The former made it easier to maintain cavalry.

Roman farming stayed prosperous in most places, but less innovative than Persia's. The gradual spread of markets and transport, a legacy from classical Greece and Carthage, encouraged ever-greater specialization. This commercialization of agriculture enabled people to make a living in stony hill country where only olives would grow. During the third and fourth centuries CE, this process was still advancing, and Roman agricultural output was still growing, especially in the farther reaches of the empire: Syria, North Africa, and Britain. In Italy itself, by contrast, food production slumped—perhaps due to loss of tax exemptions, perhaps to adverse climate change.

In Egypt, Rome's primary breadbasket, the Nile floods became less reliable in the late second century because of climate shifts. The empire's cities and armies became more reliant on food supplies from places other than Egypt and Italy. The most important agricultural innovation took place in the eastern empire, in the sixth century if not before, when Byzantine villagers in northern Syria began to raise silkworms. These changes in Roman and Byzantine agriculture had smaller impacts than those in Sassanian Iran. The growing specialization inadvertently deepened a vulnerability for Italy and the city of Rome: if Rome's empire lost access to its distant provinces, the city of Rome and Roman armies would starve.

Disease Outbreaks and Climate Change

Just about everyone, whether in Roman or Persian territory, became more vulnerable to epidemics. This resulted from both denser settlement and continuing urbanization on the one hand, and further development of long-distance connections on the other. One of the consequences of the tightening Old World web was faster and wider circulation of infections. Beginning in 165, as we've seen, the Antonine Plague (possibly an outbreak of smallpox) killed off 10 to 15 percent of the Roman Empire's population. During the years 249–260, another epidemic ripped through the Mediterranean. Cyprian, a bishop in Carthage at the time, observed that "the human race is wasted by the desolation of pestilence." Such disease disasters, long a feature of life in densely settled parts of the world, came more frequently to the Roman (and probably Persian) realms, and on bigger scales, after the late second century. The tighter networks of transport put in place mainly by Rome helped spread the outbreaks, and they, more than anything else, held population in check.

Climate shifts and shocks also weakened Rome after 150 CE. Through the last century of the Republic and the early years of the empire, most Roman regions prospered in part because of an unusually stable, warm, and moist climate. Those conditions were especially favorable for Rome's northern provinces: vineyards thrived in Britain. The Nile floods were consistently good, rarely too low or too high, so Egypt pumped out grain to the empire. But after 150 CE, and especially after 200, a cooler, dryer, and more unstable climate brought disappointing harvests. Climate change led to more hunger, less tax revenue, and less military manpower, all of which contributed to the fiscal and military crises the empire endured in the third century CE. Climate conditions improved for Roman agriculture in the fourth and fifth centuries, although never achieving the stability enjoyed during the early empire.

Unruly nature brought unprecedented calamities in the sixth century. Beginning in 535 or 536, the whole Northern Hemisphere experienced the sharpest climate shock in the previous 2,000 years. Written accounts from Ireland, Byzantium, and China speak of dark sky at noon and snow in midsummer. A Byzantine chronicler wrote that "the sun became dark and its darkness lasted for one and a half years." Temperatures plummeted, and rainfall diminished. Tree rings show that until 551, trees in Eurasia scarcely grew at all. The likely cause was a cluster of big volcanic eruptions in Alaska and Mesoamerica, between 535 and 539, that filled the sky with tiny dust particles (sulphate aerosols), partially blocking sunshine in the Northern Hemisphere. The likely consequences included repeated harvest failures and, in places such as Ireland and northern Italy, famine. In Sweden, more vulnerable than most places to deep cold, three-quarters of all villages were abandoned about this time.

Just as the dust veils were lifting, another calamity hit. Plague, an extremely lethal disease, broke out in Egypt in 541. The Justinianic Plague, named after Justinian, the Byzantine emperor at the time, probably originated in Central Asia or northwest China, where plague had long circulated among wild rodents. Travelers and traders unwittingly brought it to Egypt along the threads of the Old World web, probably over both land and sea. Once loose in the lands of the eastern Mediterranean, it killed about a quarter of the population (some experts say half) within a few years. This was more severe than the Antonine Plague, or indeed any other epidemic in prior recorded history. One eyewitness, a historian named Procopius, wrote that it killed up to 10,000 people a day in the Byzantine capital of Constantinople, that bodies piled up in the streets like stacks of hay, and that it threatened to extinguish humankind.

This last claim was exaggeration. Plague affected people living in port cities (such as Constantinople) more than anyone else, because plague-carrying rats swarm to ships and cities, attracted by stored grain. Cities in general suffered more than villages, and villagers more than mobile herders. The urbanized societies, such as Byzantium and Sassanian Iran, suffered more than others. Plague appears also to have hit Italy hard. Pope Gregory in Rome, then a town of maybe 50,000 people, was sure the world was coming to an end shortly. The Justinianic Plague receded after a few years, but plague bouts kept flaring up every decade or so until about 750. An outbreak in 745 killed 25 to 35 percent of the population of several Arab cities.

The twin disasters—climate shocks and plague—together cast a long shadow. The enormous loss of life in the more urbanized societies tipped the military balance in favor of tribal and nomadic peoples, probably assisting in the demise of Sassanian Iran and the decline of Byzantium. The plague surely contributed to the decay of urban life from 540 to 750, especially around the Mediterranean, and to two centuries of extremely bad health.

Politics and War in Iran and Rome

Between 200 and 800 CE, some big political changes unfolded in the western region of the Old World web. A short version might be this: The Sassanian Empire rose and fell; the Roman Empire shifted to the east; and new dynasties professing a new religion, Islam, overshadowed them both.

Sassanid Iran, 224–651

The Sassanid dynasty started its political career as a tribe from southwestern Iran. We know far less about them than the Romans, because fewer texts survive and recent politics in the region has limited archeological work.

In the second century CE, Parthian power had weakened owing in part to Roman military pressure. The Sassanids finished off the Parthian dynasty and proclaimed their own in 224. They consciously modeled themselves on the Achaemenids, the dynasty of Cyrus and Darius, imitating their artwork. Explicitly anti-Greek, they opposed the Hellenization under way in Persia since Alexander five centuries before.

The Sassanids made Persia—or Iran, as they called it—into a great power, as Cyrus had done long before. Their rulers considered themselves the "king of kings," equaled only by the emperors of Rome and China. Their investments in agriculture, especially the irrigation canals of Mesopotamia, paid off in enhanced revenues. So did their encouragement of long-distance trade on land and sea. Their merchants sailed the Indian Ocean world, from East Africa to India. Sassanid coins turn up as far away as China, implying linkages all across Eurasia. Like every empire, Sassanian Iran converted economic wealth into military power, and did it successfully enough to endure for more than 400 years.

The Sassanian military had to face diverse threats, from Roman infantry to Central Asian horsemen. Beginning in 230, they fought several wars against Roman armies and enjoyed frequent success. They almost always held on to their Mesopotamian provinces, which were by far their richest and home to their capital, Ctesiphon (near today's Baghdad). Their heavily armored cataphracts—armored riders on armored horses—equipped with lances (an innovation) and supported by war elephants imported from India, proved highly formidable against anyone's infantry. Sassanian armies also developed expertise in laying siege to

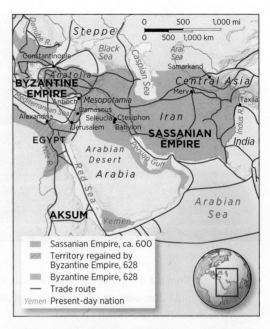

The Sassanian Empire, 224–651 CE Like the Achaemenids and Parthians before them, the Sassanid dynasts built a formidable state by controlling both the fertile farmlands of Mesopotamia and the Iranian plateau, which was well suited for grazing and specifically raising horses. The Sassanian Empire's military strength posed a stern challenge to the Roman—and later, Byzantine—Empire. Its relations with India were more peaceful, featuring much cultural exchange.

enemy fortifications. Mainly learned from their Roman enemies, siege craft helped Sassanian forces hold key cities and occasionally take Roman ones in Syria. At times, they extorted large sums of gold from the Romans in exchange for peace. When most successful in war they extended their rule to Egypt, eastern Anatolia, and parts of Central Asia. The high-water marks of Sassanian political success came in the late third, the late fourth, and the very early seventh centuries.

In addition to fighting frequent wars on its western frontier, Sassanian Iran had to keep nomadic tribes from the Eurasian steppe in check. Like China and northern India, Iran and Mesopotamia often looked tempting to the horse nomads. When they were desperate or they sensed weakness, the nomads used their superior mobility to swoop in and pillage. The Sassanians usually fared well in protecting their population and wealth, but a big exception came in 469, when a group of steppe raiders (often called the Hephthalite Huns) captured an emperor and his harem, demanding both gold and territory before returning them. Luckily for Iran, the Central Asian tribes

Sassanian Power The Sassanian rulers used art to represent their military and political strength. This rock relief, made at the height of Sassanian power in the mid-third century, shows the Roman emperor Valerian surrendering to the Sassanid emperor Shapur I in 260 CE.

and the Romans could not easily coordinate simultaneous campaigns. Sassanian diplomats could play one pastoral tribe against another, a practice at which they, like the Achaemenids before them, excelled.

The Sassanid dynasty's luck ran out in the seventh century. After a spurt of conquests and near-total destruction of their enemies, wars in the west went badly for them in the 620s, and their richest lands were devastated by Byzantine armies. Revenues plummeted, and internal quarrels turned to assassinations, civil war, and instability. In one four-year span, the empire had five rulers. By 632, what remained was governed by a boy-emperor who failed to command allegiance. Arab warriors fighting under the banner of a new faith, Islam (see below), proved irresistible. Sassanid authority crumbled. By the 640s, Sassanid forces, such as they were, scampered off toward Central Asia. The last king of kings was murdered for money by a miller in an oasis town in 651, an inglorious end to the long career of the Sassanids. His sons fled to China.

The Fall of Rome in the West, 200–476

The fate of the Roman Empire took a different course. Half of it fell, and the other half lasted another thousand years. Let's start with the fall. Few subjects have fascinated scholars as much as the fall of Rome. They have come up with hundreds of explanations, ranging from the poisoning of the elite from lead-lined aqueducts to a loss of martial vigor brought on by Christianity. In fact, the western part of the Roman Empire was accidentally toppled by people trying to take it over and preserve it for their own benefit.

Crisis in the Third Century   As we've seen, in 200 CE the Roman Empire sprawled from Britain to Iraq, a powerful state matched only by China of the Han dynasty (206 BCE–220 CE). But its fortunes quickly decayed. For two centuries, Rome had been victorious in its wars, which proved reliable sources of loot, glory, and captive slaves. But by the 230s, Rome's enemies, especially in Iran, were stronger. The early Sassanids proved much more formidable than their Parthian predecessors. And the Germanic tribes north of the Danube and east of the Rhine—undisciplined barbarians in Roman eyes—had become much more dangerous neighbors.

In effect, these tribes had become less egalitarian and fragmented, more cohesive and hierarchical, than before. In large part, it was contact with the Romans that brought these changes about. Roman trade goods helped to create or strengthen political elites among the tribes, and so did Roman diplomacy, which always sought individual leaders to bargain with. Over time, the **Germanic tribes**—Goths, Vandals, and Franks, among others—organized in larger confederations with more effective top-down command, and perhaps a stronger sense of ethnic identity as well. So their ability to mount effective attacks across the frontiers improved.

These military challenges required a vigorous Roman response. But the mines of Spain ran low on silver and gold, and emperors inflated the value of the coinage. Military manpower became harder to pay for. Bandit gangs roamed some provinces, especially Gaul, destroying property and siphoning revenue away from the state. Unpaid troops became unruly. Many army commanders tried to make themselves emperor, and some succeeded. From 235 to 284, Rome had 51 emperors or co-emperors. Almost all died violently, many of them murdered by their own troops. Civil war became the normal condition, further emboldening Rome's enemies.

Rome's military helped the empire to recover from this deep political crisis. Its navy remained supreme on the Mediterranean and along the Danube and the Rhine. Neither the Sassanians nor the Germanic tribes could contest Roman naval power. Its fortifications on the European frontiers, if amply supplied, could still hold out indefinitely. Rome's infrastructure of roads and harbors was so well built that even if poorly maintained it could still serve its purpose. The empire still had a weapons industry, and when revenues sufficed it could still churn out disciplined, trained, and well-equipped armies. By the 270s, the worst of the crisis had passed. In 283, an emperor even managed to sack the Sassanian capital of Ctesiphon—whereupon he was killed by a lightning bolt. His would-be successors launched another round of civil war.

Diocletian and Constantine That instability ended when a military man, Diocletian, became emperor (r. 284–305) and managed to re-impose unity and order with a spate of reforms. An upstart of humble background, he re-fashioned and expanded the army and bureaucracy to lower the odds of someone else seizing power (as he had done), making both institutions more obedient to him. He reformed the empire's tax system and coinage. He considered rampant greed a source of weakness and tried to fix prices for everything from silk underwear and lions to the salaries of teachers of rhetoric. (One hundred lines of writing by a scribe, decreed Diocletian, was worth the same as 12 haircuts, or one-tenth of a fattened pheasant.)

Although the price fixing did not work well, Diocletian achieved some stability during his long reign, helped by a favorable peace with the Sassanians. Unlike most of his fellow emperors, he was not murdered on the job but retired to raise cabbages at his villa. The empire, in better health than at any time in the previous 150 years, still stretched from the Sahara to Scotland, and from Syria to Spain.

Only one subsequent emperor, **Constantine** (r. 306–337), was able to hold the empire together. Born into the military and political elite, Constantine rose rapidly to positions close to Diocletian. Upon the latter's retirement, the inevitable succession

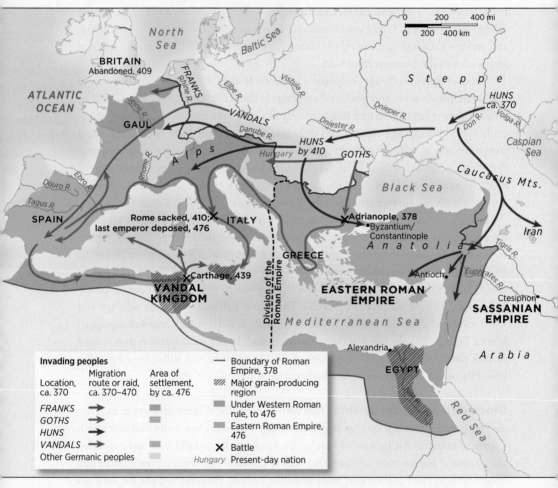

The Roman Empire, ca. 370–476 CE After Constantine's reign, the center of gravity of the Roman Empire shifted away from Italy to the east, and Constantinople gradually became more important than the city of Rome. In the west, Germanic peoples by the fifth century had acquired sufficient skills and numbers to take over much of what had been Roman territory. Rome could no longer muster the money and manpower to defend itself.

struggles began. After winning glory in campaigns on the empire's frontiers, in 324 Constantine emerged triumphant in civil wars against rival would-be emperors.

He judged the empire too large to govern solely from Rome—a place Diocletian had scarcely visited—and created a second capital in the Greek city of Byzantium, thereafter called Constantinople (today's Istanbul). It lay closer than Rome to the Iranian and Danube frontiers, where an emperor most needed to be. Thereafter, the Roman Empire had two halves, one mainly Latin-speaking and governed from Italy, and the other increasingly Greek-speaking and ruled from Constantinople. Both halves slowly became Christian. As we will soon see, Constantine himself accepted the faith during his wars.

Economic and Military Decline Upon Constantine's death in 337, his sons fought for power, launching a long period of intermittent civil war spiced by religious turmoil. A campaign against Iran ended badly for the Romans, and in 378 a battle against the Goths, one of the Christianized Germanic tribes, ended worse: two-thirds of the army was killed in Rome's worst defeat since the time of Hannibal 590 years earlier. The eastern and western halves of the empire often feuded and sometimes fought. Gradually, it became too costly to maintain garrisons in the distant provinces, and the empire began to shrink. Britain was cut loose first in 409. By 439, Rome had lost control of Spain and the breadbasket region of North Africa, overrun by Vandals, another originally Germanic tribe.

The fundamental weakness of the empire at this point was the same as during its third-century crisis: it lacked the money to pay enough men to defend its borders. Despite the economic and fiscal reforms of Diocletian and Constantine, poorer harvests, reduced trade, and renewed inflation all hampered the empire's ability to pay its army. As security weakened around the edges and in rebellious regions, trade declined further, and the fragile economic benefits of specialization and exchange crumbled. For centuries, the Roman Empire had enjoyed the fruits of a commercial economy in which farmers raised the crops that suited their lands best, and craftsmen developed specialized skills. Everyone came together through money and markets to exchange what they had for what they wanted. But this arrangement hinged on peace and order; and when disorder prevailed, the economy shrank and imperial revenues plummeted. The economic strength of the empire for so many centuries—its commercial complexity, which had sustained its formidable military against so many challenges—now became a source of weakness.

The money problem was a military problem because imperial armies depended directly on tax revenues. There were no central banks from which to borrow. There were virtually no other branches of government to starve in order to feed the military; it already accounted for the great bulk of government spending. Each year's tax haul determined how big the next year's army could be. So economic decline translated into military weakness within months.

The Huns and the Germanic Tribes   The borders became harder to defend after the 370s because the Germanic tribes were desperate to cross the Rhine and Danube to get away from formidable bands of horsemen known as the Huns. The Huns migrated from somewhere east of the Volga River. They soon began to attack everyone they could reach in Iran, and in central and southeastern Europe. Goths, Vandals, and Franks fled in fear, infiltrating or invading Roman territory sometimes as refugees, sometimes as plunderers. The movements of the Huns upset the geopolitical balance in western Eurasia, just as the rise of Achaemenid Persia, or of Rome, had done centuries before.

The migration of the Huns formed the first large-scale example of a pattern that would last a thousand years: the westward migration of mostly Turkic-speaking peoples of the steppe. (Turkic is a language group that includes modern Turkish, Uzbek, Kazakh, Tatar, and a dozen other languages.) Turkic-speakers also rode into China and India at times, often as invaders. Sometimes they were escaping long-term drought cycles, sometimes political violence—and probably in many cases both at once. They paused if they found good pasture or some opportunity for trade or plunder. Their movements were a bit like a bus: at every stop, some people got off and others joined, sometimes Turkic-speakers, sometimes not. So the farther west they went, the more polyglot and multicultural their society became. But their political core was always horsemen skilled in the arts of mounted warfare.

The Huns and other mobile pastoralists preferred grasslands in the western steppe, today's Ukraine and southern Russia. At times they kept going as far west as Hungary, where the grassland ended. Farther west the land was a patchwork of forests and fields, not suited to herders and their animals. The Huns were unusual not only for being the first of many peoples to make this trip, but also for raiding far into western and southern Europe.

When not fleeing the Huns, the Germanic tribes were often invited into Roman territory. Roman governors might hire them to fight for Rome against other tribes, or for one set of Romans against another in civil wars. Each such invitation was a rational, cost-cutting example of outsourcing. The tribesmen were cheaper than Roman legions. Collectively, however, these invitations were self-defeating. The Germanic peoples could not easily be controlled, and often they took by force what they were not freely given. Unlike previous generations of foreigners recruited into the Roman military and eventually Romanized, encouraged to marry (poor) Roman women, and granted citizenship, the Goths, Vandals, and Franks were allowed to maintain their own communities and were often discouraged from embracing Roman ways. Their rough-and-tumble conduct further eroded security within the empire and undercut its economic base. The tribes had no intention of destroying the western Roman Empire. To the contrary, they wanted to enjoy the comforts and relative safety it afforded. But in helping themselves to land and its revenues, they gradually killed the geese that laid the golden eggs.

In the early fifth century, Germanic tribes settled here and there throughout the western empire. They set up little states, demanding protection money from Roman authorities and fighting among themselves just as regularly as did the Romans. Other tribes accepted Roman gold to stay away. In 410, one group of Goths sacked the city of Rome itself, which had been free from foreign attack for 800 years. Roman slaves poured out of the city to help the Goths.

When Vandals took over North Africa and captured a Roman fleet in the harbor of Carthage in 439, the western empire lost both a crucial source of surplus grain and the inestimable advantage of peaceful seaborne trade. The Mediterranean Sea after Pompey had suppressed piracy in 67 BCE had been a tranquil Roman lake, a highway for commerce in all directions. Now the sea became a no-man's-land. The benefits of a commercial economy became still harder to reap, and increasingly each little region depended on its own resources—disastrous for areas that did not grow much food.

In the 450s, Rome's death spiral sped up when one of the Huns' chieftains, Attila, united several factions. He instantly launched a campaign of looting, sacking, and pillaging that took him to the walls of Constantinople, where an emperor bribed him to go elsewhere. In 451–452, he contemplated taking Rome itself and was dissuaded only when summer malaria savaged his forces and the Christian pope offered him all the gold he could muster. After Attila's death in 453, his confederation promptly splintered and ceased to terrorize Europe. So while the Huns battered the remaining dregs of the Roman Empire, they did not end it. When the end of the western empire finally came, traditionally dated 476, at the hands of a group of Goths, hardly anyone noticed. There was virtually nothing left to fall. Rome ended with a century of whimpers, not a bang.

The eastern empire survived, despite repeated hammerings by Goths and Huns. It had the advantages of great walls around its capital of Constantinople. Its navy kept open the routes to and from Egypt, the source of grain for cities and armies. Its revenues shrank, but modestly compared to the western empire's fiscal collapse. And eastern emperors wisely limited the degree to which they outsourced defense to Germanic tribes—especially after 399, when one tribe briefly threatened the capital. The eastern Roman Empire, known to historians as the Byzantine Empire, lasted until 1453. Its inhabitants called themselves Romans to the end.

The Byzantine Empire, 500–800

The **Byzantine Empire** included Egypt, the Levant, Anatolia, and the Balkans. In 500 CE, its population numbered about 20 million. Its cities were many and prosperous, concentrated in Egypt, Syria, Palestine, and western Anatolia. As long as it could rely on the surplus grain of Egypt and, to a lesser extent, Syria, it could maintain cities and armies. Its capital, Constantinople, sat astride the route that links the Black Sea to the Mediterranean, one of the most strategic locations on Earth. The city's gigantic walls (portions are still visible today) kept it safe from many assaults. It could be supplied by sea, so no sieges could starve it out as long as the Byzantine navy remained strong. Indeed, it outlasted a dozen sieges.

Constantinople had symbolic strengths too. Earlier emperors had built it up into a great city, with monumental architecture, streets, cisterns and water systems, and a hippodrome for chariot racing that rivaled Rome's. The emperors in Constantinople considered themselves the champions of Christianity and heirs to the entire Roman Empire. They thought the western part only temporarily escaped their control, and they sought to re-conquer it. They had no luck in that quest until the reign of **Justinian** (r. 527–565).

Justinian came from a peasant family in the Balkans but as a child was brought to the capital and received an education, including the study of Roman history and the Greek language. He spent much of his youth following the chariot races at the hippodrome, but at age 36 he helped vault one of his uncles from the imperial guard to the emperor's throne. Justinian quickly showed himself adept in palace politics and military affairs. That came in handy, because his elderly uncle soon died.

Despite a scandalous marriage to Theodora, a dancer and actress, Justinian became emperor himself in 527. He needed and got exemption from a law prohibiting marriage between high officials and actresses. Justinian and Theodora shared low origins and high ambition. Although holding opposing views about which sort of Christianity was the right one, they made a strong team. They were far from popular and barely survived riots in 532, perhaps only through the resolve and street smarts of Theodora. According to one account, she kept her head under pressure when Justinian wanted to flee the rioters. His mind changed by her advice, Justinian's troops massacred thousands of his opponents and he kept his throne.

In 533, Justinian launched a series of conquests that nearly re-constituted the old empire. His good fortune included the services of a magnificent general, Belisarius, who led Byzantine armies in the field and had organized the massacre of rioters in the capital the year before. He conquered (or re-conquered, as Justinian saw it) the

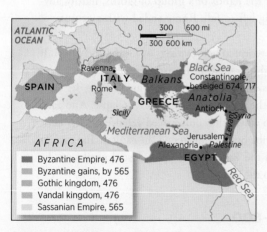

The Byzantine Empire, 476–565 CE After the final eclipse of the western Roman Empire, its successor state, the (mainly) Greek-speaking Byzantine Empire based in Constantinople, carried on Roman traditions for another millennium. Under vigorous leadership in the sixth century it recovered territories in Italy and North Africa, but its strength lay in Egypt, the Levant, Anatolia, and the Balkans.

North African kingdom of the Vandals. He added several large Mediterranean islands to that, and eventually all of Italy. For good measure, Belisarius drove marauding tribes back across the Danube, consolidating the empire's northern frontier in the Balkans. Byzantine (re)conquests almost ended then, although in Justinian's later years his armies also brought southern Spain back into the empire. Belisarius and Justinian both died in 565.

Justinian's ambition had strained the treasury. In addition to his wars, he built his great church in Constantinople, the Hagia Sophia, and employed teams of scholars to codify Roman law. He did all this in a time of diminishing resources (remember the natural disasters that began in 536), leaving his successors less to work with. They gradually lost North Africa, Italy, and southern Spain. They fought back-and-forth campaigns in the Balkans against tribes invading from the north. And they fought on the eastern front against Sassanid Iran, which they helped to bring down. After the 640s, the Byzantine Empire fought a rising power in Southwest Asia—the Arabs, of whom more shortly.

The Byzantines lost Egypt to Arab conquerors in 642, a critical defeat. Without Egypt's grain and revenues, the Byzantines were often on the defensive. Arab armies pushed into Anatolia and besieged Constantinople twice, in 674–678 and 717–718. On the latter occasion, the Byzantines survived thanks to a new military invention of theirs, Greek fire (flaming liquid squirted at enemy ships), and a storm that sank the Arab fleet. After the loss of Egypt's grain surplus in 642, the eastern empire was lucky not to follow the path of the western empire after it lost North Africa in 439.

The empire teetered on the brink of collapse, revived, and teetered again in the centuries ahead. Its army remained formidable, especially its cataphract units, modeled on the Iranians'. So did its navy. But deprived of Egypt after 642, the emperors had trouble paying troops and suffered recurrent mutinies and rebellions to go along with frequent religious schisms, palace intrigues, and usurpations. Every emperor lost territory, population, and revenue. In 800, Byzantium's empire consisted of no more than Anatolia, bits of Greece, the island of Sicily, and the southernmost tip of Italy. In 540, it had been the greatest power in western Eurasia and northern Africa, with roughly twice the population and resources of its nearest rival, Sassanid Iran. By 800, it was one of several middling powers, beset by marauding tribes and upstart neighboring kingdoms.

Religions on the Rise

The western end of Eurasia, specifically the Levant and Arabia, spawned two of the world's most successful and enduring religions—Christianity and Islam. Each now has more than a billion followers. Only north India, which gave rise to both Hinduism and

Buddhism, can offer a parallel in world history. Both Christianity and Islam followed in the traditions of earlier monotheisms.

Zoroastrianism and Manichaeism

Zorastrianism's origins are obscure. It arose around the prophecies of Zoroaster, who lived in eastern Iran sometime between the tenth and sixth centuries BCE, and sacred texts such as the *Avesta*, which had parallels to the early Vedas. Its popularity rose under the Achaemenid emperors, some of whom supported it. **Zoroastrianism** was a monotheistic religion, and many scholars think it and early Judaism influenced one another. It included concepts of a single creator-god (Ahura Mazda), angels, and the existence of human choice between good and evil. Its texts forecast a savior, born to a virgin, who would have the power to resurrect the dead. It added notions of heaven and hell, and divine judgment. After Achaemenid Persia conquered Egypt in the sixth century BCE, Zoroastrianism borrowed the concept of final judgment—one of several respects in which Egyptian culture influenced Persia. Of all world religions, Zoroastrianism was distinctive in that its priests and texts endorsed sex and marriage among siblings and between nieces and uncles, elsewhere normally regarded as incest and repugnant. The practice seems to have died out in the ninth or tenth century CE.

The Zoroastrian creed was one of several in circulation in the Achaemenid Empire, but its priesthood, the magi, enjoyed royal support. It became a genuine state religion under the Sassanids, who championed all things native to Iran and held Christianity and other creeds in contempt. Although almost eliminated in Iran in the centuries after the Sassanids' fall, Zoroastrianism still survives, with about 200,000 adherents worldwide today. The largest group, the Parsis, live in western India.

Manichaeism once rivaled Christianity and Zoroastrianism for the allegiance of millions. It derived from the preaching of Mani, born in Iran (probably in 216 CE) just

Zoroastrianism A Persian rock relief dated to around 235 CE shows the Zoroastrian god Ahura Mazda (right) assenting to the coronation of the Sassanian king Ardashir I by giving him a symbolic ring.

before the Sassanids took power. His parents were members of an obscure Christian cult. Starting at age 12 he had visions and within a few years had begun to preach an innovative blend of Christianity, Zoroastrianism, and Buddhism. Mani's teachings emphasized a code of conduct of restraint, non-violence, honesty, fasting, weekly confessions, and chastity if at all possible. Manichaeism's theology featured a permanent struggle between good and evil, light and darkness, in which everything good was spiritual and abstract, and everything evil was material and worldly. Mani seemed to have a particular loathing for human bodies and sex. In his view the only route to salvation, knowledge of the light, involved escape from the endless cycle of reincarnation—as in Buddhism—and freedom from the body.

Mani hoped his creed might become the state religion of Iran, and a Sassanid emperor, Shapur I, provided early support. A few years after Shapur died, another emperor took a different view about religion and had Mani imprisoned. He died in chains about 276, but his religion lived on. Despite vigorous persecution, Manichaeism won converts throughout the Roman Empire as far as Britain and North Africa. It did so among Zoroastrians in Iran and Buddhists in India too, and flourished along the Central Asian Silk Roads. It even spread to China, where it lasted until about 1400. In its homeland of Iran, it endured for a few hundred years, but underground and overshadowed by Zoroastrianism. Manichaeism ultimately lost out nearly everywhere to state-sponsored religions, chiefly Christianity and Islam, but not before leaving its imprint upon them both.

The Spread of Christianity, 200–800

In 200 CE, Christianity remained a minor religion in the Roman Empire and even more marginal outside it. Despite the efforts of Paul and his allies to spread the faith, its followers were few, scattered among dozens of cities and worshipping in homes or makeshift churches. It had only rickety organization, partly because most believers expected the material world to come to an end soon, so building durable institutions did not seem urgent. Christians were fewer in number than adherents of the Isis or Osiris cults emanating from Roman Egypt, or worshippers of the Persian deity Mithras. In the 270s, an emperor considered making Mithraism the state religion of the Roman Empire, which would have changed history's course, but he died before doing it. Christian population, while growing, still came to well under 1 percent of the empire's total. Roman authorities occasionally threw a few to the lions but by and large let them be, considering them an insignificant Jewish heretical cult. As of 300, nothing suggested Christianity would ever become the dominant religion of the Roman Empire.

Favorable Conditions But it did. Christianity held some appeal to the Roman masses. Pagan religions offered few specifics about any afterlife, and nothing more attractive than endless ghostly wanderings. But Christianity promised eternal salvation for those who could keep the faith. This resonated with the millions whose earthly lives included heavy doses of suffering and humiliation. In Christian belief, the poor and downtrodden had just as good a chance at heaven, if not better, than the rich and powerful. Christianity embraced sinners and offered them a fresh start.

Plagues, violence, and chaos helped Christianity on its way. As we've seen, beginning in the 160s repeated epidemics ravaged the empire. Christians distinguished themselves by their reaction, which included often selflessly caring for fellow Christians regardless of risk. As a result, they probably survived in slightly higher proportion than non-Christians, and their charitable conduct attracted admiration.

Political chaos, which peaked in the third century, helped to create Christians too. Against the backdrop of civil war, reckless ambition, and boundless greed, conscientious Christian behavior looked noble in comparison. For the many who grew discouraged by the duplicity, savagery, and sin of the visible world, an alternative universe of the spirit held strong attractions. The remarkable courage of some Christians in the face of mortal peril also provided inspiration: in Gaul about 180 CE, for instance, a slave woman named Blandina withstood days of torture with stoic calm, proclaiming her attachment to Christianity.

Like Manichaeans, Christians objected strenuously to Roman practices such as infanticide, abortion, homosexuality, and indeed sex for any purpose beyond procreation, so they might have had larger-than-average families. By 300, roughly 10 percent of the Roman Empire's population was Christian.

This modest demographic success began to worry some Roman officials. More systematic persecutions began in 250, involving confiscation of property, exile, and occasional torture and execution. Diocletian took it to another level, feeling that religious tension undermined the empire's cohesion. Seeking to use religion to bind the empire together, he had himself recognized as semi-divine and an object of worship. He banned Manichaeism for its associations with Iran, and then attacked Christianity in the final years of his rule. Romans were required to demonstrate that they sacrificed to Roman gods. Many Christians complied, but many others preferred to accept the penalties, including death. Such steadfast Christian commitment again attracted admiration. According to Christian traditions, some eagerly sought martyrdom, even if it meant a grisly death nailed to a cross or in the jaws of hungry lions, confident it would earn them a place in heaven. Diocletian retired before his persecutions had reached more than a few thousand Christians, and his successors wavered in their policy. So the Christian community easily survived, still a small minority, mainly confined to the cities.

That changed with Emperor Constantine. During the civil wars that ultimately made him emperor, he chose to become a Christian. Just how it happened is uncertain: he apparently saw visions, entrusted his fate to Christ, won several battles, and was a changed man. In any case, during the period 310–313 Constantine ended persecutions of all religions, including Christianity, in those lands he controlled.

When he assumed command of the entire empire in 324, Constantine had already become a patron of Christianity. He built churches, donated land, extended tax breaks, and otherwise supported his fellow Christians. The formerly rickety church organization became a solid edifice with institutionalized hierarchy based chiefly on regional leaders called bishops, each of whom had a specific territory (now called a diocese) to administer. He also supported Christian communities outside the Roman Empire—in Iran, for example. (That support deepened their persecution by the Sassanids.) Christianity was, suddenly, an imperial religion with the weight of the Roman Empire behind it. Without Constantine's conversion, it is hard to see how Christianity would have transcended its prior status as one among several minority religions in Roman lands.

Structure and Schism With success came both structure and **schism**. By the time of Constantine's death, there were a few hundred bishops; and the most important, in cities such as Constantinople, Antioch, and Alexandria, came to be called patriarchs. The bishop in Rome came to be called the Pope in the late fourth century and claimed primacy within the church. Bishops enjoyed power over their human flocks, church personnel, and doctrines. The other great institution of the early church was **monasticism**, which took shape first in Egypt in the third through fifth centuries. For those who sought a perfect Christian existence, free from the corruption of daily life, self-exile made good sense. Soon like-minded men and women clustered together, forming monastic communities devoted to spiritual rigor. Desert terrain was especially suitable for such conscious attempts at withdrawal. One of the first major monasteries grew up at the foot of Mount Sinai, where Christians and Jews believe Moses saw the burning bush.

At first, although Christian communities had had their arguments, by and large they were cohesive, small, and intensely loyal to one another. As they flourished, they lost some of that cohesion—as is normal with successful social movements. Rival bishops competed for authority. Points of doctrine became divisive. Most of these had to do with the precise nature of Christ, whether he was man, God, or somehow both.

In 325, Constantine summoned all the bishops he could gather to Nicaea (Iznik in modern Turkey) to sort out these questions. The prevailing view became the so-called Nicene Creed, the classic formulation of Christian belief endorsed by most churches around the world today. It required that Christians declare their faith in God, Christ, and the Holy Spirit—the Trinity of Christianity, the three forms of the same divine essence. The losing argument, that of a churchman named Arius, became a heresy. Arianism denied the Trinity, holding that Christ was the son of God but not a co-equal form of God. Although proscribed by the church, Arianism retained many followers within Christendom, including one Byzantine emperor, and lasted until the mid-sixth century.

Arianism was only the first big schism. Another arose in the mid-fifth century when a bishop, Nestorius, complained that priests and bishops ought not to refer to Mary, who in his view did not have a divine nature, as Mother of God. Another council of bishops met, argued, and then ruled in 431 that Nestorianism was a heresy. It too, however, survived official condemnation, especially outside Roman borders, and became the primary expression of Christianity in Iran and Central Asia. In fact, the bishops' ruling helped Christians in Sassanian Iran, because as disloyal heretics in Roman eyes the Nestorians were no longer suspect as enemy agents.

Yet another unorthodox view, called Monophysitism, arose in the fifth and sixth centuries. It held that Christ had only a single and divine nature. Ruled a heresy in 451, it thrived nonetheless in the eastern reaches of Christianity. Empress Theodora was a Monophysite (Justinian was not). The Coptic Church of Egypt and Ethiopia is Monophysite today. These and other doctrinal disputes preoccupied bishops and theologians and threatened to divide Christianity and Byzantium, which is why emperors needed rulings to define orthodoxy.

Fishmongers and washerwomen probably worried less about doctrine. A fourth-century bishop claimed that on the streets of Constantinople if he asked the price of bread he would hear that God the Father was greater than God the Son. But surely most ordinary folk only occasionally spared a thought for the precise nature of divinity and found the priests' theological arguments and vocabulary bewildering. They accepted Christianity because their leaders told them to, because their friends and family did, or because the simpler teachings of the church—charity, community, love, redemption—appealed to them.

By the fourth century, the experience of Christian worship and community had evolved in new directions. Christians worshipped under the guidance of trained priests (clergy), who handled the reading of sacred texts, and conducted rituals that took the place of communal meals. As the church got larger, more bureaucratic (as all state religions must), and more remote, Christians embraced local saints to provide personal, local, and intensely emotional attachments. Saints' biographies provided exemplary role models, and saints could serve as intermediaries if God or Christ seemed as remote as the emperor.

Spreading beyond Rome By the 450s, Christianity had become the majority religion within Roman borders—which still held up in the east. Tens of millions now professed the faith in one form or another. Monks, who had sought isolation at first but eventually sought converts as well, carried it far and wide. The Byzantine state promoted it in its orthodox form, both at home and abroad, while cracking down as best it could on heresies. Monarchs elsewhere in the western end of Eurasia took an interest, sometimes from curiosity, sometimes out of political calculation. In the fourth and fifth centuries, kings in Armenia, Georgia, Ethiopia, and Nubia all became Christian—and so, over many generations, did their populations. A king in what would become France followed suit in the sixth century. These were top-down conversions, like Constantine's, linking the power of the state to the fortunes of the faith. After the fourth century, this was the primary way in which Christianity spread.

Top-down conversion prevailed even in some lands that did not have kings. In the British Isles, for example, missionary monks spread Christianity to peoples with minimal political structure such as the Irish and Scots. But the monks focused their efforts on local elites—chieftains or landowners whose example would attract imitation. Beginning in the sixth century, with backing from the Pope, their efforts met gradual success.

Missionary monks, mainly Nestorians, took Christianity along the Silk Road and the Indian Ocean trade routes as far as China and India. They made converts in the oases of Central Asia and a few in China, India, and Sri Lanka. In the third and fourth centuries, Greek-speaking Christians from Egypt brought the faith to southern India, and Christians from Iran carried it to northwest India. Christianity has survived as a minority religion ever since in India. In China, Christian monks arrived by the early seventh century, a favorable time because the ruling Tang dynasty then welcomed foreigners and unfamiliar ideas. The court sponsored translations of Christian scripture into Chinese. An imperial decree referred to the "Iranian religion"—Christianity—as "mysterious, wonderful, and calm" and judged it "right that it should spread through the empire." But none of the emperors became Christians, and it did not spread widely within China.

In the absence of any overarching authority, Christianity took many forms. A king in Ethiopia or Armenia might try to root out all but his

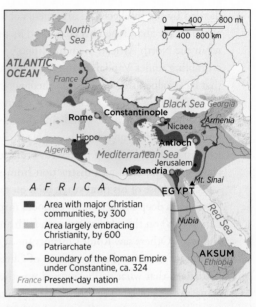

The Spread of Christianity, 300–600 CE Thanks in large part to the efforts of the Roman, and then Byzantine, Empire, Christianity gradually became the dominant religion over broad swaths of the Mediterranean world and Europe. The kings of Aksum promoted the Christian faith in what is now Ethiopia. Many Christians, mainly Nestorians, also lived in Iran and cities of Central Asia stretching (by 635) to China. Southwest India also had a small Christian community.

preferred form of the faith, but political fragmentation allowed multiple religions and sects to survive. In Latin-speaking Europe, despite plenty of political fragmentation, increasingly the intellectual heft of a North African bishop and the institutional power of popes forged a more consistent, if not quite uniform, Christianity we call Catholicism. More and more of the Germanic tribes adopted it, slowly abandoning paganism or Arianism, both of which went extinct in Europe by 600 or so.

Augustine The North African bishop was **Augustine** (354–430). In his youth a shameless libertine, in his maturity a prolific author and strict moralist, and always a deep thinker, he wrestled candidly with his unruly passions. No one other than Christ had a stronger influence upon Christianity.

Born in today's Algeria and raised by Monica, his devoutly Christian mother, Augustine left the faith and became a Manichaean for a decade, absorbing some of Mani's stern morals (although he did not live up to them, fathering a child by a slave woman) and his theology. Augustine found much to admire in Platonic thought. Then, dazzled by the intellect and arguments of a bishop in Italy, he agreed to be baptized at age 33. He abandoned his child (and its mother) and became a bishop soon thereafter in the North African town of Hippo, in the years when Roman North Africa was crumbling under Vandal assault. Somehow, he found time to write numerous books that have helped shape Christian theology ever since.

Some of his works, such as his *Confessions*, were deeply introspective, concerned with doubt, unworthiness, and sin—he was obsessed with having once stolen a pear just for fun. He renounced the waywardness of his youth and demonized the Manichaean faith he had long professed. From it, nonetheless, he took Mani's ungenerous view of womankind as a distraction from sacred pursuits. Augustine's other works, especially those of his final years, took on more political themes. The sack of Rome in 410 made a deep impact on his outlook, inspiring a long meditation (translated as *The City of God*) on the relation between faith and the material world, and between church and state. Others saw Rome's misfortune at the hand of pagan Goths as evidence that casting off traditional gods in favor of Christianity was a mistake. Augustine assured Christians that what really counted was the kingdom of heaven and one's own inner being. As he put it, "The Heavenly City outshines Rome, beyond comparison. There, instead of victory, is truth; instead of high rank, holiness; instead of peace, felicity; instead of life, eternity."

Augustine's writings helped to establish doctrines of original sin, the Holy Trinity, and the indispensability of God's grace to human freedom, all touchstones of Western Christian philosophy. He also helped to inject a neo-Platonism into Christian thought. Augustine laid the intellectual foundation for a more unified Christianity—Catholicism—in the Latin-speaking west. His ideas carried little weight in the Greek-speaking east.

Muhammad and Islam

The second monotheistic faith to spread over the western reaches of the Old World web was **Islam**. Its founder, **Muhammad** (570–632), was born to a lesser family of a ruling tribe in Mecca, an oasis and crossroads in western Arabia. Arabia was a dry, dusty, rocky land dotted with oases and coastal ports, a hard place to make a living. Its few inhabitants, organized mainly in tribes, survived by herding, trading, and raiding others' herds and trade caravans. Their main export was leather. Except for those living at the biggest oases or in the more welcoming districts of the far south such as Yemen, where there was a small kingdom, the **Arabs** were either nomadic or close to it. Despite a long tradition of oral poetry, almost nothing as yet was written in their language, Arabic (the earliest surviving inscription dates from 512). The Arabs were polytheistic, with dozens of nature deities and gods specific to individual tribes, although behind them all was a more general god, referred to as Allah.

These Arabian tribes lived on a southern fringe of the Iranian and Byzantine world, and because of trade links they often knew something of it. They also knew something of the monotheistic religions—Judaism, Zoroastrianism, Christianity—and the dualistic faith of Manichaeism through contact with the more populous lands to the north, and with Christian Ethiopia. As Arabia was drawn more tightly into the Old World web, its religious options multiplied, and Muhammad added one more.

Muhammad   His father died before Muhammad was born, and his mother died when he was six. The grandfather to whom he turned soon died as well, and from the age of eight he was raised by an uncle. Little else is known of his youth, but he somehow got work helping merchants in Mecca. At age 25, he married one of them, Khadija, a prosperous widow 15 years his senior. They had at least six children, of whom only three daughters survived childhood. By his 30s, he was well acquainted with the sorrows of this world but also a respected businessman in Mecca, known for his judgment and wisdom. At age 40, while visiting a desert cave for peace and contemplation, as Arab men regularly did, he had visions and heard a voice telling him that he, Muhammad, was the messenger of God. At first confused and frightened, he ran from the cave thinking perhaps devils had possessed him. But his wife, Khadija, and his cousin, a Christian, helped him come to terms with his vision and to see it as the revelation of God.

His closest family and friends endorsed this understanding of Muhammad as a prophet. Soon many others in Mecca did as well, but, in a common response to prophets, some thought he had lost his mind. The ruling elite, especially the merchant clans, objected to his preaching. They feared that his uncompromising denunciation of idols and paganism would be bad for business.

When he was about 50, Khadija died, as did a powerful uncle who had helped protect him. The Mecca elite now harassed him and his followers, many of whom he sent to Christian Ethiopia for safety. All seemed bleak. But one night while sleeping—as Muslim tradition has it—he was transported by an archangel to Jerusalem and then to heaven, where the sum of God's wisdom was entrusted to him. This journey, known as *Mi'raj* in Arabic, is sometimes regarded as a spiritual journey through the various levels of existence, and sometimes as an actual physical journey.

The Birth of Islam   In any case, Muhammad's earthly fortunes soon changed. A town a few days' walk to the north, Medina, where his reputation for sagacity had spread, asked him to become its judge and leader. In 622, he left Mecca just before his enemies attacked his house, and he fled to Medina. There he set up the first mosque and formed a community of followers called Muslims, a word that means "people who submit to the will of God." Muslims use this date, 622 CE, the year of the flight to Medina, as the year 1 in their calendar (a lunar calendar with 354 days to the year).

Muhammad and his followers still faced a rocky road. They took to preying upon Meccan traders returning from Syria. His enemies in Mecca, who regarded this as outright banditry, launched expeditions against him and wounded him in one fracas.

He struggled to keep his community whole, losing many men in skirmishes (and often marrying their widows, routine conduct for an Arab political chieftain). But military successes boosted his standing, and by 630 he had won over the population of Mecca. Although he generally showed mercy to those he defeated, on one occasion he either ordered or acquiesced in the execution of the males, and enslavement of the females, of a Jewish tribe that had sided against him. Many tribes of the Arabian Peninsula found it prudent to join him and become Muslims. He even invited emperors and kings of all the nearby great powers—Iran, Byzantium, Ethiopia—to join his faith, but there is no record of any response. Some of the Jews, Christians, and Zoroastrians of Arabia accepted his political authority while retaining their religions. Muhammad specifically granted them that right as "People of the Book"—a phrase that meant they had scripture.

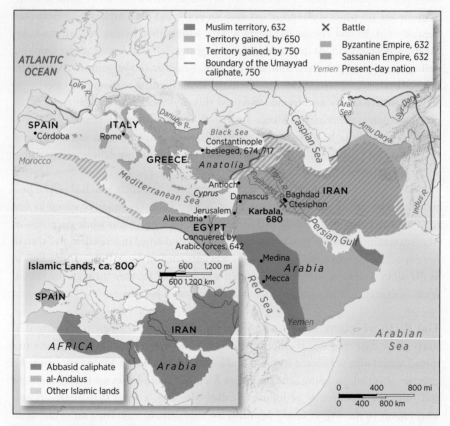

The Spread of Islam, 632–750 CE In one of the more remarkable cultural transformations of world history, the Islamic religion became the majority faith over broad areas in little more than a century. Muhammad's followers found populations weary of Sassanian and Byzantine rule willing to accept Arab leaders instead, and often ready to convert from Zoroastrian or Christian belief to Islam.

Muhammad died in 632 after a brief illness. His political achievement, beyond defeating the Meccans in battle, was to forge a community of Arabs that transcended their strong tribal identities and bonded them together in a common faith. Their political power extended throughout the western half of Arabia.

Like the several People of the Book, Islam itself had scripture, which Muslims regard as a fuller and finer—indeed, final—version of God's message. Islam's scripture, the Qur'an ("recitation"), was the text of the revelations from God as Muhammad spoke them. To believers, they are the words of God himself. The Qur'an includes a history of Jewish, Christian, and Arab prophets, exhortations to Muslims to follow only one god and to form a community of the faithful, some harsh words for unbelievers, and moral and legal guidelines for Muslims. These form the basis of divinely sanctioned law and ethics in Islam, known as **shari'a** ("the path"). The Qur'an has many echoes of the Bible, including the expectation that the day of reckoning will soon be at hand. Muhammad regarded the Qur'an, together with his family, as his most precious gifts to Muslims. He regarded himself, and was regarded by Muslims, as the last in the line of prophets stretching back to Abraham, Moses, and Jesus—just as Mani had seen himself four centuries before. Muhammad considered himself a reformer, restoring the religion of Abraham that Jews and Christians had corrupted, rather than the founder of a new religion. But a founder, in the end, is what he was.

He was the only founder of a major new religion to exercise political power directly. Jesus and the Buddha never directed armies and never had to delve far into the grimy compromises of politics. Muhammad, in contrast, left a political record that has served as one of the guides to political behavior for Muslims ever after.

The Arab Conquests The career of Islam as a political and religious movement after 632 forms one of the more remarkable stories in world history. At first, as word of Muhammad's death spread, tribes broke away, showing that their allegiance to Islam had been merely pragmatic. But soon his kin and closest companions, men such as Abu Bakr, Umar, and Uthman, forged the community of Muslims into an effective military force and broke out of the Arabian Peninsula into the richer lands then ruled by the Sassanids and Byzantines. Those great powers had just expended legions of manpower and vast fortunes in decades of pitiless warfare against one another, and at first they could not see the Arabs—mere camel herders and petty traders to them—as a threat. Many Arabs had fought as auxiliaries for both powers and had learned something of their strengths and weaknesses. They also had learned of the Byzantines' doctrine of Christian holy war and its emphasis on the importance of capturing Jerusalem.

Before the emperors knew what they were up against, the Arabs had conquered the Iranian capital of Ctesiphon (637) and the Byzantine city of Jerusalem (638). By 646, they ruled Egypt. They built navies, a new enterprise for Arabs, and seized the island of Cyprus in 649. The peoples they conquered sometimes resisted fiercely, but often they welcomed the Muslim Arabs as an improvement on their current rulers. In

Byzantine Syria and Egypt, religious schism again came into play: local elites preferred a different brand of Christianity to the one championed in Constantinople, and felt only a weak loyalty, if any, to Byzantine emperors. Islamic rule appeared to offer them greater freedom of religion. Similarly, the Jews of Egypt generally welcomed Muslim conquest, having suffered under Byzantine rule.

When they did fight, the Arabs proved remarkably formidable for men with no tradition of siege craft, infantry tactics, or naval operations. They had mastered the art of camel management, an advantage in desert environments. More decisively, they had a tremendous solidarity born of religious conviction. Their leaders convinced them that death in battle earned a ticket to paradise, a belief hardly unique to Muslims. And military campaigns promised booty and plunder beyond all imagination for poor men raised in the oases and deserts of Arabia. By 650, the Sassanian Empire was finished, Byzantium had lost its richest provinces, and the first pulse of Arab Muslim conquests was essentially complete.

In conquering Iran and Mesopotamia, Muhammad's successors echoed the conquests of Alexander the Great nearly a thousand years before. He too had molded a formidable fighting force out of an originally small and unsophisticated population, the Macedonians, and brought low the great power of Persia.

Tensions within Islam   Dividing the plunder from such conquests caused quarrels among Muhammad's followers, as it had among Alexander's. So did competition for recognition as the true successor to Muhammad, or caliph ("deputy of God"). Within just a few years of the Prophet's death, the Muslim community fractured. Should the caliph be of the Prophet's family—perhaps his closest male relative Ali, his cousin and son-in-law? Patrilineal descent was extremely important to Arab tribes. Or should the caliph be the best Muslim or the best leader—a man like Umar, a cultured and charismatic companion of Muhammad?

Discord prevailed. As it happened, the first three caliphs were not from Muhammad's family, but close companions of the Prophet who had shown their resolve and piety in many a stern test. They proved remarkably successful winning battles and converting people to Islam in Egypt, Iran, and Mesopotamia. Then, when Ali became the fourth caliph (r. 656–661), civil war resulted. The winners defeated Ali and in 661 formed the first genuine Islamic state, the Umayyad caliphate, with its capital at Damascus. Ali was murdered in prayer the following year. Here and there the partisans of Ali (known as Shi'a or Shi'ites) rose in rebellion, climaxing in a pitched battle in 680 at Karbala (in Iraq), a defeat at the hands of the Umayyads. The Shi'a champion, Hussein, a grandson of the Prophet, was killed and humiliated, and his martyrdom remains a rallying cry for Shi'a Muslims to this day. Shi'a Muslims have always been a minority within the Islamic population, and they've usually been regarded as heretics by the majority, known as Sunni Muslims.

Young religions are especially prone to schism, as the early careers of Christianity

CONSIDERING THE EVIDENCE

The Succession to Muhammad

Muhammad, the Prophet of Islam, died in 632 CE. His close friend Abu Bakr was helping to prepare the Prophet's body for burial when he was interrupted by an urgent message. At that very moment, the people of Medina were assembling to proclaim one of their own as Muhammad's successor. Although the people of Medina were called the Helpers, they actually formed the majority of the Muslim army. They had not included Muhammad's earliest converts from Mecca, known as the Migrants, in their gathering. Abu Bakr rushed to the meeting with two of Muhammad's earliest supporters. By the end of the meeting, and without consulting Muhammad's family, the assembly pledged allegiance to Abu Bakr as the first caliph, or successor to Muhammad. The following excerpt is from a compilation of recollections about the meeting that the Arab historian al-Tabari assembled around 915 CE.

When the Prophet of God . . . died, the (Medinese) Helpers assembled . . . and said, "Let us give this authority, after Muhammad . . . to Saʿd ibn Ubada [a native of Medina]." . . . Saʿd said . . . "O company of Helpers! You have precedence in religion and merit in Islam possessed by no other Arab tribe. Muhammad remained for more than ten years (here in Medina) among his people. . . . But among his own people (in Mecca) only a few men believed in him, and they were not able to protect the Prophet of God or glorify his religion. . . . Therefore keep this authority for yourselves alone. . . .

. . .

[After Abu Bakr arrived at the meeting, he said:] "God singled out the first Migrants of his people by allowing them to recognize the truth and believe in him. They consoled him and shared in his suffering. . . . They were the first in the land to worship God and to believe in God and the Prophet. They were his friends and his clan and the best entitled of all men to this authority after him. . . . Here is Umar and here is Abu Bayda [of Mecca]. Swear allegiance to whomever of them you choose." The two of them then objected: "No, by God, we will not accept this authority above you. . . . Give us your hand so that we may swear allegiance to you."

Questions for Analysis

1. What reasons did the Helpers and the Migrants present to claim leadership of the Muslim community after the death of Muhammad?

2. Why did the Helpers rush to proclaim a successor to Muhammad?

3. What were the consequences of deciding on a successor without consulting Muhammad's family, especially his son-in-law Ali?

Source: F. E. Peters, *A Reader on Classical Islam* (Princeton, 1994).

and Islam both show. Without the weight of tradition, much remains to be settled. Rival doctrines and factions compete for dominance—often violently, even in religions that preach peace. When religions acquire the powers of a state, as with Constantine's adoption of Christianity or the establishment of the Umayyads, the stakes only grow. Winners define the losers as heretics, persecute them, and if they have the means, perhaps try to exterminate them. When religions become international, as Christianity and Islam did early on, and no single state can control believers, then stamping out heresy becomes more difficult. Schisms can last for centuries or even millennia, and new ones can always develop.

Despite schism and struggle, in the first few decades of Islam the Muslim community set its rules. The most important are called the Five Pillars of Islam, which hold that a Muslim must: (1) profess that there is but one God, Allah, and that Muhammad is his messenger, (2) pray five times daily, (3) give alms to the needy, (4) fast during daylight hours during the month of Ramadan, and (5) make a pilgrimage to Mecca at least once if financially possible. On these five rules, all pious Muslims agree.

The Umayyad Caliphate   Over the next century and a half, from 650 to 800, Islam became a state religion of a sort. Caliphs claimed to be both successors of the Prophet and leaders of a political community. The Umayyad caliphs in Damascus echoed the traditions of Mesopotamian kingship and Roman emperorship. They formed no church, and by and large left the selection of religious authorities to the community of the faithful (the *umma* in Arabic). They permitted Christians, Jews, and Zoroastrians to run their own affairs, as long as they did not challenge the authority of the caliphs or denigrate Islam. They taxed non-Muslims at a higher rate than Muslims, which created an economic incentive for people to convert, and one for rulers to discourage conversion. Christianity and Judaism survived throughout the caliphate, faring better than paganism in the Christianized Roman Empire. It took centuries for Iran, Syria, and Egypt to become Muslim-majority lands.

Meanwhile, the Umayyads expanded their empire geographically. Another pulse of conquests (705–715) took Arabs and Islam into northwest India and across North Africa to Morocco, where again the Jewish population welcomed the invaders, and across the Mediterranean into Spain. Small Muslim forces raided as far north as the Loire valley in France by 732.

Governing a state with several religions, dozens of ethnicities, and newly conquered peoples was a new challenge for the Arabs. The first Umayyads relied on Arab tribes to make their wishes felt throughout their domain. As the community of Muslims grew in size and the ranks who had known the Prophet and stood with him in his struggles thinned, the loyalty of tribesmen grew less reliable. Umayyad caliphs by 680 or so, half a century after Muhammad's death, needed new sources of legitimacy.

To bolster their authority, they relied in part on "soft power" exerted in forms such as monumental architecture. The magnificent Dome of the Rock, begun in 681 on the site of the Jewish Second Temple in Jerusalem, offered an awe-inspiring reminder of Umayyad wealth and power. The Umayyads also relied on the expertise of the conquered. Like the Goths who overran the western Roman Empire or the Macedonians who conquered Persia, victorious Arabs recruited experienced specialists to sustain technical aspects of their state, such as finance, large-scale irrigation, and monumental architecture. The Dome of the Rock was built under the guidance of Greek architects and consequently shows some decorative features borrowed from Byzantine churches. Some Greeks and Iranians enjoyed considerable power and amassed fortunes working for the caliphate, which irked many Arabs and Muslims.

Managing the tribal, religious, and ethnic divisions within the Umayyad state required great skill on the part of caliphs. In time, as in the Roman Empire, some rulers came to power for whom the glitter of evenings at court outshone the allure of long days spent governing—a great liability in a state based on an ideology of piety and righteousness. By the 740s, the Umayyads were barely holding onto power.

Dome of the Rock The Umayyad caliph Abd Al-Malik oversaw the construction of this grand edifice, completed in 691–692. The site is sacred to Muslims, as it is believed to be the place where Muhammad's journey to heaven began.

The Abbasid Caliphate A rebellious faction from Iran, called the Abbasids, overthrew the Umayyads and established a new caliphate in 750. Based in a new city, Baghdad (in Iraq), the **Abbasid caliphate** boasted luxurious palaces and all the trappings of the Persian/Iranian imperial tradition. Islam was losing more and more of its original tight-knit character and becoming increasingly a religion of power—a path Christianity had followed as well. The Abbasids consolidated power over most of the Islamic world, although southern Spain became an independent Muslim state, led by the last of the Umayyad dynasts.

The Abbasids flourished for roughly a century (ca. 750–850). They rebuilt the irrigation infrastructure of the Tigris-Euphrates, which, combined with the grain surplus from Egypt, provided them with a powerful economic base. The Abbasids also tapped into the growing trade network of the Indian Ocean world, another source of prosperity. Arab and Iranian merchants roamed as far as China. And, like all Iranian or Persian states for a thousand years before them, they profited from overland trade along the Silk Roads.

The early Abbasids invested not only in palaces and military power, but in supporting scholars and artists. They took to heart the saying of Muhammad that "a scholar's ink is more precious than the martyr's blood." Jurists sorted out the finer points of Islamic law and organized various schools of jurisprudence, most of which survive today. The Abbasids underwrote translations of learned works from Chinese, Sanskrit, Hebrew, Greek, and

Abbasid Power Abbasid emirs signaled the reach of their authority across the Mediterranean by building, starting in 793, a grand mosque at Córdoba (left) in what is now Spain. Its characteristic rounded arches echo the style of the early eighth-century Umayyad mosque at Damascus (right).

Latin into Arabic and Persian. They patronized poetry and science on an unprecedented scale, and Baghdad became the greatest center of learning in the Old World web.

Their lesser rival within the world of Islam, the emirate based in Córdoba (southern Spain), flourished as well. By 800, its armies controlled most of Iberia. Arab immigrants developed irrigated agriculture there to new heights. They also reinvigorated mining. The court sponsored scholars and scientists, just as in Baghdad, and beginning in 793 successive emirs built the sprawling Córdoba mosque modeled on the Umayyad one in Damascus. Parts of Spain would remain under Muslim authority until 1492.

With establishment of the Abbasid caliphate and the survival of the Byzantine Empire, the western end of the Old World web once again featured two superpowers, as in the days of Rome and Persia. Byzantium and the Abbasids served as champions of two great religions. They often fought, like their predecessors, and generally saw themselves in implacable opposition to one another. But they were also something of a unit. Together, they housed almost all the great cities of western Eurasia and northern Africa, all the great concentrations of wealth, all the important seats of culture and learning. Together, they preserved the science and learning developed in the ancient worlds of Babylon, Persia, Egypt, Greece, and Rome. As of 800, the zones of western Eurasia that they did not control, such as Russia and almost all of Europe, were backwaters in comparison, home to petty kingdoms and wandering tribes.

Re-Centering the Old World Web

The biggest economic and social changes in the western region of the Old World web, during the period 200–800 CE, were associated with the breakup of Roman imperial unity and the re-unification of much of the Romano-Persian world under the banners of Islam.

Both processes were terribly violent. Warfare was commonplace in the days when the Roman and Parthian empires were intact, but it took place in frontier zones and involved military specialists. Parthian and Roman subjects not in the army and not living along the frontiers could expect to live in peace. Their cities needed no walls. But that security disappeared with the breakdown of the Parthian state and the incursions of Germanic tribes into Roman lands in the third century, followed by the nearly incessant civil wars among Roman generals. Pillaging armies and raiding tribesmen overran towns and farmsteads frequently, killing, raping, and enslaving as they went. Roman cities began to build walls in the third century, and by the fifth century almost every remaining city had walls. The Byzantine-Sassanid wars, especially that of 603–630, brought horrific violence to non-military populations as armies campaigned back and forth. The ideology of religious righteousness may have added extra intensity to the bloodletting in those contests. The Arab conquests too brought violence, although in the early decades the scale of their warfare was much smaller than that of the Byzantine-Sassanid struggles, which had opened the door to those Arab conquests.

The crumbling of powerful states—the western Roman Empire after 370 and the Byzantine and Sassanian empires in the 640s—allowed civil violence to spike. Brigands and gangs caused as much grief as armies did. For the millions caught in the maelstrom, this breakdown of public order was disastrous—probably more so for young women than anyone else. The scale of civil and military violence lowered population at times, although famines and epidemics normally did more damage.

Unraveling at the Western Edge

On the westernmost fringes of the Old World web—in North Africa, Iberia, Gaul, and Britain, but also in Italy and the Balkans—the end of Roman rule brought a distinct simplification of economic and social life. With heightened violence, political chaos, and the loss of security, long-distance trade withered. With it went specialized production, honed artisan skills, and the markets for both luxury goods and trade staples such as olive oil. The working of both copper and lead almost ceased. Pottery and housing styles became much more basic. Literacy declined. Money almost disappeared. Economic life became much more local and self-sufficient. By the 570s, several centuries of vibrant trade linking Mediterranean and Atlantic ports had come to an end.

Cities shriveled to little more than castles and outbuildings. In Britain, the former city of York reverted to marshland. In Italy, Rome itself became just a small town. Its population fell from nearly 1 million in 350 to 50,000 or so in 550. In Greece, by 600 or so, complex society almost vanished, after more than a thousand years. From about 400 to roughly 700 (in North Africa) or 750 (in Europe), the Old World web unraveled at its western edge.

Let's pause for a moment to consider what this unraveling meant. As with the disappearance of urban life after the Maya collapse noted in Chapter 10, this trend struck elites as the end of everything they treasured. Some Romans tried to sell their expertise to new rulers who needed bureaucratic skills. Others became beggars or brigands. For people living in the path of violent bands, the loss of organized complex society often meant the end of life.

For those lucky enough to avoid violent hordes, the breakdown of Roman networks and social complexity might have seemed a liberation, worth the price of never seeing fine buildings or good pottery again. No more taxes to pay; no more haughty aristocrats flaunting their power, wealth, and education. The average heights of ordinary people in formerly Roman lands grew in the fifth and sixth centuries, suggesting that poor people got more or better food. Falling production and trade made it harder to get rich and left almost everyone, even kings and bishops, more equal.

Like the economy, culture in the far west, and indeed almost all of Europe, became more local. Fewer people spoke Latin, and more spoke versions of Gothic languages. Over generations, these tongues melded with Latin to produce new languages. In the Balkans after 400, Slavic languages began to replace Latin.

In 200 CE the same language, Latin, had been understood from England to Egypt, and the same Roman coins accepted. Public buildings, city layouts, roads, and aqueducts looked the same. But by 600 Europe was fragmented, and no one built roads and aqueducts. It would remain culturally and politically fragmented forever after—despite the ambitions of later conquerors such as Charlemagne, Napoleon, and Hitler.

In a sense, however, the conquered Romans won the cultural battle in Europe. Most of the evolving languages, at least in western Europe, were based on Latin. The prevailing religion, after Arianism disappeared, was Catholic Christianity as formulated in Rome. The victorious Vandals in North Africa quickly opted for Roman comfort and sophistication—hot baths and silk robes, Latin speech and Christian spirituality. This outcome in Europe and North Africa resembled what typically happened when steppe people conquered China: they gradually became Chinese culturally.

It forms a sharp contrast with the Arab expansion into Iran, Syria, and Egypt—lands of wealth, power, and social complexity. The conquering Arabs, unlike Vandals and Goths, did not take up the religion of the conquered. Nor did they come to speak Persian, Syriac, Greek, or Coptic (the majority language in Egypt before 640). Instead, over time most of the conquered peoples became Muslim and, outside of Iran, shifted to speaking Arabic. One explanation for this divergent pattern is that in Europe the language of religion remained Latin, but in the newly conquered Arab lands the language of religion became the language of the conquerors, the Arabs.

Resilience in Southwest Asia

In the Byzantine, Iranian, and Arab lands, things worked out very differently from the way they unfolded in Europe after 400. Social complexity and market society survived, partly because it had deeper roots going back millennia. Imperial control broke down now and again but always revived. Urban life and economic specialization endured. Byzantine pottery retained artistic flourishes. In Byzantine Syria, villages in rocky hill country could become prosperous by producing only olive oil and trading it for all else they needed. Cities, by and large, grew. After the Arab conquests, most of the conquered cities revived, and the Arabs built new ones, such as Baghdad, soon to be among the world's biggest. In 800 the population of Baghdad topped 1 million. Córdoba in Spain, Basra in Iraq, and dozens of other cities grew from small towns into big cities. The parts of the Old World web controlled by the caliphs and Byzantine emperors did not unravel.

The volume of trade probably grew under Islamic and Byzantine rule, although we have no reliable numbers. The new Islamic caliphates provided fertile ground for the spread of ethnic trade networks, especially of Jews and Armenians. These traders formed neighborhoods in every big city and took advantage of the heightened trust that minority status usually brings within a group to conduct business with their fellows from other cities. By 800, Jewish trade networks extended from Muslim Spain to India and beyond. Armenian traders were active over almost as broad a span, and some minority sects of Islam built similar networks. Some Christian monasteries became economic centers too, specializing in skills such as wine making and beer brewing, a niche open because alcohol is forbidden to Muslims by the Qur'an. Muslim rulers were often delighted to welcome prosperous Jews and Christians, who by law were taxed at higher rates than Muslims.

The prosperity of the lands of Islam after 680 opened up new markets and trade routes, and thickened traffic on older ones. For their ambitious building projects the caliphs needed supplies of timber, which their lands largely lacked. It came from the headwaters of the Tigris and Euphrates Rivers, India, and the shores of the Adriatic Sea. Their subjects also needed fuelwood for expanding glassworks, sugar refining, and metallurgy. Damascus became a center for high-quality steelmaking, which required many tons of charcoal. The Islamic lands also needed more metals than their own mines could provide, so they imported gold from parts of Africa and Central Asia, iron from East Africa, and steel ingots from India.

The caliphates drew their slave labor from afar, because by law Muslims cannot enslave other Muslims, and the Qur'an afforded protection to People of the Book (Christians, Jews, Zoroastrians, Hindus, Buddhists, and others). That left pagans from Russia, Central Asia, or Africa as the nearest target populations legally suitable for enslavement. The Byzantines and Sassanians had had slavery and slave trades too, but on a smaller scale than the new caliphates. The intense warfare of the seventh century, and the repeated bouts of urban plague during the sixth through the eighth centuries, sharpened the demand for slaves in cities, especially women and children for textile work. The establishment of Abbasid sugar and date palm plantations in southern Iraq led to the large-scale import of male slaves from East Africa.

Islamic states also pioneered the use of slave soldiers, especially as palace guards and elite cavalry units. Called *mamluks* in Arabic, slave soldiers were common in the Muslim world until the nineteenth century. Sold or captured as boys, they underwent grueling training. Survivors of proven merit often earned privileges unavailable to other slaves or soldiers, in exchange for unstinting loyalty to their commanders. A steady supply of male slaves became important to the security of many Islamic rulers. At first, Russians and Central Asian Turks formed the largest sources of slave populations, but by 800 most slaves entering Abbasid lands came from East Africa. These slave trades strengthened some threads of the Old World web, north along Russian rivers, and south both by sea and up the Nile into East Africa.

The comparative political unity and security of life in the new caliphates encouraged urbanization, commerce, and development of new trade routes. So did the cultural unity that Islam extended from Spain to Iran. After 680, Arabs, Iranians, and other Muslims built a thicker network of trade links than the one they had inherited, integrating old sea routes with traffic on land.

Growing networks of exchange favored the accumulation of wealth and growing social inequality, as rapid economic expansion normally does. Pre-Islamic Arab society, already attuned to markets and trade, had had its inequalities. But Arabia had so little wealth in total that few could amass fortunes. On the wider Islamic canvas, which by 750 stretched from northwest India to Spain, lucky and skilled traders could become extremely wealthy. So did rulers and their financiers. This rising inequality did not sit well with Arabs who felt left behind, despite prestigious ancestry or Islamic piety. At the same time, many Iranians considered their new rulers unfit to govern a great and ancient land such as theirs. So uprisings threatened the caliphates. Securing religious legitimacy, therefore, was all the more important for caliphs. So was maintaining control over the trade routes that brought the timber, metals, and slaves to the Islamic heartlands. When the Abbasid caliphate lost its grip on those routes after the 870s (when Egypt acquired autonomy), it became a shadow of its earlier self.

Power Moving East, 200–800

In general terms, we can see an eastward drift in the center of gravity of the entire region—indeed, in all of Eurasia—with the fall of the western Roman Empire and the rise of Islam. Linkages, networks, prosperity, and centers of power in the far west weakened. The networks, merchants, and rulers in Byzantium (until the 640s) grew stronger, and those in Egypt, Iraq, and the Muslim lands generally also strengthened, especially after 660. The great isthmus of land connecting the seaborne networks of the Indian Ocean world and those of the Mediterranean once again became the leading center of wealth and power in western Eurasia—as it had been, on smaller scales, in the time of the Achaemenids, Assyrians, and pharaohs. Broad trends contributed to this, such as the rise of Indian Ocean commerce discussed in a later chapter. That was an economic tide that raised all boats, as was the expansion of caravan commerce in desert and steppe lands.

Gold Coin of Mercia
Reflecting the shift of trade and power away from Rome toward the Arab world, this gold coin, minted by an English kingdom in the eighth century, was designed in the style of Arab coins in order to ease commercial exchange.

The breakdown of authority, security, and social complexity in the western Roman Empire also played a big part in this re-centering. The re-direction of the grain surpluses of Egypt, North Africa, and Syria confirmed it. From 212 BCE, when Roman forces added Sicily to their republic, the flow of overseas grain had sustained Rome, its cities, and its armies. Its acquisition of North Africa with the defeat of Carthage, and then of Egypt, allowed enormous expansion of urban life and military power, enough to sustain an empire. With the loss of North Africa (430), and then of Syria and Egypt (640s), Rome and its successor state in the east, Byzantium, could not so easily support elaborate urban life or big armies. Those regions, instead, pumped grain into the cities and armies of the Umayyad and Abbasid caliphates. Only a few regions in the western part of the Old World web could produce vast surpluses of food, and by 710 the caliphs controlled them all.

That breakdown of authority and complexity was part of a remarkable fraying of the western edge of the Old World web. The general trend throughout history has been for webs to grow and tighten. But exceptions exist, and one of the larger ones was the experience of post-Roman Europe and Vandal North Africa. In those regions, at least at most times after 450, the linkages to the wider world withered, and life became more local, simpler, poorer, and less hierarchical—until after 800.

Social Change across the Web

Big social changes followed on the spread of Christianity and the rise of Islam. Both were moralizing, ethical religions in contrast to the paganism of the Greeks and Romans. The pagan gods rewarded humans not for ethical behavior but for making sacrifices to them. Christianity and Islam, in contrast, preached moral codes of conduct required of believers and recommended for all humankind. These codes emphasized charity to the poor, kindness to one's neighbor, and peace (in most circumstances), as well as keeping faith with one's God. Penalties for greed, lying, and civil violence ranged from fines to eternal damnation.

On balance, both religions probably improved the lot of women and children—with

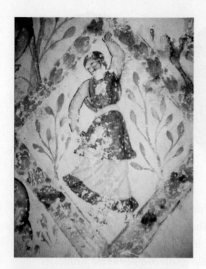

Women and the New Religions A woman dances in a fresco illustration from the ceiling of the baths in an Umayyad castle, Qasr Amra, dated to the early eighth century. Christianity and Islam both provided space for women to take on a variety of social roles and achieve a level of relative safety and security.

plenty of exceptions—given what had preceded them. In pagan Rome, women had been legally the property of husbands and fathers, although that condition softened in the early second century. In Zoroastrian Iran, women could legally be killed for refusing to marry. Zoroastrianism explicitly associated women with evil, sin, and temptation, and it encouraged social policies that constrained the damage they might do. Sexuality outside the context of procreation invited penalties in Zoroastrian society, especially for women. Christian and Muslim women had more hope of carving out safe or independent spheres for themselves than did women in pagan Rome or Zoroastrian Iran.

Christianity and Islam offered women new opportunities. Both included women in sacred roles, notably Mary in Christianity and the Prophet's daughter, Fatimah, in Islam (especially important to Shi'a Muslims). Both insisted that marriage should be consensual, although reality often departed from this ideal. Their sacred texts included rules about the proper treatment of women and wives.

The Qur'an made it clear that husbands must support their wives, and in polygamous marriages—a long tradition in Arabia—treat all wives equally. It further specified that wives should obey their husband and that females should inherit a share of their parents' property, although only half as much as their brothers. The societal expectation remained that all girls should marry, and ideally before age 18. Such provisions were probably improvements for women in Arabia, Iran, Syria, and much of the rest of the region to which Islam spread.

As for Christianity, in Rome and the Byzantine Empire, girls were also expected to marry as teenagers. Wives in Byzantine lands could inherit and own property, although sometimes there were restrictions on landed property. Theodora, once in power, tried to eliminate prostitution in Constantinople and devoted state funds to help prostitutes find husbands. A few Christian women managed to become wealthy in their own right—such as a certain Scholastica, who paid to build the public baths of the city of Ephesus in the late fourth century. By the fifth century, Christianity was making room for women who preferred female society, or sought refuge from the wider world, with the institution of convents. In the early church women had been active preachers, and many became saints for their pious or courageous conduct. Eventually the church denied all but nuns any formal religious role.

So for most women, the advent of Christianity and Islam improved their position and allowed them a little more room for maneuver in their lives. The new religions probably also improved the lot of children slightly. Both religions condemned infanticide, and Muhammad made special provisions for orphans.

None of this would likely have cheered the hundreds of thousands (perhaps millions) of women and children shipped as slaves from Africa and what is now Ukraine and Russia. The Islamic heartlands of Arabia, Egypt, Syria, Iraq, and Iran imported far more women than men in slavery, perhaps 2:1 in ratio. Most of these women were held in domestic slavery, which typically required housework, textile work, child care, and concubinage.

Christian Byzantium acquired far fewer slaves in all, mainly Slavs from the Balkans, again mostly women. For these women, the codes and norms of Christianity and Islam probably offered cold comfort. Males were not thrilled to become agricultural or military slaves either.

The success of the monotheistic religions also changed entertainments and education. Constantine banned gladiatorial combats, mock battles, and athletics, where the problem was nudity. Neither he nor later Christian emperors dared to ban chariot racing, though. The Hippodrome was the most important meeting place in Byzantine Constantinople, a place of entertainment and politics. Emperors opened the season's racing in person, just as U.S. presidents today sometimes throw out the first ball of the baseball season. Theater of the sort admired by ancient Greeks and Romans declined, but a tradition of bawdy performances (where Theodora got her start) took its place, to the dismay of the pious. Islamic societies often tried to ban alcohol, prostitution, and gambling, occasionally with success, but often without. Abbasid Baghdad apparently failed utterly in this regard.

Classical education of the sort pioneered in Athens in the fifth century BCE, with its emphasis on restless inquiry, vanished gradually after 400 CE. Learning became increasingly allied with religion, whether Christianity or Islam. In Byzantium, scholars studied the Greek of the New Testament rather than the Greek of pagans such as Homer or Herodotus. The main purpose of literacy was now to acquaint one with scripture and prevailing truths, rather than to debate with Socrates or Cicero. A Byzantine theologian of the early eighth century, promoting his own book, boasted that it had nothing new in it.

In the caliphates, education also centered on religion. Formal education featured memorization of the Qur'an and mastery of a growing body of commentaries. In taking over Iran, Iraq, and Byzantine Syria, Muslims inherited proud traditions of philosophy, mathematics, medicine, and other fields of knowledge. Reconciling them with Islamic scripture required generations of intellectual effort. Learned men enjoyed high status in Muslim societies, so many families wanted their sons to wrestle with these texts. Girls had less incentive and opportunity to do so.

The new emphasis on sacred learning meant that many ancient pagan texts were lost for good. Those that survived often lingered, little-read, in monasteries, convents, or the libraries of Islamic schools called madrassas. In later centuries, Byzantine and Islamic scholars would take a renewed interest in ancient wisdom.

All these social changes were gradual. They affected those closest to state and religious authority first, and peasants in mountain villages least of all. But in time, they affected everyone. Belief, culture, social norms, and law traveled, if slowly and irregularly, along the threads of the Old World web, leaving almost no one in Western Eurasia or North Africa untouched by 800 CE.

Conclusion

The clashes of politics, the inspiration of prophets, and the catastrophes of plague and climate change reorganized the western edge of the Old World web between 200 and 800. Rome's empire first shrank and then vanished west of the Adriatic Sea, but it survived in the east as the Byzantine Empire, with its capital at Constantinople. The city of Rome and urban life more broadly in Europe dwindled. The Sassanian Empire vanished altogether, replaced by Islamic caliphates based in Damascus and then Baghdad. Both Christianity and Islam spread rapidly, at the expense of paganism, Zoroastrianism, and other religions. The center of the entire western end of the Old World web shifted east, to Constantinople, Damascus, and Baghdad. These became the new seats of power, wealth, and learning.

Ordinary farmers, shepherds, smiths, and weavers scarcely recognized these broad and gradual trends. They knew what was going on in their village and its neighborhood, but usually little else. Few could have named the emperor or caliph in whose name taxes were collected. Fewer still could have explained the schisms within Christianity or Islam. Nonetheless, over the generations, these big shifts altered the lives of almost everyone.

Chapter Review

KEY TERMS

Umayyad caliphate p. 386

Sassanid dynasty p. 389

Germanic tribes p. 395

Constantine p. 396

Byzantine Empire p. 399

Justinian p. 400

Zoroastrianism p. 402

Manichaeism p. 402

schism p. 405

monasticism p. 405

Augustine p. 407

Islam p. 408

Muhammad p. 408

Arabs p. 408

shari'a p. 411

Abbasid caliphate p. 415

REVIEW QUESTIONS

1. What were the twin disasters that affected the Roman and Persian Empires during the third to the eighth centuries?

2. What two military threats did the Sassanids face?

3. Explain the causes and effects of the fundamental weakness of the Roman Empire in both the third and the fifth centuries.

4. How did the movements of the Huns upset the geopolitical balance in western Eurasia?

5. In what ways did the power, population, prosperity, and territory of the Byzantine Empire change between 500 and 800?

6. What were the main features of Manichaean theology?

7. Why and in what ways did the status of Christianity in the Roman Empire change between the third and fourth centuries?

8. What was Muhammad's chief political achievement, and how did he differ from Jesus and the Buddha in terms of political power?

9. What military advantages did Arab armies have over the Sassanids and the Byzantines?

10. How did the Umayyad caliphs' sources of legitimacy shift between 650 and 680?

11. In what ways were the Abbasids and Byzantines in opposition to one another, and how were they part of a greater unit?

12. What factors drove the eastward shift of power and trade into Southwest Asia between 200 and 800?

13. How did the spread of Christianity and Islam affect women, forms of entertainment, and education?

Go to INQUIZITIVE

to see what you've learned—and learn what you've missed—with personalized feedback along the way.

The East End of the Old World Web

CHINA AND ITS NEIGHBORS

200 to 1400

FOCUS QUESTIONS

1. Why was China so prosperous and stable during the Tang period?

2. How did developments in China under the Song affect the rest of East Asia?

3. How did the Mongols become the most powerful political force in East Asia?

In the fourteenth century, a Chinese author, Wang Li, commented on what he saw as a new development in the history of Eurasia:

> ...the land within the Four Seas had become the territory of one family, civilization had spread everywhere and no more barriers existed. For people in search of fame and wealth in north and south, a journey of a thousand *li* [about 300 miles, or 500 km] was like a trip next door, while a journey of ten thousand *li* constituted just a neighborly jaunt. Hence, among people of the Western Regions [meaning Central Asia and Iran, mainly] who served at court, or who studied in our south-land, many forgot the region of their birth and took delight in living among our rivers and lakes. As they settled down in China for a long time, some became advanced in years, their families grew, and being far from home, they had no desire to be buried in their fatherland. Brotherhood among peoples has certainly reached a new plane.

What Wang Li noticed was the effect of political conquests that united broad regions of Eurasia. People moved long distances more freely owing to this political unification. Merchants could travel safely across Central Asia from China to Iran along the routes of the Silk Roads. In earlier times, such voyages had been more perilous because of bandits and local rulers who would help themselves to a share of any merchant's goods.

Paradoxically, the brutal conquests of much of Eurasia by the Mongols in the thirteenth century created these peaceful and prosperous conditions—one of the major themes of this chapter. By 1300, the Old World web was humming with activity as never before. This growth in the Old World web was grafted onto the rapid intensification of web connections in East Asia that occurred especially when China was both strong and most open to foreign trade. Those moments came especially under the early Tang dynasty and the Song dynasty. The ups and downs of China's wealth and power, and how they influenced developments throughout East Asia, constitute the other main theme of this chapter.

In the course of the period from 200 to 1400 CE, all of East Asia became increasingly connected, although in fits and starts with several rollbacks. Military expansions, cultural exchanges, and diplomatic contacts all helped push this process of integration along. The rollbacks came when China grew weaker or its leaders chose to restrict foreign contact. More than anything else, it was trade that linked the regions of East Asia.

East Asia, 200–907

Merchant networks and webs of exchange develop only when and where people see opportunities that justify the risks of trade and travel. Political frameworks always matter in these calculations. Where large states keep the peace, risks are smaller and trade likelier to grow. Where they keep the peace and actively encourage commerce, which is what Wang Li observed, trade networks almost always grow. So we begin with political frameworks.

There are three related themes to note about East Asian politics in this period: China always carried the most weight in East Asian affairs; China stayed politically unified more consistently than any other country in world history; and the rhythms of unification and disunity in China tended to be mirrored in neighboring lands.

As we saw in Chapter 7, by 200 CE China dominated East Asia demographically and exerted considerable sway politically, economically, and culturally with its neighbors. That trend continued after 200, sometimes strengthening, sometimes weakening, depending mainly on the degree to which China stayed unified. The historical unity of China is so remarkable, as well as so important for the broader region of East Asia, that it deserves a closer look.

Cycles of Unity and Disunity

During the roughly 2,200 years since the formation of the Qin and Han dynasties until today, a large contiguous China, ruled by an emperor (or lately by the Chinese Communist Party), has existed about 70 to 75 percent of the time. China has been fragmented into multiple states about 25 to 30 percent of the time. No other country in world history, except for some small island states, shows anything like China's record of unity. It exceeds that of Egypt, the closest comparable case. In the first 2,200 years after Egypt's initial unification (ca. 2600–400 BCE), pharaohs ruled the entire country, or close to it, about 65 percent of the time. The durability and resilience of unity in Chinese political history are very peculiar by the standards of world history—even if today everyone takes it for granted. It is all the more remarkable given that China normally accounted for a quarter to a third of humankind, as shown in the table on the next page.

The irregular rhythms of China's periods of unity and disunity helped to shape a larger East Asian pattern that prevailed between 200 and 1400. From the end of the Han dynasty in 220 CE until the seventh century, disunity was the rule both in China and throughout East Asia. There followed an era of centralized states, anchored by China's Tang dynasty (618–907). As the Tang weakened, the pendulum shifted back toward disunity, although more briefly this time. By the mid-tenth century, unity returned again until the mid-twelfth century. Then steppe nomad confederacies conquered most of East Asia piecemeal. That brought another era of fragmentation until one nomad confederacy, under the Mongols, conquered so widely as to open another period of centralized power in China from the 1280s to the 1350s and 1360s. Broadly speaking, then, periods of consolidation and fragmentation of state power came and went in East Asia, and tended to follow similar rhythms throughout the region.

What accounts for this cyclical pattern? Climate change might have had something to do with it. The centuries from 900 to 1200 were, on average, times of better rains, fewer droughts, and more reliable rice harvests—conditions that favored stable rule. More irregular climate prevailed in the thirteenth century in East Asia, with some sharp droughts, cold spells, and unreliable harvests—conditions conducive to conflict, rebellion, and the breakdown of states. Climate change, however, at most explains only part of the story.

The demographic and economic weight of China powerfully shaped the incentives for unity and disunity in its neighborhood. When China was united, the odds improved that kingdoms elsewhere in the region would grow and centralize. If neighboring peoples wished to resist China's power,

Estimated Populations (in millions) of China and the World, 200-1400 CE

YEAR CE	CHINA	WORLD	CHINA'S PROPORTION
200	55	230	24%
400	50	200	25%
600	46	200	23%
800	53	220	24%
1000	90	275	33%
1100	125	300	42%
1200	115	400	29%
1300	85	360	24%
1400	60	350	17%

Source: Robert Marks, *China: An Environmental History* (2012), 170; Joel Cohen, *How Many People Can the Earth Support?* (1995), appendix 2, 400-401.

they needed to band together. Alternatively, if one faction in a neighboring country could gain the support of China, its chances of crushing its rivals improved. As we shall see, the Silla dynasty came to dominate Korea because it enjoyed the support of the Tang, and a modest amount of China's support could make a huge difference in a small country such as Korea.

Conversely, when China was disunited, the countries in its orbit tended to be disunited too. The defensive logic of sticking together to resist Chinese power did not apply. And China, when fragmented itself, could not easily vault one or another faction in Korea or Tibet or anywhere else into a dominant position. Thus the numerous rises and falls of states and dynasties in East Asian history between 200 and 1400, while confusing on the surface, conform to a general pattern.

China, 220-618

As we saw in Chapter 7, the Han dynasty teetered for decades and collapsed in 220 CE. A 360-year period of disunity and warfare followed, opening the door to two important shifts. The first was the establishment of Buddhism as a major cultural and religious feature in China. The second was the rise of the south, meaning the Yangzi River valley and points south.

Buddhism The collapse of the Han and the warfare that followed shook many people's faith in the value of Confucian precepts, such as the obligation of the best-educated men to serve the state. With small rival kingdoms fighting continually, bureaucrats and

officials sought to withdraw from the turbulence of political life in favor of peaceful contemplation. Daoism, which had developed within China several centuries earlier (see Chapter 7), endorsed this choice with its emphases on meditation and quests for health and longevity.

Meanwhile, beginning in the last decades of Han rule, monks from northern India crossed the Himalaya mountains bringing Buddhism to China via Central Asia. In the following centuries, Buddhism blended into the Daoist tradition in China. Both emphasized the virtues of contemplation and self-discipline. Like Daoism, Buddhism urged people to withdraw from the clamor of politics and worldly struggle in favor of the inner life. Unlike Daoism, it put high value on monasticism and celibacy—alien concepts in China, where individuals were expected to identify powerfully with their families. But many women who chafed under the Confucian expectation of submission to fathers, brothers, and husbands found Buddhism appealing. Its doctrines placed less emphasis on the authority of males over females than did Confucian tradition. Political chaos and chronic warfare in China, not to mention a brutal famine of the late 530s, invited people to reconsider their outlooks, and in this setting both Daoism and Buddhism prospered.

Buddhism already took many forms by the time it was carried to China, but it was the Mahayana school that traveled best. One reason for that was the translations by a Mahayana Buddhist monk named Kumarajiva, who was captured by Chinese forces and in 401 CE removed to a court in Chang'an, where he rendered the Buddhist sutras into elegant, philosophical Chinese texts. Although its followers initially centered around the eastern ends of the Silk Roads, Buddhism also attracted converts in southern China. It is possible that it spread by sea routes as well as overland. In China, the Zen tradition developed from the fifth century onward, one in which mastery of texts took a back seat to person-to-person teachings that emphasized meditation, self-control, and contemplation of the deeper nature of things. As we shall see, Buddhism in China continued to prosper with the advent of the Tang dynasty after 618.

Early Buddhism A leaded bronze Buddhist monk, dated to the late sixth century, depicts the simple robes worn by devotees of the newly popular religion.

Silk and the South The breakdown of central control in China after the Han collapse also led to the rise of the south. Without a unified state to oversee the production and transfers of food, people often migrated to lands where food was easier to grow and restrictions on trade were fewer. Millions moved from north China to the Yangzi River valley and farther south. The rich soils of Sichuan, on the middle Yangzi, rewarded farmers more generously than did the dusty plains of north China. Sichuan became a rice-basket, yielding vast quantities of marketable grain. Soon, Sichuan and even Tibet were linked, via the Yangzi, to seaborne trade for the first time. The river became an artery of commerce. The lower Yangzi and adjacent regions on the coast of the East China Sea became one of the world's foremost centers of wealth and population.

The warmer climate of the Yangzi valley, and of regions farther south, suited silk-worms as well as people. As we've seen, the Han dynasty had promoted silk trade to India, southwestern Asia, and the Mediterranean along trans-Asian Silk Roads. Silk exports thrived when production shifted southward to warmer climes, where the white mulberry grew well and people could raise more silkworms.

These fussy creatures, a kind of caterpillar, strongly prefer to dine on the leaves of white mulberry trees. Domesticated **silkworms** have been raised in China for 5,000 years. As they progress from larva to pupa, they secrete through their salivary glands a fine silk thread, up to a mile long, with which they build cocoons. Patient people can unspool the thread from cocoons and weave it into a lustrous and sheer cloth—silk. Silk making remained an East Asian secret for many centuries. The techniques spread to Japan in the fourth century CE and to Southwest Asia in the sixth century, but the Chinese still made more and better silk than anyone else.

Extremely laborious and requiring nimble fingers, silk making was the work of women and girls. The rise of the silk industry allowed thousands of females to produce for the market. When political unity returned to China under the Sui dynasty (581–618), the country was richer than in the time of the Han; more integrated into long-distance circuits of trade; and less centered, in demographic and economic terms, on the north—thanks in part to the nature of silkworms and the labor of Chinese women.

Re-unification under the Sui Dynasty, 581–618 The Sui dynasty, like the Qin, was short-lived but left a lasting legacy. The Sui's founder was a general from a northern regional kingdom. He overthrew the royal family, and—taking no chances—proceeded to murder 59 males of the royal lineage. In the 580s, he conquered the rest of China's many kingdoms and by 589 declared himself emperor, taking the reign-name of Sui Wendi. He launched reforms of coinage and land tenure that boosted the econ-omy, already energized by the booming silk market. Before his death, he started work on a new canal that would link the southern rice-producing regions with the northern frontier, where the bulk the Sui army stood guard against steppe raiders.

His son, Emperor Yang—or Yangdi—had a grandiose streak to match that of Alex-ander the Great, Qin Shi Huang, or any pharaoh. He launched a disastrous invasion of Korea. To supply his army, he ordered the extension of his father's canal starting in 605. Up to 5 million men and women worked as conscripts on this massive project, which opened in 609. The canal eventually stretched nearly 1,200 miles (2,000 km), linking fertile regions south of the Yangzi to the Huang He basin in the north.

The **Grand Canal**, as it is now called, stands among the world's most important public works projects ever built. It enabled the emperor—and his successors for 1,300 years—to move troops around the empire cheaply and quickly, countering rebellions.

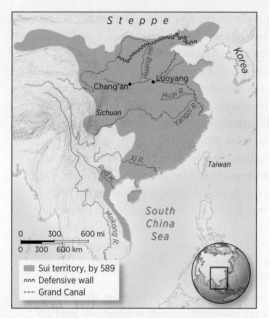

Rice from the lower Yangzi and the rich basin of Sichuan could be shipped reliably to northern frontier garrisons. China could now support bigger armies on its northern border, by far its most vulnerable.

The Grand Canal had a unifying effect in China. It was, in essence, a Nile made by human hands, binding north and south together politically. Economically, it provided merchants with a safe route for north-south trade, avoiding the open sea with its risks from storms and pirates. Easier rice transport on the Grand Canal also enabled China to support bigger cities and reduced the severity of famines. Less helpfully, the canal obliged the Chinese state to keep it dredged and in good working order ever after, because without it the northern cities and frontier armies would starve.

Yangdi also improved China's northern defenses by investing in walls. Earlier dynasties, particularly the Qin, had built walls along the northern frontiers to check the raids and invasions of

The Sui Dynasty, 581–618 CE The Sui dynasty lasted less than four decades, but it left China with two crucial legacies that affected its fortunes ever after. Both were infrastructure projects. The Grand Canal linked the Yangzi and Huang He (Yellow River) basins, allowing reliable and cheap transport between the two great centers of the Chinese economy. The walls along the northern frontier, which together ultimately became known as the Great Wall, helped protect China from its most fearsome enemies, steppe horsemen.

steppe nomads. The walls stood in disrepair when the Sui came to power, but the prosperity brought by their economic reforms enabled them to extend the barriers and link segments together into what is now called the Great Wall of China. The Great Wall was a long-term project, begun long before the Sui and continued long after, but they were among the dynasties that tried hardest to keep nomads at bay by building walls.

Hundreds of thousands died while toiling on Yangdi's public works projects, and he over-strained the treasury. His legendary excess irritated his generals to the point where they engineered his murder in a royal bath. Few lamented his death and the end of the dynasty. But Yangdi left China with the Grand Canal.

The Tang Dynasty, 618–750

The general who orchestrated the splashy assassination of Yangdi proclaimed a new dynasty in 618: the Tang. It took ten years to crush rebellions and consolidate power.

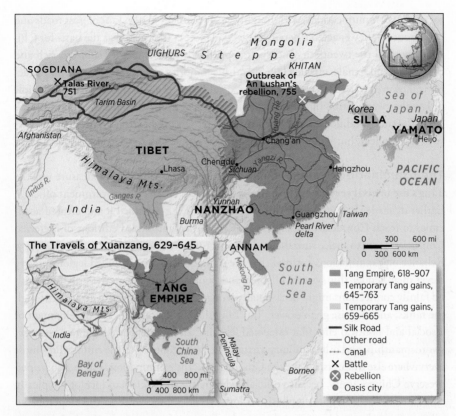

The Tang Dynasty, 618–907 CE Regarded as one of China's most effective dynasties, especially in its first century, the Tang strengthened Chinese influence in all neighboring kingdoms and in Central Asia. Traffic along the Silk Roads reached one of its peaks during Tang rule. The monk Xuanzang traveled these routes extensively, seeking out Buddhist wisdom in India to bring back to China.

Soon after, the Tang emperors set to work building the most powerful state in the world, one that later Chinese would regard as an ideal.

Early Tang Governance and Reforms The early Tang inherited an economically robust China. These were times of reliable monsoon rains and rich harvests. The Grand Canal boosted trade and improved imperial finances. The Tang built upon this inheritance. They firmed up their borders and conquered small states and tribes in Central Asia, putting all Silk Road routes as far as Afghanistan under their power by 650. Thereafter, they kept wars to a minimum.

The Tang emperors reformed the machinery of the state. Their measures included reasserting the "rule of avoidance" whereby officials could not serve in their home districts, which reduced corruption and favoritism. They organized a state postal service for official communications, with roughly 20,000 miles (30,000 km) of post roads and canal routes. They enacted a detailed legal code in 653 that served as the basis for Chinese law until the twentieth century. It applied to all the emperor's subjects, rich and poor, male and female, ethnic Han and ethnic minority alike. Punishments for infractions, however, varied depending on the social status of the transgressor—a principle of law that was routine in the deep past and is found, for example, in Hammurabi's laws. The code solidified Confucian principles: fathers might strike children or servants with little to fear, but if children struck fathers—or teachers—they courted trouble.

The Examination System   Another important and long-lasting measure was the Tang's use of **civil service examinations** as a means of selecting government officials. Earlier dynasties had pioneered this practice. The Tang extended it and created academies to teach Confucian principles. They published authorized editions of preferred Confucian texts to make sure their administrators were steeped in the right ideology. Reliance on examinations ensured that the Tang bureaucracy included legions of very clever men. Under this system, talented and bookish youths from the provinces with no family connections might occasionally win government appointments, rise through the ranks, and exercise great power. The Tang thereby encouraged the development of a social and political elite that esteemed learning and refinement above raw courage, swordsmanship, and other military virtues—a sharp contrast to the ruling elites most everywhere else in Eurasia. Like the Grand Canal, the examination system also helped preserve Chinese unity, because officials who mastered Confucian ideology typically embraced it, including its emphasis on loyalty and subservience to the emperor. No other states in the world—except those under Tang sway—would recruit administrators through written examination for another thousand years.

Wu Zetian, the Most Powerful Woman in the World   The Tang was unique among Chinese dynasties in another respect: one emperor was a woman. To most Chinese, both men and women, the notion that a woman might rule a state seemed unnatural—like "hens crowing," as they often put it. Women account for about 1.5 percent of all rulers recorded in world history, and less than that in China.

Only one woman has ever ruled China in her own name. Born in 624, **Wu Zetian** (also known as Wu Zhao) came from a prosperous and well-connected family. Her parents encouraged her to educate herself, a rarity for girls of the time. Family connections enabled her to become part of the royal household at age 13, perhaps as a concubine of the emperor Taizong (r. 626–649). Life in the imperial harem provided a political education for those keen to learn. Wu Zetian was more than keen and absorbed the evident lessons in political intrigue. She became concubine and then wife of the next emperor (Gaozong, r. 650–683), and by 655 as his health faded she came to exercise more and more power. She proved highly capable, drawing deftly on literature and history in her rulings, as was expected of an emperor. When Gaozong died in 683, she became regent for her son and then ruled in her own right from 690, proclaiming a short-lived dynasty called the Zhou. She was overthrown shortly before her death in 705. Her career was controversial, to put it mildly.

Confucian historians, aghast at the idea of a female in authority, credited her with poisoning some of her children for political purposes. They claimed she was a bewitching beauty who slept and murdered her way to the top and kept at it when in power. How much of this is true is open to question. She was surely a masterful manipulator and politician within the court. Her rivals regularly turned up dead or exiled. Her underlings operated a reign of terror, torturing anyone who might pose a challenge to her.

Wu Zetian was also the greatest patron of Buddhism in Chinese history. She supported Buddhist monasteries, commissioned Buddhist art, and encouraged the import of Buddhist texts from India. In her later years, she tried to require vegetarianism within her empire. Buddhists rewarded her efforts. They found it easier to accept a female ruler than did conscientious Confucians. Dutiful Buddhist scholars conveniently justified Wu Zetian's rule and extolled her virtues. Craven ones creatively edited sacred texts to serve her propaganda needs. The alliance between ruler and religion, important since the first states in Sumer and commonplace ever since, was fully in evidence in Wu Zetian's reign.

Wu Zetian also encouraged commerce. A merchant's daughter and an opponent of the Confucian educated elite, she felt none of their disdain for business. She had new canals dug, and docks and marketplaces erected in several cities. She lowered taxes. She allowed rich, unrefined businessmen access to the corridors of power. Her policies often appalled the Confucian literati but probably promoted prosperity in the empire.

Wu Zetian's political talents paid dividends in foreign affairs too. She kept her neighbors fighting among themselves. She doled out money, bestowed titles, and offered princes and princesses in marriage to keep her alliances in good order. She launched the Chinese tradition of panda diplomacy, donating a pair of bears to a ruler in Japan. She found ingeniously humiliating ways to execute diplomats and allies who crossed her. As the ruler of the most powerful and populous state in the world for a quarter-century, Wu Zetian was the most powerful person on Earth in her day—the only woman in world history of whom that statement is true.

Economy, Society, and Culture   Despite sordid intrigues at court, the years from about 630 to about 750 proved a prosperous and stable era for China. Reliable monsoons continued, keeping the canals in operation and the harvests bountiful. The Tang controlled food prices and oversaw the periodic re-distribution of farmland to families, reducing the ranks of landless paupers. They regulated agriculture carefully, but trade less so. The rise of the south continued: a census of 742 showed that half the population of the empire lived south of the Yangzi, whereas in 618 only a quarter did. Tea, grown in the south, became a national drink. It probably improved health in the empire: boiling tea water killed many unhealthful bacteria. Although smallpox had arrived in China (from Southwest Asia, perhaps via India) by 500 CE or so, no spectacular epidemics reversed population growth, as happened repeatedly, for example, in the Mediterranean world after the 540s. With good harvests and few epidemics, it was easier for the Tang to claim the Mandate of Heaven. (As we saw in Chapter 7, since the Zhou dynasty, rulers showed they enjoyed the Mandate of Heaven by governing well, and were shown to have lost it by disorder, natural disasters, and poverty in their realm.)

During the Tang era, Chinese families continued the settlement of the rich basin of Sichuan. Han Chinese also settled the Pearl River delta, in the far south adjacent to the South China Sea. This region provided new crops such as sugar and cotton, both introduced from India. The settlement and colonization of Sichuan and the far south were for Tang China a huge windfall, a bit like the Roman conquest of Egypt in the first century BCE or the westward expansion of the United States in the nineteenth century: a destination for people in search of better prospects, and a source of new resources and wealth for society and state. The expansion came at the expense of indigenous peoples, who had to move onto poorer lands.

The frontier settlement to the south and the expanded commerce everywhere in China during the seventh through the eighth centuries supported a surge of urbanization and a buildup of the armed forces. The main Tang capital, Chang'an, easily the largest city in the world, attained a population of perhaps 2 million. It had been the Qin, Han, and Sui capital, but the Tang rebuilt it with a grid pattern and wide avenues—like Teotihuacán but far larger. Dozens of other sizeable cities, such as Hangzhou near the mouth of the Yangzi and Guangzhou in the far south, sprang up along riverine trade routes. A more cosmopolitan urban culture developed. Market cities attracted traders from near and far, including Persians, Arabs, Malays, Japanese, Koreans, and Central Asians such as Sogdians and Uighurs. Trade, both foreign and domestic, provided more tax revenue on top of what came in the form of a grain and cloth tax levied against every male age 21 to 59. With its finances in order, the empire could afford to maintain garrisons in dusty Central Asian towns and all along the northern frontiers. Those garrisons, in turn, kept the peace and made life safe for traders. The economy and the military, in effect, supported one another.

The Tang promotion of Buddhism also helped stimulate trade. Buddhist monasteries were commercial centers: they lent money at interest, operated flour mills, owned farmland, ran inns, conducted auctions, accepted donations, and sold what we would now call tourist trinkets, especially religious icons. Until the ninth century, monasteries enjoyed special tax breaks, strengthening their commercial position. Some of the goods that China imported along the Silk Roads—gems, incense—were used in Buddhist worship rituals. Tang control of the oasis towns around the Tarim Basin, now in western China, helped foster trade with Central Asia and beyond. The city of Chang'an became the eastern terminus of the emerging camel caravan networks that made up the Silk Roads.

Tang prosperity underwrote high culture. Emperors encouraged additional translations of Buddhist texts from Sanskrit and celebrated a well-traveled monk, Xuanzang, who in 645 returned to China after fifteen years spent gathering Buddhist books and wisdom in India. Xuanzang was one of several seekers who journeyed across the forbidding Himalaya, demonstrating Chinese interest in India—that mysterious land (as Chinese saw it) of spiritual truths, magic, and medicine. The Tang, after Wu Zetian died, also established new Confucian academies and institutes of poetry.

Under the influence of Buddhism, Tang poetry and painting turned to scenes of nature, especially remote mountainous landscapes. Every literate person aspired to write poetry, even members of the imperial family. Tang poetry acquired great prestige at the time, and educated Chinese ever since have memorized its outstanding passages. Du Fu, for example, an eighth-century poet who twice failed the civil service exam, is regarded as the greatest poet-sage of the Chinese language, his lines savored for their poignancy on themes such as friendship and political turmoil. His contemporary, Li Bai, acquired an equally towering reputation as a romantic poet, reflecting on nature, loneliness, and the appeal of wine. The earliest printing, done by hand-carving into woodblocks, originated in China in the seventh and eighth centuries, and made texts more readily available and reading more popular. Tang woodblock printers specialized in poetry, agricultural and medical texts, and Buddhist scriptures.

Tang high culture was famously cosmopolitan. Foreign influences, especially from India, came in the saddlebags of sojourners on the Silk Roads. Many Tang emperors showed interest in India's longevity potions, and a few are thought to have died from overdoses of Indian elixirs. One Indian envoy in the seventh century brought sugarcane and sugar-making technology to China. The sport of polo and a new lute from Persia became popular. Camels became a new artistic motif. Foreign merchants brought new religions—Islam, Judaism, Zoroastrianism, and the form of Christianity known as Nestorianism—all of which the Tang tolerated. Foreign students from Korea and Japan flocked to Tang China.

The sphere of women expanded under the Tang, as under the Sui before them—at least, for the upper classes. Since the fall of the Han, elite women had taken larger roles in public life, and under the Sui and the early Tang this reached its height. Some women of the imperial family engaged fully in politics and exercised real power. Others, in arranged marriages to steppe chieftains or Tibetan kings, served as de facto diplomats for the Tang dynasty. Tang artwork shows elite women enjoying archery, playing polo, dancing, and doing things never depicted, and rarely done, by Chinese women under earlier dynasties.

Tang Sportswoman The Tang noblewoman in this statuette, dated to the eighth century, once held a polo mallet. Polo was one of the many high-culture pursuits that Tang elites enjoyed.

This liberty was mainly a result of the Tang rulers' descent from peoples of northwest China, among whom women typically enjoyed wider latitude.

Under the Sui and early Tang, families from prestigious lineages welcomed the birth of daughters. As brides, they could bring large gifts (brideprice) from rich families eager to boost their social standing. As one aristocrat, Yan Zhitui (d. 591) complained, "In the present age, when marriages are arranged, some people sell their daughters for the betrothal gift or buy a wife by making a payment of silk. They compare ancestry [of the two families], calculate down to the smallest sum, demand much and offer little, exactly like bargaining in a market place." Their "market" value gave young women from prestigious families some negotiating power with their parents and brothers.

However, the practice of brideprice vanished in the late Tang, and elite families once again came to prefer sons over daughters. Property and family name were transmitted through sons; women could not easily own property. Less distinguished families— of whom we know very little—normally shared the preference for sons, although in silk-producing areas hard-working daughters could bring their families useful income and enjoyed more esteem as a result.

Peasant women during the Tang worked at home much as their foremothers had done, but on average spent more time feeding mulberry leaves to silkworms, fashioning silk thread, and weaving silk cloth. Although the Tang taxed only men, a large share of tax obligations took the form of cloth, which women and girls produced. The Tang era saw an expansion not only in the market for women's work, but also for young women—as concubines whom prosperous men bought and sold. Poor families sometimes found it necessary to sell daughters to make ends meet.

East Asia at the Height of the Tang, 618–750

In foreign affairs, the Tang dominated their neighborhood. By and large, the Tang managed to prevent the rise of large nomad confederacies by playing one group off against another and bribing chieftains judiciously—much as Romans, Byzantines, and Sassanids did in western Eurasia. Small sums for the Tang would buy, or at least rent, a lot of allegiance from nomads. In this way, the Tang extended their power far into the oases of Central Asia. Sometimes they controlled these directly, although more often through local rulers whom they bribed or intimidated as necessary. They even marched an army into north India in 649, sacking the Buddha's birthplace and bringing back 2,000 slaves. Satisfactory relations with their northern and western neighbors helped boost Silk Road trade, filling state coffers and providing a steady stream of horses for Tang armies. China itself lacked enough good grassland to raise horses cheaply.

Tibet and Yunnan In the southwest, flourishing exports—in metals and animal products, for example—contributed to the rise of a **Tibetan Empire** (ca. 618–842) centered on the high, chilly plateau just north of the Himalaya. A dynasty, sometimes called

			MAINLAND	ISLAND	
YEAR CE	JAPAN	KOREA	SOUTHEAST ASIA[1]	SOUTHEAST ASIA[2]	CHINA
200	0.7	0.3	2.5	2.0	55
600	3.0	1.0	3.5	3.0	46
1000	5.0	2.5	5.0	4.0	90
1400	12.0	3.0	9.0	7.5	60

Estimated Populations (in millions) of East and Southeast Asia, 200–1400 CE

Source: Colin McEvedy and Richard Jones, *Atlas of World Population History* (1978), 166–81, 190–203.

1. Modern Burma, Thailand, Laos, Cambodia, Vietnam
2. Modern Indonesia, Philippines

Yarlung for the valley in which Tibet's capital of Lhasa is located, exerted influence from northern India to Mongolia. (See map on page 433.) Tibet's new rulers embraced Buddhism and worked to share it with their subjects, a substantial minority of whom were Christians. The Tibetans competed with the Tang and other powers in Central Asia in a geopolitical great game—with remarkable success, given the paltry population and resources of their homeland. When rebellion weakened China, Tibetan forces even occupied the Tang capital of Chang'an for two weeks in 763. Their success in war and diplomacy diminished after 830, and soon internal divisions brought an end to imperial Tibet. Never again would Tibet compete as a regional power in Asia.

A smaller kingdom, called Nanzhao, emerged in the eighth and ninth centuries in what is now China's southwestern Yunnan province. Its leadership also followed Buddhist traditions, especially Tantric Buddhism, a novel variant emphasizing faster routes to nirvana (the release from all suffering promised to those who follow the proper way) through mastery of special rituals. Brought by Indian monks, in Nanzhao it became a state religion. Nanzhao often resisted Tang China, occasionally in alliance with Tibet. At one point, Nanzhao took control of much of the rich basin of Sichuan, including its capital of Chengdu, and extended its sway southward to Burma. It dissolved in 902, just as the Tang dynasty was collapsing.

Korea, Japan, Vietnam China's neighbors to the east and south flourished partly through Tang influences. In Korea, Japan, and Vietnam, states usually recognized the Tang as overlords, although their subservience to China varied and sometimes was merely a polite fiction. (See map on page 433.)

In Korea, the Tang helped to install the Silla dynasty in 676. With Tang help, Silla conquests ended a long era of fractious politics among rival Korean kings. In cultural terms, however, China virtually conquered Korea. Elite Koreans had studied Confucian classics since the 370s. Buddhism came to Korea at about the same time, mainly via

Chinese monks, and in the northern part of the peninsula (a kingdom called Kogurgo) it became the state religion. A few Korean monks went to India to study at the birthplace of Buddhism. While Buddhism appealed strongly to elites, the masses of Korean society still found shamanism—the oldest Eurasian form of spirit worship—satisfactory. Chinese script, fashion, art, and music attracted elites in Korea too, and for a brief while in the eighth century the Silla kingdom even adopted the examination system of the Tang to select officials. Many Korean men went to China to study, and some learned Chinese and Confucian ideology so well that they passed the examinations in China and served in the Tang administration. Many more wrote Chinese poetry, or Korean-language poems in Chinese characters. Korean women were especially prized as slaves and concubines in elite Tang households.

Even as Korea absorbed more and more Chinese influences under the Silla, it retained political independence. The Tang were satisfied with the Silla rulers, who regularly had to declare their loyalty to the Tang. But the Silla elite, a formidable military class, helped preserve Korean autonomy. For them, the greatest honor was to have a son die in battle—a very different outlook from that of the Chinese literati, who raised their sons to be scholars.

Tang China also influenced Japan. Our evidence for Japanese history before 500 CE is spotty. Tiny states existed in rice-growing regions, but in much of the archipelago people continued hunting and foraging in preference to farming. Rice, iron, and horses all had been introduced from the mainland, via Korea, before 500. As elsewhere, these innovations favored state building. By the early 600s, one state in the southeast—the **Yamato region**—began to assert control over most of the populous rice-growing areas. Buddhism arrived in the sixth to seventh centuries, providing the Yamato rulers with an additional source of prestige as they mastered its rituals and knowledge. As in China, Buddhism's success provoked a nativist reaction among people who thought it threatened cherished traditions. The Yamato imported Tang city planning—they modeled their capital on Chang'an's grid pattern—temple architecture, writing, and, to some extent, laws. Yamato law codes, however, were more generous to women than the Tang's had become. Japanese women could own land, for example.

Japanese political culture retained some distinctive features. Despite an aristocratic ethos built around warfare, some of the Yamato rulers were women. Japan never adopted the Chinese notion of the Mandate of Heaven—the Yamato clan could never lose the right to rule, no matter how many earthquakes or epidemics hit Japan. No examination system was ever used, and men of learning never rivaled military men in prestige. Chronic warfare plagued Japan even after the rise of the Yamato state, keeping a premium on military skills. After crushing potential rivals within Japan, the Yamato tried to invade Korea in the early 660s. That effort failed—it was the last overseas attack Japan would launch for more than 900 years.

Vietnam felt the power of Tang China more than did Korea or Japan. Recall that the Han dynasty had conquered northern Vietnam (called Annam) but could not hold it. The Tang re-conquered Annam, and thereafter Vietnam increasingly adopted Confucian ideals, Daoism, Chinese script, and Chinese versions of Buddhism. Nonetheless, Chinese settlers never overwhelmed Vietnam—as they did what is now south China. The trickle of Chinese immigrants was absorbed and over time became Vietnamese, and the language and identity of Vietnam survived.

The Mekong Delta and Srivijaya The other lands of Southeast Asia remained essentially outside the sphere of Tang power. Small states grew up where river valleys allowed rice farming. They quickly formed their own seaborne trading webs, especially among Vietnam, the Malay Peninsula, and Java. In the Mekong delta of southern Vietnam, a state called (in Chinese texts) Funan arose around 100 to 600 CE, more influenced by India and Brahmin traditions than by China. Archeologists have found Roman coins and ceramics from Persia there, showing the reach of its seaborne connections. The script used for Sanskrit, the north Indian language of the Vedas, was used to write several Southeast Asian tongues by 500 CE. Until the fourteenth century, Indian culture, carried across the Bay of Bengal by traders and missionaries, made a stronger impression in Southeast Asia than did Chinese culture, except in the northern half of Vietnam.

The most durable of these Southeast Asian states was the Buddhist kingdom of **Srivijaya**, centered on the island of Sumatra. It emerged in the 670s and lasted until the thirteenth century. Its territory waxed and waned through the centuries, sometimes extending to the Malay Peninsula and the island of Java. Its fortunes rose and

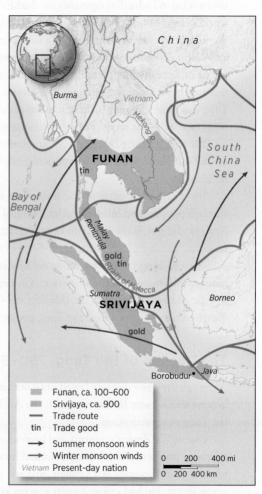

Southeast Asia, ca. 200–900 CE In the early centuries CE, Southeast Asians exploited the potential of irrigated rice production and revenues from maritime trade to build new and larger states, the greatest of which was Srivijaya. Monsoon winds allowed comparatively easy sailing to India and China, each of which exerted strong cultural influence in parts of Southeast Asia.

fell with tax receipts from trade with China and India, and especially from shipping passing through the straits between Sumatra and Malaya. The Straits of Malacca, like the straits of the Bosporus and Dardanelles where the Mediterranean and Black Seas meet, was one of the premier choke points on the map of world trade for the last 2,000 years. Control of the Straits ensured streams of revenue. Srivijaya's rulers also controlled gold exports from inland Sumatra and at times tin exports from Malaya, some of which they traded to India. For centuries, its Buddhist shrines, such as Borobudur in Java, the world's largest Buddhist temple, attracted pilgrims from as far away as India.

The Tang created something of a sinosphere in East Asia. Politically, economically, and culturally they dominated the entire region, despite frequent military defeats at the hands of Koreans, steppe raiders, Nanzhao, and Tibetans. Their script, poetry, architecture, dress, food, and religions carried prestige that rulers everywhere admired. The Tang did more than any other factor to make East Asia into a political, cultural, and economic web—or more precisely, the eastern end of the Eurasian web.

The root of Tang influence lay in relative size and strength: the Tang ruled 45 to 60 million people and had revenues to match, while other polities of the region were far smaller.

The Tang ruled parts of the sinosphere directly, and other parts they influenced through puppets and intermediaries. Some of the lands that they ruled directly, such as Annam, did not in the long run become part of China. Yunnan, the seat of Nanzhao, however, is today a southwestern province of China. But in all these lands, the cultural influence of Tang China was profound and enduring, carried by merchants, students, monks, soldiers, officials, and settlers. Chinese took up residence in many port towns of East and Southeast Asia. To this day, the Chinese word for overseas Chinatowns is *Tangrenjie*, or "streets where the Tang people live."

The Decline of the Tang, 750–907

Although the Tang dynasty lasted until 907, it teetered for most of its last 150 years. The biggest shock came in the 750s with the An Lushan rebellion, a civil war from which the Tang never recovered.

One of Wu Zetian's reforms had been to station army garrisons permanently on the northern frontier to check steppe nomad incursions. This backfired on later emperors when a general named An Lushan, himself probably of Central Asian origin, rose in revolt in 755. He had enjoyed great success keeping northern "barbarians" in line; but when he sensed court politics shifting against him, he decided, like Julius Caesar in the last days of the Roman Republic, to overthrow the state rather than lose his position. He led several hundred thousand soldiers on a rampage across north China, taking the Tang capital and forcing the emperor to flee. Emperor Xuanzong escaped toward Sichuan with his favorite consort, Yang Guifei, one of the fabled beauties of China; but on the road his imperial guard refused to protect him unless he strangled her, which

CONSIDERING THE EVIDENCE

Tang Poetry

When the An Lushan rebellion reached the Tang capital of Chang'an in 755, Du Fu was forced from his hard-won position as an official. He returned a few years later, first as a prisoner of the rebels and then as a minor official in the restored dynasty. But he left again when he was demoted to work as a provincial Commissioner of Education. His travels during and after the rebellion inspired an unusually wide range of subjects for his poetry, which is often amusingly personal. In one poem, he described his drunken fall from a horse; in another, he complained about endless paperwork. Like other Tang officials who took poetry seriously, Du Fu wrote verses critical of the hardships that the government imposed on commoners. He wrote the following poem about forced labor recruitment in 759, about halfway through the An Lushan crisis.

The Recruiting Officers at the Village of the Stone Moat

I sought a lodging for the night, at
    sunset, in the Stone Moat Village.
Recruiting Officers, who seize people
    by night, were there.
A venerable old man climbed over the
    wall and fled.
An old woman came out of the door
    and peered.
What rage in the shouts of the
    Recruiting Officers!
What bitterness in the weeping of the
    old woman!
I heard the words of the woman as she
    pled her cause before them:
"My three sons are with the frontier
    guard at Yeh Ch'eng.
From one son I have received a letter.
A little while ago, two sons died in
    battle.
He who remains has stolen a
    temporary lease of life.
The dead are finished forever.
In the house, there is still no
    grown man,
Only my grandson at the breast.
The mother of my grandson has not
    gone,

Going out, coming in, she has not a
    single whole skirt.
I am an old woman, old woman, and
    my strength is failing,
But I beg to go with the Recruiting
    Officers when they return this night.
I will eagerly agree to act as a servant
    at Ho Yang;
I am still able to prepare the early
    morning meal."
The sound of words ceased in the long
    night,
It was as though I heard the darkness
    choke with tears.
At daybreak, I went on my way,
Only the venerable old man was left.

Questions for Analysis

1. How did the official activities of the Chinese state impact commoners during the Tang dynasty?

2. Which parts of the poem suggest that Du Fu drew on a personal experience when he wrote it?

3. What do the old woman's words and actions reveal about relationships among generations and between men and women at this time?

Source: Shihao li, 石壕吏, The Recruiting Officers at the Village of the Stone Moat. Poem by Du Fu, 杜甫, trans. Amy Lowell and Florence Ayscough, in *Fir-Flower Tablets: Poems* (Boston: 1921).

he did. Their unhappy love remains one of China's favorite stories. After writing a few sad poems, Emperor Xuanzong died in 763.

An Lushan could not keep his forces united. With the rebels divided, the Tang dynasty survived, if just barely, by inviting Central Asian forces, mostly Turkic and Tibetan warriors, to help them—a strategy not so different from the one Rome had employed 400 years previously. This cost them their leading position in Central Asia, already weakened in 751 when a Tang army was crushed by Arab, Persian, and Turkic forces at the battle of the Talas River. For the next thousand years after the An Lushan uprising ended in 763, neither the Tang nor later Chinese dynasties controlled any of Central Asia.

The Tang dynasty never recovered from the An Lushan uprising. They lost a quarter of their territory and a large proportion, some say up to half, of their population. They abandoned their cosmopolitan outlook. Now they tried to undermine Buddhism as a foreign import and sought to restore what they saw as a more Chinese, more traditional, more Confucian culture that would—they hoped—restore a golden age. In the years 841 to 845 this nativist outlook, as well as ordinary greed, inspired the Tang rulers to assault Buddhist institutions, destroying 4,600 monasteries, dismissing 250,000 monks and nuns, and seizing the enormous wealth amassed by monks over the centuries—including 150,000 slaves.

Although the later Tang won some military successes, their political prestige and practical power dwindled. Without their Central Asian garrisons, the Tang lost much of their lucrative Silk Road trade. They ceased their periodic redistribution of farmland in China. They abandoned supervision of urban markets, allowing market culture to thrive but disappointing traditional Confucians who regarded unbridled pursuit of wealth through commerce as unseemly. They relied for their revenues on a new salt tax, which after the An Lushan rebellion provided more than half of the revenue. By abandoning supervision of the economy in favor of unregulated markets, the Tang inadvertently fostered an increase in wealthy merchants and landlords—as well as countless landless peasants who would provide manpower for future rebellions.

After about 820, the emperors frequently lost their hold on the palace to bands of eunuchs. These were usually men of humble origin, often sold to the court as boys by desperate parents. Once castrated, they worked as low-ranking servants to the many thousands of women in the emperor's harem. During the late Tang, about 5,000 eunuchs lived and worked in the palace. Clever and ambitious ones sometimes became bureaucrats and advisers. They used their privileged access to the imperial family to build their own networks of power, extending to influence over the palace guard. One eunuch grew so rich he could donate a billion copper coins to a monastery. At times, eunuchs ran the state through puppet emperors, executing ministers who opposed them. The eunuchs often governed better than emperors, and Tang China enjoyed a modest revival of fortunes in the mid-ninth century.

After 860, however, rebellions flared up more frequently. Rebel leaders found willing foot soldiers in the masses who had been impoverished by the Tang's liberation of the economy. Popular resentment against wealthy merchants, especially foreign ones, led to massacres. On one occasion in the 870s, according to an Arab author, an army of rebels opposed to the Tang slaughtered over 120,000 foreigners—Arabs, Persians, Jews—in Guangzhou. The rebels, led by a revenge-seeker who had failed the civil service examination, went on to take the capital, Chang'an. When someone posted a mocking poem about them, they rounded up 3,000 people deemed capable of writing clever poetry and killed them all. By 907, the shell of the Tang state shattered and China splintered.

Eunuchs A large group of eunuchs appear in a mural of palace life painted on the wall of the tomb of a Tang prince in 706 CE.

Chinese intellectuals tended to regard times when China was unified and powerful, as during the early Tang, as a golden age. Periods of disunity and weakness at the center seemed to them the unfortunate results of bad governance. For ordinary people, however, if civil wars and bandit gangs stayed away, a weak state with limited power to tax families and conscript young men could seem a liberation. As with the collapse of urban states in the tenth-century Maya world, in tenth-century China the breakdown of the state seemed a crisis to those who depended on it but may have been a boon to those whose taxes and labor supported it. China's population grew faster after the rebellion of An Lushan, despite the frequent political chaos, than it had during the glory years of the Tang, suggesting improved conditions for the masses.

East Asia in the Time of the Nomads, ca. 900–1400

With brief exceptions, the Tang had kept their northern borders under control before 750. But as their strength waned, the relative power of the nomadic tribes of Manchuria and Mongolia grew. From time to time, charismatic leaders arose among these nomads and built confederations that could exploit China's vulnerability. In the centuries following the Tang, one pastoralist group after another conquered northern China, established a dynasty, and found enough collaborators among the Chinese literati to help them rule. Southern China usually eluded their grasp and remained independent, but typically had to pay large sums to the nomads to stay that way.

As the Tang weakened, China and East Asia fragmented politically: the Chinese call this era the period of Five Dynasties and Ten Kingdoms. Fragmentation was contagious. The Tibetans' empire had already fallen apart by 842. The Silla kingdom in Korea did so by 892, and Nanzhao in Yunnan followed suit in 902. Vietnam again won its independence from China.

As warlords, kings, and would-be emperors battled it out, new powers arose to the north. One of these, a band of nomads from Manchuria known as the Khitan, outmaneuvered rivals and built a state in north China in the early tenth century. The Khitan were true nomads. They lived in tents and on horseback, and they chose their leaders every three years—until an especially ambitious one canceled further elections. When he died in 926, his lieutenants suggested his wife ought to pay her respects by joining him in the grave, as hundreds of his warriors were obliged to do. She declined, citing a mother's obligations to small children, but offered to cut off her arm and place it in her husband's coffin as a sign of wifely respect. Negotiations continued, and in the end she sliced off only one hand. She then ruled the Khitans herself with an iron fist, led the conquest of Chinese territory around Beijing, and under the reign name Shulü (also known as Chunqin) oversaw the formation of the Liao dynasty, which dominated northeast China for two centuries (926–1125).

The Song Come to Power

Another military force from the north formed around a general whose innovative battle tactics enabled him to conquer all rivals, unify much of China, and proclaim the Song dynasty (traditionally 960–1279), taking as his reign name Song Taizu.

From their capital at Kaifeng, near the Huang He in the north China plain, the Song ruled a much smaller empire than had the Tang or Han. They could not dominate their frontiers and frequently fought a new power in Vietnam, the Ly dynasty, which arose soon after 1000. In the northwest, another state, called Xi Xia, comprising only 3 million people (called Tanguts) posed further problems. But the most formidable neighbor was the Liao, with their seemingly endless supply of horses and horsemen. When not fighting the Liao, the Song were usually paying them protection money in silk and silver—if the Song didn't want to fight, they had to pay. They often paid off the Tanguts too. In the 1120s, another pastoralist group called the Jurchen, whose homeland was Manchuria, overran the north, eliminated the Liao, built an even bigger state, and confined the Song to the region south of the Yangzi. The Southern Song, as they are called, had to pay the Jurchen even more to leave them in peace.

Reforms This embattled situation gave the Song rulers every incentive to maintain an efficient state, economy, and war machine. Internally, the rulers insisted on civilian rule to prevent regional generals, like the dynasty's own founder, from seizing power. Compared to the early Tang, the Song were politically and militarily weak. But economically and demographically, they oversaw tremendous expansions despite the compromises this required in Confucian principles. They let businessmen profit, however distasteful that felt, in order to maximize their tax revenue and pay for their military. They deftly combined state ownership and high taxation in some sectors of the economy with unregulated markets in others. To oversee their nuanced policies, the Song needed a reliable and skilled bureaucracy, which drove them to promote Confucian ideology.

The Song relied heavily on examinations to fill the ranks of officialdom. Some 100,000 men took the civil service exam in 1150, and in 1250 about 400,000 did—maybe 0.1 to 0.3 percent of the total population. Aspirants had to study for a minimum of 300 days, and most chose to prepare far longer. The average age of an exam taker was about 30. After reforms to combat grade inflation in 1009, the pass rate varied from around 1 to 3 percent. In the entire population, about 1 in 10,000 held the qualification needed to work in the bureaucracy. Only the top-graded exam takers

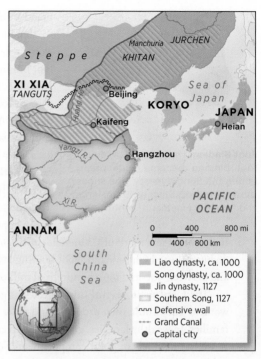

The Liao and Song Dynasties, 926–1279 CE After 900, a series of peoples from the north established ruling dynasties in northern China, a pattern that would continue for many centuries to come. The most important dynasty, however, the Song, was established by a Chinese general who re-unified China after the fragmentation that followed the Tang collapse. After 1127, the Song ruled only the southern half of the country, but its record stands out in Chinese history for the development of commerce, the arts, and science.

could enter the civil service—most of the rest became teachers. The Song's reliance on examinations resulted in a more talented cadre of administrators than existed under the Tang, who at times had accepted aristocratic birth as a qualification.

The Song's social policy was inconsistently Confucian. A revival of orthodoxy constrained women's roles, but not dramatically. Manuals of proper behavior for girls and women emphasized deference to males and to their elders. Girls were expected to learn to cook, clean, care for children, make silk, embroider, and sew. Upon marriage, they moved in with their husband's family and took orders from their in-laws. Widows found it nearly impossible to remarry.

The distinctively Chinese custom of foot binding became widespread during the Song. It first arose among elite women during the late Tang, around 900. This painful

Foot Binding The practice of female foot binding became widespread during the Song dynasty. The shoes shown here are 3.5 inches (9 cm) long, and from the nineteenth century.

practice involved tightly wrapping small girls' feet so that, as they grew, the bones broke, leaving women to hobble through life. Printed evidence of foot binding begins to appear in texts in the 1140s, and objections to it a hundred years later. Tiny, stunted feet became regarded as dainty and erotic, especially in the upper classes. A hobbled wife who couldn't work in the fields or roam away from home became a status symbol for a husband. Paradoxically, mothers often imposed this practice (usually overseen by grandmothers or elderly women who worked as foot-binding specialists) on their daughters in hopes of improving their marriage prospects. It also became a mark of Chinese identity, something that foreign barbarians did not do but cultured Chinese did. Foot binding lasted into the twentieth century in China, and between 900 and 1900 hundreds of millions of Chinese girls underwent the ordeal.

The Confucian revival during the Song contained a mixed legacy for Chinese women. They could own property, and older women exercised some authority within families. In wealthy families, girls were often encouraged to study history and literature, as well as manuals of good comportment. Some found it possible to take on a more public role through writing—most enduringly perhaps Li Qingzhao (ca. 1080–1150), a poet and scholar whose verses remain admired today for their emotional intensity. She got her start writing poetry as a teenager, grew fond of books and ancient artifacts, but lost her collections when the Jurchen overran her home. She and her husband fled to the south, where he soon died, and she lived out her days modestly, writing taut verses often on the theme of loss.

Economy The Song needed a robust economy. Military costs ate up about three-fourths of their budget. Theirs was the first state in East Asia to create a standing navy, always an expensive undertaking, which they deployed chiefly on rivers and canals against the Liao and other northern foes. For their army, which reached 1.25 million men at times, they spent fortunes on armor and arrowheads.

To meet their military requirements, the Song built the world's first military-industrial complex. After 1020, they developed iron-mining, mainly in government-owned mines. The mines yielded 10,000 to 20,000 tons of iron per year, mainly for weapons. This was more iron than the entire world produced as late as 1700. To smelt it (to extract metal from surrounding rock), they first used charcoal; but because the mines were mainly in the north where trees were scant, the Song soon turned to coal—the first major use of fossil fuels in world history. In the 1070s, when iron production peaked, they also mined more than 13,000 tons of copper—more than the whole world mined as late as 1800. Gold and silver mining increased too. Taken as a whole, the Song mining and metallurgy complex was of an entirely different order of magnitude than anything achieved anywhere before in world history. As we shall see, it did not last.

Agriculture almost kept pace with mining and metallurgy. Under the Song, a new variety of rice called champa entered China from Vietnam. **Champa rice** had spread in Southeast Asia in the eighth through the tenth centuries, helping to sustain the trading state of Srivijaya. In the early eleventh century, a Song emperor fostered its spread, first into southern China and then the Yangzi basin. Champa rice matured quickly, allowing two or even three harvests per year. It also resisted drought well and could ripen at higher and cooler elevations. It soon became the standard crop in most of China's rice-growing regions. Champa rice is probably the first instance in world history of a government promoting an improved crop variety.

Combined with an extension of irrigation systems under the Song, champa rice proved an enormous windfall that translated into rapid population growth. The capital, Kaifeng, swelled to 1.4 million people by 1100. Hangzhou held 2 million. Before the Jurchen conquests of the 1120s, the Song realm held perhaps 125 million people, China's largest population to this point.

Foreign trade matched the booms in mining and agriculture. By 1130, half of state revenues came from taxes on trade—a much higher proportion than under the Tang. The Song deliberately fostered markets and commerce, despite the irritation of Confucian traditionalists who resented uncouth, upstart tycoons. With overland trade to western and South Asia difficult because of hostile powers on China's western and northern frontiers, the Song turned to the sea. One emperor, Gaozong (r. 1127–1162), explained Song trade policy: "The profit of maritime trade contributes much to the national income. Therefore, pursuing the former custom [perhaps referring to the early Tang] the people of faraway countries should be encouraged to come and sell an abundant supply of foreign goods."

Foreigners did come. Languages such as Arabic, Persian, Tamil, and Malay were again heard in the streets of south China's cities. A dramatic expansion of trade to the Indian Ocean world took place after 1200 or so. China exported porcelain, an invention of the Tang era that the Song mass-produced, and, as usual, silk. China imported pearls, elephants, ivory, and precious metals. Shipbuilding boomed, and ship technology improved. Chinese shipwrights invented bulkheads—watertight compartments of a ship's hull that allowed it to sustain damage without the vessel sinking. Chinese ships also started using a rudimentary compass no later than 1117. Overseas trade networks, which had prospered under the early Tang but withered after the 750s, recovered in Song times. The Song lacked the tendrils of trade and power reaching into Central Asia that had distinguished the Tang, but after 1200 China's seaborne links to Southeast Asian and Indian Ocean coastlands strengthened.

The Song also allowed new forms of business and new forms of money. Merchant groups found ways to spread their risk in far-flung operations, combining assets, selling shares, and insuring voyages. Primitive banks popped up, issuing promises of payment

Song Economy Advanced wood-block-printing technology enabled the Song to produce the world's first paper money. This banknote, dated to the eleventh century, would have been about a foot (30 cm) long and 8 inches (20 cm) wide.

called flying money. Paper money appeared about 990, first made from the bark of mulberry trees. This was another revolutionary development. The Song economy grew so fast that they could not mint enough iron, copper, silver, and gold coins to grease the wheels of commerce. Besides, they needed all the iron and copper they could get for military production. The solution was paper money. Because of high demand for the books that prepared men for the exams, the Chinese already had good woodblock printing technology that could mass-produce images on paper. With paper money, merchants no longer had to carry heavy strings of iron coins on long voyages. Song currency notes were as large as a shoebox top, but still a major step forward in convenience. They included helpful notices to the effect that counterfeiters would be beheaded. For two centuries, paper money helped nourish the Song economic boom and the creation of a true market society. This market revolution confirmed China's place as the center of East Asia's economic webs, and indeed Eurasia's. Paper money was not used in Japan until the 1330s and in Europe until the 1660s.

The needs and incentives of a market society helped to generate several technological advances of economic importance. In addition to the compass and paper money, Song China witnessed the development of printing with moveable type, astronomical clocks, and, for doing calculations quickly, the abacus. Shipping improved with the bulkhead and the sternpost rudder, which enabled captains to steer their vessels more easily. Silk manufacture now featured looms with 1,800 moving parts. Of less economic importance, but ultimately of great consequence for world history, Chinese of the Song also invented gunpowder weapons. For the millions of tax-paying peasant families on whom Song power and prosperity largely depended, none of these innovations mattered as much as champa rice. More reliable food supply, not paper money or clocks, was the biggest change the Song brought to the masses.

Despite these successes in business, the economy, and technology, the Song proved militarily inferior to the Jurchen. The Jurchen were hunters, farmers, and horse breeders in Manchuria who had been vassals of the Liao. Early in the 1100s, they asserted their independence by making a deal with the Song to attack the Liao. That worked well, but the Jurchen then turned on their ally and overran much of north China. The Song retreated south of the Yangzi and made Hangzhou their new capital. The Jurchen, now called the Jin dynasty, ruled from Kaifeng, dividing China uneasily with the Southern Song. The Jin dynasty lasted in north China until it was demolished by a Mongol confederation in 1234.

The Song's Neighborhood, ca. 960–1240

From the early eleventh century on, the rise of market society and of steppe nomad power in the form of the Khitans and Jurchen affected almost all of East Asia. Korea, perhaps, felt these developments most because it stood on the doorstep of the steppe peoples' homeland.

Korea After the Silla kingdom fell apart in 892, Korea remained divided for a generation. But the rise of the Khitans inspired some Koreans to put aside their differences and join forces behind a single warlord. He forged a new kingdom, called **Koryo** (or Goryeo, 918–1392), from which our word *Korea* comes. The new state quickly extended its sway over the whole peninsula. It consisted of a de facto alliance of aristocratic families—called *yangban* in Korean—who spearheaded successful resistance to Khitan and Jurchen attacks. After 1170, the state weakened and the alliance frayed under the impact of revolts by soldiers, slaves, and Buddhist monks. Local warrior-aristocrats grabbed more power, and the central state held less. The Mongols (see below) began occasional attacks on Korea in 1217.

In its first century, Koryo was more isolated from the wider world than the Silla kingdom had been. Relations with the Khitans and Jurchen were often violent, although Korea did trade iron and grain to the Khitans for horses. With Song China less devoted to Buddhism than the early Tang dynasts, cultural relations between Korea and China diminished somewhat. But by the late eleventh century, when Koryo was firmly established and Song China was booming economically, commerce revived. Koreans imported horses from the steppe and Chinese goods, both for their own use and for re-export to Japan. Muslim traders from Southwest Asia came to Korea too. During the Koryo dynasty, despite the social dominance of old *yangban* families, Korea, like China, gradually grew more market oriented.

Korean society evolved in response to the changing political and economic environment. After 1100 or so, aristocratic families enhanced their influence, Korea's class structure rigidified, and slavery increased in importance. Nowhere else in East Asia was slavery as prevalent as in Korea. In late Koryo times, perhaps a third of the population were slaves. Most were farm laborers, often working on estates owned by *yangban* families. Some were in effect household servants. Several slave revolts broke out, the largest in 1198. Despite sharp class cleavages, Korea became more linguistically and ethnically uniform in Koryo times, in part through the frequent struggles against foreign invaders.

In the early years of the Koryo dynasty, Korean society allowed freedoms to women that shocked Chinese visitors. Korean women not only owned and inherited property, but they could mingle freely with men in public spaces and were not confined to households. Upon marriage, a husband usually moved in with his wife's family—the opposite of Chinese practice. Widows could remarry. Prosperous women might even take more than one husband, a rare custom in world history. However, as contacts with the Song expanded, Confucian influence seeped into Korea. After 958, Koryo used Confucian examinations to recruit bureaucrats, helping to promote Confucian ideals in high places, which narrowed the opportunities open to women.

Chinese influence appeared also in the most iconic product of Koryo culture, a type of glazed pottery called celadon. It first developed in China, but Korean potters refined the technique and produced a blue-green glaze that elites throughout East Asia, and collectors to this day, came to prize.

While Korean culture grew more Confucian in some respects, Korean religion remained Buddhist on the top rungs of society. Lower classes often retained their attachment to shamanist beliefs and practices, disdained by the elite as unsophisticated and akin to the religion of the Khitans, Jurchen, and other enemies.

Japan   In Japan, no steppe nomads battered at the door. China was farther away. So the incentives to cooperate against foreign enemies were weaker, and the costs of disunity among Japanese were smaller than for Koreans. The Yamato state only slowly consolidated its rule. The capital was shifted to Heian (modern Kyoto) around 794, so historians refer to the following centuries as **Heian Japan** (794–1185). Its politics were dominated by struggles between the center (meaning the imperial court and the Fujiwara clan that served as the power behind the throne) and landowning aristocratic families in the countryside. The Fujiwara family provided all the wives to emperors; and since children were raised in their mothers' families, the Fujiwara clan nurtured child emperors and influenced adult ones.

The Japanese elite had long promoted foreign religions from China such as Buddhism and Daoism. But after the power of the Tang waned, the influence of China fell accordingly, and Japanese culture became more distinctive. Japan's elites proved skillful at melding revived indigenous religious traditions, notably Shinto, with imported ones to create an ideology that undergirded their dominance. **Shinto** ("the way of the gods") was, and is, a bundle of practices and beliefs that extols ancient traditions—and supposed traditions—and emphasizes folklore, shrines, and monuments. Shinto followers diligently performed rituals honoring a multitude of gods or spirits and linking the present to the past. Gods were often associated with natural features such as rocks, streams, or trees. Shinto appeared first in written documents in the eighth century, although its practices must surely be much older. Its followers often practiced Buddhism as well, and the two religions swapped features back and forth.

The result was a tremendous religious creativity in Heian Japan, with new sects popping up all the time. Charismatic religious leaders, often women, competed for followers, often by offering easier routes to nirvana—a belief adopted in many versions of Shinto.

These evolving religious ideologies convincingly supported and justified social hierarchy. The aristocratic social order in Japan remained remarkably stable despite frequent civil wars and the slow rise of a class of swordsmen-for-hire who in later times loomed large in Japanese politics—the samurai.

Courtly life in Heian Japan featured leisure and refinement that later ages admired. A few thousand residents of the Heian court lived insulated lives of privilege, devoting themselves to poetry, parties, and pleasure. They honed the arts of bodily beautification to novel heights that included silk costumes, plucked eyebrows, and carefully blackened teeth—the epitome of elegance. Courtiers spent their nights in romantic intrigues and their days in literary idylls. Men aspired to write poetry in Chinese. Women typically wrote in Japanese, using a syllabic script called *kana*, which made their work appealing to nationalistic Japanese in modern times.

The first substantial body of literature written by women anywhere in world history comes from the Heian court. The most famous female Japanese author of any age is Murasaki Shikibu (a pseudonym—her real name is unknown), an aristocrat of the early eleventh century. She wrote the *Tale of Genji*, a story of a handsome and chivalrous prince with a varied and troubled love life. Much of it is devoted to the complicated protocols and manners of the Heian court. Today, many Japanese regard it as the high point of their national literature, much as the English see Shakespeare's plays. Several other women wrote novels or memoirs. It is mainly through such literature that we get glimpses of social life in Heian Japan, and it refers only to the courtly elites.

In one respect, Japan decisively joined the East Asian web in the eighth century. Until then, its island location had kept it safe from many epidemics. Moreover, its small and dispersed population could not sustain crowd diseases. But with denser population and urban growth, and more frequent contact with mainland Asia, Japan both received and sustained more lethal infections. Smallpox made its first appearance in 730, killing perhaps a quarter of the archipelago's population. The emperor's response was to commission a giant Buddha statue, 60 feet (18 m) tall and coated in gold. That did not suffice: wave after wave of epidemics followed. Other crowd diseases ravaged Japan as well (measles arrived in the 990s), an unhappy consequence of its closer ties with China and Korea.

This sharp change in Japan's disease environment contributed to the religious experimentation of the Heian period. Everyone wanted supernatural protection, and none of the established practices seemed to deliver it. The new fear of epidemics may have helped motivate the exquisite culture of the court: escapism was a normal response to anxiety.

A woman in the Heian court remarked on a measles outbreak of 998 that claimed "victims of all ages and classes" and left survivors feeling "depressed and uneasy." Not until about 1200 did the spate of epidemics abate, and diseases such as smallpox become endemic, childhood diseases.

Southeast Asia, 900–1400

The surplus production of rice by farming families in river valleys supported several Southeast Asian states. Migrants from Tibet formed a state in Burma in the ninth century along the Irrawaddy River. People moving south from China to the Chao Phraya Basin created a Thai state in the eighth to the tenth centuries. Seaborne links between these states and India proved powerful: kings and courts adopted Buddhist and Hindu beliefs, rituals, and trappings and often declared themselves incarnations of the Hindu god Shiva or, if they preferred, Buddhist bodhisattvas. They hired Brahmin priests, advisers, and astrologers to help them to behave prudently and to impress their subjects and neighbors—exercising a type of soft power.

Ordinary folks, as usual, were more concerned with rain, crops, food, and social relations in their family and village than with kingdoms. In most Southeast Asian settings, men worked the fields. Buying and selling was often the work of women. They could own property, and some got rich enough to endow monasteries. Women could also divorce unsatisfactory husbands. Southeast Asian women before the fifteenth century lived less constrained lives than did women in those parts of East Asia more attached to Confucian ideals.

Southeast Asia, ca. 900–1400 CE Southeast Asian rulers extended their power after 900, building larger states such as that of the Khmer, which flourished from the ninth through the fifteenth century. Irrigated rice production underpinned every Southeast Asian kingdom. So did the support of either Hindu or Buddhist priests.

In terms of territory and probably population, the largest Southeast Asian state was the Khmer Empire of the ninth through the fifteenth centuries. At its height, it held sway in most of mainland Southeast Asia. It relied on efficient rice production, taking advantage both of the champa strain of rice and of innovative irrigation techniques. Chinese visitors reported that much of the farm work was done by forced labor and that prominent families might own as many as 100 slaves.

At first, the kings of the Khmer state were Hindu in religion. Early in the twelfth century, they employed some 70,000 stonemasons to build the sprawling temple complex of Angkor Wat, the carvings on which follow Hindu artistic motifs and styles. But by 1200 or so, Buddhism had superseded Hinduism and the

Angkor Wat This temple in Angkor Thom, built in the twelfth century as a Hindu temple before being converted for Buddhist worship, is the largest religious complex in the world. Building it required the labor of some 70,000 stonemasons.

temples became Buddhist places of worship (as they are today), showing a religious fluidity common in Southeast Asian history.

The capital city of the Khmer, Angkor Thom, contained a few hundred thousand people in the fourteenth century. Its surrounding irrigation network of reservoirs and canals covered about 400 square miles (1,000 sq. km). The liberty accorded women in Angkor Thom offended Chinese visitors, one of whom noted with disdain that here "it is women who are concerned with commerce." Women also took part in the poetry and musical performances at the Khmer court, and in rare cases even served as Buddhist sages.

The Khmer state fell apart early in the fifteenth century for reasons that remain obscure. A recent hypothesis is that a deep drought deprived the Khmer of the water needed for irrigated rice, provoking widespread famine and political disorder. There is strong evidence from tree rings for such droughts, especially around the years 1345–1360 and 1400–1430. Whether that ended the Khmer Empire or not remains uncertain, but it could not have helped.

The Mongols, ca. 1200–1368

The most powerful political force in East Asia by 1220 was not the elegant aesthetes of the Heian court or the master farmers of Angkor or even the mighty Jin or Song, but illiterate, unschooled Mongol herders. How did that happen?

Over the centuries, the Tang and Song dynasties had improved their frontier defenses, mastered the craft of fortification (including ditches that horses couldn't cross), and the subtle art of setting one group of steppe people against another. So in the centuries before the Khitans' success, by and large the Chinese enjoyed the upper hand with respect to northern "barbarians." By the tenth century, the wheel of geopolitical fortune had turned once more. The Khitans were learning a lot from the Chinese. They drove hard bargains for the horses they sold for iron weapons, helmets, and other armor. They mastered siegecraft—the techniques of laying siege to fortified cities. And they learned the subtle art of pitting one group of Chinese, some unhappy generals perhaps, against another. The Jurchen and the Mongols learned all this too.

So from the tenth century through the fourteenth, the Khitan, Jurchen, Mongols, and others enjoyed frequent success in their military struggles with China, conquering north China three times, all of China once, and making life anxious for the Song all the time. They also posed recurrent threats to Korean security.

The Mongols, who numbered about 1 million in 1200, conquered almost all of East Asia—indeed, about half of Eurasia. At first glance, their feats seem impossible, considering that over 250 million people dwelt in Eurasia then. Let's look at the Mongols more closely.

Mongol Ways of Life

The Mongols lived as mobile pastoralists on the steppe grasslands to the north of China. They raised horses, sheep, and goats, keeping on the move in search of lush grass and good water for their herds. Warm and wet spring seasons, good for grass and grazing animals, suited them perfectly. Drought, deep snowfalls, or long spells of extreme cold threatened their animals and themselves. The Mongols took great pride in their riding skills. Women as well as men learned to ride horseback from childhood. Mongols conducted periodic hunts involving the coordinated movements of thousands of riders, honing skills they would use in warfare.

As with all mobile peoples, Mongol material culture was spare. They had to carry everything with them and be ready to break camp and move within minutes when enemies galloped over the horizon. Just about everything they needed they made from animal hide, bone, or sinew. But they also traded animals for iron and grain from Koreans and Chinese. Their religion was no more elaborate than their material culture. Although some had begun to experiment with Buddhism, most preferred shamanism, revering a sky god and lesser gods of rivers, rocks, and other landscape features. Shamans had neither temples nor sacred texts—indeed, no texts at all. The Mongolian tongue was not a written language until the thirteenth century.

Mongol politics consisted of the constant struggles among charismatic men seeking to build bigger followings. They succeeded by promising their followers protection against rivals and loot from successful raids. Mongol chieftains, if they wished to remain chieftains, needed to hand out the spoils of war—normally women and livestock—frequently. In a sense, it was an informal democratic system for males: men gave their allegiance to the leaders they chose. Women and children followed husbands and fathers. Family and clan mattered for survival. Everyone needed the protection of adult males, and among adult males the most admired were those most skilled in the military arts.

Genghis Khan and the Mongol Conquests

Genghis Khan, or Temujin as he was called in his youth, was born into this rough society about 1165. Little is known of his early life. His father, apparently, was a minor chieftain who arranged for nine-year-old Temujin's marriage to a girl from a related clan—a political match. Before the marriage took place (Mongols married as teenagers), Temujin's father was poisoned. Since no one wished to give allegiance to a mere boy, Temujin, his mother, and his several siblings were abandoned to fend for themselves. Keeping a family alive without an adult male and without a larger kin network was an unusual feat, but his mother had what it took. Temujin and his siblings learned all there was to know about charming strangers, stealing horses, and living off roots, fruits, berries, and small game.

Temujin was a difficult child with burning ambition. He killed one of his half-brothers in a quarrel and allegedly refused to apologize to his mother. He aimed to re-capture his dead father's stature as a chief. In his teenage years, Temujin managed to acquire support among blood brothers of his father, as well as from the clan of his betrothed, whom he married when he was about 16. He acquired a reputation for luck, skill, cunning, and cruelty to his enemies—just the sort of man Mongols wanted to follow.

In his 20s, Temujin kept defeating rivals and attracting more followers. By 1206, he had brought most Mongols into his fold and led them against neighboring peoples. Recognizing the importance of clans and kin in Mongol society, and its potential to undermine loyalty to him, he re-organized his fighting forces. Men no longer rode and fought with their kinsmen, but in units of tens, hundreds, and thousands—a decimal system of military organization he borrowed from the Khitans and the Jurchen. This helped focus Mongols' allegiance on their commanders, men chosen for their loyalty to the man now known as a "supreme leader," or *khan*—Genghis Khan.

Genghis led his armies to victory after victory, first on the steppe, and then against the Tanguts—the Tibetan-speaking people of the Xia state northwest of China. By 1215, the Mongols had crushed the Jurchen and dominated north China. They then headed west to Central Asia, where by 1220 they had taken the Silk Road cities of Bukhara and Samarkand. For another five years, Genghis and his generals campaigned in Central Asia, northern India, Iran, the Caucasus, Russia, and Ukraine. They won almost every battle and conquered every city they assaulted.

Mongolia enjoyed a favorable climate during Genghis Khan's years of conquest. From 1211 to 1225, Mongolia experienced an unprecedented run of wet and warm years,

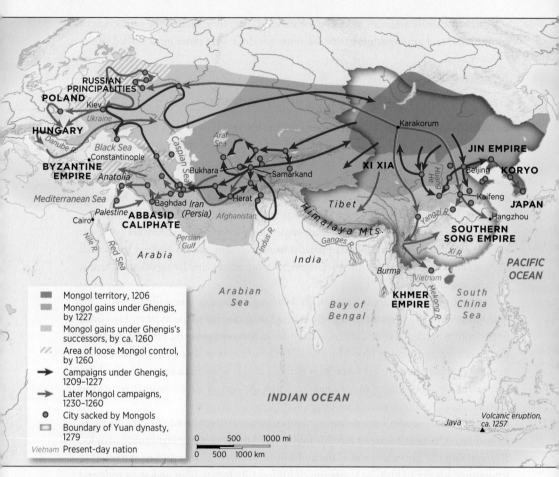

Mongol Campaigns and Empire, 1206–1260 CE   Genghis Khan, his sons, and grandsons mounted extraordinarily successful assaults on most of the richest societies in Eurasia, creating a giant, if short-lived, land empire. Its influence included flourishing trade and cultural exchanges along the Silk Roads, as Mongol authority, once established, kept the peace and discouraged brigands.

allowing grass and herds to flourish. With more animals there was more food, and with more food, more Mongols. Simultaneous surges in population growth of sheep, goats, horses, and humans helped propel Mongol expansion.

Genghis commanded 70,000 to 130,000 Mongol men on his campaigns of the 1210s and 1220s. They brought their families with them, which meant that if they lost a battle their wives and children would be killed or enslaved. That probably sharpened their motivation. Their mobility and military skills, especially as bowmen, brought consistent success.

So too did the Mongols' justified reputation for ruthlessness. A Persian historian of the thirteenth century wrote that in their conquest of Herat, in today's Afghanistan, the Mongols killed every person, cat, and dog, and flattened the city. As a matter of policy, Genghis and his generals committed legendary acts of cruelty, routinely ordering the slaughter of all adult males in conquered populations. Their goal was to acquire a bloodthirsty reputation that would tempt people to surrender without a fight. Those who did so often met lenient treatment if they offered up their horses, young women, skilled artisans, and treasure to the Mongols. Genetic evidence strongly suggests that the Mongols engaged in wholesale rape of captive women: today, roughly 8 percent of the population of Inner Asia, and 0.5 percent of all humans, are descended from a single male ancestor, probably someone from Mongolia who lived about 1,000 years ago.

When it came to religious politics, the Mongols employed a more tolerant approach. They felt no need to force anyone to adopt their gods. Peoples who submitted to Mongol authority were left free to worship as they pleased, provided they gave the Mongols what they wanted. In his sunset years, Genghis Khan took an interest in Daoism, especially its promised avenues to immortality. In the 1250s, one Mongol khan, Mongke, a grandson of Genghis, invited wise men of several faiths to his tents to make their cases for Buddhism, Islam, Daoism, or Christianity. In the end, he and his advisers concluded that God had given different people different religions just as he had given people hands with multiple fingers. Some khans supported Buddhism, and grateful Buddhist sages found ways to justify the Mongol khans' rule. Showing remarkable intellectual flexibility, some sages declared generous khans to be reincarnations of the Buddha.

The Mongol Empire   After Genghis died on campaign in 1227, his sons, nephews, and grandsons continued the family business. They raided and conquered from Korea and Vietnam in the east to Palestine and Poland in the west. The Mongols controlled half the world's horse population— perhaps 20 million beasts. Their success extended wherever their horses could find nutritious grass. When they reached forested landscapes in Central Europe or Russia, they lost their edge, although they could still move with astonishing speed in winter on frozen rivers. (Several brutally cold winters in the mid-thirteenth century made their campaigning a little easier in this respect.) Their campaigns amid the tropical forests of north India, Burma, and Southeast Asia were beset by unfamiliar diseases, probably malaria chief among them. By about 1260, their run of conquests in Central and West Asia was coming to an end. They had built the largest empire in world history, conquering north China, the Abbasid caliphate, and nearly everything in between. Now, however, the descendants of Genghis Khan increasingly fought among themselves.

One grandson of Genghis, Khubilai, after emerging victorious in struggles within his family, needed more loot to reward his followers. Out of appealing options in western Eurasia, he turned the Mongol war machine back east. Beginning in 1260, he oversaw the Mongol conquest of China's Southern Song state. Mongol cavalry struggled in Chinese terrain with its rivers, canals, and mountains. Song officials had come to rely upon the Yangzi River as their Great Wall, too wide for Mongol ponies to cross. But the Mongols showed great capacity to innovate militarily, developing naval skills to fight along the Yangzi and other rivers. By 1276 the last Song resistance flickered out, and three years later Khubilai Khan declared himself the Son of Heaven, emperor of all China, and founder of a new dynasty, the Yuan.

The Mongols as Chinese Emperors: The Yuan Dynasty, 1279–1368

Like other steppe conquerors of other agrarian empires, Khubilai faced one big problem. He had several thousand Mongols at his back, almost all illiterate, almost all expecting regular handouts of war plunder, and none prepared for the desk work necessary to administer a sprawling empire. He needed to rule perhaps 75 million Chinese subjects who regarded him and his men as barbarians. Khubilai almost solved the problem.

Governing Strategies   Khubilai moved his center of operations south, out of Mongolia to Beijing, which he made into China's capital. He hired Chinese literati to handle the routine paperwork of governing, but he eliminated the practice of staffing top posts with men selected by written examination. He prized loyalty over literary skill, so the highest offices went to Mongols. He occasionally appointed other foreigners such as Tibetans and Persians—men with administrative skills but without Chinese loyalties.

Khubilai did, however, wish to benefit from Confucian ideology with its emphases on duty and deference. He patronized Chinese sages and painters. He promoted Buddhism too. Having nothing in their religious tradition that demanded conformity, the Mongols in China, as elsewhere, allowed all religions free rein. In short, Khubilai did all he could to win over the Chinese elite while keeping it from the highest rungs of power. He found enough educated Chinese willing to collaborate with "barbarians" to govern effectively.

Khubilai Khan A painting on silk—made in China in the thirteenth or fourteenth century, sometime after Khubilai's death—shows the ruler hunting with members of his court.

Nonetheless, the **Yuan dynasty** was short-lived. Khubilai spent fortunes on palaces and wars, including two unsuccessful invasions of Japan, three of Vietnam, and one of the distant island of Java. These failures damaged Mongol prestige and drained their resources. Khubilai managed to conquer Korea, but at great cost. Moreover, the Yuan had to spend immense sums to extend the Grand Canal north to Beijing, to ensure that the new capital got enough rice. With the Yuan in financial straits, in 1294 the world's "mightiest man," as the Venetian trader Marco Polo called him, now an obese alcoholic, having long lost the hardy self-discipline so esteemed among Mongols, died peacefully.

Power Struggles, Rebellions, Epidemics After Khubilai's death, violent power struggles divided his family. Whereas in the Chinese tradition the imperial throne normally went to the eldest son, the Mongols expected sons, brothers, and nephews of a dead leader to fight for power. This principle was common among steppe and Central Asian peoples. It ensured that no weaklings came to power—but it carried the cost of intermittent civil war. Khubilai's successors, like all Mongol chiefs, were distinguished by their military competence and political cunning more than bureaucratic skills.

As Chinese emperors, the Mongol leaders faced continued financial struggles and frequent rebellions. They printed too much paper money too fast, inflating the currency to the point where no one would voluntarily accept it. When troops and canal laborers were paid with paper money, they often rebelled. As foreign "barbarians" in Chinese eyes, the Yuan had trouble convincing people that they enjoyed the Mandate of Heaven.

The Yuan emperors, unlike their ancestor Genghis, also suffered from bad climate luck. Not only did storms sink their two invasion fleets of Japan, but in the thirteenth century big volcanoes around the world were erupting like popcorn, spewing sulfate particles into the upper atmosphere and blocking out some of the sun's warmth. Six major eruptions took place between 1227 and 1284, and a gigantic one in either 1257 or 1258 ejected more sulfates than any other eruption in the previous 7,000 years. The climate impacts—cooler and dryer weather—were global in scope. Crops failed here and there around the world, and people starved. In China, natural disasters were political—evidence that rulers, first the late Song and then the Yuan, had lost the Mandate of Heaven.

By the 1270s, just when the Yuan were finishing their conquest of China, cold weather set in with a vengeance. It was the beginning of the Little Ice Age, a worldwide shift to cooler temperatures that lasted for 600 years (ca. 1250–1850). The 1290s were particularly frigid. The cold itself reduced harvests, and in north China cold years were usually also drought years. They also coincided with outbreaks of locust swarms, a frequent danger to crops in China. To make matters still worse, the freezing of rivers and canals paralyzed most commerce for much of the year, making it harder to transport food to famine areas. While cold and dry years became normal after the 1270s, in rare wet years monsoon rains were often extra strong, as in 1295–1297, years of torrential flooding. Often flood soaked one part of China while drought parched another.

By the 1330s, a wave of epidemics compounded the Yuan's difficulties. China had long suffered from occasional epidemics, but especially devastating ones burned through the country in 1331, 1344–1345, and 1356–1360. No one knows for sure what diseases were involved, but one (much disputed) possibility is that the bubonic plague was among them. In western Eurasia, as we shall see, a plague pandemic killed off about one-third of the population between 1346 and 1352. In China, population plummeted as well, whether from plague or other infections. Before the Mongol conquest, the total population stood around 100 to 120 million. By 1350, it had dropped to 70 million; by 1400, to perhaps as little as 60 million. Certainly, the Mongol conquest killed many, but famines and epidemics played larger roles in what was by far the worst population crash in Chinese history.

Culture, Society, and Economy Under these strains, Chinese culture and society changed considerably. With the elimination of the civil service exams, even brilliant literati could not look forward to careers in high office. When the exams were restored in 1315, they were given in two versions, an easy one for Mongols and a harder one for Chinese. Most Chinese literati abandoned the hope of a government career and sought other ways to make a living and demonstrate their distinction. Some turned to playwriting, leading to an outpouring of popular drama including works that remain among China's most popular, such as the irreverent love comedy *Romance of the Western Chamber* written by Wang Shifu. Others took up mathematics, medicine, or philosophy. Arabic numerals came into use under the Yuan (about the same time they took root in Europe). Persian and Arab astronomers were appointed to a state-sponsored observatory. Religious thought flourished in the absence of persecutions, and many new Buddhist texts were translated into Chinese. The Yuan dynasty was a time of troubles for China, but a time of scientific and cultural creativity as well.

The adverse climate, epidemics, and other trials may have contributed to an upturn in female infanticide and a resulting shortage of women. In most Chinese families, only males could perform religious rituals honoring the ancestors, and every family desperately wanted at least one male heir. Female children were valued less for this reason, and for economic ones as well: upon marriage, women's labor would be lost to their parents and would serve their new in-laws. In Yuan times, the imbalance between male and female in the population reached about 20 percent, implying widespread female infanticide and meaning that about a fifth of all males could not marry. For Chinese men, failure to marry and produce male heirs was a crushing disappointment. The cultural prohibition on widows remarrying (in Confucian tradition, a wife should serve only one husband) weakened because of the bride shortage.

The Chinese economy reflected the demographic and social stresses of the Yuan era but also the opportunities presented by enforced peace along the Silk Roads. The Yuan oversaw a continued commercialization of Chinese society except for seaborne trade, which they banned from time to time. They relied on tax farmers—entrepreneurs who paid the emperor for the right to collect taxes—and on forced labor for major engineering works such as the extension of the Grand Canal to Beijing. In these circumstances, economic inequality expanded. Fortunes were rapidly made and lost. The iron and coal industries of early Song times, in sharp decline after 1100, nearly disappeared. Social mobility increased, and what remained of the grand old aristocratic families of Tang times vanished altogether. Chinese society became more entrepreneurial, unstable, and unequal. The goods produced—rice, millet, wheat, silk, porcelain—remained much the same as before, but everything else was changing.

The Mongols and the Webs of East Asia Mongol rule in China encouraged trade and cultural exchange all across East Asia. With their conquests, not only were China, Mongolia, Korea, Burma, and Tibet brought under the same rule, but regions farther afield—including Japan, Vietnam, Java, and the Khmer Empire of mainland Southeast Asia—were drawn into the commercial and cultural orbit of Yuan China. When the Mongols were strongest (ca. 1250–1350), the East Asian web grew both larger and tighter than ever before.

More broadly, the Mongols' conquests and promotion of trade throughout lands they controlled brought the East Asian web into more regular contact with the rest of Eurasia. The Han-Rome linkages, the first Old World web, had weakened after 200 CE, to be strengthened during the early Tang. But the Mongols took the Old World web to another level, speeding up the movement of religious ideas, crops, technologies, and disease pathogens, among other things, throughout Eurasia. They oversaw trade and travel along the Silk Roads directly, encouraging it as best they could. Genghis Khan and his successors turned the Silk Roads into silk superhighways.

After their conquests, the Mongols intimidated almost all of Asia into peace, sometimes called the Pax Mongolica. Peace reduced risk and cost for merchants and travelers. Whereas Chinese rulers usually regarded exports as bad for the economy (after all, useful goods left the country), Mongols deliberately encouraged foreign trade. Part of the appeal of controlling China was the ease with which the Mongols could amass silk and other Chinese manufactures for trade to Central Asia and points west. In the case of porcelain, the Yuan invested in large government-sponsored factories that churned out the blue-on-white styles that today we call china. The style was originally Persian.

As Indians, Iranians, and Arabs acquired more knowledge of China and Korea, and more interest in East Asian silk and porcelain, sea links along the shores of the Indian Ocean grew as well—as we will see. The Mongols had no direct impact on the Indian Ocean trade networks, but they helped them grow tighter nonetheless by stimulating demand for goods from exotic places. In this way, the Silk Road traffic provoked Indian Ocean traffic. Together, they formed

Yuan Porcelain This rectangular wine flask from the Yuan dynasty (1279–1368), decorated with cobalt-blue mythical creatures, was manufactured in one of many government-sponsored porcelain factories.

the main connecting strands of the bigger and tighter Old World web, stretching by 1280 from Japan and Java to Spain and North Africa.

These trade networks helped make some Chinese cities into metropolises. According to the Venetian merchant Marco Polo, the Chinese city of Hangzhou, not far from modern Shanghai, was the world's most magnificent city. He marveled at the countless canals and bridges, and the sprawling market squares where one might buy "game of all kinds, such as roebucks, stags, fallow deer, hares and rabbits . . . partridges, pheasants, francolins, quails, common fowls, capons, and such numbers of ducks and geese as can scarcely be expressed." He also remarked upon the prostitutes "who are here in such numbers as I dare not venture to report."

Yet Mongol power in East Asia proved fleeting. By the 1350s, the Yuan had lost control of most of China and Korea. Various native rebellions arose and easily found recruits among young men facing dismal marriage prospects. Violent chaos prevailed until new dynasties managed to crush all rivals. These were the Ming in China (founded 1368) and the Choson in Korea (1392). We will meet them again in later chapters.

The legacy of Mongol rule in China and East Asia was strong. Their violence left a trail of ruin. Their rough manners, illiteracy, and disdain for calligraphy, poetry, and other refinements left the Chinese elite more convinced than ever that they were culturally superior to everyone else—and that elegant literary and artistic expression was the highest form of human endeavor.

Beyond that, Mongol rule brought new foreign influences into Chinese culture. It had long been Mongol practice to capture artisans in warfare and bring them back to Mongolia, so skills and styles from India and Southwest Asia—such as Persian styles in porcelain—filtered into China. So did a few new crops, such as carrots, almonds, and pistachios, and administrative techniques, such as a courier system. The Mongols also invited Muslims, Christians, and others into their realms, including Yuan China, adding to East Asia's cultural diversity. Mongol rule in China left a legacy of religious toleration and experimentation. Finally, some of their customs allowing a wider sphere for elite women lingered on, to the dismay of proper Confucians. The Ming emperors, as we shall see, found little of this legacy to their taste and tried to undo foreign influences on China.

Conclusion

When the Han Empire fell apart after 220 CE and China fragmented, long-distance trade and travel in East Asia temporarily diminished. But by the time of the Sui dynasty, Buddhist monks were bringing new ideas from India. Buddhist outlooks and institutions favored commerce. By the time of the Tang dynasty, connections between China and its neighbors had grown much stronger. Goods, merchants, missionaries, monks, armies, students, and microbes were on the move by land and sea. This heightened interconnectedness, combined with a unified China, favored the emergence of unified states in Korea, Tibet, Japan, and, less directly, Southeast Asia. By 750, Tang China presided over a humming East Asian web, with strong threads tied deep into Central Asia, revitalizing the Old World web.

After the horrors of the An Lushan rebellion (755), the Tang rulers turned their backs on the outside world. Their xenophobia extended to Buddhism and foreign trade. The power, prestige, and unity of the Tang dynasty faded; and as it did so, part of the logic of unity in Korea, Tibet, and elsewhere disappeared—with no threat from the Tang, political division more often prevailed in other East Asian societies. At the same time, connections among societies weakened as a result of the Tang's nativist policy after 755.

The tempo of interaction in East Asia revived with the arrival of the Song dynasty in China and the economic boom it fostered. Japan, Korea, Vietnam, and other East Asian societies such as Srivijaya and Angkor were again more connected to China, and to one another. The East Asian web was again growing thicker.

The nomadic invasions that began with the Khitan in the early tenth century heralded a new era for East Asia. Indeed, for most of the following millennium, most Chinese were ruled most of the time by dynasties from the steppe. At first, with the Khitans, the impacts seemed confined to north China and Korea. But as steppe peoples learned more and more from their neighbors—one of the results of heightened interaction—they tipped the balance of power in their favor. This was most conspicuous with the Mongols under Genghis Khan and his offspring.

The Mongols' Eurasian Empire strengthened the Old World web and in so doing tightened trade and cultural connections both within East Asia and between East Asia and other lands. Despite the vast destruction and loss of life in a half-century of Mongol conquests, the peace they later imposed, and their support for trade and cultural exchanges, left East Asia resurgent.

Chapter Review

KEY TERMS

REVIEW QUESTIONS

1. What were the two important shifts that followed the collapse of the Han, and why did they occur?

2. In what ways did early Tang rulers reform the state?

3. In what ways did the Tang dominate the regions in the sinosphere?

4. What cultural influence prevailed in Southeast Asia to 500, and what form did this influence take?

5. When did the Tang dynasty begin to fall, and what were its main hardships?

6. Identify the forms of business, economic measures, and technologies that the Song introduced, and their effects.

7. What impacts did the relationship between the Song and the steppe nomads have on Korean and Japanese religion, culture, and politics?

8. Why and how did the Chinese relationship with steppe nomads shift around the tenth century?

9. What environmental factors, motivations, and military tactics facilitated the Mongols' successes in warfare?

10. What were the main reasons that the Yuan dynasty was short-lived?

11. How did the strength of foreign connections change from the Tang to the Song to the Yuan?

12. Explain how and why both unity and disunity in China influenced the politics of its neighbors.

Go to INQUIZITIVE

to see what you've learned—and learn what you've missed—with personalized feedback along the way.

Forging an Indian Ocean World

SOUTH ASIA, SOUTHEAST ASIA, AND EAST AFRICA

ca. 200 to 1400

FOCUS QUESTIONS

1. Why does it make sense to define this region by water—the Indian Ocean—rather than land?

2. What major social, cultural, and political changes occurred in India between 200 and 1400?

3. What were the major components of trade in the Indian Ocean world?

4. How did the connections of trade foster a cosmopolitan culture across the Indian Ocean world?

In 1325, a 21-year-old Moroccan from a family of Islamic scholars, Abū 'Abd Allāh Muhammad ibn 'Abd Allāh al-Lawātī al-Ṭanjī ibn Batūtah (1304–1368)—Ibn Battuta for short—set out on one of the longest road trips of all time. He left his family "as a bird forsakes its nest," as he put it, intending to make the pilgrimage to Mecca that is expected of Muslims. He took detours that lasted 22 years. In the course of his journey, he visited Egypt, Arabia, Southwest and Central Asia, East

CHRONOLOGY

ca. 45 Greek sea captain first codifies use of monsoon winds in Periplus of the Erythraean Sea

ca. 300–400 First evidence of Indian cultural influence in Southeast Asia

ca. 330–550 Height of Gupta kings in India

by ca. 400 Iron tools and farming spread to southern Africa

ca. 500–900 Heyday of Nalanda monastery in India

ca. 600–900 Cattle raising spreads more widely in Southern Africa

ca. 600–1200 Bhakti movement flourishes in India

ca. 700–800 Earliest mosques are built in East Africa; gold production begins in southern Africa

ca. 800–900 Scale of commerce along Swahili coast expands

868–883 Zanj revolt in Iraq

ca. 970–1215 Height of Chola kingdom in South India

ca. 1000 Mahmoud and the Ghaznavids begin raids in India and Iran

ca. 1050–1250 Conversion to Islam on the Swahili coast peaks

ca. 1175 Mapungubwe arises in southern Africa

ca. 1206–1400 Delhi sultanate rises and falls in India

ca. 1250–1450 Great Zimbabwe flourishes in southern Africa

Africa, India, Southeast Asia, and China. In middle age in the 1350s, he decided to cross the Sahara from Morocco and visit West Africa. In all he walked, sailed, or rode about 75,000 miles (121,000 km), equivalent to almost three times around the Earth. When he got home, he dictated an account of his experiences and claimed, with some justice, to be the greatest traveler of the age.

Just about everywhere he went, Ibn Battuta found Muslims happy to host him and sometimes to employ him. He visited out-of-the-way islands such as the Maldives (off the western coast of India), where a local ruler kept him against his will while employing him as a judge. He went to great capitals—such as Constantinople, where he met a Byzantine emperor, and Delhi, where he also worked as a judge. His employer there, a sultan, asked him to head an embassy to China, where he arrived in 1345 during the final decades of Yuan rule. He didn't care for China much but admired Hangzhou, the Chinese city that 60 years before had so impressed Marco Polo. Ibn Battuta said it was the biggest city he had seen, noting with admiration the sails and ships filling the canals and the thriving community of Muslim merchants. He stayed with a family of Egyptian origin.

On his journeys he was robbed by brigands, hit by an arrow, and shipwrecked several times. But despite his mishaps and his mileage, Ibn Battuta was no trailblazer: he was following the beaten path. By the middle of the fourteenth century, the lands he visited were all part of a series of trade circuits, linked inside the Old World web.

This chapter tells the story of how the lands on Ibn Battuta's itinerary came to be connected in a single web during the millennium before his birth. It deals with the southernmost, and most maritime, parts of the Old World web. It says more about India than any other land, because India stood at the center of the watery web built on Indian Ocean travel and trade.

ca. 1275 First large stone structures are erected at Great Zimbabwe

ca. 1300 Main mosque at Kilwa on Swahili coast is built

1304–1368 Lifetime of Ibn Battuta

The Indian Ocean World: An Overview

We normally understand the world as divided into continents and regions within continents. But there are times when regions can, with equal or better logic, be understood differently—not as lumps of land, but as lands situated around a body of water. Historians habitually refer to the "Mediterranean world," for example. In recent decades, historians have seen a similar connectedness in the lands, economies, and cultures surrounding the Indian Ocean, at least after about 100 CE.

Mastering the Monsoon

The key reason the Indian Ocean world could become a coherent region after 100 CE is the accumulation of knowledge about the monsoon. Chapter 4 described the seasonal alternation of the monsoon winds and the geophysics behind it. Only gradually did mariners come to understand how to use that alternation for sailing purposes. That understanding was first codified about 45 CE by a Greek sea captain who probably lived in an Egyptian port along the Red Sea. His text, the *Periplus of the Erythraean Sea*, describes coasts and ports from East Africa to India. It explains that the winds reliably blow in a northeasterly direction across the Arabian Sea in the summer months and in a southwesterly direction in the winter. With this knowledge, sea captains could schedule their voyages so as to lose little time waiting for favorable winds. In addition, they could sail from East Africa or Arabia directly to India (and back) without having to hew close to the coastline. Sailing out in the open sea was rare before 100 CE, but it cut time from voyages and reduced risks of pirate attack.

The regularity of winds in the Arabian Sea was mirrored by those of the Bay of Bengal. The strength of the monsoon petered out below the equator, so the connected space of the Indian Ocean world extended only to northern Mozambique on the African coast and Java in Southeast Asia. After the first century CE, sailors, traders, travelers, missionaries, navies, and armies increasingly knit together the coastlands and hinterlands of the Indian Ocean world, building ties bound by the monsoon winds. The strength of the Asian monsoon made the Indian Ocean fundamentally different as a

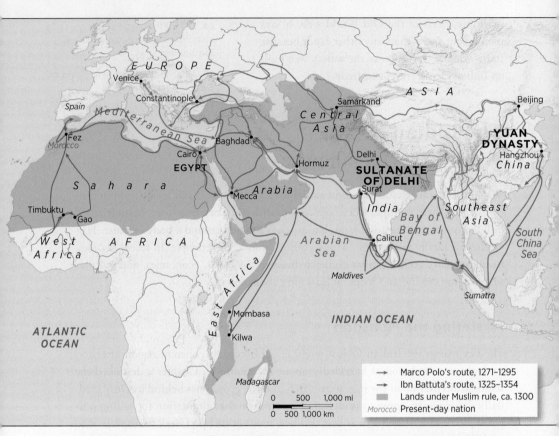

The Routes of Marco Polo and Ibn Battuta Marco Polo and Ibn Battuta never crossed paths because they were travelers of different generations. But their routes intersected in places such as Samarkand, Hangzhou, Calicut, and Constantinople. Both men criss-crossed the expanding Old World web of the thirteenth and fourteenth centuries, and together their routes give a good idea of the overland and maritime connections that held the web together.

sailing sea from the Atlantic and the Pacific. Only the Indian Ocean (and the South China Sea) has winds that make direct back-and-forth journeys, as opposed to long circuitous routes, simple. Once the monsoon knowledge became widespread, the costs and dangers of sailing in the Indian Ocean world plummeted.

Although easier to sail in than the Atlantic or the Pacific, the Indian Ocean pre-sented its share of challenges to mariners. The powerful monsoon wind itself posed dangers for the unwary. Any ship caught on the western coast of India in summer was likely to be dashed on reefs or rocks. Storms in the Bay of Bengal could swallow up a ship in a minute. Many warm-water coasts had coral reefs, which could punch a hole in a ship's hull. The characteristic ship design of the Indian Ocean was the **dhow**, with slanting, triangular sails and planks sewn together with coir, or coconut fiber, rather than nailed together. This made hulls a bit more flexible and less likely to be crushed on a reef. The Indian Ocean was easy to sail only if you knew what you were doing, and when to do it. Dozens of authors helpfully wrote treatises on winds, currents, harbors, reefs, and stars to aid with navigation.

Dhows This boat type, the dhow of the Arabian Sea, has been in use for at least 1,000 years. Small dhows, like the one pictured here, carried coastal trade from port to port. Larger ones crossed the sea linking East Africa, Arabia, the Persian Gulf, and India. Carrying one or two masts, usually rigged with triangular sails well suited to the reliable monsoon winds, the bigger dhows required crews of 12 to 30 sailors.

Trade in the Indian Ocean World

Above all else, trade defined the Indian Ocean world after 200 CE. Reduced costs and dangers encouraged an enduring boom in seaborne trade from South China to East Africa. The goods traded were mostly luxuries—silks, porcelain, spices, ivory, gems, gold, horses, slaves—used only by social elites. But they were extremely important to the identity, and indeed the formation, of elites. In the Indian Ocean world, as everywhere else, to be a king you had to live like a king, showing off your wealth and power with luxury goods.

Undergirding the long-distance trade in luxuries was a set of more local trades linking nearby ports—called **cabotage**. This trade involved goods for daily use such as salt, rice, mangrove poles, leather, cotton cloth, or pottery. Such items almost never traveled the breadth of the Indian Ocean. But they sustained merchants, ports, and ordinary people in every part of the Indian Ocean world.

Choke Points To understand the history of the region, a bit more geography is useful. While sailors could make it from one side of the Arabian Sea, or of the Bay of Bengal, to the other, they could not easily cross the whole Indian Ocean—5,000 miles (8,000 km). Everyone had to pause somewhere in southern India or Sri Lanka for water and food if they wanted to reap the rewards of trading from one half of the Indian Ocean world to the other. Thus the ocean had two halves, and India divided it. India's southernmost tip and Sri Lanka formed a **choke point** for long-distance navigation.

Along the eastern edge of the Indian Ocean stood another choke point for long-distance trade, the Straits of Malacca. Anyone aiming to trade between China and the Indian Ocean almost necessarily had to pass through the waters between Sumatra and the Malay Peninsula. The other options were slow and costly: either trans-shipping across the neck of the Malay Peninsula, or sailing to the south of Sumatra before heading north again. When and where catching the monsoon was involved, days and weeks lost could easily dictate a wait of many months.

The Indian Ocean world as a whole, counting the South China Sea as well as the Bay of Bengal and Arabian Sea, had three parts, with south India and the Straits of Malacca as the two main hinges. The bigger the trade grew, the more was at stake in controlling the good harbors of southern India and the Straits of Malacca.

India and Africa as Regions   Now a word or two about India and Africa as regions. India, historically, encompassed the subcontinent of South Asia, not just the part that forms the modern country of India. At times, the term *India* has included what is now Afghanistan and adjacent lands of Central Asia. The heart of India after 500 BCE was always the Ganges basin, with its cheap transport, good soils, easy irrigation, and dense population, home to most of the powerful states in Indian history.

Africa, in the centuries before 1400, was highly diverse in every respect and exhibited no unity of culture, language, politics, or anything else. I will treat eastern Africa as part of the Indian Ocean world. West Africa, as we shall see, was a world apart, although increasingly influenced by its trans-Saharan contacts with the Mediterranean world and Egypt. So, like East Africa, West Africa's history after 800 or so was powerfully shaped by its growing participation in the giant web that stretched from the Mediterranean to Japan.

India: Population, Society, and Culture

India stood at the center of the Indian Ocean world not only in terms of geography, but in demography as well. The texts from the centuries before 1400 say next to nothing about population, so archeology is our best guide.

Population and Health

India was the population heavyweight of the whole region, excluding China. The table on the next page presents some estimates of the evolution of population in parts of the Indian Ocean world, with China included for comparison. Sub-Saharan Africa, for which population figures in this period are sheer guesswork, might have had 10 to 12 million people in 200 CE and 30 to 35 million in 1400.

These population figures, even for 1600, are only 10 to 15 percent of today's figures. Much land remained sparsely inhabited. More than half of India in 1400 was forest. The population was also growing much, much more slowly than today. Between 1000 and 1600, for example, India's population grew by only 0.1 percent per year, and China's by 0.085 percent. China's population showed the most dramatic fluctuations, a reflection

Population (in millions) in the Indian Ocean World, 200–1600 CE

YEAR CE	INDIA	EAST AFRICA[1]	SOUTHEAST ASIA[2]	CHINA
200	40	0.5	3.5	55
600	51	1.0	5.0	46
1000	75	3.5	7.0	90
1400	94	6.5	12.0	60
1600	125	8.0	14.0	150

Sources: Colin McEvedy & Richard Jones, *Atlas of World Population History* (1978), 182–203, 250–53; Irfan Habib, *Man and Environment: The Ecological History of India* (2010), 88; Tim Dyson, *A Population History of India* (2018), 43–44, 61–62.

1. Modern Tanzania, Kenya, Somalia, Uganda; not just the Swahili coast
2. Modern Malaysia, Indonesia, Thailand, Cambodia, Laos, Vietnam

of the havoc caused by steppe invaders—the Mongols above all—as well as a spate of epidemics and adverse climate change.

As everywhere, famines and epidemics kept population growth in check. Sanskrit texts first mention what appears to be smallpox in the seventh century, although it likely afflicted India well before. Other deadly infections, such as malaria and cholera, were probably also widespread. In the case of malaria, genetic evidence offers a powerful clue: many South Asian populations have a high rate of sickle-cell trait, a genetic adaptation to the presence of malaria, implying that their ancestors for many generations lived in the presence of the disease. We still don't know if the Black Death, the plague pandemic of the mid-fourteenth century, affected India.

Family, Marriage, and Society

In Chapter 5, we considered family life in ancient India as revealed by the Vedic texts. Marriage was nearly universal, arranged by families, begun at or before puberty, and ended only by death. It took place within caste groups and frequently between close relatives. Cousin marriage was common in India, as in many rural societies. Uncle-niece marriage, taboo almost everywhere else, was acceptable. (There are often health disadvantages to children of marriages between close relatives, but it's a good practice for keeping property in the family.) Females lived under the authority of fathers, then husbands, then, if widowed, of their sons. Family property was held jointly by adult males.

None of that changed much in the centuries after 200 CE, but a little more variety is evident from the greater number of sources. For example, in parts of south India, the customary practice was to trace descent matrilineally—through the female line. Among one aristocratic group, the Nayar, women routinely had multiple husbands at the same time, none of whom was expected to take an interest in children. In other parts of India—Orissa and Kashmir, for example—women served as rulers, of which there is no hint in earlier times. One custom associated with Hinduism, *sati*, arose by the fifth century and spread throughout India by the tenth. Sati (or suttee) refers to the practice of widows leaping onto their dead husbands' funeral pyres and burning themselves to death. It was understood as a show of respect to the deceased and his family, and as a way to cancel his sins and improve his standing in the afterlife. The arrival of Islam in India (of which more later) brought further changes in marriage and family, such as the expectation that married women should seclude themselves behind veils. Muslim rulers from the fourteenth century also sought to suppress the practice of sati and held no objections to widows remarrying.

In most Hindu communities, caste remained the central social institution. It was, as before, a hierarchy of social groups based on their ritual purity and mainly rooted in men's occupations. But the broad fourfold categorization explained in Chapter 5 (Brahmins, Kshatriya, Vaishya, and Sudra), which Sanskrit texts presented as unchanging since the dawn of time, grew more elaborate. Sub-castes merged, others split, and new ones were created in response to the absorption of new peoples or the emergence of new professions. Tribals (to use the Indian term) from rain forests or mountainous landscapes were increasingly brought into the caste system as their forests were burned and turned to farmland. Even foreign raiders and invaders were folded into the caste system. Caste proved remarkably flexible, adjusting to changing times.

A further social change came with the rise of slavery in India after the twelfth century. As far as we know, slavery was rare in early Indian history. But with the arrival of Islam it became more common, although still less so than in Korea, Egypt, or West Africa, for example. In India, slaves came most often from Central Asia, but some from as far afield as Ethiopia and the coasts of the Black Sea. They worked as servants in court or aristocratic households, or as soldiers—we will soon return to the curious case of India's military slaves. One sultan of Delhi apparently owned 180,000 slaves.

Religion, Culture, and Science

As we saw in Chapter 5, in the twilight of the Mauryan dynasty (321–187 BCE), India in the second century BCE was a land of multiple religions. Hinduism, with its Vedic texts and traditions of fire sacrifice, had begun to take shape. Buddhism and Jainism, with their emphasis on renunciation and the endless cycle of death and rebirth, had spread widely partly in reaction to unpopular features of Hindu lore and practice. In the centuries between 200 CE and 1400, religion in India changed dramatically. Buddhism almost went extinct. Islam became a major faith and Zoroastrianism a minor one.

Remember that in India, unlike many other lands, authorities rarely tried to suppress novelties in religious belief or practice. Rulers tended to support all versions of faiths, rather than to suppose that only one represented the truth. Hinduism had no institutional structure to enforce orthodoxy, so new innovations within it popped up frequently and sometimes caught on. Yoga, the practice of meditation aiming at tranquility, enlightenment, and health, provides a good example. It existed in Mauryan times but became more important and took many new forms, some influenced by Buddhist and Jain traditions that were folded into Hindu practice, in the second to the eighth centuries. Variety, cross-fertilization, and change prevailed in Indian religion.

The Bhakti Movement The biggest change in Hinduism came with the rise of intense, emotional cults of the **Bhakti movement**. Between the seventh and the twelfth centuries, first in the south of India, people began to practice personal dedication to one god, such as Shiva or Vishnu, or increasingly Devi, a composite of all female divinity. There was no need for learned Brahmin priests or Buddhist austerity—just intense devotion. The Bhakti movement was spread by charismatic "preachers" who disregarded caste, often discarded the learning of Brahmins, and taught their truths in local languages such as Tamil and Tegulu rather than Sanskrit, the language of the Vedas. Many of these "saints" were of humble origin, low-caste by birth, and scorned by Brahmins. At least one, named Andal, was a woman—unthinkable to those steeped in Vedic tradition, in which women could not become religious specialists. Like India's Muslims, Bhakti followers opposed sati, a perspective that probably appealed to women. The Bhakti message found a wide audience, altering and reinvigorating Hinduism.

The Bhakti revival helped to drive Buddhism to the margins of Indian society. Its innovations enabled Hinduism to appeal to a broader slice of the population, including women and downtrodden low-caste men. Rich merchants found more justification for their wheeling and dealing, something that mercantile classes had formerly found more often in Buddhism. Fewer and fewer rulers supported Buddhist monasteries and monks. By the twelfth century, Buddhism was confined to pockets of eastern India; and with the rise of Islam, it soon lost most of its remaining foothold there too. Where it survived, it took forms increasingly similar to Hinduism. Ironically, Buddhism in these centuries was thriving in Southeast Asia and surviving in East Asia, while all but disappearing in the land of its birth.

Jainism survived a bit better, especially among traders and in the highly commercialized region of Gujarat (northwest India). But it too lost followers. In one case, a ruler of a small southern kingdom decided to abandon Jainism for the cult of Shiva; and following the advice of his spiritual counselor, he demonstrated his new

Bhakti Saints Sambandar was a seventh-century Bhakti child saint devoted to the god Shiva. He performed miracles and wrote devotional hymns, and is said to have attained *moksha*, or final release from the cycle of death and re-birth, at age 16. He is depicted here in a figurine from the eleventh century.

commitment by impaling on stakes the heads of 8,000 Jain teachers. Evidently, the rule of religious toleration in India had its exceptions.

India acquired new religions from abroad as well. A community of Zoroastrians migrated from Persia during the seventh through the tenth centuries, fleeing persecutions by newly Islamized rulers there. They clustered in western India, where they are called Parsis (meaning "Persians"). A community of Christians emerged in southwest India, called St. Thomas Christians, who believed that St. Thomas the Apostle had visited their shores in the first century CE. (Firm evidence suggests Christianity was practiced there by about 300 CE.) Jews from Iraq and Arabia took up residence in west India's ports as well.

Starting in the early eighth century, Islam joined India's portfolio of religions. Arab traders had brought Islam to western Indian ports in the mid-seventh century. Then in 711, the same year that Arab armies crossed into Spain, forces of the Damascus-based Umayyad caliphate conquered the region of Sind in what is now southern Pakistan. They got no further, owing to deserts and formidable foes, but in short order they managed to Islamize Sind.

The Spread of Islam in India   A more powerful force for the **Islamization** of India came from Central Asia beginning around 1000. With the weakening of China's Tang dynasty and the Abbasid caliphate in the eighth and ninth centuries, Turkic peoples in Central Asia acquired more power. Some of them also adopted Islam. A group of slave soldiers, from a part of Afghanistan called Ghazna, began a program of conquest in Iran and India. Under a warlord named Mahmoud, they launched 17 raids into northern India, plundering cities and temples. The Ghaznavids were skilled horsemen and indiscriminate plunderers, sacking Hindu and Buddhist temples alike and assaulting Shi'a Muslims whenever an opportunity arose. An eleventh-century Central Asian scholar, al-Biruni, wrote of Mahmoud that he "utterly destroyed" northern India. That was exaggeration, but the long history of friction between Hindu and Muslim in India dates chiefly from the raids of Mahmoud and his fellow horsemen.

As we shall see below, other Turkic horsemen followed the Ghaznavids and set up durable states in northern India. Usually, the rulers of these new states were Muslim. But the villagers remained overwhelmingly Hindu except in two regions, the Punjab and Bengal. In the Punjab, Muslims enjoyed especially high prestige because they led the battle against Mongol invaders—descendants of Genghis Khan who after 1240 tried and failed several times to add India to their empire. In Bengal, which was a thinly populated frontier forest region, Islam became dominant because rulers granted land to Muslims who would clear forests and start up new farming communities.

By and large, despite the occasional massacre of Buddhists or Hindus, the new Muslim overlords preferred not to interfere in their subjects' religious affairs. Muslim doctrine and law afford respect and protection to Peoples of the Book, which until this time had meant Jews, Zoroastrians, and Christians. But the Turkic sultans found it easy enough to extend this special status (called *dhimmi* in Arabic and Islamic law) to Hindus, Buddhists, and Jains. They had financial incentives not to press conversion to Islam, because by Islamic law Muslims were taxed at lower rates than non-Muslims. Although Hindus and Buddhists, conversely, had financial incentives to become Muslims, over the centuries of Muslim rule in north India (i.e., 1206–1857) only about a quarter of the population did so, and far less than that outside of the Punjab and Bengal.

The changes in religion encouraged linguistic change in India. The rise of Bhakti worship involved the use of local languages rather than Sanskrit. Tamil, Telugu, Bengali, Gujarati, and Marathi became literary languages and tongues used in religious ritual. They gradually became major regional languages of India, as they remain today. Sanskrit lost some of its prestige and market share. Although still spoken by small numbers of Indians, Sanskrit's fate is a bit like Latin's in Europe: it is an ancestor of many living tongues but now survives mainly as a language of priestly ritual and ancient literature.

Science and Learning in India The centuries between about 500 and 1000 CE proved especially fertile in several areas of learning. One was linguistics, the study of language itself. For Hindu rituals in which certain prayers had to be said in just the right way, detailed knowledge of Sanskrit was helpful. Science in India, as almost everywhere at the time, was part of religion. So was medicine, an active area of scientific work. Indian medical thought—the ayurvedic tradition, as it is known—dealt with everything from toxicology to sexual potency. It typically explained illness in spiritual terms but sought cures both in that realm and through drugs extracted from plants, including opium. Animal fats also served as salves. Ayurvedic medicine has ancient roots, but between 500 and 1200 CE it became codified. It has followers around the world today, attracted by its holistic approach.

Another vibrant field of science was astronomy and astrology, which in distant times were united, not only in India but in Mesopotamia, China, Europe, and elsewhere too. Indian astronomers figured out that eclipses are shadows cast by the Earth and moon upon each other.

Astronomy and astrology were closely linked to mathematics in India, as in ancient Sumer and among the Maya. Indian texts from the fifth through the eighth centuries show a growing experimentation with new concepts in mathematics. They pioneered algebra, or at least basic quadratic equations. Indian mathematicians also explored trigonometry and developed the concept of zero and the first base 10 numerical notation. They calculated π as far as 3.1416—as far as you need to go for practical purposes. Indian math had drawn on Mesopotamian and Greek precedents, and in turn it would later influence Arab mathematics, which in turn influenced European math and eventually became globalized. Indian math texts were typically written as poems, a practice that sadly did not translate into other cultures.

Nalanda The scale of the ruins of the monastery at Nalanda, which flourished between the sixth and ninth centuries CE, speaks to the site's importance as a center of knowledge and learning.

Indian science and learning were concentrated in royal courts and in the remaining Buddhist monasteries. The greatest of these monasteries was **Nalanda** (in northeast India), which attracted students from China, Korea, Tibet, Southeast Asia, and Persia. According to one Chinese visitor in the seventh century, it had 1,500 instructors and its towers and temples "soared above the mists in the sky." Some 200 villages devoted their surplus food to supporting the monks and 10,000 hungry students at Nalanda in its heyday, which extended from the sixth through the ninth centuries. Its curriculum emphasized both Buddhist and Hindu philosophy, logic, linguistics, and medicine. When in 1193 Turkic Muslims sacked it, three months were needed to burn all the manuscripts kept at Nalanda. Today, the governments of India, China, Japan, and Singapore are spending vast sums to create a new university there.

Great Powers in India

In the aftermath of the Mauryan Empire in 187 BCE, most of India fragmented politically into tiny kingdoms or loose states dominated by a handful of adult males. But over time, kingdoms became both more common and larger, a pattern found in many places around the world. In India this trend was reinforced by the Vedic texts, which present kingship as the best political format. Kings in India were in theory responsible only to the gods. But in practice, like kings everywhere, they had to tread carefully. The councils of elders that ran the affairs of castes, for example, could not be disregarded lightly. Kings could pronounce edicts carrying the force of law, but human law, even kingly law, always carried less prestige than dharma, the righteous path in Hindu belief.

Most Indian kingdoms were in effect franchises. A successful king would leave matters such as justice and policing to lesser rulers, treated as vassals. He demanded tribute from them in the forms of money, war elephants, or soldiers, and required formal declarations of obedience. In exchange, he would protect them from attack. Hundreds of states rose and fell in India in the centuries between 200 and 1400. The three most important for world history are the Gupta, the Chola, and the Delhi sultanate.

The Gupta, ca. 330–550 The most successful kings in India after the Mauryans were those of the **Gupta dynasty**. Like most big powers in Indian history before and since, they got their start in the Ganges basin. Through astute marriages they expanded their domain. Via warfare they forced rulers throughout north India to pay them tribute in their capital, Pataliputra (present-day Patna). Samudragupta reigned for four decades (r. 335–375) and conquered at least 14 other kings, a record comparable to that of Alexander the Great or Qin Shi Huangdi. His successor, Chandragupta II (r. 375–415), ruled just as long and conquered almost as widely, even into Central Asia. As one of his boosters delicately put it, "he unburdened the sacred earth of the barbarians." The Gupta kings managed no enduring conquests in south India, but they enjoyed authority throughout the north. Although smaller than the Mauryan Empire, the Gupta state was probably the largest and most populous in the world by the end of Chandragupta's reign. (China at the time was divided among several states, and the Roman Empire was a shell of its former self.)

The Gupta kings claimed semi-divine status and enjoyed strong support from the Brahmins. They were, by all accounts, pious Hindus, but nonetheless patronized Buddhist and Jain monasteries and temples. The Guptas often granted religious leaders forest land to clear and till, accepting one-sixth of the religious merit earned by holy men instead of taxes. Taking a cut of religious merit earned by specialists in virtue allowed the kings the moral latitude to use violence, trickery, and other routine tools of statecraft without unduly jeopardizing their own souls. These deals, granted

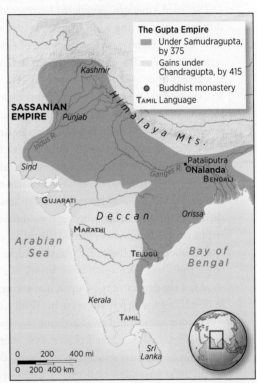

The Gupta State, ca. 330–550 The Gupta state grew by leaps and bounds in the late fourth and early fifth centuries, ultimately holding sway over half of the Indian subcontinent. Like the Mauryans a few centuries before, its kings controlled the two richest river basins, the Ganges and the Indus, and the surplus rice and wheat that peasants produced. The Gupta state was, for a while, the most powerful in the world. Its patronage of art and science brought creative results still admired inside and outside India.

for "as long as the sun and moon endure," served both rulers and religious leaders, and cemented the alliance between them.

In addition to religious institutions, the Gupta kings supported the math and science noted above, and the work of artists and poets as well. The court hosted literary lions called the Nine Jewels, who wrote poetry that later ages came to regard as the best in the Sanskrit language. The most famous and widely translated literary work of the Gupta age (early drafts probably date to the first or second century) is the *Kama Sutra*, a guide to refined living that includes one of the most thorough and unabashed studies of human sexual conduct ever written. Faxian, a Chinese Buddhist monk, visited Gupta lands in Chandragupta II's time and found what he thought was a happy and satisfied kingdom, populated by vegetarians and teetotalers. Perhaps he had some difficulty interpreting what he saw: he also reported venomous dragons that spat out snow in the Himalayas. But the work of Gupta sculptors and architects, as well as of writers and scientists, inspired modern Indians to regard the fourth and fifth centuries as a golden age.

The Gupta kings, however golden their legacy, soon ran into trouble. Despite their military strength, based on war elephants and archers, by the 450s they could no longer reliably defend their northern frontiers against Central Asian horsemen. One charismatic warlord, named Oprah, built a large following and in the 480s broke through Gupta defenses. After that, Gupta vassal rulers increasingly defected, declaring their allegiance to Oprah and other Central Asian chieftains. Soon almost no one was paying tribute to the Gupta anymore, and with lower revenues they could no longer defend their remaining vassals against anyone. Like most other agrarian states adjacent to the steppe lands, the Gupta eventually faced an enemy too mobile, militaristic, organized, and formidable for them. By 550, the Gupta dynasty ruled only a tiny kingdom, and north India was once again a patchwork of rival polities.

After the decline of the Gupta, many kings struggled for power, but none succeeded in re-uniting the rich Ganges basin. With its dense population, fertile farmland, iron and copper mines, and good riverine transport network, it remained the grand prize in Indian geopolitics. Small powers took shape in Bengal and, in the form of invading Arabs, in Sind (today's southern Pakistan). But in the absence of a great power in the north, India after 550—rather like China—experienced a slow rise of the south. Major new centers of wealth and power arose in the Deccan (west-central India) and the southeast, the Tamil-speaking region of India. The greatest of these was the Chola kingdom.

The Chola Kingdom, ca. 970–ca. 1300 For centuries merely a local dynasty in the Kaveri River basin of southeastern India, the **Chola kingdom** after 970 burst forth to become a transcontinental power. They sponsored new irrigation techniques that improved harvests. In the 980s, their kings started gobbling up neighboring lands on both the Coromandel (southeastern) and Malabar (southwestern) coasts. They built a navy and gradually took the islands of Sri Lanka and the Maldives.

More than any other major state in Indian history, the Chola drew their revenues from seaborne trade. Once they controlled the south Indian coasts and Sri Lanka, all shipping in transit across the Indian Ocean had to stop in their harbors—and pay for the privilege. Larger trends around the Indian Ocean world helped make the Chola rich and powerful. The rise of the Song in China and their commercial orientation buoyed long-distance trade, as did the simultaneous rise of a powerful and prosperous dynasty in Egypt, the Fatimids. The burgeoning trade helped rulers throughout the Indian Ocean world, but especially those situated at its choke points, such as the Chola.

The Chola state was in part an alliance of **merchant trading guilds**, not so different from the merchant families that many centuries earlier had dominated Carthage and its seaborne empire of the Mediterranean. Sea traders banded together to pool resources and share risk. The big guilds included hundreds of merchants. As their wealth grew, they used it to influence kings who needed their money. An inscription from 1055 gives a sense of the role of one of the merchant guilds and their pride in themselves:

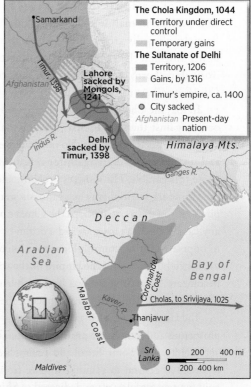

The Chola Kingdom and the Delhi Sultanate, 1044–1400 The Chola kingdom was a maritime empire, supported by revenues from seaborne trade. The Delhi sultanate was a terrestrial empire, held together by cavalry forces. While neither one dominated India to the extent that the Mauryans or the Gupta had centuries before them, each was the greatest Indian state of its day.

Famed throughout the world, adorned with many good qualities, truth purity ... and prudence, born to be wanderers over many countries...; ... by land and sea penetrating into the regions of the six continents, with superior elephants, well-bred horses, large sapphires, moonstones, pearls, rubies, diamonds...cloves, sandalwood, camphor musk, saffron, and other perfumes and drugs; by selling wholesale or hawking about on their shoulders, preventing the loss by custom duties, they fill up the emperor's treasury of gold, his treasury of jewels, and his armory of weapons.

Under Rajendra I (r. 1012–1044), the Chola grew yet more ambitious. They enhanced their position in maritime trade by taking Indian ports to the north as far as Bengal. Rajendra allegedly arranged to have some holy water from the Ganges brought south to his kingdom. Next he started sending trade missions to China in 1016, bringing ivory, rhino horn, brocade, glassware, and other goods the Chola merchants expected Chinese markets to value.

In 1025 the Chola launched a naval expedition across 2,500 miles (4,000 km) of open ocean against the state of Srivijaya, the maritime powerhouse controlling the Straits of Malacca (see Chapter 12). No one had ever done anything like this in world history, and no one would do it again for centuries. We don't know exactly why Rajendra I chose this gamble. His motives probably included trying for better terms of access to the China trade. Srivijaya's sea captains were traders if you abided by their terms and pirates if you didn't, so perhaps the Chola understood their mission as pirate control. In any case, Rajendra's navy sacked a dozen or more Srivijayan cities but did not attempt to impose enduring control. He wasn't interested in building, or perhaps knew he was unable to build, a seaborne empire of the sort that Carthage had created in the Mediterranean. Soon Srivijaya was back in business, sending additional trade missions to China by 1028. The long-term impact of the Chola naval attack was nil.

The Chola stayed with their formula of commercial and naval activity, remaining prosperous and formidable until after 1100. They patronized the arts, especially literature and architecture. Some Tamil and Telugu literary classics, and versions of Sanskrit epics regarded as central to Hinduism, date from their reign. Chola kings and merchants paid for new temples, often dedicated to Shiva, such as that at Thanjavur, in its day the biggest in India. Chola bronze statuary earned the admiration of future ages.

Chola Art Under the sponsorship of Chola rulers, art and architecture flourished—ranging from immense Hindu temples such as this one in present-day Tamil Nadu, built around 1010 CE, to smaller-scale ornate bronzes such as this sculpture of the god Shiva, made in the same period.

Chola power slipped in the late twelfth century. But the merchant guilds of southeastern India remained active in overseas trade. The Chinese city of Guangzhou features a Hindu temple in the Chola style, with a Tamil-language inscription from 1281, implying a substantial resident Tamil population. One of the Chola ports had a Chinese pagoda, built in 1267. The commercial and cultural connections between south India and Southeast Asia waned somewhat in the fourteenth century, but never disappeared.

The Sultanate of Delhi, ca. 1206–ca. 1400 Like China and Persia, India stood adjacent to the steppe corridor of Eurasia. It too experienced its share of nomad incursions, including those who helped bring low the Gupta state in the sixth century, and the Ghaznavids who brought Islam into the heart of India around 1000 CE. Other Turkic peoples from the steppe followed, drawn by the prospect of loot. As horsemen, they enjoyed a great advantage operating in north India, which for lack of good grasslands could not raise powerful steeds. Increasingly, these Turkic horsemen chose to settle in north India, where they could hope to live well off of taxes gathered from peasants.

The Turkic invaders brought with them the peculiar institution of slave soldiery. In Central Asia, families often sold excess boys to the armies of caliphs and sultans. No shame was attached to this form of slavery. Most of these boys lived out their lives as cavalrymen or in a palace guard. Occasionally, they used their military skills to overthrow their masters and install themselves on thrones. But most died anonymously—as unknown **slave soldiers**.

In the 1190s, a new band of Turkic soldiers from Central Asia began raiding north India. Like the Ghaznavids before them, most were nominally slaves. The various princes of north India could never unite against the invaders. They also lacked the horses to match their enemies' cavalry. Soon the entire Ganges basin as far east as Bengal was paying tribute to new masters, who set up a capital in Delhi, formerly a backwater town. In 1206 these Turkic horsemen established the sultanate of Delhi.

The new sultans became a new military aristocracy. Indians called their new overlords *ashvapati,* or "lords of the horses." The sultans of Delhi tried to monopolize the importation of horses in order to field cavalry in a land where no one else had enough horses. The sultans' forces clustered in garrison towns and left the villages alone, as long as they turned over taxes and conscripts. In that respect, their rule was ordinary.

In other respects, it was not. After the 1220s, when the Mongols had begun their assaults on Iran, many educated and skilled Persians fled either to Delhi or to Egypt, the main states still under Muslim rule. The language of administration and high culture in Delhi gradually became Persian, and art and architecture reflected powerful Persian influences. A new Indo-Islamic culture evolved, fusing elements of Indian tradition with Turkic, Persian, and Arabic contributions. Its most enduring features were palace and mosque architecture and poetry in the Urdu language, a blend of Hindi and Persian.

The **Delhi sultanate** was distinctive in another respect: one of its early rulers was a woman, Rayiza, whose father, a slave soldier who became sultan, judged her to be the most fit to rule among his offspring. Her brothers disagreed, and others in high places found the concept of a woman ruler too much to bear. So she faced continual rebellion—against which she sometimes led her troops on horseback—and was killed fleeing her enemies after four difficult years on the job (r. 1236–1240).

The Delhi sultanate endured despite political instability. It featured five dynasties in rapid succession, with a heavy dose of poisonings, assassinations, and coups d'état. Slave soldiers often seized power. The competition for succession among brothers, sons, and nephews of dying sultans resembled that of the Mongol and Central Asian world from which they came. To complicate matters, the Mongols themselves kept attacking through Afghanistan into the Punjab from the 1240s onward. Against the odds, the Delhi sultanate survived and prospered.

The sultanate's good fortune rested on its ability to loot temples and palaces to its south, in the Deccan and central India. This enabled it to buy new horses, pay Turkic cavalry, and hire Persian bureaucrats. Sultans ruled the Ganges heartland directly and extorted payment from princes elsewhere. Powerful sultans could make this formula work and keep the Mongols at bay. Lesser or less lucky ones found Indian princes inclined to rebel rather than pay up, sapping the sultans' financial strength and diverting their military efforts. On one occasion, the sultanate was too weak to prevent the Mongols from sacking Lahore, a rich city in the Punjab. On other occasions, the productive lands of Bengal slipped from the sultans' control.

After 1306 the Mongol onslaught on north India slackened, and the sultanate reached the pinnacle of its power. It expanded its control of surrounding regions, notably under Alauddin Khalji, who murdered his way into the top job in 1296. He led winning campaigns against large Mongol attacks, inspiring him to compare his own record to Alexander the Great's. Unlike Alexander, and unlike his own contemporaries in Yuan China, Alauddin embarked on a program of direct state control over the economy. He curtailed the role of markets, fixing prices for everything from needles to horses. This worked as a short-term strategy to maximize revenue and the sultan's military power. After beating back the Mongols, Alauddin turned his well-tuned war machine against his neighbors, expanding the sultanate's frontiers in India. He earned a fearsome reputation for demolishing temples and wreaking homicidal vengeance upon his enemies and their families, especially anyone bold enough to question the justice of his rule.

The majority of Indians under the Delhi sultanate remained Hindu. Many temples were destroyed or converted into mosques. But the sultans could not afford to see all Hindus become Muslims, because by Islamic law non-Muslims paid twice the tax of Muslims. When one faction of zealous Muslim clerics asked a sultan's permission to force Hindus to convert to Islam, they were rebuked by the sultan with political arithmetic. We Muslims, he said, are only like the salt on a dish of food. By and large, outside of Bengal and the Punjab, only garrison towns became predominantly Muslim.

The sultanate's fortunes turned after Alauddin's death in 1316. Less skilled, if no less ruthless, sultans followed. Ibn Battuta described one of them, his boss, as addicted to both gift giving and the shedding of blood. The stream of plunder slowed, and sultans had to raise taxes, inviting internal revolts and banditry. By 1350, the Delhi sultanate was only one state among several in north India. Yet another Central Asian conqueror, Timur, swooped in to sack Delhi in 1398, slaughter thousands, and carry off its treasures and skilled craftsmen to his own capital, Samarkand, in today's Uzbekistan. The Delhi sultanate limped on until finally extinguished in 1526—by yet another troop of Central Asian horsemen, the Mughals, whom we shall save for another chapter.

For toiling peasants hovering just above starvation, the advent and decline of the sultanate of Delhi didn't mean much: someone else collected their taxes. For Brahmins, the sultanate was a disaster: they lost their positions as advisers and ministers to upstart Persians and other foreigners—including Ibn Battuta, who worked as a high judge in Delhi despite not knowing Persian or Hindi. For Buddhists, too, the sultanate was bad news: its forces sacked their temples and monasteries and drove Buddhism to the verge of extinction in India. For elite women, it meant further restrictions upon their conduct and appearance, Rayiza's example notwithstanding. More broadly, the sultanate meant the integration of northern India into the world of Islam, which by 1400 stretched from Morocco, the home of Ibn Battuta, to Java.

The Indian Ocean World, 200–1400

In 1944, in the Wessel Islands off the northern coast of Australia, a World War II radar team found a handful of old coins. The coins were well worn but still carried faint Arabic inscriptions. It turned out the coins had been minted sometime between 1000 and 1300 (old coins rarely had dates on them) in Kilwa, an island off Africa's eastern coast. In the same year of 1944, on the island of Zanzibar—not far north of Kilwa—a hoard of 250 Chinese copper coins was unearthed. Four of them dated to the Tang dynasty (618–907), and the newest was from the reign of a Song emperor who died in 1275. Just how and when East African coins got to islands off the coast of Australia, and Chinese coins got to islands off of East Africa, is unknown. But they are tangible evidence of a web of interaction connecting the shores of the Indian Ocean.

The Indian Ocean world for many centuries was one of the main arenas of interaction in world history, beginning no later than 2000 BCE. By 100 CE, together with the Silk Road traffic across the steppe, its routes helped to weave together the existing (yet still developing) webs of East Asia and Southwest Asia, in effect creating the Old World web. So, after 100 CE, it was, at the same time, its own watery web and a sub-unit of the larger Old World web. The Indian Ocean world became a cosmopolitan space, an archipelago of interacting ports and, to varying degrees, their hinterlands. Although trade and cultural exchange were linked processes, here we will treat them one at a time.

THE HUMAN WEB

The Indian Ocean World

ca. 1400

BY THE EIGHTH CENTURY, the Abbasid caliph al-Mansur was able to boast of the bounty of goods that traveled the sea connections joining Baghdad, his future capital, to faraway China. The maritime networks of the Indian Ocean world had become at least as important as the centuries-old overland Silk Roads.

The East African coast (or Swahili coast by ca. 800 CE) illustrates the region's growing web links. Sailors from Arabia, Iran, India, and East Africa traded throughout the western Indian Ocean. The Swahili coast exported elephant ivory, mangrove poles, animal skins, slaves, and, by 1250, gold. Its main import was cloth from India. Traders brought more than cloth, however, to East Africa. Arabic and Persian combined with Bantu tongues to form a new language, Swahili. Simplified trading languages that blended several linguistic traditions developed at all the crossroads of the Indian Ocean world.

Along with the goods and languages of trade, four great religions spread along the pathways of the Indian Ocean world—Hinduism, Buddhism, Christianity, and Islam. Hinduism and Buddhism moved into East and Southeast Asia. Coptic Christianity expanded its footprint in northeast Africa. Islam filtered into East and West Africa, parts of India, and Southeast Asia. Local religions retreated as these major ones spread and developed new variations suited to new locations. Nonetheless, the larger pattern of web building held for the Indian Ocean world: increased contacts meant decreased cultural variety overall.

KEY

- ▩ Core area
- ◉ City
- ➤ Web connection
- ⌇⌇ Swahili language area
- Transfers via trade routes
- *ISLAM* Religion
- ʙᴀɴᴛᴜ Language
- silk Trade good; color indicates exporting region

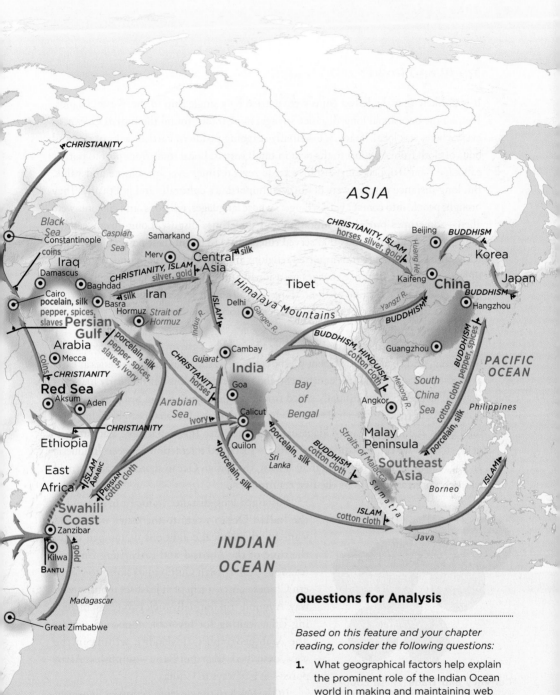

CHRISTIANITY

Black Sea

Constantinople

coins

Caspian Sea

Samarkand

Merv

CHRISTIANITY, ISLAM
silver, gold

Central Asia

silk

CHRISTIANITY, ISLAM
horses, silver, gold

Beijing

BUDDHISM

Korea

Japan

ASIA

Iraq

Damascus

Baghdad

Cairo

pocelain, silk
pepper, spices,
slaves

Persian Gulf

Arabia

Mecca

coins

CHRISTIANITY

Red Sea

Aksum

Aden

CHRISTIANITY

Ethiopia

East Africa

ISLAM
ARABIC

PERSIAN
cotton cloth

Swahili Coast

Zanzibar

Kilwa

BANTU

gold

Madagascar

Great Zimbabwe

Basra

silk

Iran

Hormuz

Strait of Hormuz

ISLAM

Indus R.

Delhi

Ganges R.

Himalaya Mountains

Tibet

Kaifeng

Huang He

China

Hangzhou

BUDDHISM

BUDDHISM

Guangzhou

Yangzi R.

porcelain, silk
pepper, spices,
slaves, ivory

Gujarat

CHRISTIANITY
horses

Cambay

India

Goa

Calicut

ivory

Quilon

porcelain, silk

BUDDHISM, HINDUISM
cotton cloth

Bay of Bengal

Sri Lanka

porcelain, silk

Arabian Sea

BUDDHISM
cotton cloth

Straits of Malacca

Angkor

Mekong R.

Malay Peninsula

Southeast Asia

Sumatra

ISLAM
cotton cloth

Java

South China Sea

BUDDHISM

cotton cloth, pepper, spices

porcelain, silk

ISLAM

Borneo

Philippines

PACIFIC OCEAN

INDIAN OCEAN

Questions for Analysis

Based on this feature and your chapter reading, consider the following questions:

1. What geographical factors help explain the prominent role of the Indian Ocean world in making and maintaining web connections across Eurasia?

2. How did the web connections of the Indian Ocean world change religious life on the East African coast and in Southeast Asia?

Trade and Power

It is unlikely that the Kilwa coins were carried by a single ship to the Wessel Islands. Despite the occasional long-distance voyage, most trade around the Indian Ocean, as everywhere, was local. Traders, essentially seagoing peddlers, carried sacks of rice and bolts of cloth from one port to the next in small vessels. Local trade from port to port—cabotage—outstripped long-distance trade several times over by volume and value. But long-distance voyages were of outsized importance culturally and politically. They brought people into contact with strangers whose languages, religions, and customs were alien—sometimes provoking imitation and sometimes disgust. Long-distance trade brought exotic luxury goods that served rulers' need to flaunt their power and wealth. Kings also sometimes found imported religions and customs useful to underscore their right to rule. Long-distance voyages occasionally brought crops and pathogens to new places. Cabotage did none of these things, so although larger in quantitative terms, it did less to affect the cultural and political history of the Indian Ocean shores—or world history.

Component circuits of the Indian Ocean world had grown up over millennia. As we've seen, trade had linked ancient Mesopotamia and the Indus valley societies as early as 2500 BCE. An ancient Greek author, Strabo, wrote that in his day (the early first century CE) some 120 ships annually sailed from a single Egyptian Red Sea port to India. Austronesians from Borneo had traveled the breadth of the Indian Ocean bringing their food crops and language to Madagascar before 400 CE. This remarkable feat (an accident, so far as we can tell) did not give rise to sustained interaction between Indonesia and Madagascar. But to some degree, at least, the Indian Ocean shores already formed a loosely connected world by the first centuries CE.

Currency and Trade These copper coins—minted in Kilwa in East Africa sometime between the eleventh and the sixteenth centuries—bear inscriptions in Arabic, the common language of the educated classes of the Islamic world, including Kilwa.

Sustained long-distance traffic from one end of the Indian Ocean world to the other waxed and waned with political conditions. It ramped up in the time of the Abbasid and early Tang Empires (ca. 600–750). Persian Gulf traders sailed to southern Chinese ports, a trip of at least six months each way. A round-trip normally took two years, including time waiting for favorable monsoon winds. The Arab geographer al-Maqdisi, writing in the 980s, described Aden and Basra—southwest Asian ports—as gateways to China.

In the tenth to the eleventh centuries, however, through traffic was already becoming rare, even while total trade climbed. The naval forces of the Chola and the Srivijaya kings insisted that ships dock at their ports and part with a share of their cargoes. In these circumstances, Indian Ocean traders came to specialize in shorter round-trips. Rather than wait weeks for the winds to change, one could schedule these shorter voyages to minimize port time—just sail for a few weeks and on arrival sell one's wares, and then head home.

The eventual decline of Chola and Srivijayan power encouraged through voyages once again after about 1250. One merchant from Aleppo (in Syria) made five sea trips from Yemen to China in the early fourteenth century. Marco Polo, probably in 1290, took ship in South China for Iran on a voyage with 600 fellow travelers, including a 17-year-old "extremely handsome and accomplished" Mongol (Yuan) princess named Kogatin. The point of the expedition was political: to give her in marriage to an elderly Mongol khan in Iran. They were held up for months in Sumatra, waiting for the monsoon to shift, and by the time they made it to Iran the khan had inconveniently died. So she, perhaps feeling relieved, was given to the dead man's son. In 1290 at least, the best-informed people in China judged a sea voyage safer and cheaper than a land one.

We don't have enough quantitative evidence to chart the ups and downs of the Indian Ocean trade reliably. But textual evidence and archeology suggest that it peaked three times: around the years 600–800, 1000–1150, and 1250–1350. In the first and last of these three periods, through voyages took place regularly. In the 1000–1150 upturn, they did not, owing to the power of the Chola and Srivijaya. The ups and downs reflected the demand for exotic goods around the Indian Ocean, which in turn reflected political developments. New states and ambitious rulers wanted exotic goods to bolster their claims to power.

The occasional downturns in Indian Ocean trade differed from the fraying of the Old World web in western Europe after 450 CE or in the Maya lowlands after 900 CE. Urban life and long-distance exchanges around the Indian Ocean survived these downturns, even if diminished in quantity, and the pace resumed after a century or two. In this respect, the Indian Ocean world's web connections were more resilient, based as they were on the vast populations and economies of China, India, and Egypt.

That resilience also reflected the enduring infrastructure of ports and ships and the knowledge behind them. Most ships in the Indian Ocean trade were built to carry a dozen or two sailors and a few tons of merchandise. The biggest known, a Gujarati ship used in the early sixteenth century to ferry pilgrims to Jiddah (the port nearest Mecca), weighed about 800 tons. This was roughly eight times the size of Columbus's biggest ship, the *Santa María*, but smaller than Chinese ships that sailed the Indian Ocean in the early fifteenth century. Both Marco Polo and Ibn Battuta wrote of ships that could carry more than 500 passengers. As noted above, these ships' hulls were built for Indian Ocean conditions. Everything else about Indian Ocean sailing, from the technical sophistication of rigging and sails to the navigational skills of sea captains, was highly developed and in wide circulation. Skills and technologies could survive a commercial downturn.

To some extent, the maritime traders competed with the caravan masters of the Silk Roads, and often at an advantage. Even a small vessel such as the dhow of the Arabian Sea could travel three times as fast as a camel caravan, carry 1,000 times as much as a single camel, and needed fewer men to manage it than did a caravan—camels are stubborn beasts. And camel transport was the most efficient land transport going.

There was risk to consider as well as cost. An Egyptian merchant hoping to sell goods in India or China had to guess whether pirates at sea or brigands on land posed the greater threat, using information that was weeks or months old. Marco Polo and his shipmates made similar calculations when escorting Kogatin to her wedding.

But sea and land routes were not always in competition. The arrival of exotic goods by one route could provoke envy and stimulate demand for more such goods coming via any route. When trade was brisk, both camels and ships were busy. Moreover, different routes presented different commercial opportunities. If you wanted to add cinnamon to your inventory, you would take a sea route and stop in Sri Lanka. If you thought you could do better dealing turquoise, you would take a land route and buy some in Central Asia.

Goods and Routes

Archeology and the surviving texts tell us a lot about the goods traded in the Indian Ocean world. The prosperity of Roman Egypt gave rise to a flurry of exchange with India in luxury goods during the first century CE. Romans sent silver, Mediterranean wine, and Greek slave women to India in exchange for pearls and pepper. Roman authors such as Pliny complained that the empire was squandering its wealth so patrician women could wear pearls. By 200 CE this trade had fallen off, but other routes in the Indian Ocean soon carried increasing traffic, which reached a plateau after 600.

While changes took place in particulars of production and trade, some basic patterns held for the whole period from 600 to 1400. Only western India and southern China offered important manufactures to the marketplaces of the Indian Ocean world. People elsewhere contributed mainly raw materials. China's main exports were porcelain and silk, although al-Idrisi, a Moroccan-born scholar, reported in the 1150s that Chinese ships carried leather, iron, swords, and glassware to Indian Ocean ports. Porcelain from the Tang and Song dynasties has turned up all around Indian Ocean shores, including East Africa. Western India sold ships, made from its once-plentiful teak forests, and Gujaratis (in northwest India) marketed colorful cotton clothing, worn from Kilwa to Java. Thousands upon thousands of spinners and weavers turned Gujarati raw cotton into commercial gold. Gujarat was, in effect, the workshop of the Indian Ocean world.

Among raw materials traded around the Indian Ocean, **spices**—the taste that launched a thousand ships—took pride of place, as silk did on the Silk Roads. Most spices, like nutmeg, cloves, cinnamon, and a variety of peppers, came from Southeast Asia or southern India. They added welcome flavor to dull dishes. According to Marco

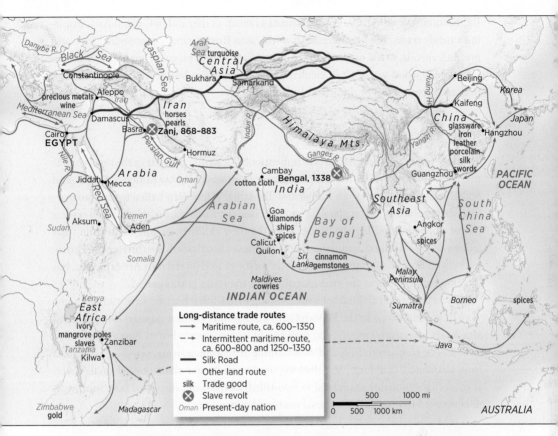

Indian Ocean Trade, ca. 600–1350 Sailing ships and camel caravans carried goods and people—and therefore ideas, artistic styles, pathogens, and much more—throughout the Old World web. Only luxury goods could justify the cost of transport over thousands of miles, and most trade was local. But the longer journeys were more important for world history because they did more to stimulate new ways of thinking, building, cooking, writing poetry, doing mathematics, weaving cloth, and so forth.

Polo, for every shipment of spices that reached Europe, either 10 or 100 shipments went to China (he offers conflicting figures at different points in his book). Egypt, Arabia, and Iran also imported boatloads of spices. At times, merchant families in southern Arabia—Oman and Aden especially—held leading positions in the western Indian Ocean spice trade.

But the spice trade was not the half of it. India also sold precious stones, notably diamonds. Sri Lanka traded rubies, emeralds, sapphires, and more cinnamon than anywhere else. Iran sold pearls, gathered by specialist slave divers, and horses, which India always needed. According to Marco Polo, one Coromandel port purchased 5,000 horses annually from Iran, of which 4,700 would die within a year. And according to

Ibn Battuta, horses in India cost 200 times as much as they did in Central Asia, inspiring a steady trade. The Mediterranean world, as in Roman times, contributed wine and precious metals, often in the form of coins. East Africa exported mangrove poles to Iraq (where wood was scarce), elephant ivory everywhere but to India above all, and iron and slaves to Egypt, Iraq, and India.

Indian Ocean Slavery

The slave trade from East Africa is first mentioned in written sources in the seventh century, but it existed earlier. Most captives came from what are now Ethiopia, Sudan, and Somalia, but some were from Kenya and Tanzania. A few even hailed from Madagascar, where according to one book of sailors' tales (the *Kitab Ajab al-Hind*) Arab traders "never stopped swindling the natives, stealing their children, buying them from their fellows with . . . trinkets and dates." One Chinese chronicle of the thirteenth century refers to "thousands and tens of thousands" of slaves sold on the East African coast, but it is impossible to know the true magnitude of the trade in this period.

Slaves performed all kinds of work. Among males, a few became slave soldiers. Some worked as pearl divers in the Persian Gulf, a dangerous job that exposed them to shark attacks. In the ninth century, the majority of slaves exported from East Africa toiled in southern Iraq, extending and maintaining irrigation systems, scraping salt crusts from abandoned farmland, and working on date and sugar plantations. Females, who at most times probably amounted to two-thirds of the slaves imported into Southwest Asia, worked mainly as domestic servants and concubines.

East Africa and the Slave Trade This image from a thirteenth-century Yemeni manuscript shows a transaction in a slave market in which two Arab merchants negotiate a price for an African youth. From the seventh century to the early twentieth, the Arabian peninsula, like Egypt and Iraq, imported slaves from East Africa, roughly two-thirds of whom were female. Slave trades were a common feature of the Old World web.

Plantation slavery on a large scale existed only in southern Iraq and only in the ninth century. It led to results no one wanted to see again. Working conditions on the date and sugar plantations, often carved out of swamps, were miserable. Africans encountered systematic prejudice, judging from the writings of al-Jahiz of Basra, a scholar born of an African mother. Several small slave rebellions broke out in the eighth and early ninth centuries, all crushed. A massive one, sometimes called the **Zanj revolt** for the word Arabs used to describe Africans, shook the Abbasid caliphate during the years 868–883. It involved tens of thousands of slaves led by an Arab said to be "eloquent... a natural poet." The slaves managed to form their own army, control Basra and southern Iraq, kill hordes of their oppressors, sell thousands of captured Arab and Iranian women to slave merchants, carry the revolt into Arabia, and even mint coins—the privilege of a sovereign ruler—before their final military defeat.

As slave rebellions go, this ranks among the largest in world history, on the scale of Spartacus's uprising in Roman Italy but much longer-lasting. By some accounts more than a million people lost their lives in it, although no figures are trustworthy. The damage to southern Iraq, combined with the simultaneous massacres of Iranian and Arab merchants in South China's ports, severed the link between the Persian Gulf and China. Thereafter, the economic engine of the Islamic world shifted to Egypt. The revolt brought an end to large-scale plantation slavery in the Indian Ocean world until the nineteenth century.

The Delhi sultanate also imported African slaves into India, usually for military duty. Some managed to take over Bengal in 1338. Rich merchants in southern China during the Tang and Song also purchased slaves from East Africa. Some Arab and Chinese texts even suggest merchants came to East Africa all the way from Indonesia to buy slaves in the eighth century. A different and more localized slave trade existed in Southeast Asia in which captives were traded from one island to another, but almost never outside the region.

Commercial Culture

Trade around the Indian Ocean, whether for slaves, cotton, horses, or ceramics, usually used money rather than barter. Often, the currency involved took the form of cowrie shells, the preferred variety of which came from the Maldive Islands. Cowries made a good currency: they are durable, lightweight, and appealing to the eye. The Maldives traded millions of them for rice and other necessities. Silver money often came from Mediterranean lands via Egypt. Gold, after the tenth century at least, came above all from the Zimbabwe plateau in southern Africa, but also from West Africa via Egypt. Copper coins came from almost everywhere.

The merchants operating around the Indian Ocean hailed from certain places more than others. In the western region, Persians and later Arabs and Gujaratis were prominent. In the eastern reaches, Malays, Tamils, and later, Bengalis, were notably active, as were Chinese. They typically worked within social networks of kinfolk, people from their home village or clan, or their co-religionists. Sometimes, as in the Chola kingdom, they organized formal merchant guilds. In the case of Indians, these networks involved people from the same caste—although normally not Brahmins, who had religious objections to travel across the sea. Successful traders had to know whom to trust; and the more people they could safely trust, the better their chances of making profits. So they had every reason to try to maintain their ties to kin and co-religionists, and to join every network that would admit them. For them, an ethnic identity as Persian or Arab or Tamil probably mattered less than other identities of kin, religion, or guild.

As a result of the need for trustworthy trading partners, much of the trade took place within commercial colonies. Faxian, the Chinese monk, noted Yemenis living in Sri Lanka in 414. By the seventh to the eighth centuries, the Malabar Coast in India hosted Jewish and Arab trading communities. Documents from a Cairo synagogue show Jewish traders operating in family networks in India after 950. Benjamin of Tudela, a Spanish rabbi of the twelfth century, found Jewish communities everywhere he traveled on his 12-year trek to India and back, and he claimed that 23,000 Jews lived in Sri Lanka (which he did not visit). Persians took up residence on the East African coast and throughout Indonesia—although we can probably discount Ibn al-Faqih's claim that even the parrots spoke Persian in Indonesia. Chinese traders settled in Sumatra, Java, and Indian ports, but almost never further west.

These merchant communities then served as brokers, helping their countrymen with languages, customs, loans, and legal complexities. Commercial agents were typically men. They often married local women, producing bilingual or multilingual children whose cross-cultural skills greased the wheels of commerce. One Persian author noted the "Chinese children" of India's Malabar Coast, for example. Traders riding the monsoon winds needed local agents to handle their business, because they had, in effect, a dated return ticket. Without local partners, they would grow desperate to sell their goods before the winds changed—and everyone knew it. In this way, the monsoon helped shape the social context and business procedures of Indian Ocean trade.

By and large, ports welcomed long-distance traders. Ports had to earn reputations as hospitable cities if they wanted merchants to return. In Calicut, in southwestern India, the ruler made foreign traders his guests for up to 90 days while they waited for favorable winds. His guards prevented looting from any merchant vessel, even shipwrecks. Other rulers took the trouble to enforce fair dealing in the marketplace or provide free warehouse space. Cheating or robbing foreign traders, however tempting, yielded only short-term rewards. The same was true of high taxes on trade, which would propel sea captains elsewhere.

The table on the next page gives an idea of the population in 1400 of some of the seaports and riverports involved in commerce around the Indian Ocean. Cairo and Chinese ports outstripped the rest.

Ports competing with one another to welcome traffic sometimes had to restrain their overlords' rapacious instincts. In 912, for example, a Jewish trader returned home to Oman after 30 years away, bringing a rich cargo of Chinese goods. At first the caliph, in faraway Baghdad, ordered the cargo confiscated and the trader arrested. This promised a nice windfall for the caliph's treasury. But Omani merchants and the local governor protested vigorously, pointing out the costs to Oman of such heavy-handed seizure. They argued that continued trade promised more revenue in the long run. Ultimately, the caliph reversed himself. But not all rulers could be equally far-sighted: many exceptions to the rule of port city hospitality occurred where political authority was weak or rebellions were under way—as in the massacres of Muslims in South China in the late ninth century.

CITY (BY REGION)	POPULATION
NORTH AND EAST AFRICA	
Kilwa	30,000
Aksum	30,000
Cairo	360,000
SOUTHWEST ASIA	
Mecca	35,000
Basra	60,000
Hormuz	50,000
INDIA	
Cambay	60,000
Goa	40,000
Calicut	50,000
Quilon	60,000
SOUTHEAST ASIA AND CHINA	
Angkor	40,000
Guangzhou	150,000
Hangzhou	240,000

Estimated Population of Indian Ocean World Port Cities, 1400 CE

Source: Tertius Chandler, *Four Thousand Years of Urban Growth* (1987), 266, 269, 286, 313–14, 317, 321, 358–59, 369, 387–88, 406, 418, 425–26.

Port cities also catered to sailors' interest in women. Like port cities everywhere, those around the Indian Ocean hosted brothels, usually illegal. Most Muslim communities allowed the practice of short-term marriages that visiting merchants might enjoy for a few weeks or a few years. Port traders also sold slave girls to merchants embarking on sea voyages. (Ibn Battuta repeatedly took advantage of both of these traditions.) The Islamic legal custom that a man might have up to four wives at a time suited sailors nicely. Some no doubt exceeded the quota. In the collection of stories called *Sinbad the Sailor*, set in the eighth century, the hero has no trouble finding a new wife whenever he wants one on the shores of the Indian Ocean.

Surviving texts imply an unusually peaceful world of commerce in the Indian Ocean, with refreshingly little in the way of massacres of minorities, sacking of cities, and naval warfare. Rulers had to enforce law and security, and treat traders well if they wanted to

CONSIDERING THE EVIDENCE

Merchant Solidarity in the Indian Ocean World

The Abbasid caliphate in the tenth century CE included Oman on the southeast coast of Arabia. The caliphs appointed a governor there to collect taxes and customs dues from merchants. Most of Oman's merchants remained in the western part of the Indian Ocean world. However, a few of them attempted the treacherous two-year journey to China, including a Jewish merchant named Ishaq. Buzurg ibn Shahriyār recorded the story of Ishaq's return to Oman in *Kitab Ajab al-Hind (The Book of the Marvels of India)*, a collection of true and fanciful sailors' stories about the Indian Ocean that he completed around 953 CE.

Ishaq, son of the Jew...came back to Oman...from China.... In order to avoid the customs and the payment of the tithe, he came to an arrangement with the Governor of Oman...which involved a sum of more than a million *dirhems*.... Such a prodigious fortune made a noise about the country, and roused the envious. A mischievous person...went to Bag[h]dad and [told the Caliph that the Governor] had levied a toll on him of [only] five hundred thousand *dinars* worth of merchandise.... The Caliph [sent his eunuch to arrest the] Jew....

[The Governor of Oman] commanded that the Jew was to be seized, meanwhile secretly warning the merchants of it.... [T]hereupon, the markets closed. Papers of protest were signed by the people of the town and by strangers, declaring that, after the Jew had been arrested, ships would no longer put in at Oman, the merchants would leave, and that they would advise others by no means to land on the coast of [Abbasid] Iraq, where a man's property was not safe.... The merchants made an uproar in the city.... [They] brought their ships to the quay-side [the port] and put on board their goods, with the purpose of removing them, and [they exclaimed]: "We shall be deprived of all means of livelihood, when ships put in here no more; Oman is a place, whose citizens get everything from the sea. Sultans are like fires, which eat up all they touch. We can't resist them, and our best plan is to take ourselves out of their way." The eunuch and his men squeezed [just] two thousand *dinars* from the Jew, and then retired [back to Baghdad].

Questions for Analysis

1. Why did the merchants of Oman think Ishaq's arrest would threaten their livelihood?
2. What specific actions did the merchants take to protest the arrest of a fellow merchant?
3. Why did the governor of Oman, an appointee of the caliph, secretly inform the merchants of the order to arrest Ishaq?

Source: Buzurg ibn Shahriyār, trans. L. Marcel Devic and Peter Courtney Quennell, *The Book of the Marvels of India* (London, 1928).

enjoy the rewards that commerce afforded them—wealth and power they needed to fight neighboring kings and overawe subjects when necessary. In effect, peace and prosperity at sea enabled kings to invest more heavily in war and destruction on land.

Piracy and Pirates

Of course, life at sea was not always peaceful. The flourishing trade of the Indian Ocean world invited piracy. It was essentially another business practice, normally pursued by full-time specialists but sometimes by part-timers who found cabotage or fishing insufficiently rewarding. Few states had much in the way of naval power to suppress pirates. And the predictability of merchants' sailing routes, thanks to the winds and the geography of the Indian Ocean, made piracy tempting to those with ships, weapons, and fearless seafaring men at their disposal.

Merchant ships, therefore, had to be prepared to defend themselves. The Roman author Pliny noted that ships on the Red Sea in the first century CE carried archers to fend off pirates. The Chinese monk Faxian, while en route from Sri Lanka to Java in 413 CE, feared pirates in the Bay of Bengal (his ship encountered violent storms but no pirates). Eight centuries later, Marco Polo described how pirates plied their trade off southwestern India's Malabar Coast. They placed their ships in a line, reaching many miles out to sea, and used fires and smoke signals to alert their fellows when they spied a merchant vessel. Polo, like Pliny, noted that merchants had to arm their ships to fend off pirates, as did our friend Ibn Battuta.

Marco Polo also explained the cozy deals occasionally made between pirate chiefs and landlubber princes. In one case on the Malabar Coast, the local prince gave pirates free rein provided they gave him all the horses they captured. Since this deal ensured that no traders would voluntarily visit the prince's domain, it shows how precious horses were in southern India.

Pirates lurked at the choke points, where merchants had to go: the Straits of Malacca, where as we have seen local traders functioned as pirates when it suited them; the seas around southern India; and the entrances to the Persian Gulf and the Red Sea. Ibn Battuta ran afoul of pirates several times on his Indian Ocean voyages. Only storms outranked pirates among the worries of seagoing merchants. Other thriving commercial seas, such as the Mediterranean or the South China Sea, also had active pirate populations.

Piracy This image found in a fifteenth-century manuscript shows pirates attacking a merchant ship in the Indian Ocean. The pirates board the ship and kill its crew, throwing their bodies into the sea below.

Religion and Power in the Indian Ocean World

Overseas traders always brought more than merchandise with them. They and other travelers brought ideas and beliefs, some of which they communicated to people in the lands they visited. The chief exports in this category were Hinduism, Buddhism, and Islam, and the languages and culture that went with them.

The monsoon and its sailing routines helped to encourage a cosmopolitan culture around the Indian Ocean. Few voyages allowed quick turnarounds. In most cases, crews spent weeks or months waiting for the winds to change, which obliged them to interact with local people. They learned languages, made friends, sought romance, married, told stories, played chess (which originated in India around 500 CE), and talked about the weather, politics, or religion. Arab or Persian sailors going to the East African coast, for example, rode the monsoon winds south in December or January, but they had to wait until April to go home again. Many of them did it year after year.

The Spread of Indian Religions in Southeast Asia

India, the center of the Indian Ocean world demographically and geographically, was a primary exporter of culture and religions. Its cultural exports went east more than west. As we've seen, Buddhism was India's main cultural gift to China. Buddhism, together with Indian ideas of kingship, astronomy, and medicine, also took root in Central Asia and Tibet.

Neither Buddhism nor Hinduism, however, had much impact along the western shores of the Indian Ocean. Neither religion fit well with political circumstances in Southwest Asia, where rulers already had longstanding partnerships with religious authorities dating back to ancient Mesopotamia and pharaonic Egypt. At no time were either rulers or populations there eager for imported religions. In East Africa, the failure of Buddhism and Hinduism to take root was probably more a matter of timing. In the early centuries before 1000 CE, contact between India and the African coast remained sporadic. By the time that contact had grown into more sustained exchanges, sultanates had formed with Islam as the religion of rulers and traders. Religion and power were already in firm alliance.

Southeast Asia, however, proved a fertile field for Buddhism and Hinduism both. Seaborne contacts with India existed from the first century CE at the latest. Evidence of Indian cultural influences date from the fourth century. The intensity of interactions with India grew large enough, early enough, that Buddhism and Hinduism both had become entrenched before Islam reached the region—the opposite of the sequence in East Africa. The political condition of Southeast Asia in the first few centuries CE made it more receptive to novel religions. States and kingship were new concepts, and ambitious rulers needed ideologies and rituals that would help undergird their power. Therefore, Indian examples (and in Vietnam, Chinese ones) served as useful models to be borrowed and adjusted to local conditions.

The young kingdoms of Southeast Asia, forming where river valleys and irrigation allowed surplus rice production, lapped up Indian culture. Rulers enhanced their power by controlling the distribution of Indian cloth, and they bolstered their prestige by adopting Indian religions, court rituals, architecture, art, and dance styles. Indian-style monumental architecture was especially useful in this regard. Rulers relished Sanskrit texts that justified kingship, and they supported Indian scholars who copied, interpreted, and taught such texts. Sanskrit's alphabet became the basis for several Southeast Asian scripts such as those used for Thai and Cambodian.

In some respects, the spread of Indian culture to the courts of Southeast Asia was merely an overseas extension of the prior spread of the Vedic culture of northern India to southern India. The remarkable spread of Indian influence to Southeast Asia peaked from the eighth to the thirteenth centuries.

As always, those doing the adopting made a few changes to suit themselves. Southeast Asian kings such as the Khmer (based at Angkor Wat in today's Cambodia) claimed divinity for themselves, something that kings in India almost never tried. In India, Hindu Brahmins and Buddhist scholars had firm ideas about distinctions between gods and kings. The best a king could do was claim to be the most devoted follower of Buddha, Vishnu, or Shiva. In Southeast Asia, Brahmins were few and kings supported and selected the religious scholars, making it easier to blur the distinctions and promote kings to divine status.

The partial Indianization of Southeast Asian states was based on contact and emulation rather than conquest and settlement. This process stands in sharp contrast to the Hellenization of Southwest Asia that followed Alexander's phalanxes, or the spread of Chinese language and culture that came with the military expansion of the Qin, Han, and Tang dynasties. Even Vedic culture within India itself had often spread by war, conquest, and the colonization of hill and forest districts. Aside from the brief Chola expedition of 1025, no Indian state projected its power into Southeast Asia. No large-scale settlement took place, although a few traders and scholars did take up residence in Southeast Asian towns and courts. Instead, Southeast Asians, their rulers above all, wanted culture fit for newly centralized and hierarchical societies—and, except in Vietnam, Indian models were the ones at hand. Scholars, missionaries, and traders, as much as soldiers and kings, could extend and tighten the world's webs—especially when riding reliable monsoon winds.

Trade and Islam on the Swahili Coast

Another momentous cultural shift promoted by Indian Ocean trade and travel webs was the Islamization of coastal East Africa. In the centuries before 1400, a distinctive cosmopolitan culture developed along the East African coast, tightly linked to the

Indian Ocean trade, if also connected to the East African interior. *Swahili* in Arabic means "people of the shore," so scholars use the term *Swahili coast*, at least for periods after 1000 CE.

Traders from the Red Sea shores had sailed the waters of the Swahili coast since at least the first century CE. The *Periplus* noted that sailors were familiar with this region, learned its languages, and married local women. Mariners had learned how far south they could go without being marooned for months waiting for the monsoon to change. The southern limit for a quick round-trip voyage was Zanzibar, or at most Kilwa. More northerly ports such as Mombasa, Malindi, or Lamu were more convenient for sailors, but their sparse hinterlands made them less attractive to merchants. By and large, the long-distance voyages from East Africa to Arabia, the Persian Gulf, and India were undertaken by traders from those latter lands, while the port-to-port cabotage on the Swahili coast was handled by East Africans. The scale of trade before the seventh century remained modest, but archeologists have found pre-Islamic ceramics from Arabia and Iran as far south as northern Mozambique.

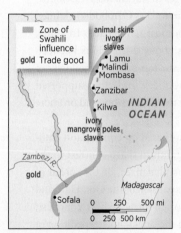

The Swahili Coast, ca. 1000–1400
Between 1000 and 1400 the trading cities of the Swahili coast became more enmeshed in the Indian Ocean's commercial circuits. Swahili merchants funneled ivory, mangrove poles, slaves, animal skins and other trade items to markets in India and Southwest Asia, often dealing with Arab and Persian merchants. Among the results of these commercial connections was the consolidation of Islam as the majority religion on the Swahili coast.

The scale of commerce along the Swahili coast expanded in the ninth century, especially in slaves and ivory. The Abbasid caliphate's intensive agricultural development of southern Iraq relied on slave labor, leading to the slave trade described above. By the tenth century, rising prosperity in Fatimid Egypt, southern India, Song China, and elsewhere spurred demand for African ivory statuettes and jewelry. African elephant tusks are both bigger and easier to carve than those of Asian elephants, and so commanded higher prices. In India, brides from respectable families needed ivory bangles for their wedding ceremonies, ensuring a steady export market for East African ivory.

By the eleventh century, gold came to rival ivory as a magnet for foreign traders. Gold, gathered from streambeds, came only from the hilly country south of the Zambezi River. Local traders brought it to the coast at Sofala, in today's Mozambique. That was too far south for Arab and Persian Gulf sailors. So Kilwa and Zanzibar grew up as seaports connecting the long-distance trade with a cabotage trade between Sofala and Kilwa. The volume and value of the Swahili trade continued to grow during the twelfth through the fifteenth centuries, fed by the flow of African gold.

Arab and Persian men settled in the trading towns from Somalia south to Kilwa. They married local women and learned local Bantu languages, and local Africans learned theirs. The interplay of African languages and Arabic, and to a lesser extent Persian, over centuries produced a new tongue, Swahili, originally mainly a trading language. It gradually became the native tongue for almost all who lived along the coast, and (since about 1800) the second language of many inland Africans as well. Swahili, a living artifact of the Indian Ocean's web, was written in the Arabic alphabet until the twentieth century.

Islam on the Swahili Coast Built from coral, the Kilwa mosque was completed by the end of the thirteenth century. It represents the mounting influence of Arab and Persian merchants and the growing popularity of Islam among the Africans on the Swahili coast.

Arab and Persian traders who settled along the Swahili coast also encouraged the practice of Islam. Many Swahili rulers wanted to burnish their Islamic credentials to help legitimate their rule—just as Southeast Asian monarchs found Hinduism or Buddhism politically useful. Swahili rulers always claimed descent from Arabia and Persia, sometimes from the Prophet himself. They supported religious scholars and architects who brought skills still rare along the Swahili coast. The earliest mosques in East Africa date from the eighth century, but big ones were built only after 1200. The main mosque at Kilwa, built of coral, dates to 1300 or so.

Conversion to Islam on the Swahili coast peaked between 1050 and 1250. When the Arab traveler and geographer al-Masudi visited in the early tenth century, he thought the local Africans "have no religious law . . . every man worships what he pleases, be it a plant, an animal, or a mineral." By the time Ibn Battuta turned up in the 1330s, all the rulers and elites along the Swahili coast were Muslims. Their Islam incorporated prior religious practices of the coast, such as veneration of local ancestors and use of the local agricultural calendar, which survived side-by-side with the Muslim one. The process of religious conversion here, as in most cases, was a melding of old and new.

Along the Swahili coast, as elsewhere throughout the Indian Ocean, trade promoted Islam and Islam promoted trade. At the heart of the equation were trust and law. Where commerce involved different languages and cultures, the umbrella of Islamic law permitted a degree of trust that fostered long-distance trade.

Of course, Africans on the Swahili coast accepted Islam for many reasons, not merely for commercial advantage. Rulers—usually big traders themselves—had other calculated reasons to become Muslim. But they, like many others, sometimes found the doctrines of Islam more satisfying than the religious practices of their ancestors. Religious conversion here, as everywhere, proceeded from a handful of motives and inspirations.

As in India, the filtration of Islam into East African society had geographical limits. No evidence exists for mosques or Islam except along the coast until well after 1400. The

African traders who supplied ivory, slaves, mangrove poles, and iron to Swahili cities were local operators, active in cabotage and in the immediate hinterlands of the cities. The ocean-going merchants from the Red Sea, Persian Gulf, or Gujarat—the vehicles of Islamization—left the hinterland alone. The residents of the coastal cities treated the interior as a source of goods and slaves, but otherwise unworthy of their attention.

The spread of Islam and Swahili culture also reached Madagascar—but just barely. The Malagasy language contains many Bantu and a few Arabic words grafted onto its Austronesian base. Archeology reveals beads and pottery from Arab lands. These items were probably brought mainly by Swahili merchants. Madagascar was too far south for Arab and Persian Gulf traders unless they wanted to invest two years in their voyage. The few texts that say anything at all about the linkages between Madagascar and the Swahili coast refer to Malagasy slave raiding on the mainland and enclaves of Swahili traders in northernmost Madagascar. Madagascar, like Borneo in Southeast Asia, was at the southernmost fringe of the Indian Ocean web.

The extension of Islam into East Africa, like that of Hinduism into Southeast Asia, narrowed the scope somewhat for local religions. Like the contemporaneous spread of Christianity into Europe or Buddhism into Central Asia, these amount to expansions of the world's great religions at the expense of smaller, more local ones. The networks of trade and power around the Indian Ocean promoted a form of cultural homogenization, reducing slightly the region's—and the world's—cultural diversity.

Great Zimbabwe and Southeastern Africa

After 800, another thread of the Indian Ocean web reached into the interior of Africa, to the goldfields of the Zimbabwe plateau. Iron tools and farming had spread to southern Africa by 400 CE, but population remained sparse and social hierarchy simple. By the period 500–600, more and more people were taking up cattle raising, well suited to the region's semi-arid grasslands. With cattle as a form of storable food, like cereals elsewhere, the first signs of social hierarchies beyond those of age and gender appeared. In southern Africa, where farming brought inconsistent rewards due to unreliable rains, cattle assumed great importance in economic and political life. People with cattle could exert power over people without by providing or withholding meat in times of need. Cattle keeping led not only to greater status hierarchy, but also to the first efforts at state building. These efforts brought modest results: aspiring rulers could control only a few hundred people because there was too much empty space into which unhappy subjects might wander off.

The slow build-up of population over the centuries made it harder to wander off to empty land and easier for ambitious men to extend their authority over larger numbers. (Remember that in most of Africa, political power consisted of control over people more than over territory.) Continued growth in the cattle population meant more opportunity to amass power and wealth, more reason to struggle over access to good pastureland, more conflict, and a more male-dominated social order. Ingenious historical linguists have inferred the emergence after about 800 CE of an expanded vocabulary for things having to do with cattle, such as 6 new terms for various shapes of cattle horns, and at least 17 new words for colors of cattle hide. Clearly, people were taking a deep interest in cattle.

Meanwhile, traders had extended the Indian Ocean web to the coasts of Mozambique and, weakly, up the river valleys of the Limpopo and Zambezi. The first signs of these trade links appeared about the period 700–800. Gold production began about this time too. In 916, al-Masudi, wrote—rather imaginatively—of "meadows of gold" in the Zambezi basin. The Zimbabwe plateau also developed iron mines and, like most parts of Africa, an ivory trade. Slowly but surely the economy and population grew, and with growth came better opportunities to amass political power.

The first sizeable state in southern Africa, called Mapungubwe, arose about 1175. Its rulers derived their authority from cattle keeping. But it also produced gold for export and imported beads made in India and Egypt. Mapungubwe did not last long, but the links to the wider world did.

A new power center arose about 1250 in a reasonably well-watered area good for cattle and better for controlling gold exports. **Great Zimbabwe** (*Zimbabwe* means "stone houses" in the Shona language) was based on cattle wealth, but with an international twist. Leaders who owned large herds let poor people eat if they gathered gold dust. Great Zimbabwe's ruling lineages traded that gold down to the coast for prestige items, including beads, cowries, and ceramics from as far away as China. They must have exercised unusual authority because starting about 1275 they erected stone buildings larger than anything else in sub-Saharan Africa for many centuries to come. The two biggest of these granite structures stand about 33 feet (10 m) tall, and their walls are up to 16 feet (5 m) thick. Someone put over a million flat stones into position to build them. About 300 smaller stone buildings are scattered around the nearby plateau.

At its peak from 1300 to 1350, as many as 18,000 people lived in one cluster at Great Zimbabwe. (Kilwa at the time had perhaps 30,000 inhabitants, and the world's biggest cities roughly 400,000 or 500,000.) The gold trade reached as much as 1 ton (907 kg) per year, partly in gold dust collected from streambeds but, as the pickings grew sparser, increasingly from mines. Some mineshafts went down 100 feet (30 m), which testifies to considerable technical skill as well as determination. Skeletons indicate that women and children did much of the dangerous underground work.

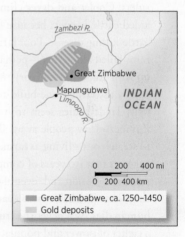

Early States of Southern Africa, ca. 1175–1450 Cattle keeping and gold production distinguished the first states to arise in southern Africa. Great Zimbabwe in particular took part in the commercial exchanges of the Indian Ocean world, supplying a goodly portion of the gold in circulation there. These polities formed the southernmost frontier of the Indian Ocean world.

Great Zimbabwe Massive stone walls—up to 16 feet (5 m) thick—remain on a hillside at Great Zimbabwe, probably built during the city's heyday between 1275 and 1350. Artifacts found at the Great Zimbabwe site include this wooden sculpture of a human form from the same period.

These were happy times for the ruling lineages. Soapstone statues of birds suggest they exercised some form of spiritual power. Judging by the chemistry of bones left behind, the elite at Great Zimbabwe feasted on prime beef. Everyone else was lucky to get mutton or stringy beef.

Climate change deepened the plight of the poor and confirmed the power of the rulers. Cooler and dryer climate after 1290 or so made agriculture less rewarding. It aided cattle keepers because it reduced the domain of the tsetse fly, which carried a cattle-killing disease. Poor farmers grew more dependent on the cattle kings. When the rains failed altogether—perhaps one out of every four or five years—they had to come up with gold, iron, or ivory to swap for a cow if they were to eat.

By 1450, the stone buildings at Great Zimbabwe were abandoned. No one knows why. Trade routes seem to have shifted to the north. New gold strikes closer to the Zambezi drew people away. Better rains might have made it possible for poor people to scratch out a living as farmers at a safe remove from the cattle kings. Some evidence suggests that 150 years of comparatively dense population and intensive land use led to rapid soil erosion and, eventually, poor pasturage for cattle. Shona oral tradition has it that Great Zimbabwe was abandoned when people there ran out of salt, essential to the human diet. Whatever the truth of the matter, although Great Zimbabwe vanished as a center of power and population, the principle of complex, hierarchical society dominated by men who hoarded cattle lived on. And so did the gold trade. In 1497, when the first European to visit the shores of Mozambique sailed to the mouth of the Zambezi, he found Arab dhows loading up on gold dust.

Conclusion

Everywhere around the Indian Ocean from 200 to 1400 CE, the broad trend was much the same. Ports grew bigger, richer, more numerous, more active, more commercially sophisticated, and more culturally cosmopolitan. They served as the crossroads of cultural exchange, where people rubbed shoulders and swapped goods, ideas, and infections with strangers from other lands. At times, patches of this Indian Ocean web might fray for a century or two, overall volumes of trade and exchange might decline, but urban life and long-distance linkages never vanished.

India stood at the center of this watery web. Its religious and political landscapes evolved partly in response to challenges and opportunities emanating from around the Indian Ocean, but from Central Asia and its horsemen too.

New centers of political power emerged where none had existed before, especially in Southeast Asia and southern Africa. Rice and cattle, respectively, helped make this happen, serving as the storable surplus that enabled the haves to control the have-nots more efficiently than before. So did trade. Whatever their attitudes toward money-driven merchants, rulers everywhere could see that the extension of markets and long-distance trade offered them a chance to fill their treasuries, display exotic prestige goods, and build their power.

Long-distance seaborne trade transformed the Indian Ocean world culturally as well as economically. Buddhism and Hinduism colonized Southeast Asian kingdoms, and Islam spread to the Swahili coast and parts of India. Local religions continued to give way to the world's dominant religions, although Hinduism, Buddhism, and Islam (like Christianity) continued to fragment and evolve as they had done since their beginnings. This process of religious change reduced the world's cultural diversity somewhat and made it a bit easier for traders and travelers to interact peaceably with one another.

These religious changes were part and parcel of the formation of cosmopolitan cultures around the Indian Ocean shore, especially in the bigger port cities. People in Mombasa and Cambay, 3,000 miles apart, had more in common by 1400 than did Mombasans and the people living three days' walk into the interior of Africa. Now connected to island Southeast Asia and to East Africa, the Old World web had become bigger and tighter than ever before.

||||||||||||||||||||||||||||||||||||||||||||||||||||||||||||||||||||||||||||||||||||||||||||||||||||||||||||||||||||||||||||||||||||||

Chapter Review

KEY TERMS

dhow p. 471

cabotage p. 471

choke point p. 471

Bhakti movement p. 475

Islamization p. 476

Nalanda p. 478

Gupta dynasty p. 479

Chola kingdom p. 480

merchant trading guilds p. 481   **Zanj revolt** p. 493
slave soldiers p. 483   **Swahili coast** p. 500
Delhi sultanate p. 484   **Great Zimbabwe** p. 503
spices p. 490

REVIEW QUESTIONS

1. What constituted the Indian Ocean world, and what was the key reason it became a coherent region around 100 CE?

2. How did sailing in the Indian Ocean differ from sailing in the Atlantic and the Pacific?

3. In what ways did the rise of the Bhakti movement affect Indian religion?

4. What were the economic bases of the Gupta dynasty, the Chola kingdom, and the Delhi sultanate?

5. What was the largest impact of Delhi sultanate rule?

6. Compare and contrast the volume, value, frequency, and wares of long-distance trade versus cabotage.

7. What were the major contributing factors to the three peaks of sustained, long-distance trade in the Indian Ocean world between 600 and 1350?

8. Why were networks of kinfolk and hospitable port cities important for Indian Ocean traders?

9. What were the main reasons that some areas in Southeast Asia adopted Indian religions and the Swahili coast adopted Islam?

10. Why and how did cattle assume importance in economic and political life in southern Africa at this time?

11. How did Great Zimbabwe's gold trade function?

12. What were the broad trends around the Indian Ocean world from 200 to 1400?

Go to IN**Q**UIZITIVE

to see what you've learned—and learn what you've missed—with personalized feedback along the way.

The West End of Eurasia and West Africa

800 to 1400

FOCUS QUESTIONS

1. In what major ways did material conditions improve in western Eurasia roughly from 800 to 1300?

2. Why were the great empires that dominated the region for a time so fragile?

3. Why were the settled societies of western Eurasia subject to invasion during this period?

4. For what reasons did this period of turmoil also experience economic and cultural growth?

5. Why was the fourteenth century such a calamity in western Eurasia?

A round 960, Hasdai ibn Shaprut, a Jewish physician, foreign minister, and adviser to a Muslim emir of Córdoba, in southern Spain, wrote a letter. Curious about a Jewish kingdom he had heard about in what is now southern Russia, he wrote to the king in question. Several merchants conveyed the letter to a *kagan*, or king, named Joseph, who wrote back explaining that indeed there was a Jewish kingdom—**Khazaria**, as it is now known.

CHRONOLOGY

ca. 300 Berber-speaking people in and around the Sahara acquire camels

by ca. 700 Berbers regularly cross the Sahara

ca. 700–900 Khazaria flourishes

ca. 700–1050 Ancient Ghana flourishes

ca. 750–843 Rise and division of Carolingian rule

750–1258 Rise and fragmentation of Abbasid caliphate

ca. 800–1050 Height of Viking pillaging, conquering, and expansion

ca. 800–1100 Agricultural revolution in northern Europe

890–900 Magyars cross into grasslands of modern-day Hungary

ca. 900–1170 Fatimids, Almoravids, and Almohads conquer land in North Africa, Spain, and Egypt

929–1031 Rise and fall of the Córdoba caliphate

ca. 980–1090 Formation and dissolution of Seljuk Turk Empire

1096–1231 Waves of Crusades

ca. 1200–1500 Height of the spread of Sufism

1204–1261 Crusaders rule Constantinople

1219–1260 Mongol western campaigns

ca. 1240–1450 Mali kingdom emerges and falls

ca. 1250 Start of Little Ice Age

Khazaria arose in the 640s in the grasslands between the Volga and the Dniepr Rivers. It reached its height in the eighth and ninth centuries and lasted until about 970. Mainly Turkic-speaking, the Khazars were farmers, herders, smiths, and traders. Their merchants made connections along the Silk Roads to China and Byzantium, and along water routes such as the Caspian Sea and Russian rivers north to the Baltic Sea and south to Mesopotamia. Archeological digs in the region have turned up belt buckles with Chinese dragons and amber beads from Sweden. The Khazars had a formidable cavalry and fought wars with Byzantine emperors and Arab caliphs. Many Khazars were Muslims, some Christians, some sky-worshipping shamans—and a growing number of them were Jews, often refugees from persecution in Byzantine towns. By most accounts, the leadership of the Khazars embraced Judaism in the ninth century; thus Joseph described his multireligious kingdom as Jewish when writing to Hasdai ibn Shaprut in Spain.

In the same centuries, Spain too contained a swirling multicultural mix of Muslims, Christians, and Jews. At times they were ruled by one Muslim polity, the emirate (after 929, the caliphate) of Córdoba, but at others they were divided into several emirates and kingdoms, none of them led by Jews. Those ruled by Muslims made up the region known as **al-Andalus**. Thus by 750 the western region of the Old World web contained societies, such as al-Andalus and Khazaria, in which Muslims, Christians, and Jews lived and worked together.

Like Chapter 11, this chapter treats the western region of the Old World web, from Iran and Russia all the way to the Atlantic shores of Europe and West Africa. Many places were Christian at some times and Muslim at others, such as Anatolia, Sicily, and Spain. Most Islamic lands were home to many Christians and Jews, and some

Christian-ruled lands had Muslim minorities. So any distinction between Muslim and Christian lands is fuzzy.

It is conventional to divide Christendom and Islamdom on the grounds that their dominant religions make them distinct. However, there are better reasons to see them together within the western region of the Old World web, especially during this period. Each experienced an agricultural revolution that improved the food supply and helped spur population growth. Both enjoyed a cultural flowering, which in fact depended on contacts between Muslims and Christians. Both were terrorized by invaders. And both simultaneously suffered the worst epidemic in human history.

1260–1350 Pax Mongolica

1314–1322 Very wet growing seasons and harvest failures in northwestern Europe; widespread livestock disease in Eurasia

1342 Major rain and flooding in central Europe

1346–1351 Plague pandemic

1453 Byzantine Empire falls

1492 al-Andalus falls

Five main themes run through this chapter. First is the heightened instability of population and ecology, as the west end of the Old World web underwent demographic growth until the fourteenth century and then catastrophe. Second is the political fragmentation that overcame giant empires such as those of Charlemagne and the Abbasids. Third is the mobilization of conquerors and migrants who helped undermine the giant empires, people such as the Vikings, Turks, and Mongols. Fourth is the economic quickening and cultural flowering of the ninth to early thirteenth centuries. And fifth, tying them all together, is the further expansion of the Old World web into northern Europe and West Africa.

The chapter covers a period that historians, drawing on European tradition, conventionally call medieval. Because specialists apply the term differently in various regions of Eurasia (and occasionally for Africa), I will use the term sparingly to mean roughly the period 500–1400.

Population, Ecology, and Agriculture

From 800 to the early fourteenth century, on average, the human condition improved in the western region of the Old World web. There were exceptions, of course, in some places and at certain times. But until 1315 the trend was broadly favorable.

Population Growth

One strong indication of improving conditions was that more people survived longer and reproduced. In the region as a whole, population almost doubled between 800 and 1300, from about 60 million to roughly 120 million. By far the fastest growth took place in regions of western, central, and northeastern Europe, places that had hitherto been

Estimated Population (in millions) in Selected Lands of North Africa and Western Eurasia								
YEARS	IRAN	ANATOLIA	EGYPT	ITALY	IBERIA	BRITAIN AND IRELAND	RUSSIA	TOTAL*
800	4	6	4	4	4	1	3.5	60
1000	4.5	7	5	6	4.5	3	4	85
1300	3.5	7	4.5	12	9	7	9	120

Source: Colin McEvedy and Richard Jones, *Atlas of World Population History* (1978), 41–49, 78–82, 99–109, 133–35, 152–54, 226–29; Paolo Malanima, "Energy and Population in Europe" (2010) at: www.paolomalanima.it/default_file/Papers/MEDIEVAL_GROWTH.pdf

*Western Eurasia and North Africa

thinly populated. The table above shows the regional variation in estimated population size in selected places. The main reason that population climbed between 800 and 1300 was improvements in agriculture.

Agricultural Revolutions

Until recently, farmers usually did the same things year in, year out. But the late medieval centuries included some exceptions, times and places where many farmers experimented with new crops and technologies. After 800, the Old World web spawned three agricultural revolutions: one in China, a second in the Mediterranean and Mesopotamia, and a third one in northern Europe. In Chapter 12, we saw how Chinese farmers doubled their yields by planting champa rice from the eleventh century onward. In both the second and third cases, as this chapter will show, farmers figured out how to grow more crops on old fields and bring new lands under the plow.

Mediterranean and Mesopotamia In the Mediterranean and Mesopotamia, important new crops from South and Southeast Asia came via Indian Ocean networks. Some were food crops, such as spinach, eggplant, watermelon, coconut, bananas, oranges, and perhaps most important, sugarcane. Others, such as cotton, provided a new fiber for clothing. All were established by 1000. The food crops brought a small improvement in nutrition, but nothing dramatic. Sugar and cotton, however, stimulated industry. Because both crops require processing, they inspired businesses dedicated to sugar refining and cotton spinning. The main markets for sugar and cotton cloth were urban populations, often located far from the fields. So the sugar and cotton businesses stimulated long-distance trade and the cultural exchange that always goes with it. The most important consequence of the agricultural revolution in Mesopotamia and the Mediterranean was more commerce and exchange. Population growth and better nutrition, while real, were secondary.

The agricultural revolution in these lands was closely linked to irrigation and to slavery. Most of the new crops required irrigation to yield well. From southern Spain to Iran, old irrigation systems were revived and new ones built. The best technologies, such as *qanats* and waterwheels, spread throughout. With efficient irrigation, farmers could harvest four crops of eggplant or spinach annually.

Building and maintaining irrigation systems was hard and hazardous. It often involved draining swamps and converting them into date palm or sugar plantations. Everywhere it increased the risk of malaria, carried by mosquitos that thrive around stagnant water. As so often occurred in world history, dangerous work fell to slaves. Scholars estimate that between 700 and 1500, perhaps 5 to 10 million slaves—mainly from Africa, Central Asia, and Russia—were sold to markets in North Africa and Southwest Asia, chiefly Iraq and Egypt. Perhaps a quarter of them worked in agriculture.

Northern Europe The other agricultural revolution of this period occurred in northern Europe, from Britain to today's Poland. Before 800, farming in northern Europe took place in patches amid forests and swamps. Yields were low and surplus small, which is why no sizable cities existed after the Roman trade networks disintegrated. But between 800 and 1100, crucial changes took place that more than doubled farm output.

New technologies were part of the turnaround. Although oxen still pulled most plows, the horse collar, perhaps acquired from China, allowed horses to pull with all their might without choking themselves. That made plowing more efficient. So did the widespread adoption of the moldboard plow with a curved iron plowshare, which turned a deep furrow and permitted fruitful use of heavy, clayey, wet soils. A new crop rotation was just as important. European farmers replaced a two-field rotation, in which half their farmland stood fallow in any given year, with a three-field rotation often involving rye or barley as a winter crop and oats in summer. Under this system, only one-third of farmland stood fallow. Rye did well in the chilly north, especially along the Baltic shores.

Livestock also contributed to northern Europe's farming revolution. Since the arrival of Neolithic farming over 6,000 years before, European farmers had raised cattle and other farm animals. With the turn to oats, and with the new horse collar, they had good reason to raise more horses than before. They were creating a system of mixed farming in which livestock grazed in pastures and, after harvest time, on the stubble in grain fields. Animal manure helped to offset the depletion of soil nutrients.

Agricultural Innovation This twelfth-century Italian manuscript shows farmers using a moldboard plow drawn by oxen. The curved blades lift and turn aside the soil, creating a central furrow that enables farmers to plant seeds more efficiently and successfully.

In addition to making farming more productive, northern Europeans extended farming over a broader area. Between 1100 and 1300, they increased the cultivated area by one-third. An order of Catholic monks, the Cistercians, specialized in opening up new farmlands. Along the shores of the Baltic, German-speakers pushed east, cutting forests, draining swamps, and planting fields. In what is now the Netherlands, long years of toil created new land by building sea walls and draining the soggy earth behind them. Europe's rising population both required new farmland and made it possible to do the work necessary to create it.

The surge in grain production created incentive to adopt watermills and windmills (an invention acquired from Iran) to grind grain into flour. Formerly this was women's work, done by hand. In England in 1086 (when an inventory called the Domesday Book was made), there were more than 5,000 mills. This technological shift freed women from some drudgery and made flour cheaper. It also opened the door to using water power in other ways, such as in sawmills.

Comparing the Agricultural Revolutions A comparison of the agricultural revolutions in northern Europe and in the Mediterranean and Mesopotamia points to three contrasts, one in causes and two in consequences. One of the contributing causes to the greater success of farming in northern Europe after 900 was better weather. Warmer and wetter climate bathed northern Europe from around 900 until about 1300. It became possible to grow rye in northern Norway and to raise grapes in England. Farmers could use higher elevations by as much as 200 feet (60 m). In the Mediterranean and Mesopotamia, however, while climate warmed it also became dryer, making agriculture more difficult and irrigation more necessary.

Whereas the agricultural revolution in the Arab and Persian lands led to more commerce and industry, it didn't generate much population growth. While the data are poor, it seems that population grew until 1150 or 1200 and then fell. In northern Europe, where the data are better, the new farming methods did boost population, as well as industry and commerce. The European agricultural revolution did not entail slave labor on any significant scale. It relied more on animal power and both wage laborers and serfs, peasants legally bound to a specific land or landowner.

A comparison also shows some characteristics that the two agricultural revolutions shared. Both extended the area of cultivation, and both involved supreme efforts to control water. In Europe, this usually involved drainage—getting excess water out of the fields. In Mesopotamia, Egypt, and the Mediterranean, it meant drainage but also irrigation—getting sufficient water onto the fields. When and where people could control water and land, whether in the wetlands of Mesoamerica or in the rice paddies of East Asia, they could grow much more food. In 1400, there were only a few landscapes around the world in which people had the expertise and labor power to regulate land and water so as to maximize farm output.

Fleeting Empires

In 800, the west end of the Old World web contained great monarchies: the Abbasid caliphate based in Baghdad, the Byzantine Empire with its capital at Constantinople, and—much less imposing in terms of power and wealth—Charlemagne's kingdom, sometimes known as the Carolingian Empire in Europe, and the state of Ghana in West Africa. By 1400, little of them remained.

The Abbasid Caliphate

As we saw in Chapter 11, the Abbasids overthrew the Umayyad caliphate in 750 and set up their own based in Baghdad. They hunted down and killed every member of the Umayyad clan except one, who slipped away to Spain. For roughly a century after 750, most of the Islamic world except southern Spain was under loose Abbasid control. The first few Abbasid caliphs fared well, using wealth from reinvigorated irrigation agriculture in Mesopotamia and Egypt. After a clash with Tang armies in Central Asia in 751, they forged good relations with China, enhancing revenues from Silk Road trade. As we will see, they also oversaw a magnificent flowering of arts and sciences.

Later caliphs could not hold the sprawling state together, although it nominally lasted to 1258. The Abbasids originally counted both Arabs and Iranians among their supporters, and both Sunni and Shi'a Muslims. Soon after taking power, however, they endorsed orthodox Sunni theology, alienating Shi'a supporters. The Abbasids also consciously modeled their state upon the pre-Islamic Sassanids of Iran, choosing showy grandeur over pious simplicity. This too irritated some followers. Like the Sassanids, they relied on a chief minister, called a vizier, to run the day-to-day business of government. He, in turn, relied on provincial governors whose loyalty to the Abbasid clan proved flexible.

Soon provincial governors were setting up their own smaller states, pretending loyalty to the Abbasids when they had to, ignoring them when possible. Morocco broke away first, under a clan called the Idrisids in 793. Others followed in rapid succession during the ninth century, in Afghanistan, eastern Iran, Egypt, and Sicily. Soon the Abbasids controlled little but the neighborhood of Baghdad.

And they scarcely controlled that after the 840s. More and more they relied on slave soldiers from Central Asia, most of them Turkic-speakers, for their military and palace guard. Outsourcing defense in this way put them at the mercy of their slaves. Beginning in 842, military slaves killed or blinded several caliphs. The power behind the Abbasid throne now consisted of rough horsemen from Central Asia—whose broader role in the history of Eurasia we will consider again below.

The Abbasid caliphate illustrates a recurrent pattern in Islamic history. Its political elite was raised in a multicultural, multilingual, and multireligious environment, by no means strictly Arab and Muslim. Elite males could afford not only up to four wives (the legal maximum) but many concubines as well. Concubines were often Greek, Ethiopian, or Armenian in language, and Christian or sometimes Jewish in religion. They bore and raised many of the children of the Abbasid political elite, including most of the caliphs. A similar pattern held for other Islamic dynasties discussed in this chapter, such as the Fatimids. Among the common people, however, no men could afford multiple wives and concubines, so the likelihood of multicultural upbringing was minimal. This pattern opened the possibility of cultural chasms between elites and commoners, and it invited religious reformers to denounce caliphs and emirs as bad Muslims unfit to rule.

After Abbasid authority fell apart in the early ninth century, the Islamic world remained politically fragmented—as it remains today. Roughly 200 regional dynasties rose and fell over the next millennium, most of them aspiring, all unsuccessfully, to restore Islamic unity of the sort presided over by the first Abbasids.

The Byzantine Empire and al-Andalus

The Byzantines, as explained in Chapter 11, had lost the Levant and their richest province, Egypt, by the 640s. They held on to Anatolia, most Aegean islands, and Greece, but little else. Steppe peoples threatened from the north. Their eastern neighbors, the Umayyads, almost annihilated them in 717–718. The Byzantine state barely survived. In the ninth through the tenth centuries, the Byzantines won back some lost territories during the reign of the all-too-aptly named Basil the Bulgar-Slayer, who oversaw successful military campaigns against the Khazars, neighboring Muslim dynasties, and the small Bulgarian Empire in southeastern Europe.

But over the next 400 years, Byzantine fortunes turned for the worse. Attacks by Russians, Turks, and Latin Crusader knights (of whom more below) took their toll. The Byzantine Empire shrank until all that remained was the capital, a few walled ports, and a scattering of islands. In 1453, a new group of Turks, the Ottomans, besieged and took Constantinople; with that final blow, the imperial tradition tracing back to Justinian, Constantine, and Augustus came to an end.

A similar fate befell a younger empire based in Córdoba and later Granada in Spain. Founded by the last of the Umayyads, it flourished in the tenth century, controlling almost all of Spain, the northern tip of Morocco, and some offshore islands. It became known as the Córdoba caliphate because in 929 one of its leaders, much to Abbasid dismay, claimed to be the rightful caliph. Like the Byzantine emperors and the Abbasids, the caliphs of Córdoba presided over a sophisticated cultural and intellectual scene, funded by a lucrative combination of irrigation agriculture and long-distance trade. Córdoba's mosque, which featured Roman, Byzantine, and especially Syrian motifs, could hold 40,000 worshippers. But as a united empire the Córdoba caliphate lasted only a century, splintering by 1031 into a handful of lesser kingdoms, never long at peace with one another.

Fragmented authority enabled the Christians of northwestern Spain to begin

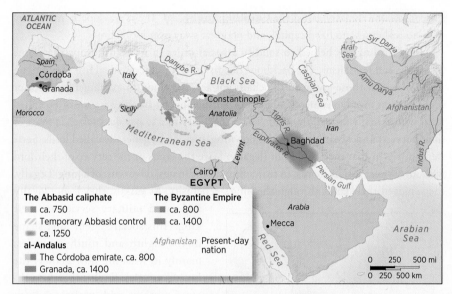

The Decline of Western Empires, ca. 750–1400 The broad political trend in the west end of the Old World web in the centuries between 750 and 1400 was one of fragmentation. Big, populous states such as the Abbasid caliphate, the Byzantine Empire, and the emirate of Córdoba (a caliphate after 929) dominated politics for centuries. But provinces broke away while bands of mounted raiders assaulted the frontiers. These three empires shrank and then vanished altogether, replaced by new and smaller monarchies.

what Spaniards call the Reconquista, the slow restoration of Christian rule. The Reconquista featured shifting coalitions of Christians and Muslims, often mercenaries, fighting under petty kings who were allies one year and enemies the next. By 1250, Muslim rule ebbed quickly, ultimately confined to the southeast of Spain and based in the city of Granada. The end for al-Andalus came in 1492, when Granada succumbed to Christian armies—just four decades after Byzantine Constantinople fell to Muslim ones.

Charlemagne's Empire

The Abbasids, Byzantium, and al-Andalus were based on centuries of urban refinement, court culture, and underneath it all, rich farmlands and bustling trade. In contrast, Charlemagne's empire was a crude upstart. But it met a similar fate: external pressures brought internal fragmentation.

After the dissolution of the Roman Empire in western Europe in the fifth century, a handful of small kingdoms slowly emerged. One of them, known as the kingdom of the Franks—one of the Germanic tribes that contributed to Rome's end—came under the control of a dynasty called the **Carolingians** by 750. Theirs was a petty monarchy with no real cities, no fixed capital, and no great sway over local elites.

The Carolingians helped to solidify a social order in western Europe that some historians call feudalism. The backbone of this order was hierarchical linkages among males in which those lower on the chain got access to land in exchange for labor or other services owed to someone higher up. At the bottom stood peasants, often called serfs, who actually farmed the land. To do that, they had to pay dues (often, a share of their harvest) and swear loyalty to landowning aristocrats, generally called lords. Serfs were unfree in that they could not (legally) leave the lands or the service of their lord without his permission. Lords, in turn, were subordinates, or vassals, of a king. Legally, they enjoyed their lands through the king's generosity. As vassals, they swore loyalty and owed military service to their king. This social system took shape in the eighth and ninth centuries, mainly in what are now France, the Low Countries, England, and northern Germany, with variations from place to place. It was codified into law and embraced by the church. Kings, including the Carolingians, always had to keep an eye on ambitious lords who might wish to become kings.

Compared to the caliphates or Byzantium, the Carolingian state was poor and simple in structure—and yet it was the most powerful polity in western Europe. In 768, a young man came to the throne who would become known as Charles the Great, or Charlemagne. Born in the mid-740s, he was clever, devious, aggressive, and imposingly tall. He rode, hunted, drank, and womanized as elite males were expected to do. But at the same time, he took pains to try to learn Latin and was a devout Christian.

In the early decades of his long reign (r. 768–814), Charlemagne built his kingdom into an empire,

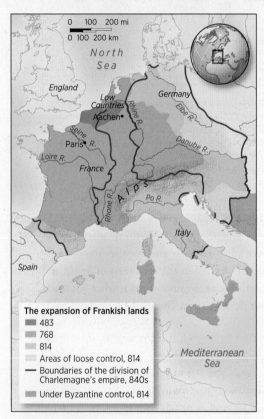

The Frankish Kingdoms, 483–843 The Carolingian dynasty built the most powerful state in western Europe by 800. It proved fleeting, however, confirming the long-term pattern in Europe of political fragmentation. Charlemagne's grandsons divided the empire as shown in the 840s.

conquering much of central Europe and Italy. He forced Christianity on pagans with calculated brutality and became the political protector of the Pope. His steadfast efforts on behalf of the church were rewarded on Christmas Day in the year 800, when the Pope crowned him emperor of a renewed Roman Empire—to the irritation of Byzantine emperors, who considered themselves the sole heirs of the Roman tradition.

Building an empire was, as usual, easier than holding it together. Charlemagne's expanded state remained a rural kingdom, consisting of hundreds of farming villages overseen by local lords who handled the administration of justice, tax collection, and other state functions. It had little in the way of urban life, long-distance trade, or sophisticated manufacturing. Its tax revenue consisted of what loyal lords could provide. Charlemagne built a capital, Aachen in today's Germany, but preferred to stay on the move, keeping up his ties to his lords and campaigning on his frontiers. He had the skill and prestige to maintain such a flimsy state, but his grandsons divvied it up in the 840s, and by the 870s lords everywhere went their own ways. The first European union lasted only two generations.

Empires of the Sahel: Ghana and Mali

Far to the south of the Carolingian lands, a more durable empire arose in West Africa. The western **Sahel** is a strip of semi-arid grassland between the Sahara's southern edge and the forest belt further south (*Sahel* means "shore" in Arabic). The Sahel climate undergoes swings of dryer or wetter spells that can last decades. By and large the soils are poor for farming, but in the floodplains of the rivers—the big ones are the Senegal and the Niger—soils are rich. Centers of population grew up along the rivers.

In an environment as unstable as the Sahel's, everyone needed friends who would help in time of drought and hunger. Ideally, that included friends far away whose crops and animals might survive when those close by withered. People of the Sahel built a social order that emphasized kinship, lineage, reciprocity, and obligation—in effect, a social safety net. The people of the Andes and the Altiplano, as we've seen, did something similar. In the Andes, people had to walk everywhere they went. In the Sahel, sometimes they could go by boat. The Niger River was excellent for big canoes and sailing boats. It was an artery of exchange and travel for millennia, like the Nile or the Ganges, giving people access to broad networks of kin and friends.

Permanent settlements along the Niger began as early as 250 BCE. People raised millet, sorghum, and rice and kept cattle, sheep, and goats. Some people focused on fishing or iron working. After 700 CE, a few centuries of wetter climate brought better harvests, more fish, and expanding human populations. A considerable tradition of urban life developed along the Niger valley, especially at Gao, which thrived after 700. It was in these circumstances that the first large monarchy in West African history, Ghana, emerged.

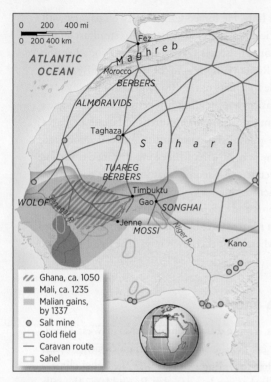

Ghana and Mali, ca. 1050–1337 The first big states in West Africa were Ghana and Mali. Both relied on combinations of river-basin farming, pastoralism, and long-distance trade. Controlling river ports along the Niger and the Senegal Rivers, as well as desert ports—the southern ends of trans-Saharan trade routes—enabled rulers of both states to amass wealth and power on a scale previously unknown in West Africa.

Ancient Ghana, ca. 700–1200

Ancient Ghana lay in the Sahel between the Senegal and the Niger Rivers (far from today's country of Ghana). We gather what we know of ancient Ghana from oral traditions, from written accounts by Arab authors who based their work on reports by visitors to Ghana, and from scattered archeological remains.

A key step in the emergence of ancient Ghana came with a transport revolution in the Sahara based on camels. Berber-speaking peoples living in and around the Sahara acquired camels by 300 CE, enabling them to colonize the desert's oases and live as semi-nomads. As they gradually mastered the arts of camel breeding and camel management, they acquired a mobility in the desert that made them both formidable raiders and traders. It took centuries to learn the best routes between oases across 1,000 miles (1,600 km) of desert. Errors were often fatal. But just as sailors gradually mastered the monsoon system of the Indian Ocean, so Berbers learned to navigate the Sahara. By 700 or so, they regularly crossed the Sahara between the Maghreb and the Sahel. Like the maritime incorporation of East African coastlands into the Indian Ocean world, this trans-Saharan link brought more of Africa into the Old World web.

To understand how camel drivers connected West Africa to the Old World web, you need to know something about camels—one of world history's most important beasts, and one of the animal kingdom's most persnickety. Camels are distant cousins of llamas, which we encountered in the Andes. They come in two main varieties, one native to Central Asia (Bactrian camels, with two humps) and one to Arabia and northern Africa (dromedaries, with one hump).

Healthy adult dromedaries weigh over 1,000 pounds (450 kg) and can carry twice the load of oxen at twice the pace. They can walk over rough terrain and can cover 40 to 60 miles (65 to 95 km) per day. They can drink 25 gallons of water (95 L) at a time and then not drink anything for a week. They can binge on huge meals and then go weeks without food. Part of their secret is they don't regulate their body temperature as much as most mammals do; instead, they allow it to rise and fall so they don't need to sweat water. And they have enzymes no other mammal has that enable them to metabolize their fat (that's what the hump is made of) without losing any muscle. The camel is justly called the ship of the desert.

Transport Revolution These camels were drawn in the thirteenth century by the Iraqi artist al-Wasiti. Although camels were first used to navigate deserts in Southwest Asia, by the fourth or fifth century CE camel drivers had begun to cross the Sahara, linking Africa's Mediterranean shores with West and Central Africa. Trans-Saharan caravans were rare until the eighth or ninth century, and the desert crossing always remained perilous.

Camel-riding raiders and traders from the Sahara brought new incentives for state formation in the Sahel. Ancient Ghana took shape around 700 or 800 as heads of kin groups (lineages) negotiated alliances. United, they stood a better chance of repelling camel-riding raiders, just as Chinese elites did when confronting horse nomads of the steppe. These lineage heads also found that they could monopolize lucrative trans-Saharan trades, providing wealth they could then distribute to followers in exchange for loyalty. Whether their state should be considered an empire, a kingdom, or something else—a confederation of allied linages, perhaps—is the subject of scholarly debate.

One of those lucrative trades was in gold, which was found in several spots in West Africa. Arab authors wrote that gold grew "like carrots in the sand" in Ghana. As early as 804, North African states minted coins using Sahelian gold. Ibn Haukal, writing in the 970s, said the king of Ghana was the richest man in the world (almost surely wrong), and al-Bakri, a century later, claimed the Ghanaian king had a 40 pound (18 kg) golden knob on a post to which he hitched animals. In addition to gold, Ghanaian rulers sold a few thousand slaves taken annually from the Sahel to North African markets.

The most valued import to Ghana was salt, allegedly sometimes exchanged for gold on a pound-for-pound basis. In the middle of the Sahara, at Taghaza, sat a dried-up salt lake. There slaves—with miserably short life expectancies—dug out rock salt, which camels then carried south to the Sahel. Ibn Battuta spent a long week in Taghaza in 1352 and complained that its water tasted bad, that its dwellings and mosque were made of rock salt and roofed with camel hide, and that it had more flies than any place he'd ever seen—and he had been around. West Africa has little salt of its own and has a climate in which people need lots of salt to replace what they sweat out. Like bolts of silk in Central Asia, the salt of the Sahara served as currency because everyone would accept it. If the trade routes of Central Asia deserve the name Silk Roads, then the trans-Saharan routes were salt roads.

The trans-Saharan routes tapped into a lively world of farming, fishing, herding, and trade in the Sahel. As almost everywhere else, most trade here was local. It involved foodstuffs—especially rice and dried fish—leather, jewelry, iron, copper, slaves, and salt. Most people lived in villages, but there were dozens of small towns of a thousand or more people. The most carefully excavated city, Jenne, on the Niger, had 20,000 or 25,000 inhabitants in 800. At times it was part of Ghana, at times independent. Ghana's capital, according to al-Bakri in the eleventh century, had 15,000 people. Ancient Ghana as a whole contained perhaps a million people.

The rulers of ancient Ghana were overlords, like the Gupta in India or Charlemagne in Europe, who took tribute from local rulers. When Ghana was strong, central rulers controlled all the "desert ports" in the Sahel between the Senegal and the Niger Rivers, so no one else could amass wealth and power on the basis of trade. They had a standing army of up to 200,000 soldiers, according to al-Bakri (likely an exaggeration). Ghana's rulers enjoyed religious authority too, although just how this worked is uncertain. Like pharaohs, when they died many slaves were buried with them.

Islam filtered into Ghana across the Sahara starting in the eighth century. It offered an alternative to local religions based mainly on spirits and gods connected to features of nature. Ghana's rulers did not immediately take to Islam (they wanted their subjects to consider them divine), but other members of the social elite found it attractive. The state could use the literacy and numeracy skills that came with becoming an educated Muslim. Some traditions were incompatible with Islamic customs. In Ghana, a ruler was succeeded by his sister's son, whereas Muslim societies normally trace descent through fathers, not mothers. By 1000 or so, Ghana's merchant elite generally practiced Islam, although in its own ways, melding it to local religious traditions and cultural norms. But the ruling families, and the common folk, preferred the religions of their ancestors.

The Ghanaian state reached its apex in the early eleventh century, but its wealth attracted enemies. In the 1070s, a Muslim dynasty of western Morocco, the Almoravids, either infiltrated and influenced—or perhaps attacked—Ghana from across the Sahara. The Almoravids hoped to secure the trans-Saharan salt and gold trade for themselves. Perhaps they were also offended by the standard of Islam practiced in Ghana. By 1076, most of Ghana's elite, including its rulers, accepted an Almoravid style of Islam. The Almoravids held several of Ghana's towns into the 1080s before withdrawing to Morocco. Recent archeology tells us that Ghana's population, and that of the Sahel region generally, fell after about 1100.

Ghana survived, now a more orthodox Islamic polity, but less powerful than before. Lineages and local rulers peeled off. By 1200, political authority in the Sahel was fragmented once again.

Ancient Mali, ca. 1240–1450 The political fragmentation of the West African Sahel did not last long. By the 1240s, a kingdom was forming in the region of the Niger bend. It would develop into a genuine empire, much larger and more centralized than Ghana. Thanks to archeology, oral traditions, and the texts of many Arab authors (including the ubiquitous Ibn Battuta, who visited in 1352–1353), we know a fair bit about ancient Mali.

Unlike Ghana, Mali was a conquest state built by a charismatic military figure. Sundiata, like his near-contemporary Genghis Khan, had a difficult childhood. He was born to an elite family, but political enemies killed all 11 of his siblings, trying to extinguish his lineage and its claim to a minor kingdom. He was spared, perhaps because he was unable to walk and seemed harmless. However, he grew into a vigorous and vengeful teenager and claimed his royal right, probably in 1230. By 1235, he had won a series of battles and was king of an expanding state along the upper Niger with access to the trans-Saharan trade routes. His story is still told as an oral tradition in modern Mali.

Mali's economic base resembled Ghana's but with a larger role for slave trading. Most people worked as farmers, herders, or fisherfolk, but many also fashioned iron and some mined gold. Under Sundiata, Mali acquired access to new goldfields on the upper Niger. North African merchants crossed the Sahara to get the gold, which in turn they traded to Egypt, and eventually shipped an increasing share across the Mediterranean to Europe, where states such as Florence (Italy), France, and England started minting gold coins in the 1250s. From 1250 to 1500, West Africa accounted for about half or two-thirds of the world's gold mining. Until about 1400, most of that went through Mali.

In addition to gold, Mali exported slaves, probably several thousand per year on average. Most were female. When Ibn Battuta returned from Mali to Morocco in 1353, he traveled with 600 slave women destined for North African markets. Mali's slave dealers, chief of whom was its king, raided neighboring peoples for captives to sell across the Sahara.

In exchange for gold and slaves, Mali imported salt, which everyone in West Africa needed, and big horses, which Mali's kings needed to enforce their rule and raid for slaves. As the table here shows, Mali's "desert ports" by 1400 flourished as substantial cities, buoyed by the salt, gold, and slave trades.

Politically, Mali was built on horse power. Its kings relied on a cavalry corps, perhaps 10,000 strong. Malian cavalry rode powerful horses, capable of carrying armor and a rider. It was nearly impossible to raise big horses in West Africa because of disease carried by tsetse flies, so Malian kings bought

Estimated Population of Cities of West African Sahel in 1400	
Gao	40,000
Kano	30,000
Timbuktu	20,000

Mansa Musa A map in the Catalan Atlas of 1375 illustrates Mali with an image of its most renowned ruler, Mansa Musa. He holds out a gold nugget, the source of his empire's wealth.

their horses from Morocco. Like the sultans of Delhi, Mali's kings sought to monopolize horse imports, and thereby the political power that came from fielding cavalry when no one else had any.

Like Ghana in its later years, Mali was a Muslim state. Sundiata considered himself a Muslim. Most of the population in the "desert port" cities was Muslim. As in Ghana, the skills that came with a Muslim education, literacy first and foremost, were useful in running a bureaucracy. Kings always sought the approval of Muslim clerics, which conferred a firmer legitimacy in the eyes of the elite. In rural villages, however, Muslims were a small minority and everyone else followed local religions.

Sundiata died about 1255, but Mali continued to thrive. In the next century, it doubled or tripled the lands under its sway. Its apex of power came under Mansa Musa (r. ca. 1312–1337), a grandson of one of Sundiata's half-brothers. Mansa Musa was more devout than earlier Malian kings, and in 1324–1326 he undertook a religious pilgrimage to Mecca (*hajj* in Arabic). Arab chronicles claim, with some exaggeration no doubt, that he brought along 60,000 companions. Ibn Battuta, who interviewed some of the companions 30 years after the fact, wrote that the royal party brought 12,000 slave women. In Cairo, apparently, Mansa Musa spent so much gold that its value sank for a decade.

On his return from Mecca in 1326, Mansa Musa brought architects and scholars with him. He funded young Malians eager to study Islam in North Africa's centers of learning. His imported architects built grand mosques and palaces. His building spree focused on Timbuktu, a modest town on the Niger bend. After 1326, it became a growing metropolis and a center of Islamic scholarship. Timbuktu eclipsed the other cities of Mali in both trade and cultural influence, becoming the chief desert port and link to North Africa. By 1352, according to Ibn Battuta, Timbuktu welcomed several trans-Saharan caravans weekly, and ordinary people wore Egyptian cloth.

Ibn Battuta also admired the standard of justice and security, writing that Malians "are seldom unjust and have a greater abhorrence of injustice than any other people. There is complete security in their country. Neither traveler nor inhabitant in it has anything to fear from robbers or men of violence." This remark suggests the authority of the state was powerful indeed, even 15 years after the death of Mansa Musa.

Not long after Ibn Battuta's visit, Mali's fortunes began to fade. The state lost control over some of the desert trade. With less salt and fewer horses, Mansa Musa's successors found people re-calculating their loyalties to Mali. By the 1430s, the cities of

Gao and Timbuktu slipped away. Peoples to the east, the Mossi and Songhai, pressed attacks that the kings could not repel. In the west, Wolof and Tuareg groups seized towns and trade.

Archeological evidence suggests that population throughout the Sahel continued to fall. Perhaps the trans-Saharan traffic brought new diseases that became raging epidemics. A few statues show human bodies covered with what might be the pustules of smallpox or even the buboes of bubonic plague. Other evidence suggests that moister climate after 1400 favored the tsetse fly at the expense of horses, undercutting Malian military power. In any case, Mali by 1450 was just one of many states in West Africa.

But the Sahel, thanks to sustained trans-Saharan trade links, had joined the Old World web during the reign of the kings of Ghana and Mali. Even a breakdown of imperial authority would not change that.

Marauders and Invaders, 850–1260

The decline or collapse of big states such as those of the Abbasids, Byzantines, Carolingians, the caliphs of Córdoba, Ghana, and Mali derived partly from the inherent difficulty of retaining the loyalties of ambitious governors, generals, and vassals. This problem spelled trouble for less forceful rulers. In most of these states, a second threat added more trouble: the arrival of formidable tribes or bands from steppes, deserts, or the far north—people accustomed to hardship and eager to plunder wealthier lands.

In earlier chapters, we saw that in the tenth and eleventh centuries tribes of horse nomads such as the Khitans and Ghaznavids took over the northern parts of China and India. They had learned enough about agrarian societies to besiege cities, outfox diplomats, and use their mobility to trade and fight on their own terms. Their equivalents on the western steppe did similar things to agrarian kingdoms in Mesopotamia and eastern Europe. So did Berber tribes from the Moroccan desert. And, in a variation on this theme, the Vikings of Scandinavia, using ships rather than horses, pillaged and conquered far and wide as well. Between about 850 and 1260, the settled agrarian societies of western Eurasia, like those of China and India, regularly faced raid or invasion from more mobile peoples in poorer lands.

Turks and Magyars from the East

Turkic-speakers of Central Asia began to put their stamp on world history in the ninth century, but they began inauspiciously as slaves. Muslim polities, including the Abbasid caliphate from the 830s, started purchasing captured Turkic boys, often ages 10 through 12, by which time they already knew riding and archery. As slaves, they usually converted to Islam and trained to become elite troops. A ninth-century Iraqi scholar, al-Jahiz, wrote that Central Asian Turks were to warfare what Greeks were to philosophy and Chinese to craftsmanship. A tenth-century Arab geographer, Ibn Hawqal, wrote that Turkic boys and girls brought the highest prices of any slaves.

These slave soldiers often used their skills to promote themselves to general or governor. As we saw, by the mid-ninth century Turkic soldiers had become the power behind the throne in Baghdad, killing and selecting caliphs as they saw fit. In some cases, they set up dynasties, ruling directly as the Ghaznavids and the Delhi sultans did in India, or as one group, the Mamluks, did in Egypt after 1250. Thus a few tens of thousands of enslaved Turkic warriors, and their descendants, became rulers in several Muslim states of India, Iran, and Egypt.

A different form of Turkic power came with the arrival en masse of the **Seljuk Turks** from Central Asia. They were a pastoral people whose leaders embraced Sunni Islam in the 980s. They began to raid successfully—against fellow Muslims—in eastern and northern Iran, gathering people to their banners as they went and slowly adopting Iranian culture. Their growing numbers and military skills enabled them to take Baghdad (1055) and to smash Byzantine armies in eastern Anatolia (1071). They even formed a loose empire for a few decades, but by the 1090s it split up into petty kingdoms.

Perhaps a million Seljuk Turks, men, women, and children, walked and rode into Anatolia over the next 200 years, setting their herds loose on pastures and fields. Slowly, they occupied most of the peninsula, pushing Byzantine frontiers back to the vicinity of Constantinople. This was more than the ebb and flow of frontiers between Christian and Muslim powers. It was an enduring change, a Turkification and Islamization of a major region of the eastern Mediterranean. Greek and Armenian Christian populations remained, sometimes under Byzantine authority but increasingly under one or another Seljuk ruler. Turks, Greeks, Armenians, and others mingled in Anatolia until the twentieth century, often peacefully, sometimes violently. It became, together with Spain, Sicily, Syria, and others, one of the lands in which Muslim and Christian lived side-by-side for many generations, sometimes intermarrying, always learning from one another's ways.

Seljuk Cavalry Two Seljuk horsemen joust in this plaque from twelfth- or thirteenth-century Iran. They are practicing the cavalry skills that were key to Seljuk expansion from Iran into the eastern Mediterranean.

The Magyars, the ancestors of today's ethnic Hungarians, were yet another pagan and pastoralist tribe from southern Siberia and Central Asia pushing westward from the sixth century onward. In the 890s, they crossed into the broad grasslands of today's central and eastern Hungary, a good landscape for flocks and herds. They displaced or absorbed the small existing population and mounted destructive raids on nearby lands, ranging from today's Denmark to Spain, for the next few generations. They pillaged southward, into the Balkans, until the 970s. But their leaders, like so many others before and since, gradually found that the charms of settled life surpassed the rewards of spreading terror on horseback. By 1000, they had converted to Christianity and set up a kingdom, one of the larger ones in Europe, and given up roaming and raiding in favor of taxing.

Fatimids, Almoravids, and Almohads from the West

Horsemen from the steppe overran and conquered the settled societies of Iran, Anatolia, and east-central Europe in the centuries after 850. Horsemen from the desert edge of the Moroccan Sahara did the same to North Africa, Spain, and Egypt starting about 900, and Ghana soon after.

First came the Fatimids. They began as exiled Shi'a Muslims who took refuge in Morocco's oasis town of Sijilmassa. They gathered followers from other Shi'a populations throughout the Maghreb and formed a state based in today's Tunisia. They won victory upon victory in North Africa and in 969 took Egypt. For a few generations, their empire, now based in Cairo, stretched from Arabia to Morocco and included the island of Sicily. Like the Seljuks or the Khitans, they went from inconsequential tribe to imperial dynasty in less than a century. From Cairo their ocean-going merchants roamed as far as China. Theirs was generally a tolerant and multicultural Shi'a state in which Christian and Jewish populations prospered. But within a few generations, dynastic quarrels, combined with terrible droughts and harvest failures along the Nile, brought down the Fatimids.

The Almoravids and Almohads also came from the Moroccan margins of the Sahara. The Almoravids promoted Islam with the zeal of new converts and practiced desert warfare with the skill of long-time inhabitants of the Sahara. In 1086, the Almoravids accepted an invitation from Muslim kings in Spain to help battle Christian armies, and soon they took control of the southern half of Iberia. At its height around 1100, their state also included almost all the Maghreb too. Over the generations, their rulers became more sedentary, urbanized, and worldly, and like the Magyars they gave up the strenuous life on horseback.

The Almohads, a collection of Berber tribesmen convinced that Almoravid rule had degenerated into sinful luxury, burst out of the mountains of Morocco in the 1130s, conquering Almoravid territory in North Africa by 1147 and ruling Islamic Iberia by

CONSIDERING THE EVIDENCE

Religion and Diplomacy in Khazaria

As Turkic-speakers entered the western region of the Old World web, their leaders often converted to Christianity or Islam. Sharing the religion of their neighbors did not guarantee peace, but it could strengthen diplomatic ties and improve their access to wider networks of commerce and communication. Conversely, Muslim and Christian rulers promoted their religion to the conquerors and migrants who threatened to overwhelm their countries.

This chapter's opening mentioned a remarkable correspondence between a Jew who served as a royal advisor to a Muslim ruler in Spain and King Joseph of Khazaria, a Jewish kingdom located near the Caspian Sea between the Volga and the Dniepr Rivers. In his 960 CE letter, King Joseph explains the surprising decision of his ancestor to reject the entreaties of Muslim Arabs and Christian Byzantines in favor of Judaism.

[King Bulan] was a wise and God-fearing man ... [who] expelled the wizards and idolaters from the land. ... The kings of the Byzantines[,] and the Arabs ... sent their envoys and ambassadors with great riches and many great presents to the King as well as some of their wise men with the object of converting him to their own religion. But the King ... [also] sent for a learned Israelite. ...

[H]e called all the sages together and said to them: "Speak and argue with one another and make clear to me which is the best religion." They began to dispute with one another without arriving at any results until the King said to the Christian priest: "What do you think? Of the religion of the Jews and the Moslims, which is to be preferred?" The priest answered: "The religion of the Israelites is better than that of the Moslims."

The King then asked the [Muslim qadi]: "What do you say? Is the religion of the Israelites, or that of the Christians

preferable?" The kadi answered: "The religion of the Israelites is preferable."

Upon this the King said: "If this is so, you both have admitted with your own mouths that the religion of the Israelites is better. Wherefore, trusting in the mercies of God and the power of the Almighty, I choose the religion of Israel, that is, the religion of Abraham. If that God ... will aid me, He can give me without labor the money, the gold, and the silver which you have promised me. As for you all, go now in peace to your land."

Questions for Analysis

1. Why did the Byzantines and the Arabs send ambassadors to try to convert the Khazar king to their respective religions?

2. What reason did King Bulan give for choosing Judaism?

3. Considering Khazaria's location, what unstated political factors may have motivated King Bulan to avoid choosing Islam or Christianity?

Source: *The Jew in the Medieval World: A Sourcebook, 315–1791*, 2nd printing (New York, 1972).

1172. Like the Almoravids before them, they intended to spread their righteous Islam to the degenerates and to do battle with infidels wherever they could be found—which in practice chiefly meant Spain. For a while, the Almohads united the fractured Muslim societies of southern Spain and mounted effective resistance to the several Christian kingdoms of the north.

Deteriorating climate as well as religious fervor and opportunism drove the peoples of Central Asia and the Moroccan Sahara to become conquerors. The same rearrangement of the Earth's climate system that brought warmer and wetter weather to northern Europe led to more drought elsewhere. From the 950s, it appears, the frequency and duration of droughts in both the Maghreb and Southwest Asia increased markedly. Herders living in semi-arid lands more frequently found only withered grasses, putting herds and herders at risk of starvation. Desperation drove them to attack neighboring cultivated and populated landscapes.

At the same time, dryer climate after 950 weakened neighboring agrarian states. Smaller harvests meant less revenue with which to pay their bureaucrats and soldiers, and thus less loyalty and more rebellion. In the eastern Mediterranean, the key, as usual, was Egypt. Its water came from rains in Ethiopia delivered by the annual monsoon, a different climate system from that of the Mediterranean. Egypt's water supply, the Nile, almost never failed for more than a year or two at a time. So Egypt, since the time of the pharaohs, had served as insurance against famine for cities and armies throughout the region. But after 950, Nile floods failed more often, just when droughts afflicted the eastern Mediterranean. Starvation resulted in villages and cities alike. Food became so scarce in the 950s in Iraq, according to the Armenian chronicler Matthew of Edessa, that "Many went mad, attacking one another mercilessly and savagely, devouring each other.... Many villages and regions became uninhabited." Drought and famine peaked in the years 1051–1072, when Nile floods failed half the time. The Seljuks, whose victories over the Abbasids and Byzantines came in these decades, were emboldened by desperation borne of drought, which simultaneously weakened their enemies.

Vikings from the North

Neither religious zeal nor adverse climate propelled the **Vikings** out of their farmsteads in the few patches of good land in Scandinavia. Before 790, the Norse (as stay-at-home Vikings are called) society was growing more complex, with more trade opportunities emerging from the slow restoration of commerce in post-Roman northern Europe. A few ambitious Norse were trying to set up kingdoms. Losers in these struggles sometimes preferred to leave home rather than submit to the winners. They became merchants and pirates, trading, looting, conquering, and settling widely in Europe in the ninth to the eleventh centuries. The Norse Sagas, oral epics written down a couple of centuries after the events they describe, are full of family feuds leading to emigration.

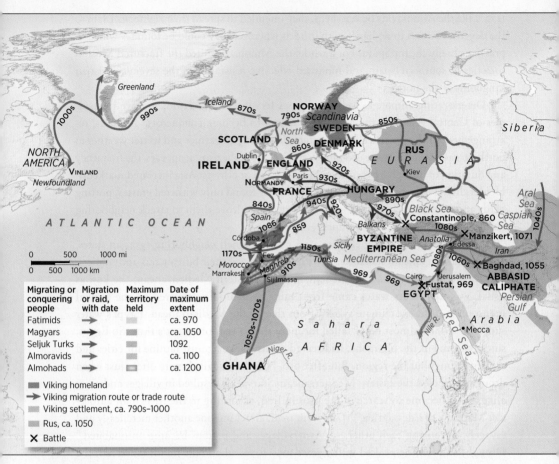

Mobile Conquerors and Political Changes, 700–1200 Over the 500 years between 700 and 1200, the settled agrarian states in the west end of the Old World web came under intense pressure from highly mobile warrior bands. Several of these—Almoravids, Almohads, Magyars, and Seljuk Turks among them—became conquerors, typically using horses or camels to achieve superior mobility. Another warrior band, the Vikings, used ships. The successful conquerors set up their own states, or in the case of the Vikings took part in the creation of one, called Rus. The Fatimids, never a warrior band but a religious minority (Shi'a Muslims), also used superior mobility to take over existing states.

In addition, the Vikings may have felt overcrowded. According to a Christian chronicler writing about 1020,

[Viking males] live in outrageous unions with many women and then in shameless and unlawful intercourse breed innumerable progeny. . . . The young quarrel with their fathers and grandfathers, or with each other, about property, and if they increase too greatly in number . . . a large group is selected by the drawing of lots according to ancient custom, who are driven away to foreign peoples and realms.

The account depicts the Vikings as voyaging to new lands when population growth made resources scarce, much as Polynesian Islanders did.

The Vikings enjoyed certain advantages as pirates and looters. They could forge weapons, armor, and helmets (alas, the horned Viking helmet is a modern myth) from the plentiful iron in Scandinavia's bogs. Their longships proved sturdy in heavy weather, maneuverable under sail or oars, and could sail up shallow rivers. They could sail from Norway to Iceland in three days, as fast as any vessel before the age of steam. Their ships were like the horses of the steppe and desert tribes. Like the Khitans, Magyars, or Almoravids, Viking raiders could appear without warning and, if necessary, flee just as quickly.

Raiding and Slaving Starting in the 790s, Vikings began their reign of terror with attacks on the east coast of Britain. They specialized in pillaging gold and silver from Christian churches and monasteries. Burgeoning trade connections enabled them to sell all the valuables they could steal in order to get things they really wanted. (Looting and piracy make more sense as a business strategy where there are markets nearby; otherwise you can end up with piles of useless goblets and chalices.) The Vikings also learned that slaves brought good prices in distant markets, so they organized a business based on kidnapping women in Britain and Ireland. They founded Dublin as their main port for slave exports.

The Vikings quickly expanded their enterprise, looting and slaving along the coasts of Atlantic France and inland as far as Paris. By 859, they had sailed into the Mediterranean. They sold slaves as far afield as Córdoba, Constantinople, and Baghdad. Simultaneously they raided and traded eastward, along the Russian rivers well suited to their longships, and in 860 even attacked Constantinople, the capital of the Byzantine Empire.

Settlements and Trade By the late ninth century, Viking chiefs had become rulers in parts of Britain and in northern France (Normandy is named for Norse settlers). In the 870s, they began to settle Iceland, previously uninhabited. Genomic evidence has recently revealed that almost all the early generations of females in Iceland came from the British Isles and the males from Norway, which strongly suggests that mass abductions (or purchases) of British women were part of the settlement scheme. In the 990s, a few Vikings also established

Viking Invaders A tenth-century Norse manuscript shows a fleet of Vikings disembarking from their ships, on one of their many raids along the east coast of England.

small colonies on the giant island of Greenland, where a warming climate brought a few green patches around the edges of its thick glaciers.

The Greenland settlements served as the springboard for a brief effort to settle on Newfoundland, the northeastern edge of North America, around 1000 CE. Within a year or two, violent encounters with the local Amerindians caused the Vikings to abandon the colony, called Vinland. But before they did, Snorri Karlsefnisson was born—the first baby in the Americas not descended from Asian migrants. He would also be the last for nearly 500 years.

The Greenland Norse, never more than a few thousand in number, were linked to the Old World web although they were situated on its farthest fringes. They traded walrus ivory to Europe for centuries, became Christians, and even sent the Pope a polar bear in the 1050s. But as the Little Ice Age took hold after 1250, their lives grew ever grimmer and their connections to Scandinavia ever weaker. Elephant ivory from Africa replaced Greenland's chief export to Europe, leaving the Greenland Norse destitute, victims of both climate change and economic integration. The last of them either packed up or died out in the 1420s. The Old World web no longer included Greenland.

But elsewhere the Vikings, like the Turks, Fatimids, and others, thickened the Old World web. Their traders enduringly linked Scandinavia to Russia, Byzantium, and the Arab world along the river routes between the Baltic and Black Seas. Some Viking graves include coins minted in Afghanistan, Iran, and Iraq. An Arab traveler, Ibn Fadlan, visited a settlement on the Volga River (in today's Russia) in 921 and found the people tall "like palm trees, fair and reddish" but "the filthiest of Allah's creatures." These were probably Vikings. To judge by Ibn Fadlan's account, a large part of their economy consisted of selling female slaves. Some Vikings helped set up the first state in the region, based at Kiev, called Rus, in the tenth century. Others became mercenaries for Byzantine emperors. Through their work as merchants, warriors, and pirates, the Vikings helped to extend the Old World web into the Atlantic and Russia, and to tighten it elsewhere.

Everywhere they settled, from Russia to Greenland, the Vikings gradually came to prefer Christianity to their Norse gods. Frequently, Christian wives converted kings who then encouraged or obliged their subjects to take up Christianity. By 1050, the Vikings were almost all Christians. Like the Magyars, Almoravids, and others, the Vikings gradually found the dangerous life as raiders less appealing than steadier work as farmers, soldiers, businessmen, and, in some cases, rulers.

Women and Social Hierarchy   With male mortality especially high among warriors and pirates, women far outnumbered men in Viking societies. The Viking Sagas show us women as merchants, missionaries, and occasionally warriors. There is also a grave site in Sweden with a woman's skeleton surrounded by weapons and armor.

Women in Viking society had no political rights and were barred from assemblies and courts. But in domestic life they enjoyed some power, managing money and choosing their husbands for themselves. They could own property and sue for divorce. In the sagas, a grandmother named Aud the Deep-Minded led a settlement expedition from Scotland to Iceland, building and commanding a longship. Another grave in Sweden includes among a woman's funeral objects some scales and weights used in market transactions. A woman of Viking extraction, Olga of Kiev, ruled the polity of Rus in the mid-tenth century, negotiating effectively with foreign powers including the Byzantine Empire. One chronicle records her rejecting a marriage proposal by burying alive the emissaries who brought it.

Viking society showed sharp inequalities of social class. Leaders enjoyed plenty of food and drink, decorative objects from afar, piles of silver and gold, and many slaves. One tenth-century household owned a Buddha figurine from India. But most people in Viking Scandinavia were poor farmers, and many were slaves. A thirteenth-century law from an island in what is now Sweden captures some of this hierarchy. It assessed penalties for murder: 10.6 pounds (4.8 kg) of silver if the victim was a freeborn local; 4.4 pounds (2 kg) of silver in the case of freeborn foreigners; and a tenth of that for slaves. As in Hammurabi's laws from ancient Mesopotamia or those of Tang China, murder penalties varied with the status of the victim.

Crusaders from the West

Beginning in the 1090s, at the same time that Christian warriors in Spain were pushing against the frontiers of al-Andalus and re-taking Sicily from Muslim rule, Christian knights from western Europe launched the first of several waves of invasions of the Levant. These invasions were part pilgrimage to the Holy Land and part military campaign. Their motives included both religious merit, to be earned by taking Jerusalem from Muslim rule, and plunder. The undertaking is called the **Crusades**, part of the larger Mediterranean tug-of-war between Muslim and Christian rulers taking place in Spain, Sicily, and Anatolia.

The immediate origins of the Crusades lay with a response to the Seljuk Turks, who, as we've seen, threatened Christian Byzantium when they drifted into Anatolia after 1071. A Byzantine emperor asked the Pope for help. In 1095, the Pope, Urban II, called for volunteers from the length and breadth of Christendom to wrest the Holy Land from Muslims. In response, Christians flocked to Crusader banners, driven by religious zeal and attracted by the hope of rewards in this life and the next.

The Pope's recruiters promised that all who died in the venture would have their sins washed away and a clear path to Heaven. Popes had used this recruiting device since about 850 to inspire Christian warriors fighting against Muslims in Spain, against pagan Vikings, and on occasion against fellow Christians at odds with the Papacy. The Muslim caliphs had used similar promises too.

It is important to grasp that the Crusades, as a whole, were not a titanic struggle between a united Christianity and a united Islam—although they are often remembered

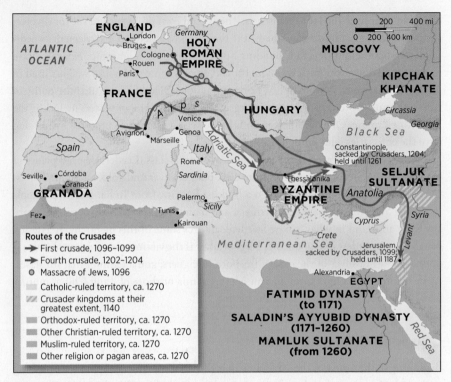

The Crusades, 1096–1291 Over two centuries, some 200,000 European Christians went to the Levant on crusades, hoping to take Jerusalem and the Holy Land from Muslim rulers and claim them for Latin Christendom. The map shows the routes of two crusades, revealing the multiple motives behind them. Along the way Crusaders sometimes assaulted Jewish communities in Europe and in 1204 sacked the Greek Orthodox Christian city of Constantinople. Once in the Levant, Crusaders met with initial success, set up small kingdoms, but soon quarreled among themselves and eventually faced foes, such as Egypt's Mamluks, who proved far too strong for them.

as such. Rather, they amounted to a series of small-scale wars, often raids or sieges. Christians fought Christians and Muslims fought Muslims, and all parties sought allies where they could find them.

Crusaders—mainly French, Germans, and English—began arriving in the Levant by land and sea in 1097. Some paused en route to plunder the Jewish quarters of European towns. Once arrived, they stepped into a fragmented political world in which all major powers—Seljuk Turks, Fatimid dynasts in Egypt—were warring among themselves. None took much notice of the Crusaders for more than 50 years.

Meanwhile, the Crusaders redeemed Jerusalem for their faith in 1099. Indeed, they sacked it, massacring thousands of its Muslim, Jewish, and eastern (Greek Orthodox) Christian inhabitants and looting its treasures. As one Christian scribe described it:

Our men rushed around the whole city, seizing gold and silver, horses and mules, and houses full of all sorts of goods, and they all came rejoicing and weeping from gladness to worship at the Sepulchre of our Savior Jesus. . . . Next morning they went cautiously up on the Temple roof [where locals had been granted protection by some knights] and attacked the Saracens [Muslims], both men and women, cutting off their heads. . . . No one has ever seen or heard of such a slaughter of pagans, for they were burned on pyres like pyramids, and God alone knows how many there were.

Ambitious Crusaders built castles, recruited followers, and called themselves kings. They declined to accept papal control or recognize Byzantine authority. Fortunately for them, they seemed too insignificant to the warring Turks and Fatimids to be worth expelling.

The several waves of Crusaders brought some 200,000 Europeans to the Levant over a two-century period (1096–1291), mostly adult males, but also many women and children. This migration paled next to that of Turks from Central Asia flowing into the same general region. And mortality among the Europeans, from violence and disease, ran high. Soon the Crusader kingdoms quarreled among themselves and began to seek allies among the Muslim powers.

When Fatimid Egypt looked like it might fall apart and Crusaders seemed keen to grab it, a Sunni Muslim warlord, Ṣalāḥ al-Dīn Yūsuf ibn Ayyūb, known as Saladin, conquered Egypt for himself by 1171. He soon added parts of Syria. To firm up his hold over these lands, he launched a holy war against the Crusader kingdoms, crushing several and taking Jerusalem in 1187. Part of Saladin's success came from division among the Crusaders, just as their initial success had derived from division among Muslims. He noted in a letter to an Abbasid caliph that among Italian Crusaders "not a single one of them does not [sell] us weapons." Those Crusader states that survived Saladin, who died in 1193, were much weakened. His dynasty, the Ayyubids, based in Egypt and Syria, thrived until shattered by Mongol armies in 1260.

After Saladin's campaigns, a new wave of Crusaders in 1204 chose to skip the Holy Land altogether and pillage Constantinople, the Christian world's richest city. This was the first time since the city had erected its defensive walls 900 years before that it had fallen to attack. Its defenders had not expected an attack by their fellow Christians. In 1261, Greek Christians managed to oust the Crusaders and re-establish Constantinople as the capital of what remained of the Byzantine Empire.

Greek and other eastern Christians were attacked by all sides during the Crusades. After decades of persecution under Crusader rule, many (perhaps most) of them chose to convert to Islam when the Crusaders left—an ironic unintended consequence of the whole enterprise.

Later Crusaders often targeted Egypt rather than the Holy Land but met with only fleeting success. Slave soldiers, called Mamluks, took over Egypt by about 1250. The Mamluks, when not preoccupied with greater threats, carved up Crusader forces.

The Crusader kingdoms teetered from the time of Saladin but did not fall until the mid- and late thirteenth century. The geopolitical situation turned briefly in their favor when Mongol armies clattered into the region, bent on destroying all Muslim powers. The Mongols, in effect, briefly served as protectors of Crusader kingdoms, helping them to hang on until 1291, when the last one fell—to Mongol and Mamluk forces. Ultimately, the Crusaders were too few and too divided to survive if the locals ever united against them.

Mongols from the East

The Mongols, as we saw in Chapter 12, built a confederacy of pastoralist peoples on the Mongolian and Central Asian steppes under the command of Genghis Khan in the early thirteenth century. Soon after, they rode west.

Mongol western campaigns began in the years 1219–1222, led by Genghis Khan and sons. They ventured into India, the Caucasus (the lands between the Black and the Caspian Seas), and Russia before Genghis decided to go back to Mongolia. His grandson, Batu, led another campaign in 1236–1241 against Russia, Poland, and Hungary, before he scurried home to defend his interests when one Great Khan died and another was to be chosen. Many of his soldiers stayed behind and settled on the grasslands north of the Black and the Caspian Seas. The third and last campaign, led by another grandson, Hulegu (probably a Buddhist), came in 1256–1260 against Iran and Syria, where Mongols briefly helped Crusader kingdoms. Like Batu, Hulegu had to head home to deal with a change of Great Khans. A remnant of his army lost a battle to the Mamluks in 1260, in Palestine. The Mongols went no further in the west.

As in East and Central Asia, in western Asia the Mongols sowed terror. Their skills as mounted archers impressed even Turks and Hungarians, who came from the same steppe tradition. They had learned siege warfare in their struggles against China. Their habit was to demand that cities surrender and to starve out or assault those bold enough to refuse. They then killed all the men, perhaps excepting skilled craftsmen, and enslaved the women and children. Many cities—indeed, entire kingdoms such as Armenia—preferred to submit without a fight. The Mongols let them be as long as they handed over enough treasure, horses, and young women. Their conquest of Baghdad in 1258, still legendary in the Arab world, left several hundred thousand people dead and reduced a once-great city to the status of provincial market town. This calculated use of terror worked. By 1260, Mongol power extended from the Black Sea and Russia all the way to Mongolia.

Like the Abbasids and Carolingians, the Mongols could not hold their empire together for long. The world's largest land empire, by the end of the 1260s, had fractured into four parts. China, not yet fully under Mongol control, was the richest and most populous fragment of the empire. The Chagatai Khanate, in Central Asia, much

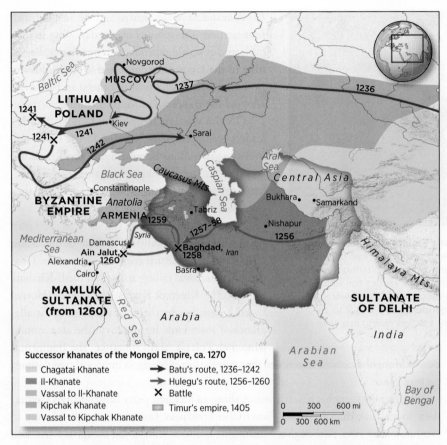

The Western Campaigns of the Mongols and the Mongol States, ca. 1236–1400 Operating thousands of miles from home, Genghis Khan's descendants, especially his grandsons Batu and Hulegu, led campaigns of conquest in Central and western Asia and into eastern Europe. Their mobile style of warfare suited the grasslands of the steppe but proved less effective in forested landscapes. The resulting Mongol Empire quickly fragmented into three khanates: Chagatai, Kipchak, and Il-Khanate. After the Mongol conquest of China, it became a fourth khanate in 1279.

weaker and poorer, struggled to survive between China and another strong Mongol state in Iran, called the Il-Khanate. The last of the four, called the Kipchak Khanate or the Golden Horde, was based in the steppe lands north of the Black and the Caspian Seas, where Batu's men had settled in the 1240s. It was almost always at war with the Il-Khanate.

Mongol warriors in the west, as in China, were vastly outnumbered by the peoples they conquered. They often married Iranian or Turkic women, and after about two generations they had largely assimilated to local culture. In Iran, the Il-Khanids,

Timur's Empire This illustration in a fifteenth-century Persian book shows Timur's army employing the ingenious military tactics for which they were renowned. They lower soldiers in a gondola down a cliff to surprise enemy soldiers hiding in a cave.

like Alexander's Macedonians and the Seljuk Turks, soon settled into roles as overlords, living luxuriously and governing through intermediaries. Beginning in the 1290s, they converted (from Buddhism in some cases, shamanism in others) to Islam and adopted the trappings of Muslim culture.

On the western steppe, the Golden Horde's leaders embraced Islam, starting in the 1320s, and over the generations became more Turkic and less Mongol. But here, unlike in Iran, there was no elaborate urbanized culture to seduce them, and they remained closer to their nomadic heritage.

The Mongol successor states suffered their own political troubles, usually in the form of succession crises abetted by outside enemies. By 1307, the Chagatai Khanate was falling apart, and the Il-Khanate by 1335. The Kipchak Khans (the Golden Horde) lasted longer, but by the 1330s were losing the allegiance of local lords in Muscovy (the area around Moscow), Poland, and Lithuania. The fragmentation of Mongol successor states, and the assimilation of Mongols into local populations, gathered pace.

Then a new Genghis Khan arose. A sheep rustler and petty brigand from Central Asia, more Turk than Mongol, Timur (also known as Tamerlane) fought his way to local power by 1380. Although a Muslim, he modeled himself on Genghis Khan and married a descendant of Genghis to bolster his prestige. Like his idol, he must have been a political and military genius, because over the next 23 years he gathered legions of followers—Turks, Mongols, Arabs, Bulgars, and many others—and forged them into a formidable fighting machine. He and his polyglot armies conquered far and wide, from India to Anatolia. He in effect re-united the fractured Chagatai, Kipchak, and Il-khanates, creating a new empire. By some calculations, his campaigns reduced world population by 5 percent, though this is hard to verify. In 1405, he died while on his way to attack China. So he fell short of re-creating the Mongol empire at its height.

Economy and Culture

Crumbling empires and rampaging invaders brought frequent turmoil to the western end of the Old World web from 800 to 1400. In such circumstances, you would not expect economic growth or cultural flowering. But economic growth and cultural efflorescence occurred in spite of turmoil, and perhaps also because of it.

Commerce and Economic Growth

The economic quickening began shortly before 800, at different rates in different places. To a large extent, the quickening followed from the population growth and agricultural revolutions discussed at the start of this chapter. But state and religious policies, new technologies, more coin and credit in circulation, and greater exchange and specialization all contributed.

We can't forget, however, the tremendous economic destruction wrought by wars and invasions. The Vikings, Turks, Magyars, Almoravids, Crusaders, and Mongols and others like them at first were bad for business. They burned cities and destroyed irrigation systems. In the wake of the Mongol invasions in Southwest Asia, ceramic and metal production fell for decades because workshops were destroyed, raw material supply chains disrupted, and artisans killed or taken to Mongolia.

People who lived through such destruction felt only misfortune. But in the longer run, the brutal conquests of Vikings, Mongols, and others promoted commerce. At first, the conquering peoples needed to nurture markets in order to dispose of loot and captives. But in time they learned to live off taxing trade. The biggest boost to trade came from the Mongols. Their empire became a huge free-trade zone extending across almost all of Eurasia from the Black Sea to the Yellow Sea. Historians use the term *Pax Mongolica* (the "Mongolian Peace") to refer to this situation, on the analogy of the Pax Romana in the Mediterranean during the high point of Roman power. The Pax Mongolica was not entirely peaceful, but Mongol power and intimidation made the period 1260–1350 more peaceful along the Silk Roads than usual.

Throughout their realm, the Mongols built a system of **caravanserais**—rest stops for caravans—to support commerce. The Silk Roads became, more so than ever, a superhighway system for caravans laden with silks, furs, brocades, ceramics, and fine metalwares. Mongol khans and their Russian underlings extended the trade networks north to the Baltic, where iron, amber, slaves, and other goods entered circulation. Even after the Mongol Empire broke up, its four successor states tried to maintain trade networks. The Il-Khanids in 1320 negotiated a commercial treaty with Venice, a trade-oriented Italian city-state. So while extremely destructive in the short run, in the long run the Mongols helped propel commercial and economic growth throughout Eurasia.

Other peoples also played important roles in promoting commercial growth. In eastern Europe, for example,

Silk Road Travel This thirteenth-century medallion functioned as a passport for travel on the Silk Road routes within Mongol lands. Its inscription, written in the Mongolian language, reads, "By the strength of Eternal Heaven, an edict of the Emperor. He who has not respect [for this pass] shall be guilty."

Jews and Armenians accelerated the monetization of economic life. Their religio-cultural emphasis on literacy made them good candidates for merchant and estate-managing duties, roles into which a small minority of each people moved. They helped to mobilize grain exports via the Baltic Sea ports and long-distance trade along the east European rivers. In the fourteenth and fifteenth centuries, many Jews from German lands chose to move east into what is now Poland and Ukraine. By 1500, Jews made up less than 1 percent of the population there, but every big town had dozens of Jewish families, a few of which did well in commerce.

Technological changes also favored growth. The most important ones came in agriculture—the horse collar, the moldboard plow, and crop rotations. Improved ship design, especially on the shores of northwestern Europe, helped trade. Mechanical clocks, building on water clocks in use in both China and Iran, were becoming routine in the fourteenth century and enabled people to coordinate their lives a little better.

Financial innovations spurred commerce too. In the Mediterranean, merchant guilds—mutual aid associations—developed forms of marine insurance. Primitive banking emerged too, with various subterfuges created to get around the moral and sometimes legal prohibitions against usury (lending at interest) found in both Christian and Islamic societies. Where Jews were permitted to follow their own laws and regulate their own affairs, they sometimes took up banking—many other economic roles such as landownership were prohibited to them—because lending at interest was acceptable practice in their communities. Big cities with Jewish populations eventually became financially linked through networks of family banking houses.

In addition to greater credit through banks, commerce quickened because it acquired more coin. Mining techniques spread to Central Asian lands previously unexploited, raising the silver supply. New technologies permitted older silver mines in central Europe to raise production levels. Egyptian links south of the Sahara brought more West African, Nubian, and Ethiopian gold into circulation. By 1400, roughly half the gold lubricating commerce in the Old World web came from West Africa.

Urban Growth The quickening of commerce spurred urban growth, and urban markets in turn stimulated commerce. Cities could grow big only where farming produced a surplus and transport costs were low. In 1000, the big cities of western Eurasia lay in Byzantine and Arab lands (including al-Andalus). Baghdad, as we have seen, may have attained a population of 1 million under the early Abbasids. It was smaller, but still a sizeable city when the Mongols burned it in 1258. Cairo probably had half a million inhabitants in 1300, and Constantinople about 200,000. By 1300 western Europe was urbanizing fast, creating new cities and expanding older ones.

New cities, albeit small ones, sprang up in lands that previously never had any, such as Russia, Scandinavia, Scotland, and Ireland. Starting in the thirteenth century, around the Baltic and the North Seas, a group of cities led by Lübeck and Hamburg banded together as the Hanseatic League to preserve their independence and merchants' privileges against kings and dukes eager to tax them. Their political success ensured flourishing maritime trade across northern European waters.

The Hanseatic cities also helped develop oceanic fisheries as never before. In 900, almost all fish eaten in northern Europe came from lakes and rivers; by 1300, it almost all came from the sea, and dozens of towns and cities specialized in harvesting cod, herring, and other marine fish. Here climate change played a role too: as the North Atlantic cooled, cold-loving fish were able to migrate south, closer to the urban markets of Europe. Where oceanic fishing thrived, cities depended less on agricultural surpluses.

The most rapidly urbanizing lands of all after 1300 were the formerly swampy plains of the Low Countries (Belgium and Holland) and the Po valley in northern Italy. Successful drainage opened the way to bountiful farming and cheap transport, making urban life more feasible. Perhaps 30 percent of the population in these formerly sodden landscapes lived in cities such as Bruges or Venice. In southern Spain, the urban proportion might have reached 20 percent. Elsewhere in Europe and Southwest Asia, 5 to 10 percent was normal.

Web Building The single biggest factor behind the commercial growth and urbanization in the western region of the Old World web was the extension and tightening—in some places, re-tightening—of networks of transport, trade, and communications. By 1300, northern Europe from Ireland to Russia joined larger trade circuits as never before. Trans-Saharan links to West Africa strengthened. And thanks to the Pax Mongolica, trans-Asian links tightened, bringing the Chinese and Indian economies into closer contact with those of western Eurasia. Moreover, many regions within western Eurasia, such as northern Italy, southern Spain, and the Low Countries, developed intensive networks of specialization and exchange to match, or nearly match, the older ones in Egypt and Iraq. So, economically speaking, the western end of the Old World web grew both tighter and bigger through 1300 and a little beyond.

It is important to note how uneven this web-building process was. Invaders (and routine warfare) wrought greater destruction on Southwest Asia than on Europe, at least after about 950 when the Vikings and Magyars settled down. And because European societies were poorer, with less in the way of elaborate infrastructure such as irrigation systems, they could rebound a bit more quickly from destruction. In 1100, European lands were still poorer, their populations less skilled, than those of Egypt, Syria, or Byzantium; the Crusaders were awed by the sophistication, especially the artisans' skills, they encountered around the eastern Mediterranean.

But by 1340, European societies, especially in Italy and the Low Countries, were growing rapidly. In population and productivity, skill and sophistication, they were growing much faster than the Islamic heartlands, Byzantium, or anywhere else in the western region of the Old World web.

Step back for a moment and think of the entire Old World web, from Japan to Morocco. In 800, the great centers of population, wealth, and power lay in northern

The Arab World The Arab geographer Muhammad al-Idrisi made this map in 1154 for the king of Sicily. It is oriented with North at the bottom and shows all of Europe, Asia, and North Africa. The map demonstrates awareness of the whole Indian Ocean world and even China.

China, northern India, Mesopotamia, and the eastern Mediterranean. By 1250, although that remained the case, now southern China under the Song and western Europe (under many kings) were the most dynamic regions of the Old World web, powered by agricultural revolutions and commercialization.

Cultural Flowering

Here and there throughout the western regions of the Old World web, especially in cities, courts, madrassas, and monasteries, high culture flourished despite all the violence and destruction. Thousands of leisured men, and a few women too, created lasting monuments to human ingenuity and wisdom in poetry, architecture, astronomy, mathematics, law, and other fields. Almost all of this cultural growth took place under the intellectual umbrella of either Islam or Christianity, stretching these traditions in new directions. A great deal of it took place because migrations, commerce, or refugee flows exposed thinkers to new ideas and practices and shook their faith in inherited ways. And it could take place because in some locations some people amassed enough wealth to sponsor art and science.

Baghdad One example was Baghdad under the early Abbasids, where Muslims, Jews, and Christians of many sects interacted. It was one of several courts competing for prestige in the Islamic world. The Abbasid court, especially under the caliph Harun al-Rashid (r. 786–809), gathered sages, artisans, and artists together. Silk Road connections to China brought exposure to Tang-dynasty porcelain, which Baghdad craftsmen adapted. Paper, also from China, helped the literary arts to prosper. Baghdad became a center of translation of philosophical and scientific texts from Greek, Sanskrit, Syriac, Persian, and other languages into Arabic. Arabs had little in the way of their own science and thus proved especially open to the mix of new ideas. The slave trades from Africa, Russia, and Central Asia brought new cultural influences. Connections to India led to the importation of mathematical concepts such as decimal notation and the use of zero.

The great scholar al-Farabi (ca. 872–951), for example, came from somewhere in Central Asia but lived most of his adult life in Baghdad. He learned several languages, including ancient Greek, and studied Aristotle with a Christian theologian. Al-Farabi wrote over a hundred treatises, including influential commentaries on logic and science, melding Aristotle with other philosophical strains and seeking to reconcile it all with Islamic principles. He wrote on sociology, math, psychology, and music too. He allegedly played music so well he could move people to tears at will. Islamic philosophers regarded him as the "second teacher"—with Aristotle being the first.

When the Seljuks (1055) and then the Mongols (1258) took Baghdad, many of its intellectuals fled. Some found sanctuary at courts in Cairo or Delhi, bolstering those cities as centers of literature and science.

Córdoba Córdoba, and al-Andalus generally, was another creative melting pot of culture. It was less hospitable to Christians than Baghdad was, but welcoming to Jews. Hasdai ibn Shaprut, whom we encountered at the outset of this chapter, oversaw the collaboration of Byzantine Greek, Arab, and Jewish scholars on medical texts. The court gathered intellectuals from all over and employed translators and copyists. A tenth-century emir allegedly had 400,000 books. The city had 70 libraries and innumerable booksellers, which startled Christian visitors unaccustomed to such devotion to literature. Alvaro de Córdoba, a Jewish convert to Christianity in the ninth century, lamented:

> My fellow Christians delight in the poems and romances of the Arabs. They study the works of Muslim theologians and philosophers, not to refute them, but to acquire a correct and elegant Arabic style. Alas! The young Christians who are most conspicuous for their talents have no knowledge of literature save Arabic: they read and study Arabic books avidly.

Even after the fall of the Córdoba caliphate in 1031, the city hosted great scholars who blended philosophical traditions from far and wide. Ibn Rushd (also known as Averroes), a twelfth-century scholar, was born in Córdoba and served courts there, in Seville, and in Morocco. Like al-Farabi, he was a polymath and an interpreter of Aristotle. He was perhaps the pre-eminent philosopher of al-Andalus, a champion of rationalist thought who occasionally got himself into trouble with religious authorities. Maimonides, also born and educated in Córdoba, wrote in Arabic and became the most influential Jewish philosopher of his time. He melded Aristotle's logic with Jewish teachings. The learning of both Ibn Rushd and Maimonides would soon become influential in intellectual circles in Christian as well as Islamic lands.

Court Culture A Persian miniature showing touches of Chinese influence. It is one of several that illustrate a 1249 copy of the Persian poet al-Ferdawsi's epic poem *Book of Kings*.

Mongol and Il-Khanid Court Culture The Mongols, for all their destruction, also stirred up a tasty intellectual stew of diverse ingredients. Like the early Arabs, they had minimal formal intellectual traditions of their own to defend, and readily adopted bits and pieces from China, India, Iran, and elsewhere. The Mongols sponsored scholars, artisans, artists, and poets but didn't indulge in the fine arts much themselves until they settled down. They liked to assemble religious scholars of all traditions and hear them debate. They encouraged the transfer of technology, techniques, and scientific knowledge from China to Iran (e.g., acupuncture) and Iran to China (e.g., astronomy) and throughout their domains. The cobalt blue dye that distinguishes Chinese porcelain came from Iranian artisans about 1325.

The courts of the Mongol successor states, especially the Il-Khanids based in Tabriz in Iran, became important sponsors of the arts and sciences. Their court artists refined the tradition of miniature painting, incorporating Chinese influences. They (and their successors) supported astronomers and poets, including some of the Persian-language poets foundational to Iranian literature. Medieval Iran spawned generations of fabulous poets who blended Islamic themes with secular ones, with a notable emphasis on love and wine. Some lived shortly before the Mongol invasions, such as al-Firdawsi and Omar Khayyam, some such as Sa'di during the Mongol storm, and others such as Hafez afterward.

Sa'di (ca. 1210–1291) spent most of his adult life as a wandering refugee fleeing Mongols, which gave him a chance to experience the diversity of peoples, including Muslims, Jews, Christians, Buddhists, and Hindus of dozens of small sects. A translation of his verse celebrating the underlying unity of humankind is now inscribed on the United Nations building in New York:

> Human beings are members of a whole,
> In creation of one essence and soul.
> If one member is afflicted with pain,

Other members uneasy will remain.
If you've no sympathy for human pain,
The name of human you cannot retain!

Medieval Paris Like Tabriz, medieval Paris was a capital of culture. In Carolingian times, monasteries had served as preserves of the high culture of Roman antiquity, employing scribes whose only innovations were copying errors. But in the eleventh and twelfth centuries, with translations of Arab scholars from Spain reaching western Europe, a more creative era followed. Thomas Aquinas (ca. 1225–1274), an Italian churchman, studied and taught in Paris. Despite failing his first theological exams, he became one of Catholicism's great philosophers, drawing on translations of Ibn Rushd (Averroes) to write commentaries on Aristotle. Just as al-Farabi and Ibn Rushd tried to reconcile Aristotle and Islam, so Aquinas sought to build bridges between Aristotle and Christianity. He did it so artfully, defending Christian tenets against possible logical objections, that the church made him a saint half a century after his death.

A century later, Christine de Pizan (ca. 1363–1429), another Italian from an educated family, made her intellectual career in Paris. Widowed at age 25 and beset by grasping lawyers, she turned to writing love poems and ballads to earn her keep and feed her children. She was among the first women ever to make a living as a writer. Wealthy patrons paid her to write about their exploits—usually, daring deeds demonstrating religious piety and chivalry toward women. These poems and songs formed part of an oral culture as well, recited by professionals called troubadours. She soon got involved in literary controversies and began to write more serious works about politics and society, including law, statecraft, and military affairs. She was especially interested in the proper role of women. She argued that male writers demeaned women and took the biblical story of Eve as temptress too much to heart, and that in fact women typically have greater nobility of character than men. In her early work she too was (indirectly) heir to Islamic culture, not the interpreters of Aristotle so much as the Persian poets whose tales of love and adventure helped advance the tradition of troubadour balladry in Europe.

Christine de Pizan An early fifteenth-century French miniature shows the author at work in her study, accompanied by a canine friend.

Universities Aquinas worked at the University of Paris and Christine de Pizan at the French royal court. Courts had long housed intellectuals and artists all around the world. Universities, however, were new. Al-Azhar opened in tenth-century Cairo.

European ones opened in the twelfth century—Bologna, Paris, and Oxford were among the earliest—and by 1400 Europe had more than 40. They all used Latin even though it was no one's native tongue. At first, they operated under the authority of the Pope; but by 1241 through teachers' strikes they had become more independent and self-governing. Bologna, uniquely, was run by students, who could fine professors who turned up late for their own lectures.

European **universities** taught theology, law, medicine, and philosophy, a broader approach to learning than that which had prevailed in monasteries. A degree in philosophy required one to two years' study, and one in medicine six or eight. Theology was the least popular subject. No women were allowed in universities. They had to seek education elsewhere, typically in their homes, as Christine de Pizan did.

Universities firmly established the principle of debate and dispute as the avenue to knowledge and wisdom. Professors and students followed ideas where logic and inclination took them, sometimes clashing with the official positions of the church. That led to trouble at times, but the mobility of scholars made it harder for any bishop or king to clamp down on unorthodox thought. The comparative freedom of universities helped Christian Europe to attain a sophistication in science and the arts that previously had been scarce. Their debt to the intellectual production of Islamic centers of learning—Baghdad, Córdoba, Cairo, and many others—was enormous. Italian universities also benefited from contact with Greek scholars in Byzantine centers.

The intellectual and artistic awakening of western Europe in the thirteenth century was remarkable. Leonardo Fibonacci (ca. 1170–1250) traveled from Pisa in Italy to North Africa as a boy and later studied math in the Arab world. He did more than anyone else to introduce Arabic numerals to Europe. He sparked an explosion of work in mathematics that never would have happened had Europeans stuck with Roman numerals. Math helped make it easier to build the magnificent cathedrals that after 1150 dominated the skyline of dozens of cities. To build a structure 160 feet (50 m) tall like Beauvais Cathedral in northern France (begun 1225), you need reliable calculations about load-bearing columns.

By 1400, European mathematicians, architects, jurists, poets, accountants, mining engineers, and shipbuilders had learned enough, much of it from Muslim Spain or Greek Byzantium, that they no longer felt awed when exposed to the sophistication of Granada, Cairo, or Constantinople.

New Currents in Religion

After 800, religion remained the main framework for intellectual and cultural life in the western end of Eurasia as elsewhere. In the centuries after 800, both Islam and Christianity expanded geographically and attracted many new converts. Islam stretched into Central Asia and southern Russia, along the East African coast, and across the Sahara into West Africa's Sahel. Christianity reached into Scandinavia, eastern Europe, and

Russia. In Spain, Sicily, Syria, Anatolia, the Levant, and elsewhere, the two religions shared space—often smoothly, sometimes not.

As both religions expanded and intermingled, their followers incorporated new features. Some West African Islamic practices, such as women's dress, offended Ibn Battuta in the 1350s. Christians were horrified by paganism in the conduct of Celtic harvest festivals in Ireland such as Samhain, the root of Halloween when witches and other spirits cavort after dark.

In response to challenges from popular religion and the educated elites who embraced the teachings of Aristotle and Plato, both the Catholic Church and the Byzantine (Greek Orthodox) Church took pains to defend dogmas and standardize rituals. The two churches had split officially in 1054 and drifted apart when the Crusaders sacked Constantinople in 1204. But both employed missionaries and monasteries to try to spread approved belief and behavior. The increasingly assertive Papacy waded deeply into European politics to try to impose its views. Non-conformists, increasingly, became defined as heretics, suitable for persecution or execution. The church often permitted, and at times encouraged, assaults on Jews, notably in fourteenth-century Spain.

In Islamic domains, many rulers and the religious scholars they allied with also sought to enforce orthodoxies. Although in Islam there was no church, no Pope, no patriarch, and thus no strong institutional base from which to promote standardization within the community of Muslims, any ruler could try to do it. Many did. Sunni caliphs, emirs, and sultans energetically persecuted Shi'a communities. Shi'a states, such as Fatimid Egypt, sometimes returned the favor. The Il-Khanids, after accepting Islam, ruthlessly purged their domains in Iran and Central Asia of Buddhist influences, turning temples into mosques and driving out those suspected of Buddhist persuasions. In the West African Sahel, reformers periodically tried to enforce orthodox forms of Islam beginning with the Almoravids in the 1070s.

But religious clampdown was a losing game. As authorities tried to establish their preferred versions of Islam and Christianity, they lost the allegiance of millions. The worldly compromises (such as accumulation of wealth and power) made by the church and Islamic leaders offended many true believers for whom the attraction of religion was its other-worldliness and (in the Christian case) its embrace of poverty. Thus many new heresies arose and older ones found new followers, especially among people eager for a direct, emotional link to God. Religious refugees took their beliefs to new ground. Islamic persecution drove Zoroastrians to India and Manichaeans deep into Asia. Splinter faiths within Shi'a Islam, such as the Druze (whose origins date to the tenth century), found refuge in mountain areas of the Levant.

The Sufi Movement The **Sufi movement** in Islam is one example of popular religion defying official control. It took shape in the ninth century among people who preferred a more mystical, personal, intense form of religious devotion to the scholarly, legalistic, and ritualized traditions of Islam. Sufis, typically from the poorer classes,

Sufism Followers of the Sufi movement perform an expressive dance of spiritual ecstasy during a religious service in this illustration created by a fifteenth-century Persian artist.

scorned finery: *suf* means "wool" in Arabic, and the first Sufis wore woolen garments, not the cottons and silks of scholars and rulers. Sufism spread via missionaries and refugees throughout the world of Islam especially in the thirteenth through the fifteenth centuries—indeed, Sufi missionaries helped Islam win converts especially in India and Africa. Sufis involved song, poetry, and dance in their rituals, and frequently found that only metaphors of first love or drunkenness could express the rapture of their encounters with God. They were normally regarded as heretics by more sedate Muslim authorities, and often persecuted.

Waldensians and Cathars Within Christendom, new currents arose condemning the greed and power-mongering of the Papacy and church. Waldensians cropped up in France in the late twelfth century, urging a return to Jesus's gospel and the embrace of poverty. Cathars, in Italy, France, and Spain, regarded themselves as proper Christians and the church as the work of Satan—and so were branded as heretics. They survived in mountain regions where the power of bishops and kings barely reached. Dissent, cults, and heresy moved the church to ever-sterner efforts to enforce orthodoxy. In 1229, the Pope established the office of the Inquisition, organized to destroy all heresy by launching investigations and holding trials before church officials. Religious dissent was part of the intellectual tumult of the age, inspired both by exchanges within the Old World web and by the worldly compromises of established religions.

That tumult, whether in Baghdad in the ninth to tenth centuries, Spain in the tenth to eleventh, Iran or western Europe in the thirteenth to fourteenth, owed its existence above all to two developments. One was the economic vitality that allowed more people more leisurely lives and supported richer institutions, whether courts or universities, in which intellectual and artistic activity might flourish. The other was the constant friction of ideas among people on the move, the gathering pace of cross-cultural encounters that resulted from trade, pilgrimages, invasions, and refugee flows. This friction took place everywhere, but most heatedly on the geographic frontiers of culture zones, above all where Muslims and Christians mixed.

The Calamitous Fourteenth Century

No amount of philosophical, scientific, and religious study could prepare people to cope with the ecological turmoil of the fourteenth century, a miserable one in the western region of the Old World web. Despite the agricultural revolutions, many people were getting too little to eat; some places experienced catastrophic flooding; and a **plague pandemic** hammered almost every community.

A Starving Time

In northwestern Europe, beginning in 1314, a series of very wet growing seasons waterlogged fields and damaged harvests for eight years. Moreover, a nasty livestock disease—recorded in documents from Ireland to Mongolia—swept through, killing 60 percent of cattle and many sheep. People without reserves of food or money starved. Population in northwestern Europe fell by 5 to 10 percent, and by up to 18 percent in England. After 1322, the bad weather ceased and the animal disease abated. European population rebounded within a few decades.

Then warm, wet weather returned with a vengeance in the summer of 1342. In central Europe, half the average annual rainfall fell in one storm. The Rhine, Danube, and all their tributaries flooded, in some cases rising 30 feet (9 m) above normal. Roiling torrents washed away stone bridges, homes, and livestock. The rain came after four centuries of forest clearance in central Europe had opened the soil to erosion. It took three years for harvests to recover, during which time many people starved. Half the soil erosion of the last millennium in central Europe took place during that one flood.

The Plague

Then the plague hit. Its ravages extended much further than those of the 1342 flood or the harvest failures of 1314–1322. In western Eurasia and North Africa, population fell by 30 to 50 percent in the years 1346–1351. Perhaps other infections contributed, but recent genetic evidence gives a diagnosis of plague. Typically hosted by rodents and their fleas, bubonic plague is highly lethal to humans, killing 60 percent of those it infects, while another form, pneumonic (breath-borne) plague, kills nearly 100 percent. (Today, plague is treatable with antibiotics.)

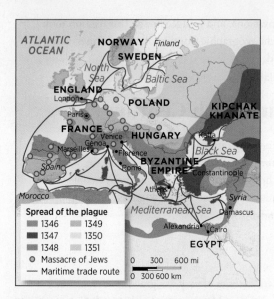

The Spread of the Plague in the Mediterranean Basin and Europe, 1346–1351 By the middle of the fourteenth century, the Old World web was sufficiently well connected and well traveled that routine movements of traders, armies, refugees, and pilgrims could efficiently spread infectious disease. Caravans and ships brought plague from Central Asia to the Mediterranean and then to northern Europe, killing tens of millions within five years.

The plague bacillus (a kind of bacterium) probably came to the western region of the Old World web from wild rodent burrows in Central Asia. Silk Road caravans carried it west. (It might also have moved east into China, and south into India, although we can't be sure.) It arrived on Black Sea shores by 1346 and soon spread throughout Syria, Egypt, and almost all of Europe by 1348. A few spots, especially Finland and regions in Poland, somehow avoided it.

Death and dying were everywhere. Ibn Khaldun, a North African scholar who lost both parents to the plague, wrote in retrospect, "Civilization [he meant the Islamic world] both in the East and the West was visited by a destructive plague which devastated nations and caused populations to vanish." A scholar in Cairo, al-Maqrizi, wrote that funeral processions could not help but collide in the streets. (Cairo probably lost about 40 percent of its population over three years.) In Florence, Italy, the author Giovanni Boccaccio described the gruesome scene:

> Such was the multitude of corpses brought to the churches every day and almost every hour that there was not enough consecrated ground to give them burial.... Although the cemeteries were full they were forced to dig huge trenches, where they buried the bodies by hundreds.

The small kingdom of Sweden lost 50 to 75 percent of its population. The havoc stretched from Egypt to England, and from Spain to Central Asia and perhaps beyond.

No one could cure plague. Many doctors believed it resulted from poisoned air, perhaps from exhalations of the Earth during earthquakes. Some thought bad air from butchered pigs caused it. Ibn Khaldun, who was not a doctor, thought overpopulation poisoned the air.

Most people didn't think in medical terms but saw the plague as divine punishment. Muslims normally believed such a major event must represent Allah's will, and they took Muhammad's sayings as evidence that pious Muslims killed by plague would be assured a place in paradise. In Christian Europe, those who didn't see it as God's wrath usually blamed witches, lepers, or Jews for the plague. In many European towns and cities, Christians who survived the plague massacred those Jews whom the plague had spared. In Islamic societies, there is no evidence of such scapegoating, perhaps because of the strength of the belief that only Allah's will could explain it.

The pandemic of 1346–1351 was only the beginning. For centuries the plague kept returning, carrying off millions more. The recurrence of plague helps explain why population in Europe did not recover until perhaps 1500 or 1550, and in Egypt, not until about 1800. This was a golden age for pathogens and a dismal one for humans.

In many places, the great calamity of the plague, piled on the earlier food crises, was a turning point economically. In Egypt and Iraq, where irrigation systems needed massive manpower, the demographic losses led to spirals of economic decline. Too few laborers meant too little water control and less food. The demand for slaves climbed.

Elsewhere, plague survivors enjoyed improved economic conditions. Scarcity of people in much of Europe, for example, pushed wages higher and rents lower. The changes were important enough that elites tried to legislate lower wages and prevent formerly poor people from dressing in fancy clothes. A spate of popular revolts resulted.

As the plague fastened its grip in the century after 1346, so did the long cold spell called the Little Ice Age, lasting from around 1250 to 1850. Europe shivered through many brutally cold winters, although the average temperature fell only about 1 degree Celsius (1.8 F) from the average of the tenth through the thirteenth centuries. The growing season shortened by about three weeks, and farmers had to abandon cultivation at higher elevations and latitudes. In the worst stretches, summers were too cold for crops to ripen. Climate-related harvest shortfalls occurred frequently, especially in the 1360s, 1410s, and 1430s, bringing widespread hunger and sporadic starvation. Never again would nature—harvest failures, floods, disease—treat the peoples of western Eurasia so brutally as it did between 1315 and 1440.

Conclusion

Between 800 and 1400, the west end of the Old World web—the lands from West Africa to Russia and from Iran to Iceland—survived some harrowing trials. Waves of invaders from the fringes—from deserts, steppes, and the far north—repeatedly assaulted the centers of population and wealth. The damage they inflicted, on property and people, was probably greatest in Iran, Iraq, and Syria. By 1260, the worst of the violence was over. But the plague followed in 1346–1351 and, like waves of invaders, kept coming back. The plague proved far deadlier than invaders, killing a third to a half of the entire region's population within five years. It was the worst demographic catastrophe in world history. Unlike invaders, it did not destroy property, only people, which meant that in some settings survivors were—in economic terms at least—better off than before.

These terrible trials preoccupied everyone who lived through them. They scarcely noticed some happier trends, such as improved efficiency in agriculture. The changes came too slowly to register, but between 800 and 1400 farmers learned how to grow more food per acre with new technologies, crops, and crop rotations. Farmers also brought new land under cultivation, especially by draining swampy lowlands. These agricultural changes, loosely parallel to others going on at the same time in China, helped population to grow, especially in Europe, despite the ravages of war. The devastation of the plague, however, overwhelmed all population growth for at least a century after 1350.

The agricultural revolutions underpinned rising prosperity, commerce, and cities. Revitalized irrigation permitted the emergence of large cities such as Baghdad and Córdoba. A surge of urbanization in Europe, centered on the Low Countries and northern Italy, also rested on improved farming. New ship technology, new financial instruments, and other advances led to humming trade circuits. Those circuits also extended into new terrain, across the Sahara or into Scandinavia. The relative peacefulness of Mongol rule after 1260 provided another boost to commerce.

The new prosperity combined with the faster pulse of cross-cultural interaction brought an intellectual and cultural awakening. The Pax Mongolica helped here too. But even more important was the ongoing dialogue between Muslim and Christian scholars in places such as Spain, Sicily, and Syria. In Europe, the formation of universities provided an encouraging environment for inquiry, usually more free than monasteries or madrassas or royal courts.

By 1400, the Old World web had extended to new lands such as the West African Sahel, Russia, Scandinavia, Iceland, even Greenland (although not for long). Its threads were longer and stronger than in 800. The spread of Christianity and Islam played a large role in tightening far-flung connections, as did refugees and traveling merchants. The world was in effect getting smaller because of these growing links within the Old World web. But the web itself, in 1400 stretching from Japan to Morocco, would soon encompass the world.

||||||||||||||||||||||||||||||||||||||||||||||||||||||||||||||||||||||||||||||||||||||||||||||||||||||||||||||||||||||||||||||||||

Chapter Review

KEY TERMS

Khazaria p. 507

al-Andalus p. 508

Carolingians p. 516

Sahel p. 517

Seljuk Turks p. 524

Vikings p. 527

Crusades p. 531

Mongol western campaigns p. 534

Pax Mongolica p. 537

caravanserais p. 537

universities p. 544

Sufi movement p. 545

plague pandemic p. 547

REVIEW QUESTIONS

1. Why is it best to view Christendom and Islamdom as part of a greater whole?

2. What were the main similarities and differences between the agricultural revolutions in the Mediterranean and Mesopotamia and in northern Europe?

3. What is the pattern in Islamic history that the Abbasid caliphate represents?

4. How did the fall of the Córdoba caliphate lay the foundation for the end of Muslim Spain?

5. What common political problem did the fleeting empires face?

6. How did the successful navigation of the Sahara change the cultural and economic connections of West Africa?

7. In what ways was Mali's state formation and economic base different from Ghana's?

8. What were the main types of Turkification that occurred during this period?

9. Compare and contrast the reasons for mobilization of the Vikings, Crusaders, and horsemen from the steppe and Moroccan desert.

10. What were the main technologies, innovations, and shifts in trade connections that led to economic growth and urbanization?

11. How did wealth, diversity, and mobility spur cultural flowering?

12. What is the connection between the imposition of religious orthodoxy and religious dissent?

13. What were the calamities of the fourteenth century and their effects?

Go to INQUIZITIVE

to see what you've learned—and learn what you've missed—with personalized feedback along the way.

15

The Americas
and Oceania

1000 to 1500

FOCUS QUESTIONS

1. What major empires and cultures developed in the Americas between 1000 and 1500?

2. What were the main developments in the Pacific islands of Oceania between 1000 and 1700?

From the earliest times, part of the standard equipment for states—especially imperial states with big, complex territories and population—was a system of writing. Storage of information was just as essential as storable food. The Inka, a giant imperial state in the Andean region of South America, is highly unusual among imperial states in world history in that it did not use writing.

The Inkas used something else for information storage and retrieval, a system of knotted and colored cords or strings, called a *quipu* (which means "knot" in the Qechua language). The Inkas did not invent *quipus*. They originated centuries before the Inkas organized their state in the fourteenth century. But the Inkas used them more than any of their predecessors.

Today, some 923 *quipus* survive, mainly in museums around the world. Each one includes several cords of llama or alpaca wool, dyed various colors, with knots of different numbers, sizes, and placements. Modern scholars still struggle to figure out exactly what they mean, as they did with Egyptian hieroglyphs, Mayan glyphs, and (unsuccessfully so far) the Indus valley script.

Most of the information kept with *quipus* was of direct interest to the imperial state and was quantitative. *Quipus* recorded population throughout the Inka realm. They also recorded transactions of goods, amounts of tribute paid to the Inkas, and some highlights of the annual calendar. Some *quipus* have up to 2,000 knots. They used a decimal system based on the placement of specific knots, and so could represent large numbers easily. According to persuasive interpretations published recently by an undergraduate, the colors of some *quipus* correspond to the names of individuals and the position of some knots records their social rank.

Those 923 surviving *quipus* illuminate the Inka Empire from within, showing us what the state officials considered important to record and something of the society they ruled. The *quipus* aren't writing and can't represent everything that writing can. But it is amazing what they did do. And future work may reveal that the *quipus* contain even more information than we now imagine.

This chapter, like Chapter 10, presents the American hemisphere together with the island world of Oceania. They were the last two big regions of the world to acquire human population. In this chapter, the saga of human occupation of the Earth reaches its conclusion with the settlement of New Zealand about 1280. The chapter deals with the indigenous histories of these regions before they came into sustained contact with people from other continents. In the case of the Americas, that means before 1492 (in the Caribbean), or 1519 (central Mexico), or the 1770s (Pacific Northwest coast). In Oceania, at least the parts considered here, it means before the 1760s. So, in a few places, the story will continue beyond 1500.

Some common themes unite the Americas and Oceania in the centuries after 1000 CE. Almost everywhere there are signs of population growth; in many cases there is evidence of state

CHRONOLOGY

ca. 800–1300 Settlement of Hawaiian archipelago

ca. 1000 Chamorro begin erecting latte stones in Guam; dependence on salmon increases on Pacific Northwest coast

ca. 1000–1300 Profusion of Polynesian voyages in South Pacific

ca. 1000–1350 Cahokia arises and empties

ca. 1000–1500 Thousands of settlements arise in Amazonia

ca. 1090–1130 Drought and collapse of Chaco Canyon society

ca. 1100–1200 Sweet potato arrives in Polynesia

ca. 1150–1300 Pacific Northwest coastal population drops

By ca. 1200 Hawaiians begin to build irrigation systems

ca. 1275–1300 Mesa Verde and Four Corners region empty out

ca. 1280 Settlement of New Zealand

ca. 1300–1500 Aztec state arises

1325 Aztecs "found" Tenochtitlán

ca. 1400–1532 Inka Empire

1428 Aztecs join Triple Alliance

ca. 1438 Pachakuti organizes resistance against Chanka people and becomes Inka chief

ca. 1460 Inkas begin building cities and monumental architecture

ca. 1450–1500 Oahu unifies into a single kingdom; bird extinction, seal scarcity, and cooling climate in New Zealand

ca. 1450–1700 Etzanoa in American Midwest emerges and disappears; Hawaiian chiefs make themselves kings

building, and in a few cases the creation of large multiethnic empires. In the Americas, there are also signs of growing and tightening interactive webs of trade and cultural exchange, although not on the same scale as in Eurasia and North Africa, which in this period were well integrated as the Old World web. In Oceania the pattern was different from that in the Americas. People spread out, settling distant new islands, and then in many cases became isolated from the rest of humanity. They formed their own tiny webs in places such as New Zealand, Hawaii, and the Mariana Islands, involving tens of thousands of people and eventually in Hawaii hundreds of thousands. But until the 1760s, when European mariners streamed into the Pacific, the islanders remained outside any and all larger webs, where most of humankind resided. They were extremely isolated from other peoples.

That extreme isolation was not quite total, however. After the migrations from Siberia into the Americas across Beringia (beginning at least 15,000 years ago), communication between the Americas and Asia languished. But some people continued to move back and forth across the Bering Strait. After their first settlement, the Pacific Islands and Australia seem to have had even less connection with Asia—and in the period treated in this chapter, none of any consequence. As we shall see, however, evidence exists to suggest—strongly—that Polynesians visited the coast of South America at least once. Otherwise, it appears the Americas and Oceania remained isolated from one another too, distinct worlds, evolving in their own directions free—for the time being—from influences and impacts of the world's largest societies, most powerful states, and most lethal diseases, those of the Old World web.

In the Americas, the absence of wheeled transport and the near-absence of pack animals (the llama in the Andes was the exception) made web building difficult in comparison to Eurasia. There was no analogue for the steppe grasslands easily traversed by horses and camels that served to bring communities together in sustained interaction. In Oceania, huge distances inhibited web building, keeping it to the archipelago scale. Most island chains, except New Zealand, had little variety within them, little complementarity that would stimulate exchange. The limited scale and pace of web building during this period in the Americas and Oceania did not reflect any lack of ambition on the part of elites, but rather greater obstacles in the form of costs, risks, and difficulties of long-distance transport.

In this chapter we will look at some societies, such as the Inka, that built sprawling states, and others that avoided state formation altogether, as in New Zealand and western North America. The state-builders left an outsized imprint on history, partly because of the power that the state apparatus conferred upon their leaders. It could be that by the end of this period, more people in the Americas and Oceania lived inside states than did not—the population history is too hazy to allow a confident judgment. But it is important not to be so dazzled by the Inkas and Aztecs as to ignore the millions who lived in petty chiefdoms, tribes, and other political structures, and who left a less visible mark behind.

The Americas

Three related trends stand out in the history of the Americas between 1000 and 1500. The first is the continued, and probably faster, growth of population. In 1000, the hemisphere had at most 50 million people, and by 1500 perhaps 70 million. These estimates are supported by archeological evidence of wider and denser settlement, spurred by the continued spread of farming and irrigation. Where populations took to farming as their main way of life, their numbers grew while their stature and health deteriorated—as happened in most other such cases in world history.

The second trend is one of increased vulnerability to climate change or military assault. Foraging and hunting peoples could walk elsewhere in search of food or run away from danger. People who had fully committed to agriculture, however, had to stay put in times of drought or brutal cold and hope for better weather in the years ahead. And they had to stand and fight rather than flee in the face of danger, lest they lose everything—lands, homes, tools, seed, and so forth. Evidence from New Zealand to British Columbia to Peru suggests increases in violence during this period, and some unexplained fluctuations in population that might indicate climate crises.

The third trend was toward larger states. The outstanding examples came in the fourteenth and fifteenth centuries: the Inkas and the Aztecs. Their careers should be seen as in parallel, but not as connected. There was nothing in the Americas like the dynamic along the steppe belts of Eurasia where agrarian states and nomad confederacies spurred one another to grow in size and power. What contact existed between Inkas and Aztecs has left next to no trace and was probably entirely trivial. Sometimes similar developments take place at the same time without any connection between them.

The Inkas

In the span of little more than a century, the **Inkas*** built a sprawling empire, the largest in the Americas before European settlement. The Inka state arose in the fourteenth or fifteenth century (precise dates are elusive in Inka history because they didn't reckon time in years, not even for people's ages) and lasted until 1532, when Spanish conquerors took it over. At its height, it contained about 10 to 18 million people. As we saw in Chapter 10, people developed complex societies very early in the Andes and along the Pacific coast of South America. The largest was that called Tiwanaku, which fell into decline before 1000 CE. All the Andean societies exploited the unique ecology of the region, with its teeming marine fisheries, its coastal deserts sliced by icy rivers, its steep slopes soaring up to the snow-capped peaks of the world's second-tallest mountain range. Andean

---

*Also spelled *Incas*, although people in the Andes tend to prefer *Inkas*.

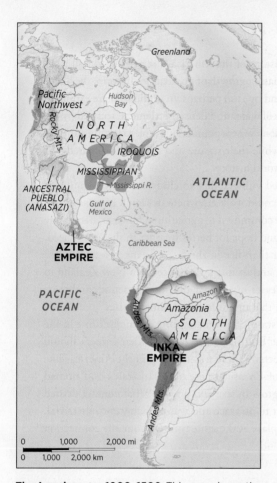

The Americas, ca. 1000–1500 This map shows the locations of peoples and cultures of the Americas considered closely in this chapter. Two of them, the Inka and the Aztec cultures, developed fully fledged empires with many millions of subjects each. Elsewhere, smaller-scale polities were the rule.

people developed intensive farming, including potatoes that could be freeze-dried into *chuño*, a food that stored well over years. Andean peoples also had to get used to natural disasters: earthquakes, landslides, and floods are common there.

The Inkas built on prior traditions and knowledge of how to use the environment. In their region, the seacoast and mountain crests are often less than 70 miles (112 km) apart. In the span of a day or two, one could walk through several ecosystems at different elevations. The equatorial sun made it possible to live at very high altitude, where the air temperature is usually chilly. Nowhere else in the world did so many people live so high up, well over 10,000 feet (3,050 m). A warm spell that lasted from around 1000 until about 1500 probably made it a little easier for the Inkas to produce food surpluses and build a large empire.

Andean social organization generally featured lineages, called *ayllus*, which elsewhere might be called clans or tribes. Andeans exploited the region's "verticality" by placing people from a given lineage in communities at every elevation. Thus every *ayllu* could hope to draw from the rich fisheries of the coast, the irrigated farming of the lowlands and foothills, and the llama and alpaca pastures of the highlands. This arrangement is sometimes called the **vertical archipelago**. Although it predated the Inkas, they developed it on a larger scale than any of their Andean predecessors because, at the apex of their power, they controlled much more territory. At its height, the Inka Empire stretched over 32 degrees of latitude, equal to the distance from Mexico City to Juneau, Alaska, in North American terms. In total area, it was among the world's largest empires in 1500.

Rise of the Inkas The early career of the Inkas is murky. Their oral traditions suggest that they migrated, perhaps from the Lake Titicaca region, to what became their capital at Cuzco, about 1200. It was then no more than a village, and the Inkas a people of no great importance, one of many in the region. But at some point, perhaps in the 1430s, they began their remarkable imperial expansion. Oral traditions say that a neighboring people, the Chanka, attacked them. The Inka leaders fled, except for a younger son who organized fierce and successful resistance. Outmaneuvering the rest of his family, he became the next chief (or Sapa Inka) perhaps in 1438. He took the name Pachakuti, which in Qechua—the main language of the Inkas and the Andes—means "shaker of the world."

Under Pachakuti and the next two rulers, the empire underwent a lightning rise, comparable to the instant empires of the Mongols or the Arabs. The Inkas, however, built theirs in much more challenging terrain and by different methods. Unlike the Mongols and the Arabs, they had no cavalry, for example, and no way to travel a hundred miles in a day.

For 30 years or more, until his death about 1472, Pachakuti oversaw the expansion of his authority through conquest, intimidation, and diplomacy. He or his sons approached local elites with offers they could not easily refuse. They offered the elites prestige goods, young women, and positions of honor within the growing Inka Empire, in exchange for a regular flow of whatever their region could produce—cloth, fish, potatoes—and laborers for the Inka elite. Local elites usually saw an advantage to themselves in these arrangements, especially because the alternative was war and likely defeat and death. Over a generation or two, most local leaders in effect swapped their independence and sovereignty for prosperous roles as protected vassals of the Inkas.

Their subjects paid a price. The flow of cloth, fish, potatoes, and labor to the Inkas required thousands of men and women to work for them, often far from home. This labor service requirement seems to have grown with time; by 1500, it often amounted to several months' work each year. The common folk got little out of these arrangements, whereas their lords, now vassals of the Inkas, got something in return for their subservience. Maintaining the allegiance of these vassals required the Inkas to dole out vast quantities of gifts, which in turn required constant production of fine clothing, jewelry, ceramics, and whatever the local lords valued. That included young women, some of whom the Inkas gathered together in special homes, called *aqllawasi*, where they were obliged to weave cloth and brew maize beer until the right political moment arose. Then they might be given to a local lord in exchange for his submission or continued loyalty.

The price of resistance to Inka expansion could be greater still. Andean chronicles tell of a coastal people, the Guarcos, who held out for three or four years until tricked into abandoning their fortifications, whereupon Inka warriors seized them. Many of the Guarcos were hanged—in the Qechua language, *guarcona* now means "hanging." Their valley was colonized by people loyal to the Inkas. Another coastal people who

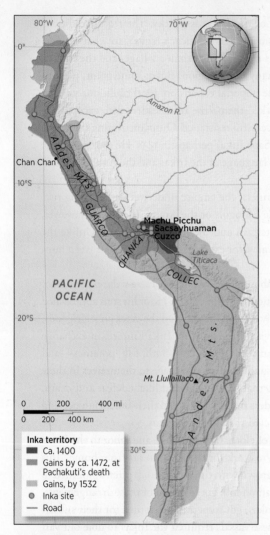

80°W
70°W
0°
Amazon R.
Chan Chan
10°S
Andes Mts.
GUARCO
Machu Picchu
Sacsayhuaman
Cuzco
CHANKA
Lake
Titicaca
COLLEC
PACIFIC
OCEAN
20°S
Mt. Llullaillaco▲
Andes Mts.
0   200   400 mi
0   200   400 km
30°S
Inka territory
▪ Ca. 1400
▪ Gains by ca. 1472, at
   Pachakuti's death
▫ Gains, by 1532
◉ Inka site
— Road

The Inka Empire, ca. 1400–1532 The Inkas came from the area around Lake Titicaca but made Cuzco, high in the Andes, their center around 1200. This map shows their political expansion into an empire in the fifteenth and early sixteenth centuries.

tried to resist Inka power and were defeated, the Collec, met a sterner fate: the Inkas killed their entire adult male population. A few such bloody conquests convinced the majority of local leaders to become Inka vassals peacefully. With this combination of generosity to elites who submitted, and brutal violence aimed at those who resisted, the Inka state expanded quickly after 1440.

Rebellions abounded nonetheless. The empire did not last long enough to replace local identities and loyalties with an imperial Inka one. Most of the local elites who accepted subservience to the Inkas chafed under Inka rule. Over time, more did so because the Inka overlords demanded ever more from their vassals.

Statecraft While skilled at violence, the Inkas were also experts in soft power. Pachakuti and his descendants claimed to be sons of the sun, long the object of worship by Andean peoples. The Inkas worked hard to enforce the use of their language, Qechua, throughout their domains. Religion, language, and culture underpinned their power, reducing the necessity to use violence. They constructed an elaborate cult of the ruler, the Sapa Inka, who commanded worship as a god. His underlings tried to ensure that no ordinary person could touch anything that the Sapa Inka had touched. Accordingly, the Sapa Inka's clothing, food scraps, even the saliva he had spat out, were collected and burnt in an annual ritual.

From the 1460s, the Inkas also built cities and monumental architecture to overawe their subjects and express their religious devotion. Cuzco, at 11,000 feet (3,400 m), acquired a giant ceremonial space, a rectangle the size of eight or nine football fields

Inka Architecture Monumental Inka buildings include the palace complex at Machu Picchu (left), built for the emperor Pachakuti in the fifteenth century; and the citadel at Sacsayhuaman (right), near the Inka capital of Cuzco, constructed from enormous boulders in the thirteenth century.

and covered in sand carried up from Pacific beaches. The Inkas used this plaza for ritual meals and big festivals where with food and drink they publicly demonstrated their generosity to those who showed them loyalty. Somehow, without draft animals, Inka engineers and laborers erected walls with giant blocks of stone cut so precisely they needed no mortar. According to one sixteenth-century Spanish visitor, the head of a pin could not fit between blocks of stone on one temple. Some 20,000 laborers worked for 20 years to build the Inka capital city. The Inkas built several other cities, usually with large plazas for ceremonial events. Their architecture tended to be simple and somber, with occasional friezes carved into the stone blocks; but unlike other Andean peoples, they used no statuary. The buildings themselves, their geometry and their settings, were impressive enough.

City building and monumental architecture were part of the program for just about every empire in world history. But Inka statecraft included a less common practice, called *mitmaq*. This amounted to the forced migration of peoples in the interest of the state. The Inkas routinely moved loyal populations into areas where they could counterbalance others with suspect allegiances; they also transplanted rebellious groups to lands where they would be surrounded by reliably loyal subjects. The Guarcos lost their valley to settlers brought in this fashion. Few if any other empires pushed people around like this as regular policy, although many, such as the Assyrians, did it from time to time.

In addition to cities and monumental architecture, the Inkas constructed a remarkable system of roads. Previous societies had built local roads and bridges in the rugged terrain of the Andes. But the Inkas built many more and unified them all into a single network. This enabled them to move goods around their domain more rapidly, essential for the politics of generosity they practiced. And, when necessary, their armies could march swiftly to any corner of the realm where generosity did not bring the compliance the Inkas wanted. The road network also helped with the frequent transfers of population the Inkas engineered. Ordinary people not on state business were not to use the roads. In all, the Inka road system stretched 20,000 to 30,000 miles (32,000 to 48,000 km)—about half the length of the Roman road network at its maximum extent—including two grand north-south trunk routes extending most of the length of the empire, one in the mountains and one below on the coastal plain. Many shorter roads ran east-west, linking the two trunk routes, often following the routes of river valleys.

Enormous labor went into building and maintaining these roads. Some were equipped with drainage ditches, and many were paved with stone. Often, the roads had to cross over rivers and gorges. Log bridges and, for long spans, rope bridges (with ropes made of vines and twigs woven together—"as thick as a leg" as one Spaniard put it) numbered in the hundreds and often had to be rebuilt after floods. The Inkas also built inns at intervals along the roads and kept them supplied with all that official travelers might need—a system similar to the state-sponsored caravanserais of Central and Southwest Asia. Theirs was an elaborate infrastructure of empire.

The Inkas used all these devices—the *quipus* we encountered at the beginning of this chapter, roads, the Qechua language, the relocation of peoples, the cult of the Sapa Inka, their "generosity," and as a last resort their army—to build and maintain their enormous empire.

Like most monarchies, the Inkas often had succession struggles that could escalate into civil war. They traced descent mainly through maternal ancestry, and Andean rulers traditionally chose a successor from among their sisters' sons, as was done in the West African kingdom of Ghana. But some rulers died before selecting a successor, leaving the field open to all his nephews and perhaps his sons as well—who could number in the dozens. Perhaps as a response to this problem, Pachakuti's successor, Thupa Inka, initiated a tradition by which the ruler married his sister (as many Egyptian pharaohs had done). This practice invited genetic defects in one's children, but it had the advantage of making some of the Sapa Inka's offspring doubly royal, and it enabled rulers to pass the throne to their own sons rather than their nephews. Thupa Inka had many wives and more than 60 sons. Succession struggles continued, playing a central role in the end of the empire beginning in 1532.

Economy and Religion The Inka economy was bound up with the reciprocity principles of the empire's statecraft. The Inkas did not use money, and markets played only a tiny role in their economy. The Inka state organized production to a remarkable degree, requiring local lords and lineages to provide legions of male laborers for months at a time in a system called the *mita*. They might work as road builders, soldiers, miners, fishermen—whatever the government wanted and wherever it wanted them. The state also commandeered some farmland from local lords, and herds of llamas from highland peoples. This arrangement allowed the Inka state to collect all the goods it needed to keep its storehouses brimming with foodstuffs, clothing, weaponry, and everything else required to supply its armies and convince almost every local lord to accept the Sapa Inka's generosity in return for submission. But the state showed an insatiable appetite for goods and labor. The Inka rulers felt enormous pressure to squeeze more production out of their population, to make people build more terraces and grow more maize and potatoes, brew more beer, raise more llamas, weave more cloth, and when this was not enough, to conquer new lands.

Spiritual life revolved around worship of a sun god, Inti, and an earth and fertility goddess, Pachamama—both of which were important throughout the Andes. Several other deities resonated locally, sometimes in a single valley or even a single household. Like many empires, the Inkas typically incorporated gods or other features of the religion of conquered peoples into their own. But they also tried to make sure conquered peoples followed Inka religious traditions—notably, worship of the Sapa Inka. Ten elite families that could claim royal ancestry oversaw proper observances of rituals and ceremonies. Religious practice included the Andean tradition of occasional sacrifice of children and llamas. Andean peoples regarded children as especially suited to intervene with ancestral spirits, and in difficult moments sometimes ritually slaughtered them. One site on the Peruvian coast near the city of Chan Chan, the capital of a polity called Chimú, yielded remains of 140 children ages 5 to 14, together with 200 llamas, killed around 1425 CE, probably at the time of a giant El Niño event. Inka child sacrifices also occurred on smaller scales involving a few youngsters, usually 4 to 10 years old, who were left on mountaintops to die after being fortified with maize beer. It was, apparently, an honor to be sacrificed in this way.

The Inka Empire was one of the two largest polities in the Americas before 1492. It formed quickly, and in extremely difficult terrain, but exerted great power from the 1430s to 1532. Then, as we shall see in a later chapter, its tendency to civil wars over succession to the throne became its undoing.

Amazonia

Large populations existed in South America outside the reach of the Inka Empire. They did not leave behind grand temples or networks of roads, nor did they develop writing. So we don't know as much about them. But they were numerous even if less visible than the Inkas.

In the rain forest of Amazonia, for example, a space as large as the lower 48 states of the United States, millions of people scratched livings from the thin, acid, and leached soils, raising crops amid the trees. Most of their domesticated plants, of which they had more than 100, were tree crops, but their staple was the root crop bitter manioc, or cassava. They also fished in Amazonia's many rivers and harvested fruits, nuts, and berries from its wide variety of wild trees.

People had lived in Amazonia already for thousands of years when, perhaps in the first few centuries CE, they began to create their own soils by intentionally gathering wastes of all sorts—the equivalent of compost piles—to enrich the naturally infertile soils. Archeologists have a name for these patches of enhanced soil: **dark earth**. They are chock full of nutrients. On these soils, people could raise crops of maize and so-called sweet manioc, a variety that cannot prosper in ordinary Amazonian soils. This technique made farming more rewarding in Amazonia and food supply less of a constraint on population growth. In the five centuries between 1000 and 1500, archeological evidence—charcoal—shows great frequency of fire, which means people were burning forest in order to plant crops. Archeology also shows a remarkable extent of dark earth, most of it on bluffs overlooking major rivers, where people lived in order to fish and use the water as their highways (as they still do in Amazonia today). In all, dark earth might cover 3 to 10 percent of Amazonia, which doesn't sound like much, but 10 percent would be about the size of France or Texas.

Scholars used to think that Amazonia was almost empty of people until modern times and that its forests were a pristine wilderness. What few people existed, scholars thought, were mobile, either hunter-gatherers or slash-and-burn farmers. But recent archeology shows how misguided that view was. By the period 1000–1500, the people of Amazonia had founded thousands of enduring settlements numbering up to 2,500 people each—large villages or small towns by global standards—in all, home to perhaps 5 to 10 million people. The first outsider to sail down the Amazon, a Spaniard in 1541, wrote that he saw many villages "less than a crossbow shot" apart on the river's banks. Thousands of villages were connected to one another, mainly by river-going canoes. Amazonia had its own loose web of connections. Much more loosely, these villages were also connected to societies outside of Amazonia, including the Inkas over the passes of the Andes.

Mesoamerica: Toltecs and Aztecs

In the fourteenth and fifteenth centuries, the Aztecs of central Mexico formed what would become the second-largest empire in pre-Columbian America. Like the Inka Empire, it lasted until Spaniards turned up in the early sixteenth century.

In Chapter 10 we saw how central Mexico had hosted complex urban society based at Teotihuacán. After its collapse in the mid-first millennium CE, urban culture diminished until the rise of the Toltecs in the tenth century. They were migrants from the north who built a city of perhaps 40,000 people, Tollan (modern Tula), including pyramids, palaces, and ball courts—squarely in the Mesoamerican tradition. Their wealth, decorative arts, military prowess, and religious devotion apparently commanded respect among neighboring peoples. The Aztecs used to say of people who excelled in every domain that they "had a Toltec heart." For unknown reasons,

CONSIDERING THE EVIDENCE

Aztec Wealth

Members of the Aztec confederation and other Nahuatl-speakers shared a myth that their people had migrated to the Basin of Mexico from Tollan (modern Tula), a city in Hidalgo, Mexico, built by Toltecs in the tenth century. The Aztecs not only imitated Toltec art but also dismantled sculptures and looted ceramics from Tula to bring back home. In the Aztec myths recorded in the *Florentine Codex* after the Spanish conquest, Nahuatl-speakers described the Toltec government, economy, and religion as ideal.

This Quetzalcoatl they considered as a god.... He was prayed to in olden times there at Tula....

And the Tolteca [Toltecs], his vassals, were highly skilled. Nothing was difficult when they did it, when they cut the green stone and cast gold, and made still other works of the craftsman of the feather worker.... [N]owhere was [too] distant... so very quickly they went that they were called "those who walked the whole day without tiring." And there was a hill [where] the crier mounted...; everywhere was heard what he said.... [T]hey knew what Quetzalcoatl had commanded the people....

Of no value was food.... It is said that the gourds [squash] were each exceedingly huge; some were quite round. And the ears of maize [corn]... could only be embraced in one's arms. ... And also the varicolored cotton grew: chili-red, yellow, pink, brown, green blue, verdigris color, dark brown, ripening brown, dark blue, fine yellow, [and] coyote colored cotton.... All of these came forth exactly so; they did not dye them.

And there dwelt all [varieties] of birds of precious feather: the lovely cotinga, the resplendent trogon, the troupial, the roseate spoonbill. And all the various birds sang very well.... And all the green stones, the gold were not costly.... In very many places there was chocolate.... They lacked nothing in their homes. Never was there famine.

...And this Quetzalcoatl also did penances. He bled the calf of his leg to stain thorns with blood. And he bathed at midnight.... [T]he offering priests took their manner of conduct from [his] life. By it they established the law of Tula. Thus were the customs established here in Mexico.

Questions for Analysis

1. Besides gold, what did the Nahuatl-speakers who told this story associate with wealth?
2. What did they admire about Quetzalcoatl's mythical rule?
3. What does this myth about the Toltecs reveal about the things that Nahuatl-speakers valued?

Source: *Florentine Codex: Book 3, The Origin of the Gods*, Second Edition, trans. Arthur J. O. Anderson and Charles E. Dibble. Monographs for the School of American Research (Salt Lake City, 1978).

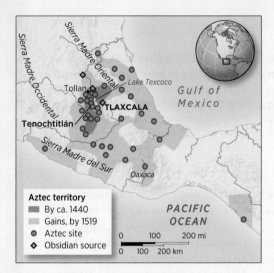

The Aztec Empire, ca. 1440–1519 The Aztecs, or Mexica, arrived in the Basin of Mexico from the north and by 1440 had begun an expansion into neighboring lands. By 1500, they ruled over 4 to 7 million people from their capital at Tenochtitlán. They dominated Mesoamerica and its 15 to 20 million inhabitants but never subdued one neighboring people, the Tlaxcalans. Obsidian, quarried at sites in the Basin of Mexico, was used for weapons and sharp-edged tools and was a major export of the Aztecs.

Tollan collapsed in the mid-twelfth century. The remaining Toltecs migrated once more, to the shores of Lake Texcoco in the Basin of Mexico, where they soon acquired the Aztecs as neighbors.

Origins The legends of the Aztecs, or Mexica, say they came from a place called Aztlan.[†] Their language, Nahuatl (or Nahua), is closest to languages spoken in northern Mexico and the southwestern United States, so it's likely that they migrated from there southward to the Basin of Mexico. The Basin—the region around today's Mexico City—is saucer-shaped, sits about 7,500 feet (2,250 m) above sea level, and is surrounded, except to the north, by much taller volcanic peaks. When the Aztecs arrived in the thirteenth to the fourteenth centuries, several interconnected lakes and swamps lay in the Basin. The Basin had fish in its waters, wildlife on its slopes, and obsidian rock everywhere, which for people relying on stone tools was a vital resource. At first, the newcomers had to accept dominion by other peoples and usually lived in the swamps and other undesirable areas on the shores of Lake Texcoco.

The Aztecs struggled for position among people already around the lake and its main island; but through war, diplomacy, and clever marriage alliances, they did well in the fierce politics of the Basin of Mexico. In 1325, they "founded" their capital city, **Tenochtitlán**—which was actually already inhabited. Until 1428, they were subordinate to other peoples in the Basin of Mexico, but in that year they joined with two other vassal peoples to create a triple alliance and turned the tables on their overlords. Thereafter, the Aztecs were the political leaders of the region. By 1440, the Triple Alliance had begun to make conquests outside the Basin of Mexico.

[†] The term *Aztec* was invented in the nineteenth century by a German geographer, Alexander von Humboldt. I use it because of its familiarity, although modern scholars sometimes prefer the term *Mexica*.

By 1500, they controlled most of central Mexico, and almost everyone else had to pay them tribute.

Statecraft A series of vigorous leaders led the Aztec conquests. Their empire grew quickly, like that of the Inkas, especially under kings guided by a political genius called **Tlacélel** (ca. 1398–1480). He was a successful advisor and general, and a brilliant propagandist. He ordered that the Aztecs destroy their enemies' historical records, which was standard practice among victors, but also their own, which was unique. That history, he felt, needed more heroic deeds and prestigious ancestry. So he invented a new past for the Aztecs—one with glorious ancestors, mainly the lords of the ancient city of Teotihuacán and the Toltec city of Tollan. He declared the Aztecs to be the linchpin of the cosmic order, responsible for its smooth working.

In particular, he recast Aztec religion so that the Aztecs alone had the sacred duty of providing the reigning sun god (that job rotated among deities) with *chalchihuatl*, the mysterious force of life, without which the sun would not continue to shine and all would soon go dark. That force of life came in the form of flowers, the first fruits of the harvest, and sacrificed human beings. So the continued harmony of the cosmos required that the Aztecs, as the people of the sun, obtain a steady supply of victims. Human sacrifice featured in many ancient cultures around the world, including all the large-scale ones of the Americas. In Mesoamerica, the tradition of sacrifice went back thousands of years. Men, women, and children of all ranks of life could be sacrificed (and some volunteered for it), but in practice the Aztecs needed prisoners of war, some of whom—the numbers are unclear—became sacrificial victims. The welfare of the world depended on continual conquests by the Aztecs and their allies: for the sun to continue to deliver its bounty, the Aztecs would have to continue to secure prisoners for sacrifice. Their religious worldview made the Aztecs militaristic.

Religion was only part of the spur to conquest. Further motivation came with a terrible drought and famine in the years 1450–1453. Aztec rulers responded by extending their domain over broader landscapes, lowlands as well as highlands, reducing the drought risk. By 1502, their reach extended throughout Mesoamerica, from Atlantic to Pacific coasts, and south to Oaxaca. One people in what is now Guatemala also paid them tribute.

The Aztecs could not dominate everyone, and like most conquerors they usually preferred to prevail without fighting. If local elites agreed to pay enough tribute, the Aztecs left them in peace. Their empire was less intrusive and meddlesome than the Inkas'. But from 1470 onward, the Aztecs were usually at war. They were mired in a stalemate with their neighbors to the west, and frequently they were fighting the people of Tlaxcala, a Nahuatl-speaking group like the Aztecs, who held out although surrounded by an Aztec-led alliance.

The formidability of the Aztecs rested on a robust economy, a large population, an efficient military, and an impressive culture.

Economic Life　Agriculture formed the heart of the economy. Maize, beans, and squash—the Three Sisters of North American farming—were the main crops, but the Aztecs raised peppers, tomatoes, and avocados too. The wetlands provided fish, turtles, and wildfowl. The Aztecs had only dogs and turkeys as domesticated animals. Fortunately for them, earlier peoples had developed the highly productive and reliable raised field agriculture, in which farmers piled up muck from the swamps into islands on which to plant their crops (see Chapter 10 for details). The Aztecs, who called the raised fields *chinampas*, refined this technique and extended it to many more lakes and swamps, multiplying the size of harvests in the Basin of Mexico. Only the deepest droughts could bring food shortages thanks to this system. Canoes, and porters using causeways, carried food into the capital city, Tenochtitlán. Human wastes, to be used as fertilizer, made the reverse trip from city to *chinampa*.

With improved food supply, especially after the droughts of the early 1450s were behind them, the Basin of Mexico was a hothouse of population growth. That provided Aztec rulers with plenty of male labor for the construction of temples, pyramids, causeways, and more *chinampas*—and with more soldiers. It also led to a larger female labor force and to growing quantities of cloth, spun by women and surrendered as tribute, which Aztec rulers used to pay for whatever they required. Cloth and cacao beans served as money in the Aztec economy.

The Aztecs built on the market traditions of Mesoamerica. Most major settlements had an outdoor marketplace open once a week (the Aztecs used a five-day week). The biggest, at Tlatelolco in the capital, was open every day and attracted 25,000 people daily. One could find cotton cloth, copper axes, aromatic woods, maguey syrup, obsidian knives, salt, turkeys, tortillas, bird feathers, rabbit fur, and—one of Mesoamerica's gifts to the world—chocolate. Tlatelolco's market must have offered a swirl of colors, sounds, and smells. Although Aztec society had a guild of long-distance merchants, most items in the markets came from nearby. Within the Basin of Mexico, goods could often move by canoe. Elsewhere, porters carried them, often over rugged terrain. The Aztecs had neither wheeled vehicles nor beasts of burden.

Aztec society included plenty of craft specialists whose work supplied these markets. With time and imperial expansion, the division of labor and degree of specialization increased. Preparing feathers and obsidian blades, for example, became full-time specializations. Cloth making was a part-time job. Men (who spent most of their time farming) prepared thread from cotton or agave (cactus), and women wove it into fabric. By 1500, the Aztecs had built one of the world's most market-oriented societies.

In addition to markets, the Aztec economy involved obligatory tribute paid by conquered peoples to the Aztec ruling aristocracy. Each province had a different obligation. Some provided laborers. Some, near the frontiers of the empire, provided war captives. Others, close to the capital, sent foodstuffs. The Aztec elite apparently had a sweet tooth, taking as tribute 15,000 jars of honey annually. Most provinces provided mainly cloth. Aztec documents show that 22 of 30 provinces also sent bird feathers as tribute to Tenochtitlán.

Archeological digs reveal that the lives of ordinary people worsened as the Aztec Empire grew. More and more production went to the urban elite and the army, leaving less and less for common folk. Houses, made of adobe brick, typically had a few ceramics, obsidian tools, and grinding stones. Earlier ones had often had some jewelry and perhaps bronze tools as well.

The Aztec economy, like those of most complex societies in world history, supported a few people lavishly and a lot of people in misery. Aztec social structure, comparatively straightforward, featured a two-fold division: a small

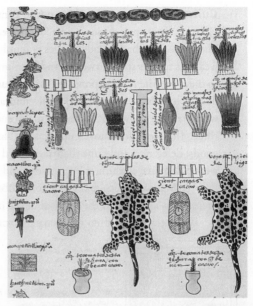

Imperial Tribute A 1553 Aztec book recorded quantities of luxury commodities—feathers, leopard skins, cocoa beans—paid in tribute to Aztec rulers. The quantities are recorded both in pictograms and (for the benefit of the king of Spain, which had conquered Mexico some 30 years before) in Spanish translation.

ruling elite responsible for administration, and a mass of common people who did all the manual labor. Life was short. Evidence from skeletons implies that death rates and birth rates were very high by global standards.

The capital city of Tenochtitlán ranked as one of the world's great cities, much larger as of 1500 than Rome or the Inka capital of Cuzco. It held 150,000 to 300,000 people, which made it larger than any city in China but Beijing. A Spaniard who saw the city in 1519 wrote:

> We were struck with the number of canoes, passing to and from the mainland, loaded with provisions and merchandise.... The noise and bustle of the marketplace below us could be heard almost a league off [a league is about 3 miles], and those who had been at Rome and at Constantinople said, that for convenience, regularity, and population, they had never seen the like.

The Aztec Empire, as of 1500, contained some 4 to 7 million people. The whole region of Mesoamerica, including peoples outside of Aztec control but connected to them by links of trade, politics, and culture, held perhaps 15 to 20 million people.

Culture In many cases, Aztec power came down to the ability to utilize organized violence. Their population and economy enabled the Aztecs to field a large military. The Aztec army had the advantages of numbers and weapons, especially obsidian-edged weapons such as spears, swords, and bows and arrows. Every male owed military service to the state. The Aztecs sponsored military academies, where males ages 15 to 20 learned how to handle weapons, build their endurance, and withstand acute pain. Successful warriors were those who captured many enemies: captives became candidates for sacrifice. These warriors moved up the social hierarchy quickly. They were rewarded with goods, deference, and fame that transferred to their descendants. They were entitled to wear distinctive clothing so everyone would know of their valor. Aztec art and literature lionized brave warriors, many of whom embraced the ideology according to which their success was essential to the survival of the cosmos—a good motivational tool.

While force was often necessary to expand the empire, religion could help hold it together. Like every other empire, the Aztecs sought to persuade subject peoples of their power, their justice, and their status as favorites of the gods. The Aztecs developed a highly complex cosmology that only well-educated priests could have mastered. The sky had 13 levels to it and the underworld 9, while the Earth stood in between. All intersected at the site of a great temple in the heart of Tenochtitlán. The Earth, itself a giant toad, rested on the back of a sea monster. A series of myths helped to explain how this cosmos evolved, as well as important questions such as the origins of the Aztec people, of maize, and of an alcoholic drink made of agave cactus sap, called *pulque*—still popular today in central Mexico. Rituals and sacrifices, done in the proper way at the proper times and regulated by priests and emperors, were expected to keep the cosmos in balance.

The Aztec pantheon was packed with gods and goddesses, and it expanded in ways that helped the empire to grow. Every town, neighborhood, and lineage

Aztec Daily Life The sixteenth-century *Florentine Codex* features numerous illustrations of Aztec daily life, such as these images of peasants harvesting, processing, and storing wheat. The text is in Nahuatl, in a writing system developed by a Spanish priest using the Roman alphabet.

had at least one god, and like Hindu gods they all could appear in different guises, often as animals. The god most venerated by the state—in effect, the tribal god of the Aztec people—was Huitzilopochtli, whose responsibilities included the sun, fire, war, and human sacrifice. Aztec gods, like ancient Greek ones, had kinfolk, suffered from jealousy and temper tantrums, and could be spiteful as well as kindly toward humans. Scholars have identified 144 gods, about two-thirds of them male. In addition to some conventional deities, such as a maize god, a moon goddess, and a god of the underworld, the Aztec pantheon included some distinctive ones, such as a god of feather workers and one who protected drunk people.

The Aztec elite oversaw the construction of monumental architecture worthy of a powerful empire. As elsewhere, such display was useful for religious rituals and for reminding ordinary people of the power of priests and rulers. Aztec ceremonial centers had stone temples decorated with elaborate carvings, often using jaguar, serpent, or eagle motifs to invoke supernatural power. The vicinity of Tenochtitlán included several large pyramids used in religious rituals that helped buttress the political order. Aztec artisans also specialized in ceramics, jade statuettes, wood carving, and colorful feather arrangements that were often used as headdresses. Art and architecture, from the layout of temples to the sequences of feathers, had religious and political meaning, and helped to legitimate the state and elite rule. The last of the Aztec rulers, Moctezuma, had a palace that accommodated about 1,000 people.

The Aztecs developed an extensive literature that built on Mesoamerican traditions. They wrote on paper made from fig tree bark. Their books, long folded sheets of animal skin, are conventionally called codices (sing. codex). Some 61 Mesoamerican codices survive, written by Aztecs or their neighbors. Nowhere else in the Americas produced books, so far as we know. Aztec books contained information on history and deeds of emperors, on tribute and laws, on rituals and gods, on medicine, botany, and poetry. The most important source for Aztec history and culture, the so-called *Florentine Codex*, compiled by a Spanish priest and his Aztec students after the fall of the Aztec Empire, is a comprehensive catalogue of some 1,200 pages.

The earliest Aztec writings used symbols that were either pictures of what they were intended to represent (pictographic) or pictures of things whose names included sounds in Nahuatl that if combined properly conveyed the intended meaning (logographic). So, to convey the sound of the name Ken, an Aztec scribe might draw a pot to indicate the *k* sounds, because the Nahuatl word for "pot" is pronounced ko-mit-el, followed by a bean and then a human head for the next sounds. It was not an easy system to learn, and only a tiny fraction of Aztecs could read. Nonetheless, in the capital, or at least its elite precincts, people recited and wrote poetry. Favorite themes included flowers, death, and the glory of Tenochtitlán.

Aztec science built on Mesoamerican traditions too. Like every pre-modern culture, they used plants as healing agents: the *Florentine Codex* lists 149 and the ailments against which they were used. Modern tests show that about 70 percent of these are actually helpful. The Aztecs were keen astronomers with a special interest in eclipses. Their most sophisticated scientific achievements lay in mathematics. They used a base 20 system and had names for numbers, formed with strings of suffixes, up to 64,000,000. They could perform complex calculations with large numbers.

Society A fair amount of textual and archeological evidence sheds light on family dynamics in Aztec society. It reveals that the broad patterns resembled those found in complex farming societies around the world, but the details were often unique. Aztec families could be simple nuclear families or joint families with several relatives living together, such as the nuclear families of two brothers. Men typically married around age 20 or 22, to brides of about age 12 to 16. Rich men could marry many wives. Divorce was legal in instances when men beat their wives or wives failed either to keep house satisfactorily or to produce children. Adultery invited stern penalties: strangling for women, and crushed skulls for men.

Parents raised children with tough love. That included plenty of lectures about the importance of honesty, industry, and proper conduct. Children who slipped up might expect to be lashed with cactus spines or forced to inhale smoke from sizzling chili peppers. Small children learned their roles and skills from their parents. But at age 15 or so, they began to attend school. Elite families sent their children to the priests' school (*calmecac*) to learn about religion and administration. Everyone else went to a *telpoch-calli* ("house of youth") to learn about war (boys) or handicrafts and child care (girls). Obligatory formal education for everyone is extremely rare in world history, and the Aztecs were among the first to require it.

Gender roles were also typical for complex agrarian societies, although women took part in marketplace culture more than in most places. At birth, baby girls received a broom, a basket, a spindle, and a bowl. Boy babies got tools or weapons. Women were expected to work in the home and its courtyard, spending long hours grinding maize, making tortillas, and weaving cloth. They raised turkeys and gathered the cactus sap needed for *pulque*. A woman's most important role was as mother, and women who died in childbirth were celebrated like fallen warriors. Aztec women did, however, venture into the marketplace and transact business on their own accounts. Some became administrators of marketplaces, responsible for seeing that everyone played fair. They could own property. Women who survived past age 50 or so (female life expectancy seems to have been about 35) retired from active work and could expect to be respectfully treated as sources of wisdom and advice; they were also permitted to drink *pulque* day and night.

The more committed to conquest the Aztec Empire became, the more its rulers needed to extoll men's military virtue and extract cloth from women. Aztec mythology and art often portrayed women as sources of discord, disrupters of cosmic harmony whose bad deeds required men to fight and die to put things right. In this respect, the Aztec culture of gender resembled that of many warrior-aristocracies in world history, including, for example, the one Homer described in the *Iliad* or that of the *Rig Veda* in India.

Like the Inka state, the Aztec Empire lasted roughly a century, using all the tools of power typical of big states everywhere in the pre-modern world. And like the Inkas, the Aztecs shared their continent with diverse peoples who lived without states and who left fewer clues about their lives. Let's look at a few examples from North America.

The Social Order In a fifteenth-century image with Spanish annotations, Aztec men and women venerate their elders—including an old woman who is shown reclining and drinking *pulque*.

The Ancestral Pueblo (Anasazi)

The **Ancestral Pueblo** lived not too far from the ancestral lands of the Aztecs, in the Four Corners area where Arizona, New Mexico, Colorado, and Utah meet today. The whole region that is now northwestern Mexico and the southwestern United States is mainly desert, much of it at high elevations. Oases and river valleys, the only hospitable landscapes where trees or crops might grow, are few. People had lived there for thousands of years, and in the few locations with enough water they had begun to raise irrigated maize by 2000 BCE. By 500 BCE, the Three Sisters—maize, beans, and squash—formed the heart of the farming system. Population ebbed and flowed with climate changes. Spring snowmelt flowing down from the mountains and high plateaus played the largest role in determining the success of irrigation farming. If the snowpack was thin and spring water scarce, crops failed and people had to live off of food reserves, survive on foraging and hunting, or migrate elsewhere.

Between 700 and 1100 or so, the Ancestral Pueblo population swelled. Wetter climate allowed more farming, food, and people, and a more sedentary existence. In a few spots they even farmed without irrigation for a while, relying on summer rains, which are often local thunderstorms. In effect, the Ancestral Pueblo placed a huge bet on agriculture, starting more than 10,000 new farmsteads between 850 and 1000. They cultivated just about every promising patch of land, hoping enough rain would fall to make the effort worthwhile. This was frontier farming, loosely analogous to expansions of agriculture into dry lands that took place in northern China or the North African

Maghreb. The scattered distribution of Ancestral Pueblo farming increased the probability that rain would fall on someone's fields and gardens. Networks of kinship and reciprocity encouraged the lucky to share with the unlucky in the knowledge that the next year their roles might be reversed. Rain didn't have to fall on everyone's crops for everyone to survive.

Since maize and beans store well, the Ancestral Pueblo could move food around as needed or keep it where the hungry could find it. An elite developed that oversaw the distribution of stored food. Its authority was probably more religious than military: there is no evidence of armies among the Ancestral Pueblo, nor of fortification. This elite also took responsibility for the rituals that the Ancestral Pueblo credited with bringing summer rain.

For centuries, this big bet on agriculture paid off. Rains in the region proved unusually good from about 1020 to 1130, according to tree ring evidence. Food was plentiful. Ancestral Pueblo women began to bear more children, and people migrated into the region as well. The Ancestral Pueblo started to carve elaborate houses into the sides of cliffs, accessible sometimes only by ladders. Their settlements also had larger ceremonial spaces, called *kivas*, often dug into the floors of buildings but sometimes at the foot of their cliff dwellings. In places such as Chaco Canyon, Mesa Verde, and Bandelier, you can still see their distinctive architecture. In the eleventh and twelfth centuries, they also built some 400 miles (650 km) of roads across the high plateau, perhaps for economic reasons—they had to drag timber a long way to their settlements—but perhaps for spiritual reasons too.

Almost all the roads led to the settlement at **Chaco Canyon** in northern New Mexico, suggesting it was the center of the Ancestral Pueblo world. Some Chaco Canyon buildings served as food storehouses. Religious and political leaders probably lived there, although no more than 2,500 of them at any one time. Several thousand other people came for ceremonies and to trade or work for food in lean times.

Ancestral Pueblo Architecture The site of a major Ancestral Pueblo settlement at Mesa Verde includes a number of the round *kiva* rooms used for religious ceremonies.

This pattern of dispersed farming settlements, ceremonial centers, and mutual aid worked well enough most years. It could not always prevent seasonal hunger (evident from skeletal remains) and—if rains failed widely—temporary catastrophe. But the network of settlements, trade links, and kin obligations connected the whole region in ways that safeguarded against starvation as long as enough summer rain fell somewhere on Ancestral Pueblo crops. Most years it did.

But not all years. A few hundred skeletons tell another side of the Ancestral Pueblo story. Roughly half of those born died by age 18, most of them in their early years from malnutrition and disease. In the eleventh century in Chaco Canyon, four out of five children had acute iron-deficiency anemia. Many women died in their late teens and twenties, presumably most in childbirth. Men lived on average seven years longer than women. Those who made it to old age usually showed signs of arthritis and osteoporosis, indicating lives of hard work. Elite Chacoans fared somewhat better. They were on average nearly 2 inches (5 cm) taller than common folk, and their children more than three times as likely to make it past age five. The elite ate more deer and antelope meat, consequently suffering far less from iron deficiency.

At its height, Ancestral Pueblo society supported some 50,000 to 150,000 people, 10,000 to 20,000 farmsteads, and 120 of their distinctive cliffside apartment complexes. The Ancestral Pueblo had energetically taken advantage of two or three centuries of above-average rainfall, and naturally enough presumed it was normal. But a cycle of drought began in the 1090s, and after a few better decades during which the Ancestral Pueblo built *kivas* and roads as never before, it returned with a vengeance around 1130. Deep drought endured for decades. Building ground to a halt. Storehouses emptied. Some people starved. Others migrated away. Few people wanted to support the elite, whose rainmaking rituals seemed to have lost their power. Chaco Canyon and its neighborhood lost most of its population.

Pottery and architectural evidence imply that some people moved north into Colorado. One settlement there, Mesa Verde, thrived until 1250 or so. Searing droughts reappeared about 1275 to 1300, by which time all the big settlements of the entire region had emptied out, and the network among them, the links of trade and power, had withered away. Fewer people remained in fewer major settlements, and the Ancestral Pueblo were less able to coordinate social action over long distances. Here the human web came and went with the rains.

Peoples of the Pacific Northwest Coast

While the Ancestral Pueblo found ways to cope with water scarcity, the peoples of the Pacific Northwest coast—from the Alaska panhandle south to Oregon—learned to exploit water's abundance. Rain and snow fell reliably along the coast and on the west-facing slopes of inland mountains, feeding hundreds of rivers. Tasty and nutritious salmon swam up these rivers to their breeding grounds in shallow streams every

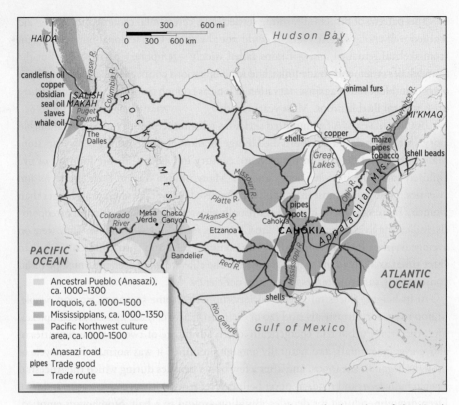

North American Cultures, ca. 1000–1500 This map shows the location of the North American cultures discussed in this chapter, together with some major long-distance trade routes. Altogether, perhaps 5 to 10 million people lived in North America in these centuries, loosely linked by trade. In the absence of pack animals or wheeled vehicles, seacoast, river, and lake transport were especially important.

summer. In a good year, 10 to 20 million salmon swam up the mighty Columbia and Fraser Rivers, and millions more up the smaller rivers

The ancestors of the Coast Salish, the Haida, and many other native peoples have lived here for 10,000 years at least, and likely more. By 1000 CE, about 30 distinct languages were spoken along the coast, but the cultures in question bore broad similarities.

They lived in permanent settlements—big villages with hundreds of people—yet they did not farm. Their homes were large cedar-plank houses that held 20 to 80 people. The sea and rivers provided abundant food. They hunted seals and other marine mammals. Some of them, like the Makah, hunted whales. Above all they fished, using weirs, baskets, and nets to capture a small share of the migratory salmon and several other fish species that frequented the coastal waters and rushing rivers. They hunted deer and gathered shellfish, berries, and edible plants too. But after 1000 CE, they relied increasingly on salmon—especially dried and smoked salmon in the winter when other foods were hard to find. The peoples of the North-west coast also conducted commerce with groups far inland, trading in slaves, copper, obsidian, and oil from whales, seals, and the candlefish (euchalon, so oily it can burn like a candle). Oil helped preserve dried and smoked fish.

These peoples lived amidst a temperate rain forest and made much of what they needed out of wood. In addition to constructing big houses, they routinely carved canoes, paddles, tools, weapons, and decorations from the abundant fir and cedar. They had no metal tools, carving instead with shells,

Pacific Northwest Peoples Haida art often featured animals that bore cultural and religious significance. This wooden dish is carved to look like both an eagle (left) and a whale (right), with the central panel serving as both the whale's fin and the eagle's wing.

stones, and beaver teeth. Their most distinctive decorative carvings, often done on poles or house-beams, represent sacred beings and family legends, and sometimes served to mark property. After 1800, when metal carving tools became available, this tradition gave rise to towering totem poles.

Social Structure Three main ranks existed in this hierarchical society: slaves, commoners, and chiefs. Slaves accounted for 20 to 40 percent of the population in some villages—broadly similar to the proportion in the ancient Roman world in the first century CE. Slaves were captives taken in raids or warfare, or the descendants of captives—slave status was hereditary. Free commoners composed the bulk of society, and a small percentage were chiefs. Chiefs could own and command slaves; indeed, they held power of life and death over slaves. A prominent chief might own dozens, partly for their labor and partly as a mark of chiefly status. But chiefs could not command free commoners. They led by persuasion. They had to be charismatic, and it helped to be skilled in the arts of war. Their authority rested in large part on their ability to distribute goods to others, often in ceremonies called potlatches.

Slaves did much of the hard and dirty work, which might include felling mighty cedar trunks, carving out a canoe with beaver teeth, or cleaning piles of fish. Commoners might specialize as carpenters, carvers, or weavers. Men fished and hunted. Women cleaned fish, wove baskets and blankets, prepared meals, and tended children. Chiefs focused on resolving disputes, conducting diplomacy with neighbors, fighting enemies, and rewarding followers. To do so, chiefs claimed ownership of fishing grounds, cranberry bogs, timber forests, and even intellectual property such as songs, stories, and dances. Commoners, who might own their own clothing, fishing tackle, and canoes but little else, gained access to other forms of property and to natural resources through the generosity of chiefs. A chief with enough property to dole out might command the loyalty of hundreds of followers. A chief who couldn't or wouldn't compete with his rivals in generosity did not long remain a chief. There was, then, considerable specialization and division of labor both among the different ranks and within the ranks of commoners—even if everyone pitched in with nets and traps during the brief summer weeks when the salmon swam past.

Warfare   In the centuries after 1000, as dependence on salmon deepened, a plague of violence haunted the Northwest coast, especially its northern stretch. War, raiding, and fortification had existed for centuries here, as we saw in Chapter 10. But now villagers built more elaborate fortifications of wood and stone atop bluffs and cliffs. They increasingly located their villages in places chosen for defense. Population dipped severely around 1150 to 1300, perhaps partly a result of heightened violence and slaving— although an unusually dry climate for two centuries might have posed an even greater problem. Small streams where salmon breed could dry up in extreme drought. In any case, after 1300, reliable rains returned and population recovered, but the scourge of warfare, like the deepened dependence on salmon, lasted.

A Local Web   Peoples along the Pacific coast lived in their own local web, aided by smooth sailing and paddling on the many bays, inlets, and straits from Alaska to Puget Sound. The rivers too were navigable for stretches, and one, the Columbia, hosted a big annual gathering at The Dalles (located 100 miles east of today's Portland) where coastal people mingled with their inland counterparts at festivals and fairs. The peoples of the coast had suitable trade goods to justify long voyages. They attacked enemies and raided for slaves hundreds of miles away at times. They stood apart from the wider world outside of North America until the 1770s, when European ships arrived.

Cahokia

The American Midwest, in 1000 CE, contained several dozen settled peoples who, unlike those of the Pacific Northwest coast, took up farming. Together they are sometimes called Moundbuilders, sometimes Mississippians. What they called themselves and one another, we do not know. Indeed, we know tantalizingly little about them, almost all of it through bones, stones, and shards of pottery. For centuries, they lived in hundreds of small villages. Then in the eleventh century, something strange happened at a place called **Cahokia**, in Illinois just across the Mississippi River from today's St. Louis. An Amerindian city sprang up.

Cahokia lay in the floodplain of the Mississippi River, which held two advantages. Its alluvial soils were fertile, and transportation along the river was easy. It also seems to have been an unusually peaceful place: the skeletons there from before 1000 CE show much lower rates of violence than those elsewhere in the American Midwest.

Cahokia, along with the rest of the American Midwest, was undergoing something of an agricultural revolution, loosely parallel to those in medieval China and northern Europe noted in earlier chapters, that dramatically boosted food supplies. The change probably had something to do with the warmer climate and longer growing season that set in around the period 900–1250 CE. It certainly had a lot to do with the development of a new form of maize: **flint maize** (*maiz de ocho*), which yielded bigger, juicier kernels and grew to maturity faster than other varieties.

With flint maize, North Americans could take fuller advantage of the nutritious combination of maize, beans, and squashes. For millennia, they had raised these crops in gardens to supplement their hunting and foraging. Now, after 800 or 900, they could become true farmers, needing little food beyond what their plots produced. Cahokia's alluvium provided excellent soils for intensive maize farming. And the timing was good too: the Mississippi experienced no huge floods between about 600 and about 1200, so Cahokia was unusually free from disaster.

In 1000, Cahokia was still just another modest settlement with a population of about 1,000 people. But by 1050, about 15,000 to 20,000 people lived at Cahokia. It became a genuine city, the largest settlement north of the Rio Grande. Pottery styles of humble cooking pots indicate that people migrated to Cahokia from what is now Missouri, Indiana, Wisconsin, and throughout Illinois. Why they came to Cahokia is unclear. Once they got there, they built ceremonial plazas and the biggest mounds in North America.

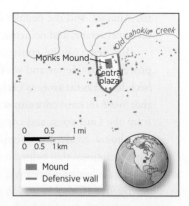

Cahokia, ca. 1050–1250 Cahokia, in today's southwestern Illinois near the Mississippi River, developed into a city of perhaps 20,000 people in the eleventh century, the largest settlement north of the Rio Grande. This map shows Cahokia's defensive wooden palisade, some of its 120 mounds, and Monks Mound, the biggest earthen structure in the Americas before 1500.

They did their building in spurts, apparently in coordinated, disciplined efforts. There are more than 100 mounds at Cahokia, of varying sizes and shapes. The largest, Monks Mound, is about 100 ft (30m) high and covers 14 acres (6 hectares—roughly 12 football fields). Archeologists reckon it would have taken 1,000 laborers about a year to pile up that much dirt. Their bosses' motivations were probably religious. Monks Mound stood next to a ceremonial space and presumably was the setting for religious rituals. Most mounds were used for sacrifices and burials. Most of those sacrificed were young women.

Cahokia was a city in the sense that many people clustered together. But most of them remained farmers. Some people specialized in craft production such as pottery and probably cloth as well. A very few might have been religious specialists and political leaders, although the political structure of Cahokia remains unclear. Burials, some of which include precious objects, indicate that the city had social hierarchy and a small elite. One man's corpse was carefully buried on 20,000 shell beads arranged in the shape of a bird and was accompanied by 53 young women apparently killed in his honor. Their skeletons imply they were poorly nourished and came from afar, perhaps as slaves. Despite its social hierarchy, Cahokia was not a state. As in Amazonia, among the Anasazi, and the peoples of the Northwest coast, Cahokia had elites but no king, no bureaucracy, and no army.

The new cultural configuration created by the surge of immigration to Cahokia proved attractive far and wide. Cahokian objects (pipes, pots, etc.) and imagery have been found as far away as Oklahoma and Minnesota, and were common in settlements that were in easy communication with the city along the Mississippi River. Shells from the Gulf coast and copper from the Lake Superior region have been unearthed at Cahokia. Evidently, Cahokia exerted some sort of power, perhaps partly economic, partly religious, that helped it spin its own thin and faint web in the heartland of North America—but only briefly.

By 1150, Cahokia was in trouble. Like people along the Northwest coast at the same time, Cahokians built fortifications of wooden walls (palisades) around the core settlement. Outer villages were abandoned. Both of these shifts suggest fear of attack— perhaps by strangers, perhaps by people unhappy about being at the bottom of the social hierarchy. Cahokians just about stopped building mounds and public buildings. Whatever central authority they had had was now too weak to organize collective undertakings. Unlike the villages of the Northwest coast, which recovered after 1300, by 1350 Cahokia was almost deserted.

Cahokia's fall remains a mystery. However, increased flooding, always a risk in the Mississippi floodplain, looks to be part of the riddle. Archeologists have found at the site much more sediment dating from around the period 1150–1250 than from either before or after. In the early 1200s an earthquake hit, knocking down part of Monks Mound. Charcoal deposits suggest parts of Cahokia burned. Droughts apparently became more common. No doubt many other things happened that contributed to the downfall of Cahokia; but however it happened, the city emptied, and the surrounding villages nearly did. No Amerindian settlement in North America since has equaled it in size. (Indeed, probably no city in North America surpassed its population until the late eighteenth century.) None of the surviving oral traditions of any Amerindian people mention anything about Cahokia.

Perhaps, however, Cahokia was not unique as a sizeable settlement in the heart of North America. Recent archeology suggests that from about 1450 to 1700 in south-central Kansas another community of perhaps 10,000 or even 20,000 people thrived as farmers, foragers, and hunters. They are probably ancestors of the Wichita, an Amerindian people. Their settlement, called Etzanoa, had vanished by 1700.

The Iroquois

In the eastern woodlands of North America, people had been foraging, fishing, and hunting since at least 10,000 BCE. Their numbers were small and grew only slowly. After 1000 BCE, some of them dabbled in horticulture, raising plants such as goosefoot and sunflowers (see Chapter 10). Then, perhaps as early as 500 CE, some groups began to experiment with maize, a new crop transmitted from one people to the next all the way from its homeland in Mexico. One such group was the Iroquois, living in what is now upstate New York, southwestern Quebec, and southeastern Ontario. Their influence extended south to Virginia and west to Ohio. The term *Iroquois* refers to a broad Amerindian language group but also to a narrower set of peoples, made up of five (after 1722, six) so-called nations—popularly known as tribes. The word *Iroquois* itself, in the Mi'kmaq language, means "killer people," which says something about how their neighbors came to regard the Iroquois.

Farming and Settlement As the Iroquois gradually took up maize farming, they became more sedentary, more numerous, and more inclined to violence among themselves and against neighboring peoples. They did not forsake hunting and foraging, and still got 40 percent of their food that way in 1400. But maize became their mainstay, as it did in Cahokia and among most Amerindians of the eastern woodlands. The shift to maize, and later beans as well, increased the food supply and boosted population. The number and size of settlements seems to have grown quickly in the thirteenth and fourteenth centuries, while Cahokia underwent decline. Population growth also made the Iroquois and their neighbors more likely to compete with one another over hunting grounds. Their investment in settlements made them less willing to flee trouble and more inclined to stand and fight in the event of conflict. This suite of changes is common in world history when peoples turn to sedentary agriculture. Whereas in 1000 the Iroquois were dispersed among hundreds of small hamlets, by 1350 they lived in larger—and fortified—settlements.

At some point before 1450 (some scholars say the mid-twelfth century), the Iroquois managed to forge a confederacy, the **League of Peace and Power**. Iroquois legend attributed this to an outsider from the north, a prince of peace born of a virgin girl. He had a speech impediment and spoke through an interpreter. Nonetheless, he persuaded the leaders of all the Iroquois to give up warfare among themselves and to unite, the better to exert power over others. Legends notwithstanding, it likely took long negotiations to create the League.

Thereafter, the Iroquois generally stuck together, and their less organized, less numerous,

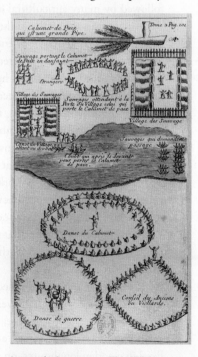

Iroquois Ceremony This 1704 engraving by a French traveler depicts several Iroquois dances and ceremonial pipes. Such pipes were used in the context of peace and war, commerce, politics, and religious rituals.

less powerful neighbors came to fear their raiders and war parties. Some neighbors migrated away out of reach, some sought to negotiate their way to safety, and others fought—usually unsuccessfully. Like many peoples, the Iroquois usually absorbed war captives into their own clans, and indeed sometimes set out to capture people to replace their own people lost to capture or death. They needed people, mainly women, to grow and grind maize.

Gender and Family   The Iroquois liked to say that the forest was the world of men and the village the domain of women. Like most peoples, they organized social life by gender, but they did it in a distinctive way. Men hunted, fished, raided, traded, and conducted diplomacy. They were often away from their villages for days or weeks at a time. Women farmed, ground maize, cooked, fetched water and firewood, and raised children—and stayed in their village almost all the time, except when butchering deer in seasonal hunting camps.

This sexual division of labor resembled that of most other North American Amerindians and, aside from women doing all the farming, resembled the arrangements followed by many agricultural societies around the world. But among the Iroquois, women also ran the affairs of their village. By the eighteenth century (for which there is plentiful documentary evidence), and probably well before that, women—or more precisely, some women—selected the chiefs of the Iroquois nations.

Life as an Iroquois woman had its struggles. After the introduction of maize, their daily routines grew tougher because grinding maize took much more effort than foraging or processing pumpkins, nuts, roots, or berries. Their skeletons show evidence of stronger musculature and more arthritis after 800 or 900 CE, when maize became the staff of life. Skeletal remains also show much higher rates of violence, which specialists see as an indication that women were commonly captured from neighboring peoples, partly in order to work grinding maize. As captives, they were sometimes roughly treated. Life expectancy for females was lower than for males. In effect, the turn to maize raised the demand for female labor, making women a scarce resource. For some women, that translated into captivity, which might resemble adoption or might resemble slavery. For other women, especially those of respected lineages, it meant power.

The turn to maize, and to sedentary ways of life in which males were often absent, encouraged the Iroquois to develop a distinctive society with a matrilineal and matrilocal tradition. Upon marriage, a husband moved in with his wife's extended family, including her sisters, mother, and aunts and their families. The Iroquois normally lived in wooden longhouses, on average 60 by 25 feet (18 by 7 m), although some were as much as 400 feet (120 m) long. Longhouses were also horizontal silos, with room for storage of maize, beans, and smoked fish or venison. As more sisters married, brought in more husbands, and families grew, the Iroquois would build additions on their longhouses. Giant pots found by archeologists indicate women cooked for many families at once.

Some scholars think the Iroquois preferred female babies over males, because upon marriage sons would contribute to another family's welfare. If true, this was an unusual preference in world history. Even if not true, the matriarchs of Iroquois society—women who by dint of ancestry, age, and personality led their longhouse or a cluster of longhouses—exerted real power and enjoyed wide respect. They helped to impose an ethic of negotiation and peace within Iroquois society, while encouraging young men to distinguish themselves by violence against other peoples. The Iroquois evolved into a society that struck its neighbors as particularly aggressive and violent but at the same time accorded women unusual authority.

Religion In religion, the Iroquois were less innovative and more conventional. Like all their neighbors, they practiced a variety of shamanism that found spirituality in nature. Their rituals included trances, tobacco and other psychoactive drugs, and large roles for dancing that would test one's stamina—all of which helped people see and communicate with the spirit world (the tobacco they smoked was stronger stuff than that sold today and could induce hallucinations). They liked to leave offerings of tobacco at choice locations, such as waterfalls and cliffs, where spirits were believed to reside. Like other Amerindian peoples from Mexico on north, they connected blood with crop fertility and thus ceremonially shed their own blood, or that of captives, to improve the harvest.

The similarity of Iroquois religion to that of other eastern woodland peoples, and indeed other Amerindians, is evidence of routine contacts among the many Amerindian peoples. The flows of migrants and captives strengthened these contacts and connections. The Iroquois did not build mounds like the Amerindians of the Midwest and Deep South, a major difference. But some of their rituals, especially those involving the sacrifice of captives, resembled practices in faraway Mesoamerica. In spiritual matters as well as in cropping patterns, Amerindians of North America showed some broad similarities, probably of Mexican origin, that indicate a loose web of interaction spanning most of the continent, especially the lands suited to maize, in the centuries after 1000 CE.

A Loose Web That loose web included trade networks in which the Iroquois took part. They swapped extra maize or tobacco to their northern neighbors in exchange for animal furs and to Amerindians in New England in exchange for shell beads (wampum). They received copper objects that originated in the upper Great Lakes region, several hundred miles away. They traded clay pipes with all their neighbors. Their trade took the form of ritual exchanges of gifts that took place now and again. They did not use money or markets.

Oceania

In the centuries between 1000 and 1700, many of the societies on Pacific islands changed under the pressures of their own success. As islanders learned how best to wring a living from their lands and lagoons, their populations grew. Their prospects improved further when some intrepid sailors ventured to South America and returned with a new crop, sweet potato. Recent genetic studies indicate that sweet potato first came to Polynesia between 1100 and 1200, from the Peru/Ecuador region, and quickly was carried to many different Polynesian islands. The sweet potato in Polynesia, like champa rice in Song China, brought about another agricultural revolution—but on a smaller scale than in China, more like maize among the Iroquois. Sweet potato yielded well in most of Oceania.

But by 1500 in most cases, abundance had given way to renewed scarcity. People organized themselves in order to defend their interests and compete for control of the best fishing grounds and farmlands. Partly in response to scarcity, several island societies took up abortion, infanticide, and celibacy and came to glory in war. In most regions of the Pacific, long-distance voyaging diminished, and isolation increased—in contrast to the situation in the Americas and in most of the world.

New Zealand: The Last Frontier

In 1000 CE, no humans lived in New Zealand. Its plants and animals were mainly remnants of the Cretaceous period (155 to 65 million years ago), almost completely isolated from the rest of life on Earth. The first people to arrive came in sailing canoes from central or eastern Polynesia, probably about 1280. They carried their distinctive biological baggage with them, as Polynesians always did when seeking new islands. The most important animals they brought in their canoes were dogs and rats. They might have set out with pigs and chickens too, as Polynesians normally did, but they must have sailed for months and perhaps ate their tastiest animals en route. They brought Polynesian food crops too, although most would not grow in the chillier climates of New Zealand. The two that did best were taro and sweet potato (called *kumara* in New Zealand—from *kumar,* a Qechua word).

The first colonists, probably about 200 in number, found a paradise of Pacific protein. New Zealand's Cretaceous creatures included the moa, a flightless bird as tall as a horse and as heavy as a pig. Dozens of other species of flightless birds flapped around too. The coasts teemed with fur seals and shellfish. New Zealand's plants were less nutritious, although the **Maori**—as the Polynesians of New Zealand are called—found a fern whose roots they turned into an edible paste. Early Maori lived where the seals and moa were, especially on the eastern coast of the South Island, usually in villages of 50 to 200 people.

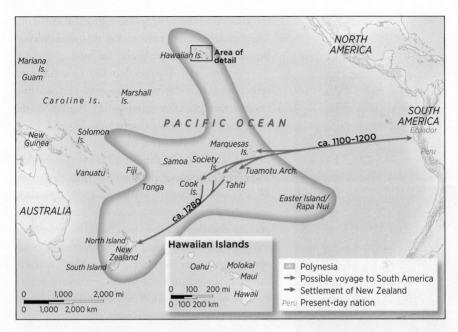

Oceania, ca. 1000–1500 Oceania in these centuries witnessed widespread population growth, a major episode of frontier expansion, and another of political development. The population growth in Oceania drew in part upon the acquisition of a new crop, sweet potato, which came from South America in the twelfth century along the routes depicted here. The frontier expansion took the form of the colonization of New Zealand after 1280, dramatically expanding the domain of Polynesian people and culture. The most notable political development was the evolution of kingship and kingdoms in Hawaii after about 1450.

While the big birds and blubbery seals lasted, the Maori ate well and flourished. Skeletal evidence shows that Maori stood taller than other Polynesians. Very few adult women did not become mothers—an indication that diet didn't limit fertility. Infant and child mortality rates came to about 20 to 35 percent, and average life expectancy for both men and women was roughly 30 years. This counts as a healthy population by world history standards. Children apparently suffered few serious beatings, although many people suffered broken bones as adults. Hunting seals among the rocks in slippery surf might explain that. Archeologists have found few weapons of war and no signs of fortification among the early Maori. Their tools were of stone, bone, and wood.

After two centuries of peace, prosperity, and abundant protein, the good times came to an end in the decades after 1450. The moas, and 30 other bird species, grew scarce and went extinct. Seals became rare. The Maori worked harder at raising garden crops, but their climate cooled as the Little Ice Age set in, which restricted the range of taro especially. Still, by 1500, garden crops accounted for half of their food because

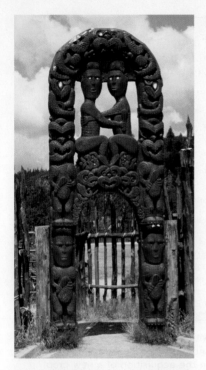

Maori Tribal Life A ceremonial arch decorates the entrance to a traditional *pa* (a Maori fortified village), its spiked fence a defense against would-be invaders.

the yields from hunting and foraging had tailed off. The population, now a few tens of thousands strong, began to compete more keenly for food.

Families and lineages banded together into larger units for defense. Weapons and warfare became routine. Like chiefs on the Pacific Northwest coast a few centuries before, Maori leaders began to build elaborate earth-and-wood fortifications (called *pa* in the Maori language) behind which their supporters huddled in times of danger. Maori chiefs eventually built about 6,000 *pa* sites, and no one could remain a successful leader without one. As elsewhere in Polynesia (and the Americas), warfare included spiritual dimensions that encouraged victors to eat parts of the vanquished, whereas the first two centuries of Maori settlement betray no signs of cannibalism. New Zealand's population between 1500 and 1750 probably grew only a little, reaching maybe 100,000 or 150,000.

The late Polynesian voyaging in the South Pacific (ca. 1000–1300) bears comparison to the Vikings in the North Atlantic (ca. 850–1100). Both required extraordinary maritime skills and resolute courage. Both Polynesians and Vikings seem to have sailed to America, staying there only briefly, affecting it negligibly, and bringing away nothing of consequence except sweet potato in the Polynesian case. With the settlement of Iceland after 874 by Vikings and New Zealand after 1280 by Polynesians, all the world's large inhabitable spaces were populated. The long saga of migration and human colonization of the Earth that had begun on African savannas about 300,000 years ago ended on a New Zealand beach.

Hawaii

Some 5,000 miles north in the central Pacific, a similar story unfolded on the islands of the Hawaiian archipelago. There the first human settlers arrived about 800 to 1300 CE—the most recent archeological evidence suggests between 1220 and 1260. Genetic evidence implies a tiny founding population, maybe 100 people—only two or three full canoes. They came from central Polynesia, like the first New Zealanders. They brought the standard Polynesian biological baggage, which was well suited to Hawaii's warm climate, and soon located the best fishing grounds and garden spots for their crops (only about 5 to 10 percent of the islands' area is good for farming).

For a few centuries Hawaiians prospered, thanks mainly to seafood. Population grew quickly. They began to build irrigation systems to get higher yields in their taro and yam gardens, and to settle in larger numbers inland. They maintained contact with other parts of Polynesia via long voyages in sailing canoes. By 1300 or so, they added fishponds to their economy, especially on Oahu. Some fishponds were nearly a mile long. The earliest Hawaiians lived in small villages. Like all Polynesian peoples, they were intensely aware of their ancestry and organized themselves into lineages or clans, led by chiefs, as was normal throughout the Pacific.

By 1400, Hawaii was starting to look less and less like a Pacific paradise. As in New Zealand, abundance gave way to scarcity once every patch of good land and every rich fishing ground was in use. Chiefs began to compete to control the good lagoons and irrigable plains. Population growth slowed, and perhaps ceased about 1450–1500. Hawaiians lost touch with other Polynesian islands and were thereafter among the world's most isolated populations, fully dependent on their own resources. To 1400, Hawaii's trajectory looked a lot like New Zealand's.

But something strange happened between 1450 and 1700 in Hawaii—well, strange by Pacific standards but normal in world history. Some of the chiefs made themselves into kings. Archeology and oral tradition agree that by the late fifteenth century Oahu was unified into a single kingdom. Soon Maui, Molokai, and most of the big island (called Hawaii) became kingdoms too. Each island now had a ruling class, organized into a bureaucracy with professional administrators. The kings organized the common people to work on monumental architecture, building bigger palaces and larger temples, and adjusted religious belief to make themselves divine or semi-divine. They encouraged royal cults, making religion into a state ideology legitimating the ruler. Kings claimed (although in practice did not easily exert) absolute power, including that of life and death over their subjects. Hawaiians could be executed for sneezing at a king's court.

With the rise of rival kings and kingdoms, Hawaii became a more violent place. The **Hawaiian kings** of the four main islands competed for power over the archipelago, resulting in continual warfare. When a king died, war for succession to the throne normally followed. Hawaiian society became more male-dominated and more martial in culture—just like New Zealand's. But Hawaii was the only one of roughly 30 Polynesian societies around the Pacific to develop kingdoms.

Hawaii's population stood at an estimated 400,000 to 500,000 in the period 1500–1750. Other islands in the Pacific had much smaller populations. Almost all followed a similar trajectory of early expansion and plenty, followed by scarcity and conflict, and painful adjustments to the stern realities of limited space.

Once again, it is instructive to compare the Polynesian and Viking experience. The inhabitants of islands, whether Hawaii or Iceland, sooner or later faced starkly limited resources. Hawaiians and Icelanders responded by limiting their population, achieved through a combination of later marriages and increased abortion or infanticide. Icelanders, however, also maintained long-distance seaborne connections, which Hawaiians—who had much longer distances to travel to the nearest populated places—lost by about 1300. So Icelanders could benefit economically from participation in trade networks. This enabled them to specialize in certain activities and exchange what they were good at producing (sealskins, fish) for what they were bad at producing (grain). The benefits of specialization and exchange, for Hawaiians, were available only within their archipelago. This was a much more limited field of operation, mainly because the Hawaiian islanders produced similar things. Hawaii may have been warmer and sunnier than Iceland, with tasty tropical fruits, but when it was isolated from the rest of humankind, its population lived with stricter limits.

Guam

The first people arrived on Guam, an island in the Mariana chain in the western Pacific, about 4,000 years ago. Their descendants, the Chamorro, like most peoples in the Americas and Oceania, had no writing, so our understanding of their history is uncertain and relies mainly on archeology. The imperfect evidence implies that between 1000 and 1500 they were growing more numerous and more hierarchical, and were interacting culturally with far-flung people more frequently.

After about 1000 CE, the Chamorro began to erect pillars with semi-spherical caps on top, like mushrooms with the caps inverted. Called **latte stones**, they were quarried out of limestone, sandstone, or basalt, although sometimes the caps were of coral. Big ones, more common as time went on, stood 15 feet (5 m) tall and weighed 20 tons (18,000 kg).

Latte Stones Latte stones, such as these on the island of Guam, were erected on several of the Mariana Islands—but nowhere else—after about 1000 CE. They probably served as foundation posts for public buildings or homes of the highest-ranking community members.

Nobody knows for sure why the Chamorro went to the considerable trouble of quarrying and erecting latte stones. As we've seen, in ancient times from Korea to England, and in Mesoamerica as well, people found reasons to put up megaliths—dolmens, Stonehenge, the Olmec heads—even if we today can't be sure what those reasons were. The leading hypothesis for the latte stones is that they served as the corner-posts or bases of buildings. They normally exist in pairs framing a rectangular space, and some sixteenth-century Spanish texts (Spanish sailors visited Guam in 1521) refer to buildings atop stone pillars. Some of the rectangles included as many as 20 latte stones and probably represent either a community building—maybe a structure for storing boats—or more likely the home of someone of especially high rank. The presence of latte stones and their rectangles in all sizes suggests that Chamorro society after 1000 was developing a new status hierarchy or finding a new way to mark social status. Spaniards wrote about a Guamanian society with three classes, living in communities segregated by social rank.

Latte stones also exist on several other islands in the Marianas, despite the hundreds of miles of ocean dividing them. This tells us that these islands, between about 1000 and 1521, hosted an interacting cultural community. Although almost entirely isolated from the larger world, the people of the Marianas were building their own modest, seaborne web like the Hawaiians—but on a smaller scale. Similar patterns were evolving on other Pacific archipelagoes, without the telltale latte stones.

Conclusion

Before 1492, the peoples of the Americas lived almost entirely isolated from the rest of humankind. Peoples of Oceania did as well, until an even later date. To some extent they forged their own webs of interaction, especially in the Andes and Mesoamerica, although always smaller and usually less integrated than those of Eurasia and North Africa. The main reason for that was the absence of suitable transport in the Americas, and in Oceania the tremendous distances and dangers of sailing in canoes.

Amerindians and Pacific Islanders found their own solutions to the problems of subsistence, social life, and dealing with the spirit world. In some instances, their solutions were unique to themselves. The Amerindian Three Sisters of agriculture existed nowhere outside the Americas. *Chinampas* existed only in Mesoamerica. Amazonian dark earths, the Iroquois League, and Polynesian sailing canoes were, if not unique solutions, then highly distinctive ones.

But many of the practices adopted in the Americas and Oceania resembled ones arrived at by peoples in China, India, Africa, or Europe, especially where leaders created states and empires. They made pots of clay, like people almost everywhere. They worshipped gods associated with nature, like many (by no means all) people. They divided work into male and female spheres. They irrigated their crops to improve yields. Imperial leaders in Mexico and the Andes used religion, architecture, and brute force to maintain their power. Amerindians and Pacific islanders arrived at these commonplace solutions quite independently, with no significant interactions with Africa or Eurasia. It is interesting to ponder the parallels among peoples who, thus far, were not in contact with one another.

After 1492, a new era in world history commenced. No longer would big regions such as the Americas or Oceania follow their own courses, nearly free from influence from further afield. In the next few chapters, Part 4 of this book, we will see how the breakdown of isolation and the formation of a single worldwide human web would affect the different people and places of the planet.

|||||||||||||||||||||||||||||||||||||||||||||||||||||||||||||||||||||||||||||||||||||||||||||||||||||||||||||||||||||||||||||

Chapter Review

KEY TERMS

Inka p. 555

vertical archipelago p. 556

dark earth p. 562

Tenochtitlán p. 564

Tlacélel p. 565

Florentine Codex p. 569

Ancestral Pueblo p. 571

Chaco Canyon p. 572

Cahokia p. 576

flint maize p. 577

League of Peace and Power p. 579

Maori p. 582

Hawaiian kings p. 585

latte stones p. 586

REVIEW QUESTIONS

1. How did *quipus* convey information, and what did they record?

2. How and why did the connections among people in the Americas and Oceania differ from those in Eurasia and North Africa?

3. What were the three important and related trends in the histories of the Americas?

4. What were the main forms of soft and hard power that supported Inka rule?

5. How did the people of Amazonia make a living?

6. How did the Aztec religious worldview underpin its militaristic society?

7. Describe and compare the economic bases of the Inkas and the Aztecs.

8. What were the subsistence methods of the Anasazi and the peoples of the Pacific Northwest coast?

9. In what ways did flint maize change societies in North America?

10. What did the Pacific Northwest coast, Cahokia, and the Four Corners region look like in the year 1300, and why?

11. How and why was the role of women in Iroquois society distinctive?

12. Identify the causes and effects of societal change in New Zealand at the end of the fifteenth century.

13. What was the common trajectory of many islands in the Pacific?

14. What do latte stones tell us about cultural exchange in the Marianas?

Go to INQUIZITIVE

to see what you've learned—and learn what you've missed—with personalized feedback along the way.

WEAVING THE GLOBAL WEB

1400 to 1800

C hapters 16 through 20 cover world history between 1400 and 1800. During that period, human history became genuinely global for the first time. Events in South America, such as a discovery of silver, affected China, and changes in Chinese tax policies affected silver miners in South America. The regional webs featured in Part 3 fused into a single global web.

The great economist Adam Smith in his famous work, *The Wealth of Nations* (1776), wrote that:

> The discovery of America, and that of a passage to the East Indies by the Cape of Good Hope, are the two greatest and most important events recorded in the history of mankind....By uniting, in some measure, the most distant parts of the world, by enabling them to relieve one another's wants, to increase one another's enjoyments, and to encourage one another's industry, their general tendency would seem to be beneficial.

Now, two and half centuries after Adam Smith, it's a bit easier to see the full significance of "uniting, in some measure, the most distant parts of the world." In Part 4 we focus on just how this "uniting" happened, and its consequences—economic, political, intellectual, social, and biological. From here on in the book, as history became more globalized, our portrayal of it also becomes more global in scope.

The First Pulse of Globalization

Before starting in, one further point is worth establishing. Although Smith refers to the discovery of America, in fact America—the Western Hemisphere—already had tens of millions of people in it, and neither the Vikings nor Columbus actually discovered it. What Columbus did discover was a practical route between Europe and America. What he and dozens of other mariners collectively discovered was how to sail the world's oceans by exploiting the prevailing winds and currents. Before the fifteenth century, almost all sailors except Polynesians and Vikings hugged the shorelines. Polynesians in the tropical Pacific, and Vikings in the North Atlantic, had learned how to navigate and survive at sea for many weeks without sighting land. But even they did not establish enduring routes over the seas they sailed.

Between 1400 and 1800, mariners traversed all the world's seas and linked all the world's inhabited coastlines and hinterlands. They discovered oceanic routes, unlocked the secrets of the globe's wind patterns, and, armed with this knowledge, spun the first genuinely global web of humankind. That was the first pulse of true globalization, and its events belong—just as Smith said—among the most important in history.

New Crossroads

One aspect of the new global connections deserves underlining at the start. For thousands of years before the 1490s, the best place on Earth in which to learn about other places was Southwest Asia. Its connections, by land and sea, brought its peoples into at least intermittent touch with others in Africa, Europe, South Asia, and to a lesser extent Southeast and East Asia as well. Southwest Asian societies enjoyed access to the Mediterranean, Black, and Red Seas, the Indian Ocean world, and the overland routes of the Eurasian steppe. Southwest Asia was the land bridge connecting world regions, the closest thing to a center of the Old World web. This geographical position put Southwest Asian societies in a situation that was sometimes dangerous but often advantageous. Their position exposed them at times to more epidemics and perhaps more invasions than most peoples elsewhere. But it also enabled them to learn more from more places, and this they could turn to their advantage.

Southwest Asia gradually lost this dangerous but privileged position after the 1490s. Seaborne communications and trade enabled Atlantic Europeans gradually to take over this role. Increasingly they, rather than Southwest Asians, learned more about technologies in use around the world. Atlantic Europeans could now adopt useful technologies from a larger menu of options than others had done. And now they, rather than Arabs, Armenians, and Persians, knew more about relative prices in different markets, enabling them to make money in trade more reliably, buying low and selling high in different parts of the world.

Global History

In Part 3, the chapters each addressed a separate region, but they shared common themes. Here, in Part 4, with the world drawing together into a single web, the chapters address separate themes with a global scope. Chapter 16 explores the navigation advances that wove the world together and the biological exchanges among regions that resulted. Chapter 17 considers the impacts of the newly formed global web on societies previously enmeshed in smaller webs. All of these societies faced severe challenges that some survived but others did not. Chapters 18 through 20 deal with the cultural, political, and economic implications, respectively, of weaving a global web.

So how did all this weaving start? The answer lies with sailors.

16

‖‖‖‖‖‖‖‖‖‖‖‖‖‖‖‖‖‖‖‖‖‖‖‖‖‖‖‖‖

Convergence

THE DISCOVERY OF THE OCEANS AND
BIOLOGICAL GLOBALIZATION

1400 to 1800

FOCUS QUESTIONS

1. What were the major contours of world history in 1400, as shown in the regional webs of the time?

2. What were the main differences in oceanic voyaging conducted by China's Ming dynasty and the Atlantic Europeans?

3. What were the most important effects of the biological globalization initiated by the oceanic voyaging of Atlantic Europeans?

4. Why was the first global web to extend across the world a significant development?

O n the morning of October 11, 1492, Amerindians living on an island in the Bahamas (probably Watlings Island) walked to the beach and, to their astonishment, discovered Christopher Columbus. Few if any Bahamians had ever seen men wearing clothes, which was not done in their islands, let alone men in metal armor. None had ever seen ships. Columbus's ships far eclipsed the dugout canoes that plied Bahamian waters. What those astonished people made of the strangers on their shores we will never know, although it's a reasonable guess that some were curious and some were terrified. Columbus, for his part, thought he stood on an island off the coast of China.

Nearly six years later, in 1498, residents of the Indian port city of Calicut, strolling along the harbor-front, were almost as astonished to discover Portuguese ships approaching. They had seen Europeans before, although not many. But they had never seen European ships anywhere in the Indian Ocean, nor any ships carrying big cannon as these did. The ships' commander, Vasco da Gama, soon found occasion to use the big cannon.

These two encounters in the 1490s symbolize the opening of a new era in world history. Before the 1490s, the Americas and Afro-Eurasia remained essentially separate hemispheres. Before the 1490s, the Old World web relied heavily on overland connections together with the maritime links centered on the Indian Ocean. After the 1490s, the world's coastlands quickly (well, over two centuries) became integrated as never before, thanks to seaborne trade. Indeed, the world's populated coasts, with scant exceptions, came to form the first genuinely global web of human interaction, channeling the flow of ideas, technologies, goods, crops, diseases, and much else.

But before we get to the story of several sailors and the seven seas, let's pause and look at the lands on which people lived as of the fifteenth century, and specifically, the webs of interaction within which they lived. Before examining the formation of a global web, it helps to remember its constituent parts.

The World's Webs in the Fifteenth Century

As of 1400, the 350 to 450 million people on Earth spoke several thousand languages, followed several hundred religions, and recognized several hundred political rulers. (A few tens of millions of them recognized no rulers at all, although with each passing year fewer and fewer lived in

CHRONOLOGY

1291 Italian sailors attempt to circumnavigate Africa

ca. 1300–1400 European and Moroccan sailors reach the Canary Islands

1368–1644 Ming dynasty in China

1402–1424 Reign of Yongle Emperor

1402–1496 Spanish conquest of the Guanches in the Canary Islands

1405–1433 Zheng He organizes and leads seven maritime voyages

1415 Portuguese army captures Moroccan port of Ceuta

ca. 1430–1440 Henry the Navigator organizes systematic voyaging along the coasts of Atlantic Africa

ca. 1480 Knowledge of how to make great ships is lost in China; Portuguese sailors establish a fort in West Africa

1492 Christopher Columbus lands in the Bahamas

1492–1650 Populations in the Americas fall by 70 to 95 percent

1494 Spain and Portugal sign the Treaty of Tordesillas

1497 Vasco da Gama embarks on expedition to India; John Cabot makes round trip from England to Newfoundland

1500 Pedro de Cabral claims Brazil for Portugal

1519–1522 Ferdinand Magellan's surviving crew members circumnavigate the globe

ca. 1550–1750 Maize becomes a food staple in Atlantic Africa

By 1570 The Pacific Ocean wind system is deciphered

ca. 1650 Population of the Americas begins to recover

ca. 1670 Military expansion of Asante kingdom begins

so-called stateless societies.) Despite nearly 5,000 years of states, cities, and empires, and some 2,000 years of expanding, proselytizing religions, the human race remained politically and culturally fragmented. It was in no deep sense a community. Even within the Old World web, spectacular diversity prevailed—from the refined world of Confucian scholars in urban China, with its leisured philosophy and gorgeous calligraphy, to the austere and dangerous world of illiterate fisherfolk on the coasts of Scotland.

The Old World Web

That diversity resulted partly from the sheer size of the Old World web. Its frontiers, in 1400, stretched from Greenland to Japan and from Indonesia to West Africa. Three-fourths of humanity lived within it. Thousands of caravan tracks, navigable rivers, and sea routes held the web together. It included hubs or nodes, such as Malacca, Calicut, Hormuz, Cairo, Constantinople, or Venice, where people heard many languages and where the silks of China crossed paths with the ivory of East Africa or the amber of Scandinavia. But it also included spaces where people kept to themselves, deep in the forests of Siberia or high in the Himalaya mountains, minimally connected to empires, trade routes, or major religions. These people, comparatively few in number, lived within the Old World web's frontiers, but they were not part of its fabric—at least, not yet in 1400.

Interactions within the Old World Web The Old World web had two main trunk routes. The overland caravan routes, collectively known as the Silk Road, linked eastern and western Eurasia. The caravan routes flourished in times of peace, when strong empires kept brigands in check and prevented dozens of local rulers from demanding payment from traders in exchange for safe passage. The best example is the Pax Mongolica (ca. 1260–1350), when the short-lived Mongol Empire stamped out brigandage almost everywhere along routes between Korea and Iraq, making travel safer for merchants.

The second main trunk route, also in reality a series of connected routes, was by sea. It extended from the East Asian ports through the waters of Southeast Asia and into the Indian Ocean, as far west as the coasts of Africa. Via a short overland passage in Egypt, these routes connected to the Mediterranean. Mastery of the monsoon winds had opened this trunk route in ancient times.

The traffic within the Old World web, along these trunk routes and countless lesser ones, served as a homogenizing force. Cultural interaction and political conquests reduced the number of different languages spoken. Meanwhile, more and more people chose (sometimes under duress) to follow fewer and fewer religions, and so Buddhism, Hinduism, Christianity, and Islam (some people would include Confucianism as a religion too) each acquired tens of millions of believers, while many other religions disappeared. Of course, at the same time, the big religions fractured, developing internal splits such as the Sunni–Shi'a divide in Islam or the Orthodox–Catholic schism in Christianity. And the big languages fractured too, although slowly. They developed dialects, so the Arabic spoken in Morocco gradually came to seem strange to Arabs in Iraq because it sounded so different from their own. So the process of homogenization in the Old World web had its limits and counter-currents.

A Thickening Web During the fifteenth century, the eastern and western edges of the Old World web were rapidly consolidating and thickening as a result of maritime trade. In earlier centuries, mastery of the arts of camel management had boosted the connectivity of the central regions of the Old World web, making desert crossings in Central Asia, Arabia, and Africa much more practical. Mastery of the monsoon winds had given sea traders in the Indian Ocean world a precocious start in developing long-distance networks. But now, from at least 1200 onward, improving ship design and navigational skill in both western Europe and eastern Asia were fast accumulating, reducing the risks of sea travel and making trade and economic specialization yet more rewarding. Sailing the western Pacific waters from Japan to Java, or the eastern Atlantic from Scandinavia to Spain, was dangerous indeed. Both seas featured frequent, furious storms, not to mention (especially in the western Pacific) bold, enterprising pirates. But bigger and better ships helped sailors overcome their understandable fears of these hazards.

Overland and Seaborne Trade These two fifteenth-century images show contrasting sides of the long-distance trade circuits of the Old World web. The image at left shows overland transport of Chinese ceramics to Southwest Asia; the image at right shows the seaborne spice trade from Southeast or South Asia as imagined by a French painter. Only high-value items could justify the costs and risks of transport, whether by land or sea, over thousands of miles.

The rewards to risking one's life and cargo at sea were genuine and growing. Both western Europe and eastern Asia produced a wide diversity of resources and goods. Markets had sprung up offering tempting prices at which to sell scarce goods from afar, whether Spanish wine in the Netherlands or Moluccan spices in China. At times, even bulk goods such as rice, salt, and timber could justify voyages in these two sea rooms.

Both these emerging maritime worlds drew additional traffic from networks of navigable rivers. In Europe, the big rivers flow fairly evenly throughout the year and permit ship or barge traffic well inland. In East and Southeast Asia, the big rivers are more seasonal because of the pattern of summer monsoon rain. But with painstaking construction of canals, dikes, and dams, these rivers too served as reliable avenues of commerce, linking interior regions with the sea.

So, in 1400, the eastern and western edges of the Old World web were humming with riverine and seaborne trade. Knowledge of geography, winds, and currents, of ship design, cartography, and navigation, of goods, markets, and prices was growing at ever faster rates. Both regions were developing a more maritime and commercial culture. Populations were recovering from the disease and climate disasters of the fourteenth century, and cities were expanding rapidly.

Local Webs

In 1400, some 60 to 120 million people in Oceania, the Americas, and the southern third of Africa lived outside the Old World web altogether. They too, of course, took part in trade networks, military conquests, and the same sorts of activities as people in the Old World web. But their scales of operations were smaller. In Oceania, people in Polynesia and Micronesia had built their own small webs of interaction. Archipelagoes like that of Hawaii, or Tonga and Fiji, hosted constant interactions among hundreds of thousands of people. In the Caroline Islands of Micronesia by 1400 or 1450, a well-integrated exchange network had grown up, using big stone discs as money—some of them heavier than a car. But this little web probably involved at most tens of thousands of people. In demographic terms, these Oceanic networks were tiny compared to the Old World web.

Webs in the Americas

In the Americas, as we saw in Chapter 15, much larger webs had developed around the dense populations in the Andes and in Mesoamerica. In 1400, perhaps 40 to 70 million people lived in the Americas, and about half were in either the Andes or Mesoamerica. Most Amerindians, and all those in the Andes or Mesoamerica, took part in interactive webs. In the absence of pack animals (outside of llamas and alpacas in the high Andes), goods could travel only by watercraft or human porters in the American webs. Canoes and rafts linked peoples on riverbanks and shorelines. Elsewhere, people had to carry everything themselves.

So the character of the American webs was slightly different from that of the Old World web, with less bulk commerce in transit. Crops such as maize diffused widely within this web, and so did some cultural practices such as ball games and mound building. But the volume and intensity of the exchanges of goods over long distances were modest compared to what occurred in the Old World web with its caravans and shipping. Buzzing markets did exist, but mainly on the local level—as in the Basin of Mexico, the region around today's Mexico City. As in the Old World web, those societies enmeshed in the American web featured more specialization and exchange, greater wealth, greater inequality, greater military power, than those societies outside the web.

Like its counterparts, the American webs left some people out entirely. In the far south of South America and in the northern reaches of North America, scattered populations lived essentially subsistence lives. In pockets of Central American or Amazonian rain forest too, there were some people living substantially in isolation.

Webs in Africa

Most of the northern half of Africa, by 1400, lay within the Old World web. Egypt had long been one of its linchpins. Trade and cultural exchange, most notably the spread of Islam, tied the East African coast as far south as Kilwa and Sofala, the Mediterranean lands, and the West African Sahel firmly to the rest of the Old World web. Where rivers made travel easy, as along the Nile and Niger, tendrils of the Old World web reached further still.

But the southern third of Africa, like sizeable parts of the Americas, or Siberia, stood apart from any big web. People there were not importing shiploads of luxury goods from Egypt or India; they were not sending young men to study Islam in Cairo or Baghdad. They were not experimenting with Indian Ocean world technology such as sugar mills or lateen-rigged sails. Instead, they were producing food and clothing for themselves or for local use, they were following their own religions, and they were using the same technologies—perhaps with minor alterations—that their ancestors had employed for many generations. They lived outside the Old World web, but within much smaller webs of their own making.

As in the Americas, these little webs in southern Africa were better for circulating ideas than goods. Without pack animals, wheeled vehicles, or ships, people here had to move everything on their backs, on their heads, or in canoes.

So in 1400 the world included one giant interactive web in Eurasia and the northern half of Africa, a large one in the Americas, and small, local ones elsewhere. The Old World web was home to most of the world's people, and to its most formidable states and societies. It alone had sailing ships capable of carrying hundreds of tons of cargo. It alone had many kinds of pack animals suited to almost any terrain. It alone had wheeled vehicles. By 1400, it had fewer obstacles to interaction, especially to trade, than did the other, smaller webs around the world.

The Old World web was not necessarily a pleasant place to live—certainly not if life expectancy or social equality are the measures—but it is where people had built the most powerful militaries, the most efficient communications networks, and the most sophisticated technologies. Therefore, it comes as no surprise that the people who brought the world's webs together, who forged the first truly global web, came from the edges of the Old World web.

The Discovery of the Open Sea

Before 1400, as earlier chapters explained, several peoples had developed maritime cultures. The most extraordinary of these was the Polynesian, which carried colonists throughout the archipelagoes of the tropical Pacific and as far south as New Zealand. However, by 1400 its farthest outposts had become cut off and sea traffic took place mainly within archipelagoes. The Vikings, too, had a seafaring history several centuries long, although by 1400 they had stopped exploring the North Atlantic and their Greenland colony was on the verge of extinction. Many other peoples sailed routinely on more protected seas, such as the Mediterranean, the Arabian Gulf, the Bay of Bengal, the South China Sea, or the Sea of Japan. The islands of Indonesia, and adjacent coasts of Southeast Asia, hosted sizeable regular traffic by 1000 CE. The traffic in all these seas was much thicker and more regular than in the Polynesian Pacific or the Viking North Atlantic. The vessels were often larger, and some could carry hundreds of tons of cargo. The routes were well established and studded with commercial seaports. Those who plied these routes usually hugged the shores, although certain passages, such as from East Africa to India and back, took sailors far from land for a week or two.

Sailors had accumulated a considerable, if fragmented, knowledge of winds and currents. Polynesians knew how to ride the currents and the trade winds of the Pacific. People all around the Indian Ocean knew how to use the monsoon to sail north in the summer and south in the winter. Everywhere, sailors had mastered the local tides, currents, and winds for the short voyages that made up the great majority of seafaring. But no one knew the overall pattern of the planet's winds. No one knew how it might be possible, in the Atlantic and Pacific as well as the Indian Ocean, to find winds that would reliably take ships far out to sea, thousands of miles from land, and then safely home again. In the fifteenth and sixteenth centuries, people learned where to find these winds, unlocking the secrets of oceanic navigation.

The ocean winds form gigantic merry-go-rounds. In the North Atlantic, for example, the prevailing winds spin in a clockwise fashion. Its westerlies (winds are named for the direction *from* which they blow, unlike ocean currents; so a westerly wind and an easterly current are going the same way) whip across from North America to Europe. Further south, the trade winds blow along the northwestern coasts of Africa and then whistle across to the Caribbean. In the South Atlantic, the merry-go-round

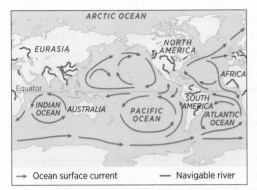
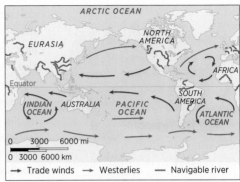

Ocean surface current — Navigable river

Trade winds → Westerlies — Navigable river

Prevailing Winds and Ocean Currents Mariners of the fifteenth and sixteenth centuries figured out the global system of winds and ocean currents, enabling them to plot the routes of sailing ships that tied the Global web together.

spins counterclockwise, so the westerlies lie far to the south and the trade winds cross from Angola to Brazil. The North and South Pacific have their own spinning wheels, as does the southern Indian Ocean. (The winds of the northern part of the Indian Ocean are governed by the monsoon.) The whole system slides north by a few hundred miles from April to August and slips back south from September to March. Thus there is a general pattern to the world's winds. But nobody knew that in 1400.

The Ming Voyages, 1405–1433

In 1400, the biggest ships and perhaps the best navigators were Chinese. Under the Song, the Yuan, and then the Ming (1368–1644) dynasties, the Chinese had rapidly developed ship and navigation technology, and Chinese merchants had taken a large role in the booming trade between East and Southeast Asia. The Ming maintained a state shipyard that employed between 20,000 and 30,000 workers. Their ships were by far the biggest in the world, capable of carrying a thousand people. Chinese tinkerers had invented the compass, and Chinese sailors used it more than sailors elsewhere. Their maritime culture was developing rapidly, thanks to constant voyaging to the islands of Southeast Asia, to Japan, and to every coast in between. By 1400, that maritime culture and Ming finances had reached a point at which they could support large, expensive, showy voyages to overawe just about everyone from Vietnam to East Africa.

Two crucial components of that maturing maritime culture were ship design and navigational tools. Chinese mariners had long used sternpost rudders and double-hulled construction. Rudders improved the steering of ships, and double hulls saved them from sinking if rammed or smashed on rocks. Chinese sailors also used the space between hulls to carry fresh water. During the Song dynasty, their seaborne trade links to the Indian Ocean acquainted them with new rigging and sails—particularly the lateen

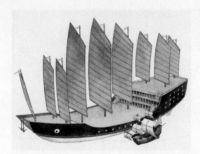

Ming Voyages As this artist's impression illustrates, the largest ships in Zheng He's fleet were 10 times the size of Columbus's flagship. The size of Ming ships was symbolic, enabling the emperor to advertise his power widely.

sail common in Arab shipping, good for sailing into the wind. Shipbuilders used these features, old and new, to design seagoing ships of 2,500 tons. They also put small cannon on these huge ships. As for navigation, Chinese sailors were already using the compass and printed sea manuals with star charts during the Song dynasty. A new emperor soon put Chinese maritime culture to new uses.

In 1402, a crafty uncle organized a military rebellion, overthrowing his nephew and becoming emperor of Ming China. Like all Chinese emperors, he took a reign name upon ascending the throne: the Yongle Emperor. To help consolidate his position, he promoted loyal eunuchs into positions of power. Eunuchs had minimal family connections of their own and therefore depended entirely on the emperor, making them highly reliable administrators. One of these eunuchs, **Zheng He**, became Yongle's indispensable adviser and political fixer. Ruling with an iron fist, Yongle moved the capital from the south to Beijing, launched campaigns against the Mongols (in which Zheng He distinguished himself), invaded and annexed part of Vietnam, and chased down and executed everyone loyal to his nephew.

Yongle also made his devoted aide Zheng He an admiral. Even though he had probably never smelled the sea, Zheng He organized a massive maritime expedition the likes of which China—and the world—had never seen. His official errand was to find and capture Yongle's nephew, who according to rumor had escaped his uncle's extermination campaign. But the scale of the undertaking indicates that Yongle had additional motives. In 1405, Zheng He set sail from Suzhou with roughly 300 ships, newly built in the shipyards of Nanjing along the Yangzi. They carried 28,000 men, both sailors and soldiers, a crew larger than the population of any city they would visit. His biggest ships, if we can believe the Chinese sources, were gigantic, about 400 feet (125 m) by 160 feet (50 m) and displacing 20,000 tons—far larger than any yet built anywhere and 10 times the size of Columbus's flagship. They were the largest wooden ships ever built.

Zheng He sailed well-traveled seas from China into the Indian Ocean. He used persuasion, intimidation, and military power to oust unfriendly rulers in Sumatra, Sri Lanka, and elsewhere, and install replacements more willing to acknowledge Yongle's overlordship and pay him tribute. In Sri Lanka he deposited a giant stone slab with inscriptions in Chinese, Persian, and Tamíl (a South Asian language in use in Sri Lanka after 1000 CE) commemorating his visit as an emissary of "the supreme overlord of kings"—lest anyone fail to appreciate Yongle's stature. Zheng He annihilated pirates—or maybe just merchant princes who failed to show proper enthusiasm for the emperor and so earned the title "pirate" in Chinese accounts. Perhaps Zheng He was also looking for allies against steppe nomads, almost always the Ming's main enemies.

Whatever his purposes, Zheng He was not attempting to find new routes. On his first six expeditions (1405–1424) he commanded similar-sized fleets, and on more than one occasion he sailed as far as the Swahili coast of Kenya. But in every case he visited ports and coasts well known to the maritime merchants of the Indian Ocean world, places where the occasional Chinese trader, and certainly Chinese goods, were familiar.

It was a traditional priority of Chinese statecraft to defend the empire's landward frontiers. Yongle mounted and personally led many expeditions into the Mongolian steppe and sent several embassies to Central Asia trying to improve the political situation on his frontiers. Overawing distant foreigners by sea ranked well behind

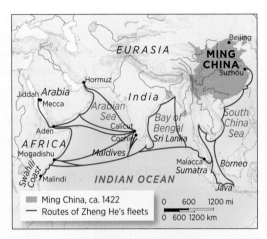

Voyages of Zheng He, 1405–1433 The Chinese admiral Zheng He led seven massive fleets into the Indian Ocean, following routes long familiar to merchants in these waters. Zheng He and his captains knew how to ride the monsoon winds, navigate with star charts, and find safe harbors. His routes extended to the far edges of the Indian Ocean world, the Swahili coast, the Arabian Peninsula, Java, and his home, China.

this priority, so the logic of doing it again and again came into question. Zheng He himself was an outsider in Chinese politics, a Muslim, a eunuch, and not even Chinese (he came from an ethnic minority population and had Persian ancestry as well). His career hinged entirely on the emperor's favor. When Yongle died in 1424, factions came to power that did not favor overseas voyaging.

Those factions eventually prevailed. Voyaging was costly and did not contribute to the security or virtue of the empire, nor much to its prosperity. Repairs to the Grand Canal, finished in 1411, made seafaring less important to the Ming state and Chinese society, since shipping could flow more safely on the canal than on the sea. Yongle's successor judged the oceanic voyaging wasteful and ended it in 1424. Under a later emperor, Zheng He and the eunuch faction prevailed one last time and launched a seventh voyage (1431–1433), again reaching Africa. But Zheng He died en route home, and his remaining supporters lost influence. The Ming eventually broke up the great fleet and sold it for fuelwood. By 1480, the skills needed to build such great ships had vanished.

The geographical and other knowledge accumulated on Zheng He's voyages found its way into Chinese charts, maps, and books. But it did not vastly expand, or fundamentally alter, Chinese understanding of the world. It temporarily lubricated the wheels of commerce that connected China to the Indian Ocean trading ports, but only for a few decades. The **Ming voyages** left scant enduring legacy.

The scale of the Ming maritime effort before 1433 suggests that the Chinese had the ships and skills to sail around Africa to Europe, or south to Australia, or across the Pacific to the Americas. But they had no good reason to try to reach Europe. They didn't yet know Australia or the Americas existed. So, instead, they sailed familiar waters in grand style with enormous government support. Then, in 1433, they stopped.

European Voyaging, 1400–1700

At the same time that the Ming were gliding into the Indian Ocean, western Europeans were probing the Atlantic. Some of them dreamed of sailing to the Indian Ocean too. They lacked the massive state support that Zheng He had enjoyed, and the states that helped them could mobilize only a tiny fraction of the resources the Ming could. These mariners were lucky if they could cobble together a tiny flotilla.

Ming Giraffe Giraffes are native to Africa, but here one appears as an illustration in a Ming manuscript, indicating the reach of Chinese maritime voyaging during the Ming period. Like other luxury goods, exotic animals could be brought back from voyages as status objects and prizes.

But European mariners usually had a good idea where they were heading. Navigational skill had accumulated slowly but surely over the centuries in Atlantic Europe. In Iberia especially, the practical experience of sailors combined with Arab mathematics and astronomy to create a more reliable—if by no means fully reliable—art of navigation. European sailors used the compass by the thirteenth century to find direction on cloudy days. By the fourteenth, they had translated Arabic texts on the use of astrolabes to help determine latitude. Soon they were authoring their own manuals on astrolabes—the English writer Geoffrey Chaucer penned one—and building the devices themselves. But even perfect navigational skill would have meant little without seaworthy ships.

Like the Chinese, Atlantic Europeans for a century or more had been rapidly refining their ship designs. More frequent connections in the fourteenth and fifteenth centuries between sailors in the North Atlantic and the Mediterranean yielded a hybrid in hull design and rigging. Shipbuilders combined the economical hull structure typical of Mediterranean ships—in which planks were nailed to ribs rather than to one another—with the sternpost rudder invented in the Baltic. This led to stronger, cheaper, and more maneuverable vessels. In addition, mariners supplemented square sails typical of northern waters with lateen sails characteristic of Arab seas to create the so-called fully rigged ship, which could sail swiftly before the wind and tack close to the wind.

Portolan Charts This innovation in cartography helped explorers to navigate the routes between ports. A 1571 Portolan chart of West Africa shows numerous ports along the coastline, with crests indicating the powers—especially Portugal, the red and white shield—that controlled them.

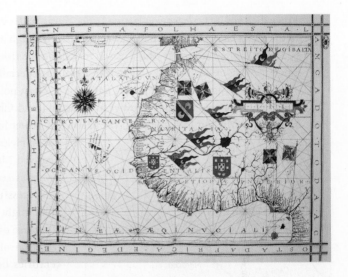

With these advances, European sailors could dispense with oars and oarsmen and rely entirely on the wind. Ships became cheaper to operate because much less was needed in the way of food, water, and wages to mount a voyage. So by the early fifteenth century, European shipwrights knew how to make sturdy, swift, and cheap ships, capable of carrying lightweight cannon and sailing anywhere in the world even in heavy weather. Their ships were far smaller than those of Zheng He, but no less seaworthy. And by 1500, they built ships large enough to carry heavy cannon capable of battering down walls or sinking any ship afloat.

Atlantic European mariners also had incentives to gamble on sailing the open seas. They, rather than the Chinese, began to unlock the secrets of the world's winds. And once they started, unlike the Ming they did not stop.

European Mariners' Motives Atlantic Europeans launched onto the high seas primarily in quest of wealth, fame, and the greater glory of their God. They started by sailing south into unfamiliar waters, looking for a practical route to African gold or Asian spices and silks, the most valuable trade goods they knew of. Merchants from Italian city-states such as Venice and Genoa had tapped into these trades, acquiring gold in Morocco or Tunisia and spices in Egypt or Syria, after the goods had changed hands many times. Merchants who could get these goods closer to the source could buy them for less and make a fortune by cutting out several middlemen.

The search for glory and fame also propelled European navigators. Fifteenth-century Europeans, especially Iberians, were steeped in a culture of adventure and chivalry as proper male pursuits. Owing in part to the centuries-long **Reconquista**—in which Christians retook Iberia from Muslim rulers—Iberian books, songs, poems, and folk tales celebrated the deeds of heroes who took daunting risks and either triumphed, or, if they died young, at least won lasting fame. Young males eager to vault several rungs up the social ladder learned that they could do so through acts of reckless heroism.

The Atlantic Europeans' third reason for taking the risks of oceanic seafaring was simultaneously religious and political. It appealed especially to Christian rulers, for whom victories against Muslim states meant more glory, political legitimacy, and support from the Pope. European voyagers who could find Christian allies in Africa or Asia against Muslim foes might tip the balance of power in favor of Christian kingdoms. Helping to find sea routes that deprived Muslim states of their trade revenues served the same purposes. If successful, quests for Christian allies might set the stage for renewed conquest of the Holy Land, in the tradition of the Crusaders of a few centuries before. For Iberians, voyaging south along the African Atlantic coast seemed an extension of the Reconquista and the loot and glory it provided. Although the last Muslim rulers in Spain were ousted in 1492, there were more targets nearby in North Africa. Indeed, the Portuguese had already begun to attack Muslim strongholds in Morocco as early as 1415.

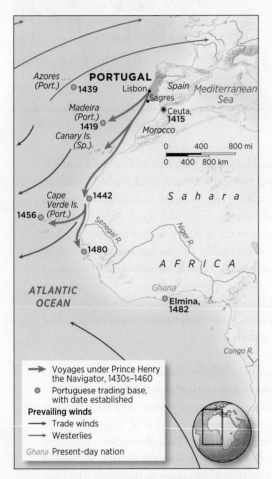

Early Exploration of the Atlantic, 1400–1480 In the fifteenth century, Iberian mariners figured out how to use the winds to venture far out into the Atlantic and get home safely. This accomplishment took navigation well beyond the familiar practice of hugging coastlines, and eventually led to successful crossings of the Atlantic and the discovery of routes linking the Atlantic and Indian Oceans.

Learning the Atlantic After about 1200, European and Moroccan mariners sailed hundreds of miles west into the uncharted Atlantic. By the fourteenth century, if not before, some stumbled across the Canary Islands, Madeira, and the Azores. The Canaries' population, called the **Guanches**, descended from North African Berber settlers who had arrived about 1000 BCE. Madeira and the Azores were uninhabited.

By the early fifteenth century, Europeans were attempting settlement of these islands, which in the Canaries required Spain to undertake military conquest of the Guanches. They fought fiercely, but their long isolation meant the Guanches had never acquired metallurgy: they used only stone, bone, and wooden weapons. Moreover, with no experience of infectious diseases by now familiar to Spaniards, they suffered repeated epidemics. The conquest of the Guanches, begun in 1402, ended in 1496. Many isolated peoples around the world would soon share their fate.

Shuttling to and from these little archipelagoes helped European sailors grow accustomed to the open Atlantic. The Canaries were crucial because they served as the entrance ramp to the northeast trade winds, which would prove to be the highway to the Americas.

At the same time as they were learning about, and starting to settle, these archipelagoes, European sailors were also edging down the coast of Africa. A pair of Italian brothers, the Vivaldis, tried to circumnavigate Africa in 1291—but they were never heard from again. Others, mainly Portuguese, followed more cautiously. The northwest coast of Africa offered little fresh water, and the northeast trade winds, which made outbound journeys simple, made it hard to get back home to Portugal. Improved ship design helped with that problem, as did the gradual discovery that sailors could follow the trade winds as far south as the Canaries and then swing north to the latitude of the Azores and catch the prevailing westerlies to get home. This was the first step in deciphering the code of the oceanic wind pattern.

African Coasts Portuguese efforts along the African coast quickened when in 1415 an army captured the Moroccan port of Ceuta. One of the leaders of that expedition, a prince known generously as Henry the Navigator, began to organize and support systematic voyaging along the coasts of Atlantic Africa in the 1430s. Henry was a seeker after honor and fame, which he once said were life's highest goals after salvation. He had strong religious convictions, influenced by chivalric notions of crusades against infidels. He also took astrology to heart and interpreted it to mean he was destined for great deeds. Henry the Navigator only put to sea two or three times in his life, but he siphoned off some of the modest resources of a threadbare dynasty in a poor country to pay for sea voyages along the northwest African coast, hoping to get at the source of West African gold.

The Portuguese voyages along the northwest coasts of Africa formed part of a larger, haphazard program that was full of failures. Several Portuguese sailors tried heading west from the Azores, out into the Atlantic, but either were pushed back by the westerly winds or lost at sea. Others tried to cross the Sahara on foot, but none returned. Henry encouraged various assaults on strongholds in Morocco, most of which failed.

All these efforts were dwarfed by the simultaneous voyaging of Zheng He, who commanded far greater resources than any Portuguese sea captain ever did. The tiny size of its investment, perhaps, explains why the Portuguese Crown did not give up and put a stop to the whole enterprise, as the Ming did with Zheng He's journeys. In

Elmina Castle The basement of the Portuguese fort of Elmina, located in present-day Ghana, was originally built as a pen to hold the enslaved people who were traded on the West African coast.

any case, the Portuguese kept at it, even after Henry's death in 1460, despite meager returns on their investment for half a century.

By the 1480s, their efforts began to pay off. Sailors reached the West African coast of what is now Ghana and established a fort—called Elmina—through which they traded for gold. Soon they found they could buy slaves on the coast and export them from Elmina to Iberia, or the sugar plantations of the Canaries or Madeira in a lucrative supplement to the gold trade. After nearly a century of meager returns, the Portuguese monarchy now had a profitable toehold in African trade. Soon every kingdom in Atlantic Europe would be sponsoring sea captains trying to get in on African commerce. One captain would also try, as several luckless Portuguese had before, to sail to China by heading west across the Atlantic.

Columbus Crosses the Atlantic In 1477, a ship broke up in a storm off the southern coast of Portugal. Almost everyone aboard drowned, but a 23-year-old sailor swam ashore. That sailor was **Christopher Columbus**.

Columbus was the son of a weaver from Genoa in northern Italy. He was a bit of a dreamer, easily lost in popular literature with its tales of adventure. He turned to the sea as a teenager, escaping the narrow horizons of an artisan's life in Genoa. As a sailor, he first roamed the Mediterranean and then made forays into the Atlantic. He became a trader too, and sometimes made lush profits in walrus tusk, whale blubber, and other items of Atlantic trade. After he washed up in Portugal in 1477, he went to Lisbon, where he had a brother working as a mapmaker. Through his brother, Columbus began to meet people with all sorts of tall tales about what lay over the western horizon.

Columbus was working in the sugar trade, shuttling between the eastern Mediterranean and the eastern Atlantic, when in the 1480s he began to peddle schemes for a voyage further west. Sometimes he said he would find new islands, as profitable as the Canaries or Madeira. Sometimes he said he would sail to China, which he claimed

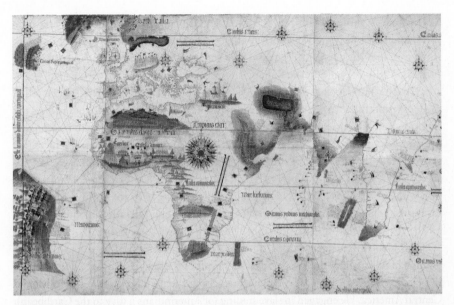

The Cantino Planisphere This Portuguese map was drawn by hand in 1502. Its rendering of the African coastline is especially detailed, an indication of how quickly and how well Portuguese mapmakers and navigators accumulated geographical information.

was a "few days" away. He had learned of the equatorial trade winds blowing to the west from Africa's northwest shores, and of the westerlies (blowing to the east) at higher latitudes. These prevailing winds, he figured, would allow a round-trip voyage to China. They would also allow him, the weaver's son, to join the titled aristocracy, which seems to have been his primary ambition. Columbus was at heart a social climber, willing to take great risks in his quest for status, wealth, and glory. But to get anywhere, he needed backers.

Like any would-be entrepreneur, Columbus pitched his schemes to anyone who would listen. He failed to convince the Portuguese monarchy to invest in his plans, so he went next door to Spain, where he proved more persuasive. Funded by Italian bankers residing in Spain, he secured permission from Ferdinand and Isabella, the king and queen of Castile (the largest region of Spain), to sail under their flag. The story that Queen Isabella pawned her jewels to finance the voyage is, sadly, mere whimsy. Some of her courtiers did invest in the voyage, using funds confiscated from Jews recently expelled from Castile.

Columbus promised the investors that he would forge a route to and from China by sailing west with the trade winds and then back home with the westerlies. He figured that Japan, which he had read about in Marco Polo's book of travels, lay about 2,500 miles (4,000 km) west of Spain. His estimate was off by about 10,000 miles. Had he calculated correctly, he surely would have stayed home.

Instead, he gathered sailors in the small Spanish port of Palos, acquired three little ships, and set out on the well-worn route to the Canary Islands. From there he ventured west into the open sea, seeing no land for 35 days before bumping into an island, perhaps Watlings Island in the Bahamas.

What he found looked nothing like Japan or China. Far from sporting silken robes, the locals stood stark naked and seemed unashamed of it. They had dugout canoes but no ships, and huts instead of palaces. Still hopeful, Columbus quickly moved on and in two weeks was in Cuba. He later stopped at the island of Hispaniola, where he met the more familiar trappings of complex society—dense populations, intensive agriculture, trade networks, and rumors of great kings. On Hispaniola, someone presented him with a few lumps of gold, something he could bring back for his investors. Upon his return home, he insisted to his backers that he had found a direct route to islands off the coast of Asia—and he probably believed it.

The Spanish Crown rewarded him with the title Admiral of the Ocean Sea and granted him broad powers to operate as he saw fit on subsequent voyages. He returned three more times to the Caribbean, even reaching the mainland shores of South and Central America. He engaged in slave trading (of Amerindians native to the Caribbean), bloody reprisals, and several sorts of atrocity in his eagerness for gold. His conduct met with rebukes among his followers and back in Spain. He hanged several Spaniards who defied his authority. A Spanish woman who reminded everyone that the Admiral of the Ocean Sea was the son of a weaver had her tongue cut out.

Columbus's Landfall In this 1493 engraving from *La lettera dell'isole*, Columbus's first account of his voyage, King Ferdinand observes from afar as Columbus and his crew land on an island in the Caribbean. The island's native inhabitants appear to flee.

Columbus's final years were filled with recriminations, lawsuits, bankruptcy, imprisonment, and bitter disappointment that he had found few riches and had not made it to China. He died in 1506, still convinced he had reached the doorstep of the Great Khan. No one else in history has had so many streets, squares, schools, and hotels named after him for making such a big mistake.

Columbus was wrong and he was brutal, but he was nonetheless a central historical figure. His voyages inaugurated a new age of connection among worlds long separate.

Soon after Columbus returned from the second of his four transatlantic voyages, another Italian, Giovani Caboto, was proposing voyages to China across the Atlantic. John Cabot, as he is known, approached merchants in Bristol, England, who were growing rich on the whale and walrus trade of the North Atlantic. Cabot also enlisted support from the English court, and in 1497 he made it across the Atlantic to Newfoundland and back in a tiny ship, about 3 percent the size of Zheng He's flagship. His crew numbered about 18. Among the treasures Cabot reported, mostly fanciful, were the very real and stupendously rich cod fisheries off of Newfoundland. Like Columbus, he recruited more investors, fitted out more and bigger ships, and set sail across the Atlantic a second time. Unlike Columbus, he never came back. Nevertheless, from soon after Cabot's time, Europeans would sail regularly to the fishing grounds off of Newfoundland, creating an enduring link—something the Viking voyaging to Newfoundland, some 500 years before, had not done.

Da Gama Sails to India In 1497, the same year that Cabot sailed, the Portuguese court fitted out an expedition of four ships and 170 men under the command of a low-ranking provincial noble named **Vasco da Gama**. Just a few years before, a Portuguese captain, Bartholomew Dias, had sailed from Lisbon to the shores of South Africa and returned safely. Dias discovered the belt of westerly winds in the Southern Hemisphere that enabled ships to sidestep adverse currents and ride into the Indian Ocean from the South Atlantic. Counting on this information, da Gama sailed way out into the South Atlantic to catch the westerlies and made it safely to the tip of South Africa and into the Indian Ocean. He worked his way up Africa's southeast coast and soon found evidence, in the form of Indian cloth and glassware, that he was where he hoped to be—in the Indian Ocean.

The ultimate prize, a practical route to and from the rich trade of Asia, lay almost within da Gama's grasp. He and his men resorted to piracy and the kidnapping of local pilots to help them find their way. On the shore of what is now Kenya they found a pilot who showed them the easiest route to **Calicut**, a trading city on the coast of India, where the Portuguese hoped to find—as one of da Gama's captains put it—Christians and spices.

The Portuguese expedition under da Gama had two main goals. The Portuguese Crown hoped to win glory, papal favor, and some practical political advantage by finding Christian allies somewhere in the Indian Ocean world, friends who would help in struggles against Muslim states of North Africa and Southwest Asia. The Crown also hoped to boost its finances by trading in spices, peppers, cloves, nutmeg, and more, items that were plentiful in India but scarce and expensive in Europe. Some Italian traders had done well in the spice trade, linking Venetian markets, through Egypt or Syria, with sources of supply in India and even further afield in Southeast Asia. The Portuguese hoped to help themselves to a share of this trade by sailing around Africa and going directly to the source of spices. Da Gama encountered no politically useful Christians in Calicut, but he found plenty of spice traders.

Da Gama and his crew did not linger long in India. The trade goods they had brought with them didn't interest the merchants of Calicut. The local prince wanted da

Gama to pay customs fees like any trader, whereas da Gama regarded himself as a royal emissary and above such things. After three disappointing months the Portuguese left, kidnapping a few Indians and sailing back toward Africa. Portuguese–Indian relations were off to a rocky start.

Da Gama left in a huff, pointing his prows into the teeth of the summer monsoon. The route that had taken three weeks with the winds at his back now took him four months on the return. Half the crew died before they reached Africa, and only 55 remained alive when da Gama returned to Lisbon more than two years after departing. He had sailed more than 25,000 miles (40,000 km), equal to the circumference of the Earth. He had confirmed the understanding of the winds of the South Atlantic and had pioneered a practical, if slow, route between western Europe and South Asia. And he had brought back enough spices to inspire investors, especially the Portuguese Crown, to send him back again.

In subsequent voyages, da Gama helped set up a lasting Portuguese presence in India and East Africa. It consisted of small trading enclaves, always fortified, sometimes under the protection of local rulers and sometimes at odds with them. The rivalries among rulers on the Indian and African coasts ensured that da Gama, and later Portuguese as well, could always find allies. Da Gama committed remarkable acts of cruelty, especially against Muslims making the pilgrimage to Mecca. He understood his mission to include piracy against Muslim shipping and did not mind making enemies. (He was not beloved by his own men either—at least, not after he ordered them to rinse their mouths with their own urine to combat scurvy, a gum disease resulting from vitamin shortage, one that often beset sailors on long voyages.)

The Portuguese commercial presence did not matter much to Indians and Africans, who continued their business much as before. But to Portugal, a poor kingdom of fewer than a million people, the occasional trading voyage to India meant infusions of riches, especially for the Crown. The trade to the Indian Ocean also affected Portuguese culture and self-image. Portuguese monumental architecture developed a distinctive style, called Manueline after Manuel I (r. 1495–1521), the king at the time of the first voyages to the Indian Ocean. It celebrates those voyages and nautical life, using artistic motifs from sailing ships and from Indian temples and mosques. The Portuguese national saga, known as *The Lusiads*, is an epic poem, first printed in 1572. It is modeled on ancient epics, especially the *Iliad*, but based loosely on the experience of da Gama and other sea captains.

One of the voyages to India missed its target. In 1500, on his swing out into the Atlantic in search of the Southern Hemisphere's westerlies, Pedro de Cabral and his fleet of 13 ships accidentally bumped into Brazil. Cabral claimed it for Portugal, despite the fact that people already lived there. After a brief look around, he continued on across the South Atlantic, around Africa, to India. Like da Gama, he ran into trouble in India with Arab merchants unhappy with competition and engaged in a vengeful massacre in Calicut before heading home in 1501.

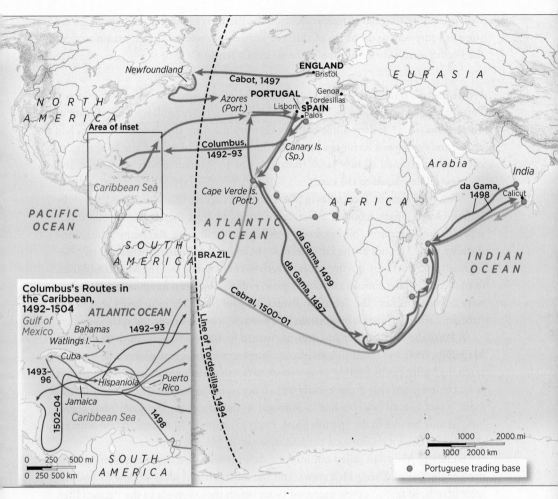

Navigation in the Atlantic and Indian Oceans, 1492–1500 This map shows the new routes pioneered by Columbus, Cabot, da Gama, and Cabral, which began the process of tying together the coasts of Europe, the Americas, Africa, and South Asia. The Line of Tordesillas, established in 1494, divided all "new" lands between Portugal and Spain.

Sailors such as Columbus, da Gama, and Cabral made the years 1492–1501 as pivotal as any decade in world history. Mariners from Atlantic Europe learned how to ride the winds back and forth between Europe and America, between Africa and America, and between Europe and South Asia. They found viable routes across the open ocean linking coastlines of continents formerly out of touch with one another.

The discovery of the oceans did not stop in the 1490s. Mariners had now solved the mysteries of the wind system of the Atlantic, as they had long ago the monsoon winds of the Indian Ocean. But the broad Pacific was another matter. Its winds and currents were even more essential to master, because the Pacific is so big that sailing against the wind is a sure way to die at sea of thirst or hunger. No one had much reason to cross the Pacific—until the beginning of the sixteenth century.

Magellan Crosses the Pacific At the end of the fifteenth century, Spain and Portugal signed what could be the most presumptuous treaty of all time, the **Treaty of Tordesillas** (1494). It drew a line halfway between the American lands Columbus had visited and Portuguese territories known as the Cape Verde Islands off the West African coast. Spain claimed all new lands (meaning new to Spaniards) west of the line, and Portugal all new lands to the east.

With the Treaty of Tordesillas in place, once Portuguese vessels were trading on the Indian Ocean, Spain acquired a motive for trying to cross the Pacific: to gain direct access to precious spices. No one knew how big the Pacific was, and many thought the distance from America to the East Indies—the islands of Indonesia where by 1515 Portuguese merchants were buying spices directly—could not be far. The Molucca Islands, in particular, where nutmeg and cloves grew, excited European imaginations as if they were diamond mines. The Treaty of Tordesillas gave Spain claim to lands west of the Americas, which, if the claim extended far enough, would include the spice islands.

A Portuguese adventurer and dreamer named Fernão de Magalhães, or **Ferdinand Magellan**, tried and failed to convince authorities in Lisbon that it would be easier to reach the **Moluccas** by finding a route south of South America and then sailing west to Asia. He imagined that if there really was an ocean to the west of the American landmass, it was a small one. No one in Portugal would listen. So, like Columbus before him, he took his idea to the Spanish court. Eager to claim the Moluccas and their spices, the Spanish Crown encouraged bankers to invest in Magellan's plans.

So in 1519 Magellan sailed out into the Atlantic with five ships, 250 men (about 1 percent the size of Zheng He's crew), and the most fanciful ideas of how to find the spice islands. Magellan's crew mutinied twice before they even got to the Pacific. Then things went south in a hurry. Magellan thought he could cross from South America to the spice islands easily, but he had been on the ocean for 14 weeks, out of food and fresh water, before his men sighted Guam—they had sailed across an ocean with hundreds of inhabited islands and by bad luck had missed them all. One of the crew explained their suffering:

> We only ate old biscuit reduced to powder, full of grubs and stinking from the dirt, which the rats had made on it when eating the good biscuit and we drank water that was yellow and stinking. We also ate the ox hides which were under the main-yard, so that the yard should not break the rigging: they were very hard on account of the sun, rain, and wind, and we left them for four or five days in the sea, and then we put them a little on the embers, and so ate them; also the sawdust of wood, and rats which cost half-a-crown each, moreover enough of them were not to be got.

CONSIDERING THE EVIDENCE

Portuguese Reasoning about Skin Color

As Portuguese ships explored the oceans, they also recorded observations about geography and people that contradicted traditions handed down from classical scholars. The Portuguese sea captain Duarte Pacheco Pereira (1460–1533) discussed some of these contradictions in his manuscript *Esmeraldo de Situ Orbis*. Pereira had voyaged nearly everywhere the Portuguese reached. He defended Portuguese forts in India, governed Elmina off the coast of West Africa, and captured a French pirate in the Atlantic. He was also the first person to mention Brazil in a navigation book. In the following excerpt, he draws on personal observations to reconsider the classical Greek assumption that skin color was determined by latitude.

[D]uring the many years we have sailed and operated in this part of the Ethiopias of Guinea [i.e., West Africa], experience has taught us how to take the height of the sun and its declination in order to tell the degrees of latitude by which each place is separated from the Equator and one of the poles. And we have found that this promontory lies directly over the Equator, and have discovered that in this place the days and nights throughout the year are equal....

Many of the ancients said that if two lands lie to the east and west of one another, both would have the same degree of sun and would be in all things alike. As to their equal share of the sun this is true, but such is the great variety employed by the majesty of nature in her work of creation and procreation that we find, from experience, that the inhabitants of this promontory of Lopo Gonçalves and of the rest of Guinea are very black, whereas the people who live beyond the Ocean Sea to the west (who have an equal amount of sun with the blacks of Guinea) are brown, and some almost white. These are the people who live in the land of Brazil.... If any want to claim that these are protected from the heat of the sun because there are many trees in that region, I would say that there are also many trees as great and as thick in this land of Guinea on the eastern side of the ocean. And if any should say that they are black because they go around naked and that the others are white because they go clothed, I would say that both of them ...go around just as they were born. So we can say that the sun does not affect one more than the others. Now it only remains to find out if they are both descended from Adam.

Questions for Analysis

1. What evidence does Pereira rely on to challenge the conclusions of "the ancients"?

2. After dismissing possible explanations for the differences in skin color between people in Africa and those in Brazil, what direction does he suggest for future research?

3. Does this excerpt suggest that the Portuguese of Pereira's time considered people whose skin color differed from theirs to be inferior in any way?

Source: "Duarte Pacheco Pereira Tries to Come to Terms with 'Difference,'" in Malyn Newitt, ed., *The Portuguese in West Africa, 1415–1670: A Documentary History* (Cambridge, 2010).

On Guam, Magellan guessed he was just off the shore of China. He was 2,500 miles (4,000 km) from it. He next blundered into the Philippines, where he got mixed up in a local war and died in battle.

Magellan's surviving crew kept going west, sailing through the islands of Indonesia, where they picked up a cargo of spices, and into the Indian Ocean, around Africa, and home to Spain. The trip had taken three years, and only about 10 percent of the crew survived. They were the first humans to circumnavigate the globe—although they had intended only to find a route to the Moluccas and spices.

It took many decades before anything practical came of Magellan's quixotic quest. Magellan had showed how big the Pacific really was, and that it—like the Atlantic— had trade winds blowing east to west. Some 40 years later, another captain showed how one could cross the Pacific west to east, from Asia to America, by riding the westerlies, found at the same latitudes as those of the Atlantic. By 1570, Atlantic Europeans had deciphered the wind system of the Pacific too.

Weaving a Maritime Web

Every coastline in the world was now more accessible than ever before to those who knew the secrets of the winds. While Magellan sailed the wide Pacific, other mariners in less dramatic fashion brought more of the world into a tighter web of connections. Portuguese captains began to visit China and Japan, following routes that Asian sailors had used for centuries. From the East African coast, Portuguese adventurers pushed inland, developing a previously small-scale trade in slaves and ivory in Mozambique and making contact with fellow Christians in Ethiopia. These Portuguese travels followed the beaten paths of Asian and African traders.

While European sailors were gathering up knowledge of routes and coasts in Africa and Asia, as far as Australia and Japan, others were adding further information from the Americas. Columbus had begun the process, but dozens of others, mainly Spaniards, followed. They sailed the coastlines, probed the river mouths, and, despite language barriers, absorbed what they could from Amerindian informants. By 1520, they had accumulated a good knowledge of the Caribbean and South America coasts. It took much longer for mariners to figure out the coasts of North America, but by 1620 sailors, mainly English and Dutch, had charted the eastern shoreline all the way north to the fogbound and iceberg-strewn coasts of Hudson Bay. To their dismay, they established that here too there was no good route to the riches of Asia. That dream died hard. As late as the 1630s, Jean Nicolet, a French fur trader, walked and canoed through Wisconsin wearing flowing Chinese robes in hopes of meeting someone who knew the way to China.

Gradually, mariners filled in the remaining blank spots on the map of the oceans. Dutch and English ship captains sailed around New Zealand and Australia in the seventeenth century, charting the coasts. But finding the Maori unwelcoming and the Aborigines poor, they left these lands alone for another 150 years. In the eighteenth

Namban Screen This six-fold Japanese screen from around 1600 likely illustrates the arrival of a Portuguese merchant ship in Japan. Portuguese sea captains began to visit Japan in 1543, bringing Christianity, guns, and Chinese silks and porcelain. They bought thousands of Japanese slaves to sell in Macao, Goa, or other Portuguese enclaves until the trade ended soon after 1600.

century, European sailors refined their knowledge of Pacific shores and blundered into most of the inhabited Pacific islands, including the remotest outposts of Polynesia in Easter Island and Hawaii. They charted the American coastlines from Alaska to Chile. By 1780, every significant coast of every ocean had been mapped, and every important island located. For all intents and purposes, the discovery of the winds and the oceans was complete.

European mariners failed in their quest to find a direct route from Europe to Asian spices and failed to find powerful Christian allies against Islamic polities. But they succeeded at something they did not consciously attempt, which was to unite the world's coasts and harbors into a single network and to build geographical knowledge so that any competent navigator, with the right equipment and ship, could go anywhere on the sea with a reasonably good idea of where he was and what lay ahead. The confidence with which merchants had long sailed the South China Sea, the Arabian Gulf, or the Mediterranean, European merchants (and for a long while only European ones) now extended to the deep oceans. The first pulse of true globalization, achieved partly by accident, was accomplished mainly by Europeans—specifically, those from Atlantic Europe.

Biological Globalization, 1492–1800

One of the most important consequences of the discovery of the oceans and their winds, and the establishment of regular traffic linking the world's shores, was a surge in **biological globalization**. This process reshuffled the continents' flora and fauna,

Waldseemüller World Map   Created by German mapmaker Martin Waldseemüller in 1507, this map was the first to encompass the full Western Hemisphere. It was also the first—on the lower portion of South America—to mention the name "America."

bringing both searing new epidemics and useful new food crops to many peoples. It changed the world's demographic balance and altered political and economic fortunes. By and large, it eased life for millions in Eurasia and Africa, and ended it prematurely for millions in the Americas and Oceania. It provides an excellent example of the fact that in world history major consequences often flow from events in ways that no one intended or foresaw.

As earlier chapters have noted, over the centuries people moved plants, animals, and microbes around the world. Sometimes they did it on purpose, like the first settlers of North America who brought dogs with them, or the Polynesians who ferried crops and animals to uninhabited Pacific islands. Sometimes they did it by accident, like the anonymous people who brought the plague bacillus from northeast Africa to the Byzantine Empire in the time of Justinian. Biological exchange has long been an important part of history, with powerful effects on food supplies and disease burdens.

The pace of biological exchange sped up whenever web connections boosted trade and migration. It slowed down when webs withered. So, for example, when the Roman and Han Empires were at their height, and trans-Eurasian trade and travel reached a temporary peak along the Silk Roads, so did biological exchange. China acquired camels, donkeys, and grapes. Mediterranean peoples added cherries, apricots, and walnuts to their gardens and diets. When commerce quickened in the Arabian Sea after 800 CE, the exchange of crops among India, East Africa, and the Mediterranean picked up speed.

Biologically, as in other respects, the Americas had remained a realm apart from these Old World web exchanges. Aside from the import of the dog (from Siberia about

15,000 years ago) and the export of sweet potato (to Polynesia about 1,000 years ago), the American hemisphere before 1492 exchanged nothing consequential with the wider world. American plants and animals included many unknown elsewhere—tobacco, armadillos, and grizzly bears, for instance. Australia and New Zealand, even more isolated, each hosted flora and fauna—eucalyptus trees, kangaroos, and moas, for example—found nowhere else on Earth.

After the voyages of Columbus, mariners linked almost every nook and cranny of the humanly habitable Earth into a biologically interactive web. The world's oceans no longer served to isolate ecosystems from one another. It became a world without biological borders, as plants, animals, and disease-causing pathogens scattered wherever ecological conditions permitted their spread. They went wherever people took them, and sometimes even further on their own.

Columbus inaugurated regular exchanges across the Atlantic in 1492. On his second voyage, he deliberately brought a ship full of species new to the Americas and brought home to Spain some biological souvenirs. Over the next few centuries, his followers did the same in an ongoing process known to historians as the Columbian Exchange. The most conspicuous result was that Amerindians acquired hundreds of new plants and animals from Eurasia and Africa, as well as a dozen devastating diseases formerly unfamiliar to them. At first, between 1492 and 1700, the spread of diseases was the most important part of biological globalization, mainly because of their horrific impact on the peoples of the Americas.

Deadly Diseases

Upon arrival in the Americas, transatlantic travelers coughed and sneezed billions of deadly microbes into the air that Amerindians breathed. Among them were the pathogens (viruses, mainly) that cause smallpox, measles, mumps, whooping cough, and influenza. All of these had become fairly widespread in the Old World web. From West Africa to East Asia, they were usually endemic, childhood diseases, sometimes now called crowd diseases (discussed in Chapter 5), that killed huge numbers of small children. But in the Old World web, most adults were survivors, and either resistant or fully immune to most or all of these viral infections. In addition to the crowd diseases, the Columbian Exchange brought some lethal vector-borne African diseases to the Americas. The two deadliest were yellow fever and falciparum malaria (the worst form of **malaria**), both spread by mosquitos.

In the Americas in 1492, none of the 40 to 70 million people had any prior experience with, and therefore no acquired immunity to, any of these diseases. Their immune systems did not instantly "recognize" and neutralize the exotic pathogens. This vulnerability was compounded by the weakening of their nutrition and health by Atlantic European colonization—which, as we'll see, included loss of farmlands, enslavement, and forced migration.

The cascade of unfamiliar pathogens brought suffering and death on the largest scale. Here is how one Amerindian, in Mexico, recalled it:

> The illness was so dreadful that no one could walk or move. The sick were so utterly helpless that they could only lie on their beds like corpses, unable to move their limbs or even their heads. A great many died from this plague, and many others died of hunger. They would not get up to search for food, and everyone else was too sick to care for them, so they starved to death in their beds.

In many Amerindian communities, the social fabric dissolved under this onslaught. People lost all hope. Few wanted to bring children into a world such as theirs had become, dominated by sickness and pain, and few were healthy enough to do so.

The scale of epidemics and death was gigantic. Between 1492 and 1650, populations in the Americas fell by 70 to 95 percent in one of the two largest-scale demographic disasters in world history. (The other was the Black Death of the fourteenth century in the Old World web.) The sharp decline in population in the Americas had many consequences that we will meet repeatedly in the chapters ahead.

The Amerindians had little in the way of lethal infectious disease that transferred to Africa and Eurasia. The first migrants to arrive in North America had passed through northeastern Siberia and Alaska during an ice age. The brutal cold probably killed off some pathogens. And since they left Siberia when no animals but dogs had been domesticated, the human infections shared with herd animals (e.g., smallpox, measles, influenza) had not yet appeared. Thus the first Amerindians arrived relatively free from infection.

Once in the Americas, Amerindians did not domesticate any herd animals other than alpacas and llamas, which seem, by chance, not to have hosted pathogens that

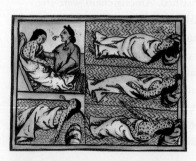

Epidemics in the Americas This illustration of Aztecs suffering and dying from the smallpox brought by Spanish colonists appears in the Florentine Codex, a Spanish missionary's sixteenth-century treatise about the Spanish conquest of Mexico in 1519–21.

evolved into agents of human disease. If Eurasia and Africa acquired any new diseases from the Americas at all (syphilis is the leading candidate, but the evidence is far from conclusive), they had trivial consequences. So, as regards disease, the Columbian Exchange was a notably one-sided affair.

The one-sidedness of the health consequences of the Columbian Exchange led Europeans who witnessed this devastation to see divine purpose at work. Francisco de Aguilar, who was present when Spaniards and their allies conquered the Aztec capital of Tenochtitlán, wrote: "When the Christians were exhausted from war, God saw fit to send the Indians smallpox, and there was a great pestilence in the city." More than a century later in New England, John Winthrop, the first governor of the

Massachusetts Bay Colony, saw the disaster as divine endorsement of the seizure of land: "For the natives, they are neere all dead of small Poxe, so as the Lord hathe cleared our title to what we possess."

Useful Animals

The Columbian Exchange was almost as one-sided with respect to domesticated animals. People transported turkeys and guinea pigs from the Americas to other continents, but nowhere did they become important. Alpacas and llamas never prospered outside their native Andes, although scattered populations do exist elsewhere. The Amerindians had little in the way of domesticated animals, and those they had did not travel well.

In contrast, Eurasian and African animal species flourished when transported to the Americas. Cattle, goats, sheep, pigs, and horses were the most important animal immigrants. They all found empty niche space in the Americas, especially cattle and horses on the vast grasslands of both North and South America. The new animals provided surviving Amerindians with new sources of hides, wool, and animal protein. Horses and oxen made plowing feasible in the Americas for the first time, allowed transportation through wheeled vehicles, and, together with donkeys and mules, provided a greater variety of pack animals. Animal-powered transport extended the potential of commerce and economic specialization, which over centuries raised overall production levels considerably.

In addition to economic growth, the new animals brought unwelcome frictions to the Americas. They munched and trampled crops, provoking quarrels between herders and farmers of the sort familiar in Africa and Eurasia but almost unknown in the Americas before 1492. In this respect, the Columbian Exchange helped make the Americas a bit more like the rest of the world, where such quarrels had long been routine.

In North America, the introduction of horses upset the political order. The Amerindians of the prairies, from Texas to Manitoba, acquired horses from newly Spanish Mexico in the seventeenth century, and some of them quickly mastered riding and horse breeding. On horseback, they became far more adept as bison hunters, solving any subsistence problems as long as the bison lasted. Moreover, those with horses easily inflicted military defeats on those without. Amerindian peoples such as the Sioux and Comanche eventually built considerable empires on the basis of mounted warfare, as Mongol and Malian horsemen had recently done in Asia and Africa. In this respect too, the Americas became less distinctive, more like the rest of the world, thanks to the Columbian Exchange and biological globalization.

Key Crops

The Columbian Exchange was more even-handed when it came to crops. The Eurasian staples of wheat, rye, barley, and rice flourished in the Americas. Some of the new crops could survive in cold and dry landscapes where the indigenous crops fared poorly: North Dakota and Saskatchewan do better growing wheat than maize. Others, such as rice, transplanted from both Asia and Africa, required heavy labor in order to produce bumper crops. Rice became a plantation crop in the Americas, worked mainly by imported African slave labor. Aside from grains, the Americas also acquired citrus fruits, grapes, and figs from Eurasia, and millets, sorghums, yams, bananas, okra, and watermelon from Africa. So the new crops extended the possibilities of American agriculture somewhat and allowed a more varied diet. But in many places they brought only a small improvement in nutrition, because people in the Americas already had maize or potatoes (or both) and plenty of fruits and vegetables.

New drug crops changed the Americas at least as profoundly as the new food crops. Sugar, originally from New Guinea but a commercial crop in South Asia, China, and the Mediterranean, came to Brazil and the Caribbean in the sixteenth and seventeenth centuries. Both a mild drug and a food, it became, as we shall see, the mainstay of a plantation economy based on African slave labor. Coffee, from Ethiopia and Arabia, also became a plantation crop in the eighteenth century. We will see the full importance of these crops in a later chapter when we encounter the plantation system in the Americas.

The Americas' contributions to global cuisine included the staples maize, potatoes, sweet potatoes, and cassava, together with tomatoes, cacao, peanuts, pumpkins, squashes, pineapples, and a handful of other food crops. Some of these crops had revolutionary consequences in sizeable regions of Africa and Eurasia. Potatoes, for example, which nicely suited soil and climate conditions from Ireland to Russia, led to a spurt of population growth in northern Europe after 1730.

Maize   This staple had a broader impact than potatoes. It did well in conditions as varied as those of southern Europe, southern and central China, and much of Africa. **Maize** allowed new lands to be brought under cultivation, because it prospered where grains and tubers would not. It soon undergirded population growth and famine resistance in China and southern Europe. But nowhere was it more influential than in Africa, where today it remains the single most important food crop. In the two centuries after 1550, maize became a staple in Atlantic Africa, from Angola to Senegambia. Different maize varieties suited the several different rainfall regimes in Africa and improved African peoples' chances of surviving drought.

While maize helped feed generations of Africans, it had bleaker consequences too. Maize stores much better than millets, sorghums, or tubers, the traditional crops in most of Africa. It thus allowed chiefs and kings to maximize their power by centralizing the storage and distribution of food. In the West African forest zone, south of the Sahel, maize encouraged the formation of larger states than ever before. The Asante kingdom, for example, embarked on a program of military expansion after the 1670s, spearheaded by maize-eating armies that could carry their food with them on distant campaigns. Maize also served well as a portable food for merchant caravans, which contributed to commercialization in Atlantic Africa, including an expansion of existing slave trades.

Slave traders could operate over longer distances if they, and their human property, had an easily portable food supply that stored well. Maize in Africa increased the practicality of the slave trade. As we shall see, it helped make slaving an intercontinental business, linking Europe, Africa, and the Americas.

Cassava Also known as manioc, **cassava** was the Americas' other great contribution to African agriculture. A native of Brazil, cassava is admirably suited to drought and poor soils, and resistant to many insect crop pests. It too did well in many parts of Africa, and like maize provided a portable, storable food that underlay state formation and expansion in West Africa and Angola. Cassava, like potatoes, need not be harvested at a particular season but may be left in the ground for weeks or more. So it is an ideal crop for people who might need to run away for their own safety and abandon their fields—for example, people routinely subject to slave raiding. In this respect, it had the opposite effect of maize: it helped peasantries to flee and survive slave raids, while maize helped slavers to conduct raids and wars.

The impact of American food crops on Africa was so great that it makes sense to think of African history, especially Atlantic African history, as divided into pre-Columbian and post-Columbian phases—as is normally done for the Americas. Maize, cassava, and a cornucopia of other crops from the Americas, including peanuts, pineapple, chili peppers, sweet potato, avocado, cacao, and a dozen others, gradually re-fashioned African cuisine and agriculture. This was the second time in African history that imported crops made a big difference—recall the impact of bananas, acquired from Southeast Asia, many centuries before.

African farmers took to the new American crops eagerly, seeing them as either useful additions or even replacements for their old ones. The greater variety of food crops provided a form of insurance against crop failure due to insect pests or bad weather. Maize had the further attraction that birds usually find it too much trouble to poke through the husks to get at the grain. Birds don't bother with cassava either. Ripe millet and sorghum, in contrast, provide tempting targets for birds, and people must defend these crops day and night if they wish to enjoy a harvest. The American crops undergirded a slow expansion of farming, state making, and perhaps even population growth in Africa after 1650—despite the demographic effects of the transatlantic slave trade.

Cassava in Africa This illustration of the cassava plant appears in a French book about Caribbean plants from 1688. Originating in the Americas, cassava became an even more successful crop in West Africa and Angola, where it was well suited to the climate, soils, and the needs of farming communities.

THE HUMAN WEB

The Columbian Exchange

1492–1800

NORTH AMERICA

EUROPE

potatoes

horses

Rocky Mts.

Appalachian Mts.

grains

cotton

Mississippi R.

Colorado R.

Danube R.

maize

maize

influenza, measles, mumps, smallpox, whooping cough
cattle, goats, horses, pigs, sheep
barley, oats, rye, wheat, citrus, cotton, figs, grapes
sugar

cassava, maize, potatoes, avocadoes, cacao, chili peppers,
peanuts, pineapples, pumpkins, squashes, sweet potatoes, tomatoes
syphilis? tobacco

Mexico

sugar

coffee
sugar

horses

Arabia

Nile R.

Ethiopia

Senegambia

Niger R.

malaria, yellow fever
rice, millets, sorghums, bananas, cotton, okra, watermelon, yams
coffee

cassava
maize

AFRICA

coffee
sugar

Amazon R.

Brazil

sugar

ATLANTIC
OCEAN

Congo R.

cassava
maize

Angola

sugar

SOUTH
AMERICA

Andes Mts.

Zambezi R.

PACIFIC
OCEAN

Andes Mts.

Paraná R.

coffee
sugar

horses

KEY

⬅ Organisms originating
in the Old World

➡ Organisms originating
in the Americas

Organism transferred

measles Pathogen

horses Livestock

maize Food and fiber crop

sugar Drug crop

Population decline due to
introduction of pathogens

☐ 90% or more

☐ Less than 90%

Areas of greatest impact
of livestock and crops

☐ Horses

☐ Food and fiber crops

☐ Drug crops

ASIA

potatoes

Himalaya Mts.
potatoes
Ganges R.

India

Huang He
Yangzi R.
maize

China

Mekong R.
potatoes

PACIFIC
OCEAN

Philippines

Guam

INDIAN
OCEAN

New
Guinea

BETWEEN 1492 AND 1800, mariners tied together the shores of the Atlantic into an especially vibrant part of the emerging Global web. Their voyages created an Atlantic world, similar in many respects to the Indian Ocean world, another lively part of a larger web, built long before. But in one respect—the Columbian Exchange—the Atlantic world had no true parallels in world history.

The Columbian Exchange of plants, animals, and lethal pathogens was the biggest pulse of biological exchange in world history. Anytime that webs extended across vast distances, people—intentionally and accidentally—carried some species to new homes. When the Silk Roads opened, for example, China acquired grapes, sorghum, donkeys, and camels from Southwest Asia. But no other such episode approaches the Columbian Exchange which suddenly united biological communities that had been separate for 50 million years.

The impacts of the Columbian Exchange included drastic changes in population, agriculture, and the economies of the Americas, Africa, and Europe. For some people, such as Amerindians, the Columbian Exchange brought disaster in the form of new diseases. For others, such as southern Europeans or southern Africans, it brought a new, high-energy food crop: maize. The introduction of maize and cassava to African agriculture and diet was so important that for Atlantic Africa at least, it makes sense to think in terms of pre-Columbian and post-Columbian phases, just as scholars routinely do for the Americas.

Questions for Analysis

Based on this feature and your chapter reading, consider the following questions:

1. Why did some peoples suffer and some peoples benefit from the Columbian Exchange?

2. What regions within the Atlantic world felt the strongest impacts of the Columbian Exchange?

Biological Globalization in the Pacific

The **Columbian Exchange** was the largest-scale, fastest, and most important set of intercontinental biological transfers in world history. But it was only part of the surge in biological globalization that followed upon the navigational exploits of Columbus's generation. A modest transpacific exchange resulted from traffic that followed Magellan's voyages, at first affecting chiefly the Philippines. That exchange intensified in the wake of later sea captains' travels throughout the world's largest ocean. The Pacific islands themselves, rather than the ocean's rim, felt the greatest effects, and as in the Americas the most striking result was sharp depopulation in the wake of repeated epidemics.

Guam, for example, in the seventeenth century became a Spanish outpost on the route between the Philippines and the Americas. Its indigenous population, the Chamorro, fell by about 90 percent within a century—mainly from the impact of smallpox, measles, tuberculosis, and other new diseases, although violence and loss of lands raised the Chamorros' vulnerability to infections. Guam also acquired many new plants and animals, such as cattle, hogs, chickens, rice, citrus trees, and a Mexican shrub tree called Tangantangan. The latter grew quickly on Guam, especially in lands no longer farmed because of the population disaster.

Later on, other Pacific islands experienced similar biological disruptions when put into sustained contact with the wider world. In every case, the demographic consequences overshadowed all others. Population declines of roughly 90 percent befell many archipelagoes, primarily a result of newly introduced diseases. A similar grim history befell aboriginal Australians after 1788 when contact with the wider world became routine. But this was a story of the eighteenth and nineteenth centuries, one that belongs to a later chapter.

The Impact of Biological Exchange

Taken together, the whirlwind of intercontinental biological exchange in the centuries between 1492 and 1800 brought astounding changes around the world. It led to long-lasting demographic catastrophes among peoples unfamiliar with the crowd diseases. In the Americas and Oceania, indigenous population size typically fell for about six or seven generations before bottoming out and beginning to recover. This rate of recovery was slow compared to the experience of Eurasian populations in the face of most epidemics. That is testimony to the terrible impact of multiple infections assaulting peoples in the Americas and Oceania in repeated hammer blows. It also reflects the significance of loss of the best lands, enslavement, and forced migration in escalating mortality and suppressing fertility. The population disasters were a part of biological globalization, but they were not just biological processes: they arose from the interaction of biological and social processes. They represent a penalty of isolation from the bigger webs of world history, a theme we have encountered before.

The surge in biological exchange eventually improved the quantity and reliability of food supplies almost everywhere. This process slowly reduced the frequency of starvation and the toll of epidemics (because well-fed people survive most diseases better than malnourished ones). The world's population almost doubled between 1500 and 1800, from about 500 million to about 950 million, and a big reason was improved nutrition thanks to food-crop globalization.

One agreeable way of thinking about the whole (admittedly often grim) subject of biological globalization in the wake of Columbus is to contemplate food. Can you imagine Italian food without tomatoes? Or Polish cuisine without potatoes? What would the South African diet be without mealie maize, or West Africa's without peanuts? Argentina's without beef? New Zealand's or southern China's without sweet potatoes? What would Korean kimchi taste like without chili peppers? If we are what we eat, then the Columbian Exchange and biological globalization not only shaped empires and demography but also helped to make us what we are.

The Beginnings of a Global Web

The oceanic voyaging of the fifteenth and sixteenth centuries united continents into a single global web for the first time in human history. The web-making process—at work from the very earliest human settlements onward—had developed an extended, multilayered fabric of connections across Eurasia and North Africa. Significant webs had developed also in the Americas, and smaller, local ones elsewhere. But for thousands of years before 1492, the Americas had largely stood apart from Africa and Eurasia, notwithstanding the brief Viking and Polynesian visits. Now the history of the Americas unfolded in continuing connection with the Old World web. Similarly, after the secrets of oceanic navigation spread and mariners sailed regularly among all the world's inhabited shores, the islands of the Pacific, the coastlands of South Africa, and a few other spots around the world became linked as never before to the new, global web now in formation.

The oceanic voyaging also tightened linkages within the Old World web. In some cases, the tighter links proved temporary, as with Zheng He's voyages to India and East Africa between 1405 and 1433. But in others they endured much longer, as with Portuguese ties to African coasts, India, and the spice islands of Southeast Asia. So the three centuries after the 1490s saw a sudden spurt in web building, one that transformed human history and inaugurated a global age in which we still live.

The spinning of the first truly global web had many consequences. The most enduring and important of these was the biological globalization that reshuffled the distribution of economically significant plants and animals around the world and brought devastating infections to the Americas and Oceania. Another important consequence flowed from the fact that it was mainly Atlantic Europeans—not Chinese,

Africans, Polynesians, or anyone else—who first fully deciphered the oceanic winds and currents. As a result, they were the first to sail the seven seas and learn of new long-distance trade possibilities. They also found new opportunities to conquer peoples less militarily formidable than themselves. The role of Europeans, especially seafaring Atlantic Europeans, in influencing world history rose to new levels. Over the prior millennia, only rarely could such a small minority of humankind exercise such out-sized influence upon world history as Atlantic Europeans would wield in the three or four centuries to come.

The penalties of isolation for societies with few or no connections to the Old World web were now felt as never before. These societies typically hosted a narrower range of infectious diseases than did peoples in the web that enveloped Eurasia and North Africa, leaving them vulnerable to shattering epidemics when European ships arrived with new pathogens. They typically possessed a less formidable array of weaponry than existed in China, India, or Europe, using less metal, no firearms, and no horses. These societies had not needed or developed institutions and technologies that equipped them to deal with the challenges posed by seafaring, horse-riding, disease-bearing, well-armed strangers.

The spinning of the first truly global web proved transformational in other respects too. It continued the longstanding process by which cultural diversity narrowed. The major religions, especially Christianity and Islam, spread to new ground. They became slightly more diverse themselves as a result, because in every case they adopted some local features; but they reduced the overall diversity of religion with their conversions in Asia, Africa, the Americas, and Oceania. The spread of Arabic, Spanish, and English also, on balance, reduced the variety of languages spoken around the world, even if the English spoken in Australia or Barbados was not the same as that spoken in London. Many languages would gradually go extinct in the centuries after oceanic voyaging linked up the world. The next few chapters will detail the formation of the global web and how it affected political, economic, and cultural life throughout the world.

Conclusion

The world in 1400 included one big web and several smaller ones. The Old World web was the big one, containing the majority of humankind and stretching across Eurasia and North Africa from Senegal to Japan. A smaller one existed in the Americas, and local ones existed in several places around the world. In the course of the fifteenth century, however, this longstanding pattern underwent a major reorganization.

Beginning early in the fifteenth century, Chinese and Atlantic European mariners undertook oceanic voyages that brought the world together as never before. The most decisive changes came with the European, mainly Iberian, voyaging. From 1460 onward, this voyaging brought an increasing number of African maritime ports (e.g., Elmina) into direct contact with communities of the Old World web. From 1492 onward, it brought the Americas and the Old World web together on a sustained basis. From the early sixteenth century onward, it brought an increasing number of Pacific islands into enduring touch with the Old World web. Thus those mariners, in seeking fortune and glory for themselves and their monarchs, created the first truly global web.

Biological globalization in some respects was the deepest of all the global web's consequences, affecting as it did the life and death of hundreds of millions of people during the sixteenth and seventeenth centuries. Exchanges of food crops resulted in changes to agriculture and diets and, in more cases than not, improvements in nutrition. People in Africa and Eurasia acquired maize and potatoes from the Americas, while those in the Americas acquired wheat, rye, barley, and new varieties of rice. Exchanges of domesticated animals brought horses, cattle, pigs, sheep, and goats (to name only the most significant) to the Americas. These plant and animal exchanges were important in the sixteenth century and remain so today.

The other major component of biological globalization was the exchange of disease pathogens. It was extremely one-sided—and extremely costly to peoples of the Americas and Oceania. Its toll varied from case to case, but generally was on the order of one-half to nine-tenths of populations affected. The population catastrophe, made more costly by violence, loss of lands, and other stresses, generally lasted for the first 150 years after sustained contact with peoples of the Old World web.

The oceanic voyaging of the fifteenth through the seventeenth centuries did not start biological globalization, which can be traced back many thousands of years. But it launched the biggest and most consequential spurt of it in world history.

Chapter Review

KEY TERMS

REVIEW QUESTIONS

1. What were the main trading routes in Eurasia and North Africa in the fifteenth century?

2. What were the other three, smaller trade networks that existed apart from the main Eurasian and North African trading routes?

3. In what two ways were the Ming voyages exceptional?

4. Identify the three main reasons European explorers sailed west into the Atlantic Ocean during this period.

5. Why was knowledge of the Atlantic Ocean's wind patterns essential for sailors?

6. What was Columbus looking for when he journeyed across the Atlantic?

7. How did the Treaty of Tordesillas spur Spanish exploration of the Pacific Ocean?

8. Why was the transfer of malaria and yellow fever to the Americas so deadly?

9. How did prairie Amerindians, such as the Sioux and the Comanche, use horses to build empires?

10. Which crops that were indigenous to the Old World web became significant plantation crops in the Americas?

11. How did maize support the growth of larger states in West Africa?

12. In what two ways did the global exchange of crops improve food supply around the world?

13. Explain the major consequences of biological globalization in the sixteenth and seventeenth centuries.

Go to INQUIZITIVE

to see what you've learned—and learn what you've missed—with personalized feedback along the way.

FURTHER READING

Chapter 1 Last Hominin Standing: Becoming Human

Robert Boyd and Joan Silk, *How Humans Evolved* (2014). A standard textbook on human evolution.

William C. Burger, *Perfect Planet, Clever Species* (2003). A highly readable account of the origins and evolution of the solar system, Earth, life, and humanity, from a biologist's viewpoint.

William J. Burroughs, *Climate Change in Prehistory* (2008). An exploration of what climate shifts meant for early humans.

David Christian, *Maps of Time: An Introduction to Big History* (2004). A historian's innovative look at the career of the human species in its fullest context.

Daniel Everett, *How Language Began: The Story of Humanity's Greatest Invention* (2017). A highly readable account that argues for a very gradual development of language beginning with *Homo erectus*.

Renée Hetherington and Robert G. B. Reid, *The Climate Connection: Climate Change and Modern Human Evolution* (2010). A look at how climate affected early humans from the onset of the last ice age to the dawn of agriculture, with a few words about the future too.

Sarah B. Hrdy, *Mothers and Others: The Evolutionary Origins of Mutual Understanding* (2011). Not an easy read, but a work that's worth the effort if you want to grasp how special humans are.

Jonathan Kingdon, *Lowly Origins: Where, When, and Why Our Ancestors First Stood Up* (2003). An interesting argument about the origins of bipedalism, grounded in geography and ecology.

Douglas Palmer, *Prehistoric Past Revealed* (2003). A geologist's perspective on the history of life on Earth, human included.

Rick Potts and Chris Sloan, *What Does It Mean to Be Human?* (2010). A lavishly illustrated work, very brief, a great starting point.

Chris Stringer, *Lone Survivors: How We Came to Be the Only Humans on Earth* (2013). A study that's especially strong on the African background of human evolution.

Chapter 2 Settling Down: Domestication and Agriculture, 30,000 to 6,000 years ago

Graeme Barker, *The Agricultural Revolution in Prehistory: Why Did Foragers Become Farmers?* (2006). A general study by one of the foremost scholars of the subject.

Peter Bellwood, *First Farmers: The Origins of Agricultural Societies* (2005). An informative work by another major authority.

John L. Brooke, *Climate Change and the Course of Human History: A Rough Journey* (2014). A scholarly synthesis, leaning toward the climatic determinist side.

Steven Mithen, *After the Ice: A Global Human History, 20,000–5,000 BC* (2003). A breezy tour through the late Paleolithic and the transitions to settled farming.

James Scott, *Against the Grain: A Deep History of the Earliest States* (2017). A broad work whose early chapters provide a readable account of domestication, mainly in Asia.

David Wengrow, *What Makes Civilization*? (2018). A compact discussion of Egypt and Mesopotamia and their neighborhood.

Yoshinori Yasuda, ed., *The Origins of Pottery and Agriculture* (2002). A work that is strong on the pottery traditions of East Asia and their relation to early farming.

Chapter 3 Building Complex Societies, 9000 to 1500 BCE

David W. Anthony, *The Horse, the Wheel, and Language: How Bronze-Age Riders from the Eurasian Steppes Shaped the Modern World* (2007). A challenging mixture of historical linguistics and archeology concerning the origins of Indo-European speakers.

Eliza Wayland Barber, *Women's Work: The First 20,000 Years* (1994). An accessible history of textiles and the women who made them.

Peter Bellwood, *The First Migrants: Ancient Migration in Global Perspective* (2013). A broad study whose later chapters are relevant here and detail some of the key farmer migrations.

Barry Cunliffe, *By Steppe, Desert and Ocean: The Birth of Eurasia* (2015). A masterful synthesis of the Neolithic in Eurasia.

Aalia Gnanadesikan, *The Writing Revolution: Cuneiform to the Internet* (2009). A work that is very good on early scripts—their origins, development, and characteristics.

Ian Hodder, *Religion at Work in a Neolithic Society: Vital Matters* (2014).

A detailed account of religion and everything else at Çatalhöyük.

Charles Maisels, *The Archeology of Politics and Power: Where, When and Why the First States Formed* (2010). A searching exploration of the origins of states and complex society.

Susan McCarter, *Neolithic* (2007). A compact and readable work, mostly on the early Neolithic in Eurasia.

Hans Nissen and Peter Heine, *From Mesopotamia to Iraq: A Concise History* (2009). A book whose first five chapters deal expeditiously with the region from the dawn of farming to the formation of big states.

Bruce Trigger, *Understanding Early Civilizations* (2003). Challenging reading, but a revealing comparative study of its subject that takes on the Americas as well as Eurasia and Africa.

Chapter 4 The Southwest Asian Web: Mesopotamia and the Indus Valley, 3500 BCE to 200 BCE

Burjor Avari, *India: The Ancient Past* (2007). A compact survey of the subcontinent from the earliest times to around 1200 CE.

Jean Bottero, *The Oldest Cuisine in the World: Cooking in Mesopotamia* (2004). A discussion of food and drink, with lots of recipes.

Glenn S. Holland, *Gods in the Desert: Religions of the Ancient Near East* (2009). A handy history of a complicated subject.

Jane McIntosh, *The Ancient Indus Valley* (2007). An accessible synthesis of Indus valley archeology

Amanda Podany, *Brotherhood of Kings: How International Relations Shaped the Ancient Near East* (2010). An analysis of war and peace in Mesopotamia, Syria, Egypt, and Anatolia from around 2300 to 1300 BCE.

Andrew Robinson, *The Indus: Lost Civilizations* (2015). A compact, popular history that touches on just about everything to do with Harappan culture.

Rita P. Wright, *The Ancient Indus: Urbanism, Economy, and Society* (2010). An authoritative scholarly synthesis of the evidence.

Chapter 5 From Nile to Ganges: An Expanding Web, 3000 BCE to 200 BCE

Nayanjot Lahiri, *Ashoka in Ancient India* (2015). A highly readable work by an archeologist, who sorts out the strange story of the Mauryan emperor who regretted his conquests.

Barbara Meertz, *Red Land, Black Land: Daily Life in Ancient Egypt* (2008). A delightfully quirky look at every aspect of life in ancient Egypt.

Ian Shaw, ed., *The Oxford History of Ancient Egypt* (2000). Mainly political history, with detailed essays on every period.

Romila Thapar, *Early India* (2004). An authoritative guide to the thickets of ancient Indian history, written by the leading scholar on the subject.

Thomas Trautmann, *India* (2011). A very compact survey by a major scholar of early India.

Marc Van De Mieroop, *A History of Ancient Egypt* (2010). A detailed survey up through the fourth century CE; more compact than Wilkinson.

Toby Wilkinson, *The Rise and Fall of Ancient Egypt* (2010). A narrative synthesis that will make you glad you don't live under the pharaohs.

Chapter 6 Building the Old World Web: Persia, Greece, and the Hellenistic World, 600 BCE to 200 CE

Lindsay Allen, *The Persian Empire* (2005). Developed to accompany a museum exhibit, this survey is strong on material culture, well illustrated, and readable.

Paul Cartledge, *Ancient Greece: A Very Short Introduction* (2011). Clear and quirky, a work by one of the world's foremost authorities on ancient Greece.

Angelos Chaniotis, *The Age of Conquests: The Greek World from Alexander to Hadrian* (2018). A survey of the sprawling Hellenistic world into the second century CE.

Charles Freeman, *Egypt, Greece, and Rome: Civilizations of the Ancient Mediterranean* (2004). The best combined overview of these three societies.

P. J. Rhodes, *A History of the Classical Greek World* (2010). The best overview of the subject up to the death of Alexander.

Carol G. Thomas, *Alexander the Great in His World* (2007). An examination of how his circumstances shaped Alexander's behavior.

Matt Waters, *Ancient Persia: A Concise History of the Achaemenid Empire, 550–330 BCE* (2013). A survey that is especially good at explaining how we know what we think we know about the subject.

Chapter 7 Weaving an East Asian Web, 5000 BCE to 200 CE

Gina Barnes, *Archaeology of East Asia: The Rise of Civilization in China, Korea, and Japan* (2015). A fine synopsis of the region.

Valerie Hansen, *The Open Empire: A History of China to 1800* (2015, 2nd ed.). A valuable summary of early Chinese history.

Charles Higham, *Bronze Age Southeast Asia* (2010). An overview by a leading archeologist.

Thomas Höllmann, *Chinese Script: History, Characters, Calligraphy* (2017). A good look at the origins and mechanics of Chinese writing.

Mark Edward Lewis, *The Early Chinese Empires: Qin and Han* (2007). The handiest place to go for information on the first imperial dynasties.

Li Liu and Xingcan Chen, *State Formation in Early China* (2003). A guide to a controversial field.

Koji Mizoguchi, *The Archaeology of Japan: From the Earliest Rice Farming Villages to the Rise of the State* (2018). A study that covers roughly 600 BCE to about 700 CE in detail.

Sarah M. Nelson, *The Archeology of Korea* (2007). Still the best general study of the subject.

Chapter 8 The West End of the Old World Web: Carthage, Rome, and the Mediterranean World, 800 BCE to 200 CE

Mary Beard, *SPQR: A History of Ancient Rome* (2016). A prominent classicist's coverage of both the Republic and the empire in accessible prose.

Brian Campbell, *The Romans and Their World* (2011). A recent and compact survey, emphasizing the military dimensions.

Nick Constable, *Historical Atlas of Ancient Rome* (2003). An overview that's great for maps and illustrations and very quick treatments of major events and themes.

Robin Lane Fox, *The Classical World* (2006). A readable survey of the Greeks and Romans through the mid-second century CE.

Robert Garland, *Hannibal* (2010). A very short and readable biography of the Carthaginian commander.

Dexter Hoyos, *Mastering the West: Rome and Carthage at War* (2015). Perhaps the best study of the Punic Wars.

Serge Lancel, *Carthage: A History* (1995). An overview by the leading archeologist of Carthage.

Richard Miles, *Carthage Must Be Destroyed: The Rise and Fall of an Ancient Civilization* (2011). Now the most authoritative study, and easy to read.

Chapter 9 On the Frontiers of the Old World Web: Africa and Europe to 200 CE

Peter Bogucki, *The Origins of Human Society* (1999). A work that is especially useful on human society in Europe.

Stanley Burstein, *Ancient African Civilizations: Kush and Axum* (2009). The most accessible recent overview.

Barry Cunliffe, *Europe between the Oceans* (2009). A comprehensive overview of European archeology and history from 9000 BCE.

Barry Cunliffe, *On the Ocean: The Mediterranean and the Atlantic from Prehistory to AD 1500* (2017). A handy and well-illustrated survey of (mainly) archeology.

Christopher Ehret, *The Civilizations of Africa: A History to 1800* (2002). The most comprehensive survey of early Africa; based heavily on historical linguistics, the book is often controversial with archeologists who prefer other methods.

Philip Kohl, *The Making of Bronze Age Eurasia* (2007). A study that is interesting on the steppe lands of eastern Europe and Central Asia, with especially rich archeological detail.

Ann Brower Stahl, ed., *African Archeology* (2005). A smorgasbord of interesting chapters, written mainly for fellow archeologists.

Chapter 10 The Americas and Oceania before 1000 CE

Karen Olsen Bruhns and Karen E. Stothert, *Women in Ancient America* (1999). An overview based on archeology and ethnography, a fair bit of which deals with more recent times than does this chapter.

Craig Childs, *Atlas of a Lost World* (2018). A breezy, journalistic travelogue focusing on the early settlement of the Americas.

Susan Toby Evans, *Ancient Mexico and Central America* (2004). A comprehensive archeological history of Mesoamerica.

Josephine Flood, *The Original Australians: Story of the Aboriginal People* (2006). A study that includes an excellent and readable chapter on early Australia.

Lynn V. Foster, *Handbook to Life in the Ancient Maya World* (2002). An excellent source of information on almost any Maya subject.

John W. Janusek, *Ancient Tiwanaku* (2008). A general synthesis of the archeology and history of Tiwanaku.

Charles C. Mann, *1491: New Revelations of the Americas before Columbus* (2005). A popular account of the controversies in pre-Columbian archeology, perhaps the best starting point.

Timothy R. Pauketat, ed., *The Oxford Handbook of North American Archaeology* (2012). A handy overview of its subject from first settlement to 1500 CE, with thematic chapters.

Dean Snow, *Archaeology of Native North America* (2010). A survey by a major figure in the field; includes Mesoamerica.

Chapter 11 The West End of the Old World Web: New Patterns of Power and Faith, 200 to 800

G. W. Bowersock, *The Crucible of Islam* (2017). A brief but thoroughly scholarly account of the context, in Arabia and beyond, in which Islam first appeared.

Touraj Daryaee, *Sasanian Persia: The Rise and Fall of an Empire* (2009). The best work in English on the subject.

Beate Dignas and Engelbert Winter, *Rome and Persia in Late Antiquity* (2007). A work that makes a compelling case for the importance of seeing these two empires together.

Fred Donner, *Muhammad and the Believers at the Origins of Islam* (2010). An accessible account of Arabia and Islam up to about 700 CE.

Judith Herrin, *Byzantium: The Surprising Life of a Medieval Empire* (2007). A readable overview, with in-depth looks at select subjects, including Greek fire.

Robert Hoyland, *In God's Path: The Arab Conquests and the Creation of an Islamic Empire* (2015). A compact treatment of the first century of Islam, with good maps.

Matthew Innes, *Introduction to Early Medieval Western Europe, 300–900: The Sword, the Plough, and the Book* (2007). Useful depth on many subjects.

Robert Louis Wilken, *The First Thousand Years: A Global History of Christianity* (2012). A brilliant overview with an appreciation of the role of Islam in the evolution of Christianity.

Chapter 12 The East End of the Old World Web: China and Its Neighbors, 200 to 1400

Timothy Brook, *The Troubled Empire: China in the Yuan and Ming Dynasties* (2010). A readable survey of the thirteenth through the seventeenth centuries by one of the major historians of China.

Valerie Hansen, *The Open Empire: A History of China to 1800* (2015). An insightful interpretative survey that emphasizes China's links to the world.

Dieter Kuhn, *The Age of Confucian Rule: The Song Transformation of China* (2009). An authoritative account of the tenth through the thirteenth centuries, emphasizing economic changes.

Soyoung Lee and Denise Patry Leidy, *Silla: Korea's Golden Kingdom* (2013). A lavishly illustrated look at the history, archeology, and art of Korea.

Mark Edward Lewis, *China between Empires: The Northern and Southern Dynasties* (2009). A general account of the period from around 200 to 600 CE.

Timothy May, *The Mongol Empire* (2018). A compact and excellent general study.

Morris Rossabi, *The Mongols and Global History* (2010). A useful overview with translations of relevant documents.

N. Harry Rothschild, *Wu Zhao: China's only Woman Emperor* (2008). A brief, readable account of the extraordinary life of Wu Zetian.

Edward Seidensticker, ed., *The Gossamer Years: The Diary of a Noblewoman of Heian Japan* (1989). A short, frank account of a woman struggling as a second wife in an unhappy marriage in tenth-century Japan. The author is unknown, referred to only as the "mother of Michitsuna."

Michael Seth, *A History of Korea* (2011). A survey that places Korea in a world context.

Zhenping Wang, *Tang China in Multi-Polar Asia: A History of Diplomacy* and War (2013). A systematic presentation of China's relations with its neighbors.

Chapter 13 Forging an Indian Ocean World: South Asia, Southeast Asia, and East Africa, ca. 200 to 1400

Catherine Asher and Cynthia Talbot, *India before Europe* (2006). Good on the twelfth through the eighteenth centuries, and attentive to cross-cultural interaction.

Satish Chandra, *History of Medieval India* (2007). The first ten chapters deal with the years 800–1400 CE in detail.

K. N. Chaudhuri, *Trade and Civilisation in the Indian Ocean: An Economic History from the Rise of Islam to 1750* (1985). A classic that did much to define the Indian Ocean as a unit of study and that is still useful on commerce.

Innocent Pikirayi, *The Zimbabwe Culture: Origins and Decline in Southern Zambezian States* (2001). A careful study of Great Zimbabwe and its contexts.

Patricia Risso, *Merchants and Faith: Muslim Commerce and Culture in the Indian Ocean* (1995). A compact introduction to a complex subject.

Abdul Sheriff, *Dhow Cultures of the Indian Ocean: Cosmopolitanism, Commerce and Islam* (2010). An excellent, thorough treatment of the western Indian Ocean.

Chapter 14 The West End of Eurasia and West Africa, 800 to 1400

Robert Bartlett, *The Making of Europe, 950–1350* (1993). An excellent synthesis.

Amira Bennison, *The Great Caliphs* (2009). A work focusing mainly on the early Abbasids.

Michael Gomez, *African Dominion: A New History of Empire in Early and Medieval West Africa* (2018). The latest synthesis of the history of ancient Ghana and Mali; attentive to questions of slavery, race, gender, and religion.

Gwyn Jones, *A History of the Vikings* (2001). A classic that stands out among the dozens of Viking books.

Hugh Kennedy, *Mongols, Huns, and Vikings* (2002). Brief but beautifully illustrated chapters on several of the peoples discussed here, including Arabs and Turks as well as those of Kennedy's title.

Janet Martin, *Medieval Russia, 980–1534* (2008). A detailed and authoritative study.

W. Montgomery Watt and Pierre Cachia, *A History of Islamic Spain* (2006). A brief, readable overview.

Chapter 15 The Americas and Oceania, 1000 to 1500

Manuel Aguilar-Moreno, *Handbook to Life in the Aztec World* (2006). A reference work more than a narrative, with chapters on just about every aspect of Aztec life.

William Engelbrecht, *Iroquoia: The Development of a Native World* (2005). A brief and readable overview of the archeology.

Patrick Kirch, *How Chiefs Became Kings* (2010). An anthropological and archeological history of Hawaii up to the time of European contact.

Craig Morris and Adriana von Hagen, *The Incas: Lords of the Four Quarters* (2011). A recent overview and amply illustrated.

Maria Rostworowski de Diez Canseco, *History of the Inca Realm* (1999). A brief overview by one of the great authorities, although a bit dated now.

David Stuart, *Anasazi America* (2014). A handy overview, mainly of the Chaco Canyon Anasazi.

Camilla Townsend, *Fifth Sun: A New History of the Aztecs* (2019). The latest overview by a top authority in the field.

Dirk van Tuerenhout, *The Aztecs* (2005). A very accessible survey, perhaps the best starting point on the subject.

Gary Urton, *Inka History in Knots: Reading Khipus as Primary Sources* (2017). Ingenious interpretations of what can be gleaned from the Inka information storage system.

Chapter 16 Convergence: The Discovery of the Oceans and Biological Globalization, 1400 to 1800

John Logan Allen, ed., *A New World Disclosed* (1997). A detailed account of European voyaging to, and into, North America from the Vikings to about 1680.

Judith Carney, *Black Rice* (2002). A detailed study of how African rice got to the Americas.

Alfred Crosby, *The Columbian Exchange: Biological and Cultural Consequences of 1492* (1972). A classic analysis that essentially invented the idea of the Columbian exchange of plants and animals.

Edward Dreyer, *Zheng He: China and the Oceans in the Early Ming Dynasty, 1405–1433* (2007). The best general treatment of the Ming voyages.

Felipe Fernández-Armesto, *Pathfinders* (2006). A general (and well-written) history of exploration, with several chapters on European maritime efforts from 1400 through 1800.

Linda Newsom, *Conquest and Pestilence in the Early Spanish Philippines* (2009). A careful analysis of how some of this chapter's themes worked out in one archipelago.

GLOSSARY OF KEY TERMS AND PRONUNCIATION GUIDE

AH *a* sound, as in *far*
IH short *i* sound, as in *hit*
OO long *o* sound, as in *snooze*
UH short *u* sound, as in *cup*
A short *a* sound, as in *tap*
EE long *e* sound, as in *sneeze*
OH long *o* sound, as in *bone*
EH short *e* sound, as in *very*
AY long *a* sound, as in *say*
EYE long *i* sound, as in *white*
OW diphthong *o* sound, as in *how*
AW diphthong *a* sound, as in *saw*

Emphasis: Syllables in capital letters receive the emphasis. If there is no syllable in capitals, then all syllables get equal emphasis.

1918 flu pandemic: A flu mutation that spread worldwide after World War I, killing 50 to 100 million people mostly between the ages of 15 and 40. Due to tighter global connections, it spread quickly and widely.

Abbasid caliphate [ah-BAH-sihd KA-lih-fayt]: The Islamic successor state (750–1258) to the Umayyads. Based in Baghdad, the Abbasids consolidated power over most of the Islamic world, profited from widespread trade, supported scholars and artists, and had learned works from Chinese, Sanskrit, Hebrew, Greek, and Latin translated into Arabic and Persian.

Abdelkadir [ab-dehl-KAH-dihr] (1808–1883): A Sufi scholar and the leader of the biggest revolt against French rule in Algeria, which reached its height in the 1830s. The French captured and exiled Abdelkadir in 1847.

aboriginal Australians: Also known as Aborigines, aboriginal Australians were mobile hunter-foragers. They spoke 200 to 250 related languages and shared consistent animist religious beliefs across the continent.

Achaemenids [ak-KEE-muh-nids] (559–330 BCE): A dynasty that came from what is now southwestern Iran. They conquered all major powers from Egypt to northwest India, making their empire unprecedented in size.

Adi Granth [ah-dee GRAHNTH]: The scripture of the Sikhs. Written in Punjabi, it is a collection of Nanak's hymns, or teachings, as well as some additional hymns.

Adolf Hitler (1889–1945): The fascist head of the Nazi Party who became chancellor of Germany in 1933. Wanting to return Germany to great power status, he introduced social and economic reforms, including national purification, which targeted Jews, Slavs, and Roma for elimination.

Ahura Mazda [uh-HOOR-uh MAHZ-duh]: A benevolent, all-knowing god and the preferred deity of the Achaemenid dynasty from Darius onward. A priesthood called the Magi led Ahura Mazda worship, which involved outdoor fire ceremonies and sacrifices.

Akbar [AHK-bah] (r. 1556–1605): A Mughal emperor who spearheaded the unification of most of South Asia. He used a combination of horses, guns, and siegecraft along with tolerant religious policy to assert and maintain power.

Aksum: An African state south of Kush that reached its peak between 300 and 500 CE. It traded African products to Egypt, the Mediterranean world, and Mesopotamia, which enabled it to amass wealth and power.

al-Andalus [al-ANN-duh-luhs] (711–1492): The Muslim-controlled part of Spain that the last Umayyad dynast founded in 711 and the Córdoba caliphate ruled from 929 to 1031. Afterward, it remained fragmented until Christian armies defeated it in 1492.

al-Qaeda: An extremist Islamist political faction begun in 1988 by Osama bin Laden that funded the September 11, 2001, terrorist attacks on the United States. It became powerful in Iraq after 2003, and its offshoots have engaged in terrorism targeting other Muslims in several countries.

Alexander II (1818–1881): The tsar of Russia who emancipated the serfs due in part to his commitment to military reform. He wanted a standing army and hoped the abolition of serfdom would lead to a cheaper and better-educated army without the risk of rebellion.

Alexander Hamilton: An American politician who prescribed tariffs to protect U.S. industry when he was secretary of the Treasury in 1791. His recommendations guided U.S. trade policy for a century and inspired the German economist Friedrich List.

Alexander the Great (356–323 BCE): Born in Macedonia to the king of Macedon, Alexander was one of the most skilled military commanders in history. He continued and completed his father's conquest of the Greek world and claimed the Achaemenid throne, uniting both regions in a vast empire.

Alexandria (founded 331 BCE): A wealthy Mediterranean seaport city during the Hellenistic age that fostered trade linkages among Egypt, Africa, the Mediterranean, and Southwest Asia. It was a center for manufacturing, medicine, mathematics, commerce, and culture.

Algerian war for independence (1954–1962): The conflict between the FLN, Algerian independence fighters, and the French Army, along with its collaborators, over France's colonial presence. It led to Algerian independence; the massacre of Muslim Algerians, known as harkis; and the mass expulsion of French settler-colonists, the pieds-noirs.

alliance networks: Two groups into which the great European powers were divided in order to uphold peace in Europe after the Napoleonic Wars. In 1914, Germany, Austria-Hungary, and Italy belonged to the Triple Alliance; and France, Russia, and Great Britain belonged to the Triple Entente.

Allies: A coalition of countries that fought against the Axis powers in World War II, most prominently the United Kingdom, United States, USSR, and China. The alliance also included many other countries, colonies, and members of the British Commonwealth.

American Revolution (1775–1781): An anti-colonial, revolutionary war between thirteen British colonies in America and the British government. The colonists won and created the United States, an independent country.

Ancestral Pueblo Inhabitants of the high-plateau Four Corners area in today's U.S. Southwest who developed a dispersed agricultural society around the ninth century. Their distinctive architectural style of cliff dwellings and ceremonial spaces called *kivas* is evident at their central settlement of Chaco Canyon. Their settlements declined in the twelfth and thirteenth centuries as a probable result of long-lasting drought cycles. They are also known as the Anasazi, which means "ancestors of our enemies" in the Navajo language.

Anthropocene: The proposed new geological age defined by the influence of humans on big natural systems, such as climate. Around 2000, many scientists started to argue that the Holocene ended in the mid-twentieth century and that we are now living in the Anthropocene.

anti-colonialism: A mass political and social movement that developed after World War I. Supporters, disillusioned with European rulers and post-war peace settlements, advocated for self-rule and the end of colonial empires.

Antônio Conselheiro [kohn-say-YAY-roo] (1830–1897): A traveling preacher in Brazil who eventually settled in Canudos. He attracted many followers with his sermons on salvation, denunciations of the state, and promise of the imminent return of Jesus Christ.

Arabs: At the time of Muhammad's birth, Arabs were a group of polytheistic, loosely connected, mostly nomadic tribes who lived in the Arabian Peninsula and made a living herding, trading, and raiding. In the seventh century, united under Muhammad, they became a formidable military force, conquering lands from India to Spain.

Asian tiger economies: Collective name for the economies of certain East Asian countries—Japan, South Korea, Taiwan, Singapore, Hong Kong, and China—that experienced massive economic growth after World War II.

Assyrian [uh-SEER-ee-uhn] **Empire** (ca. 911–609 BCE): A large and multicultural empire based in northern Mesopotamia; its power rested partly on raising horses and forging iron tools and weapons.

Augustine (354–430): A North African bishop whose prolific moralistic writings influenced the creation of a more uniform Christianity called Catholicism.

Axis: A loose coalition among Germany, Italy, and Japan. The Axis powers instigated World War II through their expansionist aims and fought against the Allies during the conflict.

Bantu [BAN-too]: A language group that originated in the area of the modern-day Cameroon-Nigerian border. It is made up of 600 related languages now spoken in East, central, and southern Africa.

Battle of Stalingrad (1942–1943): A brutal, months-long conflict between Soviet and German armies on the eastern front. The German loss of the battle was a major turning point in World War II and part of a broader Axis decline.

Beatriz Kimpa Vita (ca. 1684–1706): A young woman in Kongo who was drawn to Catholicism, became a preacher, and sought the re-unification of Kongo. She gained thousands of followers by telling them God spoke through her, but her movement threatened other aspirants to power and she was burned at the stake as a witch and heretic.

bell beaker ware: Clay containers shaped like an upside-down bell that became popular across Europe and North Africa between around 2900 and 1800 BCE. Used mainly for beer, their widespread presence points to commercial and cultural connections among elites in Europe.

Benito Mussolini (1883–1945): The fascist and authoritarian ruler of Italy who took power in 1922. He manipulated the media, promoted Italian nationalism, and capitalized on Italians' anxieties, particularly about communism, to build support.

Bhakti [BAHK-tee] **movement**: A popular form of Hinduism that emerged in the seventh century in India and appealed to a broad segment of the population. The religion stressed intense, personal devotion to one god (usually Shiva, Vishnu, or Devi) and used local languages (not Sanskrit) spoken by the common people.

Big Bang: The origin of our universe and the start of time, space, and energy. It occurred about 13.8 billion years ago, and the universe has been cooling and expanding since that time.

biological globalization: A worldwide exchange of plants, animals, and microbes that followed the discovery of the oceans and of which the Columbian Exchange was a part. It led to connections among ecosystems and a change of flora, fauna, and diseases across the world.

biological old regime: Conditions of human health that preceded the Vital Revolution. Deadly crowd diseases, gastrointestinal infections, high infant mortality, malnutrition, and starvation defined it.

bipedalism: The ability to stand upright that evolved 6 million to 4.5 million years ago; a trait that distinguishes hominins from apes and ape-like ancestors.

Bourbon Reforms: Changes reflecting Enlightenment thought that the Spanish Crown introduced in Spanish America to revitalize its empire. They included new taxes, strengthened fortifications, administrative reorganization, and freer trade.

British Raj [rahj] (1858–1947): British colonial rule in India, which relied on the cooperation of local Indian elites and the exploitation of existing societal divisions. It reordered the Indian economy with the introduction of free trade and new infrastructure.

bronze: An alloy, or combination, of the two metals copper and tin; used in many cultures for armor and weapons as well as for ornamentation.

Byzantine [BIHZ-ann-teen] **Empire**: The eastern part of the Roman Empire and all that remained of the empire after 476. At its height in the sixth and seventh centuries, it included Egypt, the Levant, Anatolia, and the Balkans; it lasted until 1453.

cabotage: Port-to-port, local trade links. In the Indian Ocean world, shorter-distance cabotage trade in everyday goods supported long-distance trade in luxuries.

Cahokia [kuh-HOH-kee-uh] (ca. 1000–1350): A large Amerindian city that was located in the floodplain of the Mississippi River in present-day Illinois and home to mostly farming people. Cahokians engaged in coordinated efforts to build ceremonial plazas and over 100 mounds used mostly for sacrifices and burials.

Calicut: An important commercial port city on the southwest coast of India. Its merchants traded various spices that were highly sought by Arab, Persian, and European merchants.

caravanserais: In Eastern countries, inns along major trade routes that accommodated large numbers of traders, their animals, and their wares.

carbon dioxide (CO_2): Released by burning fossil fuels, it is one of the most important greenhouse gases. The rise of fossil fuel use since around 1840—especially since 1950 or so—has contributed to increased concentrations of CO_2 in the atmosphere and, in turn, the current pulse of climate change.

Carolingians (ca. 750–843): A dynasty that ruled a comparatively modest and poor state in western Europe and introduced feudalism. The state became an empire during the reign of Charlemagne (r. 768–814) but fell apart after his death.

Carthage: A Phoenician colony on the Mediterranean Sea's North Africa coast that became a formidable seaborne empire based on commerce. Carthage flourished between approximately 800 and 146 BCE.

cassava [kuh-SAH-vuh]: Native to Brazil, as part of the Columbian Exchange cassava (also called manioc) became a staple food in many parts of Africa. It is drought resistant, does well in poor soils, and remains edible even if left in the ground for long periods of time.

caste system: A hierarchical and hereditary division of society that developed in the Ganges basin. The early caste system split people into four main tiers: Brahmins, Kshatriya, Vaishya, and Sudra.

Catholic Reformation: Also called the Counter-Reformation, a period of major reforms in the Catholic Church undertaken in response to the Protestant Reformation. The Catholic Church became more centralized and standardized; popes, bishops, and abbots cut back on high living; efforts were made to root out heresy and ban certain books.

Celts: A loose grouping of various peoples in Atlantic Europe who spoke similar languages and shared cultural features. They emerged between 1300 and 700 BCE. They migrated south from the Alps and Danube in droves during the fifth to third centuries BCE.

Chaco Canyon: A settlement in northern New Mexico that was likely the center of the broader Ancestral Pueblo (Anasazi) region spread throughout the Four Corners area. All roads built by Ancestral Pueblo led to Chaco Canyon, and it was the home of religious and political elites until its collapse due to drought in the twelfth century.

champa rice: A variety of rice that matures quickly, is drought resistant, and ripens at higher and cooler elevations than other strains. After the Chinese imported it from Vietnam in the eleventh century, it became a reliable food supply that spurred massive population growth.

chariot: A two-wheeled carriage pulled by horses and often used as a weapon of war. Chariots appeared first in western Asia around 2100 BCE and were widespread in Eurasia by 1500 BCE.

chartered joint-stock companies: Companies to which governments grant monopoly rights by charter and in which hundreds or thousands of investors own shares. These innovative measures, developed during the sixteenth century, helped share the risks and increase the scale of long-distance trade.

Chinese Civil War (1945–1949): Conflict between the Chinese Communist Party, led by Mao Zedong, and the nationalist Guomindang. The CCP won and created the People's Republic of China.

Chinese Revolution (1880s–1910s): A long revolution that ultimately overthrew the Qing dynasty. Yuan Shikai, an army general, along with Sun Yatsen and other revolutionaries, took advantage of an army mutiny to force the last Qing emperor to abdicate.

choke point: A narrow route providing strategic, affordable passage from one large body of water to another—such as the Straits of Malacca between Sumatra and the Malay Peninsula, or the strait between India's southern tip and Sri Lanka. Those who controlled choke points often were able to profit economically and politically.

Chola [CHOH-lah] **kingdom** (ca. 970–1300): A state that arose in southeastern India and ultimately controlled Indian Ocean trade passing along south Indian coasts and Sri Lanka. Partly an alliance of merchant trading guilds, the Chola flourished through commercial and naval activity, and even attacked Srivijayan cities while under the expansionary rule of Rajendra I (r. 1012–1044).

Christopher Columbus: Born in Genoa, Italy, Christopher Columbus secured funding from the king and queen of Castile (a powerful state in Spain) to sail west from Europe and find a route to China in 1492. He instead found islands in the Caribbean and inaugurated a new age of global interconnection.

Cimmerians: Horse nomads from the Russian and Ukrainian steppe who began arriving on the Hungarian plain around 900 BCE, bringing with them steppe traditions. Many waves of nomads and semi-nomads followed, migrating from the steppes to eastern Europe in subsequent centuries.

city: A large settlement with elaborate divisions of labor, social hierarchies, tightly packed living spaces, open public areas, and large buildings. Trade, exchange, and markets feature prominently in cities.

civil service examinations: The use of written examinations on Confucian ideology to select public administrators in China (and in Korea while under Tang influence). This system fostered cultural unity and an educated elite.

classic Hinduism (begun ca. 400 BCE): An evolution of Vedic traditions of caste, ritual, and sacrifice. Hindus added several new beliefs to Vedic foundations, including the endless migration of souls based on moral conduct, or *karma*.

climate change: Recent, rapid change in Earth's climate patterns that is unprecedented in human history and largely human-caused. It is due mainly to a significant increase in fossil fuel use in the past 30 to 40 years, which created high concentrations of greenhouse gases in the atmosphere and caused Earth's temperature to rise.

Clovis points (ca. 12,000–11,000 BCE): Stone spearheads used throughout North America; their broad dissemination indicates widespread cultural and technological diffusion across the continent.

coal: A fossil fuel made up of ancient plant remains that can be converted into motor power. Cheap, low-lying coal gave rise to the Industrial Revolution in Britain and fueled industrialization around the world.

coaling stations: Pacific ports where imperial powers' naval ships refueled during the late nineteenth century. European powers seized Pacific islands largely for their strategic use as coaling stations and the low cost of controlling them.

Cold War (1945–1991): An ideological and political struggle, primarily between the United States and the USSR, that led to a proliferation of nuclear weapons and pervasive propaganda campaigns. It also intensified conflicts around the world through the two countries' participation in proxy wars.

Columbian Exchange: The transfer of plants, animals, and microbes among Eurasia, Africa, and the Americas that followed Columbus's initiation of contact.

Comanche [kuh-MAN-shee] **Empire** (1730–1870): The Comanche rule of the southern plains of the present-day United States, resulting from their near monopoly of the regional gun trade and mastery of horses.

comfort women: Hundreds of thousands of women that the Japanese army captured from various places, including Korea, China, and the Philippines, and forced to work as sex slaves in occupied areas.

commercial revolution: The increased commercialization and specialization, coupled with frontier expansion and territorial conquest, that occurred especially in China and Atlantic Europe during the period 1500–1800. In combination, these factors caused the regions' economies to grow and their societies to become richer.

communism: A broadly appealing international movement and political theory based on the ideas of Karl Marx and Vladimir Lenin. Communists opposed capitalism and private property and believed that inevitable revolution would bring about a prosperous, equitable world.

Communist Manifesto (1848): A political pamphlet co-authored by Karl Marx and Friedrich Engels arguing that class struggle propels history. It describes the inevitability of a communist revolution and calls for the working classes around the world to join together in the struggle against the ruling elite.

complex society: A social unit characterized by a large hierarchical society, regulatory institutions, and a complex division of labor. Complex societies often developed states and cities.

Confucius [kuhn-FYOO-shuhs] **(Kong Qiu)** (ca. 551–479 BCE): A *shi* whose followers wrote down his ideas in the book *Analects*, which emphasized ethical conduct, ritual, social hierarchy, and the importance of scholars.

Constantine (r. 306–337 CE): A Roman emperor who established a second Roman capital in Byzantium (modern-day Istanbul), renamed it Constantinople, and split the Roman Empire into two halves. He converted to Christianity, ultimately making it an imperial, state-supported religion.

containerization: The transition to the use of shipping containers for the transport of goods that led to decreased shipping and labor costs as well as shorter shipping times. Containers facilitated the connection between East Asian export economies and large North American markets.

containment strategy: An approach guiding U.S. Cold War policy toward the USSR based on defeating it with patience and endurance rather than military strength. The strategy was based on the belief that Soviet communism would collapse if the United States prevented its spread.

cotton: Lightweight and durable cloth woven from the cotton plant. During the early modern period Atlantic Europeans expanded the trade of cotton to new markets in Africa, Europe, and the Americas, and it became an essential global trade commodity.

cotton gin: A machine, invented in the United States and patented in 1794, that separated cotton seeds from cotton fiber, thereby easing cotton production. It contributed to the rise of cotton manufacturing and the spread of cotton production and slavery in the U.S. South.

COVID-19: An easily transmittable infectious disease caused by the novel coronavirus (SARS CoV-2), which apparently originated in bat colonies before mutating into a human pathogen in or near Wuhan, China, in late 2019. In 2020, COVID-19 quickly spread around the world, causing a global pandemic that killed hundreds of thousands.

creole cultures: Societies in the Americas, particularly in the plantation zone, that blended various features from Africa and Europe to create hybrid cultures, religions, and languages.

crowd diseases: Infections such as smallpox, mumps, or measles that require large populations in order to stay in circulation. In large populations, these pathogens mostly affect children.

Crusades (1096–1231): Waves of small-scale wars and attacks on the Levant that were motivated by both religious and military aims. Over 200 years, Crusaders of mostly French, German, and English origin established small kingdoms that all fell by the thirteenth century.

culture of imperialism: Celebratory literature, theater, music, and public ceremony that supported the belief in the right and duty of one group to rule over others. It was most prominent in Britain but also existed in the United States, France, Germany, Italy, and Japan.

cuneiform: The earliest known form of writing, cuneiform developed in Uruk around 3400 to 3300 BCE and consisted of scratches made on wedges of clay.

Darius (r. 522–486 BCE): A lance-bearer who staged a coup d'état and became an Achaemenid king. He introduced many innovations that helped him effectively manage the vast Achaemenid territory.

dark earth: Human-made patches of nutrient-rich soil in Amazonia. People used these areas to raise crops that supported thousands of settlements.

declines in fertility: The global drop in birth rates since about 1960 due to growing urbanization, the spread of female education, and the increased use of birth control.

de-industrialization: During the Industrial Revolution, the decline of industries that could not compete with the price and quality of factory-made products.

Delhi sultanate (ca. 1206–1400): A military aristocracy established in northern India by Turkic horsemen from Central Asia who fostered an Indo-Islamic culture fusing Indian, Turkic, Persian, and Arabic elements. Its legacy includes palace and mosque architecture, and Urdu poetry—a blend of Hindi and Persian.

demographic dividend: A shift in fertility patterns that aids economic growth and development. Demographic dividends in East Asia after 1950 contributed to the Asian tigers' economic success.

demokratia [day-moh-kra-TEE-uh]: After 508 BCE, a form of government that the Athenian *polis* introduced wherein all citizens directly participated in governance. It was based on an elected ruling council of 500 that was responsible to a larger assembly of all free Athenian men over age 18 who had completed military training.

Deng Xiaoping [DUHNG show-pihng] (1904–1997): The head of China beginning in 1978 and leader of its economic transformation. His economic reforms, which essentially replaced socialism with capitalism, included the end of the commune work-unit system, re-introduction of profit motives, and encouragement of export-oriented industry.

dhows [dows]: Ships used by Arab seafarers in the Indian Ocean. Dhows featured slanting, triangular sails to efficiently capture the wind and hulls sewn with coconut fiber for maximum flexibility.

disease disasters: As a result of entry into the expanding Global web, the introduction of deadly diseases to previously isolated areas of the world that had no experience with them. In combination with violence and declining fertility, these diseases led to devastating demographic collapses in the Americas, Siberia, many Pacific Islands, and parts of southern Africa.

dolmens: Stacks of stones, erected mainly between 1500 and 500 BCE, that mark burial sites and imply growing social stratification. Although they were built in many places in Eurasia, Korea contains almost half the world's dolmens.

domestication: The genetic modification of plants or animals through human selection or breeding. Domestication enables humans to produce food instead of searching for it.

domino theory: Conjecture among U.S. policymakers that if one country fell to communism, then the countries surrounding it would follow. This theory drove U.S. involvement in the Vietnam War because officials feared that if Vietnam became entirely communist, the rest of Southeast Asia would too.

dreamtime: One of the religious beliefs of aboriginal Australians according to which a distant past linked to the birth of the world when supernatural entities crossed Australia, forming the continent and tracing paths that became "songlines."

Dutch East India Company (VOC): A very successful chartered joint-stock company created to control the Dutch spice trade. During the seventeenth and eighteenth centuries, the VOC's heavily armed ships dominated the Indonesian archipelago as the company used force and violence to gain advantageous trade terms.

economies of scale: Economies of scale occur when a producer's costs per unit of output decline as the scale of the enterprise grows. This condition, which exists in only some industries such as sugar production, benefits large-scale enterprises.

Eiichi Shibusawa [ay-EE-chee shih-boo-SOW-ah] (1840–1931): A Japanese government official and businessman who was passionate about bringing industrialization to his country. He set up Japan's first modern cotton mill in Osaka with the help of Takeo Yamanobe.

emancipation for serfs (1861): A labor liberation granted by a statute that, in theory, liberated serfs by granting them freedoms they previously lacked. In practice, it introduced many new legal constraints to which former serfs remained subject.

encomienda [ehn-koh-mee-EHN-dah]: Granted by Spanish rulers to colonizers in Spanish America, the legal right to conscript Amerindians as unpaid laborers.

Epic of Gilgamesh: A long poem written down around 2100 BCE in cuneiform and the oldest surviving epic poem in world history. It is about a legendary Uruk king, Gilgamesh, who lived around 2600 BCE.

Eurasian steppe: A broad grassland that stretches from eastern Europe to East Asia.

fascism: A political movement and ideology that formed the basis of Benito Mussolini and Adolf Hitler's governments. It emphasized militant nationalism, purification of the nation, a cult of the leader, and showy displays of national strength.

Ferdinand Magellan: A Portuguese explorer whom the Spanish Crown funded to find a route to the Moluccas by sailing west from Europe and along the southern coast of South America in 1519. He died in the Philippines after crossing the Pacific, but his crew became the first people to sail around the world and attained knowledge of the vastness of the Pacific Ocean.

field artillery and fortifications: Large and heavy mobile guns and cannon deployed in the field, and the highly engineered structures used to defend against them. These elements increased the cost and intricacy of war during the early modern period.

financialization: The rise in the prominence, prevalence, and profitability of finance worldwide due to de-regulation and digital technology. It has eased the global flow of money and contributed to increased economic volatility.

firestick farming: Intentional burning of landscapes and methodical use of fire that promotes the growth of edible plants and attracts animals for hunting. Aboriginal Australians employed firestick farming to increase their food supply.

flint maize: A form of maize, developed in the American Midwest around the ninth or tenth century, that matured faster than other varieties and with bigger kernels. It boosted food supplies and enabled North American farmers to subsist mainly on agricultural crops and less on hunting and foraging.

Florentine Codex: A comprehensive catalogue of Aztec history and culture, complied between 1545 and 1590 by a Spanish priest and his Aztec students. The *Codex* incorporates about 2,000 illustrations of Aztec daily life along with text in Nahuatl expressed in the Roman alphabet.

fractional reserve banking: The practice of banks lending out more money than they have in their reserves in order to create money in the form of credit. The Bank of Amsterdam pioneered this practice, which promoted commerce by reducing its costs.

free trade: De-regulation of trade beginning in the 1980s that Ronald Reagan and Margaret Thatcher spearheaded. Free trade policy spread around the world, leading to bigger multinational corporations and globalized supply chains.

French Revolution (1789–1799): A political revolution within France aimed at reforming the hierarchical social order. It led to sweeping changes, descended into terror and dictatorship, and was largely reversed when the monarchy was re-established in 1814.

Friedrich List (1789–1846): An economist born in Germany who wrote newspaper articles and books that guided state-sponsored industrialization. He advocated for protectionist policies and the construction of railroads.

Ganges [GAN-jeez] **basin**: Rich alluvial lands surrounding the Ganges River that supported the development of a new Indian culture and complex society starting around 1500 BCE. It is also known as the Gangetic plain.

Genghis Khan (ca. 1165–1227): Born as Temujin, Genghis Khan was the founder and leader of the Mongol Empire. Under his command, the Mongols conquered territory from China to Ukraine.

germ theory of disease: The scientific theory developed after 1850 that pointed to bacteria's role in infection. It led to sanitation reforms that reduced death and illness from water-borne diseases and paved the way for understanding infections.

Germanic tribes: Groups originating from east of the Danube River and north of the Rhine River in Europe, including Goths, Vandals, and Franks. Beginning in the 370s, the Germanic tribes migrated to Roman territory as they fled from the Huns, or when the Romans hired them to fight against other tribes or to fight for one set of Romans against another in civil wars.

Ghost Dance: A spiritual movement that arose in response to disruptions in Amerindian life during the nineteenth century. Inspired by Wovoka's prophecy, participants performed a community circle dance in hopes that this ceremony would bring the return of peace, joy, and plenty.

Glorious Revolution (1688–1689): The nearly bloodless replacement of James II with William of Orange on the throne of England, organized by Protestant British elites. It cemented the increased power of Parliament in relation to the monarchy.

Göbekli Tepe [goh-behk-LEE teh-peh]: A site in southeastern Turkey; likely a religious temple that a sedentary or semi-sedentary group built around 9000 BCE and abandoned by 7000 BCE.

gracialization: The thinning and shrinking of skeletons through evolution. Humans underwent this process as social groups grew and relied less on their physical strength for survival.

Grand Canal: A massive public works project, started under the Sui dynasty (581–618), that linked north and south China, promoting unity and enabling emperors to move troops and food quickly and easily.

Great Leap Forward (1958–1961): Mao Zedong's massive and disastrous campaign to improve China's industry and agriculture. He called for citizens to produce steel in their own backyards, the output of which proved to be useless, and introduced new agricultural policies that caused a devastating famine.

Great Zimbabwe (ca. 1250–1450): A city and center of power in southern Africa based on cattle wealth and a thriving gold trade. The rulers at Great Zimbabwe had enough authority and wealth to erect great stone buildings beginning in 1275.

gross world product (GWP): The size of the world economy, which is calculated by using the combined value of all goods and services produced worldwide. Between 1500 and 1800, the GWP almost doubled.

Guanches [GWAHNCH-ihz]: Descendants of North African Berbers, the Guanches were inhabitants of the Canary Islands who fought against Spanish conquest and settlement from 1402 to 1496. Spanish weapons technology and the diseases they carried with them eventually led to the defeat of the Guanches.

Gulf Stream: The counterclockwise movement of North Atlantic Ocean currents that warms the climates of western Europe's coastal areas from Portugal to Norway.

Gupta [GOOP-tah] **dynasty** (ca. 330–550): A dynasty that ruled the north of India and supported religious institutions, math, science, and arts. Samudragupta (r. 335–375) and

Chandragupta II (r. 375-415) were two successful Gupta kings.

Habsburgs (1282–1918): Originating as Swiss and German nobles, the Habsburgs extended their territory with military force and advantageous political marriages. They built a global empire and became a major European power but were unable to unify Europe.

Haitian Revolution (1791–1804): An anti-colonial, political, and anti-slavery revolution rooted in racial tensions and led primarily by Toussaint L'Ouverture, a former slave. It began with the largest slave rebellion in history and ended in victory, but it left Haiti fractured in its aftermath.

Hammurabi [hahm-uh-RAH-bee] (r. 1792–1750 BCE): A king of Babylon who formed a short-lived empire; he erected a stone monument inscribed with 282 laws that survives today.

Han dynasty (206 BCE–220 CE): Emperor Gaozu founded the Han dynasty following Qin rule. Han rulers expanded Chinese territory and promoted Confucian ideology; under their leadership the economy and population grew, and land and maritime trade flourished.

Hannibal Barca (247–ca. 182 BCE): A member of the Carthaginian Barca clan who transformed Carthage's presence in Spain into an empire there. Hannibal led the fight against Rome in the Second Punic War and gained renown for his skills as a military commander.

Harrapans [hah-RAP-puhnz] (ca. 2600–1700 BCE): The name of the Indus valley populations and culture; its two largest cities were Harappa and Mohenjo Daro.

Hawaiian kings: Between 1450 and 1700, several Hawaiian chiefs responded to shortages of resources and increased competition by making themselves kings, thereby initiating a ruling class, an administrative bureaucracy, and struggles for succession to the throne. Kings and kingdoms were unique in the Pacific world; no other Polynesians outside of Hawaii had them.

heavy cavalry: One of Darius's military innovations. Instead of arming mounted warriors with only light equipment, heavy cavalry rode on large, strong horses with full armor and weaponry.

Heian [HAY-ahn] **Japan** (734–1185): A period of rule in Japan, based at Heian (modern Kyoto), during which Chinese influence waned, indigenous religious traditions (especially Shinto) became dominant, aristocratic social order prevailed, and refined courtly life produced the first substantial body of literature written by women anywhere in world history.

heliocentric system: The idea, which Nicholas Copernicus wrote down in 1514, that planets rotate around the sun as opposed to the idea that the sun moves around the Earth. Johannes Kepler, Galileo Galilei, and Isaac Newton built on this work, and the heliocentric system won acceptance in 1687.

Hellenistic age (323–31 BCE): The age of Greek and Macedonian rule in Greece, Egypt, and Southwest Asia. It began after Alexander died and his generals Ptolemy, Antigonus, and Seleucus divided his empire among themselves.

herders: People who mainly lived off of domesticated grazing animals that they raised in arid and semi-arid grassland and scrubland regions.

hieroglyphs [HEYE-ruh-gliphs]: The primary Egyptian writing system, which eventually contained nearly 1,000 symbols; it developed around 3000 BCE, possibly influenced by Sumerian cuneiforms.

Hiroshima and Nagasaki: Two Japanese cities and centers of military production onto which the United States dropped nuclear weapons in August 1945. The bombs killed 105,000 people immediately and were the first, and so far only, nuclear weapons used in warfare.

HIV/AIDS: The infectious and deadly disease that spread from chimpanzees to humans in the 1940s and caused a global pandemic beginning in the 1980s. Africa was the hardest hit. As of 2020, the disease has killed 30 million people.

Holocaust: The outcome of a Nazi-led effort to racially purify Germany through the mass murder of groups Hitler deemed inferior, particularly Jews. During the Holocaust, Nazis murdered millions of Jews, as well as Roma (Gypsies), the mentally ill, and the physically disabled.

Holocene: The name given to the roughly 11,700-year period beginning with the end of the Younger Dryas and continuing until today.

hominins [HAWM-ih-nihms]: The term used to describe all humans, extinct human branches, and ape-like human ancestors who have lived in the last 7 million years. Fossil hunters have discovered 18 species of hominin so far.

Homo erectus [HOH-MOH ee-REHK-tuhs]: A hominin species that emerged 1.5 million years ago and went extinct 190,000 years ago. *Homo sapiens*, Neanderthals, Denisovans, and Flores Island "Hobbits" are all probably descended from *Homo erectus*.

Homo sapiens [HOH-MOH SAY-pee-uhns]: A type of hominin and the name for our species, human beings. *Homo sapiens* emerged 300,000 to 200,000 years ago in Africa.

Hyksos [HICK-sohs]: A group of people, probably from the area of modern-day Lebanon, who migrated to and invaded Egypt. They ruled Egypt from around 1700 to 1500 BCE.

imperial consolidation: The general trend during the early modern period of empires growing bigger and more powerful at the expense of smaller powers.

income inequality: The growing divergence in incomes beginning in the 1980s. Globalization caused a vast share of the world's wealth to be concentrated in the hands of the few, creating the mega-rich class.

indentured labor: Commitment to a fixed period of bonded labor, usually between two and eight years. Although signing indenture contracts was technically voluntary, labor recruiters often used predatory practices to secure laborers.

Indian Ocean monsoon: Regular and predictable alternating winds that made the Indian Ocean relatively easy to sail.

Indian Rebellion (1857–1858): A rebellion that began with an army mutiny and spread to include many regional revolts. The rebels' aims were to get rid of British rule and restore old regimes; but many Indians remained loyal to Britain, and the rebellion collapsed.

Indus River: A river 2,000 miles (3,000 km) long that runs from the Himalayan glaciers to the Arabian Sea. The Indus was central to agriculture and trade for the complex Indus valley cities.

Industrial Revolution: A monumental switch to factory-scale production using machinery driven by water power and fossil fuels instead of human muscle and hand tools. It began in Britain in the late eighteenth century and spread to other countries and continents, with global consequences.

information technology (IT): Innovations in information storing, processing, and sharing, particularly via the Internet and computers. IT reduces the costs of transportation and production, thus aiding in the growth of globalized supply chains.

Inka (ca. 1300–1532): An empire located in the Andean region with its capital in Cuzco. Using a combination of military force and cultural influence, it quickly became one of the two largest polities in the Americas prior to 1492.

international institutions: Governmental, non-governmental, and illicit organizations that operate internationally due to the rise of challenges, problems, and opportunities that are global in scale. Prominent examples include the United Nations, Amnesty International, and drug cartels.

international migrants: People who live in a country other than that in which they were born. Since the 1970s, the majority of migrants have moved to Western Europe, North America, and the Arabian Gulf; by 2019, international migrants made up about 3.5 percent of the global population.

iron: Made from a relatively common ore, iron was cheaper and better than bronze in many ways. However, it required a lot of fuel to smelt and highly skilled ironsmiths to shape it into useful objects.

iron working: The complex process of transforming a raw material, iron ore, into a metal useful for tools and weapons. It appeared in Europe around 1000 BCE and in Africa at roughly the same time.

irrigation: The process of diverting water from lakes, streams, and rivers and supplying it to fields and gardens to ensure crop growth. Irrigation enabled farmers to cultivate land that was otherwise too dry for growing crops.

Islam: A monotheistic religion established in the seventh century whose followers are called Muslims. Its scripture is the Qur'an, which contains God's revelations to Muhammad.

Islamization: The widespread conversion to, and adoption of, Islam. India underwent Islamization beginning in 1000; coastal East African Islamization mostly occurred between the seventh and thirteenth centuries.

Istanbul [ihs-tan-BOOL]: Formerly named Constantinople, it was the capital of the Ottoman Empire from 1453, after Mehmet the Conqueror seized it from the Byzantine Greeks. Istanbul gave the Ottomans control of profitable trade routes and was a launching point for several successful attacks in the Balkans and along the Black Sea coasts.

Jack Gladstone: A slave in British Guiana who led the Demerara revolt of 1823 with his father, Quamina. Gladstone believed that legal abolition had passed in London and called Guiana's slaves to freedom, causing 10,000 slaves to revolt.

Jacobins: A political faction made up of mostly middle-class lawyers who increasingly dominated the government of revolutionary France. They ended elections in 1793, introduced wide-reaching reforms, and ushered in the Terror—a period of widespread suspicion and public executions.

James Watt (1736–1819): A Scottish-born engineer who designed and built more efficient steam engines. He was among a group of engineers who made steam engines more appealing to and useful for manufacturers.

janissaries [JAN-ih-sehr-eez]: Slave soldiers who formed an elite infantry under the Ottoman sultan and developed volley fire with muskets. They were taken as young boys from Christian homes in the Balkans and trained in warfare and administration.

Jawaharlal Nehru [jah-WAH-hah-lahrl NAY-roo] (1889–1964): Instrumental leader of the Indian independence movement and first prime minister of India. Next to Gandhi, he was the second most important figure in the Indian National Congress.

Jenne: An archeological site in West Africa where either a cluster of villages or a city stood by 450 CE. It offers evidence of long-distance trade along the Niger River.

Jesuits: Founded in 1540 in Spain, an order of priests in the Catholic Church dedicated to evangelizing non-Catholics and to rigorous education. During the sixteenth and seventeenth centuries, Jesuit missionaries worked to counter Protestantism in places as varied as Poland, Germany, Japan, China, India, and the Americas.

Jomon culture: A group that became sedentary around 7000 BCE, mostly along the east-central Pacific coast of Japan. They lived off of shellfish,

fish, acorns, and chestnuts and were among the first inventors of pottery.

José Aponte [HOH-say uh-POHN-tay]: A Yoruba-speaking free black who led a slave revolt in Cuba in 1812. This revolt was part of a rise in resistance in Cuba and Brazil due to the growing number of Yoruba-speaking slaves being shipped to these slave markets.

Josef Stalin (1878–1953): The leader of the USSR who consolidated power in the years 1927–1928. He introduced policies of industrialization and collectivization and headed state-led mass terror and brutal coercion.

Julius Caesar (100–44 BCE): A skilled military commander who gained prominence and the loyalty of legions of soldiers, which he refused to disband when the Roman Senate instructed him to. This decision led to civil war, from which Caesar emerged successful and then ruled as dictator from 49 BCE until his assassination five years later.

Justinian (r. 527–565): A Byzantine emperor who built the famous church Hagia Sophia in Constantinople and sought to reconstitute the old Roman Empire by re-conquering territories the Romans had once controlled. He was militarily successful, but he drained the empire of money and his successors lost many of his gains.

keiretsu [kee-REHT-soo]: Large, often family-based Japanese corporate conglomerates made up of banks, trading companies, and industries. They led Japan's post–World War II economic miracle by spearheading technological innovation, assembly-line production, and miniaturization.

Khazaria [kuh-ZAHR-ee-uh] (ca. 640–ca. 970): A Turkic-speaking, multireligious kingdom located in the grasslands of the North Caucasus. The leaders converted to Judaism in the ninth century.

Khoi [KOH-ay]: African hunters and cattle raisers who lived in the southern tip of Africa and clashed with Dutch colonists. Many Khoi eventually died, and their culture largely disappeared due to dispossession and disease epidemics.

King Afonso (r. 1506–1543): A king in Kongo, West Central Africa, whose father, also a king, had converted to Catholicism. Afonso learned to speak, read, and write Portuguese, and as king he made Catholicism the state religion in Kongo. His power grew with the help of Portuguese advisers and military technology.

King Kamehameha [kah-MAY-hah-MAY-hah] (r. 1782–1819): A ruler who unified Hawaii as a single kingdom by using imported military and sailing technology that he strictly controlled. His monarchy lasted a century.

Kongo monarchy: Elected rulers of the kingdom of Kongo whose legitimacy and backing largely rested on protecting their subjects from enslavement.

Korean War (1950–1953): A conflict that began when Soviet-backed, communist North Korea invaded U.S.-backed South Korea. Chinese and United Nations forces joined the fight, which became a war of attrition until a cease-fire was agreed to in 1953.

Koryo [KOHR-yoh] (918–1392): A kingdom in Korea that was based on an alliance of aristocratic families known as *yangban*. It was started due to the threat of steppe nomads.

Kwame Nkrumah [KWAH-may n-KROO-mah] (1909–1972): An influential anti-colonial agitator and chief negotiator in the Gold Coast's transition from British colony to the independent country of Ghana. He was Ghana's first leader and ruled in an increasingly authoritarian way until his ouster in 1966.

La Marseillaise [MAHR-say-yehz]: The song chosen as the French national anthem in 1795. It inspired many countries to designate national anthems, which became a part of growing nationalist cultures around the world.

Lakshmibai [lahk-SHMEE-beye]: A local Indian ruler, also known as the Queen of Jhansi, in north-central India who continued to rule in defiance of British East India Company armies until she died in combat. She remains a national hero in India.

land empires: Empires that used industrial technologies and/or nationalist ideas to extend control over large areas of land rather than overseas. These empires included Russia, the United States, Canada, Brazil, and Argentina. The Comanche Empire in North America and the Ethiopian Empire in northeastern Africa were secondary land empires.

land reform: In South Korea, the transition from the majority of peasants renting land from wealthy landowners to the majority owning their own land. Pursued under pressure from the U.S. military during the post–World War II occupation, land reform laid the foundation for South Korea's economic growth.

Lapita: An Oceanic group that sailed out into the Pacific Ocean from the Bismarck Archipelago around 1300 BCE. They settled most of Remote Oceania, including Fiji, Tonga, and Samoa.

latte stones: Large stone pillars erected on several islands of the Marianas that probably formed the bases of buildings. The Chamorro of Guam began to build latte stones around 1000.

League of Peace and Power: An Iroquois confederacy forged sometime before 1450 among the five Iroquois nations; the League united them and stopped them from warring among one another.

Legalism: A political philosophy that emphasized law, punishment, regimentation, and the power of the state. Lord Shang (390–338 BCE), one of Legalism's chief advocates, promoted intimidation as an ideal governing method.

Levant: The eastern Mediterranean coast and its hinterland. It forms the western edge of the Fertile Crescent and is the location of the first strong evidence of farming.

Lucy: Discovered in 1974 in Ethiopia, a fossilized skeleton of a hominin called *Australopithecus afarensis* who lived 4 million to 3 million years ago.

Magdalenian culture: A semi-settled group that lived between Portugal and Poland and intercepted seasonal migrations of reindeer for sustenance. Magdalenians painted the famous cave art at Lascaux and Altamira.

maize [mayz]: A staple food crop indigenous to the Americas; also known as corn. Part of the Columbian Exchange, maize flourished in southern Europe, China, and western and southern Africa.

malaria: A disease originating in Africa that is transmitted by mosquitos and was particularly deadly in warm, humid, and populous locations. Malaria spread widely around the world, including to the Americas, as part of the Columbian Exchange.

Mandate of Heaven: A cultural formula positing the divine authority that allowed kings to rule. It was a provisional legitimacy that rulers had to convince their subjects they maintained.

Manichaeism [man-ih-KEE-iz'm]: A dualistic religion derived from the preachings of Mani around the third century CE. A blend of Christianity, Zoroastrianism, and Buddhism, it emphasized a struggle between good and evil and a code of conduct including non-violence, fasting, and restraint.

Mao Zedong [MOW tsay-TOHN] (1893–1976): Head of the Chinese Communist Party beginning in World War II and founder of the People's Republic of China. He developed a novel perspective on Marxist theory, arguing that peasants, not just industrial workers, could lead a communist revolution.

Maori [mow-ree]: Polynesians who live in New Zealand. They arrived from central or eastern Polynesia around 1280 and experienced two centuries of peace and prosperity until population growth led to scarcity and warfare at the end of the fifteenth century.

Mauryan [MAWR-yuhn] **Empire** (ca. 321–230 BCE): Indian prince Chandragupta Maurya united the Indus and Ganges valleys for the first time and established the Mauryan Empire; it ended after his grandson Ashoka's reign.

Maya [MEYE-uh] (ca. 600 BCE–900 CE): A complex hierarchical Mesoamerican society that was culturally and linguistically united but politically fragmented. Its rulers amassed wealth through the export of products such as salt, jade, and obsidian, and the Mayan glyphs were the most complete Mesoamerican writing system.

Meiji [MAY-jee] **Restoration** (1867–1868): A political revolution in Japan that ended in the reinstatement of rule by emperor and the introduction of a new elite. Meiji reformers were committed to strengthening Japan and promoting its industrialization.

Menelik II [MEHN-eh-lihk] (1844–1913): Architect and ruler of the Ethiopian Empire who used foreign military technology and skills to conquer surrounding lands and defeat Italian forces at the Battle of Adowa. He also introduced foreign technologies and institutions, such as railroads and public schools.

menhirs: Large oblong stones, standing upright, that began appearing in Europe in about 5500 BCE, marking a shift in spiritual practices that spread across the region. One example is Stonehenge, built around 2500 BCE in southern England.

merchant trading guilds: Formal organizations of groups of traders who worked together to facilitate trade and ease the risks associated with it. An alliance of merchant trading guilds formed the foundation of the Chola kingdom's power (ca. 970–1300).

Meroë [MEHR-oh-wee]: A kingdom in Kush located on the Nile between Egypt and sub-Saharan Africa that reached its peak around the first century BCE. It was the center of iron working in Africa and controlled the export of African goods to Egypt.

Mesopotamia: A largely agricultural region in the Tigris and Euphrates river valleys where Sumer, Akkad, Assyria, and Babylon were located.

metallurgy: The process of separating metals from ore—the rock in which they are found—and then fashioning metals into objects.

Mexican Revolution (1910–1920): A social and national revolution that remade Mexico. It began when a succession struggle led to the jailing of presidential candidate Francisco Madero, which sparked insurgencies across the country and led to a decade of fighting.

Middle Passage: The months-long journey of slave ships between Africa and the Americas. Slaves were tightly packed below deck, usually naked and in chains, and many died due to unsanitary conditions and violence.

Mikhail Gorbachev [mihk-HEYEL gohr-bah-CHUHV]: The reform-minded final leader of the USSR who came to power in 1985. He introduced policies of perestroika ("restructuring") and glasnost ("openness"), defused international tensions, and pursued nuclear arms reduction treaties but ultimately could not prevent the collapse of the Soviet Union.

military revolution: An increase in the complexity and expense of war between 1450 and 1800. It comprised several innovations in weaponry, defense, technique, and administration.

millenarian movements: Religious movements whose adherents believe that spiritual or divine intervention will transform the world for the better.

millet system: The Ottoman Empire's tolerant religious policy: the Ottomans taxed non-Muslims at a higher rate than Muslims but also welcomed Christians and Jews and left them alone to oversee their own communities.

Minamata disease: The effects of mercury poisoning that those who ate seafood from the Minamata bay in Japan developed due to pollution from a nearby chemical plant. It was one among many acute pollution disasters in the 1950s and 1960s that arose from East Asia's rapid industrialization.

Ming voyages (1405–1433): Seven large maritime voyages arranged by Zheng He under the Yongle Emperor of China during the Ming dynasty. The extent of the voyages and the size of their wooden ships were unprecedented, and they served to project power as far as East Africa.

mita [MEE-tah]: The forced labor draft imposed on Andean peoples by the Inka. Under Spanish rule in South America, the *mita* provided unfree labor to work in the brutal conditions of the silver mines.

Mohandas K. Gandhi (1869–1948): The Indian anti-colonial activist who developed the practice of non-violent civil disobedience called *satyagraha*. His activism led to a widespread nationalist movement in India and contributed to the end of British rule in 1947.

Moluccas [moh-LUH-kuhz]: Part of the islands of Indonesia, also known as the East Indies, where nutmeg and cloves grew. Because Europeans placed great value on these spices, trade connections to these islands were very attractive to merchants.

monasticism: A way of life long prominent in Christianity and Buddhism that involves voluntary withdrawal from society, including a rejection of marriage and family, in favor of dedication to rigorous spiritual work.

Mongol western campaigns (1219–1260): A series of campaigns beginning under Genghis Khan and carried on by his grandsons Batu and Hulegu. By 1260, Mongol rule stretched from Russia and the Black Sea to Mongolia.

monotheism [MAW-noh-thee-iz'm]: A religious system that espouses a belief in one god, or the oneness of God. Judaism, Christianity, and Islam are all monotheistic religions.

Muhammad [muh-HAH-mehd] (570–632): The founder of Islam who was born in the city of Mecca in Arabia and had visions at age 40 telling him he was God's prophet. He subsequently gathered a group of followers, called Muslims, and embarked on a successful military campaign in 622, establishing Islam as both a political and a religious movement.

Mulla Sadra [MOO-lah SA-drah] (1571–1640): An influential Shi'a theologian living in Safavid Iran. His writings attempted to reconcile Sufi mysticism with Islamic philosophical traditions and helped create an intellectual foundation for the Safavid theocracy.

multiethnic empire: A polity comprising different linguistic and religious groups and containing many ethnic minorities and multilingual people. The Habsburg, Russian, and Ottoman empires were all multiethnic.

Muslim League: The organization of Muslims in British India that advocated for the division of post-colonial India into a Muslim state and a Hindu state. Muhammad Ali Jinnah, who became the first head of Pakistan, was its leader.

Mustafa Kemal [MUHS-tah-fah kuh-MAHL] (1881–1938): Leader of Turkey's nationalist revolution and its first president. Also known as Atatürk, he introduced a set of educational and legal policies, the Atatürk Reforms, aimed at strengthening and secularizing Turkey.

Nalanda: A Buddhist monastery in northeast India that was a center of learning and science in the Indian Ocean world, reaching its height in the sixth to the ninth centuries. Nalanda was part of the thriving intellectual scene in India between 500 and 1000.

Napoleon Bonaparte (1769–1821): A military man who ascended to power in France in 1799 by way of a coup d'état and became a dictator. He won numerous military victories against foreign armies but abdicated in 1814 after a string of disastrous campaigns.

Narmer: The first ruler of Upper and Lower Egypt who completed unification around 2950 BCE; also known as Menes.

National Policy: A Canadian program that was launched in 1879 to stimulate industrialization. It involved the introduction of tariffs on foreign goods and investment in railroads.

nationalism: A set of beliefs, ideas, and attitudes that provides a sense of solidarity for a group. The group usually occupies a defined territory and claims to share language, culture, ethnicity, ancestry, political values, civic values, or some combination of these.

Natufians (ca. 12,500–9,500 BCE): Sedentary residents of the Levant who showed the earliest known signs of plant cultivation and farming.

natural selection: The process whereby organisms that are better adapted to their environments pass down advantageous genetic traits through generations.

Neanderthals [nee-ANN-duhr-tawls]: An extinct "cousin" of human beings that lived from 400,000 to 40,000 years ago in Europe, Siberia, and southwestern Asia.

neo-Confucianism: An ideology originating in the Song dynasty (960–1279) that emphasized rigorous study and academic learning as the path to morality and righteousness. In the sixteenth century, Wang Yangming—also considered a neo-Confucianist—claimed that book learning was not necessary for obtaining wisdom and acting ethically.

new imperialism: A pervasive and widespread form of empire that arose after 1870 due to the power and wealth gaps that industrialization caused and the popular support that nationalism stirred.

Nile River: A river 4,000 miles (nearly 7,000 km) long that flowed through Nubia and Egypt, bringing precious water and fertile silt.

Norte Chico (ca. 3100–1600 BCE): The collective name for a group of roughly 25 settlements in the Andes. Norte Chico was the earliest complex society in the Andean world, and its elites' power was based on the control of dried fish, a staple in the food supply.

Nubia [NOO-bee-uh]: A region south of Egypt and upriver from it on the Nile. Egypt mostly traded with or ruled over Nubia, but on occasion Nubia asserted control over parts of Egypt.

Oceania: The Southeast Asian region that includes the islands in the Pacific Ocean, including Melanesia, Micronesia, and Polynesia. Near Oceania consists of New Guinea, the Bismarck Archipelago, and the Solomon Islands; Remote Oceania reaches as far as Hawaii and Easter Island.

Octavian (Augustus): Caesar's grandnephew, adopted son, and heir, who became emperor of Rome and changed his name to Augustus. He was a ruthless emperor who ruled for 40 years, consolidated the Roman state, and built a strong administrative foundation for subsequent emperors.

Oda Nobunaga [oh-DAH noh-boo-NAH-gah] (1534–1582): A Japanese warlord who unified southern Japan and may have invented volley fire. He met his political aims by militarizing peasants and arming them with widely produced Japanese guns.

Olmecs: Concentrated in the urban centers of San Lorenzo (ca. 1600–900 BCE) and La Venta (ca. 900–300 BCE) in southern Mexico, the Olmecs were the first Mesoamerican group to develop complex hierarchical societies. They were builders of giant basalt heads and pioneers of pyramid construction in the Americas.

oracle bone inscriptions: The first evidence of Chinese writing, oracle bone inscriptions are questions posed to the gods written on turtle shells and cattle bones. Diviners heated the bones until they cracked and then interpreted the gods' answers using the fragments.

Paleolithic: The period lasting from 2.6 million years ago to 13,000 years ago; the latter part, the late Paleolithic, saw a profusion of cultural change.

pan-Africanism: The call for Africans and people of African descent to liberate Africa and end racism through unified political action. The movement also supported literary and cultural revitalization. W.E.B. Du Bois and Marcus Garvey were prominent pan-Africanists.

Parliament: A British legislative body comprising elected officials and hereditary nobles. Following the British Civil Wars and Revolution, Parliament became the chief governing authority in Britain.

Parthians (247 BCE–224 CE): Successors of Seleucid rule that emerged from a group of mobile pastoralists. They are particularly notable for successfully cultivating long-distance trade.

partition of Africa: The dividing up of African lands among Britain, France, Germany, Belgium, Spain, and Portugal between 1874 and 1890. It began as an informal process, until the Berlin Conference convened to officially partition the African continent in 1884–1885.

patío **process**: A technology involving the use of mercury to separate silver from its surrounding rock. This process made the task of silver extraction easier in the sixteenth and seventeenth centuries, thus increasing the value of lower-grade silver ores.

Pax Mongolica (ca. 1260–1350): Meaning "Mongolian Peace," a relatively calm period during which the Mongolian Empire boosted trade along the Silk Road by creating an environment of largely peaceful exchange.

pharaohs [FARE-ohs]: Egyptian kings; there were about 170 pharaohs between around 2950 and 30 BCE.

Phoenicia [fih-NEE-shuh]: The Greek name for the cities on the eastern coast of the Mediterranean, including Tyre. The word *Punic* is derived from *Phoenicia* and is used to describe things Carthaginian.

pirates: Seafaring bandits who took advantage of periods when long-distance trade was widespread and navies were weak. The beginning of global trade was a very lucrative period for pirates such as the Zhengs and those organized by the North African beys.

plague pandemic (1346–1351): A disastrous outbreak of plague that is historically unmatched in its death toll. At the time incurable, plague killed 30 to 50 percent of the Eurasian population and continued to return regularly for centuries.

plantation zone: An area stretching from the Chesapeake to Brazil where the majority of African slaves were used. Plantations grew tobacco, rice, and sugar on a large scale as part of the transatlantic economy.

plebeians [plih-BEE-uhns]: Roman citizens who did not come from elite families. Plebeians were commoners who often performed the same work as slaves, although plebeians were reimbursed for their labor whereas slaves were not.

plow agriculture: The use of large domesticated animals to pull plows—a piece of farm equipment that tills soil. Farmers could cultivate five times more land using plows.

polis [POH-lihs]: A political institution, a type of city-state, developed by the Greeks around 700 BCE, that included governance by magistrates, citizenship for adult males, and required military duties for citizen-soldiers.

political decentralization: The weakening of centralized kingdoms and the diminishing of links among transatlantic empires, all as a result of the Atlantic revolutions.

Pontiac's War (1763–1765): An Amerindian uprising against the British. Named after one of the uprising's leaders, the Ottawa chief Pontiac, it was a military standoff but resulted in the designation of all North American lands between Appalachia and the Mississippi River as an "Indian reserve."

population surge: A nearly twofold growth of the global population in the three centuries between 1500 and 1800.

Porfiriato [POHR-fihr-ee-AH-toh] (1876–1910): The decades of Porfirio Díaz's authoritarian rule in Mexico. During this period the Mexican economy grew rapidly, as did increasing inequality, due to Díaz's encouragement of foreign investment and support of dispossessing poor peasants.

Potosí [poh-toh-SEE]: Site of large-scale, dangerously deadly silver mining in the Andes under Spanish authorities during the sixteenth and seventeenth centuries; laborers were mostly conscripted Amerindians and, later, African slaves who suffered harsh conditions, frequent accidents, and mercury poisoning. Silver was the most valuable transatlantic commodity.

praetorian guard: A select group of 4,500 men that Augustus created in order to protect the emperor. On five occasions, the praetorian guard assassinated emperors deemed ineffectual or corrupt, including Caligula and Elagabalus.

Prague Spring (1968): A Czechoslovak reform effort that called for less censorship and more freedom during post–World War II communist rule. The Soviets repressed it with a violent military invasion, causing widespread criticism of communism and the USSR.

printing press: A device invented by Johannes Gutenberg in the mid-fifteenth century that involved the use of movable metal type. It allowed for easier, faster, and cheaper production and dissemination of written information.

Protestantism: A branch of Christianity, initiated by the monk Martin Luther (1483–1546), that took issue with the Catholic Church. Luther's writing and preaching emphasized scripture over tradition and salvation by inner faith. Many variations of Protestantism arose, but all denominations generally emphasized the importance of individual relationships with God.

proxy wars: Local conflicts around the world in which the United States and the USSR supported rival factions, with each superpower indirectly engaging the other as part of broader Cold War competition. There were at least 50 proxy wars, including the Korean War, the Vietnam War, the Angolan Civil War, and the Soviet-Afghan War.

Punic Wars (264–241 BCE, 218–201 BCE, 149–146 BCE): A series of three wars between the Romans and the Carthaginians. Rome won all three wars and razed Carthage after the Third Punic War.

pyramids: Monumental tombs, containing provisions for an eternal afterlife, that Old Kingdom pharaohs used conscripted peasants to build. The largest was Khufu's Great Pyramid at Giza.

Qin [chihn] **dynasty** (221–207 BCE): A state, under the ruthless leadership of Shi Huangdi, that conquered the Warring States, expanded to the south, and made unifying reforms that left a legacy of a large and united China.

Qing [chihng] **dynasty** (1644–1911): An imperial dynasty descended from a group of Manchu elite. Using innovative military techniques such as banners (units that cut across kin lines) and improved centralized command, the Qing vastly expanded Chinese territory and power.

Quakers: A Protestant sect originating in England that began the organized antislavery movement. Quaker beliefs stress the fundamental equality of all human beings, and their moral objections were instrumental to antislavery efforts in Britain and the United States.

Queen Boudica: A British queen who led an uprising against the Roman Empire in the years 60 to 61 CE. The Roman army ultimately defeated Queen Boudica and her followers.

railways: Transportation infrastructure that was central to industrialization and an outgrowth of the coal and iron industries. Railways and locomotives lowered transportation costs, connected markets, and linked countries together.

raised-field agriculture: A labor-intensive and very productive, early farming technique used in the Americas from today's Bolivia to Mexico. It is a form of amphibious agriculture that involves creating islands in wetlands and raising crops on them.

Reconquista [ray-kohn-KEE-stah]: A centuries-long Christian campaign to retake Iberia from Muslim rulers. Europeans, especially Iberians, viewed sailing expeditions as a way to continue the Reconquista in new lands by spreading Christianity and depriving Muslim states of wealth from trade.

Renaissance: A fascination among European elites with the intellectual and artistic traditions of the ancient Greeks and Romans. Humanism, the focus on human bodies and experiences, was a defining feature of the Renaissance.

rising merchant classes: Those of modest backgrounds who traded goods in the Atlantic world and became wealthy. With their newly accumulated fortune, they sought liberties and political voice to ease their commerce and preserve their position.

Russian Revolution of 1917: The overturning of imperial rule in Russia that started with a coup d'état led by the Bolsheviks, a minority Marxist faction. They eventually seized control of the government and set out to reform Russia based on the ideology of communism.

Saadians [SAHD-ee-ihnz]: Dynasts who successfully used guns and cannon to unify Morocco and defeat the Songhai in West Africa. They ultimately were unsuccessful in further attempts to gain wealth and power.

Safavids [SAH-fah-vihds]: A dynasty that originated as a Sunni-Sufi brotherhood but adopted Shi'a Islam and then conquered Iran and most of Iraq. They made Shi'a Islam the state religion, reformulated its theology, and pursued mass conversions.

Sahel: An area of semi-arid grassland that stretches east to west and is located on the southern edge of the Sahara Desert. The Senegal and Niger rivers are in the western Sahel, and ancient Ghana and Mali were located in their floodplains.

Sargon of Akkad: A king who pioneered the political format of empire and united the city-states of southern and central Mesopotamia around 2340 BCE; he built the first professional army, promoted trade, and reigned for about 56 years.

Sassanid [suh-SAH-nid] **dynasty** (224–651 CE): Successors of the Parthians and leaders of the Sassanian Empire who popularized the term *Iran* to refer to Persia. They built up irrigation works, introduced new agricultural crops, promoted long-distance trade, and made Iran into a great regional power.

schisms [SIH-zuhms]: Formal divisions generally based on opposing beliefs, especially within young religions. Early Christian schisms included Arianism, Nestorianism, and Monophysitism. Islam split into Shi'a and Sunni branches soon after its inception.

Scientific Revolution: The adoption of mathematics, observation, and systematic experimentation to understand the world instead of relying solely on scripture and ancient texts, as had been done previously.

sedentary: A term that describes people who stay in one place and form settlements instead of moving around.

self-determination: U.S. president Woodrow Wilson's idea that every

European nationality had the right to its own, self-ruled nation. This concept was an important feature of the post–World War I peace treaties and an inspiration for anti-colonialists.

Seljuk [sahl-JYOOK] **Turks** (ca. 980–1090): A pastoral, Sunni Muslim group that rode into Iran, took Baghdad, and conquered Byzantine territory in Anatolia. They spearheaded the lasting Turkification and Islamization of the eastern Mediterranean.

serfs: Peasants who worked as forced labor on large, grain-producing estates for the gentry in Prussia, Poland-Lithuania, and Russia. Landlords of these estates controlled the movement, economic activity, and personal lives of serfs.

Sergei Witte [SAYR-gay VIHT-tee] (1849–1915): A Russian statesman who was deeply involved in the country's industrialization. He directed the government to build railroads, create technical schools, and introduce protectionist tariffs.

settlement houses: During the Industrial Revolution, institutions that elite and middle-class women set up to research and help improve the conditions in which poor and working-class people lived and labored.

settler colony: A form of imperialism in which migrants from a conquering nation establish colonies in conquered lands. Settlers often seek land and dominance, and settler colonies are more violent than colonies without settlers.

shabti [SHAH-tee]: Miniature figurines buried with pharaohs to aid them in the afterlife. Pharaohs sacrificed humans to be their otherworldly attendants until 2600 BCE, after which the use of *shabti* supplanted this practice.

shamanism [SHAH-mah-niz'm]: A broad set of religious beliefs and practices, including direct communication with the supernatural realm and a belief in the existence of a spirit world where the dead live.

Shang dynasty (ca. 1600–1046 BCE): A highly militarized and hierarchical society based in the lower Huang He basin that worshipped the deity Di. During Shang rule, Chinese writing was invented.

shari'a: Meaning "the path" in Arabic, shari'a is the body of Islamic holy law and ethics that governs every aspect of Muslim life. Originally developed on the basis of the Qur'an and accounts of Muhammad's life, it has evolved to form the basis of several schools of Islamic legal practice today.

shi: A cultural elite that emerged under the Zhou and consolidated much of Chinese culture. During the Warring States period, they transformed from being just scholars, to being both scholars and men of war.

Shi Huangdi [shee HWAHNG-dee] (259–210 BCE): Also known as King Zheng and Qin Shi Huang, Shi Huangdi was a successful military commander who conquered vast amounts of land, put an end to the Warring States period, and began the Qin dynasty. He promoted Chinese unity and created a base of unification for subsequent dynasties.

Shi'a [SHEE-ah] **Islam**: An orthodox branch of Islam that was adopted as the state religion in Iran under the Safavid dynasty in the sixteenth and seventeenth centuries. Followers of Shi'a Islam believe that only members of Muhammad's lineage can hold religious and political authority.

shifting agriculture: A type of farming in which farmers cleared land, farmed it for a few years, and then moved to a new patch of land once soil was depleted; often used in forest zones with poor soils.

Shinto [SHIHN-toh]: Meaning "the way of the gods," Shinto is an indigenous Japanese religion that is animistic and polytheistic. It emphasizes ritual and is based on tradition, folklore, shrines, and monuments.

Siddhartha Gautama [sih-DAHR-tuh GOW-taw-mah]: A Kshatri caste prince, born in the sixth or fifth century BCE, who rejected his privileged background and became the Buddha (the Enlightened One); his followers established the religion known as Buddhism.

Sikhism [SIHK-ihzm]: A religion that developed in India in the sixteenth century based on the teachings of Nanak (1469–1538), who asserted that Hinduism and Islam were one and the same. Nanak rejected elaborate ceremony and the caste system, promoted pacifism, and stressed the importance of humankind over other living creatures and the equality of all people before God.

Silk Road: Relay trade routes that crossed the steppes and deserts of Asia from China to the shores of the Mediterranean; named after one of the most valuable commodities transported on these routes—Chinese silk.

silkworms: Domesticated caterpillars that provided the raw materials for the silk industry in China. Women and girls produced silk, a lucrative trade item, from the threads that silkworms excreted.

silver trade: The worldwide buying and selling of silver that sustained the global economy and grew increasingly important as more people used silver as money. In particular, governments and merchants sought silver to engage more easily in state spending or long-distance trading.

Simón Bolívar [see-MOHN boh-LEE-vahr] (1783–1830): A Venezuelan creole revolutionary leader who fought the Spanish Crown and hoped to found a united states of South America.

Simon Kimbangu [KIHM-ban-goo] (1887–1951): The Congolese founder and leader of the independent African Kimbanguist Church, whom the Belgians imprisoned for 30 years until his death. He preached faith healing, non-violence, monogamy, and sobriety.

slave soldiers: Slaves used in the military; most had been sold by their families in Central Asia to the armies of caliphs and sultans. A few slave soldiers managed to overthrow their masters and install themselves on thrones. The Ghaznavids and Turkic horsemen who established the Delhi sultanate were slave soldiers, and they spread the practice of slave soldiery into India.

slave-and-sugar plantations: Profitable, extensive commercial sugar farms in Brazil and the Caribbean that were larger and more efficient than their predecessors. They relied on the brutal exploitation of slaves who worked in notoriously unhealthy conditions and faced a life expectancy shorter than that of slaves anywhere else in the Americas.

Slavery Abolition Act (1834): Passed in Britain, the first large abolition of slavery. When the Whig Party took power in British Parliament, it introduced the act with widespread support from petitioners. It inspired abolitionists around the world.

smallpox inoculation: The intentional infection of humans with cowpox to produce an immunity against smallpox. It replaced riskier methods of inoculation, quickly spread around the world, and reduced worldwide deaths from smallpox.

social Darwinism: The pseudo-scientific application of Charles Darwin's ideas to subsets of the human species. Arguing that some humans were more fit than others, social Darwinism appealed to science to support racism and racial hierarchies.

socialists: People who sought to alter social and political institutions with an emphasis on the rights of the working class. They often supported ideas such as strong unions, worker cooperatives, and communal ownership of industry.

Sons of Africa: A London-based abolitionist organization. It was made up of former slaves, including Ottobah Cugoano and Olaudah Equiano, who wrote detailed descriptions of their experiences as slaves to strengthen the anti–slave trade movement.

spice trade: The exchange of spices that became increasingly widespread in the early modern period and acted as a driving force of global trade. Portuguese, English, and Dutch merchants dominated the spice trade after 1511.

spices: The most frequently traded raw materials in the Indian Ocean world. Spices—including nutmeg, cloves, cinnamon, and a variety of peppers—largely came from Southeast Asia and southern India; the greatest importers were China, Egypt, Arabia, and Iran.

spread of democracy: The shift from the world having twice as many authoritarian states as liberal democracies in 1974 to the reverse by 2010 due to a rise in interest rates, the end of the Cold War, and the power of example.

Srivijaya [sree-VIH-juh-yuh] (ca. 670–1300): A Southeast Asian, Buddhist kingdom based in Sumatra that Indian culture influenced. It controlled the Straits of Malacca, gaining income from taxes on Indian and Chinese shipping.

state: A territorial unit and political community with a formal government. States always have bureaucrats, judges, and soldiers, and usually have ideologies.

steam engine: A machine that converts the chemical energy in fossil fuels into mechanical energy, called steam power. Steam engines powered the defining technologies of the Industrial Revolution and vastly expanded production levels.

steppe nomads: Mobile peoples, including Khitans, Jurchens, and Mongols, who came from the steppe grasslands north of China. Often clashing militarily with the Chinese, they conquered north China three times and all of China once.

suffragism: A mass political and ideological movement that sought to give women the right to vote. It originated in the nineteenth century, and World War I greatly facilitated its progress and success.

Sufi [SOO-fee] **movement**: A form of mystical Islam that sprang up in the ninth century in response to official attempts to enforce orthodoxy. Instead of following scholarly traditions, Sufism promoted a more personal relationship with God and incorporated song, poetry, and dance into its rituals.

Sukarno [soo-KAHR-noh] (1901–1970): Javanese aristocrat, Indonesian independence activist, and founder of the nationalist Partai Nasional Indonesia. He became the first president of Indonesia after collaborating with the Japanese during World War II and then fighting off the return of Dutch colonialism.

Sumer [SOO-mehr]: The region and culture of southern Mesopotamia, located in today's southern Iraq; the early cities Ur and Uruk were in Sumer.

Sun Tzu [suhn-zoo]: Attributed author of *The Art of War*, possibly written in the sixth or fifth century BCE. The classic work gives insight on military strategy, diplomacy, statecraft, and espionage.

Sun Yatsen [suhn YAHT-suhn] (1866–1925): A physician and revolutionary who opposed the Qing and wanted to reform China in the image of powerful Western countries. He led the Chinese Revolution and became president of China's new constitutional republic until his ouster and exile to Japan in 1913.

Swahili [swah-HEE-lee] **coast**: The coast of East Africa where Arab and Persian traders interacted with local Africans. A distinct Swahili culture and language rooted in Indian Ocean trade developed along this coast.

Tacky's War (1760): An uprising in Jamaica of nearly 1,500 slaves, led by Akan-speaking slaves from what is now Ghana, that lasted for several months before it was brutally suppressed.

Taíno [TAY-noh]: The indigenous population of the Spanish-controlled Caribbean island of Hispaniola. Disease, violence, and enslavement led to a demographic catastrophe among the Taíno.

Taiping [TEYE-pihng] **Rebellion** (1850–1864): A large rebellion led by Hong Xiuquan and his army, the Taiping. Motivated by political, nationalist, and Christian goals, the Taiping managed to control much of the Yangzi Valley for 10 years until their defeat and Hong's death.

Tenochtitlán [thuh-NOCH-tee-tlahn]: The large, populous capital of the Aztec Empire located on an island in Lake Texcoco in the Basin of Mexico.

textiles and metallurgy: The two main industries at the forefront of industrial revolutions around the world. Both cloth making and iron making were well suited to steam-powered mass production.

third pulse of decolonization: The comparatively rapid emergence of around 100 new countries that occurred between 1945 and 1975, mainly in Africa, Asia, and the Caribbean.

Thirteenth Amendment (1865): Introduced at the end of the Civil War, an amendment to the U.S. Constitution that abolished slavery. It led to the liberation of 4 million people, making it the largest emancipation in world history.

Thomas Clarkson (1760–1846): A member of the Anglican elite and a staunch anti–slave trade and abolitionist activist. He allied with the Quakers to publicize the atrocities of the slave trade and was influential in the British abolition of the slave trade and slavery.

Tibetan Empire (ca. 618–842): Also known as Yarlung, the Tibetan Empire was located north of the Himalaya, and its influence spread from India to Mongolia. It was a formidable competitor to the Tang.

Tigris and Euphrates Rivers: Twin rivers that flow into the Persian Gulf; they supported agriculture and trade in Mesopotamia.

Tiwanaku [tee-wahn-AH-koo] (ca. 100–1100 CE): An Andean city and empire that amassed wealth and power through its control of the supply of llamas. The city was a religious center located near Lake Titicaca in what is now Bolivia; its empire and influence reached as far as northern Chile, lowland Bolivia, and the Peruvian Andes.

Tlacélel [tlah-KAY-luhl] (ca. 1398–1480): A successful and influential Aztec king who fortified the cultural legacy and importance of the Aztecs. He invented a glorious Aztec history and strengthened the Aztecs' religious importance by putting them in charge of sustaining the sun god.

Tokugawa shogunate [TOH-koo-GAH-wah SHOH-guh-nayt] (1600–1868): A ruling dynasty in Japan made up of the descendants of Tokugawa Ieyasu, who completed the task of unifying Japan in 1600.

Toussaint L'Ouverture [TOO-sahn LOO-vehr-toor] (ca. 1743–1803): The main leader of the Haitian Revolution. He was born a slave on St. Domingue but was freed around age 30, after which he led the Haitian slave insurrection and became a successful commander in the Haitian army.

Toyotomi Hideyoshi [tohih-yoh-TOH-mee hee-day-OH-shee] (1537–1598): Oda Nobunaga's successor; a Japanese warlord whose soldiers liberally employed guns and nearly united all of Japan. He invaded Korea, enslaving thousands, but retreated from a failed invasion in China.

transatlantic slave trade (1519–ca. 1860): The transportation by European traders of 12 to 14 million slaves from Africa to the Americas, mainly to work on plantations. This trade constituted the largest forced migration in world history.

transition to agriculture: The switch between human populations finding or cultivating food and settled human populations producing food through domestication. This process occurred in various places independently of one another.

Trans-Siberian Railway: A railway from Moscow to the Pacific Ocean that was completed in 1903. A remarkable feat of engineering and construction, the almost 6,000-mile-long railway built by 9,000 laborers was a defining symbol of the Russian Industrial Revolution.

Treaty of Tordesillas (1494): Spain and Portugal used this agreement to demarcate a line halfway between Columbus's discoveries in the Americas and the Cape Verde islands off the coast of West Africa. It gave all lands west of the line to Spain and all lands east to Portugal.

Treaty of Versailles [vehr-SEYE] (1919): A peace treaty written by the victorious Allies that imposed strict and punitive policies on Germany in the aftermath of World War I. The treaty provoked outrage in Germany due to its reparations and war guilt clauses, as well as among Chinese because it gave German concessions in China to Japan.

Treaty of Waitangi [weye-TANG-ee] (1840): A treaty in which the Maori of New Zealand agreed to become British subjects in exchange for land guarantees. British settlers soon broke this treaty, fought the Maori for land, and ended Maori independence.

tsar [ZAHR]: The title Russian rulers adopted after 1547. The tsars, particularly Ivan the Terrible (r. 1547–1584) and Peter the Great (r. 1682–1725), built an expansive and centralized Russian empire by modernizing the military and asserting control over the Russian elite.

Túpac Amaru II [too-pak ah-MAHR-oo] (1738–1781): A Jesuit-educated mestizo revolutionary descended from the Inka ruling family. He led a tax revolt in the Andes beginning in 1780 and emphasized justice and the end of ethnic oppression.

Tyre: A merchant town that linked the trade of Egypt, northern Mesopotamia, Syria, and Anatolia and specialized in a highly desirable maroon-purple dye. In order to expand their metals trade, Tyre's merchants established Carthage as well as several other colonies along the Mediterranean coast.

Umayyad caliphate [oo-MEYE-ahd KA-lih-fayt]: The first genuine Islamic state (661–750), based in Damascus and led by caliphs ("deputies of God") who claimed to be successors of the prophet Muhammad. They expanded their empire through conquests and exerted "soft power" through monumental architecture such as the Dome of the Rock mosque.

universities: The first opened in Cairo in the tenth century, followed by several in Europe in the twelfth century. European universities, as comparatively free spaces of inquiry and debate, prompted the development of science and art.

university of war: The state of constant military competition and chaos in Europe during the early modern period. These conditions increased the power of successful states and made them skilled in warfare, efficient at tax collection, and able to adapt quickly to innovations.

Vasco da Gama: A low-ranking Portuguese noble who led an expedition in 1497 around the southern tip of Africa and into the Indian Ocean in search of Christian allies and valuable spices for the Portuguese Crown. He helped set up a lasting Portuguese presence in India and East Africa.

Vedas [VAY-duhs]: Four texts, which probably originated as oral traditions, that are the earliest existing examples of literature in Sanskrit and the oldest sacred texts of Hinduism. The culture of the Ganges basin is called Vedic after them.

vertical archipelago: The system by which Andean clans, called *ayllus*, placed people from a given lineage in communities at each elevation level of the mountains in order to exploit the resources of the different environments. The Inkas did not invent this system, but greatly expanded it.

Vietnam War (1965–1975): A proxy conflict between communist North Vietnam, aligned with China and the USSR, and anti-communist South Vietnam, aligned with the United States. The United States committed hundreds of thousands of troops to the domestically unpopular war, which the North Vietnamese ultimately won.

Vikings: A group of seaborne marauders from Scandinavia that looted, slaved, and conquered nearby territories beginning around 800 CE. They settled land from Russia to Greenland and established several enduring trade links.

Vital Revolution: The steady improvement of human health and life expectancy after 1750. Better nutrition, microbial unification, control of smallpox, and sanitation reform contributed to this shift.

Vladimir Lenin (1870–1924): A Russian-born revolutionary and influential member of the Bolsheviks. He consolidated power by 1921 and was the first leader of the USSR.

Wang Yangming [wang YAHN-mihng] (1472–1529): A Chinese philosopher who challenged prevailing neo-Confucian thought and gained followers by arguing that ordinary people could attain moral perfection through inherent knowledge rather than through book learning.

Wangari Maathai [wahn-GAH-ree MAH-theye] (1940–2011): A prominent political, environmental, and women's rights activist. The first woman in the history of East Africa to earn a PhD, founder of the Green Belt Movement, member of the Kenyan parliament, and Nobel Peace Prize laureate.

witch hunts: The spike in accusations of witchcraft between 1500 and 1700, which resulted in the widespread use of torture and execution of accused witches. Unmarried women over age 40 were the main targets.

working class: A section of society, formed during the Industrial Revolution, that comprised factory and mine workers who performed shift work for wages. Workers' lives at this time were precarious and dangerous, and they were politically divided between seeking reform and inciting revolution.

World War I (1914–1918): A conflict between the Central Powers (Germany, Austria-Hungary, the Ottoman Empire) and the Entente or Allied Powers (France, Russia, Britain, Italy) fought mainly in Europe. Many smaller European nations joined in, as well as ultimately the United States. The war required mass mobilization of populations and resources and led to unprecedented violence and destruction.

World War II (1937–1945): The most expansive and deadliest war in history, fought between the Axis powers and the Allies. It involved four overlapping wars, fought primarily in Europe, China, the Pacific, and North Africa.

Wu Zetian [woo ZAY-shihn] (624–705): The only woman who both ruled China in her own name and was the most powerful person on Earth when in power. Wu was a controversial ruler who was ruthless toward her enemies, adept at foreign affairs, a great patron of Buddhism, and a supporter of commerce.

Yamato race theory: A fictional idea developed in the 1930s. It held that all Japanese people shared a common ancestry to an ancient race that was superior to other nearby peoples, including Koreans and Chinese.

Yamato region: A state in the southeast of Japan that began to expand its influence in the 600s. It ruled several rice-producing regions, emphasized military skill, adopted Buddhism, and imported cultural ideas from the Tang.

Yangzi [YAHNG-zuh] **River**: A river in China whose valley was home to the second transition to agriculture, which occurred about 7000 BCE and was rice-based.

Yermak [yehr-MAHK]: A Cossack who pioneered the expansion of the Russian fur trade into Siberia during the 1580s. His success also spearheaded the introduction of disease and practices of brutality that ultimately killed many native Siberians.

Yoshinogari [yoh-shih-noh-GAH-ree]: A site on Japan's southern island of Kyushu where evidence of weaving, bronze casting, and other crafts has been found, as well as mainland trade goods such as Korean-made bronze daggers and Chinese bronze mirrors.

Young Turk Revolution (1908): A coup d'état in the Ottoman Empire that nationalist army officers, called the Young Turks, led. They were frustrated with foreign encroachment on Ottoman territory and successfully imposed a constitution.

Younger Dryas (10,700–9,700 BCE): A severe cold and dry period that temporarily reversed the process of slow global warming that occurred after the coldest part of the last ice age.

Yuan [yoo-AHN] **dynasty** (1279–1368): The dynasty established by the Mongols after the defeat of the Song by Khubilai Khan. Despite their rough-edged steppe-nomad nature, the Yuan allowed religious diversity, promoted scientific creativity and cultural exchange, and encouraged trade throughout the many lands they controlled.

Zanj revolt (868–883): A massive uprising of slaves from East Africa who worked on plantations in Iraq. One of the most successful slave rebellions in world history, it dealt an immense blow to southern Iraq and ended the practice of plantation slavery in Iraq for around a millennium.

Zheng He [SHENG-hah]: An admiral and an important ally of the Yongle Emperor. He arranged and led the Ming voyages during the fifteenth century.

Zhou [JOH] **dynasty** (1045–256 BCE): The dynasty that began the process of Chinese unification, developed irrigation, promoted iron farm tools, and began using chariots in war. In 771 BCE, Zhou rulers lost much of their territory; only part of their kingdom, the Eastern Zhou, survived until 256 BCE.

ziggurats [ZIG-uh-rahts]: A pioneering form of monumental architecture, ziggurats are temple-palaces dedicated to local gods.

Zoroastrianism [zohr-oh-ASS-tree-ahn-iz'm]: A monotheistic religion that arose in Persia around the prophecies of Zoroaster sometime between the tenth and sixth centuries BCE. With priests called magi, it emphasized the creator-god Ahura Mazda, human choice between good and evil, and divine judgment.

TEXT CREDITS

PHOTO CREDITS

Stock Photo; p. 238: ERIC LAFFORGUE/ Alamy Stock Photo; p. 240: Cultural Relics Publishing House (Wenwu), Beijing, China; p. 243: akg-images/Bildarchiv Steffens; p. 245: Science & Society Picture Library/Getty Images; p. 246 : akg-images/Pictures From History; p. 252: DGP_travel/Alamy Stock Photo; p. 255: The Picture Art Collection/ Alamy Stock Photo; p. 257: DeAgostini/ Getty Images; p. 260: Werner Forman/Art Resource, NY.

Chapter 8: Page 269: album/Alamy Stock Photo; p. 272 (left): Musee National de Carthage, Carthage, Tunisia/Bridgeman Images; (right): Peter Horree/Alamy Stock Photo; p. 273: EnriquePSans/Alamy Stock Photo; p. 275: Andrej Privizer/Alamy Stock Photo; p. 277: Scala/Art Resource, NY; p. 280: Alinari/ Art Resource, NY; p. 284: bpk Bildagentur/ Antikensammlung, Staatliche Museen, Berlin/ Art Resource; p. 285: Scala/Art Resource, NY; p. 290 (left): De Agostini/G. Berengo Gardin/Getty Images; (right): Museo della Civilta Romana, Rome, Italy/Bridgeman Images; p. 292: Werner Forman Archive/Bridgeman Images; p. 301: Alpineguide/Alamy Stock Photo; p. 302: Scala/Art Resource, NY; p. 303: akg-images.

Chapter 9: Page 310: Ashmolean Museum, University of Oxford, UK/Bridgeman Images; p. 314: akg-images; p. 316: Peter Horree/ Alamy Stock Photo; p. 318: De Agostini Picture Library/C. Sappa/Bridgeman Images; p. 326: Fratelli Alinari/akg-Images; p. 330: PRISMA ARCHIVO/Alamy Stock Photo; p. 331: Album/Alamy Stock Photo; p. 333: Ashmolean Museum, University of Oxford, UK/ Bridgeman Images; p. 336: Album/Alamy Stock Photo; p. 340: HIP/Art Resource, NY.

Chapter 10: Page 349: Department of Anthropology, National Museum of Natural History, Smithsonian Institution, A581650; p. 352: Werner Forman/Universal Images Group/Getty Images; p. 355: Indianapolis Museum of Art at Newfields, USA/Gift of Bonnie and David Ross/Bridgeman Images; p. 359: CM Dixon/ Print Collector/Getty Images; p. 363 (top): DeAgostini/Getty Images; (bottom): Justin Kerr; p. 365: Erich Lessing/Art Resource, NY; p. 368: Michael Rooney/Alamy Stock Photo; p. 372: Jean-Michel COUREAU/Gamma-Rapho via Getty Images; p. 376: Suzanne Long/Alamy Stock Photo; p. 380: Douglas Peebles Photography/Alamy Stock Photo.

Chapter 11: Page 388: akg-images/Rainer Hackenberg; p. 390 (top): Erich Lessing/Art

Resource, NY; (bottom): Musee des Antiquites Nationales, St. Germain-en-Laye, France/ Bridgeman Images; p. 394: Hemis/Alamy Stock Photo; p. 402: Westend61 GmbH/Alamy Stock Photo; p. 415: Bridgeman Images; p. 416 (left): akg-images/Bildarchiv Monheim; (right): Umayyad Mosque, Damascus, Syria/ Bridgeman Images; p. 421: © The British Museum/Trustees of the British Museum; p. 422: Qusayr 'Amra, Jordan/Bridgeman Images.

Chapter 12: Page 430: Artokoloro Quint Lox Limited/Alamy Stock Photo; p. 437: Pictures from History/Bridgeman Images; p. 445: The Picture Art Collection/Alamy Stock Photo; p. 448: Daniel Schwen/Pictures From History/ Newscom; p. 450: FLHC 16/Alamy Stock Photo; p. 455: akg-images/Dirk Radzinski; p. 460: GRANGER — All rights reserved; p. 463: Marco Secchi/Alamy Stock Photo.

Chapter 13: Page 471: pixel shepherd/Alamy Stock Photo; p. 475: Tomas Abad/Alamy Stock Photo; p. 478: imagebrOKER/Alamy Stock Photo; p. 482 (left): robertharding/Alamy Stock Photo; (right): © RMN-Grand Palais/ Art Resource, NY; p. 488: Christine Osborne Pictures/Alamy Stock Photo; p. 492: Art Collection 3/Alamy Stock Photo; p. 497: Heritage Images/Getty Images; p. 501: Jason Gallier/ Alamy Stock Photo; p. 504 (left): Christopher Scott/Alamy Stock Photo; (right): Heritage Image Partnership Ltd/Alamy Stock Photo.

Chapter 14: Page 511: Album/Alamy Stock Photo; p. 519: akg-images/Pictures From History; p. 522: akg-images/Pictures From History; p. 524: DEA Picture Library/Getty Images; p. 529: Index Fototeca/Bridgeman Images; p. 536: Roland and Sabrina Michaud/ akg-images; p. 537: age fotostock/Alamy Stock Photo; p. 540: akg-images/WHA/ World History Archive; p. 542: Werner Forman/Art Resource, NY; p. 543: British Library, London/Bridgeman Images; p. 546: Pictures from History/Bridgeman Images.

Chapter 15: Page 559 (left): Michele Burgess/Alamy Stock Photo; (right): De Agostini Picture Library/G. Dagli Orti/Bridgeman Images; p. 567: akg-images/Universal Images Group; p. 568: akg-images/De Agostini Picture Library; p. 571: akg-images/WHA/ World History Archive; p. 572: Ian Dagnall/ Alamy Stock Photo; p. 575: Werner Forman Archive/Bridgeman Images; p. 579: Bibliotheque Nationale, Paris, France/Bridgeman Images; p. 584: Universal Images Group North America LLC/DeAgostini/Alamy Stock Photo;

p. 586: Douglas Peebles Photography/Alamy Stock Photo.

Chapter 16: Page 595 (left): Topkapi Palace Museum, Istanbul, Turkey/Bridgeman Images; (right): Bibliotheque Nationale/De Agostini/Bridgeman Images; p. 600: Gregory A. Harlin/National Geographic Image Collection/Bridgeman Images; p. 602: The Picture Art Collection/Alamy Stock Photo; p. 603: Pictures from History/Bridgeman Images; p. 606: Sabena Jane Blackbird/Alamy Stock Photo; p. 607: Alamy Stock Photo; p. 608: Granger Collection; p. 615: Album/Alamy Stock Photo; p. 616: The Picture Art Collection/Alamy Stock Photo; p. 618 : Granger Collection; p. 621: akg-images.

INDEX

Page numbers in **bold** refer to glossary terms.
Page numbers in *italics* refer to illustrations.
Page numbers followed by *c, m, b,* or *t* refer
to chronologies, maps, boxes, or tables,
respectively.

Portolan chart, *603*
pottery of, 67*c*
region of, 472
savanna and, 311, 321
sedentary peoples in, 52
similarities of frontier Europe and, 309–11
slavery and, 310
social fluidity in, 323–25
social hierarchy in, 517
southeastern, 502–4
vegetation and fossil sites of, 9*m*
violence in, 324
Zheng He's voyages to, 601
See also specific regions and countries
African ivory, 500
Afro-Asiatic language family, 313
afterlife, belief in, 159, *162*, 162–63, 206
Agamemnon, 199
agave cactus, 568
Agni, 174
agriculture, 109*c*, 308*c*
  Abbasid caliphate and, 416
  and accumulation of wealth, 63
  Achaemenid Persia and, 195–96
  in Africa, 52, 53, 56, 308*c*, 315–16, *316*, 320–21, 323
  in Amazonia, 561–62
  in Americas, 345*c*, 351–54, *352*, 619–23
  Ancestral Pueblo and, 571–72
  Aztecs and, 566–67
  biological exchange and, 616, *622*, 624
  biological globalization and, 619–23
  Carthage and, 274
  cereal based, 55–56
  in China, 50, 51, 56, 449
  climate and, 46–47, 384, 512
  commercial, 390, *390*
  daily routines and, 62–63
  diet and, 51, 55, 59–60, 84, 165
  disease and, 56–58, 102
  early villages and, 68–74
  in Egypt, 152–53
  energy and, 62
  environment and, 58
  in Europe, 331–34
  expansion by displacement, 56–58
  expansion by imitation, 58
  families and, 63
  farming and, 60
  favorable conditions for, 45–48
  in Fertile Crescent, 56–56
  fertility rates and, 60
  firestick farming, 375–76
  herding vs., 67*c*, 74–77, *85*
  and human biological evolution, 82–87
  improvements in, 384
  Inka and, 560–61
  innovation in, 384, 510–12, *511*, 537, 550
  intensive, 115
  inventions of, 34, 44–55, 46*m*
  Iroquois and, 578–80
  irrigation and, 89–91, 102, 114–15, 122

  Jomon culture and, 58
  in Korea, 226*c*, 238, 261
  maize based, 54–55
  in Mesoamerica, 54–55
  in Meso- and North America, 54–55
  in Mesopotamia, 114–15, 133
  migration and, 77–80
  in New Guinea, 226*c*
  new species in, creation of, 86–87
  in Oceania, 377
  origins of, 34, 44–55
  in Persia, 389–90
  population and, 59
  raised-field, 351–52
  regime, 58–59
  religion and, 63
  rice based, 55
  Roman Empire and, 295–96, 390
  Sassanian Empire and, 392
  Shang dynasty and, 233–34
  shifting, 73–74
  in South America, 54
  in Southeast Asia, 51–52, 237, 259–60, *260*
  spread of, 55–59, 57*m*
  stature and, 59–60
  three-field crop rotation, 511
  Tiwanaku, 372
  transitions to, 46–50, **48**, 59–63, 64
  transition to, 34*c*, 48–50
  Zhou dynasty and, 242
  See also climate change; diet; farming; irrigation; *specific regions and countries*
Aguilar, Francisco de, 618
Ahura Mazda, **195**, 218, 222, *402*
Ainu, 44
Akkadian Empire, 109*c*, 119–20, 121*m*, *197*
Akkadian gods, 129*b*
Aksum, 309*c*, 320*b*, **326**, 326–27
Alalgar, 116
al-Andalus, **508**, 509*c*, 514–15, 515*m*, 541
  See also Iberia; Islam; Spain
Alaska, 22, 23, 347, 355, 380
al-Azhar, 543
al-Bakri, 519, 520
Aleuts, 345*c*, 380
Alexander the Great, 189*c*, **213**, *214*, 431
  Aristotle and, 210, 213–14, 216, 247
  conquests of, 189, 219*m*, 222, 251, 412, 484
  death of, 216, 219*m*, 252
  divine status of, 216
  empire of, 214–16, 215*m*
  leadership of, 216–17
  money and, 220
  as Persian king, 213–17
  in Tyre, 273
  upbringing of, 213–14
Alexandria, 189*c*, **221**, 221–22, 284
alfalfa, 195, 389–90
al-Farabi, 541
al-Ferdawsi, *542*
Algeria, *63*
al-Idrisi, Muhammad, *540*

WORLD POLITICAL MAP

GREENLAND
(Denmark)

ICELAND

Faroe
(Denma

ALASKA
(U.S.)

CANADA   Hudson
Bay

U
KIN

Bering Sea

Gulf of
Alaska

IRELA

Aleutian Is.

F

PORTUGA

UNITED STATES

Azores
(Portugal)

Bermuda (U.K.)

Madeira Is.
(Portugal)   MORO

Canary Is.
(Spain)

WESTERN
SAHARA

HAWAII
(U.S.)

Gulf of
Mexico   THE BAHAMAS

MEXICO   CUBA   DOMINICAN REPUBLIC
PUERTO RICO (U.S.)

MAURITANI

JAMAICA HAITI   SAINT KITTS AND NEVIS
ANTIGUA AND BARBUDA

BELIZE   Caribbean Sea   DOMINICA

CAPE VERDE   SENEGAL

GUATEMALA   ST. VINCENT SAINT LUCIA

GAMBIA

EL SALVADOR   AND THE GRENADINES BARBADOS

GUINEA BISSAU   GUINEA

HONDURAS   GRENADA

PACIFIC OCEAN   NICARAGUA   TRINIDAD AND TOBAGO

SIERRA LEONE

COSTA RICA   VENEZUELA

LIBERIA

PANAMA   GUYANA FRENCH GUIANA
(France)

ATLANTIC

COLOMBIA   SURINAME   OCEAN

KIRIBATI

Galapagos Is.
(Ecuador)   ECUADOR

SAMOA   FRENCH POLYNESIA
(France)

PERU   BRAZIL

TONGA

BOLIVIA

Easter I.
(Chile)   CHILE   PARAGUAY

Chatham Is.
(N.Z.)

URUGUAY

ARGENTINA

Falkland Is.
(U.K.)

S. Georgia
(U.K.)

S. Sandwich Is.
(U.K.)

Abbreviations			
ARM.	Armenia	**K.**	Kosovo
AUS.	Austria	**LUX.**	Luxembourg
AZ.	Azerbaijan	**MO.**	Montenegro
BEL.	Belgium	**NETH.**	Netherlands
B.H.	Bosnia and Herzegovina	**N.MAC.**	North Macedonia
CR.	Croatia	**SE.**	Serbia
CZ.	Czech Republic	**SLK.**	Slovakia
GEO.	Georgia	**SLN.**	Slovenia
HUNG.	Hungary	**SWITZ.**	Switzerland